Mind in Life

Mind in Life

BIOLOGY, PHENOMENOLOGY,

AND THE SCIENCES OF MIND

◆ ◆ ◆

Evan Thompson

THE BELKNAP PRESS OF

HARVARD UNIVERSITY PRESS

Cambridge, Massachusetts

London, England

First Harvard University Press paperback edition, 2010

Library of Congress Cataloging-in-Publication Data

Thompson, Evan.
Mind in life : biology, phenomenology, and the sciences of mind / Evan Thompson.
p.   cm.
Includes bibliographical references and index.
ISBN 978–0–674–02511–0 (cloth : alk. paper)
ISBN 978-0-674-05751-7 (pbk.)
1. Consciousness.   2. Philosophy of mind.   3. Phenomenology.   4. Mind and body.
5. Experience.   I. Title.
B808.9.T45   2007
128'.2—dc22   2006050713

To

Gabriel Cohen Varela
Maximilian Todd Williams
Gareth Todd Thompson

Contents

Preface

THE THEME OF THIS BOOK is the deep continuity of life and mind. Where there is life there is mind, and mind in its most articulated forms belongs to life. Life and mind share a core set of formal or organizational properties, and the formal or organizational properties distinctive of mind are an enriched version of those fundamental to life. More precisely, the *self-organizing* features of mind are an enriched version of the self-organizing features of life. The self-producing or "autopoietic" organization of biological life already implies cognition, and this incipient mind finds sentient expression in the self-organizing dynamics of action, perception, and emotion, as well as in the self-moving flow of time-consciousness.

From this perspective, mental life is also bodily life and is situated in the world. The roots of mental life lie not simply in the brain, but ramify through the body and environment. Our mental lives involve our body and the world beyond the surface membrane of our organism, and therefore cannot be reduced simply to brain processes inside the head.

The chapters to come elaborate these ideas using material drawn from three main sources—biology, phenomenological philosophy, and psychology and neuroscience. The book as a whole is intended to bring the experimental sciences of life and mind into a closer and more harmonious relationship with phenomenological investigations of experience and subjectivity.

The principal motive behind this aim is to make headway on one of the outstanding philosophical and scientific problems of our time—the so-called explanatory gap between consciousness and nature. Exactly how are consciousness and subjective experience related to the brain and body? It is one thing to be able to establish correlations between consciousness and brain activity; it is another thing to have an account that explains exactly how certain biological processes generate and realize consciousness and subjectivity. At the present time, we not only lack such an account, but also are unsure about the form it would need to have in order to bridge the conceptual and epistemological gap between life and mind as objects of scientific investigation, and life and mind as we subjectively experience them.

In this book, I offer no new or original theory or model of consciousness, no new conceptual analysis of physical and phenomenal concepts, and no new speculative metaphysical synthesis to unify consciousness and nature. My aim and approach are different. To make real progress on the explanatory gap, we need richer phenomenological accounts of the structure of experience, and we need scientific accounts of mind and life informed by these phenomenological accounts. Phenomenology in turn needs to be informed by psychology, neuroscience, and biology. My aim is not to close the explanatory gap in a reductive sense, but rather to enlarge and enrich the philosophical and scientific resources we have for addressing the gap. My approach is thus to bring phenomenological analyses of experience into a mutually illuminating relationship with scientific analyses of life and mind.

Acknowledgments

I CANNOT HELP but think of this book as exemplifying what philosophers call the bundle theory of personal identity. According to the bundle theory, there is no single and permanent self that persists through time; the self is rather a bundle of constantly changing and psychologically continuous experiences or mental episodes. Similarly, this book began many years ago and has undergone so many transformations since its inception that I cannot say with any confidence that it is the "same" book I started work on more than ten years ago.

Originally, this book (or its textual ancestor) was supposed to be co-authored with Francisco Varela. We had hoped to write a follow-up to our book (co-authored with Eleanor Rosch), *The Embodied Mind: Cognitive Science and Human Experience* (MIT Press, 1991). When we began planning our new book (in 1994), Francisco had just learned that he was chronically ill with Hepatitis C. Thus, from the beginning, a sense of urgency lay over this book. Eventually it became clear that Francisco would need a liver transplant. At this time (in 1998), Francisco decided to step back from the project and encouraged me to continue on my own. I thus set about to revise the book by myself. After the success of the transplant, Francisco felt new enthusiasm for the project, and we tried to resume our collaborative efforts. Sadly, his illness returned not long afterward, and Francisco died on May 28, 2001, at his home in Paris. The obituary I wrote a few days later for the online journal *Psyche* can be read at: http://psyche.cs.monash.edu.au/v7/

psyche-7–12-thompson.html An abridged version was also published in *Journal of Consciousness Studies* 8 (2001): 66–69.

After Francisco's death, I tried to continue writing this book as a co-authored one. But there was still a large amount of writing to be done, and as time passed it became clear that the book needed to be completely recast and rewritten by me alone. I reorganized and rewrote the chapters, and changed the title twice, before the book finally took its present form. Thus, although the enormous influence of Francisco's thought will be evident to anyone who reads this book, I bear full responsibility for this work's contents, and all shortcomings and errors are mine.

Over the long and difficult time it has taken to produce this book, I have had the support and encouragement of many people.

No one has given me more encouragement, aid, and love, and shared more in the tumultuous life of this book, than Rebecca Todd. The love and gratitude I feel are beyond expression. In addition to living with my long periods of self-absorption while struggling with this book, she has read numerous drafts and helped me improve my thinking and writing immeasurably. I cannot imagine having written this book without her.

Our sons Maximilian Todd Williams and Gareth Todd Thompson have had to endure my working on this book for almost their entire lives. My gratitude to them is boundless. I dedicate this book to them, and to our dear family friend, Gabriel Cohen Varela, son of Francisco Varela and Amy Cohen Varela, and the same age as my younger son.

Gail Thompson, William Irwin Thompson, and Hilary Thompson have given great support in ways too numerous to detail. I am deeply grateful to them.

I also express deep thanks to John and Nancy Todd for their encouragement over many years.

Amy Cohen Varela's enthusiasm for this book, and her unhesitating support and encouragement when I decided to transform it into a single-authored work after Francisco's death, are deeply appreciated.

Alva Noë's friendship and intellectual companionship during the writing of this book are greatly valued. I express my gratitude to him also for comments on early versions of several chapters, and for his reading and commenting on the penultimate version of the entire manuscript.

Many people over the years have read various portions of this book and given helpful advice along the way: Giovanna Colombetti, Diego Cosmelli, Isabela Granic, Robert Hanna, Marc Lewis, Antoine Lutz, Susan Oyama, Michael Silberstein, Dan Zahavi, and Phil Zelazo.

For helpful discussions on a wide variety of topics related to this book, I thank Lisa Adams, Ralph Adolphs, Michel Bitbol, Maria Botero, Paul Bourgine, Richie Davidson, Natalie Depraz, Jean-Pierre Dupuy, Frans de Waal, Adam Engle, Michel Ferrari, Shaun Gallagher, Vittorio Gallese, Tom Hollenstein, Evelyn Fox Keller, Uriah Kriegel, Jean-Philippe Lachaux, Connie Lamm, Alex Lamey, Dorothée Legrand, Michel Le Van Quyen, Luigi Luisi, Jun Luo, Eduard Marbach, Barry McMullin, Bernard Pachoud, Slobodan Perovic, Claire Petitmengin, Jean Petitot, Ljiljana Radenovic, Franz Reichle, Eugenio Rodriguez, Andreas Roepstorff, Jean-Michel Roy, David Rudrauf, Brian Cantwell Smith, John Stewart, Steve Torrence, Joel Walmsley, Mark Wexler, and Arthur Zajonc.

The penultimate version of this book served as the main text for a graduate seminar in "Phenomenological Philosophy of Mind" I taught during the Fall Term 2005, in the Department of Philosophy at the University of Toronto. I am grateful to everyone who attended that seminar—especially Ranpal Dosanjh, David Egan, Cathal Ó Madagáin, Joshua Ben Nichols, Adrienne Prettyman, and Joel Walmsley—for their critical responses to the text.

Helena De Preester, at short notice, read the penultimate version of the text and sent me numerous detailed and insightful comments that helped my final revisions considerably.

Mike Wheeler also read the entire manuscript and helpfully called attention to several places where my arguments could be improved.

I am particularly thankful for the patience of Lindsay Waters at the Harvard University Press. His encouragement and speedy efficiency when the manuscript finally arrived on his desk are much appreciated.

I am grateful to several institutions and individuals for their support. During March and April 2003, I stayed as a visting Mâitre de Recherche at the Centre de Recherche en Epistémologie Appliqué (CREA), at the Ecole Polytechnique, Paris. I wish to thank its director, Jean Petitot, for this opportunity, which greatly aided me in writing this book. I also thank Dan Zahavi, director of the Center for Subjectivity Research at the University of Copenhagen, for inviting me to visit for two weeks in

June 2004 and June 2005, and for numerous productive exchanges during this time. Finally, I am grateful to the McDonnell Project in Philosophy and the Neurosciences, its director, Kathleen Akins, and my fellow project members, for their interest in and support of my work.

For financial support, I am grateful to the Social Sciences and Humanities Research Council of Canada for a Standard Research Grant (1998–2001) and a Canada Research Chair (2002–2007); York University for a Faculty of Arts Research Fellowship (2001–2002); the McDonnell Project in Philosophy and Neuroscience; the Center for Consciousness Studies at the University of Arizona, Tucson; and the University of Toronto for a Connaught Start-up Research Award.

An earlier version of Chapter 9 was published as the article "Sensorimotor Subjectivity and the Enactive Approach to Experience," in *Phenomenology and the Cognitive Sciences* 4 (2005): 407–427 (© Springer-Verlag). Chapter 10 is an expanded version of "Look Again: Phenomenology and Mental Imagery," in *Phenomenology and the Cognitive Sciences* (in press; © Springer-Verlag), and of "Representationalism and the Phenomenology of Mental Imagery," in *Synthese* (in press; © Springer-Verlag). I am grateful to the editor of these journals for permission to use this material in revised form here.

Finally, I am grateful to my former colleagues at York University and my new colleagues at the University of Toronto for their encouragement and interest in my work.

◆

PART ONE

The Enactive Approach

ONE

❖ ❖ ❖

Cognitive Science and Human Experience

COGNITIVE SCIENCE—that part of the science of the mind traditionally concerned with cognitive processes—has been described as having
"a very long past but a relatively short history" (Gardner 1985, p. 9).
Scientific concern with the mind can be traced all the way back to
Plato and Aristotle, but the term *cognitive science* did not arise until the
late twentieth century, as a name for the new, modern, scientific research progam that integrated psychology, neuroscience, linguistics,
computer science, artificial intelligence (AI), and philosophy. What
united these disciplines, and set cognitive science apart from earlier
approaches in psychology and philosophy, was the goal of making explicit the principles and mechanisms of cognition. Cognitive science,
in providing a whole new array of concepts, models, and experimental
techniques, claimed to be able to provide rigorous scientific knowledge of the mind beyond what earlier forms of psychology and philosophy had offered.

In recent years, however, it has become increasingly clear to many
researchers that cognitive science is incomplete. Cognitive science has
focused on cognition while neglecting emotion, affect, and motivation
(LeDoux 2002, p. 24). In addition, a complete science of the mind
needs to account for subjectivity and consciousness.

With hindsight it has also become evident that, in the passage from
traditional philosophy and psychology to modern-day cognitive science, something was lost that only now is beginning to be reclaimed.
What was lost, in a nutshell, was scientific concern with subjective ex-

perience. In 1892 William James quoted with approval George Trumball Ladd's definition of psychology "as the description and explanation of states of consciousness as such" (James 1985, p. xxv; emphasis omitted). Consciousness was supposed to be the subject matter of psychology, yet cognitive science has had virtually nothing to say about it until recent years. To understand this neglect we need to consider the development of cognitive science since the 1950s.

Three major approaches to the study of the mind can be distinguished within cognitive science—cognitivism, connectionism, and embodied dynamicism. Each approach has its preferred theoretical metaphor for understanding the mind. For cognitivism, the metaphor is the mind as digital computer; for connectionism, it is the mind as neural network; for embodied dynamicism, it is the mind as an embodied dynamic system. Cognitivism dominated the field from the 1950s to the 1970s. In the 1980s, connectionism began to challenge the cognitivist orthodoxy, followed in the 1990s by embodied dynamicism. In contemporary research, all three approaches coexist, both separately and in various hybrid forms.[1]

Cognitivism

Cognitive science came into being in the 1950s with the "cognitive revolution" against behaviorist psychology. At the center of this revolution was the computer model of mind, now known as the classical conception of cognitive processes. According to this classical model, cognition is information processing after the fashion of the digital computer. Behaviorism had allowed no reference to internal states of the organism; explanations of behavior had to be formulated in terms of sensory stimuli and behavioral conditioning (on the input side), and overt behavioral response (on the output side). The computer model of the mind not only made reference to internal states legitimate, but also showed it to be necessary in accounting for the behavior of complex information processing systems. Even more important, the computer model was taken to show how content or meaning could be attributed to states inside the system. A computer is supposed to be a symbol-manipulating machine.[2] A symbol is an item that has a physical shape or form, and that stands for or represents something. According to the computer model of the mind, the brain, too, is a computer, a "physical symbol system," and mental processes are carried out by the manipulation of symbolic representations in the brain (Newell and Simon 1976; Pylyshyn 1984). A typical cognitivist model takes the form of a program for solving a problem in some domain. Nonsymbolic sensory inputs are transduced and mapped onto symbolic representations of the task domain. These representations are then manipulated in a purely formal or syntactic fashion in order to arrive at a solution to the problem. Cognitivist explanations focus on the abstract problem-solving characterization of cognitive tasks, the structure and content of symbolic representations, and the nature of the algorithms for manipulating the representations in order to solve a given problem. Cognitivism goes hand in hand with functionalism in the philosophy of mind, which in its extreme computational form holds that the embodiment of the organism is essentially irrelevant to the nature of the mind. It is the software, not the hardware, that matters most for mentality.

Cognitivism made meaning, in the sense of representational semantics, scientifically acceptable, but at the price of banishing consciousness from the science of the mind. (In fact, cognitivism inherited its consciousness taboo directly from behaviorism.) Mental processes, understood to be computations made by the brain using an inner symbolic language, were taken to be entirely nonconscious. Thus the connection between mind and meaning, on the one hand, and subjectivity and consciousness, on the other, was completely severed.

Long before cognitivism, Freud had already undermined any simplistic identification of mind and consciousness. According to his early model, the psyche is composed of three systems, which he called the conscious, the preconscious, and the unconscious (Freud 1915, pp. 159–222). The conscious corresponds to the field of awareness, and the preconscious to what we can recall but are not aware of now. The unconscious, in contrast, Freud considered to be part of our phylogenetic heritage. It is thoroughly somatic and affective, and its contents have been radically separated from consciousness by repression and cannot enter the conscious–preconscious system without distortion. (Later, Freud introduced a new structural model composed of the ego, id, and superego; see Freud 1923, pp. 339–407.)

The cognitivist separation of cognition and consciousness, however, was different from Freud's model. Mental processes, according to cognitivism, are "subpersonal routines," which by nature are completely inaccessible to personal awareness under any conditions. The mind was divided into two radically different regions, with an unbridgeable chasm between them—the subjective mental states of the person and the subpersonal cognitive routines implemented in the brain. The radically nonconscious, subpersonal region, the so-called cognitive unconscious, is where the action of thought really happens; personal awareness has access merely to a few results or epiphenomenal manifestations of subpersonal processing (Jackendoff 1987). Thought corresponds to nonconscious, skull-bound, symbol manipulation. It takes place in a central cognitive module of the brain separate from the systems for perception, emotion, and motor action. The cognitive unconscious is neither somatic nor affective, and it is lodged firmly within the head.

This radical separation of cognitive processes from consciousness created a peculiar "explanatory gap" in scientific theorizing about the mind.[3] Cartesian dualism had long ago created an explanatory gap between mind and matter, consciousness and nature. Cognitivism, far from closing this gap, perpetuated it in a materialist form by opening a new gap between subpersonal, computational cognition and subjective mental phenomena. Simply put, cognitivism offered no account whatsoever of mentality in the sense of subjective experience. Some theorists even went so far as to claim that subjectivity and consciousness do not fall within the province of cognitive science (Pylyshyn 1984). Not all theorists shared this view, however. A notable exception was Ray Jackendoff, who clearly formulated the problem facing cognitivism in his 1987 book *Consciousness and the Computational Mind*. According to Jackendoff, cognitivism, in radically differentiating computational cognition from subjective experience, produced a new "mind-mind" problem, in addition to the classical mind-body problem. The mind-mind problem is the problem of the relation between the computational mind and the phenomenological mind, between subpersonal, computational, cognitive processes and conscious experience (Jackendoff 1987, p. 20). Thanks to cognitivism, a new set of mind-body problems had to be faced:

1. The phenomenological mind-body problem: How can a brain have experiences?

2. The computational mind-body problem: How can a brain accomplish reasoning?
3. The mind-mind problem: What is the relation between computational states and experience?

Each problem is a variant of the explanatory gap. The cognitivist metaphor of the mind as computer, which was meant to solve the computational mind-body problem, thus came at the cost of creating a new problem, the mind-mind problem. This problem is a version of what is now known as the "hard problem of consciousness" (Chalmers 1996; Nagel 1974).

During the heyday of cognitivism in the 1970s and early 1980s, cognitivists liked to proclaim that their view was "the only game in town" (Fodor 1975, 1981), and they insisted that the computer model of the mind is not a metaphor but a scientific theory (Pylyshyn 1984), unlike earlier mechanistic models, such as the brain as a telephone switchboard. The cognitive anthropologist Edwin Hutchins (1995), however, has argued that a confused metaphorical transference from culture to individual psychology lies at the very origin of the cognitivist view. Cognitivism derives from taking what is in fact a sociocultural activity—human computation—and projecting it onto something that goes on inside the individual's head. The cognitive properties of computation do not belong to the individual person but to the sociocultural system of individual-plus-environment.

The original model of a computational system was a person—a mathematician or logician manipulating symbols with hands and eyes, and pen and paper. (The word "computer" originally meant "one who computes.") This kind of physical symbol system is a sophisticated and culturally specific form of human activity. It is embodied, requiring perception and motor action, and embedded in a sociocultural environment of symbolic cognition and technology. It is not bounded by the skull or skin but extends into the environment. The environment, for its part, plays a necessary and active role in the cognitive processes themselves; it is not a mere contingent, external setting (Clark and Chalmers 1998; Wilson 1994). Nevertheless, the human mind is able to idealize and conceptualize computation in the abstract as the mechanical application of formal rules to symbol strings, as Alan Turing did in arriving at his mathematical notion of a Turing Machine. Turing successfully abstracted away from both the world in which the mathematician computes and the psychological processes he or she uses to perform a computation. But what do such abstract formal systems reflect or correspond to in the real world? According to the cognitivist "creation myth," what Turing succeeded in capturing was the bare essentials of intelligent thought or cognition within the individual (all the rest being mere implementation details).

The problem with this myth is that real human computation—the original source domain for conceptualizing computation in the abstract—was never simply an internal psychological process; it was a sociocultural activity as well. Computation, in other words, never reflected simply the cognitive properties of the individual, but instead those of the sociocultural system in which the individual is embedded. Therefore, when one abstracts away from the situated individual what remains is precisely not the bare essentials of individual cognition, but rather the bare essentials of the sociocultural system: "The physical-symbol-system architecture is not a model of individual cognition. It is a model of the operation of a sociocultural system from which the human actor has been removed" (Hutchins 1995, p. 363; emphasis omitted). Whether abstract computation is well suited to model the structure of thought processes within the individual is therefore questionable. Nevertheless, cognitivism, instead of realizing that its computer programs reproduced (or extended) the abstract properties of the sociocultural system, projected the physical-symbol-system model onto the brain. Because cognitivism from its inception abstracted away from culture, society, and embodiment, it remained resistant to this kind of critical analysis and was wedded to a reified metaphor of the mind as a computer in the head.[4]

The connectionist challenge to cognitivism, however, did not take the form of this kind of critique. Rather, connectionist criticism focused on the neurological implausibility of the physical-symbol-system model and various perceived deficiencies of symbol processing compared with neural networks (McLelland, Rummelhart, and the PDP Research Group 1986; Smolensky 1988).

Connectionism

Connectionism arose in the early 1980s, revising and revitalizing ideas from the precognitivist era of cybernetics.[5] Connectionism is now widespread. Its central metaphor of the mind is the neural network. Connectionist models of cognitive processes take the form of artificial neural networks, which are virtual systems run on a digital computer. An artificial neural network is composed of layers of many simple neuron-like units that are linked together by numerically weighted connections. The connection strengths change according to various learning rules and the system's history of activity.

The network is trained to convert numerical (rather than symbolic) input representations into numerical output representations. Given appropriate input and training, the network converges toward some particular cognitive performance, such as producing speech sounds from written text (as in the famous NETtalk system of Sejnowski and Rosenberg 1986), or categorizing words according to their lexical role (Elman 1991). Such cognitive performances correspond to emergent patterns of activity in the network. These patterns are not symbols in the traditional computational sense, although they are supposed to be approximately describable in symbolic terms (Smolensky 1988). Connectionist explanations focus on the architecture of the neural network (units, layers, and connections), the learning rules, and the distributed subsymbolic representations that emerge from the network's activity. According to connectionism, artificial neural networks capture the abstract cognitive properties of neural networks in the brain and provide a better model of the cognitive architecture of the mind than the physical symbol systems of cognitivism.

The connectionist movement of the 1980s emphasized perceptual pattern recognition as the paradigm of intelligence, in contrast to deductive reasoning, emphasized by cognitivism. Whereas cognitivism firmly lodged the mind within the head, connectionism offered a more dynamic conception of the relation between cognitive processes and the environment. For example, connectionists hypothesized that the structural properties of sequential reasoning and linguistic cognition arise not from manipulations of symbols in the brain, but from the dynamic interaction of neural networks with symbolic resources in the external environment, such as diagrams, numerical symbols, and natural language (Rummelhart et al. 1986).

Despite these advances, connectionist systems did not involve any sensory and motor coupling with the environment, but instead operated on the basis of artificial inputs and outputs (set initially by the designer of the system). Connectionism also inherited from cognitivism the idea that cognition is basically the solving of predefined problems (posed to the system from outside by the observer or designer) and that the mind is essentially the skull-bound cognitive unconscious, the subpersonal domain of computational representation in the mind-brain. Connectionism's disagreement with cognitivism was over the nature of computation and representation (symbolic for cognitivists, subsymbolic for connectionists).

With regard to the problem of the explanatory gap, connectionism enlarged the scope of the computational mind but provided little, if any, new resources for addressing the gap between the computational mind and the phenomenological mind. Subjectivity still had no place in the sciences of mind, and the explanatory gap remained unaddressed.

Embodied Dynamicism

The third approach, embodied dynamicism, arose in the 1990s and involved a critical stance toward computationalism in either its cognitivist or connectionist form.[6] Cognitivism and connectionism left unquestioned the relation between cognitive processes and the real world. As a result, their models of cognition were disembodied and abstract. On the one hand, cognitive processes were said to be instantiated (or realized or implemented) in the brain, with little thought given to what such a notion could mean, given the biological facts of the brain and its relationship to the living body of the organism and to the environment. On the other hand, the relationship between the mind and the world was assumed to be one of abstract representation: symbolic or subsymbolic representations in the mind-brain stand for states of affairs in some restricted outside domain that has been specified in advance and independently of the cognitive system. The mind and the world were thus treated as separate and independent of each other, with the outside world mirrored by a representational model inside the head. Embodied dynamicism called into question all of these assumptions, in particular the conception of cognition as disembodied and abstract mental representation. Like connectionism, embodied dynamicism focuses on self-organizing dynamic systems rather than physical symbol systems (connectionist networks are examples of self-organizing dynamic systems), but maintains in addition that cognitive processes emerge from the nonlinear and circular causality of continuous sensorimotor interactions involving the brain, body, and environment. The central metaphor for this approach is the mind as embodied dynamic system in the world, rather than the mind as neural network in the head.

As its name suggests, embodied dynamicism combines two main theoretical commitments. One commitment is to a dynamic systems approach to cognition, and the other is to an embodied approach to cognition.

The central idea of the dynamic systems approach is that cognition is an intrinsically temporal phenomenon and accordingly needs to be understood from the perspective of dynamic systems theory (Port and van Gelder 1995; van Gelder 1998). A dynamic systems model takes the form of a set of evolution equations that describe how the state of the system changes over time. The collection of all possible states of the system corresponds to the system's "state space" or "phase space," and the ways that the system changes state correspond to trajectories in this space. Dynamic-system explanations focus on the internal and external forces that shape such trajectories as they unfold in time. Inputs are described as perturbations to the system's intrinsic dynamics, rather than as instructions to be followed, and internal states are described as self-organized compensations triggered by perturbations, rather than as representations of external states of affairs.

The central idea of the embodied approach is that cognition is the exercise of skillful know-how in situated and embodied action (Varela, Thompson, and Rosch 1991). Cognitive structures and processes emerge from recurrent sensorimotor patterns that govern perception and action in autonomous and situated agents. Cognition as skillful know-how is not reducible to prespecified problem solving, because the cognitive system both poses the problems and specifies what actions need to be taken for their solution.

Strictly speaking, dynamicism and embodiment are logically independent theoretical commitments. For example, dynamical connectionism incorporates dynamicist ideas into artificial neural networks (see Port and van Gelder 1995, pp. 32–34), whereas autonomous agents research in robotics incorporates embodiment ideas without employing dynamic systems theory (Maes 1990). Nevertheless, dynamicism and embodiment go well together and are intimately related for many theorists. As Randall Beer notes: "Although a dynamical approach can certainly stand alone, it is most powerful and distinctive when coupled with a situated, embodied perspective on cognition" (Beer 2000, p. 97).

Embodied dynamicism provides a different perspective on the cognitive unconscious from computationalism. No longer is the cognitive unconscious seen as disembodied symbol manipulation or pattern recognition separate from emotion and motor action in the world. Instead, the cognitive unconscious consists of those processes of embodied and embedded cognition and emotion that cannot be made experientially accessible to the person. This characterization of the cognitive unconscious is offered not as a hypothetical construct in an abstract functionalist model of the mind, but rather as a provisional indication of a large problem-space in our attempt to understand human cognition.

At least four points need emphasizing in this context. First, as a conceptual matter, the relations among what is nonconscious, unconscious, preconscious, and conscious (in any of the innumerable senses of these words)—or in a different, but not equivalent idiom, what is subpersonal and personal—remain far from clear. Second, as an empirical matter, the scope and limits of awareness of one's own psychological and somatic processes have yet to be clearly mapped and undoubtedly vary across subjects. Third, the key point still stands that most of what we are as psychological and biological beings is in some sense unconscious. It follows that subjectivity cannot be understood without situating it in relation to these unconscious structures and processes. Finally, these unconscious structures and processes, including those describable as cognitive and emotional, extend throughout the body and loop through the material, social, and cultural environments in which the body is embedded; they are not limited to neural processes inside the skull.

The emergence of embodied dynamicism in the 1990s coincided with a revival of scientific and philosophical interest in consciousness, together with a renewed willingness to address the explanatory gap between scientific accounts of cognitive processes and human subjectivity and experience. A number of works on embodied cognition were explicitly concerned with experience and challenged the objectivist assumptions of computationalism.[7] Some of these works were also explicitly dynamical in orientation.[8] In particular, the enactive approach of Varela, Thompson, and Rosch (1991) aimed to build bridges between embodied dynamicist accounts of the mind and phenomenological accounts of human subjectivity and experience. The present book continues this project.

The Enactive Approach

Enaction means the action of enacting a law, but it also connotes the performance or carrying out of an action more generally. Borrowing the words of the poet Antonio Machado, Varela described enaction as the laying down of a path in walking: "Wanderer the road is your footsteps, nothing else; you lay down a path in walking" (Varela 1987, p. 63).

The term *the enactive approach* and the associated concept of enaction were introduced into cognitive science by Varela, Thompson, and Rosch (1991) in their book *The Embodied Mind.* They aimed to unify under one heading several related ideas. The first idea is that living beings are autonomous agents that actively generate and maintain themselves, and thereby also enact or bring forth their own cognitive domains. The second idea is that the nervous system is an autonomous dynamic system: It actively generates and maintains its own coherent and meaningful patterns of activity, according to its operation as a circular and reentrant network of interacting neurons. The nervous system does not process information in the computationalist sense, but creates meaning. The third idea is that cognition is the exercise of skillful know-how in situated and embodied action. Cognitive structures and processes emerge from recurrent sensorimotor patterns of perception and action. Sensorimotor coupling between organism and environment modulates, but does not determine, the formation of endogenous, dynamic patterns of neural activity, which in turn inform sensorimotor coupling. The fourth idea is that a cognitive being's world is not a prespecified, external realm, represented internally by its brain, but a relational domain enacted or brought forth by that being's autonomous agency and mode of coupling with the environment. The fifth idea is that experience is not an epiphenomenal side issue, but central to any understanding of the mind, and needs to be investigated in a careful phenomenological manner. For this reason, the enactive approach maintains that mind science and phenomenological investigations of human experience need to be pursued in a complementary and mutually informing way.[9]

The conviction motivating the present book is that the enactive approach offers important resources for making progress on the explanatory gap. One key point is that the enactive approach explicates selfhood and subjectivity from the ground up by accounting for the autonomy proper to living and cognitive beings. The burden of this book is to show that this approach to subjectivity is a fruitful one.

To make headway on this project, we need to draw from biology, neuroscience, psychology, philosophy, and phenomenology. In this book, I try to integrate investigations from all these fields.

One common thread running through the following chapters is a reliance on the philosophical tradition of phenomenology, inaugurated by Edmund Husserl and developed in various directions by numerous others, most notably for my purposes by Maurice Merleau-Ponty (Moran 2000; Sokolowski 2000; Spiegelberg 1994).[10] My aim, however, is not to repeat this tradition's analyses, as they are found in this or that author or text, but to present them anew in light of present-day concerns in the sciences of mind. Thus this book can be seen as contributing to the work of a new generation of phenomenologists who strive to "naturalize" phenomenology (Petitot et al. 1999). The project of naturalizing phenomenology can be understood in different ways, and my own way of thinking about it will emerge later in this book. The basic idea for the moment is that it is not enough for phenomenology simply to describe and philosophically analyze lived experience; phenomenology needs to be able to understand and interpret its investigations in relation to those of biology and mind science.

Yet mind science has much to learn from the analyses of lived experience accomplished by phenomenologists. Indeed, once science turns its attention to subjectivity and consciousness, to experience as it is lived, then it cannot do without phenomenology, which thus needs to be recognized and cultivated as an indispensable partner to the experimental sciences of mind and life. As we will see, this scientific turn to phenomenology leads as much to a renewed understanding of nature, life, and mind as to a naturalization of phenomenology (Zahavi 2004b).

There is also a deeper convergence of the enactive approach and phenomenology that is worth summarizing briefly here. Both share a view of the mind as having to constitute its objects. Here constitution does not mean fabrication or creation; the mind does not fabricate the world. "To constitute," in the technical phenomenological sense, means to bring to awareness, to present, or to disclose. The mind brings things to awareness; it discloses and presents the world. Stated in a classical phenomenological way, the idea is that objects are disclosed or made available to experience in the ways they are thanks to the intentional activities of consciousness. Things show up, as it were, having the features they do, because of how they are disclosed and brought to awareness by the intentional activities of our minds. Such constitution is not apparent to us in everyday life but requires systematic analysis to disclose. Consider our experience of time (discussed in Chapter 11). Our sense of the present moment as both simultaneously opening into the immediate future and slipping away into the immediate past depends on the formal structure of our consciousness of time. The present moment manifests as a zone or span of actuality, instead of as an instantaneous flash, thanks to the way our consciousness is structured. As we will see later, the present moment also manifests this way because of the nonlinear dynamics of brain activity. Weaving together these two types of analysis, the phenomenological and neurobiological, in order to bridge the gap between subjective experience and biology, defines the aim of neurophenomenology (Varela 1996), an offshoot of the enactive approach.

The enactive approach and phenomenology also meet on the common ground of life or living being. For the enactive approach, autonomy is a fundamental characteristic of biological life, and there is a deep continuity of life and mind. For phenomenology, intentionality is a fundamental characteristic of the lived body. The enactive approach and phenomenology thus converge on the proposition that subjectivity and consciousness have to be explicated in relation to the autonomy and intentionality of life, in a full sense of "life" that encompasses, as we will see, the organism, one's subjectively lived body, and the life-world.

It will take some work before these ideas can stand clearly before us in this book. In the next chapter I introduce phenomenological philosophy in more detail, before returning to the enactive approach in Chapter 3.

TWO

The Phenomenological Connection

THIS CHAPTER INTRODUCES a number of themes from phenomenological philosophy that will appear throughout this book. Phenomenology is important here for two main reasons. First, any attempt to
gain a comprehensive understanding of the human mind must at
some point consider consciousness and subjectivity—how thinking,
perceiving, acting, and feeling are experienced in one's own case.
Mental events do not occur in a vacuum; they are lived by someone.
Phenomenology is anchored to the careful description, analysis, and
interpretation of lived experience. Second, the enactive approach
puts the organism and the body center-stage in mind science, but the
human body, unless it is dead, is always the *lived body*. Phenomenology, in one of its strongest currents flowing from Husserl and
Merleau-Ponty, is a philosophy of the lived body. For these reasons,
phenomenology can guide and clarify scientific research on subjectivity and consciousness, and provide a philosophical framework for
assessing the meaning and significance of this research for our self-
understanding.

This chapter has two purposes. First, it introduces some core ideas
of Husserl's phenomenology, in particular the phenomenological
method of investigating the structure of experience, known as the phenomenological reduction, and the phenomenological concept of intentionality. Second, it sketches three phases of phenomenology,
known as static, genetic, and generative phenomenology.

Static phenomenology analyzes the formal structures of consciousness, whereby consciousness is able to constitute (disclose or bring to awareness) its objects. Static phenomenology takes these intentional structures and their correlative objects as given and analyzes them statically or synchronically.

Genetic phenomenology is concerned with how these intentional structures and objects emerge through time; therefore, it cannot take them as given. Instead, it analyzes how certain types of experience motivate later and more complex types—for example, how implicit and prereflective experiences motivate attentive and reflective experiences. From the perspective of genetic phenomenology, experience has a sedimented structure, and the process of sedimentation needs to be understood in relation to the lived body and time-consciousness. Some of the key guiding phenomena for genetic phenomenology—affect, motivation, attention, habit—are familiar from the perspective of mind science, especially developmental psychology, emotion theory, and affective-cognitive neuroscience. These points of convergence and mutual illumination will be taken up in later chapters.

Whereas time-consciousness and the lived body are the guiding threads for genetic phenomenology, for generative phenomenology the guiding thread is the life-world. The subject matter of generative phenomenology is the cultural, historical, and intersubjective constitution of our human world. The importance of generative phenomenology for mind science and the enactive approach in particular will be taken up in the last chapter of this book.

Phenomenology with an Attitude

Phenomenology, in its original Husserlian inspiration, grows out of the recognition that we can adopt in our own first-person case different mental attitudes or stances toward the world, life, and experience. In everyday life we are usually straightforwardly immersed in various situations and projects, whether as specialists in scientific, technical, or practical knowledge or as colleagues, friends, and members of families and communities. Besides being directed toward these more-or-less particular, "thematic" matters, we are also directed at the world as an unthematic horizon of all our activity (Husserl 1970, p. 281). Husserl calls this attitude of being straightforwardly immersed in the world "the natural attitude," and he thinks it is characterized by a kind of unreflective "positing" of the world as something existing "out there" more or less independently of us.

In contrast, the "phenomenological attitude," arises when we step back from the natural attitude, not to deny it, but in order to investigate the very experiences it comprises. If such an investigation is to be genuinely philosophical, then it must strive to be critical and not dogmatic, and therefore it cannot take the naïve realism of the natural attitude for granted. Yet to deny this realistic attitude would be equally dogmatic. Rather, the realistic positing of the natural attitude must be suspended, neutralized, or put to one side, so that it plays no role in the investigation. In this way, we can focus on the experiences that sustain and animate the natural attitude, but in an open and nondogmatic manner. We can investigate experience in the natural attitude without being prejudiced by an unexamined view of things, which is characteristic of the natural attitude.

Yet how exactly is such an investigation to proceed? What exactly are we supposed to investigate? Husserl's answer is that our attention should be directed toward the world strictly as we experience it. We are to attend to the world strictly as it appears and as it is phenomenally manifest. Put another way, we should attend to the modes or ways in which things appear to us. We thereby attend to things strictly as correlates of our experience, and the focus of our investigation becomes the correlational structure of our subjectivity and the appearance or disclosure of the world.

The philosophical procedure by which this correlational structure is investigated is known as the *phenomenological reduction*. "Reduction" in this context does not mean replacing or eliminating one theory or model in favor of another taken to be more fundamental. It signifies rather a "leading back" *(reducere)* or redirection of thought away from its unreflective and unexamined immersion in the world to the way in which the world appears to us. To redirect our interest in this way does not mean we doubt the things before us or that we somehow try to turn away from the world to look elsewhere. Things remain before us, but we envisage them in a new way, namely, strictly as experienced. Thus, everyday things available for our perception are not doubted or considered as illusions when they are "phenomenologically reduced," but instead are envisaged and examined simply and precisely *as perceived*. Remembered things are examined strictly and precisely *as remembered*, imagined things *as imagined*. In other words, once we adopt the phenomenological attitude, we are interested not in *what* things are in some naïve, mind-independent or theory-independent sense, but rather in exactly *how* they are experienced, and thus as strict relational correlates of our subjectivity.[1]

As a procedure of working back from the what to the how of experience, the phenomenological reduction has to be performed in the first person. As is true of any such procedure, it is one thing to describe its general theoretical character and another to describe it pragmatically, the concrete steps by which it is carried out. The main methodical step crucial for the phenomenological reduction Husserl called the *epoché*. This term derives from Greek skepticism, where it means to suspend or refrain from judgment, but Husserl adopted it as a term for the "suspension," "neutralization," or "bracketing" of both our natural "positing" attitude and our theoretical beliefs and assertions (whether scientific or philosophical) about "objective reality." From a more embodied and situated, first-person perspective, however, the epoché can be described as the flexible and trainable mental skill of being able both to suspend one's inattentive immersion in experience and to turn one's attention to the manner in which something appears or is given to experience (Depraz 1999b; Depraz, Varela, and Vermersch 2000; Steinbock 2004). Suspending one's inattentive immersion in experience implies the capacity to notice such immersion, and thus implies what psychologists call meta-awareness (awareness of awareness). Being able to redirect one's attention to the manner in which something appears implies flexibility of attention; in particular it implies being able voluntarily to shift one's attention and stabilize or sustain it on a given mode of presentation. The ultimate aim is not to break the flow of experience, but to reinhabit it in a fresh way, namely, with heightened awareness and attunement.[2]

Within the phenomenological tradition one can discern a certain ambivalence regarding these theoretical and practical or existential dimensions of the epoché. On the one hand, Husserl's great concern was to establish phenomenology as a new philosophical foundation for science; thus for him the epoché served largely as a critical tool of theoretical reason.[3] On the other hand, because Husserl's theoretical project was based on a radical reappraisal of experience as the source of meaning and knowledge, it necessitated a constant return to the patient, analytic description of lived experience through phenomenological reduction. This impulse generated a huge corpus of careful phenomenological analyses of human experience—the perceptual experience of space (Husserl 1997), kinesthesis and the experience of one's own body (Husserl 1989, 1997), time-consciousness (Husserl 1991), affect (Husserl 2001), judgment (Husserl 1975), imagination and memory (Husserl 2006), and intersubjectivity (Husserl 1973), to name just a few.

Nevertheless, the epoché as a practical procedure—as a situated practice carried out in the first person by the phenomenologist—has remained strangely neglected in the phenomenological literature, even by so-called existential phenomenologists such as Heidegger and Merleau-Ponty. They instead took up and then recast in their own ways the method of the phenomenological reduction (see Heidegger 1982, pp. 19–23; Merleau-Ponty 1962, pp. xi–xiv). For this reason, one new current in phenomenology aims to develop more explicitly the pragmatics of the epoché as a first-person method for investigating consciousness (Depraz 1999b; Depraz, Varela, and Vermersch, 2000, 2003; Varela and Shear 1999b). This pragmatic approach also involves comparing the epoché to first-person methods in other domains, especially Buddhist philosophy and contemplative mental training (Depraz, Varela, and Vermersch, 2003; Lutz, Dunne, and Davidson, 2007). In addition, it explores the relevance of first-person methods for producing more refined first-person reports in experimental psychology and cognitive neuroscience (Lutz and Thompson 2003). This endeavor is central to the research program known as neurophenomenology, introduced by Francisco Varela (1996) and discussed extensively later in this book.

Let us return to the phenomenological reduction in its original philosophical context. Here the reduction, in its full sense, is a rich mode of analysis, comprising two main steps. The first step leads back from the natural attitude to the phenomenological attitude by neutralizing the realistic positing of the natural attitude and then orienting attention toward the disclosure or appearance of reality to us (this step corresponds to the epoché). The second step leads from this phenomenological attitude to a more radical kind of philosophical attitude. More precisely, this step leads from phenomenology as an empirical and psychological attitude (phenomenological psychology) to phenomenology as a transcendental philosophical attitude (transcendental phenomenology).

The term *transcendental* is used here in its Kantian sense to mean an investigation concerned with the modes or ways in which objects are experienced and known, and with the *a priori* conditions for the possibility of such experience and knowledge. Husserl casts these two aspects of transcendental inquiry in a specific form that is clearly related to but nonetheless different from Kant's (see Steinbock 1995, pp. 12–15). First, transcendental phenomenology focuses not on *what things are* but on the *ways in which things are given*. For Husserl, this means focusing on phenomena (appearances) and the senses or meanings they have for us, and then asking how these meaningful phenomena are constituted (brought to awareness). Second, to address this constitutional problem, transcendental phenomenology tries to uncover the essential formal laws under which experience necessarily operates in order to constitute a meaningful world.

In the natural attitude, reality is taken for granted as being simply there without any active engagement on the part of consciousness. In other words, there is no thought that reality involves acts or processes of constitution. Grasped phenomenologically, in the transcendental phenomenological attitude, reality is that which is disclosed to us as real, whether in everyday perception or scientific investigation, and such disclosure is an achievement of consciousness. The point here is not that the world would not exist if not for consciousness. Rather, it is that we have no grip on what reality means apart from what is disclosed to us as real, and such disclosure necessarily involves the intentional activity of consciousness. The point of the transcendental phenomenological reduction is to gain access to this activity and the constitutional role it plays.

It is often said that whereas Husserl's orientation is transcendental in this way, Heidegger and Merleau-Ponty reject the transcendental standpoint and identify the constitutional structures unearthed by phenomenology with existential structures of "being-in-the-world." (The hyphens indicate that "being," "in," and "world" are not ontologically separable, but form one irreducible and unified structure.) But this interpretation is simplistic. First, both Heidegger's "Dasein" (his term for individual human existence) and Merleau-Ponty's "lived body" (a concept that comes straight from Husserl) are transcendental in the relevant sense, for they are ways of characterizing that which makes possible the disclosure or manifestation of the world as meaningful.

Second, although Husserl in the most well-known portions of his work (the writings published in his lifetime) did focus largely on the constitutional structures of "egological" consciousness (consciousness at the level of the individual reflective "I" or "ego"), recent scholarship indicates that these analyses are not fully representative of his mature philosophical investigations.[4] As his thought developed, he greatly expanded his investigations, analyzing constitutional structures belonging to the "nonegological" (or "pre-egological") depths of the lived body, time-consciousness, and intersubjectivity, as well as the terrain of historical and cultural life.[5] The point here is more than an interpretive or textual one; it is philosophical. Transcendental phenomenology cannot be limited to—and indeed goes far beyond—a philosophy of "egological" consciousness or subjectivity. "Transcendental" signifies a radical attitude, one that aims to regress back to the very roots (conditions of possibility) of our experience of a meaningful world. These roots ramify far beyond individual consciousness into the depths of our lived bodies and out into our social and cultural worlds.

The remainder of this chapter sketches a few of these developments of phenomenological thought. My aim is not to give a detailed scholarly account of any particular aspect of phenomenology, but to set forth some themes and ideas important for the chapters to come.

Intentionality

A good place to begin is the phenomenological doctrine of the intentionality of consciousness. According to phenomenology, consciousness is intentional, in the sense that it "aims toward" or "intends" something beyond itself. This sense of intentional should not be confused with the more familiar sense of having a purpose in mind when one acts, which is only one kind of intentionality in the phenomenological sense. Rather, *intentionality* is a generic term for the pointing-beyond-itself proper to consciousness. (It comes from the Latin *intendere*, which once referred to drawing a bow and aiming at a target.)

Phenomenologists distinguish different types of intentionality. In a narrow sense, they define intentionality as object-directedness. In a broader sense, they define it as openness to the world or what is "other" ("alterity"). In either case, the emphasis is on denying that consciousness is self-enclosed.[6]

Object-directed experiences are those in which we are conscious *of* something in a more-or-less determinate sense. When we see, we see something; when we remember, we remember something; when we hope or fear, we hope for or fear something. These kinds of "transitive consciousness" are characterized by the intending of an object (which need not exist). "Object" in its etymological sense means something that stands before us. Something standing before us lies beyond, over against, or outside of us. Object-directed experiences can thus be understood as experiences in which we are conscious of something distinct from ourselves as a present subject, whether it be a past event remembered, something perceived in the settings around us, a future event feared or hoped for, something imagined, and so on.

Many kinds of everyday experience, however, are not object-directed in this sense. Such experiences include bodily feelings of pain, moods such as undirected anxiety, depression, and elation, and absorbed skillful activity in everyday life. These experiences are not or need not be "about" any intentional object. They are not directed toward a transcendent object, in the sense of something experienced as standing over against oneself as a distinct subject. Put another way, they do not have a clear subject-object structure.[7]

Philosophers who think of intentionality simply as object-directedness would deny that experiences like these are intentional. Nevertheless, such experiences do qualify as intentional in the broader phenomenological sense of being open to what is other or having a world-involving character. Thus bodily feelings are not self-enclosed without openness to the world. On the contrary, they present things in a certain affective light or atmosphere and thereby deeply influence how we perceive and respond to things. A classic example is Sartre's discussion of feeling eyestrain and fatigue as a result of reading late into the night (1956, pp. 332–333).[8] The feeling first manifests itself not as an intentional object of transitive consciousness but as a trembling of the eyes and a blurriness of the words on the page. One's body and immediate environment disclose themselves in a certain manner through this feeling. In the case of moods, although they are not object-directed in the same way intentional emotions are—such as a feeling of sympathy for a loved one or a feeling of envy for a rival—they are nonetheless hardly self-enclosed without reference to the world. On the contrary, as Heidegger analyzes at length in *Being and Time*, moods reveal our embeddedness in the world and (as he sees it) make possible more circumscribed forms of directedness in everyday life. Finally, in absorbed skillful activities, such as driving, dancing, or writing, one's experience is not that of relating to a distinct intentional object but of being engaged and immersed in a fluid activity. Such experience takes on a subject-object structure only during moments of breakdown or disruption (see Dreyfus 1991, 2002; Dreyfus and Dreyfus 1986).

In phenomenology, intentional experiences are described as mental *acts*—acts of perceiving, remembering, imagining, empathizing, and so on. Phenomenology conceives of mental life as a temporally extended and dynamic process of flowing intentional acts. These acts are animated by precognitive habits and sensibilities of the lived body. Intentional acts are performances of a person, a living bodily subject of experience, whose cognitive and affective life is constituted by communal norms, conventions, and historical traditions. Mental life is animated by an intentional striving that aims toward and finds satisfaction in disclosure of the intentional object. In this way, intentionality is teleological (Held 2003, p. 14).

Given this conception of intentionality, it follows that neither the mental act nor that which it intends can be understood in isolation. Every mental act is the very act it is in virtue of that which it intends, and every object is constituted in and through the temporally extended course of intentional experience. As Donn Welton explains:

> There is a genuinely new conception of mental acts here in play . . . On the one hand, acts do not belong to a closed interior realm available only to introspection. Rather, they have their being by virtue of their relationship to that which transcends them. On the other hand, the determinations of "the given" can be fully clarified only by seeing them in relation to certain acts that contribute to their configuration. It is neither the subject nor the object but the relationship that is primary. (Welton 2000, p. 17)

Phenomenologists call this relation the correlational structure of intentionality. "Correlational" does not mean the constant conjunction of two terms that could be imagined to exist apart; rather, it refers to the invariant structure of intentional act/intentional object. Object-directed intentional experiences necessarily comprise these two inseparable poles. In Husserlian phenomenological language, these two poles are known as the "noema" (the object in its givenness) and the "noesis" (the mental act that intends and discloses the object in a certain manner).[9]

We need to keep this framework in mind when we think about the relation between the phenomenological conception of intentionality and what philosophers of mind today call *mental representation*. In a broad and theoretically neutral sense, a mental representation is supposed to be a mental structure (concept, thought, image) with semantic properties (content, truth conditions, reference), or a state or process involving such a structure. Usually, a mental representation is not considered to be an object of cognition or awareness, but rather that by which one cognizes or is aware of something in the world. Many phenomenologists would agree that intentional experience is representational in this broad sense of having descriptive content— that in intentional experience the world is represented in some particular way or other. Nevertheless, the phenomenological conception of intentional experience has certain other distinctive features. First, in phenomenology, as mentioned earlier, intentional experiences are conceptualized not as *states having content* but as *acts having directedness*. These two conceptions are not necessarily incompatible, but their theoretical orientation and emphasis are different. Second, "re-presentation," in its technical phenomenological sense, applies only to certain types of intentional acts, namely, those that mentally evoke or bring to presence something that is not present in its bodily being.

Phenomenologists thus draw a crucial distinction between intentional acts of *presentation (Gegenwärtigung)* and of *re-presentation (Vergegenwärtigung)* (see Marbach 1993). On the one hand, perceptual experience is presentational: in this type of experience the object is given as present in its very being. In memory or imagination, on the other hand, the object imagined or remembered is not given as present in its very being, but rather as both phenomenally absent and as mentally evoked or called forth. In this way, memory and imagination are said to be re-presentational. Note that the definitive feature of re-presentational experience is that the object is given as absent and as mentally evoked, but not necessarily as *re*-evoked or called forth *again*. Re-evoking belongs to memory but not necessarily to visualizing or fantasizing. Note also that re-presentational experiences do not float freely, as it were, but arise in relation to ongoing presen-

tational experiences of one's surroundings. I discuss this phenomenological conception of mental re-presentation in connection with
mental imagery in Chapter 10.

Let us return to the connection between phenomenology and the
enactive approach. As we will see in Chapter 3, the main explanatory
tool of the enactive approach is the theory of self-organizing and autonomous dynamic systems. Such systems bring forth or enact
meaning in continuous reciprocal interaction with their environments. "Inner" and "outer" are not preexisting separate spheres, but
mutually specifying domains enacted or brought forth by the structural coupling of the system and its environment. This subpersonal account of cognitive systems echoes the personal-level account of the
correlational structure of intentionality.[10] As Jean-Pierre Dupuy writes
in his philosophical history of cognitive science, discussing the "missed
encounter" between phenomenology and mind science in the cybernetic era:

> A given [autonomous] network usually possesses a multiplicity of self-
> behaviors (or, as they are sometimes called, "attractors" . . .) and con-
> verges toward one or another of them depending on the initial condi-
> tions of the network. The "life" of a network can thus be conceived as a
> trajectory through a "landscape" of attractors, passing from one to an-
> other as a result of perturbations or shocks from the external world.
> Note that these external events come to acquire meaning in the context
> of the network as a result of the network's own activity: the *content*—the
> meaning—that the network attributes to them is precisely the self-
> behavior, or attractor that results from them. Obviously, then, this con-
> tent is purely endogenous and not the reflection of some external
> "transcendent" objectivity.
>
> It should be obvious, too, that this line of argument . . . provides us
> with at least the germ of a very satisfactory model of what Brentano
> called "immanent objectivity" . . . The attractor is an entity that both
> fully participates in the activity of the network and yet in some sense, by
> virtue of the fact that it results from a higher level of logical complexity,
> transcends the activity of the network. The dynamics of the network
> may therefore be said to *tend toward* an attractor, although the latter is
> only a product of these dynamics. The network is thus an *intentional*
> creature in Brentano and Husserl's sense. Systems theory was to coin

another term to describe this paradoxical relationship between the dynamics of a system and its attractor, referring to it as "autotranscendence." This is not very different, really, from Husserl's notion of "transcendence within immanence." (Dupuy 2000, pp. 104–105)

Because this notion of transcendence-within-immanence is often misunderstood, it bears clarification here. It does not mean that what appears to be beyond or outside the sphere of mental activity is really contained within the mind (in some idealist or internalist sense). Rather, the crucial point is that the transcendent is given as such by virtue of the intentional activities of consciousness. Thus it falls within the sphere of what is phenomenologically constituted (disclosed or brought to awareness by consciousness). Clearly, this point makes sense only at a transcendental level, for at this level the transcendent is understood as a *mode of givenness* or disclosure (one characterizing things in the world, but not one's own consciousness). Thus, at a transcendental level, what is *really or genuinely transcendent* is also *phenomenologically immanent* (see Crowell, in press, for further discussion).

The correspondence between phenomenology and dynamic systems theory to which Dupuy is pointing should therefore be understood as follows. External events are *really transcendent,* for they are certainly not contained within the system, nor are they a mere product of what goes inside the system. Nevertheless, they are *intentionally immanent,* in the following sense: they do not arrive already labeled, as it were, as external events; instead they are constituted or disclosed as such, and with the significance they have, by virtue of the network's autonomous (self-organizing) dynamics. In other words, their status as external events for the system (as opposed to their status for an observer of the system) is a function of the system's own activity. Their meaning or significance corresponds to an attractor of the system's dynamics (a recurrent pattern of activity toward which the system tends), which itself is an emergent product of that very dynamics. The external world is constituted as such for the system by virtue of the system's self-organizing activity. Dupuy's proposal, in a nutshell, is that *constitutional intentionality corresponds to a kind of self-organization.* This proposal, as we will see in later chapters, is one of the key guiding intuitions of the enactive approach and neurophenomenology.

From Static to Genetic Phenomenology

This convergence between phenomenology and the enactive approach can be taken further. The correlational structure of intentionality belongs to what Husserl called static phenomenology. As his thought progressed, however, Husserl found that he needed to articulate a *genetic phenomenology,* that is, a phenomenology whose point of departure is not the explicit correlational structure of intentional act (noesis) and intentional object (noema), but rather the genesis of intentional experience in time. From the standpoint of genetic phenomenology, we need to account for the correlational structure of intentionality developmentally by understanding how it emerges from inarticulate experience that does not have a clear subject-object structure. One wellspring of this kind of experience is the lived body *(Leib);* another is time-consciousness. The shift from static to genetic phenomenology thus marks a turn toward the lived body and time-consciousness. Thus it enables us to deepen the connection between phenomenology and the enactive approach.

Static phenomenology makes use of two methodological strategies (Steinbock 1995, pp. 38–39). The first is static analysis or the analysis of invariant formal structures of experience, such as the correlational structure of intentionality, or the difference between presentational and re-presentational mental acts and the ways the latter presuppose the former. The second strategy is constitutional analysis—the analysis of how things are disclosed or brought to awareness by virtue of the intentional activities of consciousness. From a transcendental perspective, the invariant formal structures of experience uncovered by static analysis are precisely the essential formal laws under which experience necessarily operates in order to constitute its objects. An example is Husserl's investigation in his 1907 lectures, "Thing and Space," of the conditions of possibility for the perceptual experience of things in space (Husserl 1997). Husserl shows that visual perception depends constitutively on certain invariant functional interdependencies between visual sensation and the experience of moving one's body (which he calls kinesthesis). These analyses anticipate recent enactive or dynamic sensorimotor accounts of perception (discussed in Chapter 9). According to these accounts, to perceive is to exercise one's skillful mastery of the ways sensory stimulation varies as a result of bodily movement (Noë 2004; O'Regan and Noë 2001a).

Unlike static phenomenology, genetic phenomenology does not take the already disclosed intentional object as its point of departure, nor is it content to stay at the level of analyzing formal and constitutive structures of experience. Instead, it investigates the genesis and development of those structures themselves. After all, we do not simply drop into the world and open our eyes and see. What we see is a function of how we see, and how we see is a function of previous experience. For genetic phenomenology, what we experience is not a fixed given but something that has come to be given—something *emergent*—out of previous experience (Bernet, Kern, and Marbach 1993, pp. 200–201). In Chapters 11 and 12, I discuss phenomenological analyses of time-consciousness and affect produced from this genetic orientation and relate them to research in psychology and neuroscience.

Genetic phenomenology also brings with it a different way of thinking about the conscious subject. From a static viewpoint, the "I" is thought of as a kind of "ego-pole" of the noetic-noematic structure, in contraposition to the "object-pole."[11] A fuller articulation of the correlational structure of intentionality would thus be [ego] noesis-noema (I intend the intentional object). From a genetic standpoint, however, this way of thinking remains abstract because it ignores the temporal development and individuation of the subject. The "I" or "ego" is not a mere "empty pole" of selfhood in experience but a concrete subject having habits, interests, convictions, and capabilities as a result of accumulated experience. In other words, the subject has to be seen as having a "life" in all the rich senses of this word—as formed by its individual history, as a living bodily subject of experience *(Leib)*, and as belonging to an intersubjective "life-world" *(Lebenswelt)*.

Genetic phenomenology distinguishes between active genesis and passive genesis. In active genesis subjects play an active and deliberate, productive role in the constitution of objects. The products of active genesis are tools, artworks, scientific theories, experimental interventions, logical judgments, mathematical propositions, and so on. Active genesis, however, always presupposes a passivity by which one is *affected* beforehand. It must be stressed that "passive" in this context does not mean a state of inactivity, but rather a state of being involuntarily influenced and affected by something. In particular, it means being influenced and affected on an aesthetic level, in the original Greek sense of *aisthesis* as sense perception, including especially the perception and felt experience of what is attractive and unattractive. Thus the thought behind the active / passive distinction is that our active orientation toward things in practical or theoretical reason, or artistic creation, presupposes a deeper and more fundamental openness to the world. It is an openness to being sensuously affected and solicited by the world through the medium of our living body, and responding by attraction and repulsion. Investigating these sensorimotor and affective depths of experience leads phenomenology to the notion of passive genesis. In passive genesis, the lived body constitutes itself and its surrounding environment through the involuntary formation of habits, motor patterns, associations, dispositions, motivations, emotions, and memories.

At this level of "passive synthesis" in experience, the relevant notion of intentionality is not so much object-directedness as openness to the world, here in the bodily form of an implicit sensibility or sentience that does not have any clear subject-object structure. Intentionality at this level functions anonymously, involuntarily, spontaneously, and receptively. Husserl distinguishes between receptivity and affectivity (2001, pp. 105, 127). As Dan Zahavi explains, "Receptivity is taken to be the first, lowest, and most primitive type of intentional activity, and consists in responding to or paying attention to that which is affecting us passively. Thus, even receptivity understood as a mere 'I notice' presupposes a prior affection" (Zahavi 1999, p. 116; see also the Translator's Introduction to Husserl 2001). Affection here means being *affectively influenced* or *perturbed*. The idea is that whatever comes into relief in experience must have already been affecting us and must have some kind of "affective force" or "affective allure" in relation to our attention and motivations. Whatever exercises affective allure without our turning to it attentively is said to be "pregiven," and whatever succeeds in gaining attention is said to be "given." Thus the given—the mode or way in which something appears to object-directed consciousness—has to be understood dynamically and teleologically as emergent in relation to the pregiven. Object-directed intentional experiences emerge out of the background of a precognitive "operative intentionality" (Merleau-Ponty 1962, p. xviii) that involves a dynamic interplay of affective sensibility, motivation, and attention. This affectively "saturated intentionality" (Steinbock 1999) provides our primordial openness to the world.

The phenomenological terrain of "passive synthesis" is rich in potential for illuminating and being illuminated by research in psychology and neuroscience on emotion and cognition. Some of these connections are already discernible in Husserl's description of passive synthesis as operating according to a principle of association (Husserl 1960, pp. 80–81; 2001, pp. 162–242). For Husserl, association is an intentional process whereby experiences are built up or synthesized into larger, patterned wholes. Using the terminology of emergence, we could say that association is the process by which coherent patterns of experience emerge from conjoined and reciprocally affecting experiences. Here are a few vivid examples given by William James in his *Principles of Psychology:*

> Let a person enter his room in the dark and grope among the objects there. The touch of the matches will instantaneously recall their appearance. If his hand comes in contact with an orange on the table, the golden yellow of the fruit, its savor and perfume will forthwith shoot through his mind. In passing the hand over the sideboard or in jogging the coal-scuttle with the foot, the large glossy dark shape of the one and the irregular blackness of the other awaken in a flash and constitute what we call the recognition of objects. The voice of the violin faintly echoes through the mind as the hand is laid upon it in the dark, and the feeling of the garments or draperies which may hang about the room is not understood till the look correlative to the feeling has in each case been resuscitated . . . But the most notorious and important case of the mental combination of auditory with optical impressions originally experienced together is furnished by language. The child is offered a new and delicious fruit and is at the same time told that it is called a "fig." Or looking out of the window he exclaims, "What a funny horse!" and is told that it is a "piebald" horse. When learning his letters, the sound of each is repeated to him whilst its shape is before his eye. Thenceforward, long as he may live, he will never see a fig, a piebald horse, or a letter of the alphabet without the name which he first heard in conjunction with each clinging to it in his mind; and inversely he will never hear the name without the faint arousal of the image of the object. (1981, pp. 524–525)

According to the empiricist philosophers Locke and Hume, such associations happen in a completely mechanical way. Association operates as a kind of connective force in the mind that links impressions and ideas simply in virtue of their simultaneous occurrence, proximity, or repeated succession. Hume's analysis of causation provides a famous example of this way of thinking about association. Hume argued that causal connections are neither directly observable nor provable by reason, but are objects of mere belief based on habit and custom. The belief in a causal connection between A and B arises from the association or "constant conjunction" of A and B in past experience: experiences of A constantly conjoined to experiences of B make the mind habitually expect that the occurrence of A will be followed by the occurrence of B.

For Husserl (and James), however, association is not meaningless and mechanical, but thoroughly intentional. Association is not the mechanical aggregation of complex experiences out of preexisting experience-atoms. Husserl, like James, completely rejects this atomistic conception of experience. Like emergent processes in a self-organizing system, associated experiences reciprocally strengthen and reinforce each other and thereby give rise to new formations that supersede their prior separateness. Association also involves the retention and anticipation of sense or meaning. Earlier experiences are affectively "awakened" by later ones on the basis of their felt similarities, and they motivate the anticipation that what is to come will cohere with the sense or meaning of experience so far. In Husserl's terminology, there is an "analogical transfer of sense" from earlier to later experience: what is present now is passively apprehended within a sense that has its roots in earlier experience and that has since become habitual (Bernet, Kern, and Marbach 1993, p. 202).

The notion of habit is central to Husserl's conception of passive genesis, as he states explicitly in a lecture from 1927: "As Hume correctly teaches, habit is not only our nurse, rather it is the function of consciousness that shapes and constantly further shapes the world" (quoted by Bernet, Kern, and Marbach 1993, p. 203; see also Welton 2000, p. 243). Husserl mentions Hume, but the notion of habit was very important to James as well. In his *Principles of Psychology* James declared that habit is the ground of all association in the stream of consciousness and in brain activity (thereby anticipating Donald Hebb and connectionism).[12] Later, in 1945, Merleau-Ponty introduced his notion of the habit-body in his *Phenomenology of Perception* while discussing the experience of the phantom limb: "our body comprises as it were two distinct layers, that of the habit-body and that of the body at this moment. In the first appear manipulatory movements which have disappeared from the second, and the problem how I can have the sensation of still possessing a limb which I no longer have amounts to finding out how the habitual body can act as guarantee for the body at this moment" (1962, p. 82). To say that the habitual body acts as guarantee for the body at this moment is to say that one's lived body is a developmental being thick with its own history and sedimented ways of feeling, perceiving, acting, and imagining. These sedimented patterns are not limited to the space enclosed by the body's membrane; they span and interweave the lived body and its environment, thereby forming a unitary circuit of lived-body-environment (Gallagher 1986b).

In Part III, I will explore this convergence of genetic phenomenology and enactive cognitive science in greater detail. For now let me simply point out how important the dynamic coupling between one's lived body and the surrounding world is to both perspectives. In this coupling, the motivating undercurrent is the habitual and associative linkage of affective, sensorimotor, and imaginative bodily experiences.

From Genetic to Generative Phenomenology

Late in his life Husserl began to move in still another direction—from genetic phenomenology to *generative phenomenology*. Already in genetic phenomenology intersubjectivity had arisen as an important theme, in the form of the dynamic coupling between self and other on the basis of their lived bodily presence to one another. Generative phenomenology, however, widened the scope of this genetic analysis beyond the self-other relation to include the parameters of birth and death as well as the interconnectedness of generations.

In this context, the term *generative* has a double meaning: it means both the process of becoming and the process of occurring over the generations (Steinbock 1995, p. 3). Generative phenomenology concerns the historical, social, and cultural becoming of human experience. If static phenomenology is restricted in scope with respect to genetic phenomenology, then genetic phenomenology is restricted in scope with respect to generative phenomenology: the subject matter of generative phenomenology is the historical and intersubjective becoming of human experience, whereas genetic phenomenology focuses on individual development without explicit analysis of its generational and historical embeddedness.

In shifting from a genetic to a generative register, the notion of the lived body is complemented with that of the *life-world* (Husserl 1970; Steinbock 1995, pp. 86–122; Welton 2000, pp. 331–346). The life-world is the everyday world in which we live. It is "always already pregiven," serving as the horizon of all our activities, practical and theoretical. Two important aspects of this rich and multifaceted notion need to be mentioned here—the back-and-forth circulation or exchange within the life-world between empirical science and everyday human life, and the life-world as the pregiven horizon and ground of all human activity.

The life-world comprises the everyday world and the things that can be directly experienced within the everyday world—our living bodies, our natural surroundings, and our cultural creations (tools, artworks, and so on). The life-world is subject-relative in the sense that it is relationally bound to human subjectivity. This is in contrast to "objective nature" as conceived by science, which is arrived at through logical and theoretical abstraction. *Nature* so construed is an objectification and has as its cognitive correlate the objectifying intentional attitude adopted by a community of theorizing subjects. *Objective nature* presupposes the life-world as its evidential source and ground. In principle it cannot be experienced directly because it is the product of abstraction and idealization. Nevertheless, the propositions, models, logical constructs, and experimental techniques of the sciences are clearly experienceable in another sense: they are human accomplishments that have experiential validity for members of the scientific community, and their effects flow into the everyday world and become tangibly experienced in the form of technology and social practice. Our life-world encompasses science, in addition to other spheres of experience such as art, philosophy, and religion. Hence, there is a necessary "circulation" between everyday experience and scientific experience (Varela, Thompson, and Rosch 1991, pp. 10–14). On the one hand, everyday experience provides the sensuous, material contents from which and with which science must work. On the other hand, the scientific analyses built from these contents contribute to the formation of our life-world and provide important leading clues for phenomenological analyses of how our experience of the world is genetically and generatively constituted.

In taking up these phenomenological analyses, Husserl initially conceived of the life-world as a synthetic totality. Hence he treated it on the model of an object, albeit a peculiar all-encompassing one (see Steinbock 1995, pp. 98–102; Welton 2000, pp. 336–346). Eventually, however, it became clear to him that the life-world cannot be given as any kind of intentional object, for it is always already there, pregiven rather than given.[13] Thus, in a crucial and famous passage from his last work, *The Crisis of European Sciences and Transcendental Phenomenology* (1970, §37, pp. 142–143), he wrote that the world is always already there, existing in advance for us, as the "ground" and "horizon" of any human activity. He then asserted that the way we are conscious of the world and the way we are conscious of things or objects, though inseparably united, are fundamentally different. We can be conscious of things only as things within the world horizon, and we can be conscious of the world horizon only as a horizon for existing objects. Yet the world is not any kind of entity, nor is it simply the totality of entities, precisely because it is the horizon presupposed by any entity or any totality. It is tempting to say "the world is one," except that, as Husserl puts it, the world "exists with such uniqueness that the plural makes no sense when applied to it." In other words, the world is not one in any sense in which it could have been two. To put it another way, to describe the world as "unique," such that "every singular and every plural drawn from it, presupposes the world horizon," means that the notion of counting makes no sense or has no application here.[14] Given this difference between the manner in which any object is given and the manner in which the world horizon is given (namely, as always already pregiven), it follows that there must be "fundamentally different correlative types of consciousness for them."

Husserl's terms *horizon* and *ground* are metaphorical, at once visual and geological. A horizon is not a thing "out there" but rather a structure of appearance. It therefore implicates or points back to the perceiver for whom appearances are so structured. In phenomenological language, "horizon" taken noematically as a structure of appearance necessarily implicates "horizon" taken noetically as a structure of consciousness. One could say that a horizon is the precondition for the appearance of anything, except that "precondition" is too static. Stated in a genetic register, a horizon is a dynamic structure of disclosure in which both the object (noema) and consciousness (noesis) partake (Steinbock 1995, p. 107). Anything that comes forth, manifests, or emerges does so in an open clearing or expanse, delimited by a horizon. The horizon of every possible horizon is the world. Yet the world-horizon cannot be the synthesis, totality, or mereological sum of all these possible horizons because it is pregiven or *a priori* with respect to any of them and thus is *sui generis*. Similarly, to describe the life-world as ground *(Boden)* is not to say that it is a static foundation; rather, it is the pregiven soil out of which everything is generated and nourished. This soil includes one's forebears and culture. We human beings constitute and reconstitute ourselves through cultural traditions, which we experience as our own development in a historical time that spans the generations. To investigate the life-world as horizon and ground of all experience therefore requires investigating none other than generativity—the processes of becoming, of making and remaking, that occur over the generations and within which any individual genesis is always already situated.

Generative phenomenology brings to the fore the intersubjective, social, and cultural aspects of our radical embodiment. Individuals are born and die, they develop and constantly change, and they emerge from their forebears and perpetuate themselves in generations to come. Individual subjectivity is from the outset intersubjectivity, originally engaged with and altered by others in specific geological and cultural environments (Depraz 1999c, p. 482; Steinbock 1995). Individual subjectivity is intersubjectively and culturally embodied, embedded, and emergent.

Classical cognitive science, to the extent that it operated under the assumption that the individual self comes first and the other second, simply left out intersubjectivity and culture. Indeed, it had no real means to analyze their contributions to the "cognitive architecture" of the human mind. As a result, classical cognitive science has offered abstract and reified models of the mind as a disembodied and cultureless physical symbol system or connectionist neural network in the head of a solitary individual. As we will see in the last chapter of this book, however, the enactive approach, particularly when guided by genetic and generative phenomenologies of the lived body, intersubjectivity, and the life-world, offers a different vision. I will argue that self and other enact each other reciprocally through empathy and that human subjectivity emerges from developmental processes of enculturation and is configured by the distributed cognitive web of symbolic culture.

THREE

◆ ◆ ◆

Autonomy and Emergence

ACCORDING TO THE ENACTIVE APPROACH, the human mind emerges from self-organizing processes that tightly interconnect the brain, body, and environment at multiple levels. The key ideas on which this proposition is based are those of *autonomous systems* and *emergence* or *emergent processes*. In this chapter, I explain these ideas. In the next chapter, I explore some connections between these ideas and phenomenological ideas about form, in particular forms or structures of behavior. These two chapters will lay the groundwork for the enactive strategy of addressing the explanatory gap by going back to the roots of mind in life and then working forward to subjectivity and consciousness.

In the first section of this chapter, I review some basic ideas about dynamic systems that form a background for the enactive approach. In the second section, I explain the notion of an autonomous system. A distinctive feature of the enactive approach is the emphasis it gives to autonomy. In brief, an autonomous system is a self-determining system, as distinguished from a system determined from the outside, or a heteronomous system. On the one hand, a living cell, a multicellular animal, an ant colony, or a human being behaves as a coherent, self-determining unity in its interactions with its environment. An automatic bank machine, on the other hand, is determined and controlled from the outside, in the realm of human design. The paradigm for interaction with a heteronomous system is input/processing/output, in which deviations from desired outputs are seen as system errors. The paradigm for interaction with an autonomous system is a conversation, in which unsatisfactory outcomes are seen as breaches of understanding (Varela 1979, p. xii). According to the enactive approach, living beings and cognitive agents need to be understood as autonomous systems. I discuss the implications of this autonomy perspective for how we think about information in the third section.

In the fourth section, I turn to emergence, a now familiar notion that describes the arising of large-scale, collective patterns of behavior in complex systems as diverse as cells, brains, ecosystems, cities, and economies. Emergence is closely related to self-organization and circular causality, both of which involve the reciprocal influence of "bottom-up" and "top-down" processes. For example, a tornado emerges through the self-organization of circulating air and water particles; it reciprocally sucks those particles into a particular macroscopic configuration, with devastating effect for anything in its path. In this section, I sketch a way of thinking about emergence that I call dynamic co-emergence. Dynamic co-emergence means that a whole not only arises from its parts, but the parts also arise from the whole. Part and whole co-emerge and mutually specify each other. A whole cannot be reduced to its parts, for the parts cannot be characterized independently of the whole; conversely, the parts cannot be reduced to the whole, for the whole cannot be characterized independently of the parts. I discuss philosophical issues related to this conception of emergence in Appendix B.

Dynamic Systems

In recent years growing interest in the dynamics of cognition and emotion has given rise to a distinct dynamical approach in mind science (Kelso 1995; Lewis and Granic 2000; Port and van Gelder 1995; Thelen and Smith 1994). The central idea of the dynamical approach is that natural cognition—cognition in evolved, living agents—is a dynamic phenomenon and accordingly needs to be understood from the perspective of the science of dynamic systems. This perspective includes dynamic-systems theory (a branch of pure mathematics), dynamic-systems modeling (mathematical modeling of empirical systems), and experimental investigations of biological and psychological phenomena informed by these tools.

The first important concept we need to introduce in this context is that of a *dynamic system*.[1] In simple terms a dynamic system is one that

changes over time. The term *system*, however, is ambiguous, in that it
can refer either to an actual system in the world, such as the solar
system, or to a mathematical model of an actual system. In the case of
the actual world, the term *system* does not admit of precise definition.
In general, a system is a collection of related entities or processes that
stands out from a background as a single whole, as some observer sees
and conceptualizes things. The classic example from the history of science is the solar system. Its components are the sun, moon, and
planets, and its states are their possible configurations. What changes
over time is the state of the system. A dynamic system in the sense of a
model, however, is a mathematical construction that aims to describe
and predict the way an actual system changes over time (the paths of
the planets, and events such as eclipses, in the case of the solar
system). To this end, some aspects of the actual system are singled out
as being especially important and are mathematically represented by
quantitative variables. Specifying the numerical values of all the variables at a given time indicates the state of the system at that time. A dynamic system includes a procedure for producing such a description
of the state of the system and a rule for transforming the current state-
description into another state-description for some future time. A dynamic system is thus a mathematical model for the way that a system
changes or behaves as time passes.

   If the passage of time is considered to be continuous (like the
sweeping second hand of an analogue clock), then the dynamic system
is a differentiable one: the variables change in a smooth and continuous way, and the rules or "evolution equations" that govern the
changing state of the system take the form of differential equations. If
time is considered to pass in evenly spaced, discrete jumps (like a digital clock), then the system is described by a difference equation or a
mapping (a function repeatedly applied or iterated in discrete time
steps). Some differential equations have an analytical solution, which
means they can be exactly solved by mathematical formulas. Given the
starting values of the variables (the initial conditions), then all future
states of the system can be known without recalculating the state of the
system for each time increment. Most differential equations, however,
cannot be solved in this way. When the equations contain nonlinear
terms—functions in which the value of the output is not directly proportional to the sum of the inputs—then such a solution is impossible.

Therefore a different mathematical approach has to be taken from
that of finding a formula that makes possible the prediction of a future
state from a present one.

This other approach, introduced by Henri Poincaré in the nineteenth century, is known as the *qualitative* study of differential equations (or of nonlinear differentiable dynamic systems). One thinks of
the space of all possible states of the system as a geometric space,
known as state space or phase space, and the way that the system
changes or behaves over time as curves or trajectories in this space. Instead of seeking a formula for each solution as a function of time, one
studies the collection of all solutions (corresponding to trajectories in
phase space) for all times and initial conditions at once (Norton 1995,
p. 46). This approach is said to be qualitative because it uses topological and geometrical techniques to study the general or global character of the system's long-term behavior (its behavior in phase space),
instead of seeking to predict the system's exact future state (the specific values of its variables at a future time). It is precisely this qualitative approach to dynamics that goes by the name of dynamic systems
theory.

We need to introduce one more related notion—that of complexity.
The term *complexity* describes behavior that is neither random nor ordered and predictable; rather, it is in between, exhibiting changing
and unstable patterns. Of particular importance in the context of recent nonlinear dynamic-systems approaches to the brain and behavior
is the notion of *complexity as dynamic instability* or *metastability*—"the successive expression of different transient dynamics with stereotyped
temporal patterns being continuously created and destroyed and re-
emerging again" (Friston 2000b, p. 238). Recent science indicates that
complexity of this sort can be found at numerous scales and levels,
from the molecular and organismic to the ecological and evolutionary,
as well as the neural and behavioral.[2] In every case the message seems
to be that complexity, instability, or metastability is necessary for self-
organization and adaptive behavior.

We can now return to the dynamical approach in mind science. The
fundamental dynamical hypothesis of this approach is that natural
cognitive agents (people and other animals) are dynamic systems (or,
more precisely, that the cognitive systems agents instantiate are dynamic systems), and that accordingly action, perception, and cogni-

tion should be explained in dynamic terms (van Gelder 1998). Proponents of the dynamical hypothesis contrast it with the cognitivist hypothesis, which states that cognitive agents (or the cognitive systems they instantiate), whether natural or artificial, are digital computers or physical symbol systems and that accordingly cognition should be explained in symbol-processing terms.

To illustrate these ideas, we can turn to research on neural and behavioral coordination dynamics by Haken, Kelso, and colleagues (Bressler and Kelso 2001; Kelso 1995). One case they have studied is rhythmic finger movement (Haken, Kelso, and Bunz 1985). The experimental task was to move the two index fingers at the same frequency from side to side. At low speeds, there are two comfortable coordination patterns (the system is bistable): either the fingers move in-phase (equivalent muscle groups in each hand contract simultaneously) or anti-phase (equivalent muscle groups alternate in their contraction and expansion). As the speed gradually increases, the in-phase pattern becomes unstable, and eventually at a certain critical frequency the fingers spontaneously switch to an anti-phase pattern (the system undergoes a bifurcation). As the speed decreases, the in-phase pattern becomes stable again, but it does so below the original switching point (this delayed return to a previous state is known as hysteresis).

Haken, Kelso, and colleagues devised a dynamic-systems model to describe and predict these properties of motor behavior. The model describes how the relative phase relation between the two fingers evolves over time. Relative phase is an example of a "collective variable"—one whose value is set by the relation between the values of other variables, in this case those describing the individual finger movements. A collective variable describes a high-level or global characteristic of a system that emerges as a coherent and ordered pattern from the interactions of the system's components. This macrolevel pattern is also known as an order parameter because it reduces the degrees of freedom of the system's components by organizing them into a coherent and ordered pattern. When the fingers move in-phase, the collective variable or order parameter of relative phase is zero; once the critical transition or bifurcation to anti-phase happens, the relative phase becomes nonzero up to some maximum value. Because the phase transition occurs at a certain critical frequency of finger oscillation, the frequency acts as a "control parameter" for the system. The control parameter does not dictate or prescribe the collective variable or order parameter (the emergent pattern of relative phase). Rather, its changing values lead the system through a variety of possible patterns or states (Kelso 1995, p. 7). Thus the model mathematically describes how the control parameter of finger-movement frequency leads the system through different patterns of finger coordination.

In the language of dynamic-systems theory, this kind of description gives the state space of the system—the abstract and multidimensional space that represents all possible states of the system by specifying all possible values of the system's variables. The temporal evolution of the system corresponds to its trajectory through this space. The model predicts the observed switching from one phase to another without positing any internal motor program that directs the switches by issuing symbolic instructions. Instead, the phase transitions occur spontaneously as emergent properties of the system's self-organizing dynamics. Kelso and colleagues have extended and developed this type of phase-transition model to apply to a wide variety of cognitive domains, such as motor skill learning, speech perception, visual perception, and the dynamic coordination of activity among cortical areas of the brain (Bressler and Kelso 2001; Kelso 1995).

One of the key points relating to the dynamical approach is its emphasis on time. Traditional computational models are static in that they specify only a sequence of discrete states through which the system must pass. In contrast, dynamic-systems models specify how processes unfold in real time. As Tim van Gelder states, "Although all cognitive scientists understand cognition as something that happens *over* time, dynamicists see cognition as being *in* time, that is, as an essentially temporal phenomenon (van Gelder 1999a, p. 244). Van Gelder (1998) describes this contrast as one between *change* versus *state; geometry* versus *structure; structure in time* versus *static structure; time* versus *order; parallel* versus *serial;* and *ongoing* versus *input/output.*

Whereas computationalists focus primarily on discrete states and treat change as what happens when a system shifts from one discrete state to another, dynamicists focus on how a system changes state continuously in time. Dynamicists conceive of state changes geometrically, in terms of their position and trajectory in phase space, whereas computationalists focus on the internal formal or syntactic structure of combinatorial entities. Computationalists think of these structures as laid out statically (like snapshots), as either present all at once or not, and hence of cognition as the rule-governed transformation of one such static structure into another. For dynamicists, cognitive structures are laid out as temporally extended patterns of activity, and cognition is seen as the flow of complex temporal structures mutually and simultaneously influencing each other. Dynamicists are therefore interested in the timing (rates, periods, durations, synchronies) of processes, whereas computationalists have traditionally been interested only in the order of cognitive states. Moreover, computationalists tend to think of this order as being the serial or sequential progression of sense → perceive → think → act, whereas for dynamicists cognition unfolds as the continuous coevolution of acting, perceiving, imagining, feeling, and thinking. Finally, whereas computationalists think of cognitive processes as having an input-output structure—the system receives an input, proceeds through a sequence of internal operations, produces an output, and then halts—dynamicists think of processes as always ongoing, with no clear starting or end points. The goal is not to map an input at one time onto an output at a later time, but always to maintain appropriate change (van Gelder 1998).

Autonomous Systems

The dynamicist idea that cognitive processes are always ongoing with no clear starting or end points can be deepened by introducing the distinction between autonomous and heteronomous systems. *Autonomy* and *heteronomy* literally mean, respectively, self-governed and other-governed. A heteronomous system is one whose organization is defined by input-output information flow and external mechanisms of control. Traditional computational systems, cognitivist or connectionist, are heteronomous. For instance, a typical connectionist network has an input layer and an output layer; the inputs are initially assigned by the observer outside the system; and output performance is evaluated in relation to an externally imposed task. An autonomous system, however, is defined by its endogenous, self-organizing and self-controlling dynamics, does not have inputs and outputs in the usual sense, and determines the cognitive domain in which it operates (Varela 1979; Varela and Bourgine 1991).

In general, to specify any system one needs to describe its organization—the set of relations that defines it as the system it is. In complex systems theory, the term *autonomous* refers to a generic type of organization. The relations that define the autonomous organization hold between processes (such as metabolic reactions in a cell or neuronal firings in a cell assembly) rather than static entities. In an autonomous system, the constituent processes (i) recursively depend on each other for their generation and their realization as a network, (ii) constitute the system as a unity in whatever domain they exist, and (iii) determine a domain of possible interactions with the environment (Varela 1979, p. 55). The paradigm is a living cell. The constituent processes in this case are chemical; their recursive interdependence takes the form of a self-producing, metabolic network that also produces its own membrane; and this network constitutes the system as a unity in the biochemical domain and determines a domain of possible interactions with the environment. This kind of autonomy in the biochemical domain is known as *autopoiesis* (Maturana and Varela 1980). Figure 3.1 illustrates the basic organization required for autopoietic autonomy.

Autopoiesis is the paradigm case of biological autonomy for two reasons. It is empirically the best understood case, and it provides the core "biologic" of all life on Earth. To qualify as autonomous, however, a system does not have to be autopoietic in the strict sense (a self-producing bounded molecular system). An autopoietic system dynamically produces its own material boundary or membrane, but a system can be autonomous without having this sort of material boundary. The members of an insect colony, for example, form an autonomous social network, but the boundary is social and territorial, not material.

In exploring the notion of autonomy, we can take two complementary approaches—a top-down approach and a bottom-up one (Ruiz-Mirazo and Moreno 2004). Both approaches see autonomy as a relational, system-level property, but there is a critical difference between the two. Whereas the top-down approach focuses on the relational organization proper to autonomy, the bottom-up approach emphasizes the energetic and thermodynamic requirements for autonomy.

Varela takes the top-down approach in his 1979 book, *Principles of Biological Autonomy*.[3] In this work he defines an autonomous system as a system that has organizational closure (later called operational closure) (Varela 1979, pp. 55–60). Here closure does not mean that the system is

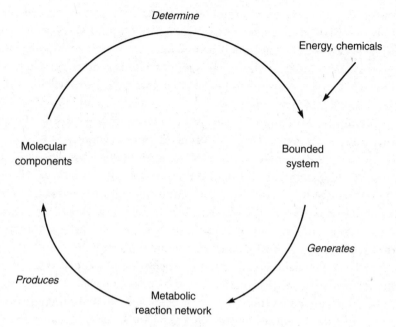

Figure 3.1. The basic autopoietic organization.

materially and energetically closed to the outside world (which of course is impossible). On the contrary, autonomous systems must be thermodynamically far-from-equilibrium systems, which incessantly exchange matter and energy with their surroundings. *Organizational closure* refers to the self-referential (circular and recursive) network of relations that defines the system as a unity, and *operational closure* to the reentrant and recurrent dynamics of such a system.[4] An autonomous system is always structurally coupled to its environment. Two or more systems are coupled when the conduct of each is a function of the conduct of the other. (In dynamic-systems language, the state variables of one system are parameters of the other system, and vice versa.) "Structural coupling" refers to the history of recurrent interactions between two or more systems that leads to a structural congruence between them (Maturana 1975; Maturana and Varela 1987, p. 75). Thus the state changes of an autonomous system result from its operational closure and structural coupling. The result of any state change is always further self-organized activity within the system, unless its closure is disrupted and it is no longer able to carry on its coupling, in which case it disintegrates. Systems described as autonomous in this sense abound throughout the living world—single cells, microbial communities, nervous systems, immune systems, multicellular organisms, ecosystems, and so on. Such systems need to be seen as sources of their own activity, specifying their own domains of interaction, not as transducers or functions for converting input instructions into output products. In other words, the autonomous character of these systems needs to be recognized.

The second, bottom-up approach to autonomy builds on these notions of organizational and operational closure, but tries to work out the energetic and thermodynamic requirements for the instantiation of "basic autonomy" in the physical world. From this perspective, basic autonomy is "the capacity of a system to manage the flow of matter and energy through it so that it can, at the same time, regulate, modify, and control: (i) internal self-constructive processes and (ii) processes of exchange with the environment" (Ruiz-Mirazo and Moreno 2004, p. 240). This capacity brings with it specific and demanding physical-implementation requirements: the system must have certain types of components, specifically a semipermeable active boundary (a membrane), an energy transduction/conversion apparatus (an energy currency such as adenosine triphosphate (ATP) in living cells, which transfers energy from chemical bonds to energy-absorbing reactions within the cell), and at least one type of component that controls and facilitates the self-construction processes (catalysts) (Ruiz-Mirazo and Moreno 2004, p. 252).

Figure 3.1 depicts the basic autopoietic organization for a living cell. A cell stands out of a molecular soup by creating the boundaries that set it apart from what it is not and that actively regulate its interactions with the environment. Metabolic processes within the cell construct these boundaries, but the metabolic processes themselves are made possible by those very boundaries. In this way, the cell emerges as a figure out of a chemical background. Should this process of self-production be interrupted, the cellular components no longer form a unity, gradually diffusing back into a molecular soup.

Figure 3.1 can be compared with Figure 3.2, which depicts the minimal form of organizational closure for a nervous system. Any nervous system operates according to a basic "neurologic," a pattern that continues and elaborates the biologic of autopoiesis. The fundamental

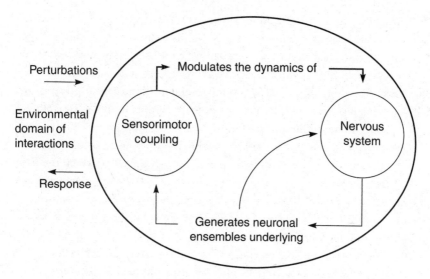

Figure 3.2. Organizational closure of the nervous system.

logic of the nervous system is to couple movement and a stream of sensory activity in a continuous circular fashion (Maturana and Varela 1987, pp. 142–176). Wherever movement is essential to a multicellular organism's mode of life, there is the corresponding development of a nervous system. A nervous system links sensory surfaces (sense organs and nerve endings) and effectors (muscles, glands) within the body. In this way it integrates the organism, holding it together as a mobile unity, as an autonomous sensorimotor agent.

This neurologic underlies all the variations on sensorimotor coordination found in the animal kingdom. In all animals, neuronal networks establish and maintain a sensorimotor cycle through which what the animal senses depends directly on how it moves, and how it moves depends directly on what it senses. No animal is a mere passive respondent; every animal meets the environment on its own sensorimotor terms. Merleau-Ponty recognized this crucial point in his first work, *The Structure of Behavior*:

The organism cannot properly be compared to a keyboard on which the external stimuli would play and in which their proper form would be delineated for the simple reason that the organism contributes to the constitution of that form. When my hand follows each effort of a struggling animal while holding an instrument for capturing it, it is clear that each of my movements responds to an external stimulation; but it is also clear that these stimulations could not be received without the movements by which I expose my receptors to their influence . . . When the eye and the ear follow an animal in flight, it is impossible to say "which started first" in the exchange of stimuli and responses. Since all movements of the organism are always conditioned by external influences, one can, if one wishes, readily treat behavior as an effect of the milieu. But in the same way, since all the stimulations which the organism receives have in turn been possible only by its preceding movements which have culminated in exposing the receptor organ to the external influences, one could also say that the behavior is the first cause of the stimulations.

Thus the form of the excitant is created by the organism itself, by its proper manner of offering itself to actions from outside. Doubtless, in order to be able to subsist, it must encounter a certain number of physical and chemical agents in its surroundings. But it is the organism itself—according to the proper nature of its receptors, the thresholds of its nerve centers and the movements of the organs—which chooses the stimuli in the physical world to which it will be sensitive. "The environment *(Umwelt)* emerges from the world through the actualization or the being of the organism—[granted that] an organism can exist only if it succeeds in finding in the world an adequate environment." This would be a key board which moves itself in such a way as to offer—and according to variable rhythms—such or such of its keys to the in itself monotonous action of an external hammer. (1963, p. 13)[5]

This passage clearly expresses an autonomy perspective. Organisms display patterns of behavior that require us to see them as autonomous. Varela tries to characterize this autonomy at an abstract level in terms of a generic dynamic pattern or form, namely, organizational and operational closure. Hence Varela gives us his "Closure Thesis," which states, "Every autonomous system is organizationally closed" (Varela 1979, p. 58).[6]

Figure 3.1 illustrates the minimal form this closure takes for life at the single-cell level, and Figure 3.2 illustrates the minimal form it takes for the nervous system. Whereas autopoietic closure brings forth a minimal "bodily self" at the level of cellular metabolism, sensorimotor closure produces a "sensorimotor self" at the level of perception and action. In the one case the passage from network closure to selfhood (and correlative otherness) happens at the level of an active semipermeable boundary or membrane, which regulates interaction with the outside environment. In the other case it happens at the level of behavior and intentional action. In both cases we see the co-emergence of inside and outside, of selfhood and a correlative world or environment of otherness, through the generic mechanism of network closure (autonomy) and its physical embodiment (Varela 1997a; see also Moreno and Barandiaran 2004).[7]

In addition to these cellular and sensorimotor forms of selfhood, other forms of selfhood arise from other organizationally and operationally closed systems. The immune system, for instance—understood as an autonomous immune network that establishes a coherent somatic identity for the organism, rather than as a mere mechanism of defense—brings forth a dynamic, somatic identity at a distributed cellular and molecular level (Coutinho 2003; Varela and Coutinho 1991). The animate form of our living body is thus the place of intersection for numerous emergent patterns of selfhood and coupling. Whether cellular, somatic, sensorimotor, or neurocognitive, these patterns derive not from any homuncular self or agent inside the system organizing it or directing it, but from distributed networks with operational closure. In Varela's image, our organism is a meshwork of "selfless selves," and we are and live this meshwork (Varela 1991; Varela and Cohen 1989).

Let me forestall an objection that might arise at this point. The nervous system is clearly embedded in the body of the organism, and the organism in its environment (Chiel and Beer 1997). This fact seemingly contradicts the statement that the nervous system is an autonomous system and that the organism is an autonomous agent. The thought here would be that the operation of the nervous system loops through the body (via sensory and motor surfaces), and therefore it is not possible that the nervous system has operational closure (that the product of every process within the system stays within that system). Similarly, because the bodily activity of the organism loops through the environment (motor activity affects the sensory stimulation one receives back from the environment), the organism cannot have an operationally closed dynamics.

A number of points, both methodological and epistemological, need to be made in reply. The first point is that, strictly speaking, system, autonomy, and heteronomy are heuristic notions—they are cognitive aids or guides in the scientific investigation and characterization of observable phenomena and patterns of behavior. As heuristic notions, they (implicitly) refer back to and implicate the interpretive and explanatory stance of an observer (or observer community). What counts as the system in any given case, and hence whether it is autonomous or heteronomous, is context-dependent and interest-relative. For any system it is always possible to adopt a heteronomy or external-control perspective, and this can be useful for many purposes. Nevertheless, this stance does not illuminate—and indeed can obscure—certain observable patterns of behavior, namely, patterns arising from the system's internal dynamics rather than external parameters. An organism dynamically produces and maintains its own organization as an invariant through change, and thereby also brings forth its own domain of interaction. (Although living organisms are paradigmatic in this regard, nothing apparently rules out the possibility of artificial autonomy.) A heteronomy perspective does not provide an adequate framework to investigate and understand this phenomenon; an autonomy perspective is needed.

The second point is that in any given case or for any candidate system we need to distinguish between, on the one hand, the operation of the system as such, which is a function of both its organization (the set of relations that defines it as a system) and physical structure, and, on the other hand, its performance in relation to whatever wider context in which it is observed. For example, if we wish to characterize the organization and operation of the nervous system as a finite neuronal network, then we need to characterize the nervous system as organizationally and operationally closed, such that any change of activity in a neuron (or neural assembly) always leads to a change of activity in other neurons (either directly through synaptic action or indirectly through intervening physical and chemical elements). Sensory and effector neurons are no exception because any change in the one leads to changes in the other, such that the network always closes back upon itself, regardless of intervening elements (Maturana and Varela 1980, p. 127). Nevertheless, the domain of states available to the nervous system (as an operationally closed network) is clearly a function of its history of interactions with the rest of the body (and the environment). Hence, besides characterizing the nervous system's operation as a closed network, we need to characterize its performance in its structural coupling with the rest of the body (and the environment). Similarly, to characterize the organism as a finite cellular or multicellular entity, we need to characterize it as an organizationally and operationally closed system. At the same time, we need to characterize the organism's performance or behavior in its structural coupling with the environment.

We can also shift perspectives and characterize the nervous system as a heteronomous system—that is, as a component system with various functions defined in relation to the organism (such as registering sensory changes or guiding movement). Notice, however—and this is the third point—that in so shifting perspectives we are *ipso facto* no longer talking about the same system. The system with which we are now concerned is no longer the nervous system as a finite neuronal network, but rather the larger system of the organism (in which the nervous system is seen as a component). Similarly, we can also shift perspectives and characterize the organism as a heteronomous system subject to the control of the environment (for instance, other organisms). Once again, in thus shifting perspectives we are *ipso facto* no longer dealing with the same system. The system now is the larger system of organism-plus-environment, not the organism as a finite cellular or multicellular entity.[8]

These considerations show us that there is no inconsistency between characterizing the nervous system and organism as autonomous and emphasizing their somatic and environmental embeddedness. We do, however, have to keep our logical and conceptual accounts clear, so that we know which explanatory heuristic is in play at any given time. In any case, for the enactive approach it is the autonomy perspective on natural cognitive agents that remains the reference point for understanding mind and life, not a predefined input-output task strucure.

Information and Meaning

Adopting an autonomy perspective also brings with it a certain way of thinking about semantic information or meaning. For enactive theorists, information is context-dependent and agent-relative; it belongs to the coupling of a system and its environment. What counts as information is determined by the history, structure, and needs of the system acting in its environment.

According to the received view in cognitive science, in order to explain cognitive abilities we need to appeal to information-bearing states inside the system. Such states, by virtue of the semantic information they carry about the world, qualify as representations. Cognitivists conceive of these representations as symbols in a computational "language of thought," and connectionists as constrained patterns of network activity corresponding to phase space "attractors" (regions of phase space toward which all nearby trajectories converge). In either case there is a strong tendency to adopt an objectivist conception of representation: representations are internal structures that encode context-independent information about the world, and cognition is the processing of such information.

This objectivist notion of information presupposes a heteronomy perspective in which an observer or designer stands outside the system and states what is to count as information (and hence what is to count as error or success in representation). Information looks different from an autonomy perspective. Here the system, on the basis of its operationally closed dynamics and mode of structural coupling with the environment, helps determine what information is or can be.

A neurobiological example can help to illustrate these ideas.[9] Certain kinds of cortical neurons are often described as feature detectors because they respond preferentially (fire above their base rate) to various types of stimuli, such as edges, lines, and moving spots. Such neurons are identified by recording their individual activity with a microelectrode and determining the sensory stimulus to which the neuron is most sensitive. Such neurons are said to "represent" features of objects and to make that information available for futher processing by various systems in the brain. This view lies behind the standard formulation of the so-called binding problem. This problem concerns how distinct features (shape, color, motion), as represented by cell populations in spatially distributed and functionally segregated neural pathways, can be bound together to form a complete and accurate representation of the object (so that the right shapes go with the right colors and motions). This way of thinking about the brain treats it as a heteronomous system: object features outside the organism provide informational inputs to the brain, and the brain's information processing task is to arrive at an accurate representation of the objective world and produce an adaptive motor output.

From an autonomy perspective, it is crucial to distinguish between information about stimuli as they are defined by an observer and information in the sense of what meanings the stimuli have for the animal. Only the latter play a significant role in the brain's operation. The notion of an object "feature" is defined by an observer who stands outside the system, has independent access to the environment, and establishes correlations between environmental features and neuronal responses. The animal's brain has no access to features in this sense (and *a fortiori* has no access to any mapping from features to neuronal responses). As Freeman explains, "In the view from neurodynamics, neurons that respond to edges, lines, and moving spots are manifesting the local topological properties of neuronal maps, which extract local time and space derivatives in automatic preprocessing for spatial and temporal contrast enhancement. No objects or features are manifested at the level of the single neuron, assuredly not those used by an observer" (Freeman 1995, p. 54). From an autonomy perspective, individual neurons do not detect objectively defined features. Rather, assemblies of neurons make sense of stimulation by constructing meaning, and this meaning arises as a function of how the brain's endogenous and nonlinear activity compensates for sensory perturbations. From this perspective, the feature-binding problem is not the brain's problem, but the brain theorist's problem; it is an artifact of a certain way of looking at the brain. Freeman's description of the alternative view, based on looking at the brain as an autonomous system operating according to nonlinear causality, is well worth quoting here:

> In this view the experimenter trains a subject to co-operate through the use of positive and negative reinforcement, thereby inducing a state of expectancy and search for a stimulus, as it is conceived by the subject. When the expected stimulus arrives, the activated receptors transmit pulses to the sensory cortex, where they elicit the construction by nonlinear dynamics of a macroscopic, spatially coherent oscillatory pattern that covers an entire area of sensory cortex . . . It is observed by means of the electroencephalogram (EEG) from electrode arrays on all the sensory cortices . . . It is not seen in recordings from single neuron action potentials, because the fraction of the variance in the single neu-

ronal pulse train that is covariant with the neural mass is far too small, on the order of 0.1 percent.

The emergent pattern is not a representation of a stimulus . . . It is a state transition that is induced by a stimulus, followed by a construction of a pattern that is shaped by the synaptic modification among cortical neurons from prior learning. It is also dependent on the brain stem nuclei that bathe the forebrain in neuromodulatory chemicals. It is a dynamic action pattern that creates and carries the meaning of the stimulus for the subject. It reflects the individual history, present context, and expectancy, corresponding to the unity and wholeness of intentionality. Owing to dependence on history, the patterns created in each cortex are unique to each subject. (Freeman 1999b, pp. 149–150)

The distinction between autonomous meaning-construction and heteronomous information processing needs to be placed in the broader context of the embodied dynamicist way of thinking about information. To explain this way of thinking, it will be helpful to go back to ideas introduced by Howard Pattee (1977). Pattee made an important distinction between two modes of description of a complex system—the *linguistic mode*, which describes the system in terms of discrete, rate-independent, symbolic elements, and the *dynamical mode*, which describes the system in terms of continuous, rate-dependent processes, and thus explicitly includes the flow of time. Pattee raised the following question: "How do we know we are not intepreting certain structures as descriptions, only because we recognize them as consistent with rules of one of our own languages?" (1977, p. 262). In other words, how do we know our linguistic descriptions are not simply observer-relative, but rather correspond to symbolic structures that belong to the system itself and play a role in its operation? And he answered: "we must further restrict our model of a complex system to remove the case of the external observer reading a message that is not really in the system itself. This restriction is achieved by requiring that a complex system must read and write its own messages" (1977, p. 262).

Pattee's example is a living cell. When we describe DNA triplets as "coding for" amino acids, we employ the linguistic mode of description. Which amino acid a given DNA triplet specifies is supposed to be rate-independent—it does not matter how fast the triplet is "read" in the course of protein synthesis. It is also supposed to be arbitrary, in the sense that "[i]t is hard to see why a code in which GGC means glycine and AAG means lycine is either better or worse than one in which the meanings are reservsed" (Maynard Smith 1986, p. 19). According to Pattee, the linguistic mode of description in this case is not observer-relative because the cell is a self-describing system that "reads and writes its own messages." The writing of its own messages corresponds to DNA replication (the production of a complement of the original DNA molecule through a template); the reading of its own messages corresponds to protein synthesis (DNA "transcription" to RNA and RNA "translation" to protein).

Pattee then makes a number of crucial points. First, for the code to be read there must ultimately be a transduction or conversion within the cell from the linguistic mode to the dynamical mode. This conversion occurs when the rate-independent linear array of amino acids folds to become a three-dimensional enzyme. Within the life cycle of the cell, there is thus a transformation from the enzyme as something designated in the genome to the enzyme as an operational component of metabolism. Second, this transformation (the protein folding) is not itself linguistically described in the cell, but rather happens according to physical law (under the higher-order constraint of the DNA-specificed amino acid sequence). Third, if the transformation were linguistically described, the speed and precision with which it is accomplished would be considerably compromised. Pattee's conclusion is that "we would not expect a complete formal description or simulation of a complex system to adapt or function as rapidly or reliably as the partially self-describing, tacit dynamic system it simulates" (1977, p. 264).

Pattee emphasizes the complementarity of the linguistic and dynamical modes of description, but also suggests that symbolic information emerges from and acts as a constraint on dynamics. This idea is important for embodied dynamicism and the enactive approach. Let us return to the example of the cell. In general, nucleotide triplets are capable of predictably specifying an amino acid if and only if they are properly embedded in the cell's metabolism, that is, in a multitude of enyzmatic regulations in a complex biochemical network. This network has a chicken-and-egg character at several levels. First, proteins can arise only from a DNA/RNA "reading" process, but this process cannot happen without proteins. Second, the DNA "writing" and "reading" processes must be properly situated within the intracellular environment, but this environment is a result of those very processes. Finally, the entire cell is an autopoietic system—that is, an autonomous system defined by an operationally closed network of molecular processes that simultaneously both produces and realizes the cell concretely in the physical space of its biochemical components.

Now, when we employ the linguistic mode of description and state that DNA/RNA "codes" for proteins, we restrict our focus to one particular sequence of this overall circular causality. We abstract away from the many intervening and necessary causal steps in the actual dynamic process of protein synthesis, and we bracket out the essential participation of many other molecular elements (such as RNA polymerase enzymes, and positive and negative regulatory proteins). We "thus reduce our description to a skeleton that associates a certain part of a nucleic acid with a certain protein segment. Next we observe that this kind of simplified description of an actual dynamic process is a useful one in following the sequences of reproductive steps from one generation to the other, to the extent that the dynamic process stays stable (i.e., the kinds of dynamics responsible for bonding, folding, and so on) . . . A symbolic explanation, such as the description of some cellular components as genes, betrays the emergence of certain *coherent patterns of behavior to which we choose to pay attention*" (Varela 1979, p. 75). It is the emergence of such coherent dynamic patterns that underwrites the symbolic informational level of description: "An object or event is a symbol only if it is a token for an abbreviated nomic chain that occurs *within the bounds of the system's organizational closure.* In other words, whenever the system's closure determines certain regularities in the face of internal or external interactions and perturbations, such regularities can be abbreviated as a symbol, usually the initial or terminal element in the nomic chain" (Varela 1979, pp. 79–80). Thus, when we talk about DNA "coding" for proteins we are not referring to a special type of symbolic causal relation or a special type of intrinsically informational molecule that rises above the dynamic fray. Rather, we are abbreviating a lengthy but remarkably stable dynamic pattern of biochemical events. It is precisely the stability and predictability of the entire pattern that allows us to telescope it in a linguistic mode of description by treating nucleotide triplets as in effect "standing for" amino acids.

This mode of description is unobjectionable (and has heuristic value) as long as it is remembered that the genetic code is no more than a rule of causal specificity based on the fact that cells use nucleic acids as templates for the primary structure (amino acid sequence) of proteins (Godfrey-Smith 2000b; Thompson 1997). Yet it is unacceptable to say that DNA contains the information for phenotypic design, because this statement attributes an intrinsic semantic-informational status to one particular type of component and thereby divests this component of its necessary embedding in the dynamics of the autopoietic network. It is this network in its entirety that specifies the phenotypic characteristics of a cell, not one of its components, and it is this network as a whole that serves as the precondition and causal basis of DNA replication ("writing") and protein synthesis ("reading") (see Moss 1992). Information is not intrinsic to the static linear array of the DNA sequence, but is rather dynamically constituted in and by the cell as an autopoietically organized, three-dimensional entity—by the cell as a *body*. In summary, the linguistic mode is emergent from the dynamical mode, and information exists only as dynamically embodied.

With these points having been made, we return to the difference between autonomous meaning-construction and heteronomous information processing. Information is formed within a context rather than imposed from without. Gregory Bateson used to say, "information is a difference that makes a difference" (Bateson 1972, p. 315). We could elaborate this insight by saying that information, dynamically conceived, is the making of a difference that makes a difference for some-*body* somewhere (see Oyama 2000b). Information here is understood in the sense of *informare*, to form within (Varela 1979, p. 266). An autonomous system becomes informed by virtue of the meaning formation in which it participates, and this meaning formation depends on the way its endogenous dynamics specifies things that make a difference to it (Kelso and Kay 1987; Turvey and Shaw 1999).

For another example we can return to the finger coordination study of Haken, Kelso, and Bunz (1985). There the switching from in-phase to anti-phase happens without any command from a motor program; rather, it occurs spontaneously as an emergent property of the system's self-organizing dynamics. The collective variable or order parameter of relative phase is informational in the sense that it specifies coherent patterns or relations that inform the system and that can be physically or physiologically realized in multiple ways. As Kelso explains:

> Instead of treating dynamics as ordinary physics using standard biophysical quantities such as mass, length, momentum, and energy, our *coordination or pattern dynamics* is informational from the very start. The order parameter, ϕ [relative phase], captures the *coherent relations* among different kinds of things. Unlike ordinary physics, the pattern dynamics is context dependent: the dynamics are valid for a given biological function or task, but largely independent of how this function is physiologically implemented. Thus, if we accept that the same order parameter, ϕ, captures coherent spatiotemporal relations among different kinds of things, and the same equations of motion describe how different coordination patterns form, coexist, and change, it seems justified to conclude that order parameters in biological systems are functionally specific, context-sensitive *informational* variables; and that the coordination dynamics are more general than the particular structures that instantiate them.
>
> Notice, coordination dynamics is not trapped (like ordinary physics) by its (purely formal) syntax. Order parameters are semantic, relational quantities that are intrinsically meaningful to system functioning. What could be more meaningful to an organism than information that specifies the coordinative relations among its parts or between itself and the environment? This view turns the mind-matter, information-dynamics interaction on its head. Instead of treating dynamics as ordinary physics and information as a symbolic code acting in the way that a program relates to a computer, dynamics is cast in terms that are semantically meaningful. (Kelso 1995, p. 145)

Let me connect these points to the autonomy perspective. As we have seen, from the autonomy perspective a natural cognitive agent— an organism, animal, or person—does not process information in a context-independent sense. Rather, it brings forth or enacts meaning in structural coupling with its environment. The meanings of an autonomous system's states are formed within *(informare)* the context of the system's dynamics and structural coupling. Therefore, if we wish to continue using the term *representation*, then we need to be aware of what sense this term can have for the enactive approach. Representational "vehicles" (the structures or processes that embody meaning) are temporally extended patterns of activity that can crisscross the brain-body-world boundaries, and the meanings or contents they embody are brought forth or enacted in the context of the system's structural coupling with its environment.

Another way to make this point would be to say that autonomous systems do not operate on the basis of internal representations in the subjectivist/objectivist sense. Instead of internally representing an external world in some Cartesian sense, they enact an environment inseparable from their own structure and actions (Varela, Thompson, and Rosch 1991, p. 140). In phenomenological language, they constitute (disclose) a world that bears the stamp of their own structure. As Merleau-Ponty puts it, quoting Goldstein, in the passage cited earlier: "the environment emerges from the world through the being or actualization of the organism." In the case of animal life, the environment emerges as a sensorimotor world through the actualization of the organism as a sensorimotor being. The organism is a sensorimotor being thanks to its nervous system. The nervous system connects anatomically distant sensory and motor processes, subsuming them in operationally closed sensorimotor networks. Through their coherent, large-scale patterns of activity these networks establish a sensorimotor identity for the animal—a sensorimotor self. In the same stroke, they specify what counts as "other," namely, the animal's sensorimotor world.

This idea of a sensorimotor world—a body-oriented world of perception and action—is none other than von Uexküll's original notion of an *Umwelt*. An *Umwelt* is an animal's environment in the sense of its lived, phenomenal world, the world as it presents itself to that animal thanks to its sensorimotor repertoire: "all that a subject perceives becomes his perceptual world and all that he does, his effector-world. Perceptual and effector worlds together form a closed unit, the Umwelt" (von Uexküll 1957, p. 6). The logic of this co-emergence is depicted in Figure 3.3.

In this figure, information is the intentional relation of the system to its milieu, established on the basis of the system's autonomy (organizational-operational closure). One of the main scientific tasks for embodied dynamicism and the enactive approach is to explain how the

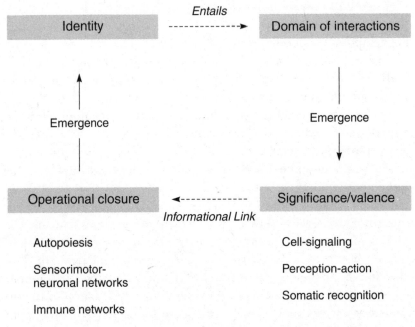

Figure 3.3. Co-emergence of autonomous selfhood and world.

pattern dynamics of brain, body, and behavior are informational in this sense (see Kelso 1995, p. 288).

Emergent Processes

Another key idea of the enactive approach that needs elaboration here is the idea of *emergence* or *emergent processes*. In complex systems theory, an emergent process is one that results from collective self-organization. An emergent process belongs to an ensemble or network of elements, arises spontaneously or self-organizes from the locally defined and globally constrained or controlled interactions of those elements, and does not belong to any single element. The enactive approach builds on this notion of emergence but reformulates it as "dynamic co-emergence," in which part and whole co-emerge and mutually specify each other.

Let me first introduce emergence in the complex systems sense. A standard example of this kind of emergence is the formation of "Bénard cells," a dynamic geometrical pattern of fluid flow, in liquids or gases subject to an imposed temperature gradient (see Kelso 1995, pp. 7–8; Solé and Goodwin 2000, pp. 13–17). The emergence of Bénard cells can be seen in the behavior of cooking oil in a frying pan. Applying heat to the pan increases the temperature difference between the cooler layer of oil at the top and the hotter layer of oil at the bottom. When the temperature difference between top and bottom is small, there is no large-scale or global motion of the oil, but eventually when the difference becomes large enough instability occurs and the liquid starts to roll in an orderly fashion known as convection rolls. In other words, the system undergoes a state transition, described mathematically as a bifurcation, as the new self-organizing behavior and spatial structures of convection rolls emerge. As the temperature gradient is increased still further, the convection rolls undergo another transition or bifurcation and give rise to an array of hexagonal up-and-down flow patterns called Bénard cells.

This example illustrates several basic points about collective self-organization and dynamic emergence. The temperature gradient is the *control parameter* for the transitions or bifurcations. It leads the system through a variety of possible states but does not dictate, prescribe, or code for the emerging flow patterns. Nor is there any homunculus or program inside the system determining those patterns. In Kelso's words: "Such spontaneous pattern formation is exactly what we mean by self-organization: the system organizes itself, but there is no 'self,' no agent inside the system doing the organizing" (Kelso 1995, p. 8). The *order parameter* of the system is the amplitude of the convection rolls. It is created by the interactions of the fluid molecules, but at the same time it governs or constrains their behavior by drastically reducing the immense number of degrees of freedom of motion that the individual molecules would otherwise have.

Emergence through collective self-organization thus has two aspects. One is local-to-global determination, as a result of which novel macrolevel structures and processes emerge. The other is global-to-local determination whereby global structures and processes constrain local interactions. These global-to-local influences do not take the same form as the local-to-global ones: they typically manifest themselves through changes in control parameters (the temperature gradient in the example above) and boundary conditions rather than through changes to the individual elements (the fluid molecules). Coherent and ordered global behaviors, which are described by collective variables or order parameters, constrain or govern the behavior of the individual components, entraining them so that they no longer have the same behavioral alternatives open to them as they would if they were not interdependently woven into the coherent and ordered global pattern. At the same time, the behavior of the components generates and sustains the global order. This two-sided or double determination is known as circular causality (Haken 1983).

Emergence and circular causality are crucially important in the context of neurodynamics. Neuroscience indicates that cognition, emotion, and action require the transient integration of numerous, widely distributed, and constantly interacting brain regions and areas. An outstanding question for neuroscience today is to determine the mechanisms of this large-scale integration. From a dynamic-systems perspective, large-scale integration corresponds to the formation of transient dynamic links between widespread neural populations (Varela et al. 2001). On the one hand, large-scale dynamic patterns emerge from distributed local neuronal activities. On the other hand, large-scale patterns constrain these local activities. According to a number of theorists, dynamic instability or metastability is crucial to large-scale integration because it permits a flexible repertoire of global states without the system becoming trapped in any one particular state.[10]

Emergence and circular causality can also be illustrated by neurodynamical studies of epilepsy (Thompson and Varela 2001). Focal epileptic seizures originate in specific parts of the cortex; they can remain confined to those areas or spread to other parts of the brain. Their clinical manifestations depend on the cortical area in which they originate, how widely they spread, and how long they last. Local epileptic activity can modify the subject's mental competencies and give rise to various kinds of mental experiences, such as visual or auditory illusions and hallucinations, and memory phenomena involving the vivid actual recall of a past event or déjà-vu illusions. These mental phenomena can also be induced by direct electrical stimulation of the temporal lobe in epileptic patients, as classically described by Wilder Penfield (1938). Thus local neuronal activity at the level of an epileptogenic zone can produce large-scale effects, eventually influencing the global level of a moment of consciousness. This is a case of local-to-global emergence in the brain.

The converse—global-to-local influence—though less documented and more controversial, seems also to be the case. The basic idea is that cognitive activity, which reflects large-scale integration in the brain, can affect local activity. For example, the subject can voluntarily affect local epileptic activity, as indicated by numerous patient reports and a few clinically reported cases (see Le Van Quyen and Petitmengin 2002). As long ago as 1954, Penfield and Jasper described the blocking of a parietal seizure by the initiation of a complex mathematical calculation (Penfield and Jasper 1954), and recently more extensive observations have confirmed such cognitive influences (Schmid-Schonbein 1998). We can assume that such intervention is possible because the epileptogenic zones are embedded in a complex network of other brain regions that actively participate in the large-scale integration underlying cognitive acts. It also seems reasonable to assume that these global patterns of integration can influence local events, including eventually the local epileptogenic zones, whose activity can thus be taken as an indication of the global influence.

Experimental work by Michel Le Van Quyen, Francisco Varela, and their colleagues provides evidence for such global-to-local influence in the case of a patient with an unusually focal and stable occipitotemporal epileptic discharge.[11] This patient showed no evidence of cognitive impairment and was willing to participate in simple cognitive tasks of visual and auditory discrimination. For the visual task, he was asked to press a button when the target stimulus appeared, but not when the two other nontarget stimuli were shown. The temporal intervals between successive discharges of the epileptic spike pattern were analyzed. Dynamical inspection (in the form of a phase space known as a first-return map) showed that the distribution of the intervals followed a particular kind of unstable dynamic pattern. The spikes displayed a distinct periodic activity for a short time before they diverged away along another unstable direction, a kind of dynamic pattern known as an unstable periodic orbit. Furthermore, this activity covaried with the specific mental state of the patient during the perceptual task and appeared to be modulated by the gamma frequency (30–70 Hertz) activity associated with his cognitive states. (Gamma frequency activity is widely reported to be associated with a variety of cognitive processes,

including attention, perception, and memory.) These findings suggest
that the patient's act of perception contributed in a highly specific way
to "pulling" the epileptic activities toward particular unstable periodic
orbits. Such global-to-local influence mobilized by cognitive activity
might open up possibilities for cognitive strategies of control of
epileptic seizures (Le Van Quyen and Petitmengin 2002).

Let me conclude this chapter by linking these ideas about circular
causality and emergence back to autonomy. An autonomy perspective
brings with it a certain way of thinking about emergence. What
emerges in the case of an autonomous system such as a cell is a self-
producing entity that also brings forth its own domain of interactions
(see Figure 3.3). This sort of emergence takes a major step beyond dynamic pattern formation in physical dissipative systems:

> [A]lthough the phenomenon of self-organization always involves the
> generation and maintenance of a global (or high-level) pattern or cor-
> relation that constrains the (low-level) dynamics of the components of
> the system, in standard dissipative structures this occurs only provided
> that the system is put under the appropriate boundary conditions. If
> those (externally controlled) conditions are changed (in particular, if
> the input of matter or energy is outside a certain range), the self-
> organizing dynamic vanishes. Therefore, there is an important differ-
> ence between the typical examples of "spontaneous" dissipative struc-
> tures and real autonomous systems: in the former case, the flow of
> energy and/or matter that keeps the system away from equilibrium is
> not controlled by the organization of the system (the key boundary con-
> ditions are externally established, either by the scientist in the lab or by
> some natural phenomenon that is not causally dependent on the self-
> organizing one), whereas in the latter case, the constraints that actually
> guide energy/matter flows from the environment through the constitu-
> tive processes of the system are endogenously created and maintained.
> (Ruiz-Mirazo and Moreno 2004, p. 238)

An autonomous system, such as a cell or multicellular organism, is
not merely self-maintaining, like a candle flame; it is also self-
producing and thus produces its own self-maintaining processes, including an active topological boundary that demarcates inside from
outside and actively regulates interaction with the environment. In the
single-cell, autopoietic form of autonomy, a membrane-bounded,

metabolic network produces the metabolites that constitute both the network itself and the membrane that permits the network's bounded dynamics. Other autonomous systems have different sorts of self-constructing processes and network topologies. Whether the system is a cell, immune network, nervous system, insect colony, or animal society, what emerges is a unity with its own self-producing identity and domain of interactions or milieu, be it cellular (autopoiesis), somatic (immune networks), sensorimotor and neurocognitive (the nervous system), or social (animal societies).

Dynamic co-emergence best describes the sort of emergence we see in autonomy. In an autonomous system, the whole not only arises from the (organizational closure of) the parts, but the parts also arise from the whole.[12] The whole is constituted by the relations of the parts, and the parts are constituted by the relations they bear to one another in the whole. Hence, the parts do not exist in advance, prior to the whole, as independent entities that retain their identity in the whole. Rather, part and whole co-emerge and mutually specify each other.

Biological life, seen from the perspective of autopoiesis, provides a paradigm case of dynamic co-emergence. A minimal autopoietic whole emerges from the dynamic interdependence of a membrane boundary and an internal chemical reaction network. The membrane and reaction network (as well as the molecules that compose them) do not pre-exist as independent entities. Rather, they co-emerge through their integrative, metabolic relation to each other. They produce and constitute the whole, while the whole produces them and subordinates them to it. We will come back to this paradigm case of dynamic co-emergence in Part II.

FOUR

The Structure of Behavior

THE NOTION OF EMERGENCE presented in the previous chapter can be linked to ideas developed by Merleau-Ponty in his first and underestimated book, *The Structure of Behavior,* published in 1942. What I am calling dynamic co-emergence is the sort of emergence that best describes what Merleau-Ponty means by *form,* namely, a whole that cannot be dislocated from its components but cannot be reduced to them either. Merleau-Ponty uses the notion of form to characterize what he calls the three orders of matter, life, and mind. He states that matter, life, and mind "participate unequally in the nature of form," that they "represent different degrees of integration and . . . constitute a hierarchy in which individuality is progressively achieved" (1963, p. 133). Reviewing these ideas and connecting them to more recent theoretical and empirical developments will help lay the groundwork for the enactive strategy of addressing the explanatory gap by going back to the roots of mind in life and then working forward to subjectivity and consciousness.

Form and Circular Causality

Merleau-Ponty's goal in *The Structure of Behavior* is "to understand the relations of consciousness and nature: organic, psychological or even social. By nature we understand here a multiplicity of events external to each other and bound together by relations of causality" (1963, p. 3). Merleau-Ponty's concern is for what we today would call the explanatory gap between consciousness and nature. His strategy is to introduce a third term, something that does not fit the (Cartesian) consciousness/nature dichotomy in modern philosophy and science, something that will force us to revise how we think about matter, life, and mind. This third term is *behavior:* "taken in itself, it is neutral with respect to the classical distinctions between the 'mental' and the 'physiological' and thus can give us the opportunity of defining them anew" (1963, p. 4). A thorough investigation of behavior will reveal that we need to conceive of natural processes (material, living, and mental) as unities or structured wholes rather than simply as multiplicities of events external to each other, bound together by efficient causal relations. The word "behavior," of course, is not Merleau-Ponty's; he uses the French *comportement,* which better conveys his thought in the present context. The behaviorist connotations of "behavior" are strong in Anglophone philosophy and psychology, and Merleau-Ponty is no behaviorist. On the contrary, *The Structure of Behavior* (*La Structure du Comportement*) includes an extensive critique and rejection of behaviorism. He states the reason for this critique at the outset: "By going through behaviorism . . . one gains at least in being able to introduce consciousness, not as psychological reality or as cause, but as structure" (1963, p. 5).

"Structure" in Merleau-Ponty's usage is synonymous with "form" (a concept he takes from Gestalt psychology, though he thinks Gestalt psychology does not understand it properly). He states, "there is form whenever the properties of a system are modified by every change brought about in a single one of its parts and, on the contrary, are conserved when they all change while maintaining the same relationship among themselves" (1963, p. 47). According to this conception, "[f]orm . . . possesses original properties with regard to those of the parts that can be detached from it. Each moment in it is determined by the grouping of the other moments, and their respective value depends on a state of total equilibrium the formula of which is an intrinsic character of 'form'" (1963, p. 91). Thus organizational closure, in which processes recursively depend on each other for their own generation and realization, and constitute a system as a unity, is a type of form in Merleau-Ponty's sense.

By analyzing certain psychological and physiological theories of his time, Merleau-Ponty argues that behavior cannot be decomposed into parts understood as separate elements, whether these be stimulus and conditioned response according to behaviorism or isolable nerve circuits according to neurophysiology. He calls such decompositional explanation "realistic analysis" or "mechanical thinking"; it treats wholes as exhaustively analyzable into parts externally related to one another. Neither life processes (the province of biology) nor mental processes (the province of psychology) can be understood through realistic analysis because (i) these processes are nondecomposable structures of behavior or forms of comportment; (ii) form or structure is constituted by the reciprocal determination of whole and part; and (iii) such reciprocal determination is recognizable only to "dialectical thinking," but not mechanical thinking.

The claim that behavior has to be understood dialectically brings us to Merleau-Ponty's conception of dialectical relations.[1] As is clear from the way Merleau-Ponty opposes mechanical and dialectical relations, part of what it is to be mechanical is to be linear, and part of what it is to be dialectical is to be nonlinear. Early in the book he writes: "the relations between the organism and its milieu are not relations of linear causality but of circular causality" (1963, p. 15). Later he gives the following definition of mechanical relations:

> A mechanical action, whether the word is taken in a restricted or looser sense, is one in which the cause and the effect are decomposable into real elements which have a one-to-one correspondence. In elementary actions, the dependence is uni-directional; the cause is the necessary and sufficient condition of the effect considered in its existence and its nature; and, even when one speaks of reciprocal action between two terms, it can be reduced to a series of uni-directional determinations. (1963, pp. 160–161)

Hence a mechanical relation between A and B is one in which (supposing A to be the cause of B): (i) A determines B (A is the necessary and sufficient condition of B); (ii) B does not determine A (uni-directional dependence); and (iii) every element of A that is causally efficacious on B stands in a one-one mapping with some resulting element of B (one-to-one correspondence). Conditions (ii) and (iii) make the relation a linear one. By contrast, a dialectical relation is one in which: (i) A determines B, and B determines A (bi-directional dependence or reciprocal determination); and (ii) neither A nor B is analyzable into discrete, causally efficacious elements that stand in a one-to-one correspondence (nondecom-posability). Furthermore, dialectical relations are dynamic, not static. Hence (iii) A alters B, and B alters A; (iv) A is altered by B *as determinant of B,* and B is altered by A *as determinant of A;* and (v) it makes sense deriva-tively to speak of A making what A is via B, and B making what B is via A (Priest 1998, p. 163). Given these kinds of close interdependencies, A and B can also be regarded as parts of a larger global whole or pattern when they are dialectically related. Hence (vi) what A is a part of is what B is a part of (Priest 1998, p. 43).

It is on the basis of this conception of dialectical relations that Merleau-Ponty can assert: "The genesis of the whole by composition of the parts is fictitious. It arbitrarily breaks the chain of reciprocal deter-minations" (1963, p. 50). That such reciprocal determination implies what complex systems theory today tries to describe in terms of non-linearity, self-organization, circular causality, and structural coupling is evident in what Merleau-Ponty goes on to write immediately after his explanation of mechanical relations quoted above:

> On the contrary, as we have seen, physical stimuli act upon the or-ganism only by eliciting a global response which will vary qualitatively when the stimuli vary quantitatively; with respect to the organism they play the role of occasions rather than of cause; the reaction depends on their vital significance rather than on the material properties of the stimuli. (1963, p. 161)

To say that the organism's global response varies qualitatively when the stimuli vary quantitatively is to say that stimuli act upon the or-ganism as control parameters, which upon reaching a certain critical threshold induce a global qualitative discontinuity in the organism (a bifurcation in phase space). To say that stimuli play the role of occa-sions rather than cause is to say that they act as triggering conditions but not as efficient causes. To say that the organism's reaction depends on the vital significance of the stimulus is to say that the informational stimulus is not equivalent to the physical stimulus. The latter is defin-able independently of the organism; the former is not. The informa-tional stimulus is the stimulus as informed by (the form or structure of) the organism. It cannot be described as "input" definable inde-pendently of the organism because it is already relational, definable only in relation to the organism, or specifiable only against the back-

ground of the organism's structural coupling with its environment.
Thus Merleau-Ponty continues:

> Hence, between the variables upon which conduct actually depends
> and this conduct itself there appears a relation of *meaning,* an *intrinsic
> relation* [emphasis added]. One cannot assign a moment in which the
> world acts on the organism, since the very effect of this "action" ex-
> presses the internal law of the organism. The mutual exteriority of the
> organism and the milieu is surmounted along with the mutual exteri-
> ority of the stimuli. Thus, two correlatives must be substituted for these
> two terms defined in isolation: the "milieu" and the "aptitude," which
> are like two poles of behavior and participate in the same structure.
> (1963, p. 161)

These remarks can be related to my earlier discussion (in Chapter 3)
of meaning and information, understood from the perspective of autonomous systems. Something acquires meaning for an organism to the
extent that it relates (either positively or negatively) to the norm of the
maintenance of the organism's integrity (De Preester 2003, p. 202).
Such maintenance is a function of what Merleau-Ponty calls the "internal law of the organism," which, in our terms, means the organism's
autonomy. Biological autonomy thus necessarily includes the bringing
about of norms. To appreciate this point we can refer back to Figure 3.3
(see Chapter 3). This figure attempts to depict how organizational-
operational closure generates a circular and dialectical relation between an autonomous system and its correlative domain of interactions
or milieu. On the one hand, operational closure is the mechanism
(principle of pattern formation) for an emergent identity or "self." On
the other hand, the realization of a "self" through closure is simultaneously also the specification of a correlative environment, a domain of
interactions or milieu. This milieu constituted through closure is intrinsically meaningful for the "self" that is also so constituted. Meaning
is intrinsic to the coupling of organism and milieu, and thus surmounts
their mutual exteriority.

When Merleau-Ponty writes that the two poles of behavior (organism and milieu) participate in the same structure, he means, first,
that behavior or comportment is a structured whole, a dynamic pattern, and, second, that milieu and organism participate in this structure not as stimulus and reaction but as situation and response. Be-

havior is a kind of dialogue in which the organism has an "aptitude" to respond to situations as in effect questions that need answering. Behavior is, as it were, dialogical and expresses meaning-constitution rather than information processing. It follows that behavior does not exist *in* the nervous system or *in* the body (1963, p. 161) any more than a conversation exists in the individual speakers (or their brains) or a jazz improvisation exists in the individual instruments or soloists.

These points can be linked to theoretical and empirical developments that have taken place since Merleau-Ponty's time. Merleau-Ponty's first point, stated in contemporary language, is that behavior is *morphodynamic*. Morphodynamics is a branch of dynamic systems theory concerned with the emergence of form or structure (Petitot 1992, 1995, 1999). The basic idea is that "structures are essentially dependent on *critical phenomena,* i.e., on phenomena of symmetry breaking which induce qualitative discontinuities (heterogeneities) in the substrates . . . Discrete structures emerge via qualitative discontinuities . . . a system of qualitative discontinuities in a substrate is called a *morphology* and dynamic theories of morphologies belong to what is called *morphodynamics.* There is therefore a close link between the concept of 'structure' and morphodynamics" (Petitot 1995, p. 231; emphasis in original).

A contemporary formulation of Merleau-Ponty's second point is that behavior is a collective phenomenon comprising brain, body, and environment, not something that resides inside the nervous system. It therefore needs to be characterized by collective variables and order parameters that cut across the brain, body, and environment. This idea is an important theme of research in embodied dynamicist cognitive science (Chiel and Beer 1997; Thelen and Smith 1994; Thelen et al. 2001). Kelso's work can serve as a useful example. In certain experimental paradigms involving intentional motor behavior and cortical activity (Bressler and Kelso 2001; Kelso et al. 1998), he has shown that the same collective variable of relative phase expresses "an abstract order parameter isomorphism between brain and behavioral events that cuts across the fact that different things are being coordinated" (Kelso 1995, p. 276). In other words, at a morphodynamic level, the same form or structure is taken to characterize certain sensorimotor behaviors and brain activities. Merleau-Ponty's thesis that "behavior is a form" (1963, p. 127) can thus be mathematically elaborated and empirically substantiated by morphodynamical science. Merleau-Ponty's thought toward the end of his life also moved in this morphodynamical direction, when he spoke in his 1959–1960 lectures of a "phenomenal topology" of nature (2003, p. 264).

The Physical and Living Orders

In the penultimate chapter of *The Structure of Behavior*, Merleau-Ponty sketches a rudimentary phenomenal topology of matter, life, and mind, or as he calls them, the three orders of the physical, the vital, and the human. He begins by considering the notion of form or structure in physics. A physical form, like a soap bubble or a convection roll, is a structural stability established in relation to given external conditions (1963, p. 145) and thus stands out as a qualitative discontinuity in the material substrate. Already at this level, analytical reductionism is to be rejected:

> [E]ach local change in a [physical] form will be translated by a redistribution of forces which assures us of the constancy of their relation; it is this internal circulation which is the system as a physical reality. And it is no more composed of parts which can be distinguished in it than a melody (always transposable) is made of the particular notes which are its momentary expression. Possessing internal unity inscribed in a segment of space and resisting deformation from external influences by its circular causality, the physical form is an individual. It can happen that, submitted to external forces which increase and decrease in a continuous manner, the system, beyond a certain threshold, redistributes its own forces in a qualitatively different order which is nevertheless only another expression of its immanent law. Thus, with form, a principle of discontinuity is introduced and the conditions for a development by leaps or crises, for an event or for a history, are given. (1963, p. 137)

This description of physical form as introducing a principle of discontinuity and the conditions for development by "crises" has been borne out by theoretical developments after Merleau-Ponty. Particular developments are René Thom's "catastrophe theory," which mathematically describes abrupt transitions and qualitative discontinuities in physical systems (Thom 1975), and Jean Petitot's (1992) extension of Thom's work to a morphodynamical "physics of phenomenality," which aims to bridge the gap between the microphysical substrate and the macrophysical, phenomenal modes of manifestation of matter (see Petitot and Smith 1996).

Whereas the physical order is characterized by the emergence of physical forms as qualitative discontinuities in a material substrate, the vital order is characterized by the emergence of living structures in the physical order. Like physical structures, living structures, too, obtain stability in relation to external influences, but they do so in a different way:

> The physical form is an equilibrium obtained with respect to certain given external conditions . . . Doubtless certain physical systems modify the very conditions upon which they depend by their internal evolution . . . But action which is exercised outside the system always has the effect of reducing a state of tension, of advancing the system toward rest. We speak of vital structures, on the contrary, when equilibrium is obtained, not with respect to real and present conditions, but with respect to conditions which are only virtual and which the system itself brings into existence; when the structure, instead of procuring a release from the forces with which it is penetrated through the pressure of external ones, executes a work beyond its proper limits and constitutes a proper milieu for itself. (1963, pp. 145–146)

This transition from physical structures to living structures is the transition from matter to life, from physics and chemistry to biology. The simplest living structures are metabolic structures. If we combine Merleau-Ponty's account with the theory of biological autonomy (Ruiz-Mirazo and Moreno 2004; Varela 1979, 1997a), then we can say that a living cell differs from a dissipative physical structure in three main respects. First, a living cell dynamically produces and maintains itself through the continual chemical synthesis and breakdown (anabolism and catabolism) of material compounds, including those that make up its own membrane boundary. In so doing, it also endogenously controls and regulates its own external boundary conditions, whereas a dissipative physical structure (such as a candle flame) does not. Living structures are self-producing and self-regulating unities, and so they have a qualitatively different type of morphodynamics from dissipative physical structures. In a living cell, the endogenously produced organization of the system also actively controls the flow of matter and energy that keeps the system away from thermodynamic equilibrium.

Second, the material and energetic demands of this entire process orient the cell of necessity toward the environment, not simply in the sense of real and present conditions, but also in the sense of conditions that need to be actualized (effected or procured)—in other words, *virtual conditions*. Organisms shape the physicochemical environment into a milieu (an *Umwelt*). A milieu, from the standpoint of what is present and real at the physicochemical level, is virtual, something needing to be actualized, and actualized moreover at another level, the level of vital *norms* and *meaning*.

This last point brings us to the third respect in which living structures differ from mere physical structures: whereas physical structures can be expressed by a law, living structures have to be comprehended in relation to norms: "Thus each organism, in the presence of a given milieu, has its optimal conditions of activity and its proper manner of realizing equilibrium" (1963, p. 148). A living cell or organism "modifies its milieu according to the internal norms of its activity" (1963, p. 154).

Bacterial (prokaryotic) cells, the simplest autopoietic systems on Earth, can be used to illustrate this conception of living structures. *Escherichia coli (E. coli)* is a kind of bacteria that has motile, rod-shaped cells. When swimming in the presence of a sucrose gradient, these cells will tumble about until they hit upon an orientation that increases their exposure to sucrose. At this point they will swim forward, up-gradient, propelled by their flagella, toward the zone of greatest sucrose concentration. While sucrose is a real and present condition of the physicochemical environment, the status of sucrose as a nutrient is not. Being a nutrient is not intrinsic to the physicochemical structure of the sucrose molecule; it is a relational feature, linked to the bacterium's metabolism. In Merleau-Ponty's terminology, the status of sucrose as food is virtual. It is something actualized at another level. Specifically, it is enacted or brought forth by the way the organism, given its autonomy and the norms its autonomy brings about, couples with the environment. Sucrose belongs to the physical order; sucrose-as-nutrient belongs to the living order. Sucrose has meaning and value as food but only in the milieu that "the system itself brings into existence" or "constitutes for itself."

In order to give a full and complete account of the bacterium's activity in swimming up the sucrose gradient, it is not sufficient to refer simply to the local molecular effects of sucrose as it traverses the membrane and gets taken up internally. Although these local effects are indeed crucial, they are at every step subordinated to and regulated by the global maintenance of autopoiesis. In other words, the local molecular effects happen as they do because of the global and organizational context in which they are embedded. And it is this global level that defines the bacterium as a biological individual and sucrose as food.

Living structures are thus ontologically emergent with respect to mere physical structures. They constitute a new order of nature that is qualitatively distinct from the merely physical order. This new order is marked by two generic characteristics. The first is that an organism is an individual in a new and precise sense that goes beyond the earlier notion of physical individuality. Although Merleau-Ponty earlier stated that "the physical form is an individual" (1963, p. 137), he now states that an organism "is an individual in a sense which is not that of even modern physics" (p. 154). A physical form is an individual in the sense of being an invariant topological pattern in a changing material substrate (like a convection roll or soap bubble). Individuality in this case corresponds to identity of form through material change. A living form, in the autopoietic sense, is one whose own organization (defining network of relations) is the fundamental, morphodynamic invariant through material change. An autopoietic system is a circular network whose constituent molecular processes both produce and embody that network. Individuality in this case corresponds to a *formal self-identity*—to an invariant dynamic pattern that is produced, maintained, and realized by the system itself, while the system undergoes incessant material transformation and regulates its external boundary conditions accordingly. An autopoietic system is thus an individual in a sense that begins to be worthy of the term *self*. The second generic characteristic marking the living order is that the relation between organism and environment is meaningful and normative. As Figure 3.3 depicts, meaning (or significance or information) is implicated once there is the coupling of a co-defined self-pole and environment-pole, and such coupling is intrinsically normative (in the biological sense of norms discussed above).

I will develop this account of life in more detail in Part II. It can be summarized now, using the theory of autopoiesis to elucidate Merleau-Ponty's account, by saying that living structures are those based on autopoiesis.

The Human Order

Merleau-Ponty's third order is the human order. The human order has originality in that its most typical structures and forms of behavior are symbolic.[2] Symbols or symbolic structures do not exist in isolation but belong to symbol systems. In these systems each symbol is related not simply to what it symbolizes—the thing or event, for instance, for which it stands—but also to other symbols. These lateral relations among symbols open up the possibility of varied expressions or representations of the same thing. Symbols imply the mental ability to grasp something as an invariant under a diversity of aspects and perspectives. Thus symbols imply the ability to grasp something as an *object*, in the phenomenological sense of something that remains invariant through perspectival variation and is graspable by the subject as also being available to other subjects. Yet what is especially distinctive about human symbolic behavior for Merleau-Ponty is that it is directed not toward things or objects as such but toward "use-objects"—things endowed with culturally constituted meanings. Thus symbolic behavior implies the enactment of a whole new kind of milieu. This milieu is no longer vital situation-response but "perceived situation-work" (1963, p. 162).[3]

The pair "perceived situation-work" comprises more than the pair "perception-action"—even as this second pair is understood today by dynamic sensorimotor theories, which maintain that perception and action constitute one another instead of being merely instrumentally related as means to end (Hurley 1998; Noë 2004; O'Regan and Noë 2001a). The difference between the two sets of pairs is that the structure "perceived situation-work" is essentially intersubjective.

By "perceived situation" Merleau-Ponty means perception of the actions of other subjects, upon which is founded the perception of things as cultural use-objects. Merleau-Ponty maintains that the "original object" of human perception, both developmentally (first in ontogenetic time) and phenomenologically (the most fundamental or primordial in the constitution of experience), is the intentional action of another human subject (1963, p. 166). Human perception is primarily directed toward how intentions are expressed in other human beings rather than toward objects of nature and their sensory qualities. Human perception grasps intentions as "experienced realities," not as objects in a detached or intellectual sense. As Merleau-Ponty points out, anticipating subsequent research in developmental psychology, the infant's first experienced realities in visual perception are the face and gestures of the mother or caregiver. The mother's face is not an object or a mere collection of sensory qualities, but a center of intentional expression and action (see, for example, Meltzoff and Moore 1998; Stern 2000; Trevarthen and Aitken 2001). Perception is thus first and foremost physiognomic, and later it is directed toward things as use-objects. Perception never loses its physiognomic quality; it remains physiognomic not simply in its nascent phases, but in its mature phenomenal character (an idea that gains importance in Merleau-Ponty's subsequent writings).

By "work," Merleau-Ponty means activities (ensembles of intentional actions) that transform physical and living nature and thereby modify the milieu or produce a new one (1963, p. 162). Work is forward-looking and creative or productive. By altering the present milieu, work in effect negates it in favor of a new one. (Merleau-Ponty uses the word "work" instead of "action" precisely to convey this Hegelian idea.) The correlative form of perception required for work is perception that presents its object not as something simply there now (something present and actual), but as something of use that can change other things (something oriented in relation to the future and possibilities).

Whereas living structures are ontologically emergent with respect to physical ones, the human structure "perceived situation-work" is emergent with respect to living structures. It represents a new kind of dialectical relation between organism and milieu, or self and world. For this reason, Merleau-Ponty states: "although all actions permit an adaptation to life, the word 'life' does not have the same meaning in animality and humanity; and the conditions of life are defined by the proper essence of the species" (1963, p. 174). A key feature of human life is the ambiguity of its dialectical relation to its milieu. The human milieu is social and cultural, and it is created by human beings themselves. Our symbolic forms of behavior enable us to create social and

cultural structures to which we are committed. Yet we refuse to let ourselves become identical to them; we are always trying to pass beyond
them and create new things. In Merleau-Ponty's words: "use-objects
and cultural objects would not be what they are if the activity which
brings about their appearance did not also have as its meaning to reject them and to surpass them" (1963, p. 176; emphasis omitted). This
self-surpassing mentality is a structural precondition for cultural forms
in the first place (even while it is always already reciprocally constituted by them in any of its concrete instances). Exemplified in the
human order, this mentality is emergent not simply in relation to the
living order overall, but also in relation to higher animals (1963, pp.
175–176).

   With these ideas, Merleau-Ponty passes from a static and genetic
phenomenology of form or structure to a generative phenomenology
of intersubjectivity and culture (or from a phenomenal topology of nature to a phenomenal topology of culture.)

   In this book, I follow Merleau-Ponty's lead, beginning with life, development, and evolution (Chapters 5–7), then proceeding on to consciousness (Chapters 8–12), and finally discussing empathy and enculturation (Chapter 13).

Consciousness and the Structure of Behavior

Let me return to the overall goal of *The Structure of Behavior*, which is to
bridge the explanatory gap between consciousness and nature by revising how we think about matter, life, and mind. The burden of
Merleau-Ponty's argument has been to show that the notion of form
can both integrate the orders of matter, life, and mind and account for
the originality of each order. On the one hand, nature is not pure exteriority, but rather in the case of life has its own interiority and thus
resembles mind. On the other hand, mind is not pure interiority, but
rather a form or structure of engagement with the world and thus resembles life.

   The first side of this story begins with matter and life. Given the notion of form as Merleau-Ponty presents it, we can no longer understand nature in Cartesian fashion as simply "a multiplicity of events external to each other and bound together by relations of causality"
(1963, p. 3). This conception of nature as sheer exteriority (*partes extra*

partes, as Merleau-Ponty puts it) is already surpassed by the morphody-namical notion of form at the physical level. Form, so understood, "is no more composed of parts which can be distinguished in it than a melody (always transposable) is made of the particular notes which are its momentary expression" (1963, p. 137).

It is at the vital level, however, that interiority arises. Interiority comprises both the *self-production of an inside,* that is, an autopoietic individual, and the *internal and normative relation* holding between this individual and its environment (the "intrinsic relation" that surmounts the "mutual exteriority of organism and milieu"—Merleau-Ponty 1963, p. 121).

As we have seen, this sort of interiority—the self-production of an inside that also specifies an outside to which it is normatively related—arises through autopoietic closure and the thermodynamic requirements of basic autonomy. Thus autopoiesis is a condition of possibility for the dynamic emergence of interiority (Varela 1991, 1997a). As just remarked, however, this emergence of an inside is also the specification of an outside. Thus the dynamic emergence of interiority can be more fully described as the dynamic co-emergence of interiority and exteriority.

Nevertheless, there seems to be an asymmetry here, for it is the internal self-production process that controls or regulates the system's interaction with the outside environment (Varela 1991). As we have seen, the thermodynamic requirements of basic autonomy in its autopoietic form entail that the system actively regulate its external boundary conditions, that is, how matter and energy flow through the system. The capacity for such regulation in turn entails that the system be not simply an internally self-producing system, but also an interactive agent in its environment (Ruiz-Mirazo and Moreno 2004). Hence, although inside and outside are dynamically co-emergent, they do not share the same symmetrical relation. As Moreno and Barandiaran explain: "the (self) generation of an inside is ontologically prior to the dichotomy in-out. It is the inside that generates the asymmetry and it is in relation to this inside that an outside can be established. Although the interactive processes/relations are necessary for the maintenance of the system, they presuppose it (the system) since it is the internal organization of the system that controls the interactive relations" (Moreno and Barandiaran 2004, p. 17).

Merleau-Ponty's point is that once we recognize this sort of interiority and the normativity it includes, then we can no longer regard life as a mechanism in the classical sense (an arrangement of parts externally related to each other through efficient causal relations). Rather, we must then see nature as having a kind of inner life, for which the classical notion of mechanism is completely inadequate. This line of thought thus points away from Descartes, who radically severed mind from biological life, toward Aristotle, for whom mind and life belonged together under the heading of soul or psyche (see Chapter 8).

The second side of the story is the rethinking of mind, and in particular human consciousness, that runs alongside this rethinking of nature. Consciousness is not an interior state of the mind or brain that stands in a linear causal relation to sensory input and motor output. It is a form or structure of comportment, a perceptual and motor attunement to the world. In our human case, this attunement is primarily to an environment of meaningful symbols and the intentional actions of others. Merleau-Ponty uses the following example to illustrate these ideas:

> For the player in action the football field is not an "object," that is, the ideal term which can give rise to an indefinite multiplicity of perspectival views and remain equivalent under its apparent transformations. It is pervaded with lines of force (the "yard lines"; those which demarcate the "penalty area") and articulated in sectors (for example, the "openings" between the adversaries) which call for a certain mode of action and which initiate and guide the action as if the player were unaware of it. The field itself is not given to him, but present as the immanent term of his practical intentions; the player becomes one with it and feels the direction of the "goal," for example, just as immediately as the vertical and the horizontal planes of his own body. It would not be sufficient to say that consciousness inhabits this milieu. At this moment consciousness is nothing other than the dialectic of milieu and action. Each maneuver undertaken by the player modifies the character of the field and establishes in it new lines of force in which the action in turn unfolds and is accomplished, again altering the phenomenal field. (1963, pp. 168–169)

This conception of consciousness as skillful attunement to the environment resonates strongly with contemporary dynamic sensorimotor

approaches to perceptual consciousness. In these approaches, perceptual experience is the skillful exercise of sensorimotor knowledge
(Noë 2004; O'Regan and Noë 2001a). I discuss the dynamic sensorimotor approach to perceptual consciousness in Chapter 9 and return
to Merleau-Ponty's idea of skillful, attuned consciousness at the beginning of Chapter 11.

Naturalism and the Phenomenological Attitude

So far I have presented only one side of Merleau-Ponty's view, the one
he describes as "the point of view of the 'outside spectator'" (1963, p.
184). This perspective is the one adopted by the empirical sciences
(physics, chemistry, biology, and psychology) in viewing matter, life,
and mind as part of nature. Merleau-Ponty adopts this perspective in
order to enrich it with the notion of form. The other side of Merleau-
Ponty's view, however, is to step back and look at how form becomes
constituted as an object for scientific cognition in the first place. What
is the mode or manner in which form appears, and what is the epistemological origin of this mode of givenness? This question is philosophical and expresses the perspective of transcendental phenomenology. Thus the other side of Merleau-Ponty's view is that of the inside
participant, who refuses to be satisfied simply with an outsider's or
spectator's perspective on matter, life, and mind but who aims also for
a transcendental phenomenological understanding of how they come
to be constituted for consciousness.

Adopting this second perspective, Merleau-Ponty puts forward the
following argument: (i) The notion of form is borrowed from the perceived world; (ii) the notion of form is encountered in physics only to
the extent that physics refers us back to perceived things; (iii) hence,
the notion of "physical form" cannot be the real foundation of the
structure of behavior, in particular of behavior's perceptual structure;
and (iv) the notion of form is conceivable only as an object of perception (1963, p. 144). In other words, Merleau-Ponty argues that naturalism needs the notion of form (and has come to recognize this need
through its own inner development), but this notion is irreducibly
phenomenal. Hence naturalism cannot explain matter, life, and mind,
as long as explanation means purging nature of subjectivity and then
trying to reconstitute subjectivity out of nature thus purged.

There is something important in this argument, but we need to be careful. In particular, we need to guard against making it into an argument for metaphysical idealism—that physical forms are constructions out of a preexistent consciousness. Rather, the argument needs to be understood as expressing a transcendental line of thought. When we ask the constitutional question of how objects are disclosed to us, then any object, including any scientific object, must be regarded in its correlation to the mental activity that intends it. This transcendental orientation in no way denies the existence of a real physical world, but rather rejects an objectivist conception of our relation to it. The world is never given to us as a brute fact detachable from our conceptual frameworks. Rather, it shows up in all the describable ways it does thanks to the structure of our subjectivity and our intentional activities. Michel Bitbol presents a clear statement of this transcendental attitude:

> What is then the central idea of transcendental philosophy? It is to construe each object of science as the focus of a synthesis of phenomena rather than as a thing in itself. And it is to accept accordingly that the very possibility of such objects depends on the connecting structures provided in advance by the procedures used in our research activities. Thus something is objective if it results from a universal and necessary mode of connection of phenomena. In other terms, something is objective if it holds true for any (human) active subject, not if it concerns intrinsic properties of autonomous entities.
>
> Here science is not supposed to reveal anything of a preexistent underlying absolute reality, nor is it a more or less random aggregate of efficient recipes. Science is rather the stabilized byproduct of a dynamic reciprocal relation between reality as a whole and a special fraction of it. Defining this special fraction of reality qua subject is the reverse side of its actively extracting objectlike invariant clusters of phenomena.
>
> Somebody who shares this attitude is metaphysically as agnostic as empiricists, but as convinced as realists that the structure of scientific theories is highly significant. For, from a transcendental standpoint, the structure of a scientific theory is nothing less than the frame of procedural rationalities that underpin a certain research practice (and that, conversely, were constrained by the resistances arising from the enaction of this practice). (Bitbol 2003, pp. 336–337)

Bitbol's formulation acknowledges that active experiencing subjects do not remain unaffected by the objectivity they help to constitute, but are rather reciprocally affected and constituted by it. As Husserl recognized, although the life-world is the horizon and ground of all experience, and must therefore be presupposed by science, science also "streams into" the life-world (Husserl 1970, pp. 113, 138). Merleau-Ponty, however, sometimes seems to lose sight of this point, particularly in his discussion of the relation between physical form and phenomenal form in *The Structure of Behavior*. To see what I mean we need to consider his argument for the priority of the phenomenal in light of theoretical and empirical developments since his time.

Merleau-Ponty first introduces the argument midway through the book when discussing the relation between behavior and the brain. Having argued against an atomistic conception of nerve functioning and for the necessity of a dynamic and structural (morphodynamic) account of brain processes (1963, pp. 60–91)—thus anticipating views of the brain as a complex, self-organizing system—Merleau-Ponty indicates that two different meanings are possible in this analysis (1963, pp. 91–93). On the one hand, by characterizing brain processes topologically, one could aim to maintain the priority of the nervous system in relation to mind. In this view, psychological phenomena are physiologically localized, not topographically in the anatomical space of the brain's components, but topologically as dynamic forms or patterns of neuronal activity, visible as "figures" against the "background" of activity in the rest of the brain (and body). In this way, as Merleau-Ponty points out, "a rigorous 'isomorphism' could be maintained" between psychological and physiological phenomena (1963, p. 92). This thesis of psychoneural isomorphism, classically associated with Gestalt psychology (see Köhler 1947), animates today's dynamic systems approach:

> If thoughts, according to the theory, must be expressed in terms of ϕ-like [relative phase-like] collective variables that characterize dynamic patterns of spatiotemporal activity in the brain, then the following conclusion appears logically inescapable: an order parameter isomorphism connects mind and body, will and brain, mental and neural events. Mind itself is a spatiotemporal pattern that molds the metastable dynamic patterns of the brain. Mind-body dualism is replaced by a single

isomorphism, the heart of which is semantically meaningful pattern variables. (Kelso 1995, pp. 288–289)

The second meaning Merleau-Ponty discerns is that an analysis of brain and behavior using the notion of form might also refer us back to the phenomenal notion of form. Merleau-Ponty explains this line of thought as follows:

> But the very fact that we had to borrow the terms "figure" and "ground" from the phenomenal or perceived world in order to describe these "physiological forms" . . . leads us to wonder if these are still *physiological* phenomena, if we can in principle conceive of processes which are still physiological and which would adequately symbolize the relations inherent in what is ordinarily called "consciousness" . . .
>
> The function, "dot on a homogenous ground," or more generally, the function, "figure and ground," has a meaning only in the perceived world: it is there that we learn what it is to be a figure and what it is to be a ground. The perceived would be explicable only by the perceived itself, and not by physiological processes. A physiological analysis of perception would be purely and simply impossible . . . Since this structure of behavior and the cerebral functioning which supports it can only be conceived in terms borrowed from the perceived world, the latter no longer appears as an order of phenomena parallel to the order of physiological phenomena but as one which is richer than it. Physiology cannot be completely conceptualized without borrowing from psychology. (1963, pp. 92–93)

According to this line of thought, the notion of form is irreducibly phenomenal and descriptive, not physiological and causal. Nevertheless, it is impossible to characterize neural functioning physiologically without this notion. Thus the phenomenal domain supplies the meaning of physiological constructs, and hence there cannot be any one-to-one equivalence between the phenomenal and physiological domains.

Once again, there is something important in this line of thought, but we need to proceed carefully. It is true that the notion of phenomenal form is conceptually and epistemologically prior to the notions of physical and physiological form. For example, the scientific theories of morphogenesis (Thom 1975) and morphodynamics (Petitot 1992) take as their main primitive a phenomenal notion of "qualitative discontinuity" (discontinuous variations in qualities). This notion can be rigorously described phenomenologically, following Husserl's *Logical Investigations,* in terms of the distinction between "separated" and "blended" sensible qualities (Husserl 2000, vols. 2, 3: §8, pp. 448–450). But this notion can also be given a mathematical expression in topology and can then be used to give an account of perceptually salient, macrophysical forms (see Petitot and Smith 1996). This morphological account is not only descriptive, but also explanatory, because it can be used to establish a bridge between microphysical accounts of the material substrate and macrophysical, phenomenal forms.

That there is a science of "pheno-physics" (qualitative physics of phenomenal morphologies) implies that "qualitative discontinuity" and "form" do not have meaning "only in the perceived world." First, phenomenal form is mathematically describable and hence has meaning in mathematics. Second, this mathematical morphology can be given physical and physiological content, through morphodynamic models of macrophysical and neurophysiological systems (see Petitot 1994, 1999). Hence it is also not the case that the perceived is "explicable only by the perceived itself." On the contrary, the perceived is explicable by mathematical models that link brain processes and behavior at morphodynamic levels. Merleau-Ponty apparently did not envision the possibility of such developments (at least not in 1942). Here he was undoubtedly influenced by Husserl, who expressly doubted that there could be mathematical descriptions of phenomenal forms. Neither thinker, however, even Husserl the mathematician, could have foreseen the advances in topology and differential geometry that would make such a description possible (see Petitot 1999; Roy et al. 1999, pp. 54–56). These new developments can also be taken to support Merleau-Ponty when he writes, "A physiological analysis of perception would be purely and simply impossible," if by "physiological analysis" he means an analysis at a strictly neuronal level independent of any higher-order, morphodynamic level of explanation.

The issue of isomorphism is complex and will surface again at various points later in this book.[4] Suffice it to say here that if isomorphism is interpreted simply as a working hypothesis for trying to characterize neural activity in relation to psychological processes, then it is hard to see how Merleau-Ponty's assertion that the physiological cannot be completely conceptualized without borrowing from the phenomenal could stand as an objection. One can acknowledge that physiological concepts have origins in the phenomenal world, yet nonetheless maintain that there may be isomorphisms at a certain level or of a certain type between physiological phenomena and perceptual phenomena. As we have seen, morphodynamics takes this approach, as does Varela (1999) in his neurophenomenology of time-consciousness, discussed in Chapter 11. Furthermore, Merleau-Ponty seems to miss the key point that the notion of form is enlarged and enriched in meaning when extended from the phenomenal domain into mathematics, physics, and biology. This enrichment need not leave the phenomenal notion unchanged but can circulate back to modify and reshape it.

When Merleau-Ponty criticizes what he calls naturalism or realism, it is really objectivism he has in mind. Objectivism maintains that "structures can be found *in* a nature taken in-itself *(en soi)* and that mind can be constituted from them" (1963, p. 140). Objectivism tries to purge nature of subjectivity and then reconstitute subjectivity out of nature thus purged (see Husserl, 1970, pp. 20–100). The problem with this way of thinking is that it forgets that physiological processes, as describable phenomena of scientific investigation, are also constituted in the phenomenological sense. This critical point, however, holds at a transcendental level of analysis. Hence, Merleau-Ponty's argument seems best interpreted as an argument against the objectivist who would try to nullify the transcendental status of consciousness by appealing to psychoneural isomorphism.

The point here would have to be something along the following lines: because of the transcendental status of consciousness (that consciousness is always already presupposed as an invariant condition of possibility for the disclosure of any object), there is no way to step outside, as it were, of experiencing subjectivity, so as to effect a one-one mapping of it onto an external reality purged of any and all subjectivity. It is in this transcendental sense that the phenomenal world is richer than any region of scientific objects—even the presumed "universal" region of physics. And it is only from this transcendental standpoint that Merleau-Ponty's reversal of the order "physical → vital → human" or "matter → life → mind" makes sense. Mind emerges from matter and life at an empirical level, but at a transcendental level every form or structure is necessarily also a form or structure disclosed by consciousness. With this reversal one passes from the natural attitude of the scientist to the transcendental phenomenological attitude (which, according to phenomenology, is the properly philosophical attitude).

If we follow Merleau-Ponty's lead, but combine it with the more recent developments reviewed in this chapter and the previous one, then we can begin to envision a different kind of approach to matter, life, and mind from objectivism and reductionism. Starting from a recognition of the transcendental and hence ineliminable status of experience, the aim would be to search for morphodynamical principles that can both integrate the orders of matter, life, and mind, and account for the originality of each order. This approach is precisely what Varela envisioned in calling for a "neurophenomenology" in mind science (Varela 1996).

The rest of this book takes up this task. I begin in Part II by reconsidering the nature of life or living being. For phenomenology, living being is living subjectivity; for biology, it is living organisms. The subject matter of the next three chapters is living being in this full sense.

PART TWO

◆

Life in Mind

◆ ◆ ◆

FIVE

Autopoiesis

The Organization of the Living

IN LIFE EVERY BEGINNING IS UNIQUE, but none is isolated and self-contained. We start out as single cells, formed from the union of two parent cells, an egg and a sperm. Our parent cells, too, are offspring, produced in the bodies of our mothers and fathers, who owe their origins to still earlier couplings of egg and sperm. Every beginning has a beginning before it and another one before that, leading back through the receding biological past to its time and place of origin, the beginning of life on Earth.

Around four billion years stand between our time and that distant aeon of life's emergence. A number of that magnitude is hard for the human mind to comprehend. Its vastness seems to diminish the force of pointing to our common ancestry with all the living things on Earth. Closer to home are the one hundred billion nerve cells or neurons that make up the human brain. All are the progeny of a small fold of cells that emerged when we were embryos of about four weeks. Inside each one of them, in its protein and DNA, we can find a family resemblance to the genes and enzymes of all the other living cells on Earth.

We harbor the past everywhere within our bodies. To the cells inside us the chemical composition of the somatic environment plays a role reminiscent of the ocean environment where the earliest cells resided. Three billion years ago bacteria swam in the warm shallows of the Earth's primeval seas. Among their descendants today are the bacteria dwelling within our bodies, without which we could not live, while other remnants of their progeny, such as mitochondria and mobile cilia, exist inside our modern cells (Margulis 1984, 1993).

The idea that all life evolved from a common ancestor and hence that there is an underlying unity to the widespread diversity of life is central to modern biology. We are taught in school that the unity of life is based on three things: (1) all living things are made of cells; (2) the life cycles of all cells—their formation, growth, development, reproduction, and so on—are based on chemical reactions among similar sorts of molecules; and (3) the way that amino acids are put together to form proteins is specified by DNA and RNA according to a precise and nearly universal scheme.

To these points we can add a fourth, following theorists who address the question "what is life?" by searching for principles of biological organization. There is a basic formal organization of life, and its paradigm and minimal case is to be found in the single cell. A single-cell organism is a self-making or self-producing being. Self-production is different from reproduction: In reproduction, a cell divides in two; in self-production, a cell continuously produces itself as a spatially bounded system, distinct from its medium or milieu. What is remarkable about self-production is that every molecular reaction in the system is generated by the very same system that those molecular reactions produce. Some years ago the neurobiologists Humberto Maturana and Francisco Varela drew attention to this circular, self-producing organization and called it *autopoiesis* (Maturana and Varela 1973, 1980; Varela, Maturana, and Uribe 1974). My purpose in this chapter is to present some key ideas of the autopoietic approach to life.

The Cell Theory

In 1858, one year before the publication of Charles Darwin's *Origin of Species,* the German biologist Rudolf Virchow propounded what is now known as the cell theory: the basic unit of all life is the cell and all cells arise from preexisting cells. In his book *Cell Pathology* Virchow wrote:

Each day brings forth fresh discoveries but it also opens up fresh matters for discovery. Is anything positive in histology, we have to ask ourselves. What are the parts of the body whence commence the vital actions? Which are the active elements, and which the passive? These are queries which have given rise to great difficulties, dominating the field of physiology and pathology, and which I have solved by showing that "the cell constitutes the true organic unit," that it is the ultimate irreducible form of every living element, and that from it emanate all the activities of life both in health and in sickness. (Virchow 1967, p. 23)

Virchow was not the first to observe the living cell. The earliest observations of cells date back to 1674 when Anton van Leeuwenhoek, the Dutch naturalist and lens-grinder, looked at pond water through a microscope and saw tiny creatures swimming there. In Virchow's own century many naturalists observed that the tissues of living organisms are composed of cells. But many of them also believed in an idea known as "the free formation of cells"—that cells develop out of a previous noncellular material. Virchow rejected this idea about how cells come into being. He summed up his rival view in a famous Latin aphorism: "The existence of a cell presupposes the prior existence of some other cell—*omnis cellula e cellula* (every cell must come from some other cell)—just the same as a plant cannot occur except it be derived from some other plant, or an animal from some other animal" (Virchow 1967, p. 25).

It might seem that biology has moved beyond Virchow's view of the cell as "the ultimate irreducible form of every living element." Molecular biology has taken us deep inside the cell, into the microscopic universe of DNA, RNA, and amino acids. There can be no doubt that irreplaceable insight and discovery have been gained from the molecular perspective. Yet as a number of biologists have discussed in recent years, molecular biology can lose sight of the organism as a whole (Goodwin 1994; Rose 1997). Here, too, Virchow's words are worth recalling: "There is no doubt that the molecular changes occurring inside the cells are referred to some part or other composing them; the final result is, however, due to the cell from which the vital action started and the living element is not active except in so far as it presents us with a complete whole enjoying its own separate existence" (Virchow 1967, p. 23).

The idea that the cell is a complete whole and that all cells arise from preexisting cells would seem to pose a dilemma: Either life has always existed or there must have been a first cell. But if all cells arise from preexisting cells, how could life ever come into being or get started in the first place? "There is only one way to form cells," Virchow wrote, "that is by fissiparity; one element is divided after the other. Each new generation proceeds from some preceding generation" (Virchow 1967, p. 25). If life had an origin, a historical beginning, then there must have been a first generation of living cells. But how could a first generation come into being without some previous generation to rely on? How could life arise from nonlife?

According to present scientific understanding, our solar system and the Earth took form about five billion years ago, followed some billion years later by the origin of life during the Archean Aeon, with the subsequent expansion of life into the five kingdoms of living beings known today. Monera is the oldest kingdom; it comprises all the prokaryotes or cells having no nuclei (bacteria). The members belonging to the other four kingdoms are all eukaryotes or organisms made up of nucleated cells—Protoctists (e.g., amoebae and green algae), Fungi, Plants, and Animals (Margulis and Schwartz 1988).

The origin, expansion, and history of life are usually pictured as a tree with many branches, an image that provides a way of visualizing the unity of life due to evolution from a common ancestor. Living things arise from earlier living things, and thus there is an underlying continuity from the most ancient to the most modern forms of life. With the origin of life over 3.5 billion years ago, however, something novel happened, a new form or order of things emerged. Although life is composed of physical and chemical elements, living organisms are different from other sorts of physicochemical things, and the surface of a planet populated by living beings is strikingly different from a planet that has no life.

Given this naturalistic and evolutionary perspective, the only way out of the dilemma posed here is to suppose that there must have been simpler, precursor chemical systems, protocells or "Ur-cells," that led eventually to the "ancestor cells" of the oldest bacterial organisms (Morowitz 1992; see also Margulis 1984). We know that all contemporary life must derive from a universal ancestor, which might have been a single cell or population of cells, but we do not know how many independent origins of protocells there were leading up to this ancestral organism. As Harold Morowitz observes in his book *Beginnings of Cellular Life:* "The problem is not simply the origin of life, it is the physical chemical formation of the Ur-organism and a subsequent evolutionary epoch giving rise to the universal ancestor" (Morowitz 1992, p. 88).

A number of different, but interrelated, questions arise from this perspective: What were the environmental conditions of the early Earth when life arose? When exactly did life arise? Did life arise more than once, at different times and places? How did complex bacterial cells arise from simpler protocellular systems? How did protocellular life arise from nonlife? What exactly do we mean by "life" in this minimal sense?

Many scientists prefer to avoid the last question altogether because they see it as philosophical rather than empirical. But the question will not go away that easily. The question of how and when life originated is inseparable from the question of what a living system is. If the aim is to determine how and when life arose, then one needs a clear way of characterizing what distinguishes living systems from nonliving ones. Such a characterization could also serve as a standard or criterion for recognizing life elsewhere on other planets, or for determining whether anything we might someday synthesize artificially would qualify as living.

In contemporary biology, there are three main approaches to characterizing life. One approach is to characterize life on the basis of genetics and reproductive populations. One generation of bacteria makes the next generation of bacteria; one generation of fruitflies produces the next generation; and so on, for all plants and animals. From this perspective, life depends on historical continuity and evolution, on the genetically based linkage of generations and the arising of novel variants within a population as a result of various evolutionary factors.

A second way to characterize life is more ecological. From this perspective, individual organisms are seen not only as members of reproductively linked populations, but also as beings that interact constructively with their environments, and so change the world in which they and their descendants live. Organisms are "niche-constructing" beings (Odling-Smee 1988). A particularly large-scale example of this way of thinking can be found in the Gaia theory put forward by atmospheric chemist James Lovelock and microbiologist Lynn Margulis (Lovelock 1979, 1988; Lovelock and Margulis 1974; Margulis and Lovelock 1974). In their view, life is a phenomenon that can occur only on a planetary scale. Life's persistence depends on integrated processes involving the biota (the sum total of living things) and the Earth's material environment (atmosphere, rocks, and oceans). Lovelock in particular has argued that were it not for the global presence of living organisms, the Earth would be rendered uninhabitable for life.

Finally, there is a third way to characterize life, one in which the focus is on the single individual entity or organism, here and now (Luisi, Lazcano, and Varela 1996). Suppose you are looking at a single specimen. It could be a strain of bacteria, a newly discovered jellyfish, a synthetic supramolecular complex, a specimen of presumed life on a distant planet, or a new insect-like robot. You then wonder: Is this a living thing or not? This question targets an individual entity, and the evolutionary and ecological backgrounds are of less immediate importance (they could be unknown or difficult to establish). In this sort of local, here-and-now situation, the demand for a clear criterion to distinguish life from nonlife seems especially pressing.

These three ways of characterizing life are complementary, not mutually exclusive. In the case of life on our own planet—the only life we know at present—"life" in a full sense means reproductively linked populations of ecologically embedded and active individual organisms. Modern molecular biology, however, has neglected the individual characterization of life and adopted almost exclusively the genetic-population characterization. Yet the individual characterization has a certain logical priority over the reproductive one. The reason is that reproduction presupposes an individual and some process whereby that individual reproduces. Thus the individual logically and empirically precedes reproduction and the evolutionary process of selection (Fleischaker 1988; Maturana and Varela 1980, pp. 96–111; 1987, pp. 55–74). In other words, any given population or evolutionary series is secondary to the individuation of the members of that population or series. Hence a characterization of life that accounts for individuality has logical priority over one that does not.

In the history of biology, a variety of criteria for distinguishing between living and nonliving systems have been proposed—carbon-based chemical composition, nucleic acids, the capacity to move, the ability to reproduce, and so forth. A standard procedure in biology textbooks today is to list such characteristics in order to delineate the class of living things. Such lists usually include metabolism and self-maintenance, the genetic material of DNA and RNA, and evolution by natural selection. The problem with this approach is that it is descriptive, not explanatory. It takes for granted the distinction between living and nonliving, and then it lists some common characteristics of systems accepted as living. But how do we know which characteristics should be included on the list or when the list is complete? Lists describe things but do not explain them. To explain we need a theory.

According to the cell theory, all living things are made up of cells. Although this statement does provide a scientific criterion of life, it has shortcomings. It is based on the observation that no life on Earth has ever been found without cells. But in the absence of a clear characterization of what a living system is, we cannot simply assume either that noncellular life is impossible or that no such life has ever existed. Moreover, to define life in terms of cells is basically tautological: life is cellular because there is no life without the cell. To get out of the tautology we need to specify the basic properties of a cell without invoking the notion of life. In other words, we have to specify what it is about a cell that makes it living.

One strategy for meeting this demand would be to characterize a living system, such as a cell, in terms of its relational form or organization (Maturana and Varela 1980, 1987). A system's organization consists of the relations that define the system as being a member of a specific class. For something to qualify as an automobile, for instance, its parts have to be arranged or related to one another in a certain way. In specifying a system's organization, one abstracts a pattern or set of relations that defines what kind of system the system is. A system's organization is thus not equivalent to its actual structural relations and components because the same organization can be structurally realized in different ways, and a system can undergo structural change without necessarily changing its organization. Thus the organization of an automobile can be realized in different physical materials and mechanisms, and these can change during the automobile's lifetime. Similarly, a single cell, such as a bacterium, undergoes many structural changes during its life cycle without changing its organization as a unicellular organism. Is it possible to specify a definitive organization in the case of living systems? With regard to the cell theory, can one specify the organization of a cell independent of its structure?

The Autopoietic Organization

The theory of autopoiesis, formulated by Maturana and Varela (1973, 1980, 1987), addresses precisely these questions about the organization of the living.[1] Maturana and Varela focus on the single, biological individual, the living cell. A cell is a thermodynamically open system, continually exchanging matter and energy with its environment. Some molecules are imported through the membrane and participate in processes inside the cell, whereas other molecules are excreted as waste. Throughout this exchange, the cell produces a host of substances that both remain within the cell (thanks to its membrane) and participate in those very same production processes. In other words, a cell produces its own components, which in turn produce it, in an ongoing circular process. The word "autopoiesis" was coined to name this kind of continual self-production. A cell is a self-producing or autopoietic unity. Systems that do not produce themselves, but whose product is different from themselves, are said to be *allopoietic*. For example, a ribosome (a small spherical body within a living cell composed of RNA and protein, and the site of protein synthesis) is a crucial participant in the autopoiesis of a cell, but is produced by processes other than those that constitute its own operation (Varela, Maturana, and Uribe 1974, pp. 188–189). Maturana and Varela also distinguish autopoietic systems from *heteropoietic* ones, which are allopoietic systems that arise in the realm of human design, such as cars and digital computers. Maturana and Varela's fundamental proposition is that *living systems are autopoietic or have an autopoietic organization*. They are organized in such a way that their constituent processes produce the components necessary for the continuance of those same processes.

The concept of the autopoietic organization arose from an attempt to abstract from the molecular processes of the cell the basic form or pattern that remains invariant through any kind of structural change, as long as the cell holds together as a distinct entity. To understand the autopoietic organization we therefore need to view it at a cellular level.

Figure 3.1, as we saw earlier, gives a schematic illustration of the basic pattern or organization of a minimal cell. By "minimal cell" I mean a cell with a minimal organization sufficient for it to be a distinct, independent entity. A cell is spatially formed by a semipermeable membrane, which establishes a boundary between the inside of the cell and the outside environment. The membrane serves as a barrier to free diffusion between the cell and the environment, but also permits the exchange of matter and energy across the boundary. Within this boundary, the cell comprises a metabolic network. Based in part on nutrients entering from outside, the cell sustains itself by a network of chemical transformations. But—and this is the first key point—the metabolic network is able to regenerate its own components, including the components that make up the membrane boundary. Furthermore—and this is the second key point—without the boundary containment provided by the membrane, the chemical network would be dispersed and drowned in the surrounding medium. Thus the cell embodies a circular process of self-generation: thanks to its metabolic network, it continually replaces the components that are being destroyed, including the membrane, and thus continually re-creates the difference between itself and everything else.

We can approach this idea in a slightly different way: a cell stands out of a molecular soup by creating the boundaries that set it apart from what it is not. Metabolic processes within the cell determine these boundaries, but the metabolic processes themselves are made possible by those very boundaries. In this way the cell emerges as a figure out of a chemical background. Should this process of self-production be interrupted, the cellular components no longer form a spatially individuated whole and they gradually diffuse back into a molecular soup.

The pattern presented in Figure 3.1 is what Maturana and Varela mean by the autopoietic organization. Anything that realizes this organization is an autopoietic system. In Maturana and Varela's view, "the notion of autopoiesis is necessary and sufficient to characterize the organization of living systems" (1980, p. 82; emphasis omitted). They also state: "Autopoiesis in the physical space is necessary and sufficient to characterize a system as a living system" (p. 112). Some scientists have recently argued, however, that although autopoiesis is a necessary condition for life, it is not sufficient (Bitbol and Luisi 2005; Bourgine and Stewart 2004; Luisi 2003). I will take up this issue at the end of this chapter.

Maturana and Varela give several precise definitions of autopoiesis in their writings. Their original and canonical definition is of an "autopoietic machine:"

An autopoietic machine is a machine organized (defined as a unity) as a network of processes of production (transformation and destruction) of components that produces the components which:

(i) through their interactions and transformations continuously regenerate and realize the network of processes (relations) that
produced them; and

(ii) constitute it (the machine) as a concrete unity in the space in
which they (the components) exist by specifying the topological
domain of its realization as a network. (Maturana and Varela
1980, pp. 78–79)

By "machine" Maturana and Varela mean a system that is defined by
its organization and that hence can be explained in terms of the relations constituting that organization, rather than in terms of the structural components realizing that organization in a particular concrete
system. "Components" and "processes of production" are abstract ways
of characterizing what in the molecular domain are molecules and
chemical reactions. Thus, roughly speaking, a molecular autopoietic
system is one in which chemical reactions produce molecules that (i)
both participate in and catalyze those reactions and (ii) spatially indi-
viduate the system by producing a membrane that houses those reactions.

A slightly different definition of the autopoietic organization is
given by Varela, Maturana, and Uribe (1974) and then illustrated with
reference to a cell:

The autopoietic organization is defined as a unity by a network of productions of components which

(i) participate recursively in the same network of productions of
components which produced these components, and

(ii) realize the network of productions as a unity in the space in
which the components exist.

Consider for example the case of a cell: it is a network of chemical reactions which produce molecules such that

(i) through their interactions generate and participate recursively
in the same network of reactions which produced them, and

(ii) realize the cell as a material unity.

Thus the cell as a physical unity, topographically and operationally separable from the background, remains as such only insofar as this organization is continuously realized under permanent turnover of matter,

regardless of its changes in form and specificity of its constitutive chemical reactions. (Maturana, Varela, and Uribe 1974, p. 188)

One might wonder what the phrase "generate and participate recursively" means in the cellular illustration of the first condition. It seems plausible to interpret "participating" in a reaction as meaning to be a *reactant,* and "generating" a reaction as meaning to *catalyze* that reaction (McMullin 1999, p. 2). Thus the definition's first condition "is that the reaction network which characterizes the organization of the system must produce all the species of molecular component which are considered to materially constitute the system, *and* these components must themselves *generate* the reaction network, in the sense of catalysing some (or all?) of the reactions (which would otherwise occur at negligible rate)" (McMullin 1999, p. 3). The second condition is that the reaction network must also establish the system as a "unity in space," that is, demaracte the system by establishing a boundary between it and the external environment. This condition is met in a cell by the production of a semipermeable membrane.[2]

In later writings, Varela (2000a) proposed the following simplified definition of autopoiesis. For a system to be autopoietic, (i) the system must have a semipermeable boundary; (ii) the boundary must be produced by a network of reactions that takes place within the boundary; and (iii) the network of reactions must include reactions that regenerate the components of the system.

In summary, the form or pattern of the autopoietic organization is that of a peculiar circular interdependency between an interconnected web of self-regenerating processes and the self-production of a boundary, such that the whole system persists in continuous self-production as a spatially distinct individual.

The autopoietic organization captures the minimal organization of a cell without invoking the notion of life or defining life in terms of the cell. Indeed, the autopoietic organization could be realized in many different kinds of molecular system, not just in biological cells as we know them. For example, chemical reactions in living cells involve nucleic acids (RNA and DNA) and the corresponding enzymes. The autopoietic characterization of minimal life, however, is not dependent on this particular structural arrangement of nucleic acids and proteins. The autopoietic characterization is more general and so could

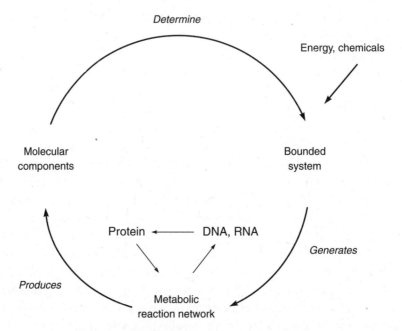

Figure 5.1. DNA/RNA version of autopoiesis.

hold for an "uncoded life"—for instance, an early terrestrial protocell (Fleischaker 1990a) or a synthesized molecular system lacking nucleic acids (Bachman, Luisi, and Lang 1992). In other words, the autopoietic characterization of minimal life, though based on the living cell, sets out the general pattern of which DNA-based life is one possible expression.

Figure 5.1 shows the autopoietic organization in relation to the DNA-based version of life found in the structure of living cells on Earth. As we have seen, the autopoietic organization is a circular one: molecular components produced by an internal reaction network assemble into a semipermeable boundary, which contains the internal microenvironment and reaction network, which again produces the molecular components, and so on continually as long as the cell holds together. Whereas Figure 3.1 depicts the autopoietic organization without specifying the type of reactions and the chemical nature of the components, Figure 5.1 explicitly shows the role played by DNA and RNA in living cells.

One advantage of characterizing life in terms of the minimal organization or pattern of autopoiesis is that we can list clear criteria for determining whether anything satisfies that organization:

1. *Semipermeable Boundary:* Check whether the system is defined by a semipermeable boundary made up of molecular components. Does the boundary enable you to discriminate between the inside and outside of the system in relation to its relevant components? If yes, proceed to 2.
2. *Reaction Network:* Check whether the components are being produced by a network of reactions that take place within the boundary. If yes, proceed to 3.
3. *Interdependency:* Check whether 1 and 2 are interdependent: are the boundary components being produced by the internal network of reactions, and is that network regenerated by conditions due to the boundary itself? If yes, the system is autopoietic.

By applying these criteria, one can determine whether any given system is autopoietic, even at a level where commonsense conceptions of life are of little help. Consider the items in Table 5.1, each of which is analyzed according to the three criteria above.

A bacterium (a prokaryote) and an amoeba (a eukaryote) are autopoietic because they satisfy all three criteria. A crystal, however, is not autopoietic because its components are not generated from within it-

Table 5.1 Determining whether an entity is autopoietic

Entity	Criterion 1 Boundary	Criterion 2 Network	Criterion 3 Interdependent	Conclusion: Autopoietic?
Virus	Yes	No	No	No
Crystal	Yes	No	No	No
Bacterium	Yes	Yes	Yes	Yes
Amoeba	Yes	Yes	Yes	Yes
Mitochondria	Yes	Yes	No	No
DNA section	No	No	No	No
Autocatalytic set	No	Yes	No	No

self. Replicative molecules, such as DNA and RNA, are also not autopoietic because they have neither a semipermeable membrane nor an internal reaction network, and thus they do not instantiate a circular, self-producing organization. Viruses are often described as living, but they do not satisfy the autopoietic criteria. A virus is a bounded structure with a protein coat, thereby satisfying the first criterion. But the second (and hence the third) is not satisfied because the molecular components of a virus (nucleic acids) are not generated inside the virus, but outside in the host cell. A virus has no metabolism of its own and thus is not self-maintaining in the autopoietic sense. Outside of a host cell, in the environment, a virus can persist, but it does not exchange matter with its environment in a continual self-producing way.

Another interesting case is autocatalytic sets of molecules. A catalyst is a molecular substance whose presence is needed for a particular chemical reaction to take place, or to speed up a reaction, but the catalyst is not changed by the reaction. Autocatalytic reactions are those in which the product of the reaction is a catalyst for that very reaction. An autocatalytic set or a collectively autocatalytic system is a chemical network made up of many self-perpetuating loops of molecular reactions. The system is composed of molecules that act as catalysts for the very reactions that produce those molecules. Such a network will be able constantly to re-create itself as long as there is a sufficient supply of food molecules. The key property of this sort of chemical network is catalytic closure. Except for the food molecules supplied from outside, every molecule in the system is produced by the autocatalytic reactions that make up the network.

Stuart Kauffman has suggested that catalytic closure is the basis of life: "Life, at its root, lies in the property of catalytic closure among a collection of molecular species. Alone, each molecule is dead. Jointly, once catalytic closure among them is achieved, the collective system of molecules is alive" (Kauffman 1995, p. 50). Kauffman sees catalytic closure as akin to autopoiesis, and he has suggested that his models of autocatalytic sets of proteins can serve as models for the molecular realization of autopoiesis (Brockman 1995, p. 217; Kauffman 1995, p. 274). But although there is a family resemblance between an autopoietic system and an autocatalytic set, the two are not equivalent (Maturana and Varela 1980, p. 94; McMullin 1999). The family resemblance is due to the second, reaction-network criterion. The difference is that in a collectively autocatalytic system there is no semipermeable boundary that spatially demarcates and contains the network (Criterion 1), and so the autocatalytic set cannot be regenerated by conditions due to such a boundary (Criterion 3). Hence an autocatalytic set does not qualify as a spatially distinct individual in the way an autopoietic system does.

A minimal autopoietic system is equivalent not simply to an autocatalytic network, but to an autocatalytic network housed within and interdependently linked to a semipermeable membrane boundary. The crucial property is that the membrane is not a mere containment device for the reaction network; rather, it is produced and maintained as a product of that network. This property is decisive for characterizing an autopoietic system as an autonomous individual (Varela 1979). A collectively autocatalytic system, because it lacks this property, does not qualify as a proper autonomous agent (*pace* Kauffman 2000; see McMullin 2001).

The three autopoietic criteria are clearly based on single-cell organisms. What about multicellular organisms? Are these also autopoietic systems?

In discussing this issue, Maturana and Varela (1987, pp. 87–89) distinguish between first-order and second-order autopoietic systems. Living cells are first-order autopoietic systems, whereas systems that include individual cells as structural components are second-order autopoietic systems. Maturana and Varela call such systems "metacellulars" and list as examples multicellular organisms, colonies, and societies. Given their definition of a metacellular as any unity in whose structure we can distinguish cell aggregates in close coupling, one could also include organs, such as the heart or liver. The crucial issue is whether any second-order autopoietic systems are also first-order autopoietic systems.

To answer this question it is not enough to point out that a second-order autopoietic system contains cells as elements of its *structure*, for the issue is whether the system's proper components (whatever they are) realize the autopoietic *organization*. For instance, one might think that a multicellular organism such as an insect is a first-order autopoietic unity because its components, including those that make up its boundary, are being constantly replaced from within itself, subject to conditions imposed by the boundary. At the same time, an insect colony might be considered merely an aggregate of autopoietic systems, but not an autopoietic unity in its own right. The thought would be that because an aggregate of human bodies in a society is not a body at a higher level, an aggregate of autopoietic systems is not itself an autopoietic system. The problem is that for this intuitive differentiation to be rigorous, it must be grounded on an explicit account of the kinds of organization proper to metacelluar systems:

> We know in great detail how a cell comes about as a molecular autopoietic unity, but how can we possibly describe in an organism the components and relations that make it a molecular autopoietic system? In the case of metacellulars, we are still ignorant of the molecular processes that would constitute those metacellulars as autopoietic unities comparable to cells . . . we shall leave open the question of whether or not metacellular systems are first-order autopoietic systems. What we can say is that they have *operational closure* in their organization: their identity is specified by a network of dynamic processes whose effects do not leave that network . . . whatever the organization of metacellulars may be, they are made up of first-order autopoietic systems and form lineages by reproducing through cells. These two conditions are sufficient to assure us that whatever happens in them, as autonomous unities, happens with conservation of the autopoiesis of their component cells, as also with conservation of their own organization. (Maturana and Varela 1987, pp. 88–89)

Given the knowledge we now have of molecular processes during the development of metazoan organisms (see Chapter 7), it seems reasonable to claim that metazoans are first-order autopoietic systems in addition to second-order ones. Nevertheless, difficulties remain, for in determining whether a given system qualifies as autopoietic, much depends on how we interpret "boundary" and "internal reaction network" in the criteria for autopoiesis. On the one hand, the theory of autopoiesis was formulated to apply to production processes in the molecular domain, and so allowing the boundary and network to be nonmolecular raises problems.[3] Here Varela's (1979) distinction between autonomy (organizational closure) and autopoiesis is pertinent. An autopoietic system is a specific kind of autonomous system—one having an organizational closure of production processes in the molecular domain—but there can be autonomous systems that are not autopoietic if their constituent processes exhibit organizational closure in their domain of operation. For example, an insect colony or animal group might qualify as autonomous in this sense. On the other hand, taking "boundary" to mean only a unicellular semipermeable membrane or even a multicellular epidermal layer seems too restrictive (plants and insects do not have a skin). Rather, the crucial matter is that the system produce and regulate its own internal topology and functional boundary, not the particular physical structure that realizes this boundary (Bourgine and Stewart 2004; Zaretzky and Letelier 2002).

Minimal Autopoiesis

According to the autopoietic criteria, the simplest living systems found on Earth are prokaryotic or bacterial cells. Unlike the structurally more complex eukaryotic cell, which contains a number of internal compartments, including a nucleus housing the cell's chromosomes and DNA, the bacterial cell has no compartments, and its coiled DNA floats within the cell. Nonetheless, a bacterial cell is already a highly complex biological entity, in which some two thousand to five thousand genes and a similar number of proteins mutually produce each other within the cell membrane they fabricate together (Margulis and Sagan 1995, p. 50).

Could one model a more streamlined molecular system that meets the three autopoietic criteria? This question is relevant not only to modeling minimal autopoiesis, but also to research on the origins of life, for one central goal of this research is to explain how protocells could have arisen and eventually led to the complex living cells we see today (Morowitz 1992; Szostak, Bartel, and Luisi 2001).

One way to approach the topic of minimal autopoiesis is through computer models, an approach central to the field known as "Artificial Life" or "Alife." One of the first computer models of minimal life was devised by Varela, Maturana, and Uribe (1974) some years before the field of Alife defined itself in the late 1980s (Langton 1989). This model has been revised and reimplemented by McMullin and Varela (1997).[4] The qualitative chemistry of the model is inspired by and represents a simplification of the kind of chemical reactions found in living cells. The chemical domain of the model occurs in a discrete, two-dimensional space. This type of model is known as a tesselation automaton or two-dimensional cellular automaton. Each position in the

space is either empty or occupied by a single particle. Particles generally move in random walks in the space. There are three distinct types
of particles, and they engage in three distinct reactions (see Plate I):

- *Production:* Two substrate (S) particles may react in the presence
  of a catalyst (K) to form a link (L) particle.
- *Bonding:* L particles may bond to other L particles. Each L
  particle can form (at most) two bonds, thus allowing the formation of indefinitely long chains, which may close to form membranes. Bonded L particles become immobile.
- *Disintegration:* An L particle may spontaneously disintegrate,
  yielding two S particles. When this disintegration occurs, any
  bonds associated with the L particle are also destroyed.

Chains of L particles are permeable to S particles but impermeable
to K and L particles. Hence a closed chain or a membrane that encloses K or L particles effectively traps them.

The basic autopoietic phenomenon predicted for this artificial
chemistry is the possiblity of realizing dynamic cell-like structures that
continually produce the conditions for their own maintenance. Such a
system would consist of a closed chain or membrane of L particles that
encloses one or more K particles. There can be continual production
of L particles because they are formed by catalyzed reactions of the S
particles that permeate through the membrane. Because they cannot
escape through the membrane, L particles in relatively high concentration will build up inside the system. From time to time, however, the
membrane will rupture as a result of the disintegration of its component L particles. Given the high concentration of L particles inside the
membrane, the probability is high that one of these particles will drift
to the rupture site and effect a repair, before the K particle escapes. In
this way the conditions that allow for the buildup of a high concentration of L particles will be reestablished precisely.

A secondary phenomenon that might occur is the spontaneous establishment of a self-sustaining system from a randomized initial
arrangement of the particles. Such spontaneous formation was reported in the original 1974 study by Varela, Maturana, and Uribe but
was not studied by McMullin and Varela (1997). Instead, they artificially introduced a putative autopoietic entity into the system and investigated whether this entity could succeed in realizing the self-

sustaining reaction network just described over a large number of time steps (the basic autopoietic phenomenon predicted for this artificial chemistry).[5]

The qualitative chemistry presented in this section corresponds to the description originally given by Varela, Maturana, and Uribe (1974). Subsequent attempts to reimplement their work, however, led to the discovery of an additional interaction, present in their original program code but not documented in the description (McMullin 1997a, 1997b). This additional interaction prevents the spontaneous and premature bonding of L particles produced within the membrane. Such bonding makes the L particles immobile and unavailable to effect a repair to the membrane. McMullin and Varela (1997) call this additional interaction "chain-based bond inhibition" and describe it as follows: "This is an interaction whereby bonding is inhibited to any free L particle which is in the immediate vicinity of another L particle which is doubly bonded. In effect then, a free L particle cannot form a bond as long as it is alongside (as opposed to at the end of) an existing chain of L particles; but it *can* form bond(s) when it is at the end of a chain; and, especially, when it is positioned at a site where a chain has broken (i.e. a rupture site)" (McMullin and Varela 1997, p. 6). McMullin and Varela (1997) show that this interaction is crucial to realizing the basic autopoietic phenomenon in the model.

Plates II–V show one of the runs of the experiment, during which an autopoietic reaction network is established and a succession of successful membrane-repair episodes occurs. The morphology that is established seems particularly robust, persisting for approximately one thousand time-steps of the model. The initial configuration, illustrated in Plate II, is a single, artificially constructed, cell-like entity—a closed membrane of L particles housing a single K particle. It is embedded in a toroidal space. Between time 0 and time 226 the initial membrane suffers two ruptures, which are repaired with no change of membrane morphology. Between time 227 and 444 there are four rupture and repair episodes, yielding the new membrane morphology shown in Plate III. This new morphology appears to be relatively robust. It persists up to time 1250, while undergoing 5 more rupture and successful repair episodes. Between time 1250 and time 1310 there are two rupture and repair episodes, which produce the new morphology shown in Plate IV. The entity persists in this morphology through two more rupture and repair episodes, until time 1741. Then there are two ruptures in quick succession, at times 1742 and 1745. At time 1746 the membrane fragments, and partially spirals into the cavity, as shown in Plate V. It is then no longer possible to recover the closed membrane through any simple process of self-repair.

Does this self-sustaining system meet all the requirements for autopoiesis? This question is actually somewhat tricky. Varela, Maturana, and Uribe (1974, p. 191) state explicitly, "Within this universe [of the model] these systems satisfy the autopoietic organization" (see also Varela 1979, p. 20). But there is one component in the model—the K particle or catalyst—that is not itself produced by any reaction in the network. Bourgine and Stewart (2004) take this feature of the model to imply that the system is not fully autopoietic. McMullin (1999), however, citing Varela, Maturana, and Uribe's (1974) criteria for determining whether a specific system is autopoietic, suggests that it may be acceptable for some of the components not to be produced by reactions in the system, as long as these components play a necessary and permanent role in the production of other components. For instance, substrate particles are not necessarily produced by the reaction network because they can traverse the membrane and enter the system from outside. Furthermore, in the case of the spontaneous generation of a self-sustaining network, the preexisting catalyst (K) would interact with the preexisting substrate (S), thereby forming a chain of bonded links (L particles). Eventually the chain would enclose the catalyst, and as a result the L particles produced within the enclosure would replace the decaying L particles of the boundary. Such a self-sustaining network would appear to satisfy the three autopoietic criteria.[6]

In a recent paper, Bourgine and Stewart (2004) expand the tesselation-automaton model from two to three dimensions and give a mathematical treatment of the model as a random dynamical system (see Figure 5.2). This approach enables them to model temporary holes in the membrane. In a two-dimensional model with a one-dimensional membrane, two holes would immediately disrupt the membrane, but in a three-dimensional model with a two-dimensional membrane, the membrane retains a topological continuity despite a substantial fraction of holes in the membrane. Their system is made up of three types of components: A-components or substrate molecules; B-components formed by a reaction between two substrate mol-

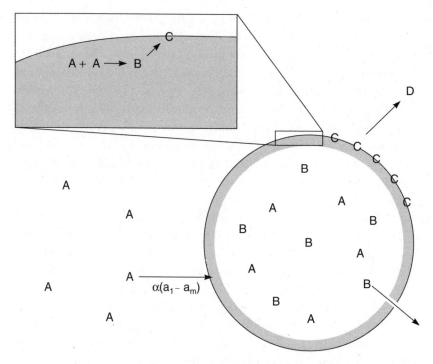

Figure 5.2. A schematic illustration of the 3D tesselation automaton model of autopoiesis. From Bourgine and Stewart (2004). The enlarged inset shows the processes occurring in a thin volume just under the membrane (catalytic production of B, and B-components entering the membrane to become C-components). The reaction C → D represents the disintegration of a C-component, leaving a hole in the membrane. B-components are normally confined by the membrane but can be lost through holes. α (a_1-a_m) gives the net flux of A across the membrane. Reprinted with permission from Paul Bourgine and John Stewart, "Autopoiesis and Cognition," *Artificial Life* 10:3 (Summer 2004), 330. © 2004 by the Massachusetts Institute of Technology.

ecules A (A+A → B); and C-components belonging to the membrane, which has the form of a two-dimensional sheet and whose inside surface catalyzes the reaction A+A → B. Within the membrane, B-components diffuse freely. If two single B-components collide, they do not combine, but if a free B-component collides with the edge of a hole in the membrane, it attaches to the surface and repairs the hole (either partially or completely depending on the hole's size). (This feature is analogous to chain-based bond inhibition.) A B-component that integrates the membrane in this way thereby becomes a C-component. C-components (at the membrane's inside surface) in turn catalyze the production of B-components. In this way, the system avoids the need for a catalyst not produced by the system itself. (C-components are formed by B-components, and C catalyzes the production of B.) Finally, each of the C-components can disintegrate, and the end-product D cannot integrate the membrane, but escapes into the outside environment, leaving a hole in the membrane (or enlarging a preexisting one).

In their mathematical treatment of this system as a random dynamical system, Bourgine and Stewart show that the crucial variable for understanding the structural dynamics of the system is the proportion of the total surface area occupied by C-components. When the value of this variable is above 50 percent, the system maintains itself dynamically, such that the rate of disintegration of the membrane $(C \rightarrow D)$ is balanced by the repair process $(B \rightarrow C)$. Below a critical point, the repair dynamics can no longer balance the formation of holes. The holes increase in size and number, there is vicious positive feedback, and the system collapses. The phase space of the system's operation thus has two qualitatively different regimes and a critical point of bifurcation. As Bourgine and Stewart note: "Like a candle-flame, the system is either 'alive' or 'dead.' If it is alive, it may waver at times (several holes may appear), but it can recover and go on as though nothing has happened. If it is dead, nothing can resuscitate it; the system collapses and disintegrates entirely" (Bourgine and Stewart 2004, p. 332).

The models we have been examining indicate that it should be possible for the three autopoietic criteria to be realized in comparatively simple chemical systems. In other words, it should be possible to realize a self-sustaining reaction network, whose boundary is produced by the network and in turn encloses the network, in a chemical system much simpler than a bacterial cell. Yet these models are not real physical systems but either computationally simulated ones (McMullin and Varela 1997; Varela, Maturana, and Uribe 1974) or abstract systems described in the mathematical framework of dynamic systems theory (Bourgine and Stewart 2004). Although the three autopoietic criteria may be necessary and perhaps sufficient to specify the organization of minimal life, for some entity to count as a living system, embodiment is required. That is, the system has to satisfy the three autopoietic criteria in the physical space (Maturana and Varela 1980, pp. 84, 112; see also Boden 2000; Fleischaker 1988). This point raises the following question: what about minimal autopoiesis in a real chemical medium?

The creation of chemical models of autopoiesis has been the research goal of chemist Pier Luigi Luisi and his colleagues since the early 1990s.[7] Working with micelles and vesicles, they claim to have succeeded in creating minimal autopoietic systems in the laboratory (Bachman, Luisi, and Lang 1992; Luisi 1993). These systems may shed light on various chemical processes of molecular self-assembly involved in the origins of life (Szostak, Bartel, and Luisi 2001).

Micelles and vesicles are three-dimensionally closed, molecular structures capable of spontaneous formation or self-assembly. Certain types of molecule, when dispersed in aqueous solutions, form clusters or aggregates in a predictable way. A micelle is a tiny droplet whose boundary is formed by such clustering. The molecules, known as surfactants (surface active agents), aggregate in the form of a sphere, thereby producing a bounded microenvironment (the interior of the droplet). In addition, certain molecules can self-assemble into double-layer aggregates called bilayers and thereby form vesicles, which are small, fluid-filled sacs with a bilayer boundary like a cell membrane. The molecular self-assembly of a bilayer membrane and its closure into a vesicle to form a "minimal cell" have served as the foundation for several scenarios for the origins of life (Fleischaker 1990a; Morowitz 1992; Morowitz, Heinz, and Deamer 1998; Szostak, Bartel, and Luisi 2001), in line with the tradition going back to the Russian scientist Alexander Oparin (Oparin 1938).

The basic idea behind using micelles and vesicles to create a minimal autopoietic system is to synthesize a bounded structure that hosts in its aqueous interior a chemical reaction that leads to the production of the surfactant, which in turn aggregates to form a boundary for the reaction. A schema for such a system is presented in Figure 5.3 (compare to Figure 5.2). One begins with a semipermeable-membrane boundary consisting of only one type of component S (Figure 5.3). A single type of nutrient A can permeate the membrane. Inside the system A is transformed into S. The system is characterized by two competitive interactions, "generation" and "decay." Generation yields S from A, and decay breaks down S into a

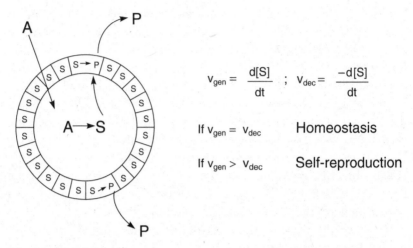

Figure 5.3. The minimal autopoietic system. Two competitive reactions—one that builds the component of the boundary and another one that destroys it—characterize the system. According to the relative value of these two velocity constants, the system can be in homeostasis, or grow, or die. From Pier Luigi Luisi, "Autopoiesis: A Review and Reappraisal," *Naturwissenschaften* 90 (2003): 53, fig. 4, © 2003 Springer-Verlag. Reprinted with kind permission of Springer Science and Business Media.

product P that leaves the boundary and enters the environment. When the velocities of these two generation and decay interactions are numerically equal, then the system is in a self-perpetuating steady state or homeostasis. When the velocity of generation is greater than that of decay, then the system can grow and eventually reproduce by splitting into two smaller systems. Finally, when the velocity of decay is greater than that of generation, then the system will become impoverished in the S-component and eventually implode.

An example of the second, reproductive mode, implemented in vesicles, is shown in Figure 5.4. It begins (top left) with a relatively static aqueous vesicle formed by the surfactant S. Then a highly lipophilic precursor of S, indicated as S-S, binds to the boundary of the vesicle, where it is hydrolyzed, yielding the same surfactant S. The vesicle grows and eventually divides into two or more thermodynamically stabler and smaller vesicles. The whole process is autocatalytic: the more vesicles are formed, the more S-S is bound and the more vesicles are formed.

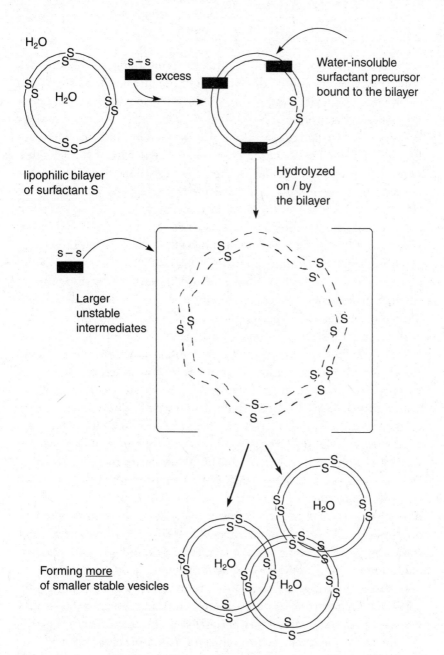

Figure 5.4. Autopoiesis and self-reproducing vesicles. Experimental procedure to obtain self-reproducing vesicles (liposomes). *S-S* represents the water-insoluble precursor of the surfactant, *S,* and *S_S* is hydrolyzed on the membrane of the micelles or of the vesicles. From Pier Luigi Luisi, "Autopoiesis: A Review and Reappraisal," *Naturwissenschaften* 90 (2003): 56, fig. 7, © 2003 Springer-Verlag. Reprinted with kind permission of Springer Science and Business Media.

Do such micelles and vesicles qualify as minimal autopoietic systems? The answer is not entirely clear. On the one hand, these systems clearly meet Criteria 1 and 2: there is a semipermeable boundary, and the boundary is produced by the system itself. There is a clear analogy between the circular organization of these systems and that of an autopoietic minimal cell. On the other hand, it is unclear whether these systems fully meet Criterion 3—the presence of an internal reaction network that regenerates itself and the boundary. As Luisi observes: "Reaction takes place on the boundary, which is part of the system, but a restricted one: the internal aqueous core is not part of the reaction system, and furthermore we are dealing with only one reaction instead of an internalized reaction network" (Luisi 2003, p. 56). (The same point can also be raised for Bourgine and Stewart's three-dimensional tesselation automaton.) Luisi maintains that these systems are the simplest possible case of experimental autopoiesis, albeit a limiting case (Bitbol and Luisi 2005). One could argue, however, that they are better described as proto-autopoietic than minimally autopoietic. Which description one chooses depends on how one evaluates these systems with respect to the third criterion. As we will see in the last section of this chapter, this issue also bears on whether autopoiesis is necessary and sufficient, or merely necessary, for minimal life.

To close this section, let me briefly connect the idea of minimal autopoiesis to research on the origins of life on Earth. In 1985, Freeman Dyson in his book *Origins of Life* (1985) pointed out that life as we know it requires both metabolic self-maintenance and the replication of nucleic acids. He proposed that living cells arose from the "symbiotic" merger of two independently evolved, prior systems—one a self-replicating system composed of nucleic acids and the other a self-maintaining, autocatalytic system of proteins. From an autopoietic perspective, however, the crucial step required for biological individuality—for an individual living system, here and now, or there and then—is that such subsystems be enclosed within a membrane that they produce together. As Margulis and Sagan observe, prior to this step neither subsystem is alive, and after this step it is the whole system that is living (and hence the word "symbiosis" to describe their merger is not quite right) (Margulis and Sagan 1995, p. 60).

In *Beginnings of Cellular Life: Metabolism Recapitulates Biogenesis*, Morowitz (1992) proposes that many features of nucleic acids and proteins evolved only after these molecules came to be enclosed within membrane-bounded units or protocells. Consistent with an autopoietic perspective, he emphasizes the importance of the membrane for establishing and stabilizing life: "It is the closure of an amphiphilic bilayer membrane into a vesicle that represents a discrete transition from nonlife to life" (Morowitz 1992, p. 9). He distinguishes between "Ur-cells" (or protocells) and ancestor cells. Vesicle formation is the key event in the transition from nonlife to life at the protocell stage. We do not know how many times this happened—how many independent origins of protocellular life there might have been. We do know, however, that all contemporary life derives from a universal ancestor, which could have been a single cell or population of cells. Thus the problem of the origins of life comprises both the chemical formation of the Ur-cells and the subsequent evolutionary sequence that gave rise to the universal ancestor (Morowitz 1992, p. 88). In Morowitz's scenario, protocells in the form of vesicles originated first, a simple form of metabolism or internal reaction network came next, then proteins developed, and genes arrived last.

The first step was the formation of vesicles in the ocean at the water-atmosphere interface some 4 to 3.8 billion years ago. This event created a three-phase system of an interior, boundary, and exterior. In the autopoietic viewpoint, this step corresponds to Criterion 1, the establishment of a semipermeable boundary separating inside from outside. The second step was the development of a simple metabolic reaction network inside the vesicles. This network could synthesize the molecules needed for self-maintenance, including the molecules of the membrane boundary. This second step corresponds to Criteria 2 and 3 and thus to an autopoietic protocell. Morowitz hypothesizes that the metabolism of these early cells was not protein-based. The protocells were also potentially self-reproducing and hence would have proliferated. What then ensued was the first evolutionary radiation leading from the protocells to the universal ancestor. This transition involved both the formation of amino acids, as a result of the protocellular metabolism becoming more complex, and the origin of nucleic acids and the so-called genetic code.

Morowitz's scenario is clearly congenial to the autopoietic view of life. The details, of course, require experimental verification. But what matters to me here are not so much the details of any single origins-of-

life scenario, but rather the overall theoretical framework. In an autopoietic framework, minimal life is not identified with any particular
molecular structure, such as RNA/DNA, but rather with a bounded,
self-producing concatenation of processes, which can in principle be
structurally realized in different ways.

Autopoiesis and Ecopoiesis

Earlier in this chapter I mentioned three different ways of characterizing life—the evolutionary, ecological, and individual characteriza-
tions. The focus of this chapter is the individual characterization. The
autopoietic characterization of life highlights the organization of an
individual living system. Models of minimal autopoiesis try to shed
light on how such a system could emerge from a prebiotic chemical
environment. We should not lose sight, however, of the ecological context of autopoiesis. As Morowitz writes:

> When we speak of the origin of life, we are referring generally to the
> rise of organisms . . . It is well to remember, however, that this can take
> place only within a global ecological system. In a certain sense, the
> origin of life refers to a transformation of the planetary surface from an
> inorganic state to one dominated by the activities of plants, animals,
> and microbes. (Morowitz 1992, p. 6)
>
> Traditional biology has tended to concentrate attention on indi-
> vidual organisms rather than on the biological continuum. The origin
> of life is thus looked for as a unique event in which an organism arises
> from the surrounding milieu. A more ecologically balanced point of
> view would examine the protoecological cycles and subsequent chem-
> ical systems that must have developed and flourished while objects re-
> sembling organisms appeared. (Morowitz 1992, p. 54)

Two points are important here. First, autopoiesis always has to be
ecologically embedded. "Self-producing" refers to the kind of circular
organization that makes the cell an individual; it does not mean that
the cell makes itself apart from its environment. Second, although life
may have begun in small, local pockets, it quickly proliferated, evolved,
and transformed the entire surface of the planet. Life as we know it is
a phenomenon of evolutionary and planetary scale. Take, for example,
the prokaryotic bacteria, which according to the autopoietic criteria

are the simplest living beings on Earth. Bacteria are hardly isolated self-makers. On the contrary, they never live as isolated individuals in nature; rather, they form microbial communities or associations (Margulis and Sagan 1986). Moreover, they can pass their genes among each other without reproducing, in effect sharing a common potential genome. For these reasons, some biologists have argued that all bacteria form one organism, or superorganism:

> [B]acteria, in addition to carrying out their individual and localized team activities, together form a planetary entity of communicating and cooperating microbes, an entity that, we think, is both genetically and functionally a true superorganism. It is at the social level—the level of their associations—that bacteria manifest their exceptional capacities and play a major role in nature. (Sonia and Panisset 1983, p. 8)

The idea that life is a planetary phenomenon is central to the Gaia theory advanced by chemist James Lovelock and microbiologist Lynn Margulis (Lovelock 1979, 1988; Margulis 1998). Their theory states that the biota (totality of living organisms), atmosphere, oceans, rocks, and soils make up a single planetary entity that is self-regulating and self-maintaining. They call the entity Gaia, which Lovelock often describes as a planetary organism or superorganism. The theory is controversial, in part because of the issues about life discussed in this chapter. For this reason, it is worth considering the theory here.

When Lovelock and Margulis first proposed their theory in the 1970s, they called it the Gaia hypothesis (Lovelock and Margulis 1974; Margulis and Lovelock 1974). The hypothesis was that the physical and chemical conditions of the Earth's surface, atmosphere, and oceans are kept within limits favorable to life and that this homeostasis is accomplished automatically by the biota through negative feedback processes. Since this original formulation, Lovelock and Margulis have expanded the hypothesis into a theory. According to the Gaia theory, the biota and their material environment evolve together, as a single "tight-coupled system," with the self-regulation of the planetary climate and atmosphere occurring as emergent phenomena. Not only is life a planetary phenomenon, but the material environment of life on Earth is in part a biological construction. As Lovelock puts it: "In no way do organisms just 'adapt' to a dead world determined by physics and chemistry alone. They live with a world that is the breath and bones of their ancestors and that they are now sustaining" (Lovelock 1991, p. 32). Lovelock and Margulis believe that this planetary system, Gaia, is the largest known biological individual:

> Gaia is best thought of as a superorganism. These are bounded systems made up partly from living organisms and partly from nonliving structural material. A bee's nest is a superorganism and like the superorganism, Gaia, it has the capacity to regulate its temperature. (Lovelock 1988, p. 15)

The assertion that Gaia is a planetary superorganism has not gone without criticism. Some of the main early criticisms came from the biologists W. Ford Doolittle and Richard Dawkins (Dawkins 1982, pp. 234–237; Doolittle 1981, 1987). They argued that Gaia should not be accorded the status of a living system because it is not a reproducing individual and hence has no hereditary lineage. They also maintained that it is unlikely that the planetary self-maintaining mechanisms that Lovelock and Margulis hypothesized could result from natural selection, and so if they exist they are "accidental."

These criticisms bring us back to the issues about life. Doolittle and Dawkins were looking at life from the perspective of evolution, reproduction, and genetics. Is this the right perspective for answering the question of whether there is a planetary biological individual? I do not think so. The right perspective is that of the individual characterization of life, the one that figures in our examination of minimal life in this chapter. As we have seen, at this level reproduction does not enter as a defining feature of the organization of a living system. Reproduction requires an individual to be reproduced, and hence is logically and empirically secondary to the processes whereby an autonomous system constitutes itself as an individual. Therefore, a self-producing but non-reproducing planetary system could count as a genuine biological individual. Furthermore, its self-producing and self-maintaining mechanisms, though not the result of natural selection acting on a population of similar systems, would nevertheless hardly be "accidental." Indeed, they would presumably reflect lawful principles of self-organization and emergence in complex systems.[8]

If Lovelock and Margulis are right, what sort of biological entity would Gaia be? Lovelock describes Gaia as a superorganism. Margulis describes Gaia as an autopoietic system like a cell:

The simplest, smallest known autopoietic entity is a single bacterial cell. The largest is probably Gaia. Cells and Gaia display general properties of autopoietic entities; as their surroundings change unpredictably, they maintain their structural integrity and internal organization, at the expense of solar energy, by remaking and interchanging their parts. Metabolism is the name given to this incessant activity. (Margulis 1991, p. 237)

Margulis's words echo something Lewis Thomas wrote in his book *The Lives of a Cell*, around the same time that Lovelock first announced the Gaia hypothesis:

I have been trying to think of the earth as a kind of organism, but it is no go. I cannot think of it this way. It is too big, too complex, with too many working parts lacking visible connections. The other night, driving through a hilly, wooded part of southern New England, I wondered about this. If not like an organism, what is it like, what is it *most* like? Then, satisfactorily for that moment, it came to me: it is *most* like a single cell. (Thomas 1974, p. 5)

Should Gaia, the whole ecosphere of the planet Earth, be considered an autopoietic system? Margulis has been a long-standing advocate of autopoiesis as the most adequate characterization of life at the individual level. Her work on symbiosis, cell evolution, and the Gaia theory has greatly enriched the autopoietic perspective (Margulis 1993, 1998; Margulis and Sagan 1995, 2002).[9] Yet whether we should count Gaia as an autopoietic system is a difficult question. The crucial issue is whether "boundary" and "internal reaction network" have a clear interpretation when we shift from the molecular to the planetary scale. We have already had occasion to notice that interpreting "boundary" to mean only semipermeable membrane or skin is too narrow. Rather, what is important is that the system produce and regulate its own internal topology and functional boundary, in whatever domain the system operates. Lovelock and Margulis make a strong case for considering the ecosphere to be a large-scale system that produces its own internal topology and functional boundary, actively regulates its boundary conditions, and continually produces the components that in turn produce it.

But to make this intuitively compelling picture precise would re-

quire both more detailed knowledge of the "geophysiological" processes that produce and realize Gaia, and more precise elaborations of
the three autopoietic criteria in nonmolecular domains. As Bourgine
and Stewart remark: "It must be an open question at present as to
whether the terrestrial ecosphere actually is a *bona fide* autopoietic
system; to answer this question, it will be necessary to put our mathematical definitions of autopoiesis in full working order, and then to
carry out the considerable task of applying them to the case of the
ecosphere. However, we can already say at this stage that we certainly
do not want to definitely rule out this possibility, simply because the
ecosphere does not have a single clearly reified membrane" (2004, p.
337).

In one of his articles Lovelock uses the term *ecopoiesis* to describe
Gaia (Lovelock 1987). This term seems just right for conveying both
the resemblance and difference between Gaia and the autopoietic cell.
The resemblance is due to the ecosphere and the cell being autonomous systems, the difference to the scale and manner in which
their autonomy takes form.

Autopoiesis and Cognition

According to Maturana and Varela, "the notion of autopoiesis is necessary and sufficient to characterize the organization of living systems"
(1980, p. 82; emphasis omitted). They also state: "Autopoiesis in the
physical space is necessary and sufficient to characterize a system as a
living system" (p. 112). My aim in the final section of this chapter is to
evaluate these necessity and sufficiency claims.

The necessity claim can be expressed as the proposition that for an
individual entity, here and now, to be characterized as a living system,
it must realize the autopoietic organization, that is, satisfy the three autopoietic criteria. In other words, no system that deserves, here and
now, to be called living can fail to be autopoietic. The way to test or
challenge this claim is to look for a putative counterexample—that is,
a system that deserves, here and now, to be called living but is not autopoietic. Given that the criteria for autopoiesis are based on living
cells and that multicellular organisms and colonies are considered to
be higher-order autopoietic systems, such a counterexample would
have to come from outside the domain of cells. Two candidates that

come to mind are viruses and replicative molecules such as RNA and DNA.

As we saw earlier in this chapter, a virus does not meet the autopoietic criteria. It does not produce from within itself its own protein coat or nucleic acids. Rather, these are produced by the host cell in which the virus takes up residence. Nonetheless, viruses are often described as living. Do they therefore pose a challenge to the necessity claim? It is important to be clear that this issue is not about the meaning of the everyday word "living." The issue is whether the theoretical concept of autopoiesis succeeds in characterizing the organization of those systems that are the definitive objects of biological investigation. Viruses are clearly objects of microbiological research. Therefore the issue comes down to whether the theory of autopoiesis can provide a good reason not to characterize them as living systems.

Such a reason is not hard to find. Viruses are not dissipative systems or metabolic entities. They do not exchange matter or energy with the environment. Outside of a host cell a virus is completely inert and is entirely subject to the vicissitudes of the environment. Inside a cell it makes use of the cell's metabolism, but it has no metabolism of its own. A virus is thus a fundamentally different kind of physicochemical entity from both prokaryotic cells or bacteria and autocatalytic protocells. The theory of autopoiesis succeeds in capturing this difference at the organizational level. Hence viruses do not pose a compelling challenge to the claim that autopoiesis is necessary to characterize the organization of a living system.

What about replicative molecules? One might argue that minimal life can be characterized or defined in terms of RNA and DNA and the molecular structures they form. For instance, certain RNA strands known as ribozymes can act as catalysts for their own replication. Ribozymes are remarkable because they have both catalytic abilities like enzymes and the template specificity of nucleic acids. In a test-tube they rapidly evolve self-replicating patterns. If such molecules deserve to be described as living, then autopoiesis is not necessary to characterize a system as living.

This line of thought presents a problem, however: it shifts tacitly from the individual, here-and-now account of life to the population and genetic-evolutionary account. A single RNA molecule does not catalyze its own replication and evolve by natural selection. Autocatalytic replication requires a large family of molecules, and evolution by natural selection requires a reproductive population. Thus the molecular description derives from the evolutionary, population level and so has no force as a counterargument to the autopoietic account at the individual level. Furthermore, the population and evolutionary perspective presupposes the individual perspective: a population is by definition composed of individual members, and evolution requires reproductive individuals. The population perspective thus cannot characterize life at the level of single individuals, here and now, especially individuals that have no genetic heritage or lack genetic material, such as synthetic laboratory entities or early terrestrial protocells (Luisi 1998).

Let me turn now to the sufficiency claim, which states that if something displays autopoiesis, then it is living. This claim has recently been called into question by two groups (Bitbol and Luisi 2005; Bourgine and Stewart 2004). It is significant that both groups are important proponents of autopoiesis and that they offer essentially the same argument: all living systems are both autopoietic systems and cognitive systems, but an autopoietic system is not necessarily a cognitive system.

This argument raises the question of the relationship between autopoiesis and cognition. Maturana and Varela (1980) originally proposed that all living systems are autopoietic systems and that all autopoietic systems are cognitive systems. "Autopoiesis" pertains to the self-producing organization of a living system, whereas "cognition" pertains to the behavior or conduct of a system in relation to its environment. According to Maturana and Varela (1980), the relation between autopoiesis and cognition has two crucial features. First, the instantiation of the autopoietic organization in an actual, concrete system entails a cognitive relation between that system and its environment. Second, this cognitive relation reflects and is subordinated to the maintenance of autopoiesis. As Maturana put it in a groundbreaking early paper: "A cognitive system is a system whose organization defines a domain of interactions in which it can act with relevance to the maintenance of itself, and the process of cognition is the actual (inductive) acting or behaving in this domain. Living systems are cognitive systems, and living as a process is a process of cognition. This statement is valid for all organisms, with and without a nervous system" (Maturana 1970, p. 13; emphasis omitted).

Bourgine and Stewart (2004) and Bitbol and Luisi (2005) accept the proposition that all living systems are cognitive systems. What they challenge is that autopoiesis entails cognition. Bourgine and Stewart take their three-dimensional tesselation automaton to be a minimally autopoietic system but not a cognitive one. Bitbol and Luisi consider autocatalytic micelles and vesicles to be minimally autopoietic systems but not cognitive ones. In each case, the system autocatalytically produces its own boundary but does not actively relate to its environment (see also Ruiz-Mirazo and Moreno 2004, pp. 244–245). There is nothing comparable to the taxic responses of microorganisms, tropisms of plants, or sensorimotor activities of animals. Hence these systems need not be described as having what Maturana and Varela call a "cognitive domain"—a domain of interactions or niche, defined by the system's organization, in which the system operates or behaves so as to maintain its viability, that is, its autopoiesis (Maturana 1970, pp. 10–11; Maturana and Varela 1980, p. 119).

For Bourgine and Stewart, cognitive interactions are those in which sensory responses guide action and action has consequences for subsequent sensory stimulation, subject to the constraint that the system maintain its viability. "Sensory response" and "action" are taken broadly to include, for example, a bacterium's ability to sense the concentration of sucrose in its immediate environment and to move itself accordingly. For a living system, viability requires maintaining autopoiesis. In the case of the tesselation automaton, however, there is no behavior guided by sensation. The system, though minimally autopoietic, is not cognitive and therefore is not a living system.

For Bitbol and Luisi, "cognition is tantamount to metabolism." They distinguish two steps or levels of cognition. The first corresponds to the normal metabolic assimilation of select compounds from the environment. The second corresponds to the incorporation of novel elements that effect a change in the structure of a living system—that is, to the existing metabolism but not to the system's organization. They liken the first step to Piaget's notion of assimilation, and the second to his notion of accommodation. In the autocatalytic micelles and vesicles, however, there is no metabolic network. Instead there is only a single type of autocatalytic reaction that takes place at the boundary of the entity, and the internal aqueous core is not part of this reaction system. These chemical systems, though autopoietic, do not arrive at even the first stage of cognition as metabolic assimilation and therefore are not living systems.

On the basis of these considerations, Bourgine and Stewart, as well as Bitbol and Luisi, conclude that autopoiesis is a necessary but not sufficient condition for a system to be a living system, whereas the union of autopoiesis and cognition is both necessary and sufficient.

The main question to raise about this line of thought is whether the tesselation automaton and the autocatalytic micelles and vesicles really qualify as *bona fide* minimal autopoietic systems rather than proto-autopoietic ones. (The tesselation automaton is of course an abstract model, not a real physicochemical system, but in its architecture and dynamics it is close to the micelles and vesicles.) One could argue that a minimal autopoietic system requires more than merely a closed and self-producing boundary; it also requires a distinct internal reaction network that regenerates both itself and the boundary, and regulates the system's interactions with the outside environment by way of that boundary. This interpretation of the criteria for autopoiesis is probably closer to Maturana and Varela's original formulation. Nevertheless, Varela maintained that the autocatalytic micelles and vesicles are minimal autopoietic systems. Also, he did not hesitate to call them living (Luisi 2003; Luisi and Varela 1989).

It would seem, therefore, that we are faced with the following choice. We can maintain that the tesselation automaton and the autocatalytic micelles and vesicles are models of minimal autopoiesis. We can also state that autopoiesis in the physical space is necessary, but not sufficient, to characterize a system as a living system. Or we can claim that these models are not autopoietic but only proto-autopoietic, for autopoiesis requires a distinct internal reaction network that regenerates both itself and the boundary, and regulates the system's interactions with the outside environment by way of that boundary. On this option, autopoiesis in the physical space entails being a cognitive system, and is both necessary and sufficient to characterize a system as a living system.

Let us remind ourselves of what cognition means in this context. Cognition is behavior or conduct in relation to meaning and norms that the system itself enacts or brings forth on the basis of its autonomy (see Chapter 4).[10] Another way to put the issue before us, therefore, is whether autopoiesis is sufficient for cognition. If autopoiesis is taken narrowly to mean internal self-production of the minimal sort that does not involve active interaction with the outside environment, then autopoiesis is not sufficient for cognition. But if autopoiesis is taken more widely to mean internal self-production sufficient for constructive and interactive processes in relation to the environment, then autopoiesis does entail cognition.

I will not presume to legislate this matter: I will leave it for the scientists to work out in whichever way is most productive for their research. For my purposes it is enough to maintain that any living system is both an autopoietic and a cognitive system, for this thesis is sufficient to establish a deep continuity of life and mind. The task before us now is to examine this deep continuity in greater detail.

SIX

◆ ◆ ◆

Life and Mind

The Philosophy of the Organism

IF AUTOPOIESIS AND COGNITION are what distinguish life from non-life, then the projects of understanding life and understanding mind are continuous. This deep continuity of life and mind holds no less for philosophy than it does for biology and mind science. As Hans Jonas wrote in the Introduction to his 1966 book, *The Phenomenon of Life:*

> A philosophy of life comprises the philosophy of the organism and the philosophy of mind. This is itself a first proposition of the philosophy of life, in fact its hypothesis, which it must make good in the course of its execution. For the statement of scope expresses no less than the contention that the organic even in its lowest forms prefigures mind, and that mind even on its highest reaches remains part of the organic. (1966, p. 1).

In mind science, the proposition that life prefigures mind and mind belongs to life has been called the strong continuity thesis of life and mind (Godfrey-Smith 1996; Wheeler 1997), or as I prefer to call it, the deep continuity of life and mind. According to this thesis, life and mind share a set of basic organizational properties, and the organizational properties distinctive of mind are an enriched version of those fundamental to life. Mind is life-like and life is mind-like. Andy Clark describes the thesis this way: "the thesis of strong continuity would be true if, for example, the basic concepts needed to understand the organization of life turned out to be self-organization, collective dynamics, circular causal processes, autopoiesis, etc., and if *those very same*

128

concepts and constructs turned out to be central to a proper scientific understanding of mind" (Clark 2001, p. 118; emphasis in original).

Jonas's proposition about the philosophy of life, however, expresses a further thought, one that is less well explored by advocates of the deep continuity thesis. This thought is that the continuity of life and mind is not simply organizational, or functional or behavioral, but also phenomenological. In other words, the continuity includes the subjective and experiential aspects of mental life as well as the cognitive aspects. For Jonas, certain basic concepts needed to understand human experience turn out to be applicable to life itself: "The great contradictions which man discovers in himself—freedom and necessity, autonomy and dependence, self and world, relation and isolation, creativity and mortality—have their rudimentary traces in even the most primitive forms of life, each precariously balanced between being and not-being, and each already endowed with an internal horizon of 'transcendence'" (1966, p. ix).

This idea of the deep continuity of life and mind is the theme of this chapter. My aim is to use the theory of autopoiesis to build a bridge between the philosophy of the organism and the philosophy of mind. Where subjectivity and experience lie along this path, and what role phenomenology must play in the philosophy of life, are matters we will need to probe along the way.

The Kantian Connection

My starting point is to examine the theory of autopoiesis in relation to Kant's classic treatment of organic nature in his *Critique of Judgment,* first published in 1790 (Kant 1987). Kant gave an original and visionary account of the organism as a self-organizing being, an account close in many ways to the theory of autopoiesis. Kant also thought, however, there were significant restrictions on the kind of scientific explanation we are able to give of organic nature. I intend to show that the theory of autopoiesis can resolve the difficulties he encountered.

Kant believed that we human beings cannot explain organic nature mechanistically but must explain it teleologically, that is, by using the concept of *end* or *purpose.* Kant's model of mechanistic explanation was Newtonian physics, which has no place for teleology, and he thought it absurd to suppose we might one day be able to comprehend organisms in mechanistic terms. Thus in a famous passage he wrote: "For it is quite certain that in terms of merely mechanical principles of nature we cannot even adequately become familiar with, much less explain, organized beings and how they are internally possible. So certain is this that we may boldly state that it is absurd for human beings even to attempt it, or to hope that perhaps some day another Newton might arise who would explain to us, in terms of natural laws unordered by any intention, how even a mere blade of grass is produced" (Kant 1987, pp. 282–283).

Kant's point was not to deny that the mechanistic explanation of nature can and will advance. Rather, it was that teleology would nonetheless remain indispensable, for the following reasons (Cornell 1986). First, to describe an entity as an organism means to conceive of it as intrinsically teleological, because an organism is a self-organizing being— an organized being that is both cause and effect of itself. Second, this teleological conception cannot be subsumed under the concept of mechanism (efficient causation in a world of inanimate matter), the two being incommensurable in principle. Finally, any extension in the understanding of efficient causes in biology would still always have to be placed within the teleological framework of the organism.

We need to ask how this reasoning fares in relation to biology today. In our time, the issue of mechanistic versus teleological explanation is more complicated. Classical mechanistic explanation has been superseded in physics (quantum theory and relativity theory) by forms of explanation that are neither strictly mechanistic in the Newtonian sense nor teleological. On the other hand, mechanistic explanation has been greatly elaborated in biology, in neo-Darwinian evolutionary theory, and in molecular biology, and has been transformed by the theory of complex dynamic systems. At the same time, biologists and philosophers have outlined "teleonomic" or functionalist forms of explanation that do not involve any of the traditional Platonic or Aristotelian components of teleology, namely, backward causation (from a future goal-state to the events leading up to it), anthropomorphism (referring to a conscious purpose), and vitalism (appealing to immaterial forces) (Lennox 1992).

Given these advances, one might suppose that Darwin's theory of evolution by natural selection, advanced in 1859 some seventy years after Kant's *Critique of Judgment*, did indeed "explain to us, in terms of natural laws unordered by any intention, how even a mere blade of grass is produced," and thus that Darwin was to be the "Newton of the blade of grass." There is a sense in which this thought is correct, for Darwin's theory, as originally advanced, is thoroughly Newtonian in character (Cornell 1986). As Weber and Depew (1996) observe, Darwin originally conceived natural selection within a framework derived from classical Newtonian dynamics: "adaptive natural selection is portrayed as a process in which an inertial tendency (Malthusian reproduction) is constrained by external, impinging forces (scarcity), rather than as the working out of an endogenous tendency that Darwin, following Lyell, tends prejudicially to speak of as 'adaptation as the slow willing of animals' (Darwin to Joseph Hooker, 11 January 1844 . . .)" (Weber and Depew 1996, p. 35).

Yet a case can be made for the view that Darwin was not the Newton of the grass blade. Kant's concern was the definitive organization of living beings, but the Darwinian theory of evolution by natural selection does not provide any account of organization at the level of biological individuals. On the contrary, the theory must presuppose biologically organized individuals that reproduce. Moreover, Darwin's Newtonian framework, in which design arises from natural selection conceived of as an external force, does not address the endogenous self-organization of the organism. This aspect of development and evolution, rooted in the organism's autonomy, had to be rediscovered in modern biology, with tools the Darwinian tradition did not provide. For these reasons, the Kantian issues cannot be resolved by appealing to Darwin but must instead be worked out in relation to theories of biological self-organization.

Let me begin by reviewing Kant's famous "antinomy of teleological judgment" (Kant 1987, §§70–71). Kant presents natural science as relying on two maxims or principles of investigation that apparently conflict but are reconcilable as long as they are understood strictly as principles that regulate or guide our investigation of nature, rather than principles that tell us about the constitution of objects in themselves. According to the first, mechanical principle: "All production of material things and their forms must be judged to be possible in terms of merely mechanical laws" (Kant 1987, p. 267). According to the second, teleological principle: "Some products of material nature cannot be judged to be possible in terms of merely mechanical laws. (Judging them requires a quite different causal law—viz., that of final causes.)" (p. 267). Mechanical laws involve only the fundamental properties of matter and efficient causality. Thus the solar system is mechanistically explicable because we can derive its existence—the formation and motions of the sun and planets—from physical processes operating according to mechanical law. But other products of nature, notably plants and animals, are "organized beings," and we cannot explicate the organization they exhibit in their structure and workings solely in terms of mechanical law. In other words, we know no way to derive their organized character from the basic properties of unorganized matter. We are thus forced to explicate organisms teleologically, that is, as ends or purposes.

Kant defines a purpose as "the object of a concept insofar as we regard this concept as the object's cause" (pp. 64–65). In the case of a purpose, "we think . . . of the object itself (its form, or its existence), as an effect that is possible only through a concept of that effect" (p. 65). Thus any product of design is a purpose: we think of a designed object as an effect that is possible only by virtue of a concept or idea, a design or plan. In other words, the action of the cause is based on the idea of the effect. But this concept of purpose is not limited to products of design or intentionally created artifacts. It applies to any object whose possibility we cannot understand unless we assume that the object was produced by a "causality that operates according to purposes"—that is, that arranges things according to the "representation of a certain rule" (p. 65).

Kant holds that organisms are purposes in this sense. We cannot explain their organized character by mechanical law, and we can understand their possibility only if we assume they are produced according to a teleological causality. We cannot explain organisms mechanistically because their organized forms are contingent, not necessary, with respect to the mechanical laws of inorganic nature. Hence these laws are insufficient to explain organisms, and we require a different sort of teleological principle:

> For when we point, for example, to the structure of birds regarding how their bones are hollow, how their wings are positioned to produce motion and their tails to permit steering, and so on, we are saying that all of this is utterly contingent if we go by the mere *nexus effectivus* in nature

and do not yet resort to a special kind of causality, viz., the causality of purposes (the *nexus finalis*); in other words, we are saying that nature, considered as mere mechanism, could have structured itself differently in a thousand ways without hitting on precisely the unity in terms of a principle of purposes, and so we cannot hope to find a priori the slightest basis for that unity unless we seek it beyond the concept of nature rather than in it. (Kant 1987, p. 236)[1]

   This line of thought involves a parallel—but a limited one, as we will see—between organisms and artifacts. The organization of an artifact, such as a watch, is also contingent with respect to mechanical laws. To explain the formation of a watch we cannot appeal only to basic properties of matter and efficient causality; we also need to invoke design. But unlike the nineteenth-century British natural theologian, William Paley (Paley 1996), who saw in this parallel an argument for viewing organisms as divine artifacts, Kant maintained that organisms are natural products, not products of divine design. Organisms are mechanically inexplicable and must be regarded as purposes, but unlike artifacts they are *natural purposes*. They are caused not by any external rational agent, but by their own formative powers.
   Kant distinguishes between two kinds of purposiveness: "intrinsic purposiveness" and "relative purposiveness" (Kant 1987, §63). Intrinsic purposiveness belongs to an effect considered directly as a purpose (that is, as an effect that is possible only through the idea of that effect), whereas relative purposiveness is the usefulness or benefit an effect has as a means to some end. Kant mentions "rivers [that] carry along all sorts of soil on which plants can grow" (1987, p. 245) and snow in cold lands, which "protects crops from frost" and "makes it easier for people to get together (by means of sleighs)" (p. 247). But he completely rejects the thought that natural products are purposes because they are useful to human beings. In the case of an organism, which is a natural purpose, its purposiveness is not relative or extrinsic but intrinsic: it is based on the organism's being an *organized* being, in apparent accordance with a concept or idea, but one that makes the organism an end unto itself.
   Kant initially defines a natural purpose in the following way: "a thing exists as a natural purpose if it is *both cause and effect of itself* (although [*of itself*] in two different senses)" (1987, p. 249). His example is a tree.

A tree reproduces over successive generations, so that each generation is an effect of the preceding one and a cause of the succeeding one. Thus the species tree is both cause and effect of itself. As an individual entity, a tree produces itself through growth and generation. Furthermore, each part of the tree is dependent on the other parts for its preservation; hence each part produces itself in mutual dependence on the others.

Kant expands his account by stating two requirements for a thing to be a natural purpose. First, "the possibility of its parts (as concerns both their existence and their form) must depend on their relation to the whole" (1987, p. 252). If a thing is a purpose, then its idea is the underlying condition for its production, and that idea must determine *a priori* everything in it, in particular the organization of the parts with respect to the whole. But, Kant notes, if something meets only this requirement, then it is merely an artifact and not a natural purpose. For something to be a natural purpose, a second requirement must be met: "This second requirement is that the parts of the thing combine into the unity of a whole because they are reciprocally cause and effect of their form" (1987, p. 252). He restates these requirements a paragraph later. First, every part exists for the sake of the others and the whole. But this condition is not sufficient because it holds also for artifacts: in a watch, each part is there for the sake of the others. Hence the second requirement: "we must think of each part as an organ that *produces* the other parts (so that each reciprocally produces the other) . . . Only if a product meets that condition [as well], and only because of this, will it be both an *organized* and a *self-organizing* being, which therefore can be called a natural purpose" (1987, p. 253; emphasis in original).[2]

This difference between an artifact and a natural purpose is important. In the case of an artifact, each part depends on its relation to the whole because the idea or concept of the whole plays a causal role in its production. This idea or concept resides outside the entity in the mind of an intelligent designer. An organism, however, is a natural product, not an artifact, and the cause of its production resides within it. An organism is self-producing and self-organizing, for each of its parts reciprocally produces the others. It follows that we cannot take the idea or concept of the organism to be a *cause of the organism itself*, for that would mean taking the organism to be an artifact and not a natural product. Rather, we must take the idea of the organism as the *ground of our cognition of it.* That is, we must view it as the basis for our ability to cognize it as an organized being and to grasp its structure and workings in a unified way. Thus, when Kant introduces the second condition that in a natural purpose "the parts of a thing combine into the unity of a whole because they are reciprocally cause and effect of their form," he immediately adds: "For only in this way is it possible that the idea of the whole should conversely (and reciprocally) determine the form and combination of all the parts, not as cause—for then the whole would be a product of art—but as the basis on which someone judging this whole cognizes the systematic unity in the form and combination of all the manifold contained in a given matter" (1987, p. 252).

Kant's account of organisms as natural purposes and self-organizing beings underlies his position that we cannot explain them mechanistically. We have seen that he maintains that the structure and workings of an organism appear contingent with respect to the mechanical laws of matter. Hence we cannot explain an organism simply in terms of the laws of matter in motion. Rather, we must explain an organism teleologically, regarding it as a purpose. In a purpose, each part exists for the sake of the others, and thus the parts are related to each other reciprocally as end and means. We cannot explain this reciprocal relation as a necessary consequence of matter in motion. But this reason for a teleological account also holds for artifacts: in a watch, each part is there for the sake of the others, and the parts are thus related to each other as end and means. An organism, however, is not simply a purpose but a natural purpose. In this case, not only are the parts there for the sake of each other, but they also produce each other, repair each other, and generally exist by means of one another. We cannot comprehend this reciprocal causality of self-production in terms of our conception of mechanistic efficient causation. Hence our only alternative is to see this causation as if it were expressive of purposive design, but a purposiveness that would have to be intrinsic, not extrinsic or relative.

Thus organisms are mechanistically inexplicable not simply because they are purposes and need to be understood teleologically, but also because as natural purposes—as self-producing and self-organizing beings—they are fundamentally different from machines (1987, p. 253). A machine is a purpose, but one in which the material parts are logically independent of and temporally antecedent to the whole they determine. In an organism, however, the parts are not logically independent of and temporally antecedent to the whole. They are determined by their presence in the whole and have properties they would not have independently of the whole. Whereas a machine can be explained by analyzing it into its parts, to explain an organism we need to grasp it as a unified whole that reciprocally determines the form and combination of every one of its parts (1987, pp. 252–253).

The resemblance between Kant's conception of self-organization and the current scientific one is striking. As Alicia Juarrero writes: "What we find anticipated in Kant is a rudimentary systems theory, the recognition of a systemic level of organization with emergent properties that cannot be reduced to an understanding of the components alone" (Juarrero-Roqué 1985, p. 111). In particular, Kant's recognition of the distinctive self-producing character of the organism, in which each part reciprocally produces the others, prefigures the notion of autopoiesis (Weber and Varela 2002).

Yet the Kantian view is that self-organization cannot be understood naturalistically. To understand the unity of the organism we must "seek it beyond the concept of nature rather than in it" (1987, p. 236). Self-organization is ultimately not naturalistically intelligible to us. It involves a reciprocal causality of self-production that proceeds as if in accordance with design, but a design that is immanent in the organism itself and does not reside in the mind of an external designer. "Strictly speaking," Kant writes, "the organization of nature has nothing analogous to any causality known to us" (p. 254).

Kant's position is subtle. Although both mechanism and teleology are indispensable for our investigation of nature, we cannot assume either that nature in itself is purposeful or that teleology is simply an illusory human projection upon a mechanical reality. We need to rely on both mechanistic and teleological thinking, depending on whether we are considering a part on its own in its efficient causality or in its role in the organism as a whole. As Cornell states, "We simply do not know what, if anything, is 'behind' life, 'causing' its basic purposive quality in some ultimate sense. Because of this epistemological limitation, because the principles of mechanism and teleology finally express only two modes of thought incommensurate but both necessary to conceive and investigate living nature, Kant stated repeatedly that it was 'indubitably certain' that no completely mechanistic explanation of life would be forthcoming" (1986, p. 408).

Kant's distinction between "constitutive" concepts and "regulative" concepts is important here. Roughly speaking, constitutive concepts tell us what something is and thus make up our knowledge, whereas regulative concepts regulate and guide an inquiry. For Kant, the concept of a natural purpose is not constitutive but regulative. It guides our investigation of organic nature and enables us to grasp the structure and workings of organized products of nature or organisms. In other words, the concept of a natural purpose is heuristic, not explanatory. We do not take the idea of the organism or the whole organized being to be the cause of the organism itself (because then the organism would be an artifact, not a natural purpose). Rather, we rely on the idea of the whole as the ground of our ability to grasp the organism in a unified way (1987, p. 252).

Kant states that "the concept of a thing as in itself a natural purpose is not a constitutive concept either of understanding or of reason. But it can still be a regulative concept for reflective judgment, allowing us to use a remote analogy with our own causality in terms of purposes generally, to guide our investigation of organized objects and to meditate regarding their supreme basis" (1987, p. 255). On the basis of this "remote analogy," we conceive of organisms teleologically, according to the following maxim or principle: "An organized product of nature is one in which everything is a purpose and also reciprocally a means" (1987, p. 255). From this principle Kant derives as a corollary the statement, "In such a product nothing is gratuitous, purposeless, or to be attributed to a blind natural mechanism" (p. 255). This principle and its corollary are also regulative, not constitutive. They tell us that we ought to proceed on such assumptions, given the teleological framework. In this way, "we expand natural science in terms of a different principle, that of final causes, yet without detracting from the principle of mechanism in the causality of nature" (1987, p. 259).

The Kantian problem of teleology is closely related to the problem of the explanatory gap between consciousness and nature. To conceive of something as an organism is to conceive of it as a natural purpose, a self-organizing being. But this conception is inexplicable in naturalistic terms and is based on an analogy to our own human experience of purpose. Kant allows that teleology and mechanism might "in the inner basis of nature itself . . . be linked in one principle" (1987, p. 268), but he believes that human reason is not in a position to comprehend this hidden unity. This position is not unlike that of today's "New Mysterians," who believe that although consciousness is an entirely natural phenomenon, the concepts needed for a naturalistic explanation of consciousness lie beyond our human ken (McGinn 1991).

We can now return to the question of how Kant's account fares in relation to biology today. Kant believed that human reason is unable to understand the causality of self-organization, but the scientific situation has changed dramatically since his day. We now have the beginnings of a science of complex self-organizing systems. The theory of autopoiesis is especially relevant to the Kantian account, for this theory gives a detailed scientific characterization of precisely that feature Kant made central to his conception of the organism, namely, a self-producing organization. Here two kinds of scientific advances have been decisive. The first advance is the detailed mapping of molecular systems of self-production within living cells. We are now able to comprehend many of the ways in which genetic and enzymatic systems within a cell reciprocally produce one other. The second advance is the invention of mathematical concepts and techniques for analyzing self-organization in nonlinear dynamic systems. Neither advance could have been foreseen in Kant's time—or even Darwin's.

The implications of these advances for the Kantian account are significant. An autopoietic system satisfies Kant's definition of a natural purpose, namely, something whose parts reciprocally produce one another and that therefore exists as both cause and effect of itself (Juarrero-Roqué 1985, pp. 118–119; Weber and Varela 2002). In an autopoietic system, the continued existence of the membrane and internal reaction network is possible thanks to their mutual self-production. What is so startling about this self-production, from the standpoint of classical linear mechanics, is that a self-perpetuating whole emerges out of local processes while subsuming those processes so that they no longer have a merely local and independent identity. It is precisely this view of circular causation and nonlinear emergence that was unavailable to Kant.

Does this modern understanding of self-organization pull the rug out from under Kant's view that self-organization is not a constitutive principle of nature, but only a regulative principle of our judgment?

Answering this question requires care. On the one hand, Kant's statement, "the organization of nature has nothing analogous to any causality known to us" (1987, p. 254), no longer seems compelling, thanks to our growing understanding of circular causality, nonlinear dynamics, and self-organizing systems. Many scientists now believe there are necessary principles of biological self-organization.[3] The advance of science seems to have rolled back the limits of reason as Kant saw them, so that there is no longer any compelling reason to regard self-organization as simply a regulative principle of our judgments about nature rather than also a constitutive principle of nature itself (Juarrero-Roqué 1985).

On the other hand, Kant's critical, epistemological point—that we are not entitled to draw conclusions about the "inner basis of nature itself" from either mechanistic or teleological explanations—still has a certain force. But this force comes into play at a transcendental level of analysis. At this level, nature as a scientific object can no longer be naïvely taken for granted. Rather, it must be seen in relation to the subjectivities and research practices of the scientific investigators to whom it is disclosed.[4]

The autopoietic grounding of Kant's notion of a natural purpose enables us to see our way clear of another major problem that puzzled Kant. Immediately before describing self-organization as foreign to any causality we know, Kant comes close to defining biological life in terms of self-organization. He backs away, however, because he cannot see how to avoid the philosophical dilemma of "hylozoism" (matter is inherently alive) versus dualism (life requires the presence of an immaterial soul):

In considering nature and the ability it displays in organized products, we say far too little if we call this an *analogue of art*, for in that case we think of an artist (a rational being) apart from nature. Rather, nature organizes itself . . . We might be closer if we call this inscrutable property of nature an *analogue of life*. But in that case we must either endow matter, as mere matter, with a [kind of] property ([viz., the property of life, as] hylozoism [does]) that conflicts with its nature . . . Or else we must supplement matter with an alien principle (a soul) *conjoined* to it. But [that also will not work. For] if an organized product is to be a natural product, then we cannot make this soul the artificer that constructed it, since that would remove the product from (corporeal) nature. And yet the only alternative would be to say that this soul uses as its instrument organized matter; but if we presuppose organized matter, we do not make it a whit more intelligible. Strictly speaking, therefore, the organization of nature has nothing analogous to any causality known to us. (1987, p. 254)

Kant sees the futility of appealing to any immaterial principle of vitality outside of nature as a way of understanding the self-organized character of life. The only other option he can envision is hylozoism, the doctrine that all matter is endowed with life. But this doctrine contradicts the very nature of matter, which according to Newtonian physics is lifelessness or inertia (1987, p. 276). Unable to get beyond this dilemma, Kant retreats to the position that self-organization can be only a regulative principle of our judgment, not a constitutive principle of nature.

This dilemma no longer seems compelling. Our conception of matter as essentially equivalent to energy and as having the potential for self-organization at numerous spatiotemporal scales is far from the classical Newtonian worldview. In particular, the physics of thermodynamically open systems combined with the chemistry and biology of self-organizing systems provides another option that is not available to Kant: life is an emergent order of nature that results from certain morphodynamical principles, specifically those of autopoiesis. According to this view, an autopoietic system is no mere analogue of life, but the minimal instance of life and the basis of every living form we know.

I have claimed that the theory of autopoiesis offers a naturalized, biological account of Kant's notion of a natural purpose. The question we need to consider now is what place teleology has in this autopoietic account.

Autopoiesis and Teleology

For Kant, as we have seen, self-organization implies intrinsic purposiveness. A natural purpose is both cause and effect of itself. Every part not only exists for the sake of the other parts, but also reciprocally produces them. The parts produce the whole, but also have their existence by means of the whole. Because of this self-organizing circularity, cause-and-effect relations are also means-end relations. A natural purpose is thus a totality of interrelated means and ends. Unlike an artifact, its purposiveness is not extrinsic (a use to which it can be put by something outside it), but intrinsic, being no other than to exist by organizing itself, by self-organizing.

In contrast, the theory of autopoiesis in its original formulation was explicitly mechanistic and antiteleological. Maturana and Varela identified living systems with autopoietic machines and denied that living systems are teleological: "Living systems, as physical autopoietic machines, are purposeless systems" (Maturana and Varela 1980, p. 86). By "machine" they did not mean an artifact; they meant any entity or system whose operation is determined by its relational organization and the way that organization is structurally realized (1980, pp. 75, 77).[5] Autopoietic machines maintain their own organization constant through material change, and thus are homeostatic or homeodynamic systems of a special sort (1980, pp. 78–79). Purposes, aims, or functions are not features of the organization of any machine; they are instead descriptive notions used to characterize a system in relation to some context of use defined by an observer (1980, pp. 85–86).

There thus appears to be a conflict between Kant's claim that organisms are not machines and are intrinsically purposive, because they produce and organize themselves, and the autopoietic thesis that organisms are physical autopoietic machines and are purposeless systems. One way to deal with this conflict is simply to point out that Kant did not know about the possibility of self-organizing machines and that his conception of a machine is obsolete (see Keller 2000, pp. 106–111). But this point leaves untouched the matter of teleology. If being self-organizing, or more precisely self-producing, is tantamount to being intrinsically purposive, then a self-producing machine would be an intrinsically purposive machine. We are thus faced with two distinct issues—the conceptual or theoretical relation between organisms and machines, and the conceptual or theoretical relation between autopoiesis and teleology.

With regard to the first issue, it will be useful to introduce another line of work in theoretical biology, the work of Robert Rosen (1991, 2000). Like Maturana and Varela, Rosen aims to give a precise account of the organization of life, and although they never mention each other in their writings, there are deep affinities between their theories

(Letelier, Marín, and Mpodozis 2003). Unlike Maturana and Varela, however, Rosen presents a rigorous argument for distinguishing between organisms and machines. An intriguing feature of this argument is that it is precisely what Maturana and Varela would call the circular and self-referential organization of the living that distinguishes organisms from mechanisms and machines. The argument is also reminiscent of Kant. The organization of an organism comprises numerous circular causal loops, such that every component is definable only in terms of the total organization to which it belongs, whereas the total organization is definable only by specifying those components.

Rosen argues that because of these self-referential loops or "impredicativities," organisms, unlike machines, cannot be completely "fractionated" or analytically separated into parts whose properties directly sum to equal the properties of the whole system, and organisms also cannot be adequately modeled by computational or algorithmic processes. In Rosen's terminology, organisms are "complex," which means they belong to the class of systems that have nonfractionable properties and Turing-incomputable models. Machines, on the other hand, are "simple," in the sense that they belong to the class of systems that have only fractionable properties, can be completely modeled by a single dynamical description (have a single "largest model"), and have only computable models.

To understand this line of argument we need to be clear about what Rosen means by "machine" (Rosen 1991, pp. 202–243). He does not mean technological entities, for he explicitly acknowledges the possibility of nonmachine technologies of complexity, for example, biological technologies. As he puts it, "If organism is not machine, then technology need not be machine either" (Rosen 2000, p. 295). Nor does he mean, unlike Maturana and Varela, any physically instantiated relational organization, for complex systems (in his sense) have a relational organization but are not machines. For Rosen, "machines" are a subclass of "mechanisms," where by "mechanism" he means the class of systems all of whose models are Turing-computable and that can be captured by a single dynamical description. A machine is a mechanism one of whose models is a mathematical machine, that is, a system in which one can distinguish between software (or program) and hardware (physical implementation).

Rosen maintains that there is a fundamental difference between machines so understood and organisms. In a mechanism (and hence a machine) "there can be no closed path of efficient causation" (Rosen 1991, p. 241). By this statement he means that for any function, in the mathematical sense of a mapping, in a relational model of a machine, one eventually needs to go outside the system to answer the question of what brings about or entails that function. In a relational model of an organism, however, every function or mapping is entailed by another function within the model. In an organism, but not in a machine, every efficient cause is produced from within the system. Organisms are thus "closed to efficient causation" and their relational models manifest "maximal entailment," whereas machines are "impoverished" in their entailment structure. It is crucial to understand that "closed to efficient causation" does not mean or imply that an organism is materially or thermodynamically closed. On the contrary, a physical system cannot be closed to efficient causation unless it is materially and thermodynamically open (Rosen 2000, pp. 5–32). Rosen's notion of being closed to efficient causation is thus analogous to Maturana and Varela's notion of organizational closure. In addition, his differentiation between organisms and machines is analogous to Varela's differentiation between autonomous systems with organizational-operational closure and heteronomous systems defined by outside control (Varela 1979).

Rosen also argues that a Turing machine cannot simulate closure and maximal entailment in an organism. More precisely, he claims to prove mathematically that a certain class of relational models, called Metabolism-Repair systems or (M, R) systems, in which every function is entailed by another function inside the system, are not Turing-computable. On this basis he argues that any material realization of an (M, R) system, such as a cell, cannot be a mechanism or machine. This result raises the question of what the relation is between Rosen's (M, R) systems and autopoietic systems. In an important article, Letelier, Marín, and Mpodozis (2003) argue that autopoietic systems are a subset of (M, R) systems: Every autopoietic system is operationally equivalent to an (M, R) system, but not conversely, because a generic (M, R) system lacks the autopoietic property of generating its own boundary and internal topology. As Letelier, Marín, and Mpodozis point out, it follows from this analysis that autopoietic systems are not Turing-computable (they have noncomputable models in addition to computable ones) and that a physical autopoietic system is not a machine (according to this abstract and powerful concept of machines).

If this argument is sound, then Rosen's work presents an important challenge to the original placement of autopoiesis in the category of cybernetic mechanism. His work also challenges the hypothesis that autopoiesis can be captured by cellular automata models of the sort I discussed in the last chapter. The point here would not be that autopoietic systems have no mechanistic models, but rather that no mechanistic model could represent all the relevant features of these systems, and hence new sorts of models would need to be developed. At the same time, Bourgine and Stewart's (2004) model of minimal autopoiesis as a random dynamical system (see Chapter 5) can be taken as a challenge to Rosen: what crucial feature of the living organization does this model leave out that Rosen's (M, R) systems succeed in capturing?

We can now return to the issue of teleology and autopoietic self-organization. In calling autopoietic systems purposeless, Maturana and Varela meant that the notions of purpose, aim, goal, and function are "unnecessary for the *definition* of the living organization, and . . . belong to a descriptive domain distinct from and independent of the domain in which the living system's *operations* are described" (Varela 1979, pp. 63–64). The position they were opposing is that living beings are essentially *teleonomic* in the sense set forth by Jacques Monod, namely, "*objects endowed with a purpose or project,* which at the same time they exhibit in their structure and carry out through their performances" (Monod 1971, p. 9, emphasis in original). Against this view that teleonomy "is essential to the very definition of living beings" (ibid.), Maturana and Varela argued as follows:

> Purpose or aims . . . are not features of the organization of any machine (allo- or autopoietic); these notions belong to the domain of our discourse about our actions, that is, they belong to the domain of descriptions, and when applied to a machine, or any system independent from us, they reflect our considering the machine or system in some encompassing context. In general, the observer puts the machines either conceptually or concretely to some use, and thus defines a set of circumstances that lead the machine to change, following a certain path of variations in its output. The connection between these outputs, the corresponding inputs, and their relation with the context in which the observer includes them, determine what we call the aim or purpose of the machine; this aim necessarily lies in the domain of the observer that de-

fines the context and establishes the nexuses. Similarly the notion of function arises in the description made by the observer of the components of a machine or system in reference to some encompassing entity, which may be the whole machine or part of it, and whose states constitute the goal that the changes in the components are to bring about. Here again, no matter how direct the causal connections may be between the changes of state of the components and the state in which they originate in the total system, the implications in terms of design alluded to by the notion of function are established by the observer and belong exclusively to his domain of description. Accordingly, since the relations implied in the notion of function are not constitutive of the organization of an autopoietic system, they cannot be used to explain its organization. (Maturana and Varela 1980, pp. 85–86)

This passage shows that the notion of purpose being criticized is a functionalist version of what Kant would call extrinsic or relative purposiveness, the idea that an entity serves an end or purpose that is external to it.[6] Maturana and Varela's main contention was that although this notion of purpose can have communicative value, it has no explanatory value in characterizing a system's organization. A functional description of a subsystem necessarily includes a larger context to which the function makes reference, namely, that of the whole system. If, on the one hand, one already possesses a complete theory of the organization of the whole system, then the functional description is explanatorily dispensable, although it can still be useful for communicative purposes. On the other hand, the indispensability of a functional description "is symptomatic of the lack of a theory for the organization or structure of the system in which the subsystem, described in functional terms, occurs" (Varela 1979, p. 65).

What bearing does this argument have on the Kantian thought that to exist by being self-organizing is to be intrinsically purposive? Three points are important here. First, the dispensability of extrinsic functional descriptions of a system's components is logically compatible with the whole system being intrinsically purposive. Extrinsic functions presuppose the larger context of the whole system, but intrinsic purposiveness pertains to the overall organization of the whole system itself. A system is supposed to be intrinsically purposive just in case each of its parts is both a product and producer of the other parts, so that the system is a self-organizing whole. As we have seen, an autopoietic system satisfies this requirement. In an autopoietic system, the mutually productive relations among the component processes define an operationally closed network. This closure means that individual components can be interpreted in both causal and finalistic terms in relation to other components and the whole.

Second, in laying down the conditions for the autopoietic organization, no reference is made to any ends, purposes, goals, or functions of the component processes or the whole system. Thus the theory of autopoiesis does not presuppose or appeal to intrinsic purposiveness in an unanalyzed way but rather explicates this notion naturalistically.

Finally, "intrinsic" in this naturalized account must be taken to mean *constitutive* and not *nonrelational* (and hence unanalyzable).[7] Intrinsic purposiveness is a constitutive property of an autopoietic system, but it is an emergent property analyzable in terms of the relational autopoietic organization.

Given this line of reasoning, it might be better to call this sort of constitutive purposiveness *immanent purposiveness*. The thought here is that purposiveness is neither a nonrelational property of something internal to the system (as "intrinsic" can misleadingly suggeset) nor a property determined by something outside the system (by something that transcends the system). Rather, purposiveness is a constitutive property the whole system possesses because of the way the system is organized.

Varela eventually came to believe that this notion of immanent purposiveness is not simply descriptive but explanatory, because it makes visible a dynamic pattern of activity proper to life that would otherwise be missed. He calls this pattern the twofold pattern of *identity* and *sense-making* (Varela 1991, 1997a). Although for many years he had rejected the idea that autopoiesis involves anything teleological, in one of his last essays he revised his view. This essay, written with Andreas Weber, concerns the relations among autopoiesis, Kant's conception of a natural purpose, and Jonas's philosophy of the organism (Weber and Varela 2002). Weber and Varela argue that autopoiesis entails immanent purposiveness in two complementary modes. The first mode of purposiveness is *identity:* autopoiesis entails the production and maintenance of a dynamic identity in the face of material change. The second mode of purposiveness is *sense-making:* an autopoietic system always has to make sense of the world so as to remain viable. Sense-making changes the physicochemical world into an environment of significance and valence, creating an *Umwelt* for the system. Sense-making, Varela maintains, is none other than intentionality in its minimal and original biological form (Thompson 2004; Varela 1997a).[8]

Varela (1997a) links identity and sense-making in the following way:

1. An organism is fundamentally a self-affirming, identity-producing process based on autopoiesis.
2. A self-affirming identity establishes logically and operationally the reference point or perspective for sense-making and a domain of interactions.

These two propositions are meant to be complementary; they are supposed to describe two sides of one emergent process (see Figure 3.3).

In a recent and important article on autopoiesis, Ezequiel Di Paolo (2005) challenges certain aspects of this framework. He argues convincingly that although Maturana and Varela's original definition of autopoiesis is sufficient for the intrinsic teleology of self-production, it is not sufficient for the projective teleology of sense-making (for related considerations see also Ruiz-Mirazo and Moreno 2004). Minimal autopoiesis entails only the general case of conservation of identity through internal material turnover and external perturbations to the system, and not the special case of active monitoring and regulation of the autopoietic network by internal homeostatic or homeodynamic mechanisms. It is this special case that sense-making requires. Sense-making is normative, but the only norm that autopoiesis can provide is the all-or-nothing norm of self-continuance, not the graded norm implied by an organism actively seeking to improve its conditions of self-production (as when a bacterium swims up a sucrose gradient).

This point recalls Merleau-Ponty's idea that vital structures have to be comprehended in relation to norms, whereas physical structures are comprehensible in relation to laws: "each organism, in the presence of a given milieu, has its optimal conditions of activity and its proper manner of realizing equilibrium," and each organism "modifies its milieu according to the internal norms of its activity" (1963, pp. 148, 154). Unlike Maturana (1975, 1980a), who refuses to countenance such normative language and insists that autopoiesis is simply the conservation of organization, Varela implicitly endorses the normative conception when he describes sense-making as arising from the constant and necessary need to supplement the autopoietic process with what it lacks to keep on going (Varela 1991, 1997a). Di Paolo agrees that a normative conception is needed; otherwise there is no way to account for such biological phenomena as stress, illness, fatigue, and health, as well as plasticity and adaptation more generally. But he makes the valid and important point that the original and canonical formulation of autopoiesis is not sufficient to ground this normative conception. Rather, a distinct capacity for "adaptivity" needs to be added to the minimal autopoietic organization so that the system can actively regulate itself with respect to its conditions of viability and thereby modify its milieu according to the internal norms of its activity.[9] In sum, although autopoiesis is necessary for sense-making, it is not sufficient, but autopoiesis and adaptivity are jointly necessary and sufficient.

This issue about normativity is closely related to the issue of whether autopoiesis is necessary and sufficient for life, or merely necessary. As we saw at the end of the last chapter, Bitbol and Luisi (2005), and Bourgine and Stewart (2004), argue that living systems are cognitive systems, but autopoiesis does not entail cognition because a minimal autopoietic system is not a cognitive system. A minimal autopoietic system lacks an internal metabolic network that makes possible flexible and adaptive responses to the environment. Such a system is *robust*—it conserves its identity through material change—but not *flexible* or *adaptive* because it has no way to assimilate and accommodate to the environment. Similarly, Di Paolo argues that sense-making requires adaptivity, but minimal autopoiesis is not sufficient for adaptivity and hence is insufficient for sense-making. Adaptivity is a special way of being tolerant to challenges by actively monitoring perturbations and compensating for them in relation to the autopoietic identity taken as an internal norm. Adaptivity needs to be established on the basis of autopoiesis; otherwise sense-making is not original to the system but merely attributed from outside. But minimal autopoiesis is not sufficient for adaptivity and sense-making.

The upshot of this discussion is that living beings embody an immanent purposiveness and this purposiveness manifests itself in the two complementary modes of autopoiesis (the intrinsic teleology of self-production) and sense-making (the projective teleology of adaptivity and cognition). Minimal autopoiesis is necessary but not sufficient for sense-making (or cognition), but an enlarged conception of autopoiesis that includes adaptivity is necessary and sufficient.

We have now come a long way toward setting forth the basis for the deep continuity of life and mind. But yet another important step needs to be taken: we need to address the phenomenological side of teleology, namely, purposiveness as a feature of lived experience. Unless we take this step, we will not have confronted a core part of the Kantian problem of teleology, which is essentially a version of the explanatory gap between mind and nature. As a result of phenomenological philosophy after Kant, particularly the writings of Hans Jonas, we now have a philosophical account that can bridge the gap between autopoietic biology and phenomenology. Although Jonas's writings predate the theory of autopoiesis, he nevertheless advances a conception of the organism that philosophically complements and phenomenologically enriches this theory. Only by intertwining these two perspectives, the biological and the phenomenological, can we gain a fuller understanding of the immanent purposiveness of the organism and the deep continuity of life and mind.

Needful Freedom and the Selfhood of the Organism

Living beings affirm their own identities by differentiating themselves from their surroundings and thus demand to be seen from an autonomy perspective. Autopoiesis is basic autonomy in its minimal cellular form: a living cell stands out from a chemical background as a closed network of self-producing processes that actively regulates its encounters with its environment. What Kant recognized as a distinguishing characteristic of organic beings—that they are unities rather than mere aggregates—finds its minimal expression in a living cell. A cell, not merely a persisting material aggregate, is a self-sustaining unity, a unity that dynamically produces and maintains its own identity in the face of what is other. Jonas has this distinctive mark of life in mind when he writes: "The introduction of the term 'self,' unavoidable in any description of the most elementary instance of life, indicates the emergence, with life as such, of internal identity—and so, as one with that emergence, its self-isolation too from all the rest of reality" (1966, pp. 82–83).

Yet self-isolation cannot mean outright independence from the world. Nor can the emergence of internal identity with life as such mean that identity is a given. The organism is in and of the world, and its identity has to be enacted in the very process of living, which is to say in the assimilation of and accommodation to the world. Autonomy, far from being exempt from the causes and conditions of the world, is an achievement dependent on those very causes and conditions. In Jonas's evocative phrase, the predicament of the organism is one of *needful freedom:*

> In this process of self-sustained being, the relation of the organism to its material substance is of a double nature: the materials are essential to it specifically, accidental individually; it coincides with their actual collection at the instant, but is not bound to any one collection in the succession of instants, "riding" their change like the crest of a wave and bound only to their form of collection which endures as its own feat. Dependent on their availability as materials, it is independent of their sameness as these; its own, functional identity, passingly incorporating theirs, is of a different order. In a word, the organic form stands in a dialectical relation of *needful freedom* to matter. (1966, p. 80)

A dialectical relation, as we have seen, is one whose terms evolve as a result of their mutual interdependence and thereby come to constitute a new unity. Richard Levins and Richard Lewontin, in their book *The Dialectical Biologist,* describe dialectical relations in the following way: "These are the properties of things we call dialectical: that one thing cannot exist without the other, that one acquires its properties from its relation to the other, that the properties of both evolve as a consequence of their interpenetration" (Levins and Lewontin 1985, p. 3). The relationship between organism and environment is dialectical in this sense. The organism cannot exist without the environment, it acquires its properties from its relation to the environment, and both it and the environment evolve as a consequence of their interpenetration.

The organism's needful freedom is one aspect of this relation. An organism is a material being, and its reality at any given moment coincides completely with its material constitution. Yet its identity cannot be based on the constancy of matter because its material composition is constantly renewed: "Every five days you get a new stomach lining. You get a new liver every two months. Your skin replaces itself every six weeks. Every year, ninety-eight percent of the atoms in your body are replaced. This nonstop chemical replacement, metabolism, is a sure sign of life" (Margulis and Sagan 1995, p. 23). Only at the level of form or pattern can we find constancy in the flux.

Jonas proposes that the sheer fact of metabolism brings with it a dialectical relation of freedom and necessity peculiar to living beings. Following in Kant's footsteps, Jonas takes the organism's self-organizing being as his starting point, but by asserting that freedom is coeval and coextensive with life itself, he takes a bold step beyond his illustrious German predecessor. For Kant, although organisms are natural purposes because they are self-organizing beings, they are not free inasmuch as they self-organize according to a predetermined pattern (inscrutable to us). Therefore, we human beings, considered as products of nature, are not free; only as rational and moral agents who transcend nature are we free. Freedom belongs to the sphere of practical reason in which reason must presuppose its own freedom in order for morality to be possible. We belong to this sphere not by virtue of our organic being but by virtue of our rational being, which transcends nature. Jonas, however, rejects this dualism:

> One expects to encounter the term ["freedom"] in the areas of mind and will, and not before: but if mind is prefigured in the organic from the beginning, then freedom is. And indeed our contention is that even metabolism, the basic level of all organic existence, exhibits it: that it is itself the first form of freedom. These must sound strange words to most readers, and I do not expect it otherwise. For what could be further from freedom, further from will and choice which are required for it by any normal understanding of the word, than the blind automatism of the chemistry carried on in the depths of our bodies? Yet it will be the burden of one part of our discourse to show that it is in the dark stirrings of primeval organic substance that a principle of freedom shines forth for the first time within the vast necessity of the physical universe—a principle foreign to suns, planets, and atoms. Obviously, all consciously "mental" connotations must at first be kept away from the concept when used for so comprehensive a principle: "Freedom" must denote an objectively discernible mode of being, i.e., a manner of executing existence, distinctive of the organic *per se* and thus shared by all members but by no nonmembers of the class: an ontologically descriptive term which can

apply to mere physical evidence at first. Yet, even as such it must not be unrelated to the meaning it has in the human sphere whence it is borrowed, else its extended use would be frivolous. (1966, p. 3)

It is the individuality or selfhood of the organism that links freedom as an "objectively discernible mode of being" in the living world and freedom in the sense of human liberty. Precisely as Maturana and Varela take the term *autonomy* from the human realm to describe the self-generating and self-maintaining organization of living systems, so Jonas takes the term *freedom* to describe "a certain independence of form with respect to its own matter" (1966, p. 81), achieved in and through metabolism. A lifeless thing does not metabolize; hence "its duration is mere remaining, not reaffirmation" (1966, p. 81). Without metabolism, there can be no "lifeline" (Rose 1997), no developmental continuity of the individual through material change. Every organism enacts a lifeline and thus is marked by a kind of freedom in relation to the materiality of the world. An organism's identity is not bound to its material constitution, for this constitution is constantly renewed; its identity is accomplished dynamically at a formal level. Yet with this freedom comes a correlative necessity: the organism has to change; stasis is impossible. The organism must eat and excrete; otherwise it dies. Without incessant metabolic exchange with the world there can be no emancipation of dynamic selfhood from mere material persistence. The organism's condition is thus one of needful freedom: "This is the antinomy of freedom at the roots of life and in its most elementary form, that of metabolism" (1966, p. 84).

Identity and Sense-Making

In the needful freedom of metabolism, according to Jonas, we find the immanent purposiveness of life. Metabolism is the constant regeneration of an island of form amidst a sea of matter and energy. Metabolism establishes a self with an internal identity marked off from the outside world and whose being is its own doing. Metabolism operates according to internal norms that determine whether otherwise neutral events are good or bad for the continuation of the organism. In these ways, metabolism is immanently teleological. An organism must subordinate every change it undergoes to the maintenance of its identity and regulate itself and its interactions according to the internal norms of its activity. Life is thus a self-affirming process that brings forth or enacts its own identity and makes sense of the world from the perspective of that identity. The organism's "concern," its "natural purpose," is to keep on going, to continue living, to affirm and reaffirm itself in the face of imminent not-being. Incessant material turnover and exchange with the environment is both a reason for this concern and the only way to meet it. Such is the immanent teleology of life: "Organic individuality is achieved in the face of otherness, as its own ever challenged goal, and is thus teleological" (Jonas 1968, p. 243).

The theory of autopoiesis can be called upon to complement this account. According to this theory, immanent purposiveness, the organism's "concern," is not any extrinsic and heteronomous purpose or adaptive function, as in neo-Darwinism, nor any special vital force or entelechy, as in vitalism. Rather, as we have seen, it is the twofold purposiveness of identity (self-production) and sense-making (adaptivity and cognition), based on autopoiesis.

This twofold purposiveness turns an indifferent physicochemical world into an environment of biological significance: "The environment *(Umwelt)* emerges from the world through the actualization or the being of the organism—[granted that] an organism can exist only if it succeeds in finding in the world an adequate environment" (Merleau-Ponty 1963, p. 13, quoting Goldstein).

In establishing a pole of internal identity in relation to the environment, the autopoietic process brings forth, in the same stroke, what counts as other, the organism's world. To exist as an individual means not simply to be numerically distinct from other things but to be a self-pole in a dynamic relationship with alterity, with what is other, with the world. This kind of relationship is not possible for nonautonomous entities. Without organizational and operational closure—without, in other words, any circular and self-referential process whose primary effect is its own production—there is no identity-producing mechanism. Hence there is no dynamic co-emergence of an individual and environment.

An environment, in von Uexküll's (1957) sense of an *Umwelt*, has meaning and value (see Merleau-Ponty, 2003, pp. 167–178). An organism's environment is not equivalent to the world seen simply through the lenses of physics and chemistry. Physical and chemical phenomena, in and of themselves, have no particular significance or meaning; they are not "for" anyone.[10] Living beings shape the world into meaningful domains of interaction and thereby bring forth their own environments of significance and valence (see Figure 3.3).

From our perspective as observers, we can constantly switch back and forth between the physics and chemistry of the world and the environments of living beings. We can manipulate physical and chemical parameters, and then describe the significance these manipulations have for the organism. For example, if we wish to analyze a bacterium swimming in a sucrose gradient, we can point to the local effects of sucrose on membrane permeability, the viscosity of the medium, the hydromechanics of flagellar beat, and so forth. We point to these particular features of the physicochemical world, however, only because the bacterium as an autopoietic unity singles them out as relevant to its identity; their biological meaning depends on the bacterium. If we ignore the perspective of the bacterium as an autopoietic individual, then all correlations between sucrose gradients and hydromechanics become mere chemical regularities devoid of any biological significance (Varela 1991).

Varela (1991, 1997a) describes this difference between the organism's environment and the physicochemical world as one of a "surplus of significance." There is no food significance in sucrose except when bacteria migrate up-gradient and metabolize sucrose molecules, thereby enhancing their autopoiesis. The food significance of sucrose is certainly not unrelated to the physics and chemistry of the situation; it depends on sucrose being able to form a gradient, traverse a cell membrane, and so on. But physics and chemistry alone do not suffice to reveal this significance. For that the perspective of the autopoietic cell is needed. For this reason, Varela states that the structural coupling of organism and environment always involves a "surplus of significance" provided by the organism. Whatever the organism encounters it must evaluate from the vantage point established by its self-affirming identity. At its simplest, this evaluation takes the form of the dual valence of attractive or repulsive and the correlative behaviors of approach or escape. In this way, sense-making "lays a new grid over the world: a ubiquitous scale of value" (Weber and Varela 2002, p. 118).

The Self-Transcendence of the Organism

Jonas traces the immanent purposiveness of life back to what he calls the self-transcendence of the organism: "By the 'transcendence' of life we mean its entertaining a horizon, or horizons, beyond its point-identity" (1966, p. 85). Identity or self-production can be achieved only "by way of a continuous moving beyond the given condition" (1968, p. 243). If the organism must change its matter in order to maintain its identity, then the organism must aim beyond itself, beyond its present condition or point-identity in the here and now.

In his essay "Biological Foundations of Individuality," Jonas (1968) links these ideas to Spinoza. The constant regenerative activity of metabolism endows life with a minimal "concern" to carry on being. Spinoza called this concern *conatus,* the effort and power of life to preserve itself, to stay in existence. "But Spinoza," Jonas writes, "with the knowledge of his time, did not realize that the *conatus* to persevere in being can only operate as a movement that goes constantly *beyond* the given state of things" (1968, p. 243). We can add that Jonas, with the knowledge of his time, did not realize that this movement is a natural consequence of autopoiesis and sense-making. Metabolism is not only the simplest form of this movement of going beyond the given state of things, but also the biochemical realization or instantiation of a crucial portion of the autopoietic organization. That organization must be homeodynamically maintained, and it can be maintained only through the incessant material flux of metabolism. In this way, the operational closure of autopoiesis necessitates that the organism be a thermodynamically open system. This dual condition of closure and openness is yet another facet of the organism's needful freedom. An organism is never bound to its material composition at any given instant, but by the same token it has to change because stasis means death.

This necessity propels the organism both forward and outward. An organism must project beyond itself, opening into the temporal horizon of its own life cycle or lifeline and the spatial horizon of the outer world. In this way, autopoiesis and sense-making enact or bring forth biological time and space: "The internal direction toward the next impending phase of a being that has to continue *itself* constitutes biological time; the external direction toward the co-present not-itself constitutes biological space. As the here expands into the there, so the now expands into the future" (Jonas 1966, p. 86).

The horizons of biological space and time have been greatly expanded over the course of evolution, particularly in metazoan organisms with nervous systems. Later in this book I will discuss phenomenological analyses of time-consciousness, as well as the relation between time and affect. Jonas finds an adumbration of this relation already at the cellular level of metabolism:

> self-concern, actuated by want, throws open as well a horizon of time that embraces, not outer presence, but inner imminence: the imminence of that future into which organic continuity is each moment about to extend by the satisfaction of that moment's want. Thus life is facing forward as well as outward and extends "beyond" its own immediacy in both directions at once. In fact, it faces outward only because, by the necessity of its freedom, it faces forward: so that spatial presence is lighted up as it were by temporal imminence and both merge into past fulfillment (or its negative, disappointment). (1966, p. 85)

Metabolism propels life outward and forward, beyond its present condition in space and time. Life must be oriented in this way because its primary condition is one of concern and want, a condition that in animal life manifests itself as appetition or desire. Concern, want, need, appetition, desire—these are essentially affective and protentional or forward-looking. The organism opens outward into space because its metabolism propels it forward in time, and this forward trajectory is fueled by want, concern, and need. As Jonas argues (1966, p. 86), if concern is the organism's primary condition, then what phenomenologists call the protention of the immediate future has a certain primacy over the retention of the just-past in the temporality of life.

Later in this book I examine phenomenological analyses of time-consciousness that stress its affective receptivity and protentional openness to the future. Jonas's relevance for these analyses lies in his observation that the forward trajectory of the organism at the cellular level of metabolism is the vital source of the protentional openness of time-consciousness.

This forward trajectory is another expression of life's immanent purposiveness. Whereas teleology for Kant was only a regulative principle for our judgments about organized nature, Jonas identifies purposiveness with "a dynamic character of a certain mode of existence, coincident with the freedom and identity of form in relation to matter" (1966, p. 86). This mode of existence is equivalent to what Merleau-Ponty calls vital structures. Vital structures modify their milieus according to the internal norms of their activities. For Jonas, such modification is an expression of the dynamic character of this type of structure, a dynamic character he calls transcendence. Here Jonas draws on his mentor Heidegger's concept of transcendence as the always-already-surpassing or being-projected-beyond-oneself in the world that is proper to human existence *(Dasein)*. Heidegger held that transcendence in this existential sense is presupposed by (and thus more fundamental than) the phenomenonological notion of intentionality as mental directedness (Heidegger 1982, pp. 161–162). Jonas, in a radical move, takes this insight of existential phenomenology down to the very roots of mind in life and the incessant self-transcendence of metabolism.[11] This move brings us back to the idea, announced at the beginning of this chapter, of the deep continuity of mind and life.

The Deep Continuity of Life and Mind

The usual way to express this idea is that the organizational properties of mind are an enriched version of those fundamental to life (Godfrey-Smith 1996; Wheeler 1997). Jonas, as we have seen, goes further. He uses phenomenological philosophy to argue that certain existential structures of human life are an enriched version of those constitutive of all life. Varela also has in mind such existential continuity when he reformulates Maturana's (1970) proposition, "living is a process of cognition," as the proposition, "living is sense-making" (Varela 1991, 1997a; Weber and Varela 2002).

For an example of what Varela means by sense-making we can revisit the now familiar example of motile bacteria swimming uphill in a food gradient of sugar. The cells tumble about until they hit upon an orientation that increases their exposure to sugar, at which point they swim forward, up-gradient, toward the zone of greatest sugar concentration. This behavior occurs because the bacteria are able to sense chemically the concentration of sugar in their local environment through molecular receptors in their membranes. They are able to move forward by rotating their flagella in coordination like a propeller. These bacteria are, of course, autopoietic. They also embody a dynamic sensorimotor loop: the way they move (tumbling or swimming forward) depends on what they sense, and what they sense depends on how they move. This sensorimotor loop both expresses and is subordinated to the system's autonomy, to the maintenance of its autopoiesis. Consequently, every sensorimotor interaction and every discriminable feature of the environment embodies or reflects the bacterial perspective.

To repeat a point made earlier in this book (see Chapter 4), although sucrose is a real and present condition of the physicochemical environment, its status as food is not. That sucrose is a nutrient is not intrinsic to the status of the sucrose molecule; it is, rather, a relational feature, linked to the bacterium's metabolism. Sucrose has significance or value as food, but only in the milieu that the organism itself brings into existence. Varela, as we have seen, summarizes this idea by saying that thanks to the organism's autonomy, its environment or niche has a "surplus of significance" compared with the physicochemical world.[12] Living is a process of sense-making, of bringing forth significance and value. In this way, the environment becomes a place of valence, of attraction and repulsion, approach or escape.

We can elaborate Varela's proposition, "living is sense-making," as follows.

1. *Life = autopoiesis and cognition.* Any living system is both an autopoietic and a cognitive system. (Henceforth, I will use "autopoiesis" widely to include cognition and adaptivity.)
2. *Autopoiesis entails the emergence of a bodily self.* A physical autopoietic system, by virtue of its operational closure (autonomy), produces and realizes an individual or self in the form of a living body, an organism.
3. *Emergence of a self entails emergence of a world.* The emergence of a self is also by necessity the co-emergence of a domain of interactions proper to that self, an environment or *Umwelt.*
4. *Emergence of a self and world = sense-making.* The organism's environment is the sense it makes of the world. This environment is a place of significance and valence, as a result of the global action of the organism.
5. *Sense-making = enaction.* Sense-making is viable conduct. Such conduct is oriented toward and subject to the environment's significance and valence. Significance and valence do not preexist "out there," but are enacted, brought forth, and constituted by living beings. Living entails sense-making, which equals enaction.

At this point one might object that the propositions "living is a process of cognition" and "living is sense-making" conflate cognition with adaptation. Margaret Boden (2000) makes this charge. She thinks it would be better to use the term *cognition* more strictly to avoid the implication that autopoiesis necessarily involves cognition.

To decide this matter, we need to attend to what we mean in using the words "adaptation" and "cognition." Adaptation is a condition, but cognition is an activity. For neo-Darwinians, evolution involves the optimization of adaptation through natural selection. From an autopoietic perspective, however, adaptation is an invariant background condition of all life (Maturana and Varela 1987, pp. 94–117), whereas cognition, in the present context, means the activity of sense-making. Cognition is behavior or conduct in relation to meaning and norms that the system itself enacts or brings forth on the basis of its autonomy. We have seen that sense-making requires more than minimal autopoiesis; it requires autopoiesis enhanced with a capacity for adaptivity or assimilation and accommodation. Adaptivity in this context means flexibility, the capacity to change in relation to changing conditions in a viable (and not necessarily optimal) way. According to the view I have been proposing, autopoiesis plus adaptivity entails sense-making, which is cognition in its minimal biological form.

This usage of "cognition" is admittedly a broad one,[13] and I certainly do not intend for it to obscure the distinctive characteristics of animal and human cognition. Nevertheless, this usage is not merely a way of speaking because it rests on an explicit hypothesis about the natural roots of intentionality: Intentionality arises from the operational closure and interactive dynamics of autopoiesis. Recall the proposal, presented in Chapter 2, that intentionality, understood broadly to mean the constitution or disclosure of the world, corresponds to a type of self-organization. We are now in position to see that the minimal form this type of self-organization can take is autopoiesis (understood to include adaptivity). Below the level of complexity of autopoiesis—for example, the level of self-organizing, physical dissipative structures—we find no analogue of the phenomenological notion of the disclosure of the world. Once we arrive at autopoiesis, however, we find the first instance of precisely this kind of analogue, namely, a system whose activity brings forth or constitutes a world.[14] In sum, intentionality first emerges in nature in the form of autopoiesis and sense-making.

In putting forward this proposal, I thus agree with Dennett when he states: "intentionality doesn't come from on high; it percolates up from below" (Dennett 1995a, p. 205). Elaborating this idea, he writes:

> When an entity arrives on the scene capable of behavior that staves off, however primitively, its own dissolution and decomposition, it brings with it into the world its "good." That is to say, it creates a point of view from which the world's events can be roughly partitioned into the favorable, the unfavorable, and the neutral. And its own innate proclivities to seek the first, shun the second, and ignore the third contribute essentially to the definition of the three classes. As the creature thus comes to have interests, the world and its events begin creating *reasons* for it—whether or not the creature can fully recognize them . . . The first reasons preexisted their own recognition. (Dennett 1991a, p. 174)

This passage could easily stand as a gloss on what I have been calling sense-making. Nevertheless, there is an important difference between Dennett's proposal and the one I am offering here. Whereas mine is based on the theory of autopoiesis, Dennett's is based on the selfish-gene theory championed by Dawkins (1989). (I criticize this theory in Chapter 7.) For Dennett, agency and meaning are born when replicating molecules arrive on the scene: "Through the microscope of molecular biology, we get to witness the birth of agency, in the first macromolecules that have enough complexity to 'do things.' This is not florid agency—*echt* intentional action, with the representation of reasons, deliberation, reflection, and conscious decision—but it is the only possible ground from which the seeds of intentional action could grow" (1995a, p. 202).

The problem with this view is that a replicating macromolecule is not a basic autonomous system. It does not produce itself from within itself, and it does not regulate its external boundary conditions. DNA and RNA are not *self*-replicating (and certainly not in the way a basic autonomous system is *self-producing*): They do not replicate themselves; they get replicated as a result of their participation in a complex network that they do not produce (though of course they play a crucial role in its self-production) (see Chapter 7). Agency and meaning require autonomy; minimal agency and meaning require minimal autonomy. Minimal autonomy *depends* on macromolecules but requires that those macromolecules be *organized* in a particular way, namely, in the autopoietic way. It is this autopoietic organization that is the ground from which the seeds of intentional action grow, not macro-molecules as such.

We have been considering issues raised by Boden's charge that autopoiesis should be sharply distinguished from cognition. At the other end of the spectrum from Boden, biologist Lynn Margulis (2001) writes about "microbial consciousness" and the "conscious cell." She and Dorion Sagan believe that consciousness is coeval and coextensive with life itself:

> Not just animals are conscious, but every organic being, every autopoietic cell is conscious. In the simplest sense, consciousness is an awareness of the outside world. And this world need not be the world outside one's mammalian fur. It may also be the world outside one's cell membrane. Certainly some level of awareness, of responsiveness owing to that awareness, is implied in all autopoietic systems. (Margulis and Sagan 1995, p. 122)

Another author who upholds this view is philosopher and phenomenologist Maxine Sheets-Johnstone, who argues that motile bacteria embody a rudimentary form of corporeal or proprioceptive consciousness (Sheets-Johnstone 1999a, pp. 52, 73).

In assessing this idea of cellular consciousness, we need to think about what consciousness is supposed to mean in this context. Margulis and Sagan describe consciousness as "awareness of the outside world," but a familiar idea from mind science is that not all forms of awareness imply consciousness in the sense of subjective experience. There are a number of different concepts of consciousness, but the one most relevant here is probably *sentience,* the feeling of being alive and exercising effort in movement. The nineteenth-century French philosopher Maine de Biran (1766–1824) wrote of the "feeling of existence" *(le sentiment de l'existence).* Neuroscientists Damasio (1999) and Panksepp (1998b) write about a primitive *feeling of self.* Thus one might describe consciousness in the sense of sentience as a kind of primitively self-aware liveliness or animation of the body. Does sentience emerge with life itself, with the first living bodies, namely, bacteria? Jonas also poses this problem in his writings:

> At which point . . . in the enormous spectrum of life are we justified in drawing a line, attributing a "zero" of inwardness to the far side and an

initial "one" to the side nearer to us? Where else but at the very beginning of life can the beginning of inwardness be located? (1996, p. 63)

Whether we give this inwardness the name of feeling, receptiveness or
response to stimuli, volition, or something else—it harbors, in some degree of "awareness," the absolute interest of the organism in its own
being and continuation. (1996, p. 69)

This "absolute interest of the organism in its own being and continuation," as we noted earlier, is what Spinoza called *conatus,* life's concern to exist or to carry on being. From the perspective of the theory
of autopoiesis, we can think of this concern as the twofold purposiveness of identity and sense-making. The point we need to make now is
that this immanent purposiveness does not entail consciousness.[15] In
support of this view are the following considerations. First, although
this point is controversial, it is reasonable to suppose that being "phenomenally conscious" of something entails being able to form intentions to act in relation to it (Hurley 1998, pp. 149–150). It is hard to
make sense of the idea of being conscious of something, in the sense
of subjectively experiencing it, while having no possibility of intentional access to it whatsoever. There is no good reason, however, for
thinking that autopoietic selfhood of the minimal cellular sort involves
any kind of intentional access on the part of the organism to its sense-
making. Second, it seems unlikely that minimal autopoietic selfhood
involves phenomenal selfhood or subjectivity, in the sense of a prereflective self-awareness constitutive of a phenomenal first-person perspective (see Chapter 9). Rather, this sort of awareness would seem to
require (in ways we do not yet fully understand) the reflexive elaboration and interpretation of life processes provided by the nervous
system. Finally, it is important to situate consciousness in relation to dynamic, unconscious processes of life regulation. This effort becomes
difficult, perhaps impossible, if one projects consciousness down to the
cellular level.

Life Can Be Known Only by Life

In this last section, let us turn our gaze back on ourselves and ask the
following question: What is that enables us, as scientists and philosophers, to cognize or grasp the phenomenon of autopoietic selfhood?

What are the conditions of possibility for our recognition and comprehension of this form of existence? Would autopoietic selfhood be disclosable from some disembodied, objective standpoint? Or, rather, are we able to cognize this form of existence because it resembles the form of our own bodily selfhood and subjectivity, which we know firsthand?

We have seen how autopoiesis gives rise, in one stroke, to inwardness and outwardness, to the self-production of an inside that also specifies an outside to which it is normatively related. I submit that this inwardness or interiority is disclosable to us because we ourselves are living beings who experience our own bodily selfhood firsthand. Let us suppose, following Jonas (1966, pp. 64–98), that we were looking at an organism from the perspective of a disembodied and purely analytical, mathematical intellect. Would we be able to recognize the organism's inwardness and purposiveness? From the disembodied, analytical standpoint, the organism would be resolved into a collection of fleeting, objective physicochemical events, "and all features of a *self-related autonomous unity* would, in the end, appear as purely . . . fictitious" (1996, p. 78, emphasis added).[16] Yet we are bodily beings ourselves, and we experience inwardness and purposiveness in our dealings with the world.[17] Thus, "*we* are able to say what no disembodied onlooker would have a cause for saying: that the mathematical God in his homogeneous analytical view misses the decisive point—the point of life itself: its being self-centered individuality, being for itself and in contraposition to all the rest of the world, with an essential boundary dividing 'inside' and 'outside'" (p. 79).

Jonas summarizes this line of thought in the proposition that "life can be known only by life" (p. 91). This proposition is a quintessential phenomenological one: before being scientists we are first and foremost living beings, and we thus possess within ourselves evidence of purposiveness (Weber and Varela 2002, p. 110). As Jonas puts it, "being living bodies ourselves, we happen to have inside knowledge" (1966, p. 79). In observing other creatures struggling to continue their existence—starting with bacteria that actively swim away from a chemical repellent—we can, through the evidence of our own experience and the Darwinian evidence of the continuity of life, view inwardness and purposiveness as proper to living being.

It is true that this view of life has a retrospective element. We retrospectively recast our biological descriptions in terms commensurable with a phenomenological analysis of our own experience. Legitimizing this procedure are the ongoing and inescapable, pragmatic circulation and mutually constraining relation between science and experience (Gallagher 1997; Varela 1996; Varela, Thompson, and Rosch 1991). Thus, in the present context, the theory of autopoiesis provides a naturalistic interpretation of the teleological conception of life originating in experience, but our experience of our own bodily being is a condition of possibility for our comprehension of autopoietic selfhood.

The proposition that life can be known only by life is also a transcendental one in the phenomenological sense. It is about the conditions for the possibility of knowing life, given that we do actually have biological knowledge. One way to articulate this transcendental line of thought is as follows: (1) To account for certain observable phenomena, we need the concepts of organism (in the Kantian sense of a self-organizing and immanently purposive whole) and autopoiesis. (2) The source for the meaning of these concepts is the lived body, our original experience of our own bodily existence. (3) These concepts and the biological accounts in which they figure are not derivable from some observer-independent, nonindexical, objective, physico-chemical description, as the physicalist myth of science would have us believe. To make the link from matter to life and mind, from physics to biology and psychology, we needs concepts such as organism and autopoiesis, but these concepts are available only to a bodily subject with firsthand experience of its own bodily life. In Merleau-Ponty's words: "I cannot understand the function of the living body except by enacting it myself, and except in so far as I am a body which rises toward the world" (1962, p. 75).

This transcendental perspective overturns the uncritical standpoint of objectivist philosophy and science. Objectivism takes things for granted, without asking how they are disclosable to human experience and knowledge, or how they come to be disclosed with the meaning or significance they have. Objectivism in biology, for example, takes the organism for granted as a ready-made object out there in the world. No concern is shown for how the category "organism" is constituted for us in scientific experience. In contrast, phenomenology traces this category back to its cognitive source, which is the lived experience of our bodily being. Objectivism refuses to take this sort of reflexive step.

In this way, it consigns itself not merely to ignorance and the unexamined life, but also to a form of false consciousness. As Merleau-Ponty states in the Preface to his *Phenomenology of Perception:* "The whole universe of science is built upon the world as directly experienced, and if we want to subject science itself to rigorous scrutiny and arrive at a precise assessment of its meaning and scope, we must begin by reawakening the basic experience of the world of which science is the second-order expression" (1962, p. viii). A critical and reflective science can embrace this phenomenological perspective because it sees that by clarifying scientific experience in this way, science itself is properly situated in relation to the rest of human life and is thereby secured on a sounder footing.

In this chapter and the previous one, we have focused on scientific knowledge of the vital order, the phenomenon of life. The point at which we have now arrived, though familiar to phenomenologists, may be less so to biologists, or at least they speak of it less readily. This point is that empathy is a precondition of our comprehension of the vital order, in particular of the organism as a sense-making being inhabiting an environment. In using the term *empathy* in this context, I anticipate the last chapter of this book. There we will see that empathy is a multi-faceted experience rooted in the spontaneous and involuntary resonance of two living bodies with each other. It is this sort of bodily empathy I am invoking now, but widened beyond the human sphere to ground our comprehension of the organism and our recognition of the purposiveness of life (Husserl 1980, pp. 94–98; 1989, pp. 170–180). Empathy in this sense encompasses the coupling of our human lived bodies with the bodies of other beings we recognize as living, whether these be human, animal, or even—particularly for biologists with a "feeling for the organism" (Keller 1984)—bacteria.

◆ ◆ ◆

SEVEN

Laying Down a Path in Walking

Development and Evolution

WE LIVING ORGANISMS are historical and developmental beings. We descend by reproduction, not only from our human ancestors, but from countless other living beings, forebears who preceded the human species, all the way back to the earliest bacterial organisms. In addition, each of us has a unique history in the form of a "lifeline" or developmental pathway through space and time (Rose 1997). We are multicellular organisms, and all our cells descend by reproduction from one particular cell, formed from the fusion of parental egg and sperm. Our history is thus shaped by reproduction at two intersecting levels: we are the offspring of our parents, and our individual cell components descend by reproduction from the embryo each of us once was.

Although our parents and ancestral organisms supply our bodies with developmental resources and help to guide our bodies on the path they tread in life, that pathway does not lie predetermined within us—in our genes or anywhere else. Rather, the path is our footsteps, laid down in walking. This image of laying down a path in walking in which there is no clear separation between path and footsteps, the way and its walking, is the guiding image of this chapter (Varela 1987).

Up to now I have discussed life only at the level of the individual, here and now. Yet the single, individual organism as it is today is in a way an abstraction, both with respect to the organism as an ecologically embedded, developmental process, a life cycle, and with respect to the organism as a member of a reproductive lineage. For this

166

reason, we need to expand our framework to encompass development and evolution.

The present chapter focuses on life as a historical phenomenon, on the evolution and development of living beings. According to the viewpoint presented here, our living body, seen as a temporally extended lifeline, is a developmental process or life cycle that initiates new life cycles through reproduction. Living beings are constituted by historical networks of life cycles, and the units of evolution are developmental systems comprising organism and environment.

Autopoiesis, Reproduction, and Heredity

To understand what makes living beings historical beings we need to begin with the phenomenon of reproduction.[1] Reproduction consists of the production of new individuals, more or less similar in form to their parent organisms, through a specific process such as cell division. In more abstract terms, reproduction consists of one unity originating another unity of the same class, that is, having the same organization. Reproduction therefore requires two basic conditions—an original unity and some process that reproduces that unity. In the case of living beings, the original unity is an autopoietic unity, and the reproductive process ends with the formation of at least one other autopoietic unity distinct from the first.

Although autopoiesis and reproduction go hand in hand in living cells, there is a logical asymmetry between the two. Reproduction presupposes autopoiesis, but autopoiesis does not necessarily entail reproduction, for a system can be self-producing according to the autopoietic criteria without being capable of reproduction. Such a case, besides being logically or conceptually possible, could well have happened in the history of early life on Earth. Perhaps the very first spontaneously self-assembling autopoietic systems were incapable of reproduction and therefore left no descendants. Subsequently, reproduction might have at first happened only through fragmentation, as a result of the early autopoietic protocells bumping into other entities. In the historical network thus produced, some variant cells might then have undergone reproductive fracture as a result of their own internal dynamics. These self-reproducing variants would have possessed a dividing mechanism and given rise to a lineage or stable historical succession. Whether or not events occurred this way, the following general point holds good: reproduction cannot be part of the minimal organization of living beings because to reproduce something, that something must first be a unity and have an organization that defines it. Therefore reproduction is logically and operationally secondary to autopoiesis.

In biological reproduction, the smallest possible parent is a single cell. In prokaryotic cells, reproduction occurs through binary fission: the mother cell divides into two portions that pull apart to become daughter cells. In eukaryotic cells, reproduction occurs through mitosis, a type of nuclear division that results in two daughter cells each having a nucleus containing the same number and kind of chromosomes as the mother cell. It is essential in either case that reproduction happen through the partition and incorporation of the original cellular unity into its offspring: the original cell undergoes a fracture that results in two new cells of the same kind.

Although there is no separation in the cell between the reproducing mother cell and the reproduced daughter cells, the daughter cells do not preexist in the mother cell. Furthermore, although the daughter cells have the same autopoietic organization as the original cell, and accordingly share structural characteristics with it, they also differ structurally from the original cell and from one another. They are smaller, and their structures derive directly from the original cell during the reproductive phase of its life cycle. Thus living cells, as a result of reproduction, form historical lineages in which there is preservation of the autopoietic organization together with variation in its structural realization.

Reproduction occurs through division and therefore depends on the prior multiplication of cellular components, that is, on the prior replication of molecules and molecular structures within the cell. Nevertheless, these two phenomena—reproduction and replication—belong to different levels and have a different logic. Reproduction takes place at the level of the whole cell as an autopoietic unity; replication takes place at the level of the molecular components within the cell. In general, for replication to take place there must be a mechanism that can repeatedly produce entities of the same class. In the case of protein synthesis, the productive mechanism is a complex molecular one, involving DNA, RNA, and ribosomes.[2] In the case of DNA replication, the mechanism involves the production of a complement of the original DNA molecule through a template.[3]

As this case illustrates, in replication (1) all the material must come from outside the original structure (the DNA strand) in the form of new material from the surrounding medium inside the cell (the necessary precursor molecules of adenine, guanine, cytosine, and thymine, which themselves must be synthesized from simpler substances); (2) the productive mechanism of replication (comprising DNA-binding proteins, the enzyme DNA-polymerase, and a variety of DNA repair mechanisms) and the product (DNA molecules) are operationally different systems; and (3) the productive mechanism generates independent elements. By contrast, in the reproduction of the whole cell, only material from within the original parental cell is required; everything happens within the unity as part of the unity, and there is no separation between the reproducing and reproduced systems.

What these differences mean, with regard to history, is that whereas reproduction necessarily gives rise to historically linked unities, replication does not. Replicas are often historically independent of one another. What happens to any one of them in its individual history does not affect what happens to those that follow it in the series of production. An important exception occurs when one replica is used to make the following replica, as happens in DNA replication. In this case, a number of historically connected entities are generated, for what happens to each of them during the time before it serves as a model determines the characteristics of the subsequent replica. Unlike replication, reproduction necessarily gives rise to historically connected unities because it occurs through the division and incorporation of the original unity into its offspring.

In any historical lineage generated by reproduction, there will be both conservation of, and variation in, the structural characteristics of the unities from one generation to another, simply as a result of the reproductive mechanism of division. In other words, wherever we find a reproductive lineage, we find the twin phenomena of heredity, in which structural characteristics belonging to one member of the series reappear in the following member, and reproductive variation, in which differences arise between parents, offspring, and siblings. The study of these phenomena of course belongs to the field of genetics.

Much of modern genetics has focused on trying to identify genes as units of heredity with lengths of DNA. For many reasons that are too complex to analyze here, the image of the gene as a molecular repository of information with a replicative agenda of its own has come to exert a great deal of influence in science and society at large, despite the efforts of many scientists to correct this fundamentally biased picture. Because this genocentric doctrine is at odds with the view of life and mind presented in this book, it is important to reveal its flaws and to sketch an alternative to it.

Genocentrism and the Received View of Evolution

Genocentrism arose in the twentieth century as a result of modifications or revisions of the so-called received view of evolution, which originated with the writings of Charles Darwin and Alfred Russel Wallace in the mid-nineteenth century. Darwin's *Origin of Species*, first published in 1859, eventually convinced most scientists of the fact of evolution—that organisms descend with modification from earlier organisms and that the paths of descent have a branching pattern, with present-day species being descended from one or a few remote ancestors. According to Darwin, the principal mechanism of evolution, though not the only one, is what he called natural selection. By this he meant the "preservation of favourable variations and the rejection of injurious variations" (Darwin 1996, p. 176) from generation to generation, on analogy with the artificial selective breeding for desired traits practiced by human beings on plants and animals.

Although Darwin did not provide an explicit, precise definition of natural selection, his own argument as well as those of subsequent scientists made clear that evolution by natural selection can be defined as a process having three basic requirements: (1) *Phenotypic variation*: there must be variation among the individuals of a population in their attributes or traits. (2) *Inheritance*: these traits must be heritable; it must be possible for them to be passed on from parents to their offspring. (3) *Differential reproductive success or fitness*: the individuals must have different degrees of reproductive success (some individuals leave more offspring than others), based at least in part on their heritable traits. In short, the process of evolution by natural selection requires that there be heritable variation in fitness (reproductive success).[4]

Let me now sketch the basic picture of how heritable variation in fitness contributes to evolution, according to the received view. Individual organisms in a population vary in their structural characteristics or traits. Some organisms, as a result of the traits they possess, are better than others at solving the problems posed by their environment. Therefore they are more likely to survive to reproductive age, and to leave more offspring, than other organisms having different traits. If the traits of the more successful organisms are (at least in part) heritable, then there will be a bias toward a greater frequency of those traits in subsequent populations. Thus the frequency distribution of traits in the population will change, and the population will have evolved.

We need to connect this notion of evolution to that of adaptation. In the picture just presented, organisms that are better adapted to their environment than their fellows have greater reproductive success. What exactly is meant by this notion of adaptation? It is tempting to suppose that adaptation means the state of being adapted, based on embodying some design or construction that matches well some pre-existent physical situation. The concept of adaptation in Darwinism, however, is not so much that of a state, but a process—the process of adapting or becoming adapted, which is linked to fitness (i.e., to survival and reproduction). According to the received view, this process of adapting, as molded by natural selection, accounts for the degree of adaptational design apparently observed in nature (Lewontin 1978).

According to the received view, for natural selection to result in adaptive change in a population, it must occur gradually and cumulatively over many generations. The likelihood of a single mutation giving rise to adaptive change is low, and single mutations having large effects are almost always injurious. Gradual cumulative selection, however, requires more than heritable variation in fitness. It also requires a low mutation rate (so that there is not too much variation, which can swamp selection) and a fairly constant direction of selection pressures over many generations. In addition, each step along the way has to be one that increases fitness. In the image of a so-called adaptive landscape, in which height represents fitness, natural selection cannot lead a population down into a valley in order to reach a higher hill beyond.

So far I have mentioned only some of the basic ideas of evolutionary theory derived from Darwin. In the twentieth century, classical Darwinism was transformed into what is sometimes called neo-Darwinism, first during the 1930s as a result of the so-called Modern Synthesis between evolutionary theory and genetics and then again with the rise of molecular biology in the 1950s. In the first decades of the twentieth century, the Darwinian theory of evolution by natural selection had actually been seen as opposed to the developing science of genetics, which was based on the rediscovery of Mendel's work at the beginning of the century. Darwinians had conceived of phenotypic traits as differing continuously from each other, but according to Mendelian genetics, the differences between phenotypic traits are discrete and are determined by discrete hereditary units or genes. Beginning in the 1930s, however, scientists such as R. A. Fisher, Sewall Wright, and J. B. S. Haldane showed how to incorporate Mendelian genetics into the Darwinian theory. The basic idea was that genes acting according to Mendel's laws would replace one another in a population over time, if they were linked to small differences in the traits that affect the survival and reproduction of organisms. As a result of these developments, as well as the subsequent identification of the cellular and molecular basis for the units of inheritance in the DNA on the chromosomes in the cell nucleus, the term *evolution* came to be used in a narrower sense than before to mean changes in gene frequencies in a population.

In summary, according to the received view, selective pressures act on the genetic variety of a population, producing adaptive shifts in the population over time. Natural selection is considered to be an optimizing force in the sense that it leads to the evolution of the fittest traits present in the population. Thus the received view goes hand in hand with the thesis known as adaptationism, which emphasizes the optimizing power of natural selection as the main factor in organic evolution. This is not to say that the received view does not recognize other well-known, important factors—for example, random genetic drift (roughly, changes in gene frequencies due to chance); the migration of individuals into and out of a population; as well as pleiotropy (one gene having two phenotypic effects) and linkage (two genes being located on the same chromosome, so that the inheritance of one is linked to that of the other), both of which can cause distinct phenotypic traits to be correlated. Rather, the point is that the received view, in particular the adaptationist thesis, downplays the importance of nonselective processes and emphasizes natural selection and adaptive change.

What is the relationship between the received view and genocentrism? Genocentrism accepts the main tenets of the received view—in particular, the adaptationist thesis—but advocates a shift in perspective to a "gene's-eye" view of evolution (Dawkins 1989; Williams 1966). According to genocentrism, the fundamental units of life are not organisms but genes. Genes vary in their characteristics, and they multiply by making copies of themselves, with some genes being more successful than others at replicating themselves as a result of their particular characteristics. Thus genes evolve as a result of competitive interaction and natural selection. In contrast, organisms are vehicles made by and for genes, which enable genes to take advantage of different environments and thereby replicate more successfully.

In this view, "replication" and "interaction" are the two processes that make up evolution. Replication is the process whereby certain entities— the "replicators"—are directly and accurately copied from one generation to the next, thus forming a lineage. Interaction is what makes replication differential: certain entities—"interactors"—interact with the environment in such a way that the replicators they contain are differentially copied into the next generation. Although in principle the same entity can be both a replicator and an interactor, interactors are typically conceived of as "vehicles" constructed by and for the replicators, genes being the paradigm replicators and organisms the paradigm interactors. Replicators (genes) compete with each other by constructing vehicles (organisms but perhaps also colonies and populations) that mediate their interaction with the environment and thereby aid replication.

Armed in this way with the replicator/interactor distinction, genocentrism (or "gene selectionism") is able to accommodate the point that natural selection does not act directly on genes (replicators) but only on phenotypes (interactors), while nevertheless maintaining that genes are the ultimate source and beneficiary of phenotypic adaptation. In summary, according to genocentrism, organisms evolve as elaborate contraptions—"robots" or "survival machines," as Dawkins calls them—constructed and controlled by genes (Dawkins 1989, pp. 19–20).

Problems with Genocentrism

The view that life is essentially a matter of the genes inside the cell nucleus is homologous to the view that the mind is essentially a matter of a computer brain inside the head. Genetic processes are described in the language of "information," "instructions," and "coding," which corresponds to the classical computationalist picture of the mind (and brain) as an information processing device or computer in the head. If the mind is a computer, then its cognitive processes are essentially abstract (algorithmic) and independent of their embodiment in the organism. In this view, the brain amounts to little more than a particular hardware implementation for the software of the mind. Similarly, if the genome is a set of coded instructions, then it, too, is essentially abstract and causally privileged in its role as a program in the cell. The cell therefore amounts to little more than a "vehicle" driven by its genes. Genocentrism and computationalism thus run on the same conceptual fuel. Both perpetuate the dualisms of hardware versus software, matter versus information, body versus mind, and both mischaracterize the role that particular subsystems play in what are fundamentally dynamic phenomena of the whole organism embedded in its environment. Although these two views dominated the scientific and philosophical scene from the middle to late twentieth century, today they are being rapidly subjected to critical examination and revision. In this section, I take a critical look at genocentrism, in preparation for my later presentation of an enactive approach to evolution.

The Weismann Doctrine

According to genocentrism, biological identity through time is based on genetic replicators, for only they are thought to survive transgenerationally. This view derives from the so-called Weismann Doctrine, named after the late nineteenth-century naturalist August Weismann, who proclaimed the Doctrine of the Continuity of the Germ Plasm. Weismann held that there is a strict distinction between the germ plasm (genome) and the somatic tissues of the organism. In the organism's development, there is an early differentiation and strict segregation of the germ line—cells that are the ancestors of the organism's sex cells—and the somatic line—cells that form the tissues and other components of the organism's body. The germ line is solely responsible for heritability; it serves as the potentially immortal bridge between generations, whereas the soma is merely a mortal vessel upon which natural selection acts. Genes in the germ-cell lines are the paradigm replicators; they are the "active germ line replicators," in contrast with the "passive replicators," which have no influence on the probability of their own replication, and the "dead-end replicators," which replicate only within the individual organism (mitotically) (Dawkins 1982, p. 83). Although each particular active germ line replicator (each token replicator) has only a finite life, it serves as the ancestor to an indefinitely long and virtually open-ended lineage of copies. Gene lineages are thus potentially immortal, whereas organisms are mortal "vehicles" that carry the gene lineage forward from one generation to the next.

The term *Weismann Doctrine* (or *molecular Weismannism*) conveys three related, but distinct, ideas: (1) *The segregation doctrine*: the germ line and the somatic line are strictly segregated during ontogeny, and hence the germ cells are insulated from any changes in the somatic cells. (2) *The inheritance doctrine*: there is no nongenetic inheritance. (3) *The causal asymmetry doctrine*: extragenetic elements and processes in the cell depend on the genes, but the genes are not similarly dependent on them. We can identify the problems with genocentrism by reviewing the problems with these three ideas (Smith 1994).

1. The Segregation Doctrine

The division between germ line and somatic line does not exist in all animals and is not applicable to plants. Indeed, the segregation doctrine does not hold for most organisms. Leo Buss, in his important book *The Evolution of Individuality*, distinguishes between three modes of development, which he calls somatic embryogenesis, epigenesis, and preformation (Buss 1987, pp. 20–22). In somatic embryogenesis, there is no distinct germ line: all cells are capable of participating in the development of the body and in the formation of gametes. Since there are no insulated germ-line cells, it is possible for mutations that arise in somatic cells to be passed on to progeny. In epigenesis, there is a clearly differentiated germ line, but it appears relatively late in development. In this case, the insulation of the germ line is not complete, for any changes in somatic tissues that occur before complete segregation of the germ line can be passed on to progeny. Finally, in preformationistic development, the germ line is terminally segregated in early ontogeny. In this case, the germ line is largely insulated from somatic influence, and the segregation doctrine basically holds.

The most common mode of development is somatic embryogenesis; it is present in plants, fungi, and protoctists. The other two modes of development are found only in animals, but even in the animal kingdom there a number of phyla in which somatic embryogenesis occurs. Therefore, although some organisms do segregate the germ line and somatic line in early development, the segregation doctrine does not hold for the majority of multicellular organisms.

2. The Inheritance Doctrine

The Weismann Doctrine is often invoked in support of the proposition that nongenetic inheritance is impossible. There are two problems with this proposition. First—and this is a conceptual problem—the proposition involves a confusion of the phenomenon of heredity with the physical mechanism of inheritance (Maturana and Varela 1987, pp. 68–69). Heredity in the widest sense is the transgenerational conservation of the resources needed for development in a lineage of historically connected unities. DNA replication, however, is a physical mechanism of inheritance. From an evolutionary perspective, there is no theoretical reason to dismiss the possibility of other extragenetic mechanisms of heredity, for evolution will occur as long as there are heritable traits, regardless of the mechanisms by which inheritance occurs. Indeed—and this is the second empirical problem—there is considerable evidence for the existence of so-called epigenetic inheritance systems—that is, systems for the inheritance of nongenetic structures within the cell involving mechanisms other than DNA replication (Jablonka 2001; see also Sterelny and Griffiths 1999, pp. 95–97).

The basic idea behind epigenetic inheritance is that cells can differ in phenotype while having identical DNA sequences, and these phenotypes can be inherited, that is, transmitted to daughter cells during cell division. The transmission of cell phenotypes requires mechanisms other than DNA replication; these mechanisms are called epigenetic inheritance systems. Three types of epigenetic inheritance system have been distinguished (Jablonka 2001; Jablonka and Szathmáry 1995):

(1) *The steady-state inheritance system* This type of system is based on the self-regulation of gene expression and gene products within the cell. The simplest example is a system in which a gene produces a product that facilitates its own continued activity. In order for such a pattern of activity or functional state to be inherited, a sufficient quantity of the regulatory gene products must be transmitted to the daughter cells during cell division.

(2) *The structural inheritance system* In this type of system, a three-dimensional structure serves as a template for identical structures in the daughter cells. For example, variations in the cytoskeletal and cortical organization of the cell can be inherited through cell division (mitosis and meiosis).

(3) *The chromatin-marking system* This type of system is based on the inheritance of chromatin marks, such as the methylation patterns on DNA.[5] A particular DNA sequence can have several different heritable methylation patterns imposed on it, and these patterns are replicated in the daughter cells by a special methylation replication system. It has been proposed that certain differences in social behavior between human males and females may derive from the inheritance of different methylation patterns. In females, a sequence of the X chromosome may be methylated, so that individuals who get only one X chromosome and receive it from their mothers cannot transcribe the genes in that region of the chromosome. Certain gene products are therefore not available to males. Even so, that sequence is demethylated in the male sperm cells, and hence females get from their fathers an X chromosome possessing the activated genes (Isles and Wilkinson 2000; Skuse et al. 1997).

Epigenetic inheritance is only one example of the general point that not all inheritance is a function of gene lineages. Another is symbiosis (Margulis and Sagan 2002). Symbiosis is defined as the intimate living together of two or more organisms of different species. Many organisms depend on other organisms that live inside them or attached to them. Hereditary symbioses, in which the symbionts remain together throughout their life cycle, are common. For example, organisms that eat and digest wood, such as termites, depend on the microbial communities of protists and bacteria in their guts to break down the cellulose and lignin into sugars and acetate. Nearly every group of organisms has members that have formed symbiotic alliances with other organisms, including humans. The patterns of symbiont inheritance typically involve the transmission from one generation to the next of whole functioning populations of symbionts, such as microbial communities, in addition to symbiont DNA (Margulis and Sagan 2002). These facts about symbiosis undermine the simplistic equation of biological identity through time with the transgenerational bridge of DNA.

One last point about inheritance needs to be made. We have seen that organisms are sense-making beings. They bring forth or enact their environments through their particular manner of structural coupling with the world. As a result, living beings structure the environment of their progeny, so that an organism inherits not simply a genome but an entire developmental matrix (Sterelny and Griffiths 1999, p. 95). In Susan Oyama's words:

> What we are moving towards is a conception of a developmental system not as the reading off of a preexisting code, but as a complex of interacting influences, some inside the organism's skin, some external to it, and including its ecological niche in all its spatial and temporal aspects, *many of which are typically passed on in reproduction* either because they are in some way tied to the organism's (or its conspecifics') activities or characteristics or because they are stable features of the general environment. (Oyama 2000b, p. 39; emphasis in original)

I will return to this important notion of a developmental system later in this chapter.

3. The Causal Asymmetry Doctrine

It is simply not true that genes are prime-movers and cells their vehicles (Moss 2003). For example, although there can be no membranes without the gene products that constitute them, genes cannot exist without membranes, and the gene products that constitute membranes are put together from an already existing membrane template. Indeed, the very term *replicator* is fundamentally misleading, for it obscures this circular causality by implying that genes are self-replicators, as if DNA could replicate all by itself. Actually, DNA replication depends on the complex orchestration of numerous intracellular processes in the global context of autopoiesis. Not only do cellular processes make possible the transmission of genes into the next generation, but many cellular elements are transmitted along with the genes and are necessary for the proper development of the cell, as we saw in the case of epigenetic inheritance systems. In the case of human gametes, these epigenetic elements include proteins and protein structures (such as microtubule organizing centers), cytoplasmic chemical gradients, organelles and lipid membranes, and DNA methylation patterns, to name just a few. In addition, some of these cellular elements alter genetic structure in causally important ways. For example, by attaching methyl groups to the DNA, cellular processes set the methylation state of the genome, thereby enabling genes to be turned on and off as needed.

It will not do for the genocentrist to reply that the genes nonetheless have causal primacy because cellular processes are carried out according to the information contained in the DNA. First, the metaphor of genes issuing "instructions" based on the "information" they "encode" is deeply problematic, as we will see shortly. Second, genes never occur apart from the epigenetic elements of the intracellular environment, nor are "naked replicators" or "naked DNA" ever transmitted, not even in the sperm (which transmits not only parental DNA but also centrioles, which are epigenetic, microtubule organizing centers involved in cell division). Moss states the general point this way: "Explorations of the mechanisms involved at the level of the DNA molecule itself, have not led to any privileged point of causal origins, but rather immediately refer back to the complex state of the cell/organism as a whole as the causal basis of the activity of the genes" (Moss 1992, p. 344; see also Moss 2003).

Let me summarize this discussion of the Weismann Doctrine. We have seen that the germ line and the somatic line are not strictly segregated in ontogeny in the majority of organisms, that there is a variety of forms of nongenetic inheritance, and that gene activation depends crucially on the cellular milieu. Thus a careful examination of the Weismann Doctrine, far from supporting genocentrism, instead leads to the fundamental point that heritability is controlled by processes of development in the "somatic ecology" of the organism (Buss 1987, p. 3). (As Buss points out, this is in fact Weismann's enduring contribution.) I will return to this view of development later in this chapter.

The Gene as Unit of Information

Another aspect of genocentrism we need to examine is the myth of the gene as a unit of pure information. One of the central tenets of genocentrism is that genes have a causally privileged status because they transmit information from one generation to the next, whereas other causes of development are merely material and have no informational status. Nowhere is this conception of the gene as a discrete unit of information proclaimed with more fervor than in Dawkins's writings. For Dawkins, a pronouncement like "Life is just bytes and bytes and bytes of digital information" (Dawkins 1995, p. 19) "is not a metaphor, it is the plain truth" (1986, p. 111).

This disavowal of metaphor is indefensible. The plain truth is that DNA is not a program for building organisms, as several authors have shown in detail (Keller 2000; Lewontin 1993; Moss 2003). In this context "program" is precisely a metaphor, and not a particularly good one at that (see Coen 1999, pp. 9–12).[6] One reason is that whereas software and hardware are independent in a computer—the hardware has to be there before the program can be run, and hardware and software do not produce each other autopoietically—DNA replication and gene activation are entirely dependent on the autopoiesis of the cell. They contribute enormously to this process, but they also owe their existence to it.

A better metaphor for development than "following coded instructions" is "laying down a path in walking." This metaphor implies that there is no separation between plan and executed action. It also evokes the similarity between organic self-organization and human creativity, discussed by Kant and revivified by geneticist and developmental biologist Enrico Coen, in his book *The Art of Genes: How Organisms Make Themselves:*

> When someone is being creative there need be no separation between plan and execution. We can have an intuitive notion of someone painting a picture or composing a poem without following a defined plan. Yet the outcomes of such creative processes—the painting or the poem—are not random but highly structured. In this respect, I want to suggest that human creativity comes much nearer to the process of development than the notion of manufacture according to a set of instructions, or the running of a computer program. (Coen 1999, p. 13)

This image of life as the creative outcome of highly structured contingencies is more accurate than the informational metaphor. In a painstaking analysis of the history of the term *information* in molecular biology, historian and philosopher of biology Sahotra Sarkar concludes that "there is no clear technical notion of 'information' in molecular biology. It is little more than a metaphor that masquerades as a theoretical concept and . . . leads to a misleading picture of the nature of possible explanations in molecular biology" (Sarkar 1996, p. 187).

The term *information* was explicitly introduced into molecular bi-

ology and defined in 1958 in a paper by Francis Crick. "By information," he wrote, "I mean the specification of the amino acid sequence
of a protein" (Crick 1958, p. 144). The concept of genetic information
is supposed to be grounded on the fact of the so-called genetic code
whereby genes specify the kinds of proteins a cell can make. More precisely, the genetic code corresponds to the system in which particular
triplets of nucleotide bases in DNA specify particular amino acids. Protein synthesis is thus said to involve "instructions" that are "written" in
DNA and then "decoded" in a complex process of molecular "transcription" and "translation." Transcription corresponds to the production, from the DNA template, of a complementary sequence of triplets
of messenger RNA molecules (mRNA); translation corresponds to the
production of a sequence of amino acids from the mRNA sequence
(accomplished by ribosomes, transfer RNA, and other molecules). It is
thus the highly stable physicochemical relation of specification between DNA and protein that lies behind the notion of the genetic
code (Godfrey-Smith 2000b; Thompson 1997).

One might think, given this stability, that the DNA/RNA-protein relationship could be expressed in the form of a look-up table from
which one could predict the amino acid sequence of a protein from a
particular chain of DNA. As Sarkar (1996) discusses at length, however, because of the complexities of eukaryotic genetics, this look-up
table would have hardly any predictive or explanatory value. The complexities are numerous, but the basic point is easy to state: the causal
chain between DNA sequences and phenotypic characteristics is too
indirect, complex, and multifaceted for there to be any robust one-to-
one relationship between them. Hence no phenotypic characteristic
can be said to be "coded for" by DNA sequences.

In more concrete terms, enzymatic processes within the cell orches-
trate DNA-to-RNA transcription and RNA-to-protein translation, such
that identical DNA sequences are connected to different phenotypic
results by different chemical states of the cell or by different cellular
environments (Moss 2003, pp. 75–116; Sarkar 1996, pp. 199–201;
Sterelny and Griffiths 1999, pp. 124–128). Thus "[w]hich protein is
made from a given gene at a given time in a given part of the body depends on the overall chemical state of the cell, which can be influenced by many elements of the developmental matrix" (Sterelny and
Griffiths 1999, p. 103). Any sense in which genes could be said to con-

tain information for the development of the organism could then
equally well be applied to other developmental features of the organism.[7]

Another problem associated with the notion of information is that it
almost invariably goes hand in hand with a dualism of matter versus information. This dualism obscures the nature of cellular dynamics.
DNA is itself a product of the cell's operation as an autopoietic system.
As we saw in Chapter 3, the statement "DNA 'codes for' protein" iso-
lates one particular sequence of events in the dynamics of the cell and
abstracts away from the many intervening causal steps that make up
that sequence. Hence the statement needs to be understood as a
heuristic abbreviation of a lengthy causal sequence of biochemical
events in an isolated portion of the metabolic network, and it should
not be taken as an accurate reformulation of the phenomenon of protein synthesis (Maturana and Varela 1980, p. 90; Varela 1979, p. 75).

The metaphor of "encoded information," like all metaphors, has
conceptual ramifications. A code is a representational system, composed of arbitrary referential relations between the symbols of the
code and the things they stand for. The molecular components of the
cell, however, are not representational in this way. Nucleic acids are
components of the autopoietic process and not arbitrary links between
independent entities (Maturana and Varela 1980, p. 102). To say that
DNA "codes for protein" is unobjectionable as long as the genetic
code is seen as no more than a rule of causal specificity based on the
fact that cells use nucleic acids as templates for the primary structure
(amino acid sequence) of proteins (Godfrey-Smith 2000b; Thompson
1997). To say that DNA "contains the information for phenotypic design," however, is unacceptable because it attributes a special semantic
or intentional status to one particular type of component. In this way,
it divests this component of its necessary interrelation with the rest of
the autopoietic network. It is this network in its entirety that specifies
the phenotypic characteristics of a cell, not one of its components, and
it is this network as a whole that is the precondition and causal basis of
DNA replication and protein synthesis.

Information is not intrinsic to the linear array of the DNA sequence.
Rather, it is constituted in and by the cell as an autopoietically organized, three-dimensional entity—by the cell as a *body*. By continuing to
think in terms of the metaphor of information encoded in DNA, one

forecloses the need to understand information as an emergent feature of the dynamic complexity of molecular and cellular processes (Fleischaker 1990b).

One genocentrist who addresses some of these critical points is Dennett (1995a). In his eyes, the critics of genocentrism are "the deconstructionists of biology, elevating the reader [the code-reading environment] to power by demoting the text [the genetic code]." To which he replies: "It is a useful theme as an antidote to oversimplified gene centrism, but in overdose it is about as silly as deconstructionism in literary studies" (1995a, p. 115, n. 10). In his view, " 'gene centrism,' the doctrine that the DNA is the sole information store for inheritance . . . was always only a handy oversimplification . . . [because] of course it is really only libraries-*plus-readers* that preserve and store the information" (1995a, p. 197). Dennett allows that the intracellular and extracellular environments complete the information encoded in DNA. As he states, "We see here a special case of a very general principle: any *functioning* structure carries *implicit* information about the environment in which its function 'works' " (1995a, p. 197).

There are a number of problems with this position. Genocentrism has always meant more than simply the doctrine that DNA is the sole information store for inheritance. Genocentrism holds that the gene is the fundamental unit of life and the primary unit of selection in evolution. This view is typically expressed in the metaphor of genes as selfish, calculating agents—a metaphor Dennett shows no hesitation in adopting (see 1995a, p. 326). I have been arguing that this claim of conceptual and empirical priority for genes as "replicators" is mistaken. Furthermore, I know of no genocentrist who has explicitly admitted that the notion of DNA as an information store "was always only a handy oversimplification." This admission therefore seems to be a major concession to the foes of genocentrism. In making this concession, Dennett tries to save genocentrism by suggesting that DNA is an explicit information store whose functioning depends on the implicit information of the environment. But trying to partition information in this way—into what is explicitly coded and what is implicitly given as a background condition—only highlights again the point that there is no clear and unequivocal notion of information at work. The main critical point remains in force: the reason that the notion of DNA as an information store is an oversimplification—and not a very handy one—is that it has little or no predictive or explanatory power, but rather obscures our understanding of the dynamics of autopoiesis, reproduction, heredity, and development. Indeed, once one starts down the road of treating information—whatever it is—as something that is distributed throughout networks of interactions (both inside and outside the cell), then the very notion of information as something stored (preexistent to the network dynamics)—either explicitly in the static linear array of nucleotides or implicitly in the environment—and transmitted from one place to another, loses sense. Dennett begins to go down this road but believes he can stop halfway. He realizes that the fact that "DNA . . . requires a continuing supply of 'readers' that it does not specify" raises the question "where does the rest of the information come from to specify those readers?" He gives this answer:

> [I]t comes from the very continuities of the environment—the persistence in the environment of the necessary raw (and partially constructed) materials, and the conditions in which they can be exploited. Every time you make sure that your dishrag gets properly dry between uses, you break the chain of environmental continuity (e.g., lots of moisture) that is part of the informational background presupposed by the DNA of the bacteria in the dishrag whose demise you seek. (1995a, p. 197)[8]

But then how is a principled line to be drawn between explicit (coded) and implicit (uncoded) information? If information from the environment is needed to make the genetic information informational in the first place, then what is the ground for holding onto the genocentric tenet that the genes are the informational prime-movers? As Oyama remarks:

> It is not clear whether Dennett senses his entire concept of information is in peril. He seems to waver between increasing and decreasing the informational load on the DNA . . . Suppose we take seriously his disclaimer that the "information store for inheritance" was never *really* meant to be confined to the genes. Was it really meant to be in damp dishrags? . . . this is not just a minimal enlargement of hereditary transmission to include other cell constituents; it reaches outside the cell itself. Once you have scattered inherited information around with the very free hand that would be needed to take care of all biological functions, what happens to the traditionally privileged channels of heredity

(genetic and, in dual-inheritance models like his, genetic and cultural)? . . . Perhaps Dennett means that information is not "out there," that it is not in the nucleus or anyplace else, that it is a way of talking about certain interactions rather than their cause or a prescription for them. If so, it cannot be carried, stored, or transmitted at all. But then Dennett would seem to have ended up in agreement with at least some of the critics he finds so obtuse. (Oyama 2000b, pp. 197–198).

Dennett invokes another oft-seen argument in these debates, the argument from parsimony: "The claim that the gene-centrist perspective is best, or most important, is not a claim about the importance of molecular biology, but about something more abstract: about which level does the most explanatory work under most conditions" (1995a, p. 327). But the genocentric metaphor of DNA as information-store does little if any real explanatory work. Moreover, once genes are put back into the dynamic context of the cell, the picture of evolution and development that emerges is not one of adult organisms linked by genetic bridges. Rather, it is one of a continuous and nonlinear causal spiral of interdependent factors at multiple levels of the life cycle, of which the genetic is only one (Keller 2000, pp. 133–148; Moss 2003; Smith 1994).

Dennett also has a peculiar conception of the role of reductionism in this debate. He notes, "it is often said that gene centrism is 'reductionistic,' " but he counters, "So it is, in the good sense. That is, it shuns skyhooks [mind-first forces or powers of design that descend from on high] and insists that all lifting in Design Space must be done by cranes [mindless mechanisms that work from the ground up]" (1995a, p. 326). This line of thought assumes that any criticism of genocentrism must be born from a hankering after skyhooks and thereby does not see that not all cranes in biology need be genocentric ones (or need be based on genocentric ones). The autopoietic perspective (which of course not all the critics of genocentrism share) makes no appeal to skyhooks. Instead, it employs only cranes in the form of principles and mechanisms of self-organization and their biochemical realization in living cells.

The deepest fault of the metaphor of DNA as program or information-store is that it implies a dualist framework of matter and information, one homologous to the computationalist and functionalist dualism of the mind as informational software and the brain as hardware. In both cases,

processes that are intrinsically dynamic (temporally orchestrated), embodied (somatic and organismic), and embedded (necessarily situated in
an environment or milieu)—whether of ontogeny, evolution, or cognition—are projected into the reified abstractions of a genetic program in
the cell nucleus or a computer program in the brain. In the one case, to
describe DNA as "coding for" phenotypic design reifies the coded content into a kind of mythical "pure information." Such information "can
be encoded, recoded, and decoded, without any degradation or change
of meaning" (Dawkins 1995a, p. 19). It is thus conceptually and ontologically distinct from its contingent material expression in the cell, organism, or body. In the other case, to describe the brain as a computer in
the head whose function is "information processing" is to reify information into something that preexists "out there," is "picked up" and "processed" by representational systems in the brain, and is independent in
principle of the body, which serves merely as its "vehicle." In both cases
we are handed not simply a dualism of matter versus pure information,
but a flight into informational space that is in many ways also a flight
from materiality and the body (Oyama 2000b, p. 198).

For these reasons, the notion of information I have been criticizing
is ultimately regressive, for it entails a form of thinking that is structurally isomorphic to vitalism and mind-body dualism.[9] Consider these
passages from Dawkins and Dennett in which this informational dualism is transparent:

> What lies at the heart of every living thing is not a fire, not warm breath,
> not a "spark of life." It is information, words, and instructions. If you
> want a metaphor, don't think of fires and sparks and breath. Think, in-
> stead, of a billion discrete, digital characters carved in tablets of crystal.[10]
> If you want to understand life, don't think about vibrant, throbbing gels
> and oozes, think about information technology. (Dawkins 1986, p. 112)

Here is Dennett's version of informational dualism:

> If you think of yourself as a center of narrative gravity [an abstraction
> defined by the brain's information processing] . . . your existence de-
> pends on the persistence of that narrative . . . which could *theoretically*
> survive indefinitely many switches of *medium*, be teleported as readily
> (in principle) as the evening news, and stored indefinitely as sheer in-
> formation. If what you are is that organization of information that has

structured your body's control system (or, to put it in its more usual provocative form, if what you are is the program that runs on your brain's computer), then you could in principle survive the death of your body as intact as a program can survive the destruction of the computer on which it was created and first run. (Dennett 1991a, p. 430)

And Dawkins again:

[The] river of DNA . . . flows through time, not space. It is a river of information, not a river of bones and tissues: a river of abstract instructions for building bodies, not a river of solid bodies themselves. The information passes through bodies and affects them, but it is not affected by them on its way through. The river is not only uninfluenced by the experiences and achievements of the successive bodies through which it flows. It is also uninfluenced by a potential source of contamination that, on the face of it, is much more powerful: sex. (Dawkins 1995, p. 4)

Despite its modern scientific garb, the informational dualism expressed in these passages is philosophically less sophisticated than the ancient form of dualism. In the ancient dualism of soul and body—as expressed, for example, in Plato's *Phaedo*—the soul *(psyche)* and the body *(soma)* interpenetrate and influence each other in the life led by the self. An impure body corrupts the soul; a pure one frees the soul. In contrast, in the new dualism, "information passes through bodies and affects them, but it is not affected by them on its way through." This notion of information as something that preexists its own expression in the cell, and that is not affected by the developmental matrix of the organism and environment, is a reification that has no explanatory value. It is informational idolatry and superstition, not science.

Developmental Systems Theory

If genocentrism is homologous to the computationalist view that the mind is a computer in the head, then developmental systems theory is homologous to the enactive view that the mind is embodied in the active organism and embedded in the world.[11] Developmental systems theory defines evolution not as change in gene frequencies but as "change in the distribution and constitution of developmental (organism-environment) systems" (Oyama 2000a, p. 77). The fundamental unit of evolution so conceived is the life cycle:

> A life cycle is a developmental process that is able to put together a whole range of resources in such a way that the cycle is reconstructed. The matrix of resources that create a life cycle is the "developmental system" from which the theory takes its name. Life cycles form a hierarchy of evolutionary units similar to that described by more conventional hierarchical views of evolution [which emphasize multiple levels of organization and units of selection, such as genes, cell lineages, organisms, colonies, superorganisms, and so on]. (Sterelny and Griffiths 1999, p. 108)

Developmental systems theory rejects dichotomous accounts of development and evolution; these accounts are conceptually structured by the causal dichotomies of internal versus external, innate versus acquired, nature versus nurture, genetic versus environmental, replication versus interaction, and information versus matter. Such accounts include not only the "interactionist consensus" of the received view, according to which all biological traits develop as a result of both genetic and nongenetic factors, but also many accounts that stress the importance of so-called intrinsic factors, namely, developmental constraints and the self-organizing properties of complex systems. These intrinsic factors are supposed to contrast with the "external factor" of natural selection (see Kauffman 1991; Maynard Smith 1998, pp. 21–40; Maynard Smith et al. 1985). According to developmental systems theory, life cycles propagate from one generation to the next by constructing and reconstructing themselves (like a path laid down in walking), instead of unfolding according to any transmitted, genetic blueprint or program. The processes of reconstruction involve numerous, interdependent causal elements, which relate to each other reciprocally as process and product, rather than belonging to the dichotomous categories of genetic nature versus environmental nurture.

To explain the conceptual shift from genocentrism to developmental systems theory, I would like to quote extensively from a text by Oyama (2000a, pp. 197–200).[12] She presents five typical rationales for genocentrism, to which she adds both a parenthesis indicating what the rationale glosses over and an expansion of the parenthesis that expresses the perspective of developmental systems theory (DST):

1. *Argument* (to be read in a stentorian voice): Genes produce organisms.

   Qualifying parenthesis: (Although they are not, of course, sufficient: raw materials must be available and conditions must be adequate.)

   DST expansion: Genes themselves don't "make" anything, although they are involved in processes requiring many other molecules and conditions. Other interactants (or resources, or means) are found at scales from the microscopic to the ecological, some living, some not. None is sufficient, and their effects are interdependent. Development never occurs (and could not occur) in a vacuum.

2. *Argument:* Shared genes are responsible for species characteristics.

   Qualifying parenthesis: (Again, as long as proper conditions are present.)

   DST expansion: Just as genes can't make organisms in general, they can't create species-typical characters in particular. Typical conditions, again at many scales, contribute to forming these characters, whose uniformity should not be exaggerated. The activity of the organism, including self-stimulation, is often a crucial aspect of species-typical development, and so are influences from other organisms. Genetic and environmental variation is often underestimated, and flexible processes can sometimes result in typical phenotypes despite atypical phenotypic resources [emphasis omitted].

3. *Argument:* Genetic variants specify the heritable phenotypes needed for natural selection.

   Qualifying parenthesis: (Of course, heritability depends on conditions, and it can be hard to separate genetic from environmental effects.)

   DST expansion: Unless nongenetic factors are excluded by stipulation, other developmental resources can also "specify" phenotypic variants, which can be heritable in a variety of senses. The genotype-phenotype correlations that warrant the talk of genetic specification may not occur under all circumstances, and may change within and across generational time. Specificity, furthermore, is a slippery matter; it depends on the question being asked, the comparison being made, and on the measure being used, as well as the developmental state of the organisms and the context of the comparison. In fact, the genotype-environment correlations and statistical interactions that plague the behavior geneticist are manifestations of just the interdependent networks that developmental systems theorists describe.

4. *Argument:* Only genes are passed on in reproduction; phenotypes, and therefore environmental effects, are evanescent, and thus evolutionarily irrelevant.

   Qualifying parenthesis: (Of course, the genes are housed in a cell.)

   DST expansion: If transmitting or "passing on" means "delivering materially unchanged," then few if any developmental resources are transmitted across evolutionary time, depending on how one measures material change. If transmission means "reliably present in the next life cycle," which is the biologically relevant meaning in DST, then an indefinitely large set of heterogeneous resources or means is transmitted. They are sought or produced by the organism itself, supplied by other organisms, perhaps through social processes and institutions, or are otherwise available. Although many developmentally important environmental features are exceedingly stable, others are noncontinuous, perhaps varying seasonally or geographically. Any definition of inheritance that doesn't privilege the nuclear or cell boundary a priori will be applicable to other constituents of the system. . . . The developmental systems perspective stresses the processes that bring together the prerequisites for successive iterations of a life cycle. . . .

5. *Argument:* If gene frequencies don't change, then evolution has not, by definition, occurred.

   Qualifying parenthesis: (Of course, the gene concept is historically recent, and other definitions of evolution are possible.)

   DST expansion: A historian could tell us how gene frequencies moved from being an *index* of evolutionary change to be *definitional,* but we needn't insist on that one definition. In fact, many branches of biology routinely speak of changes in phenotypes. If one must have a "unit" of evolution, it would be the interactive developmental system: life cycles of organisms in their niches. Evolution would then be change in the constitution and distribution of these systems. This definition embraces, but is not restricted to, more traditional ones.

Having highlighted the contrast between genocentrism and developmental systems theory, I can now present developmental systems theory in a more positive form. This presentation has five steps.

Step One is to expand the notion of inheritance. Not only genes, but many other kinds of developmental resources are inherited. These resources range from cytoplasmic components within the cell to symbionts and social traditions, which together form a widely extended developmental system. Any element of the developmental system that reliably recurs in each generation and that plays a role in constructing the evolved life cycle counts as something inherited (Gray 1992; Sterelny and Griffiths 1999, p. 97).

Step Two is to reject the "master molecule" conception of the gene. Genes are not distinctly informational causes of development different in kind from other developmental factors that do not qualify as informational. According to the "parity thesis" of developmental systems theory, the only coherent definition of information in developmental biology is one that is equally applicable to genetic and nongenetic causal factors (Griffiths and Knight 1998; Oyama 2000c).

Step Three is to reconceptualize the nature of developmental information. Information is not transmitted from one generation to the next, but is rather reconstructed in development—hence Oyama's phrase *the ontogeny of information* (Oyama 2000b). Information is what counts as information for some process at some time; hence it changes over time and is context-dependent.

Step Four is to reconceptualize "nature" and "nurture" as product and process rather than as dichotomous causal factors. "'Natures' . . . are simply developing phenotypes, whether common or rare, and they emerge and change by the constant 'nurture' of developmental interactions. This makes nature and nurture not internal and external causes or alternative sources of organic form, but rather developmental *products* (natures) and the developmental *processes* (nurture) by which they come into being" (Oyama 1992b, p. 225). "Another way of saying this is that nature is the current state of a developmental system, while nurture is its ontogenetic history" (Oyama 1993, p. 8).

Step Five is to reconceptualize evolution (phylogeny) and natural selection. Evolution is change in the constitution and distribution of developmental systems. Natural selection is not an independent, external agent or force acting on organisms, but rather the outcome of the differential propagation of developmental systems: "It is the net result of many other interactions in which organism and environment define and select each other" (Oyama 1993, p. 8). Natural selection, so conceived, "requires reliable life cycles, not static genetic programmes or organisms" (Oyama 2000a, p. 80).

This last step of the argument joins developmental systems theory to debates about natural selection and adaptationism. I leave discussion of this matter for the last two sections of this chapter, in which I will link developmental systems theory to the idea of enactive evolution. What I wish to do now is to highlight three important implications of the above line of thought.

If ecologically embedded developmental systems are the fundamental units of evolution, then it follows (1) that the replicator/interactor distinction is no longer useful for conceptualizing evolutionary processes; (2) that there is no intelligible distinction between inherited (genetic) and acquired (environmental) characteristics; and (3) that there is no intelligible distinction between nature and culture.

If, on the one hand, a replicator is defined as an entity that has the intrinsic causal power to replicate itself, then the only replicator is the reproducing organism or life cycle, which is supposed to be the paradigm interactor. On the other hand, if a replicator is defined as anything that is reliably replicated in development, then there are many replicators besides the genes. Therefore the replicator/interactor distinction has no clear application to evolution and development: "Rather than replicators passing from one generation to the next and then building interactors, the entire developmental process reconstructs itself from one generation to the next via numerous interdependent causal pathways" (Sterelny and Griffiths 1999, p. 95).

Given this account, "inherited" and "acquired" (or "innate" versus "learned") cannot name two mutually exclusive subclasses of developmental characteristics. Phenotypic traits are as much acquired as inherited, for they must be developmentally constructed, that is, acquired in ontogeny; and environmental conditions are as much inherited as acquired because they are passed on inseparably with the genes and thus enter into the formation of the organism from the beginning. The point, as Oyama stresses, "is not that genes and environment are necessary for all characteristics, inherited or acquired (the usual enlightened position), but that there is no intelligible distinction between inherited (biological, genetically based) and acquired (environmentally mediated) characteristics . . . Once the distinction between the inherited and the acquired has been eliminated, not only as extremes, but even as a continuum, evolution cannot be said to depend on the distinction" (Oyama 2000b, p. 138; see also Scholz 2002).

Finally, the usual way to distinguish nature from culture is to say that nature is that which is biologically given ("inherited," "innate," "hardwired"), whereas culture is that which is learned or "socially constructed." Often it is said that whereas biological evolution is neo-Darwinian, cultural evolution is Lamarckian.[13] These ways of distinguishing nature from culture are permutations of the nature-nurture and inherited-acquired distinctions, and rest on the dichotomy between genetically transmitted and environmentally acquired traits. Given that this dichotomy is baseless, it makes no sense to try to divide the traits of organisms into the separate categories of nature and culture.[14]

Let me close this section with some remarks about the relationship between the theory of autopoiesis and developmental systems theory. Earlier in this chapter I described how autopoietic unities can undergo sequential reproduction and generate historical lineages. We can characterize such unities in terms of their self-producing dynamics and their structural coupling with their environments. In the second case, we characterize them as ecologically embedded life cycles or developmental processes, after the fashion of developmental systems theory. Therefore a natural kinship exists between developmental systems theory and the theory of autopoiesis. Both theories, as Oyama notes, "express dissatisfaction with certain aspects of the neo-Darwinian evolutionary synthesis: a sometimes narrow, gene-centered focus, the resulting neglect of active, developing organisms, and the notion of adaptation as the solving of pre-existing environmental problems . . . Each also has quarrels with standard neo-Darwinism's treatment of inside-outside relations, in which the developmental formation of organisms is controlled from the inside (often by genetic programs), and in which evolution is largely a matter of shaping by the external environment" (Oyama 1999, p. 187). Indeed, beyond their criticisms of neo-Darwinism, the two theories support each other. The theory of autopoiesis is needed to describe the self-producing organization of living things on the basis of which development and evolution proceed, and developmental systems theory is needed to give a nondichotomous account of the structural coupling of organism and environment in ontogeny and phylogeny.[15]

Robustness and Flexibility in Developmental Systems

Having examined developmental systems theory, we can now take a fresh look at the important roles certain genes play in the developmental systems of various organisms. But first some historical context is needed.

Earlier in this chapter I reviewed the Modern Synthesis between evolutionary theory and genetics. Yet as Gilbert, Opitz, and Raff (1996) remark:

> If there were a "Modern Synthesis" between genetics and evolution, there had to have been some "*Unmodern* Synthesis" that it replaced. This Unmodern Synthesis was the notion that evolution was caused by changes in *development*. The syntheses of E. Haeckel, E. Metchnikoff, A. Weismann, W. K. Brooks, and others [in the nineteenth and early twentieth centuries] were that of evolution and embryology. Haeckel's Biogenetic Law [that ontogeny is a recapitulation of phylogeny] had superseded all the other developmental syntheses, and by the 1930s, this synthesis had become both racist and scientifically untenable . . . It was an easy target for both geneticists and embryologists (such as W. Garstang and N. J. Berrill) to destroy. But in the 1930s and 1940s, embryology had nothing new to substitute for this discredited notion. In fact, embryologists were no longer interested in evolution and had separated themselves from evolutionary biology in an attempt to become "more scientific", i.e., experimental . . . Genetics readily filled this vacuum, and the Modern Synthesis substituted genetics for embryology as the motor for evolution. Thus, embryology—which had previously been the "handmaid" to evolution . . . and which Darwin perceived as his major source of evidence—gave way to genetics. (Gilbert, Opitz, and Raff 1996, p. 358)

In the 1970s, however, the adequacy of the Modern Synthesis as an explanation for the origin of species began to be questioned: "Genetics might be adequate for explaining microevolution, but microevolutionary changes in gene frequency were not seen as able to turn a reptile into a mammal or to convert a fish into an amphibian" (Gilbert, Opitz, and Raff 1996, p. 361). This critical reexamination has led to a "New Synthesis" of developmental and evolutionary biology, known as evo-devo (see Hall and Olson 2003). The core idea of this new synthesis—that all important changes in evolution are alterations in development—goes back to earlier thinkers in the nineteenth and twentieth centuries. Yet it is now being articulated in much greater detail, through research that spans and interconnects the fields of cell biology and comparative embryology, palaeontology, and molecular genetics. The aim is no less than to explain how developmental processes become modified during evolution and how these modifications produce changes in the morphologies and body plans of animals (Arthur 2002; Coen 1999; Gerhart and Kirschner 1997; Holland 1999; Raff 1996).

One of the central ideas to have emerged from this new synthesis is that evolution is driven by robust and flexible developmental processes (Gerhart and Kirschner 1997, pp. 444–445). *Robustness* is the capacity not to change when conditions change, a capacity for self-maintenance, self-adjustment, and self-organization in the face of change. *Flexibility* is the capacity to change in relation to changing conditions, to accommodate to change. Robust and flexible developmental processes, because they allow for phenotypic variations to arise in development that are not lethal to the organism, enhance the capacity of organisms for evolutionary change. Throughout evolution, "robust flexible processes are conserved and diversified processes surround them" (Gerhart and Kirschner 1997, p. 444). This makes evolution a striking tapestry in which conservation and innovation, permanence and change, and necessity and contingency are thoroughly interwoven.

In the past few decades structures previously taken to be unrelated (independently evolved)—such as the insect eye and the vertebrate eye, often held up as a classic case of convergent evolution—have been discovered to be related at deeper levels of genetic and developmental conservation. In other words, structures that had been taken to be *analogous* (similar in appearance but evolved in different ways) were shown to be based on deeper *homologies* (derivations from a common evolutionary origin). This finding was particularly evident at the level of processes in the developing embryo involving particular clusters of genes and the transcription factors specified by these genes. (Transcription factors are proteins that increase or decrease the binding of RNA polymerase enzymes to the DNA molecule during the process of DNA-to-RNA transcription.) Thus eye development in both insects and vertebrates is associated with the transcription factor specified by the gene *pax-6*, despite the fundamental differences in eye anatomy in these two groups of animals. Mutants for this gene, called small eye in the mouse and eyeless in the fruitfly *Drosophila*, have either partial or complete loss of their eyes. Similarly, humans who have congenital abnormalities in the *pax-6* gene show reduced eye size and no iris. It has also been shown that if the mouse *pax-6* gene is transferred to the fruitfly, it causes an eye to appear wherever it is activated—the eye of a fruitfly, not a mouse. In animals as different as insects and mammals, the presence of the gene initiates a cascade of events at a particular site in the embryo that leads to the development of an eye at that site.

As Gilbert, Opitz, and Raff remark, these findings of homologous genes for analogous processes and structures have "wreaked havoc with our definitions of analogy and homology" (1996, p. 364). The classical notion of homology pertained to similarities of structure (such as skeletons or genes). The new notion of "homology of process," however, pertains to similarities of dynamic interactions at the level of developmental mechanisms. The result is that structurally analogous organs, such as the verbetrate and arthropod eye or the vertebrate and arthropod leg, can be formed by homologous processes.

In the case of eye development in arthropods and vertebrates, the homology of process has been taken to imply that the gene *pax-6* is an important regulatory gene of a conserved pathway for eye formation that arose before the separation of arthropods and vertebrates in the Cambrian, 550 million years ago. That is, present-day insect and vertebrate eyes are probably the modified descendants of a basic light-sensitive cell in a Precambrian metazoan, whose development was associated with the expression of the *pax-6* gene sequence: "Although it is hard to imagine invertebrate and vertebrate eyes as homologous, that is springing from a common 'eye' intermediate, in a deep sense they have each been generated from a conserved set of regulatory components, brought together in different settings at different times" (Gerhart and Kirschner 1997, p. 34).[16]

Some of the most striking examples of conserved regulatory components can be found at the highest level of metazoan spatial organization and cell-type specialization. This is the level of the whole animal's *phylotypic body plan,* the spatial organization the animal shares with all members of its phylum (examples of phyla are the arthropods, chordates, annelids, echinoderms, and molluscs) (see Gerhart and Kirschner 1997, Chapter 7). This organization, too, can be described not only anatomically, but at the level of homologous processes in the developing embryo.

To appreciate the depth of this way of looking at animal body plans, consider that after the origin of life and the emergence of eukaryotic cells, the next major event in life's history was the establishment of multicellularity, in the Precambrian 600–1000 million years ago. This event could not have happened unless different cell lineages could be linked together cooperatively (see Buss 1987). For a metazoan to operate as a coherent entity it has to have ways of cooperatively linking together cells that differentiate and specialize in development. For this reason, metazoan development combines differentiated cells into tight patterns of interaction through metabolic and genetic regulatory networks.

Spatial differentiation in particular, whereby cells come to have regional identities in the multicellular population that is the metazoan body, is a key advance of multicellularity. Without this advance, the various structural and functional cell differentiations (muscle, nerve, bone, and so on) would be of little use. It is now known that this establishment of regional or positional identity depends on certain genes known as selector genes.[17] These genes are activated during embryonic development before functionally specialized cell types are present, and they distinguish bodily regions from one another in the developing embryo. Thus cells that are functionally similar but located in different regions of the body may differ in their activation of selector genes.

What this means with regard to the phylotypic body plans of animals is that they can be described both anatomically and in two other ways— first, in terms of gene homology, that is, "in terms of compartments of expression of selector genes, a 'second anatomy' only visible when the embryo is treated with colored reagents that reveal the location of the RNAs and proteins encoded by these genes"; and second, in terms of the homology of process, that is, "as a spatial organization of compartmentalized developmental processes involving selector genes and reliably distributed signaling proteins" (Gerhart and Kirschner 1997, pp. 296–297). These developmental processes are known as the organism's phylotypic processes, and "the body plan is the spatial organization of phylotypic processes" (ibid.).

The body plan is formed during the course of early development and arises at the so-called phylotypic stage, the earliest stage at which the distinguishing features of the body plan are present. For example, we belong to the phylum of chordates, whose phylotypic stage is called the pharyngula, the earliest stage at which the four distinguishing features of chordates are present—the notochord (skeletal rod replaced later in development by the backbone), the dorsal hollow nerve cord, gill slits, and a tail behind the anus. There are approximately thirty modern phyla and therefore as many phylotypic body plans and phylotypic stages of development. These body plans and stages have been highly conserved in evolution, having persisted for 530 million years; at the same time there has been considerable diversification at the pre- and postphylotypic stages of embryonic development. This diversification is evident in the anatomical differences between the classes, orders, and families within a phylum. At the phylotypic stage, all members of a phylum look rather similar, though they differ earlier in development and of course diverge considerably later on. Thus early development converges on the phylotypic stage and then diverges. In Gerhart and Kirschner's image: "The phylotypic stage sits in the midst of development like an isthmus, as a conserved stage preceded and followed by greatly diversified stages" (1997, p. 380).

In the case of arthropods, the phylotypic body plan arises at the "segmented germ band" stage of the embryo (so called because of the egg's flattened, elongated shape and apparent body segmentation). This stage occurs just after the major anteroposterior and dorsoventral dimensions of the body have been established. Particular compartments of the body are defined along these two dimensions as a result of the activation of particular selector genes. Three main classes of selector genes are activated along the anteroposterior axis—the segment polarity genes, whose specified products establish the common features of all segments of the body; the terminus genes, whose specified products define the nonsegmented ends of the body; and the homeotic genes, whose specified products differentiate regions of the embryo from one another, in particular the head's anterior and posterior, the thorax, and the abdomen.

The homeotic genes have been the subject of much attention and discussion. They comprise ten selector genes, each of which is activated in a particular compartment of the body plan from front to back. Two are expressed in the anterior head of the embryo; the other eight, known as Hox genes, are activated in the posterior head, the thorax, and the abdomen. Each homeotic gene contains a DNA sequence called the homeobox, which specifies a sequence of sixty amino acids known as the homeodomain. Proteins containing this sequence belong to the homeodomain family of transcription factors and regulate gene activation in the developing embryo.

The Hox genes in particular, together with their homeodomain products, appear to operate not as a collection of individual elements but as a network with its own distinctive properties. For instance, there is one single order to their activation, based somehow on the remarkable fact that the eight Hox genes are clustered on one chromosome in an order that corresponds to the anteroposterior order of their eight activation compartments in the body plan. Once each gene is regionally activated, it becomes auto-activating and self-maintaining through a regulatory circuit that includes its specified homeodomain transcription factor. Moreover—and this discovery ranks as one of the most remarkable and surprising of recent biology—similar Hox genes, with the same type of colinear order of gene-placement on the chromosome and anteroposterior order of activation in the body—are found not only in arthropods, but also in the metazoa of other phyla, such as chordates, annelids, and molluscs. If we compare the DNA sequences of the genes at corresponding locations in different animals, we find more resemblance between them than between the sequences of genes at different locations in the same animal. The most anterior gene in the fruitfly, for example, is more similar to the most anterior gene in the mouse than it is to the other fruitfly Hox genes, and so on along the length of the body from front to back.

The conclusions that have been drawn are that the common ancestor of all bilaterally symmetrical animals possessed a series of Hox genes and that these genes have been conserved ever since in metazoan evolution. Indeed, given the antiquity and universality of the Hox genes, it has been proposed that they define a common "zootypic"

body plan for all metazoans (Slack, Holland, and Graham 1993). Thus
Hox gene networks provide a striking example of robustness and flexibility, as evidenced by their conservation in evolution as well as their
duplication and diversification, leading to a corresponding wide variety of bodily compartments and appendages along the anteroposterior dimension of modern metazoa.

We find the same robustness and flexibility, conservation and innovation, along the dorsoventral dimension of metazoan body plans. In
1820 Etienne Geoffroy Saint-Hilaire proposed that vertebrates and insects shared the same basic body layout. His proposal led to the famous
debate between Geoffroy and Georges Cuvier in 1830 before the
Académie des Sciences in Paris (see Coen 1999, Chapter 7). Geoffroy's
view, based on considerations of form, was that vertebrates and arthropods share a common dorsoventral organization, but that the layout of
one is the inverse of the other. Thus vertebrates have a ventral heart
and dorsal nerve cord, whereas arthropods have a dorsal heart and
ventral nerve cord. Cuvier's opposing view was based on considerations of function; he argued that vertebrates and arthropods must be
regarded as different types of animal because of the differences in the
functional organization of their body parts.

Although Geoffroy's position was much criticized over the years, it
turns out that he was on the right track after all, though for reasons he
could not possibly have foreseen (see Arendt and Jung 1994; De
Robertis and Sasai 1996; Gerhart and Kirschner 1997, pp. 340–343).
Whereas he based his position on skeletal considerations—in particular, on his "Principle of Connections," according to which bones
maintain the same connections in animals, regardless of their function[18]—the underlying order is rather that of the developmental processes involving selector genes and their transcription factors within
specific bounded regions. Thus the phylotypic body plans of arthropods and chordates do indeed share a common dorsoventral organization, with the body plan of one inverted in relation to that of the other.
In arthropods, the development of the *ventral* side of the body is regulated by the activation of the gene *sog* (short gastrulation); this gene is
closely related to the chordate gene *chordin*, which regulates the development of the *dorsal* side of the chordate body. The development of
the *dorsal* side of the body in arthropods is regulated by the activation
of *dpp* (decapentaplegic), and this gene is closely related to the chor-

date gene *BMP* (bone morphogenetic protein), which regulates the development of the *ventral* side of the chordate body. It has been proposed that *sog/chordin* and *dpp/BMP,* along with the Hox genes and a light-sensitive organ associated with *pax-6,* were present in the ancestor of the arthropod and mammalian lineages—a hypothetical ancient wormlike animal, dubbed "Urbilateria" (primitive bilateral animal), that lived before the "Cambrian explosion" of body plans (De Robertis and Sasai 1996).

In this chapter I have been expanding the autopoietic account of life to include developmental systems and evolution. The discussion in this section has revealed the striking pattern of *conserved unity fostering diversity* in the evolution of developmental systems. In Gerhart and Kirschner's words: "Where diversification is found, conserved flexible robust processes are nearby, selected to have those properties" (1997, p. 438). In the case of the spatially organized phylotypic processes of the body plan: "They have been conserved because of the selections on the diversifications they have allowed . . . it is the diversifiability of the body plan, its flexibility, versatility, and robustness, and not just the anatomy of the phylotypic stage, which has been continuously selected" (p. 372). The term *selected* raises a number of other issues, which we will take up in the next two sections. We can hold these issues at bay for the moment in order to summarize the main point of this section: robust and flexible developmental processes make possible the generation of diversity, and hence the process of evolution as a whole.

Enactive Evolution

I turn now to confront the contentious issues about natural selection and adaptation in evolutionary theory and the philosophy of biology. My position is that the autopoietic and developmental systems perspectives entail a reconceptualization of natural selection and adaptation.

Genocentrism and the received view are dominated by what Oyama (2000a) calls a reverberating circuit of ways of thinking about life processes, formed by the three interlocking conceptions of natural selection, innateness, and heredity. Natural selection is conceptualized as an external force whose effect is to optimize fitness; innate traits are at-

tributed to internal genetic programs of development; and heredity is
seen as the transmission of genes for traits from one organism to another. These ideas reinforce one another. Because heredity is seen as
the transmission of genes for traits, evolution is reduced to changes in
gene frequencies in a population, whereas ontogeny is supposed to be
the unfolding of a pregiven, genetically encoded, developmental program: "The idea of genetically created phenotypes then reinforces the
idea of natural selection as 'operating' on static traits . . . It is this circuit that must be broken if we are to understand the relations among
selection, development, and heredity" (Oyama 2000a, p. 78).

We have seen how developmental systems theory breaks this circuit.
First, heredity depends not on the "transmission" of genetic information
for phenotypic design, but on the reconstruction of pattern in ontogeny,
a process that involves many other developmental resources besides the
genes. Second, the innate/acquired distinction is not applicable to developmental processes. Finally, natural selection is not an external force,
but the differential propagation of developmental systems. It is this third
point about natural selection that will occupy us now.

From the standpoint of the received view, in particular from the perspective known as adaptationism, the central problem of evolutionary
theory is to explain not simply the fact of evolution—that organisms
descend with modification from other organisms—but also the widespread appearance of design in nature, or in other words, that living
things appear to be well adapted to their environments. According to
adaptationism, evolution and the appearance of design are to be explained by the process of natural selection: there is variation among
the traits of individuals in a given population; the traits are heritable;
some individuals leave more offspring than others as a result of the
heritable traits they possess; and consequently the fittest traits present
in the population tend to be "selected" from one generation to the
next. Adaptation is supposed to be a direct consequence of natural selection. Given a sufficient amount of time, organisms will tend to be
well adapted to their local environments as a result of the natural selection of the fitter variants. Yet, because the environment is never
static but always changing, natural selection will inevitably lag behind
environmental change. Therefore we should not expect organisms to
be perfectly adapted.

In 1978 Stephen Jay Gould and Richard Lewontin published a now famous article in which they criticized what they saw as the all-too-easy reliance on this picture of evolution, a picture they called the "adaptationist programme" (Gould and Lewontin 1978). Over the years this article has inspired considerable argument back and forth, but certain core points have withstood the test of time and controversy. One of these points is that adaptationists treat the organism as if it were a mosaic of separate parts when it is actually an integrated whole. Adaptationists typically atomize the organism into "traits" and try to explain these traits "as structures optimally designed by natural selection for their functions" (Gould and Lewontin 1978, p. 256). Then, when faced with the limitations of this part-by-part analysis, they pay lip service to the integration of the organism. They treat it merely as an epiphenomenon of the compromises or "trade-offs" that need to be made among the competing demands of optimizing different traits.

The theory of autopoiesis and developmental systems theory together provide a different view of the organism. Autopoietic systems (and autonomous systems generally) are unified networks of many interdependent processes. Organisms are accordingly not the sort of systems that have atomistic traits as their proper parts; such traits are the products of theoretical abstraction. Similarly, from the viewpoint of developmental systems theory, the adaptationist notion of the organism as an array of traits on which selection acts obscures development. In development, there are no static traits, but rather integrated developmental processes.

Another important point Gould and Lewontin made in their critique was that adaptationism separates the organism from the environment and sees the environment as posing problems that the organism must solve by adapting. This view of organism-environment relations, combined with the atomistic analysis of the organism into separable traits, implies that the organism is simply a passive object of selection rather than an active agent or subject of the evolutionary process (see Levins and Lewontin 1985, pp. 85–106).

Developmental systems theory offers one of the most radical rejections of the separation of organism and environment. If the unit of evolution is the developmental system, and if inherited developmental resources include not only endogenous elements (genes, cytoplasmic components, cytoskeletal and cortical cellular organization, and so on), but also structured exogenous environments—environments structured into viable niches by the organisms themselves—then there is no basis for thinking that the environment is independent of the organism. On the contrary, organism and environment construct each other in development and evolution:

> Evolution occurs because there are variations during the replication of life cycles, and some variations are more successful than others. Traditionally, variants are said to be exposed to independently existing selective forces, expressions of an independently existing environment. In the developmental systems representation, the variants differ in their capacity to replicate themselves. One variant does better than another, not because of a correspondence between it and some preexisting environmental feature, but because the life cycle that includes interaction with that feature has a greater capacity to replicate itself than the life cycle that lacks that interaction. This perspective is appropriate because many of the features of the traditional environment have evolutionary explanations. Organism and environment are both evolving as an effect of the evolution of differentially self-replicating life cycles. Life cycles still have fitness values, but these are interpreted, not as a measure of correspondence between the organism and its environment but as measures of the self-replicating power of the system. Fitness is no longer a matter of "fittedness" to an independent environment. (Griffiths and Gray 1994, pp. 300–301)

This co-determination of organism and environment is central to the concept of enaction (Varela, Thompson, and Rosch 1991). Like two partners in a dance who bring forth each other's movements, organism and environment enact each other through their structural coupling. Given this view of organism-environment co-determination, it follows that evolution should not be described as a process whereby organisms get better and better at adapting to the design problems posed by an independent environment. Central to evolution is not the optimization of adaptation, but rather the conservation of adaptation. As long as a living being does not disintegrate, but maintains its autonomous integrity, it is adapted because it is able to carry on its structural coupling with its environment (Maturana and Varela 1987). The adaptation of a living being to its environment is therefore a necessary consequence of its autonomy and structural coupling. In other words, the condition of adaptation is an invariant of life; it is necessarily conserved as long as autopoiesis and structural coupling continue.

Given adaptation as an invariant background condition, structural variations in living beings arise through reproduction and development. Many of these variations produce individuals that can survive in a given environment, and these variants are accordingly all adapted. They are capable of continuing the lineage to which they belong in their particular environment, regardless of whether or it is changing, at least for some period of time. Other structural variations give rise to lineages with differing opportunity to contribute to the variety of a population in a changing environment. We see this difference retrospectively: there are lineages that disappear, and what their disappearance reveals to us is that their structural configurations did not enable them to conserve the condition of adaptation (autopoietic organization and structural coupling) needed for their continuity. This view of evolution, centered on the conservation of adaptation through autopoiesis and structural coupling with the environment, can be called *enactive evolution.*[19]

According to this perspective, all living beings are adapted as long as they are alive. Reproductive success—the measure of fitness—is not determined by isolated traits, but by the entire life cycle. Hence assigning efficiency values to traits is misleading.

Adaptationist biologists would disagree. Dawkins, for example, thinks that as a result of cumulative selection and evolutionary "arms races" between competing lineages, living beings often become better designed or adapted to their niches over the evolutionary short term (Dawkins 1986, pp. 178–181). But even this circumscribed idea of adaptive progress has problems. First, the notion of an evolutionary "arms race" is merely a questionable metaphor taken from the realm of human affairs and projected onto the interactions between certain species in the history of life. It is an entirely observer-relative description. Second, no general variable property of adaptedness or degree of "fit" between an organism and its environment has been identified and rigorously defined in evolutionary biology. There are, to be sure, various technical definitions of fitness, but there are significant differences among them and they are used in different theoretical contexts. They are not indicative of any one variable of adaptedness (see Stearns 1982, 1986).

The idea of enactive evolution can be spelled out more fully in the following four points:

1. The unit of evolution at whatever level (genomic, cell lineage, individual, social group, and so on) is a developmental system (in the widest sense of a milieu-embedded, propagative unit).
2. Developmental systems are composed of ecologically embedded, autonomous networks, which exhibit rich repertoires of self-organizing configurations.
3. Such networks are analyzable not in terms of *optimality* of design or fittedness to the environment, but rather in terms of *viability* in the face of an unpredictable or unspecified environment.
4. Through reproductive structural coupling with their environments, these networks generate selection in the sense of the differential retention of inherited variation.

The first point implies a pluralist stand on the debate about the units of selection in evolution. Many nested units of developmental systems work in parallel. They evolve through differential propagation and retention of inherited variation, and are subject to complex "competitive" and "cooperative" interactions. These nested units include ecologically embedded genes, organisms, and social groups (see Sober and Wilson 1998).

Second, the proper parts of developmental systems are not "traits" in the typical adaptationist sense (which, in fact, has never been well defined), but rather autonomous networks. An autonomous network, as we have seen, is a network defined by its organizational and operational closure rather than by input-output information flow and external control. The paradigm is the autopoietic cell; other examples include genomic regulatory networks, morphogenetic fields in the developing organism,[20] immune networks, and neural assemblies.

Third, functioning autonomous networks are endowed with the capacity to be viable in the face of unpredictable or unspecified environments. The basic idea behind the concept of viability is that the behavior of the system is characterized by a set of possible trajectories rather than by a unique optimal one. The task of the system is to stay within the zone of viability (otherwise the system disintegrates) rather than to follow a precise trajectory determined by the requirement of optimal fitness (see Varela and Bourgine 1991). In relation to the notion of fitness, the notion of viability can be linked to so-called satis-ficing models. The term *satisficing* was introduced by Herbert Simon (1955) to describe the process of taking a solution that is suboptimal but good enough for the task at hand. Stearns describes its applica-bility to fitness models in evolutionary theory as follows:

> In an evolutionary context, the good is given by some fitness definition, and the modelling style determines what gets done with that definition. In a satisficing model, the search for an optimum is replaced by the search for a stopping rule, for a way to tell when a good-enough alter-native has been found. Such a model can accommodate several fitness measures with incommensurable dimensions, for it stipulates that search stops when a solution has been found that is good enough along all dimensions. If one adopts this view, the real task becomes to find out what organisms regard as "good enough." (Stearns 1982, p. 13)

With this shift from optimality to viability, natural selection no longer resembles a kind of "external steering" effected by independent environ-mental forces. Rather, it becomes akin to a "coarse filter" that admits any structure that is good enough (has sufficient integrity) for persistence.[21] Put another way, many of the morphological and physiological charac-teristics of organisms seem to be greatly underdetermined by the re-quirements of survival and reproduction in changing environments. When variation in such characteristics is " 'noticed' by selection, the focus of selection is not the trait *per se* but the whole organism, ultimately via its life history" (Wake, Roth, and Wake 1983, p. 220; see also Stearns 1992).

Yet I would go further and urge that natural selection be conceived of not as an independent filter or constraint on viability but rather as an emergent consequence of the structural coupling between autonomous systems and their environments. This issue brings us to the fourth point concerning enactive evolution: that the structural coupling or interac-tive dance between reproductive autonomous systems and their envi-ronments generates natural selection. By this I mean that natural selec-tion results from the "satisficing" of viable trajectories effected by the autonomous networks themselves in their structural coupling with their environments. The key point is that natural selection is not an external force or constraint impinging on the networks from an independent en-vironment; rather, it is the outcome of the history of co-determination between the networks and their surroundings.

Given this conception of selection, it might be argued that the very term *natural selection* is undesirable because of its all too easy association with the idea of an external force acting on passive objects. As Goodwin suggests, perhaps we should "simply replace the term *natural selection* with *dynamic stabilization*, the emergence of stable states in a dynamic system. This might avoid some confusion over what is implied by natural selection" (Goodwin 1994, p. 53). I admit to having some sympathy for this recommendation, but it seems counterproductive to drop the term. A different strategy is to use the term but to resituate it within an enactive framework. It is worth remembering that the concept of natural selection has been continually revised and expanded with the increase in biological knowledge since Darwin's time. As Weber and Depew observe: "while the stable core of the Darwinian research tradition is the concept of natural selection, natural selection itself has been conceived differently over time in terms derived largely from changing ideas about dynamics" (Weber and Depew 1996, p. 33; see also Weber and Depew 1995).

Yet this observation gives rise to other questions. How should we conceive of theories that stress self-organization and biological autonomy in relation to the Darwinian tradition altogether? Is the idea of enactive evolution continuous with the Darwinian tradition or is it post-Darwinian? These questions go to the heart of the different visions of life on Earth offered by biology today; addressing them serves as a fitting way to conclude this chapter and Part II.

Laying Down a Path in Walking: Between Necessity and Contingency

In their article "Natural Selection and Self-Organization," Weber and Depew put their fingers on the central issue, which is currently much debated in biology and the sciences of complex systems:

> If natural selection continues to be conceived in received ways, it will necessarily be viewed as competing with chance and self-organization. In consequence, the new dynamics may be seen as portending a coming crisis in the Darwinian tradition, and as offering new weapons to Darwinism's historical rivals in evolutionary theory, in particular the still vital "laws of form" tradition that goes back to Geoffroy de St. Hi-

laire . . . If, on the other hand, we recognize that there has always existed a vital and vitalizing connection between Darwinism and dynamics we may more easily come to see that natural selection, rather than competing with chance and self-organization, is part of a complex process that involves all three elements, and is itself a phenomenon that has evolved out of the play of the others. In this case, complex dynamics, far from portending the end of the Darwinian tradition, will have provided as vital a source for the continued development of Darwinism as dynamics has done in the past. (Weber and Depew 1996, p. 34)

Current biology and philosophy of science present an array of positions on this issue. At one end stand the process structuralists—Brian Goodwin (1994) and Gerry Webster (Webster and Goodwin 1996), Mae-Wan Ho and Peter Saunders (1984), and sometimes Stuart Kauffman (see Burian and Richardson 1996). This group maintains, in the tradition of Etienne Geoffroy Saint-Hilaire and D'Arcy Thompson, that universal "laws of form" or generative principles of order provide a better foundation for understanding biological structures than natural selection and historical lineages (see Lambert and Hughes 1988). At the other end stand the functionalists and adaptationists, such as John Maynard Smith (1993), Richard Dawkins (1986), and Daniel Dennett (1995a). They hold that the best way to study biological systems (the unavoidable way, according to Dennett) is to look for good design and that the only explanation of good design (complex adaptation) is natural selection, even if selection turns out to be greatly constrained by "forced moves" in "design space" (Dennett 1995a), corresponding to what the structuralists see as "laws of form" in "morphospace." Between these two extremes lies an array of intermediate positions. Stephen Jay Gould, for instance, advocated pluralism about both the units of selection and the causes of evolution (which, in addition to natural selection, include genetic drift, developmental constraints, and mass extinctions). He also placed special emphasis on the role of historical contingency in evolution, and hence on the need for historical-narrative forms of explanation (Gould 1989). In a different vein, Kauffman (1993), Weber and Depew (1995), and Wimsatt (1985) attempt to synthesize or marry self-organization, chance, and natural selection in evolutionary explanation.

Of these viewpoints the one most at odds with the idea of enactive evolution is the functionalist position that "biology is engineering," as

Dennett puts it. By this he means that organisms are a kind of designed entity—"natural artifacts," he calls them—and that they are to
be explained by the strategy of "reverse engineering." Through this
strategy, one tries to explain a structure by assuming that there is a
good reason for its presence and then deduce its function given that
assumption. One can choose to interpret organisms as artifacts in this
fashion, and it can be useful to do so in various circumstances.[22] It
must be remembered, however, that this notion of the organism as a
natural artifact is an explanatory heuristic, not an ontological category.
Furthermore, as a heuristic, it is tantamount to treating the organism
as a heteronomous and decomposable system. Therefore it needs to
be balanced by the autonomy perspective.

The intepretation of organisms as natural artifacts derives from the
British tradition of natural theology, in which Darwin was steeped (see
Ruse 1996). The central argument of this tradition—the Argument
from Design—states that just as a well-organized entity happened
upon by chance, such as a watch found lying on the ground, is more
likely to be the product of intelligent design than of random formation, so too are living beings more likely to be the product of an intelligent designer (namely, God) than of random formation.[23] Darwin accepted the key assumption of the argument that there is a deep
resemblance between organisms and designed entities or artifacts, as
do Dawkins (1986) and Dennett (1995a, p. 68) today. Darwin's great
contribution was to pull the rug out from under the argument by
making the case that design could arise without an intelligent designer, as a result of natural selection. The structuralist tradition on
the Continent, however, going back to Kant, had a more sophisticated
view of design, in which the autonomy of the organism occupied
center-stage. In the British tradition of natural theology, the autonomy
of the organism goes unrecognized: the organism is likened to a
watch, an entity whose parts are not reciprocally the cause and effect
of each other's form, and whose function or purpose lies outside it in
its user. Thus the Argument from Design presupposes a conception of
the organism as a heteronomous system whose purposiveness is entirely extrinsic.

Kant, however, as we saw in the last chapter, clearly recognized that
living beings are fundamentally different from designed entities because they are self-organizing beings whose purposiveness is accord-

ingly intrinsic. Whereas William Paley, in his *Natural Theology* (Paley 1996), built his argument on the resemblance of an organism to a watch, Kant had already stated that the organism is unlike a watch or any other mechanical entity. In a mechanical entity, the parts are the external conditions of each other's operation, and the cause of the machine as a whole lies outside the machine in its designer. In an organism, however, the parts exist by means of each other, and the cause of the whole resides within the system itself. It is true that Kant did eventually advance his own reasons for the thesis of intelligent design. To account for the natural teleology of the organism, the only options he could envision were "hylozoism" (all matter is inherently alive), which he thought was absurd, and theism, which postulates an intelligent Being who designedly creates organisms as "natural purposes." The point to be stressed here is that Kant recognized and formulated, probably for the first time, the autonomous organization proper to living beings. This recognition carried over into the Continental tradition of structuralism and Rational Morphology in biology, but was never adequately grasped in the functionalist tradition inherited and revolutionized by Darwin.

The enactive stand against the claim that biology is just engineering thus coincides with the structuralist tradition with respect to the need for an autonomy perspective. (The enactive approach would not agree, however, with the structuralist's privileging of ahistorical laws of form over historical pathways in evolution.) To move from the claim that organisms can be interpreted from a reverse engineering stance to the claim that they are artifacts of design is to confuse a particular heuristic or interpretive framework with the phenomena themselves.[24] Those phenomena also require an autonomy perspective.

The issue at hand is what to make of natural selection in relation to the generative principles of self-organization. Many adaptationists— the so-called Ultra-Darwinists—would endorse Dennett's description of natural selection as an "algorithmic process." An algorithm is supposed to be a mindless, formally defined, step-by-step procedure that is guaranteed to produce a certain result. One of the definitive properties of an algorithm is that it can be implemented in any material substrate, as long as the causal powers of the substrate enable the steps of the algorithm to proceed exactly as prescribed. If natural selection is algorithmic in this sense, then it is implementation-independent. Anything can evolve by natural selection as long as replication, variation, and differential survival are present. Darwin's "dangerous idea" (dangerous because it upsets cherished beliefs) would then be just this idea that natural selection is an algorithmic process that mindlessly gives rise to design. Or to use another of Dennett's formulations, Darwin's dangerous idea would be like the "universal acid" of childhood fantasy that eats through everything, including the jar you would contain it in. So too the principle of natural selection (as an algorithmic process) would threaten to leak out of biology and spread both downward, accounting for the origins of life and even the universe, and upward, accounting for human consciousness, culture, and ethics.

The problem with such an inflated notion of natural selection (besides the problem of turning Darwinism into a kind of secular ersatz religion, like the once popular and equally inflated versions of Marxism and Freudianism) is that it becomes impossible to give a fully naturalistic account of natural selection. That is, it prohibits an account of natural selection "as a natural phenomenon in its own right, whose emergence is the expected outcome of more basic dynamic and thermodynamic processes" (Weber and Depew 1996, p. 57).

According to the enactive viewpoint, natural selection is an emergent consequence of autopoiesis, not its cause. This point is both logical and historical. Natural selection requires reproduction, but reproduction presupposes autopoietic unities that reproduce. Hence autopoiesis is logically prior to natural selection. Fontana, Wagner, and Buss express this idea both succinctly and forcefully:

> Darwin posited evolution as an effect of what basically amounts to be a force: natural selection. Natural selection is a statement about kinetics: In a population, those variants of organisms will accumulate that are better able to survive and reproduce than others. If there is ongoing variation and if variation is (at least partially) heritable, then the continuous operation of selection kinetics will lead to the modification of living organizations. One would like to understand, however, how organization arises in the first place. Darwin's theory is not intended to answer this. Indeed, this is apparent upon inspection of the *formal* structure of the theory. Neo-Darwinism is about the dynamics of alleles within populations, as determined by mutation, selection, and drift. A theory based on the dynamics of alleles, individuals, and populations

must necessarily assume the prior existence of these entities. Selection cannot set in until there are entities to select. Selection has no generative power; it merely dispenses with the "unfit," thus identifying the kinetic aspect of an evolutionary process. The principle [*sic*] problem in evolution is one of *construction:* to understand how the organizations upon which the process of natural selection is based arise, and to understand how mutation can give rise to organizational, that is, phenotypic, novelty. A solution to this problem will allow one to distinguish between those features of organizations that are necessary and those that are coincidental. Such an endeavor requires a theory of organization. Yet biology lacks a theory of organization. The need for a conceptual framework for the study of organization lies at the heart of unsolved problems in both ontogeny and phylogeny. (Fontana, Wagner, and Buss 1994, p. 212)

Biology may have the beginnings of a theory of organization in the form of the theory of autopoiesis (which Fontana, Wagner, and Buss acknowledge as a forerunner to their own project) and other related theories of biological organization, such as those of Kauffman (1995, 2000) and Rosen (1991, 2000). In any case, the point is that natural selection cannot spread downward (as the Ultra-Darwinist supposes) to account for life in its minimal autopoietic form because natural selection must presuppose the autopoietic organization.

Ultra-Darwinists would disagree. If natural selection is an algorithmic process, they state, then it is implementation-independent and therefore can be dropped down a step to the chemical level. The result is that the autopoietic organization of the cell might be explainable as the consequence of natural selection operating on a population of replicative molecules. But the problem is that it is far from obvious that the substrate is neutral in the algorithmic sense. In other words, it is not clear that "selection" has one univocal meaning that is applicable to the biological level of reproducing organisms and the chemical level of molecular replication. Selection at the biological level is selection of the reproductively fit; selection at the chemical level is the selection of the energetically efficient. Similarly, the concepts species and population at the biological level refer to genealogically related individuals in time and space, whereas at the chemical level they refer to types of molecular structure.

Molecules are not individuals in the autopioetic sense. Indeed, they are not individuals at all but statistical aggregates or collections. As Fleischaker notes: "molecules are not 'related' to one another as cells are, and they cannot be: while they are physical entities, molecules are statistical 'individuals' and not genealogical—molecules have no lineage so they do not redistribute their substance, they do not reproduce themselves, and they do not have heritable characteristics . . . If we are not careful or self-conscious in our use of these terms, we will smuggle Darwinian (cellular, reproductive) concepts into non-Darwinian (molecular, replicative) domains where they can have no meaning" (Fleischaker 1994, p. 41).

This brings us to the historical point about the priority of autopoiesis with respect to natural selection. The historical phenomenon I have in mind is the origin of life on Earth. The emergence of the autopoietic cell is a central event in the origin of life. It marks the transition to basic autonomy and thus from nonlife to life. Natural selection, in its Darwinian sense of selection of the reproductively fit, does not exist before this transition. It comes into play once reproduction and heritable variation in lineages of autopoietic systems are manifest. Weber and Depew clearly present the basic logic of this point (though not specifically in terms of the theory of autopoiesis):

> It is too easy to forget that life originates in a world in which the phenomenon of natural selection properly so-called does not, by definition, exist. For natural selection, as we now understand it, requires replicative, variation, and transitional capacities that can be ascribed only to systems that we define as living. It is a sign that something has gone wrong, accordingly, when the problem is conceived as one of "bootstrapping"—finding a way for primitive information-retaining macromolecules to acquire greater replicative fidelity without having to rely on the complex catalytic enzymes on which their fidelity now depends, but which are themselves products of the very process whose origins are in question . . . [We do not] doubt that the process that led to the emergence of life was a *selection* process. But the physical imperatives of self-organization and dissipation require that the particular sort of selection process leading to the emergence of living systems was at first the selection of the stable (physical selection) and of the efficient (chemical selection) rather than of the reproductively fit (biological se-

lection). Properly posed, the problem of the origin of life is to watch the *phenomenon* of natural selection emerge out of these more basic forms of selection. From this perspective, it may be more fruitful to look at primitive proto-cellular systems as the sites of the dynamics leading to life, or at least to favor coevolution between proteins and replicating nucleic acids over a "replicators first" strategy. The more basic forms of selection that obtain in such sites are inseparable from the amplification of stochastic events by the self-organizational tendencies and propensities of open systems and dissipative structures. (Weber and Depew 1996, pp. 51–52)

Rather than speaking of physical and chemical selection, I would prefer to say that a certain kind of dynamic stabilization—the emergence of stable self-producing processes in a bounded biochemical system—is the prerequisite of natural selection. Natural selection in turn comes into play as an emergent consequence of reproductive autopoietic systems having acquired the capacity to vary and to pass on the developmental resources needed for reconstructing and propagating their life cycles. Natural selection thus understood is a process that emerges out of autopoiesis and accordingly cannot be seen as a substrate-neutral or implementation-independent algorithmic process that can be lifted out of its home base in biology.

According to the viewpoint I am proposing, self-organization and natural selection are not opposed but are actually two interwoven aspects of a single process of enactive evolution. Similar ideas have been advanced in recent years, notably by Stuart Kauffman (1993, 1995). His expression of these ideas takes different forms, with the result that his viewpoint is subject to interpretation. Sometimes he emphasizes emergence of generic stable states through self-organization, after the fashion of process structuralism. Sometimes he treats self-organization as the stable background or null hypothesis against which selection is to be measured. Sometimes he sees natural selection as a constraint on self-organization (a coarse filter on what it produces); at other times, he sees self-organization as a constraint on the force of selection.

This oscillation seems to derive from the same kind of dichotomous thinking that is the target of developmental systems theory: self-organization and natural selection are dichotomously conceived as the inner and the outer, and the notion of constraint is consequently reified into an independently existing factor imposed either from within or from without (see Oyama 1992a). The first step out of this impasse is to remember that what counts as a constraint is relative to one's explanatory frame of reference.[25] The next step is to reconceptualize self-organization and natural selection as reciprocally process and product with respect to each other. (The move here is analogous to the reconceptualization of nature and nurture as process and product in developmental systems theory.) In this way, self-organization and selection become two interwoven aspects of one single evolutionary process of organism-environment co-determination. This kind of interweaving is clear in Kauffman's models of co-evolution, in which the interactions between populations are modeled in terms of coupled fitness landscapes. In these landscapes the populations change not only their own environments but the environments of each other.

Once this step is taken, it becomes clear that opposing the necessity of self-organization to the contingency of history makes no sense. There are necessary principles of organization, but the particular manner in which they are realized or embodied is always contingent upon the evolutionary and developmental pathways history makes available.

As an empirical matter, of course, the interplay of necessity and contingency in the history of life on Earth is unclear. Gould has argued in his book *Wonderful Life* that evolution is largely a matter of contingency. He means that it is dependent on particular antecedent events whose consequences are typically unpredictable: "the 'pageant' of evolution [is] a staggeringly improbable series of events, sensible enough in retrospect and subject to rigorous explanation, but utterly unpredictable and quite unrepeatable" (Gould 1989, p. 14). At the end of his book we are told that the existence of the phylum to which we belong—the phylum Chordata, whose name comes from the notochord or hardened dorsal rod that evolved into our spinal chord—is an evolutionary accident, "a contingency of 'just history.'" It is a result of the fact that the earliest recorded chordate, *Pikaia gracilens,* survived the mass extinctions of the Cambrian period: "Wind the tape of life back to Burgess times [the time of the fossil remains from the Burgess Shale in British Columbia], and let it play again. If *Pikaia* does not survive in the replay, we are wiped out of future history—all of us, from shark, to robin, to orangutan" (Gould 1989, p. 323).

In contrast, Simon Conway Morris, in his book on the Burgess Shale, argues that "contingency is inevitable, but unremarkable" because of convergent evolution. He states that the same trait (such as flight) evolves independently in different species: "What we are interested in is not the origin, destiny, or fate of a particular lineage, but the likelihood of the emergence of a particular property, say, consciousness. Here the reality of convergence suggests that the tape of life, to use Gould's metaphor, can be run as many times as we like and in principle intelligence will surely emerge. On our planet we see it in molluscs (octopus) and mammals (Man)" (Conway Morris 1998, pp. 13–14). Conway Morris is arguing from an adaptationist perspective, but others have made a similar point in the context of computer models of self-organizing systems, in which the "tape" can be played not only twice but over and over again. Thus Fontana and Buss (1994) have devised a model based on an abstract chemistry that is endowed with a simple dynamics. They have shown that certain robust generic properties repeatedly arise in the model world, such as complex self-maintaining organizations of an autopoietic sort, which can in turn be hierarchically combined to produce new organizations that contain the lower-level ones as components.

As an empirical issue, the interplay between contingency and necessity in the history of life will remain unsettled for some time. What can be said, however, is that it is conceptually unhelpful to oppose the two. Contingency and necessity form another one of those polarities to be found at the very core of life—like being and not-being, self and other, freedom and necessity, form and matter, as Jonas has so insightfully described. Indeed, Jonas's descriptions of these polarities, made from the perspective of the "empathic study of the many forms of life" (1966, p. 2), coheres well with the scientific perspectives of autopoietic biology, developmental systems theory, evo-devo, and the theory of complex systems. These perspectives lead us to expect, on the basis of lawful necessity, that events are often highly contingent upon each other with unpredictable consequences.

The idea of enactive evolution represents an attempt to convey this interplay of necessity and contingency. Neither simply continuous with the Darwinian tradition nor a radical departure from it, the idea represents an attempt to inscribe the principles of autonomous self-organization proper to living beings in the evolutionary narratives of the Darwinian heritage. "Enaction" connotes the performance or carrying out in action of a lifeline. It evokes the image of living beings laying down historical pathways through their own dynamics and those of the environments to which they are structurally coupled. Enactive evolution is the laying down of a path in walking.

◆

PART THREE

Consciousness in Life

EIGHT

Life beyond the Gap

DESPITE ITS GREAT DIVERSITY of forms, life has brought forth only a few basic modes of being during its natural history on Earth. Unicellular autopoiesis, as we have seen, is the minimal organization of life. Multicellularity, the cooperative linking together of multiple cellular individuals to form a body, is the basis for the other modes of being. If we regard bacteria and protists as forming multicellular colonies rather than distinct individuals, then we can say that there are basically three ways of being a multicellular organism, classified on the basis of how subsistence is derived or nourishment procured: the plant mode, in which subsistence takes the form of feeding on light; the fungi mode, in which food is extracted or absorbed from a surrounding environment of other organic beings; and the animal mode, in which nourishment must be actively searched for and pursued. Animal life is thus marked by a distinctive sensorimotor way of being in the world. This sensorimotor way of being, in its full extent, comprises locomotion and perception, emotion and feeling, and a sense of agency and self—in a word, sentience.

The subject matter of Part III is consciousness, beginning with bodily sentience. Earlier in this book I described sentience as the feeling of being alive. Being sentient means being able to feel the presence of one's body and the world. Sentience is grounded on the autopoietic identity and sense-making of living beings, but in addition it implies a feeling of self and world. How to account for the emergence and presence of sentience in the natural world is one of the outstanding problems of the sciences of mind today.

221

To prepare the way for our investigation of consciousness in the remaining chapters of this book, I begin by examining some prevalent philosophical assumptions about consciousness and biological life. The point of this examination is to show that the dualistic separation of consciousness and life makes it impossible to understand consciousness in its basic form of bodily sentience. According to the enactive approach, there is a deep continuity of life and mind, including conscious mentality, and the philosophy of mind needs to be rooted in a phenomenological philosophy of the living body.

Consciousness and Life

Many philosophers of mind today believe that a profound difference exists between consciousness and mere biological life. On the one hand, consciousness, or more precisely, so-called phenomenal consciousness, is thought to be an internal, subjective, qualitative, and intrinsic property of certain mental states. Life, on the other hand, is thought to be an external, objective, structural, and functional property of certain physical systems. Given this way of thinking, the attempt to understand consciousness and its place in nature generates a special problem, the so-called hard problem of consciousness (Chalmers 1996, 2002; Nagel 1974): how is consciousness, as experienced from the inside by an individual conscious being, related to the natural life of that being, as observed and understood from the outside? In Thomas Nagel's words:

> For if the facts of experience—facts about what it is like *for* the experiencing organism—are accessible only from one point of view [the subjective point of view], then it is a mystery how the true character of experiences could be revealed in the physical operation of that organism . . . The problem is unique. If mental processes are physical processes, then there is something it is like, intrinsically, to undergo certain physical processes. What it is for such a thing to be the case remains a mystery. (1979, pp. 172, 175)

The problem is that physical accounts explain the structure and function of a system as characterized from the outside, but a conscious state is defined by its subjective character as experienced from the inside. Given this difference, physical accounts of structure and function seem insufficient to explain consciousness. In other words, there seems be an explanatory gap between physical structures and functions and consciousness (Levine 1983). Thus it is a mystery how conscious experiences could be physical processes.

According to this way of thinking, there is no equivalent hard problem about how biological life is related to physical structure and function. Thus David Chalmers writes:

> When it comes to the problem of life . . . it is just obvious that what needs explaining is structure and function: How does a living system self-organize? How does it adapt to its environment? How does it reproduce? Even the vitalists recognized this central point: their driving question was always "How could a mere physical system perform these complex functions?", not "Why are these functions accompanied by life?" . . . There is no distinct "hard problem" of life, and there never was one, even for vitalists. (Chalmers 1997, p. 5)

The thought proposed here is that although physical accounts of structure and function are conceptually and logically sufficient to account for living processes, consciousness is different. Conscious experience, though associated with various cognitive functions, such as perceiving things around one and reporting or expressing one's state of mind, seems resistant to functional analysis. Many philosophers believe that the physical structures and functions that make up a conscious being are not conceptually and logically sufficient to account for the subjective character of its experience. These philosophers think they can conceive of a system that is physically identical to a conscious being, but that either has systematically different sorts of experiences from that conscious being (an "invert") or lacks conscious experience altogether (a "zombie"). According to this way of thinking, whatever continuity exists between life and mind holds only for the functional properties of the mind and not for consciousness. There is no deep continuity of life and consciousness but rather a radical break between them. Given a complete and precise account of the physical structure and function of a living, conscious being, nothing about its conscious experience logically or conceptually follows. As Chalmers writes: "For a phenomenon such as life . . . the physical facts imply that certain functions will be performed, and the performance of those functions is all we need to explain in order to explain life. But no such answer will suffice for consciousness" (1996, pp. 106–107).

This line of thought is questionable. It is well known that sentience is deeply involved with life-regulation processes of complex organisms (Damasio 1999; Panksepp 1998b; Parvizi and Damasio 2001). We therefore ought to be suspicious of any apparently intractable dichotomy between consciousness and life. In other words, we ought to be suspicious of the concepts of consciousness and life that lie behind this formulation of the hard problem.

A historical remark may be useful at this point. Chalmers asserts that even the vitalists recognized that the concept of life is a functional concept. Hence, he says, there was no hard problem about life for vitalism, only a problem about understanding how a physical system could carry out various vital functions (metabolism, growth, repair, reproduction, and so on). This interpretation, however, seems incorrect. Some vitalists did indeed encounter a hard problem about life (Garrett, in press). Like those philosophers who think it conceivable that a physical duplicate of a conscious being could lack consciousness altogether, these vitalists thought it conceivable that organized, moving bodies, functionally indistinguishable from organisms, could lack "vitality." These vitalists asked, why are these organized movements accompanied by life? This reasoning strikes us as empty because we no longer accept the vitalist concepts of matter and life. Our concept of matter is no longer that of inanimate, minute, extended bodies governed by mechanical laws of motion, and our concept of life is no longer that of a special property of vitality. It seems reasonable to suppose that the concepts of consciousness and life that figure in the standard formulation of the hard problem are similarly inadequate.

My point in drawing this analogy is not to imply that consciousness is functionally definable in the same way materialists think that life is functionally definable. On the contrary, as I argued in Chapter 6, there is an inwardness to life that standard materialist accounts fail to recognize. My point is rather that to make headway on the problem of consciousness we need to go beyond the dualistic concepts of consciousness and life in standard formulations of the hard problem. In particular, we need to go beyond the idea that life is simply an "external" phenomenon in the usual materialist sense. Contrary to both dualism and materialism, life or living being is already beyond the gap between "internal" and "external." A purely external or outside view of structure and function is inadequate for life. A living being is not sheer exteriority *(partes extra partes)* but instead embodies a kind of interiority, that of its own immanent purposiveness. This interiority, as we have seen, comprises the self-production of an inside that specifies an outside to which that inside is constitutively and normatively related.

To borrow Heidegger's terminology, living being has a kind of "in-being," and in-being is an existential structure that cannot be adequately described in the language of external structure and function (Heidegger 1985, pp. 165–166). This kind of in-being, that of autopoietic interiority, is not a matter of material boundedness. As Heidegger points out, a living being is "in" its world in a sense completely different from that of water being in a glass (ibid.). The interiority of life is the interiority of selfhood and sense-making, which is a precursor to the interiority of consciousness. A living being enacts a milieu marked by significance and valence. Exteriority is surmounted by an internal relation of meaning and normativity between the two poles of organism and milieu. There is thus an inwardness to life that escapes a purely external conception. This inwardness underlies the deep continuity of life and mind, and is the context in which the emergence of consciousness must be understood.

The problem with the dualistic concepts of consciousness and life in standard formulations of the hard problem is that they exclude each other by construction. Hence there is no way to close the gap between them. To reduce conscious experience to external structure and function would be to make consciousness disappear (materialism); to reduce external structure and function to internal consciousness would be to make external things disappear (idealism); and to inject some third ingredient between the two is a desperate effort to bridge an unbridgeable chasm. The hard problem is thus not so much hard as impossible. The problem of making comprehensible the relation of mind and body cannot be solved as long as consciousness and life are conceptualized in such a way that they intrinsically exclude one another. For this reason, it is crucial to realize that this chasm is a philosophical construction built on sedimented and problematic ways of thinking going back to Descartes. We need to look more closely at this Cartesian legacy, for it remains a powerful force in many contemporary treatments of the problem of consciousness.

Descartes's Legacy

Descartes is mainly responsible for conceptualizing consciousness as inner experience accessible only to first-person reflection, and life as external and mechanical structure and function. Before Descartes, in the Aristotelian tradition, life and mind belonged together under the heading of soul *(psyche)*. For Aristotle, soul is not an immaterial substance, but in the broadest sense it is the capacity of the organism to be active in various ways. It thus encompasses whatever capacities or abilities belong to life, including cognitive or mental ones. In a striking image, Aristotle says that the soul is to the body as vision is to the eye: "if the eye were a living creature, its soul would be its sight" (*De Anima* II, I, 412b 19; see Mensch 1996, p. 175). In this conception, the soul is logically inseparable from the body. Precisely in the way it is inconsistent to suppose that the act of seeing can exist without the functioning of the eye, or that the eye can function properly without the act of seeing, so it is inconsistent to suppose that the soul—the vital capacities of the body—can exist without a living body or that a living body can exist without a soul. For Aristotle, exactly as seeing is the goal or purpose of the eye, so the soul is the totality of goals something must embody to be alive. Soul and body are thus two sides of the one single process of living. There are different kinds of soul, however, depending on the goals life can or must embody. These ends are nourishment and growth (the nutritive or vegetative soul); feeling and sensation (the sensitive soul); self-motion and self-direction (the volitional soul); and reason and the use of symbols (the rational or intellectual soul).[1]

With the rise of mechanistic natural philosophy in the sixteenth century, the Aristotelian view of natural phenomena as goal-directed was rejected. According to the mechanistic worldview, there are no goals or purposes inherent in the natural world; nature operates only according to the mechanical laws that govern matter in motion. To be alive is not to strive to realize a certain telos but to be a particular configuration of matter governed by mechanical principles. The Aristotelian notion of soul came to be seen as a fiction that did not apply to anything in the natural world. Instead, the soul was now equated with the rational mind, which transcends nature and whose essence is conscious thought.

Descartes played a key role in effecting this separation of mind and nature, consciousness and life. He rejected both the traditional connection between being conscious and being alive, as well as the traditional separation of living things and mechanisms (Matthews 1991). On the one hand, consciousness is a property of the immaterial mind or soul, and therefore the conscious mind per se is not alive. On the other hand, being alive is a property of the human body, which is simply a machine, and therefore the living body per se is not conscious. Consciousness and life have different natures, and no matter how closely united they are within a human person, they can nevertheless exist apart (as indeed supposedly happens after death, according to Descartes's Catholicism).

Descartes's separation of consciousness and life involved a new way of thinking about consciousness in relation to sense experience (Matthews 1991). According to the traditional Aristotelian conception, sensation and perception logically require a body. That is, the statement (1) *S senses or perceives something*, entails (2) *S has a bodily organ of sensation or perception;* and therefore (3) *S has a body (or is a body)*. Descartes, however, in the "Second Meditation" of his *Meditations on First Philosophy*, proposes a new meaning for "sense-experience" *(sentire)*, in which the entailment from sense-experience to the existence of one's body no longer holds. He writes that he can doubt whether he has a body (it is possible he is deceived), and therefore his body might not belong to his proper essence. He cannot doubt, however, that he is consciously thinking, and therefore he must be essentially a thinking thing. But what exactly is a thinking thing? It is, he states, "A thing that doubts, understands, affirms, denies, is willing, is unwilling, and also imagines and has sense perceptions" (Descartes 1986, p. 19). Yet how can a mere thinking thing, that is, a thinking thing that is supposed to have no body, also imagine and have sense perceptions, which apparently require a body? Descartes's answer is that even if none of the objects of his imagination is real, the power of imagination nevertheless belongs to his thinking. Similarly, even if none of the things he senses is real, it certainly seems to him that he senses them: "I certainly *seem* to see, to hear, and to be warmed. This cannot be false; what is called 'having a sensory perception' is strictly just this, and in this restricted sense of the term it is simply thinking [or consciousness]" (ibid.).

The upshot of this restricted sense of sense-perception, according to

Gareth Matthews's explanation, is "a new concept, consciousness, which includes thinking plus the 'inner part' (so to speak) of sensation and perception" (Matthews 1991, p. 68). Put another way, to arrive at the proper conception of consciousness, "We must (so to speak) 'peel off' from seeing, hearing, tasting, etc., the *seeming* to see, to hear, to taste, etc., which is such that one cannot do that and also doubt that one is doing it" (ibid). Such "seemings" provide the intrinsic "phenomenal contents" (as they are called today) of perception, and they do not logically entail the existence of one's body (or any other thing of nature for that matter).

Unlike the Aristotelian concept of soul, Descartes's new concept of consciousness was radically divorced from the concept of life. Yet it also had a first-person, phenomenological orientation missing from the concept of soul. Aristotle recognized the unity of soul and life only from an impersonal standpoint. He never discussed the body from an inward point of view, as one's own body (Patočka 1998, pp. 8–11). Descartes, however, established his separation of consciousness and life on the basis of a first-person starting point. Beginning from his own self-awareness, he asked what must indubitably be the case given his own experience. Sometimes this first-person impulse led him to reflect on bodily experience, in particular when he had to account for the experiential unity of mind and body in his own case. Thus, in a famous passage in the "Sixth Meditation," Descartes rejected the metaphor of the soul as a pilot of its ship:

> There is nothing my nature teaches me more vividly than that I have a body, and that when I feel pain there is something wrong with the body, and that when I am hungry or thirsty the body needs food and drink and so on. So I should not doubt that there is some truth in this.
>
> Nature also teaches me, by these sensations of pain, hunger, thirst, and so on, that I am not merely present in my body as a sailor in a ship [the French version reads: as a pilot in his ship], but that I am very closely joined and, as it were, intermingled with it, so that I and the body form a unit. If this were not so, I, who am nothing but a thinking thing, would not feel pain when the body was hurt, but would receive the damage purely by the intellect, just as a sailor perceives by sight if anything in his ship is broken. (Descartes 1986, p. 56)

Yet the undeniable fact that I and my body form a unit is precisely what Descartes's philosophy is unable to explain. The body for

Descartes is simply a mechanical thing, and any inwardness or sentience that apparently belongs to its vital functioning lies on the other side of a metaphysical divide, in the realm of immaterial consciousness. But if the conscious mind and the living body are thus completely different, then the fact that they form a distinct unity in each individual human being is incomprehensible. In particular, the fact that my mind is united to my body is entirely accidental or arbitrary, for as a matter of metaphysical principle my mind could just as easily be united to some other body. There is thus no way for Descartes to make good on his advance over Aristotle in recognizing the personal character of the living body (see Patočka 1998, pp. 9–20).

After Descartes there was a current of European thought that confronted the Cartesian separation of mind and body, consciousness and life, by reflecting once more on bodily experience (see Merleau-Ponty 2001). A prime example is the French philosopher Marie-Francois-Pierre Maine de Biran (1766–1824), who from his earliest texts in 1794 to the last pages of his *Journal* never ceased to wonder at what he called the "feeling of existence" *(le sentiment de l'existence).* Maine de Biran did not contest the disembodied Cartesian thinking ego in the name of some kind of sentimentalism. Instead he tried to grasp the very source of the personal "I," which, he held, is to be found in the bodily experience of exercising effort in movement. Jan Patočka, the noted Czech phenomenologist, describes Maine de Biran's insight this way:

> I have a primordial awareness of effort, of having certain possibilities, for instance, of moving my hand. The meaning of effort, of my purposive manipulating of my body, stems from myself. From this effort I know immediately that the movement stems from me as from an autonomous center . . . We are primordially an active I, exercising effort.
>
> Effort has its bounds: something resists it. It is not boundless energy, it is an efficacy of the body, a bodily effectiveness. Here it becomes evident that the I is possible *only as corporeal*—the I is a willing, striving I and, *consequently,* a corporeal one. This includes various modes—freshness, fatigue, exhaustion, etc. . . . An I is possible only in a biological organism. A biological organism becomes a real *person* in the moment I can do something on my own (i.e., move). (Patočka 1998, p. 25)

Maine de Biran's "feeling of existence" is another way of describing sentience, the feeling of being alive. This notion points away from the

disembodied Cartesian concept of consciousness and back to the primordial experience of exerting effort and being affected, that is, to
consciousness as bodily sentience.

Zombies: A Phenomenological Critique

Attention to sentience can also help us to see the limitations of another aspect of Descartes's legacy—the penchant for "zombies" among
many philosophers of mind today (Chalmers 1996, pp. 94–99; Moody
1994). A zombie is a fictional entity that has exactly the same physical
structure, functional mechanisms, and behavior as a conscious human
being, but has no conscious experience whatsoever. If such an entity is
logically or conceptually possible, if it is genuinely conceivable without
contradiction or some other kind of incoherence, then (so the argument goes) materialist analyses of consciousness in terms of physical
structure and function cannot be correct.

This argument is deeply Cartesian in form. Descartes argued in his
Meditations on First Philosophy that the mind is essentially conscious
thought, the body is essentially extension or the occupation of space, and
it is perfectly conceivable that conscious thought can exist apart from extension. Although Descartes concluded that the mind and the body are
not identical, his argument can be turned around, as Nagel pointed out
in one of the earliest versions of the modern zombie argument:

> The existence of the body without the mind is just as conceivable as the
> existence of the mind without the body. That is, I can conceive of my
> body doing precisely what it is doing now, inside and out, with complete
> physical causation of its behavior (including typically self-conscious be-
> havior), but without any of the mental states which I am now experi-
> encing, or any others for that matter. If that is really conceivable, then
> the mental states must be distinct from the body's physical states.
> (Nagel 1980, p. 205)[2]

With regard to these sorts of arguments, Nagel went on to observe
the following: "The real issue is whether one can know that one has
conceived such a thing . . . What must be shown, to defeat the Cartesian argument, is that when we try to conceive of our minds without
our bodies, or vice versa, we do not succeed in doing that, but instead
do something else, which we mistake for it" (1980, p. 205).

The Cartesian argument in its zombie form provides an extreme case of the radical conceptual divorce between consciousness and life. Your hypothetical zombie twin is physically and biologically identical to you; it is a complete duplicate of the biological organism that you are. It is therefore *alive* exactly as you are, with regard to every structural, functional, and behavioral detail. Nevertheless, it does not *feel alive* in the slightest; it is not sentient.

This thought seems incomprehensible. We are asked to imagine a living being, a human organism, whose bodily life is identical with respect to its physical structure and function to that of a conscious human being, but that has no bodily sentience, no subjective experience of its bodily existence and environment. In phenomenological language, we are asked to imagine a *physical living body* (a *Körper*) that is physically and behaviorally identical to a conscious being, but that is not a *lived body* (a *Leib*). It is hardly clear that this scenario is conceivable or imaginable strictly as described. The scenario requires that a physical counterpart (a molecule-for-molecule duplicate) of a given conscious subject's actual-world body have a bodily life indistinguishable from that of the conscious subject in every respect except for having no subjective experience whatsoever of its own body (Hanna and Thompson 2003).

Yet many of the perceptual and motor abilities of one's physical living body (the body as *Körper*) evidently depend on that body's being a subjectively lived body (a *Leib*). Without proprioceptive and kinesthetic experience, for example, many kinds of normal perception and motor action cannot happen. The zombie scenario requires the assumption that bodily experience is not necessary for or in any way constitutive of the relevant behavior, that exactly the same behavior is possible without bodily sentience. This assumption is quite strong and needs to be argued for independently. There is little reason to believe it. Although one can make a conceptual distinction between bodily experience from the inside and bodily functioning from the outside, it hardly follows that the latter could exist without the former.

It is worth elaborating this line of thought in relation to phenomenological analyses of perception. One of the central themes of Husserl's analyses of perception is that every visual or tactile perception is accompanied by, and functionally linked to, the sensing of one's bodily movements (hand movements, eye movements, head movements, whole-body movements, and so on) (Husserl 1997). Every aspect or profile of an object given to tactile or visual perception is not simply correlated to a kinesthetic experience of one's body but is functionally tied to that experience. When one touches the computer keys, for example, the keys are given in conjunction with a sensing of one's finger movements; when one watches a bird in flight, the bird is given in conjunction with a sensing of one's head and eye movements. Husserl argues at length that perceptual continuity—the continuity of the object through a changing manifold of appearances—depends on this linkage of kinesthesis and perception. As he states, it is through one's movement and bodily self-experience in movement that an object presents itself as a unified series of appearances. In other words, bodily self-experience in the form of kinesthesis is a constitutive condition of ordinary perception.

Behind this analysis is the idea that in order to perceive an object from a certain perspective—to take its appearance or profile from that perspective as an appearance of an objective thing in space—one needs to be aware, tacitly or prereflectively, of other coexisting but absent profiles of the object. These absent profiles stand in a certain relation to the present one: they can become present if one carries out certain movements. In other words, they are correlated to one's kinesthetic system of possible bodily movements and positions. If one moves this way, then that aspect of the object becomes visible; if one moves that way, then this aspect becomes visible. In Husserl's terminology, perception is "kinesthetically motivated."

For simplicity, we can take the case of a motionless object. If the kinesthetic experience (K_1) remains constant throughout a given time interval, then the perceptual appearance (A_1) remains constant too. If the kinesthetic experience changes (K_1 becomes K_2), then the perceptual appearance changes too (A_1 becomes A_2). There is thus a functional interdependency between the kinesthetic experiences and the perceptual ones. A given appearance (A_1) is not always correlated with the same kinesthetic experience (e.g., K_1), but it must be correlated with some kinesthetic experience or other. For this reason, perception is bound up with kinesthetic and proprioceptive experience.

The result is that prereflective bodily experience, the tacit experience of one's body, is constitutive of perception. How, then, can we make sense of the idea of a completely unconscious being, a being with no experience whatsoever of its own body, whose (functionally defined) perceptual abilities are exactly those of its (physically identical) conscious counterpart? For this scenario to make sense it must be conceivable that a being having normal human perceptual abilities could have no kinesthetic experience of its body and no prereflective experience of itself as an embodied agent. But if the phenomenological analysis is right, then bodily experience is constitutive of the perceptual function of individuating continuous objects in space through a manifold of sensory appearances. So any being that was capable of the same perceptual function would need to have an experience of its own body and hence could not be a zombie.

This line of reasoning challenges confidence in the imaginability of the zombie scenario but does not demonstrate that the scenario is inconceivable. My aim, however, is not to refute the belief in the logical possibility of zombies, as it were head-on. One does not need to demonstrate the logical impossibility of zombies by deriving a formal contradiction from the supposition to call into question this supposition's philosophical value (*pace* Chalmers 1996, p. 96). One need only reveal the problematic assumptions on which it rests—that exactly the same behavior can happen in the presence and absence of sentience, and that sentience is a strictly internal and phenomenal occurrence, whereas behavior is entirely a matter of external structure and function. Given these problematic assumptions, philosophers should not be allowed to get away with simply asserting that the zombie scenario seems conceivable to them. They must describe the scenario in sufficient detail so that it is intelligible given the apparent inseparability of a conscious subject's physical living body (its *Körper*) and its lived body (its *Leib*).

This demand requires more than what zombie aficionados provide. Jaegwon Kim, for example, simply asserts that zombies seem conceivable "without much difficulty" (Kim 1998, pp. 101–102). And Chalmers writes:

I confess that the logical possibility of zombies seems equally obvious to me [as that of a mile-high unicycle]. A zombie is just something physically identical to me, but which has no conscious experience—all is dark inside. While this is probably empirically impossible, it certainly seems that a coherent situation is described; I can discern no contra-

diction in the description. In some ways an assertion of this logical possibility comes down to a brute intuition, but no more so than with the
unicycle. Almost everybody, it seems to me, is capable of conceiving of
this possibility. (Chalmers 1996, p. 96)

I disagree. It hardly seems true that, when asked to imagine the scenario in sufficient detail, almost everyone can conceive of this possibility or that they can do so without much difficulty (see Cottrell 1999;
Dennett 1995b). What does seem true is that the scenario will seem
conceivable to anybody who is under the sway of the Cartesian concept
of consciousness and who has not thought carefully about what the
scenario, strictly described, actually demands of one's imagination, in
particular with regard to the phenomenology of bodily experience.
The putative logical possibility of zombies is therefore not like the logical possibility of a mile-high unicycle. The latter supposition involves
simply an imagined variation on the physical size and structural pro-
portions of a thing, but the former supposition involves an intellectual
extrapolation to the limit of a deeply problematic way of thinking
about consciousness and bodily life.

The Cartesian concept of consciousness also leads to an extreme
skepticism about other conscious minds. How could one ever tell the
difference between a zombie and a conscious subject? If "zombiehood" is possible, then it is possible (conceptually or logically, if not
empirically) that your spouse, child, closest friend, or lover is a zombie
without you or anyone else knowing. Such a supposition expresses at
its most extreme the Cartesian problem of other minds.[3] But it gets
even worse. As Guven Güzeldere observes: "Zombiehood brings with it
not only the problem of other minds, and thus third-person [and
second-person] skepticism, but first-person skepticism as well. If you,
the reader of these lines, suddenly turned into a zombie, no one would
notice any difference, and in a significant sense of 'noticing' [the external, functional sense], neither would you" (Güzeldere 1997, p. 43).
One problem with this kind of skepticism is that our understanding of
what it is to be a conscious subject is intersubjectively constituted
through empathy. (By "empathy" I mean the sensorimotor and affective coupling of our lived bodies as well as our mutual imaginative exchange of cognitive and emotional perspectives.) I will return to this
idea in Chapter 13.

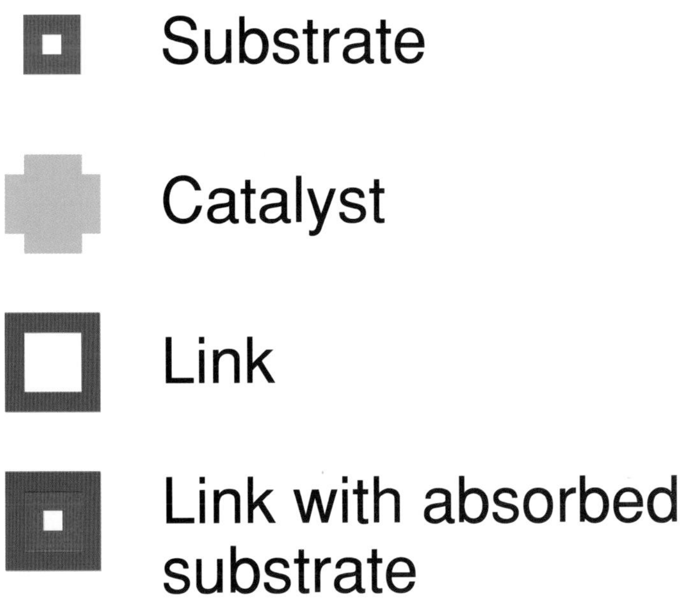

Substrate

Catalyst

Link

Link with absorbed substrate

Plate I. Computer model of autopoiesis, key to particle types in the SCL (substrate-catalyst link) artificial chemistry. Reproduced with permission from Barry McMullin, "Rediscovering Computational Autopoiesis," http://www.eeng.dcu.ie/~alife/bmcm-ecal97/.

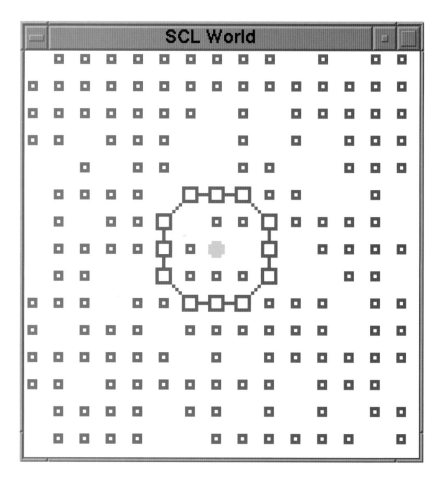

Plate II. Computer model of autopoeisis, initial configuration. Reproduced with permission from Barry McMullin, "Rediscovering Computational Autopoiesis," http://www.eeng.dcu.ie/~alife/bmcm-ecal97/.

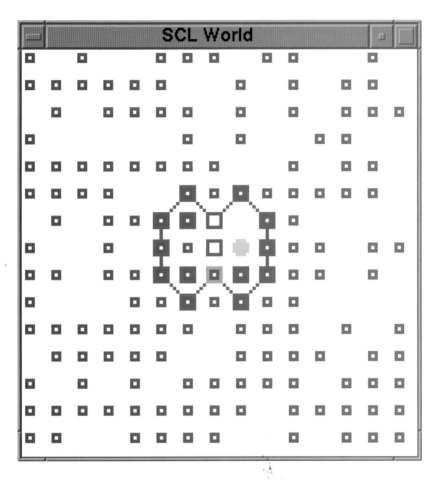

Plate III. Computer model of autopoeisis, Experiment 2, Run 1, Time 444. Reproduced with permission from Barry McMullin, "Rediscovering Computational Autopoiesis," http://www.eeng.dcu.ie/~alife/bmcm-ecal97/.

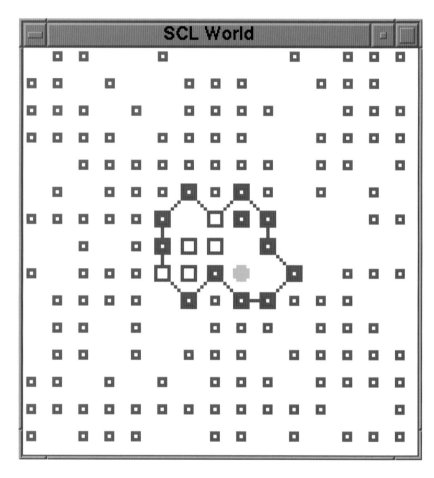

Plate IV. Computer model of autopoeisis, Experiment 2, Run 1, Time 1310. Reproduced with permission from Barry McMullin, "Rediscovering Computational Autopoiesis," http://www.eeng.dcu.ie/~alife/bmcm-ecal97/.

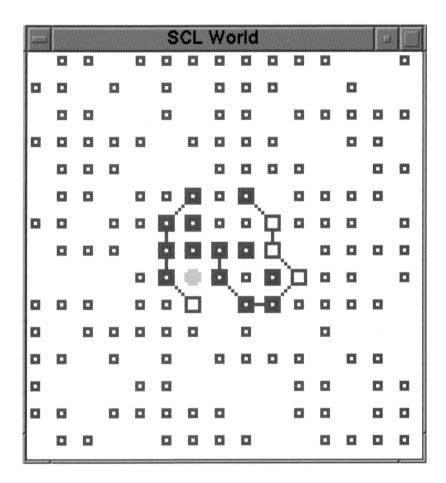

Plate V. Computer model of autopoeisis, Experiment 2, Run 1, Time 1746. Reproduced with permission from Barry McMullin, "Rediscovering Computational Autopoiesis," http://www.eeng.dcu.ie/~alife/bmcm-ecal97/.

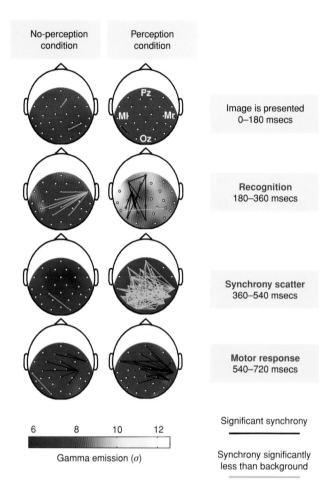

Plate VI. The shadow of a perception. Average scalp distribution of gamma activity and phase synchrony. EEG was recorded from electrodes at the scalp surface. Subjects were shown upright and upside-down Mooney figures (high-contrast faces), which are easily perceived as faces when presented upright, but usually perceived as meaningless black-and-white forms when upside-down. The subjects' task was a rapid two-choice button response of whether or not they perceived a face at first glance. Color-coding indicates gamma power (averaged in 34–40 Hz frequency range) over a given electrode and during a 180-millisecond time window, from stimulation onset (0 ms) to motor response (720 ms). Gamma activity is spatially homogeneous and similar between conditions over time. By contrast, phase synchrony is markedly regional and differs between conditions. Synchrony between electrode pairs is indicated by black and green lines, corresponding to a significant increase or decrease in synchrony, respectively. These are shown only if the synchrony value is beyond the distribution of shuffled data sets ($P < 0.01$; see methods, Rodriguez et al. 1999). Reprinted from Evan Thompson and Francisco Varela, "Radical Embodiment: Neural Dynamics and Consciousness," *Trends in Cognitive Sciences* 5 (2001): 418–425, fig. 1, © 2001, with permission from Elsevier.

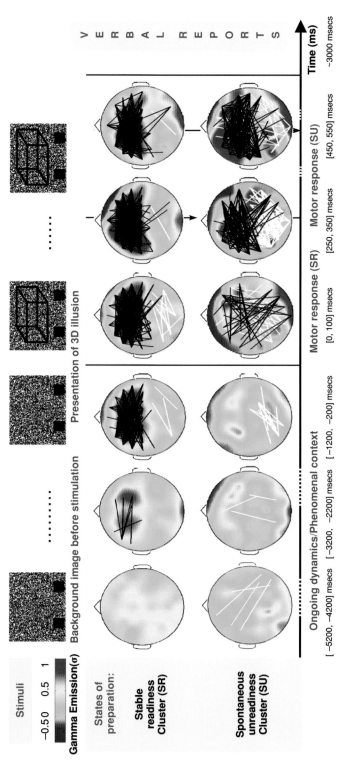

Plate VII. Dynamical neural signatures of ongoing conscious perception. Dynamical neural signatures of the prestimulation activities and the brain responses are presented for one subject during readiness with immediate perception (SR) (154 trials) and spontaneous unreadiness with surprise during stimulation (SU) (38 trials). Color-coding indicates scalp distribution of time-frequency gamma power around 35 Hz normalized compared to a distant baseline (−1800 ms, −1700 ms; 0 ms corresponds to presentation of the stereogram) averaged for trials and for time windows indicated by an arrow. Black and white lines correspond to significant increase and decrease in synchrony, respectively. Reprinted with permission from Antoine Lutz, Jean-Philippe Luchaux, Jacques Martinerie, and Francisco J. Varela, "Guiding the Study of Brain Dynamics by Using First-Person Data," *Proceedings of the National Academy of Sciences USA* 99 (copyright 2002, National Academy of Sciences, U.S.A.), 1589, fig. 2.

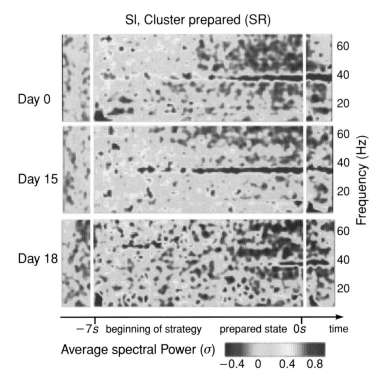

SI, Cluster prepared (SR)

Day 0

Day 15

Day 18

Frequency (Hz)

−7s beginning of strategy prepared state 0s time

Average spectral Power (σ)

−0.4 0 0.4 0.8

Plate VIII. Stability of dynamical neural signature in one subject. Stability of dynamical neural signature for recordings for one subject during steady readiness (SR) in frontal electrodes (FP1 to FT8), with significant increase at 36 Hz and decrease between 44–64 Hz during −1200 ms, −200 ms for every recording (59, 60, and 35 trials, respectively). This subject reported being globally less focused during the third recording than during the second one. Color-coding indicates scalp distribution of time-frequency gamma power normalized compared with distant baseline (−8200 ms, −7200 ms) averaged for trials and electrodes. Reprinted with permission from Antoine Lutz, Jean-Philippe Luchaux, Jacques Martinerie, and Francisco J. Varela, "Guiding the Study of Brain Dynamics by Using First-Person Data," *Proceedings of the National Academy of Sciences USA* 99 (copyright 2002, National Academy of Sciences, U.S.A.), 1590, fig. 5.

The moral of this discussion is that instead of starting from the concepts of mind and body in standard formulations of the hard problem we need to take our start from the lived body. To close this chapter I would like to reformulate the problem of the explanatory gap by taking life and the body as our starting point.

The Body-Body Problem

If on the one hand mental processes are bodily processes, then there is something it is like, intrinsically, to undergo certain bodily processes. On the other hand, if there belongs to certain bodily processes something it is like to undergo them, then those bodily processes are experiences. As Nagel (1974) puts it, they have a "subjective character," without which they would cease to be experiences. They are feelings in the broad sense that William James had in mind when he used the word "feeling" "to designate all states of consciousness merely as such" (1981, p. 185) and that Antonio Damasio has revived by describing feelings as "bearing witness to life within our minds" (Damasio 2003, p. 140). The problem of what it is for mental processes to be also bodily processes is thus in large part the problem of what it is for subjectivity and feeling to be a bodily phenomenon.

In this formulation of the hard problem, I have substituted the term *body* for *physical*.[4] Body connotes life, a living organism, and is richer in meaning than physical in the Cartesian sense. Drawing on this richness can help us to refine the terms of the explanatory gap.

Phenomenologists distinguish between two ways the body can be disclosed or constituted in experience—as a material thing *(Körper)* and as a living subject of experience or lived body *(Leib)*. We need to refine this distinction, however, for at least two reasons. First, we need to guard against the danger of reifying a phenomenological distinction between two ways our body can be disclosed into an ontological duality. The body can be disclosed as a physical body and as a lived body, but this does not imply that there are two bodies or that the body has two mutually irreducible, metaphysical properties or aspects.[5] Second, even this distinction between two modes of bodily presence, correlated with two ways of experiencing the body, is inadequate, because it does not convey the diversity of ways the body can be disclosed in our experience.

Husserl had to avail himself of a variety of terms for the spectrum of

differentiated ways the body can be disclosed, from an objective physical body to a subjective life-flow, with various notions of the body as
living or lived in between (Depraz 2001a, pp. 2–111).[6] Subsequent
phenomenologists have elaborated, enriched, and refined these
analyses. As we will see in Chapter 13, there is also a complex intersubjective structure of experience, linking how one's own body is disclosed to oneself and how it is disclosed to another (as well as how another's body is disclosed to oneself). For these reasons, "body" has to
be taken as naming an open region of investigation and analysis, not a
fixed ontological reference point in some abstract metaphysical
scheme (like "physical" and "mental" in Cartesian dualist or materialist
metaphysics).

I have argued that the standard formulation of the hard problem is
embedded in the Cartesian framework of the "mental" versus the
"physical," and that this framework should be given up in favor of an
approach centered on the notion of life or living being. Although the
explanatory gap does not go away when we adopt this approach, it
does take on a different character. The guiding issue is no longer the
contrived one of whether a subjectivist concept of consciousness can
be derived from an objectivist concept of the body. Rather, the guiding
issue is to understand the emergence of living subjectivity from living
being, where living being is understood as already possessed of an interiority that escapes the objectivist picture of nature. It is this issue of
emergence that we need to address, not the Cartesian version of the
hard problem.

To sharpen this issue, we need to refine the phenomenological distinction between the physical body and the lived body. In addition to
this basic distinction, we can distinguish between the structural morphology of the physical body and its living and lived dynamics (Cole,
Depraz, and Gallagher 2000). The morphology comprises the bodily
structures of limbs, organs, regulatory systems, brain structures, and so
on, whereas the dynamics comprises the lived flow of life, that is, the
flow of intentional movement and lived sensations (interoceptive, exteroceptive, and proprioceptive). There does not seem to be any explanatory gap in the transition from seeing the body as a physical object to seeing it in its structural morphology as a living body. But there
does seem to be a gap or discontinuity in the movement from seeing
the body as a living body to seeing it as a lived body, as a locus of

feeling and intentional activity—in short as sentient. What exactly is the nature of this gap?

Two points are important here. First, the gap is no longer between two radically different ontologies (mental and physical), but between two types within one typology of embodiment. Second, the gap is no longer absolute because in order to formulate it we need to make common reference to life or living being. For these reasons, and to highlight the contrast with the Cartesian formulation of the hard problem, we could call this explanatory gap the *body-body problem* (Hanna and Thompson 2003).

The difference between the body-body problem and the Cartesian hard problem is philosophically nontrivial. In the hard problem, the explanatory gap is absolute because there is no common factor between the mental and the physical (and there can be none given how they are defined). Hence the main options are to accept the gap as a brute ontological fact (dualism), to close the gap by reduction (materialism or idealism), or to bridge the gap by introducing some third and speculative "extra ingredient" (for which there is no scientific evidence or motivation). These options make no sense for the body-body problem. In finding our way to this problem, we have had to jettison the traditional Cartesian vocabulary of mental versus physical entities and properties. The lived body *is* the living body; it is a dynamic condition of the living body. We could say that our lived body is a performance of our living body, something our body enacts in living. An important philosophical task is to show how there can be an account of the lived body that integrates biology and phenomenology, and so goes "beyond the gap" (Bruzina 2004; Roy et al. 1999). The scientific task is to understand how the organizational and dynamic processes of a living body can become constitutive of a subjective point of view, so that there is something it is like to be that body. For the enactive approach, this task takes the form of trying to understand a lived body as a special kind of autonomous system, one whose sense-making brings forth, enacts, or constitutes a phenomenal world.

Biological Naturalism

Before ending this chapter, I would like to compare the approach to consciousness and life I have been exploring with John Searle's "biological naturalism" (Searle 1992, 2004). Searle also rejects the traditional categories of mental and physical. He writes: "If we are going to keep this terminology at all, we need an expanded notion of the physical to allow for its intrinsic, subjective mental component" (2004, p. 116). For Searle, conscious states are biological processes that are intrinsically qualitative, subjective, and first-personal. They have a subjective or first-person ontology, which means that they exist only insofar as they are experienced by a conscious animal or human subject. Conscious states are constitutively first-personal, and therefore are ontologically irreducible to brain processes described neurophysiologically, which are constitutively third-personal. At the same time, consciousness is causally reducible to the brain because it is entirely caused by lower level neurobiological processes and is realized in higher level or systemic brain activity.

I share Searle's view that consciousness is a subjective biological process and that, so described, it is irreducible to brain processes described neurophysiologically in the third person. But there are also differences between our views.

I have argued that we already need an expanded notion of the physical to account for life and to prepare the way for any further expansion needed to account for consciousness. Life is not physical in the standard materialist sense of purely external structure and function. Life realizes a kind of interiority, the interiority of selfhood and sense-making. We accordingly need an expanded notion of the physical to account for the organism or living being. Furthermore, I find compelling Robert Rosen's view that such an expanded, biological notion of the physical would be generic or typical in its application to nature rather than a special case (Rosen 1991, 2000). Although organisms are statistically rare in the class of physical systems, it does not follow that they are special or nongeneric in that class (Rosen 1991, pp. 13, 37; 2000, p. 27). Most of physics has been developed for thermodynamically closed rather than open systems, and especially not for autopoietic systems or living systems generally, which are precisely those systems for which individuality and interiority are applicable concepts. It is the closed systems that are organizationally special or nongeneric, not the open ones. Rosen makes an analogy to rational and irrational numbers in arithmetic: "We have . . . a predilection for rational numbers, a predilection that gives them weight out of all proportion to their actual abundance. Yet in every mathematical sense, it is the rational numbers that are rare and very special indeed. Why should it not be the case with physics and biology? Why could it not be that the 'universals' of physics are only so on a small and special (if inordinately prominent) class of material systems, a class to which organisms are too *general* to belong? What if physics is the particular, and biology the general, instead of the other way around?" (1991, p. 13).

I also differ from Searle in my assessment of the irreducibility of consciousness. Searle observes that, in standard cases of scientific reduction, a given type of phenomenon, such as heat or color, gets redefined in terms of its underlying microphysical causes (molecular kinetic energy or light reflectances), such that its subjective appearance (felt heat or perceived color) is excluded from its definition.[7] Thus, causal reduction of the macroscopic causal properties to the microstructural ones, and redefinition of the phenomenon in terms of its microstructure, are supposed to support ontological reduction of the phenomenon to its microstructural constituents.

This pattern of reduction depends on the appearance/reality distinction: the phenomenon is supposed to be reducible because it can be redefined in terms of the underlying reality and not the appearance. In the case of consciousness, however, we cannot make this appearance/reality distinction because "consciousness consists in the appearances themselves" (Searle 1992, p. 122).[8] Hence "the point of the reduction would be lost if we tried to carve off the appearance and simply defined consciousness in terms of the underlying physical reality" (ibid). Searle, however, thinks the irreducibility of consciousness is trivial, for it is simply "a trivial consequence of the pragmatics of our definitional practices" (ibid.). We define consciousness in terms of the subjective appearances, not the underlying physical reality, with the result that "the reductions . . . that leave out the epistemic bases, the appearances, cannot work for the epistemic bases themselves" (ibid.).

By contrast, I think the irreducibility of consciousness is not trivial and indicates that consciousness has a transcendental status in addition to an empirical one. Consciousness, considered as epistemic base, is not equivalent to the perceptual appearances, which pertain to empirical objects as given to our consciousness. Consciousness as epistemic base is equivalent to the experiential acts by which those objects are disclosed to us. From a phenomenological perspective, objects are disclosed in the ways they are—as complex structured manifolds of ap-

pearance—thanks to certain essential formal laws under which experience necessarily operates so as to disclose a meaningful world. Consciousness considered in this way is a condition of possibility for there
being any appearances at all. To understand consciousness this way is
to understand it transcendentally and not merely empirically. Thus I
take the irreducibility of the epistemic bases themselves to point
toward the need for a transcendental perspective on consciousness
(see also Rowlands 2003).[9]

The last difference I want to mention concerns Searle's view that
consciousness is causally reducible entirely to the brain. This view provides a way to see consciousness as a causally efficacious biological process. Consciousness in Searle's view is a higher level or global state of
the brain that is causally relevant to the organism's behavior and subsequent neural activity. This neurobiological conjecture coincides with
several neurodynamical proposals about consciousness (see Cosmelli,
Lachaux, and Thompson 2007; and Chapters 3, 11, and 12 of the
present volume). Nevertheless, the view that consciousness is entirely
causally reducible to the brain may be biologically premature. We
simply do not yet know whether the brain alone is the minimal causal
basis for consciousness or whether this basis also includes features of
the brain-body interface or brain-body-environment interface.

Consider the philosophical thought experiment of the brain in a
vat. Your brain is removed from your body and is artificially maintained in a chemical vat where it receives exactly the same stimulation
to all its neuronal terminals that it normally receives as you go about
your life. Would you (or your brain) notice any difference? Would you
not have qualitatively identical subjective experience? Philosophers
have used this scenario to motivate many ideas, one of which is that the
brain (or some subsystem of the brain), and nothing outside the brain,
is the minimally sufficient condition for consciousness or subjective experience. Yet this claim does not follow from the brain-in-a-vat scenario. Rather, what follows is that, whatever is the minimally sufficient
condition for consciousness, this condition has been successfully realized by the vat setup. For all we know, this condition necessarily includes as a proper part something outside the brain, provided in this
case by the vat.[10]

Notice that the vat setup would have to be capable of (1) keeping
the brain alive and up and running, (2) duplicating all exogenous

stimulation, and (3) compensating in exactly the right way for all endogenous (and self-organizing) activity. Such a setup would almost
certainly have to duplicate many of the chemical, biomechanical, and
sensorimotor properties of the body, probably even the body's sensorimotor coupling with the world. In other words, the null hypothesis is
that any vat that meets the requirements of this scenario will be a surrogate body. Hence the brain-in-a-vat thought experiment does not establish either that consciousness is entirely causally reducible to the
brain or that the minimally sufficient condition for consciousness resides exclusively within the brain. Perhaps bodily processes belong to
the minimally sufficient condition for consciousness and the "vat"
would have to be a surrogate body.[11]

One might object that we already know that direct electrical stimulation to the cortex can produce various sorts of conscious experiences. Is this fact not good reason to think that, given appropriate
background conditions in the rest of the brain and body, there must
be some neural substrate that is minimally sufficient for the instantiation or realization of consciousness?

This proposal, however, depends on empirical considerations that
are far from settled. We simply do not yet know the minimal biological
requirements for the instantiation or realization of consciousness. It is
one thing for neural activity to be the minimal sufficient condition for
the instantiation of a fleeting, episodic moment of phenomenal consciousness. It is quite another thing for neural activity to be the minimal sufficient condition for the instantiation of consciousness in the
sense of coherent and temporally extended intentional experience of
the world. As the above considerations about the brain-in-a-vat scenario suggest, such consciousness might require nothing less than a
living body engaged with the world.

Even if the minimally sufficient condition for consciousness is indeed the brain, it does not follow that we are nothing over and above
our brains. Consider these statements by Searle: "The brain is all we
have for the purpose of representing the world to ourselves and everything we can use must be inside the brain. Each of our beliefs must be
possible for a being who is a brain in a vat because each of us is precisely a brain in a vat; the vat is the skull and the 'messages' coming in
are coming in by way of impacts on the nervous system" (Searle 1983,
p. 230). Yet the brain is not all we have, and not everything we can use

for the purpose of representing the world is inside our brain. We have our body as well as resources in the environment, and it is far from obvious that any bodily process or environmental resource used in representing the world needs to be represented inside the brain. Each of us is precisely not a brain in a vat but rather a bodily subject. The body is not a vat, and any so-called vat that could duplicate or stand in for the body would most likely have to be a surrogate body. The brain is an organ, not an organism, and it is the organism, animal, or person that has conscious access to the world. As conscious subjects we are not brains in cranial vats; we are neurally enlivened beings in the world.

Although for every subjective and phenomenal change in one's conscious experience there is presumably a corresponding change in one's brain, it remains an open question to what extent these changes are explicable independent of the sensorimotor and environmental contexts of brain activity.[12] The hypothesis of the enactive approach is that the relation between experience and the brain will remain opaque unless these contexts figure explicitly in our accounts. This issue is central to the next chapter.

NINE

Sensorimotor Subjectivity

ONE OF THE GUIDING ideas of this book is that the human mind is embodied in our entire organism and in the world. Our mental lives involve three permanent and intertwined modes of bodily activity—self-
regulation, sensorimotor coupling, and intersubjective interaction
(Thompson and Varela 2001). Self-regulation is essential to being alive
and sentient. It is evident in emotion and feeling, and in conditions
such as being awake or asleep, alert or fatigued, hungry or satiated. Sensorimotor coupling with the world is expressed in perception, emotion,
and action. Intersubjective interaction is the cognition and affectively
charged experience of self and other. The human brain is crucial for
these three modes of activity, but it is also reciprocally shaped and structured by them at multiple levels throughout the lifespan. If each individual human mind emerges from these extended modes of activity, if it
is accordingly embodied and embedded in them as a "dynamic singu-
larity"—a knot or tangle of recurrent and reentrant processes centered
on the organism (Hurley 1998)—then the "astonishing hypothesis" of
neuroreductionism—that you are "nothing but a pack of neurons"
(Crick 1994, p. 2) or that "you are your synapses" (LeDoux 2002)—is
both a category error and biologically unsound. On the contrary, you
are a living bodily subject of experience and an intersubjective mental
being.

This chapter focuses on the second of these modes of bodily activity—dynamic sensorimotor activity. Earlier in this book we saw that
the fundamental logic of the nervous system, its basic "neurologic," is

243

to couple movement and a stream of sensory activity in a continuous circular fashion. The nervous system links sensory surfaces (sense organs and nerve endings) and effectors (muscles, glands) within the body. In that way, the nervous system integrates the organism, holding it together as a mobile unity, as an autonomous sensorimotor agent. The nervous system establishes and maintains a sensorimotor cycle, whereby what one senses depends directly on how one moves, and how one moves depends directly on what one senses. One manifestation of our biological autonomy is that we meet the environment on our own sensorimotor terms.

In recent years, a new dynamic sensorimotor approach to understanding perceptual consciousness has arisen in cognitive science and the philosophy of mind (Hurley 1998; Noë 2004; O'Regan and Noë 2001a). Rather than appealing to the intrinsic properties of neural activity in order to understand perceptual experience, this approach looks to the dynamic sensorimotor relations among neural activity, the body, and the world. By thus enriching our conception of the biological substrate of perceptual experience, this approach offers new resources for tackling the explanatory gap. My aim in this chapter is to draw on these resources in order to make some headway on the body-body problem—the problem of relating one's subjectively lived body to the organism or living body that one is.

Subjectivity and Bodily Self-Consciousness

The body-body problem is a non-Cartesian way of recasting the explanatory gap between the conscious mind and the physical body. As we have seen, in the body-body problem, the gap is no longer between two radically different ontologies ("mental" and "physical") but between two types within one typology of embodiment (subjectively lived body and living body). The gap is also no longer absolute because in order to formulate it we need to make common reference to life or living being.

The body-body problem concerns the relation between one's body as one subjectively lives it and one's body as an organism in the world. This problem is in turn part of the general problem of the relation between oneself and the world, for one's living body is part of the world and one's body as one subjectively lives it is part of one's sense of self.

We can thus ask two interrelated questions: how does one's lived body relate to the world, and how does it relate to itself? Addressing these questions is one way to approach the body's sensorimotor subjectivity.

The relation between one's self and the world encompasses the relation between one's self and one's body. Descartes, as we saw in the last chapter, pointed out that one's self is not located in one's body as a pilot within a ship but instead is "very closely joined" and "intermingled" with it, so that the two "form a unit." Nevertheless, self and body remain two, not one. Merleau-Ponty, in contrast, rejects this dualism. One's self is not merely *embodied* but *bodily:* "But I am not in front of my body, I am in my body, or rather I am my body" (1962, p. 150).[1] Yet Merleau-Ponty also refuses to understand the proposition "I am my body" in a materialist way, as meaning that I am (or my self is) nothing more than a complex physical *object*. Instead, he maintains the original position that I am a *bodily subject*. In this way, he rejects the traditional concepts of mind and body, subject and object, as well as the ontologies they imply (dualism, materialism, and idealism) (see Priest 1998, pp. 56–57).

To appreciate the originality of Merleau-Ponty's position, we need to consider his conception of bodily subjectivity. We can begin with Merleau-Ponty's likening the unity of the body to the unity of a work of art. He introduces this idea by way of a contrast between the perceptual unity of a physical object through its perspectival variations and the experiential unity of one's own body. A physical object, such as a cube, stands before me or over against me, and presents various facets to me; what perceptually unites these facets as facets of one and the same cube is the law of their perspectival variation. My body, however, does not stand before me or over against me, and what unites the various experiences I have of my body is not a law or rule of perspectival variation, but rather an integrated perceptual and motor "background of significance" (1962, p. 150). As Merleau-Ponty explains: "What unites 'tactile sensations' in the hand and links them to visual perceptions of the same hand, and to perceptions of other bodily areas, is a certain style informing my manual gestures and implying in turn a certain style of finger movements, and contributing, in the last resort, to a certain bodily bearing" (ibid.). It is this elucidation of one's bodily subjectivity as constituted by a certain style or bearing that leads Merleau-Ponty to liken the body to a work of art:

The body is to be compared, not to a physical object, but rather to a work of art . . . A novel, poem, picture, or musical work are individuals, that is, beings in which the expression is indistinguishable from the thing expressed, their meaning, accessible only through direct contact, being radiated with no change of their temporal and spatial situation. It is in this sense that our body is comparable to a work of art. It is a nexus of lived meanings, not the law for a certain number of covariant terms. A certain tactile experience felt in the upper arm signifies a certain tactile experience in the forearm and shoulder, along with a certain visual aspect of the same arm, not because the various tactile perceptions among themselves, or the tactile and visual ones, are all involved in one intelligible arm, as the different facets of a cube are related to the idea of a cube, but because the arm seen and the arm touched, like the different segments of the arm, together *perform* one and the same action. (Merleau-Ponty, 1962, pp. 150–151)

This passage can help us to appreciate that when Merleau-Ponty asserts, "I am my body," he does not mean that I as a subject am simply my body considered as an object. Rather, I am my body in a way not unlike the way an artwork is what it expresses. My body is an expressive being, and what it expresses is my subjectivity.

This expressive conception of bodily subjectivity points forward to Merleau-Ponty's later chapter on "The Body as Expression and Speech" (in his *Phenomenology of Perception*). At the beginning of that chapter, in a footnote, Merleau-Ponty calls attention to two senses of "being"—a "weak sense of existence as a thing, or that of predication," and a stronger "existential sense of belonging to . . . , or taking up (I am my body, I am my life)" (1962, p. 174). Clearly, the statement "I am my body," as Merleau-Ponty means it, must be taken in the existential sense. Moreover, when we understand the statement this way, it becomes compatible with a certain way we can understand the statement "I have a body." Merleau-Ponty calls attention to the two senses of "being" while discussing Gabriel Marcel's distinction between "being" and "having." Marcel uses "being" in the richer existential sense, whereas "having" "designates a proprietary relationship (I have a house, I have a hat)" (1962, p. 174). This proprietary relation is an external one, for my possessions are specifiable independently of me. Merleau-Ponty, however, points out that there is another sense of "having"—"for the relation which the subject bears to the term into which it projects itself (I have an idea, I have a desire, I have fears)" (ibid.). Here the relation is not external but internal, for what I have is not specifiable independently of me. Indeed, it "belongs" to me or I "take it up," in the existential sense. The link between these senses in which "I am a body" and "I have a body" is precisely the expressive relation between my bodily being and my subjectivity.

In keeping with this original view, which aims "to leave behind us, once and for all, the traditional subject-object dichotomy" (1962, p. 174), Merleau-Ponty maintains that the relation between self and world is not that of subject to object but rather what he calls, following Heidegger, being-in-the-world. For a bodily subject it is not possible to specify what the subject is in abstraction from the world, nor is it possible to specify what the world is in abstraction from the subject: "The world is inseparable from the subject, but from a subject which is nothing but a project of the world, and the subject is inseparable from the world, but from a world which the subject itself projects" (1962, p. 430). To belong to the world in this way means that our primary way of relating to things is neither purely sensory and reflexive, nor cognitive or intellectual, but rather bodily and skillful. Merleau-Ponty calls this kind of bodily intentionality "motor intentionality" (1962, p. 110, 137). His example is grasping or intentionally taking hold of an object. In grasping something we direct ourselves toward it, and thus our action is intentional. But the action does not refer to the thing by representing its objective and determinate features; it refers to it pragmatically in the light of a contextual motor goal effected by one's body (1962, p. 138). In picking up a teacup to drink from, I identify it not by its objective location in space but by its egocentric relation to my hands, and I grasp it in light of the goal of sipping from it.

At the same time, things in my surroundings, such as teacups, computer keys, and door handles, have motor senses or meanings, what Gibson (1979) calls "affordances," which elicit appropriate actions. Things in the world bring forth suitable intentional actions and motor projects from the subject (the subject is a project of the world), but things in the world have specific motor senses or affordances only in relation to the motor skills of the subject (the world is projected by the subject). This body-environment circuit of motor intentionality belongs to what Merleau-Ponty calls the "intentional arc" subtending the life of consciousness, which integrates sensibility and motility, perception and action (1962, p. 136). The intentional arc and being-in-the-world overall are neither purely first-personal (subjective) nor purely third-personal (objective), neither mental nor physical. They are existential structures prior to and more fundamental than these abstractions. For this reason, Merleau-Ponty maintains that they can "effect the union of the 'psychic' and the 'physiological'" (p. 80) in an existential analysis of bodily subjectivity (and its breakdown in pathology).

In the intentional arc subtending the life of consciousness, one's body is present "not as one object among all other objects, but as the vehicle of being in the world" (1962, p. 139). But if one's body is the vehicle of being in the world and is in this way a condition of possibility for the disclosure of the world, how or in what way can it too be given to experience? This question asks about how one experiences oneself as a bodily subject or how a lived body experiences itself as a lived body.

One way to approach bodily self-consciousness is to work back from the world, which transcends the bodily self, to the body as the correlate of its perceptual presence. A familiar theme of phenomenology, going back to Husserl, is that the lived body is a presupposition of the world's perceptual presence. Things are perceptually situated by virtue of the orientation they have to our moving and perceiving bodies. To pick up the teacup is to grasp it from a certain angle and to hold and manipulate it in a certain manner. To listen to the radio is to hear it from a certain vantage point, which changes as one moves about the room. To see the wine bottle on the table is to view it from a certain perspective and to see it as within or beyond one's reach. If something appears perspectivally, then the subject to whom it appears must be spatially related to it. To be spatially related to something requires that one be embodied. To say that we perceive a given profile of something, all the while aware that it has other absent but possibly present profiles, means that any profile we perceive contains references to these other profiles; each profile implicates the others. These (noematic) references correspond to our (noetic) ability to exchange one profile for another through our own free movement, by tilting our heads, manipulating an object in our hands, walking around something, and so on.

The crucial point about the lived body in this context is twofold. First, the body functions as the "zero point," "null point of orientation," or absolute indexical "here" in relation to which things appear perspectivally. Second, the lived body cannot be reduced to yet another intentional object of perception but always exceeds this kind of intentionality. The lived body manifests itself in perceptual experience, not primarily as an intentional object but as an implicit and practical "I can" of movement and motor intentionality (Husserl 1989, pp. 266–277). Husserl contrasts this "I can" with Descartes's famous "I think," for the intentional structure of bodily subjectivity is not I think a certain thought *(ego cogito cogitatum),* but rather I can and do move myself in such and such a way (1989, pp. 159, 228, 273; see also Sheets-Johnstone 1999a, pp. 134–135, 230–232). In this way among others, perceptual experience involves a non-object-directed and implicit awareness of one's lived body, an intransitive and prereflective bodily self-awareness.[2]

One can, of course, also experience one's body as an object, for example, by looking directly at it or at one's reflection in a mirror. In such cases, one is dealing with what has been called the conscious "body image" by contrast with the unconscious "body schema" (Gallagher 1986a, 1995). The body image is the body as an intentional object of consciousness. It is consciousness of the body-as-object (Legrand 2006). In the body image, the body is experienced as owned by the experiencing subject, and the image is typically a partial representation insofar as conscious awareness usually attends to only one part or area of the body at a time. The body schema, however, is not an intentional object of consciousness or a partial representation of the body, but rather an integrated set of dynamic sensorimotor processes that organize perception and action in a subpersonal and nonconscious manner.

This distinction between body schema and body image leaves out a fundamental form of bodily experience, namely, prereflective bodily self-consciousness (Legrand 2006; Zahavi 1999, pp. 98, 240). The body schema is not phenomenologically available to the subject: "The body schema . . . is not the perception of 'my' body; it is not the image, the representation, or even the marginal consciousness of the body. Rather, it is precisely the style that organizes the body as it functions in communion with its environment" (Gallagher 1986b, p. 549). One's consciousness of one's body, however, is not limited to the body image, nor is the body image the most fundamental form of bodily consciousness. On the contrary, most of the time one's body is not present as an intentional object but is experienced in an implicit, tacit, and prereflective way. This kind of experience is consciousness of the body-as-subject. It corresponds to the relation of the lived body to itself, that is, to one's experience of one's body as perceiving and acting rather than as perceived.[3] Sartre (1956, p. liii) describes this sort of self-consciousness as "non-positional" or "non-thetic" because it does not posit one's body as an object; Merleau-Ponty calls it prereflective. Authors in the analytic philosophical tradition have described it as a nonobservational form of self-awareness (Shoemaker 1968, 1984).

The term *prereflective* is useful for our purposes because it has both a logical and temporal sense. Prereflective experience is logically prior to reflection, for reflection presupposes something to reflect upon; and it is temporally prior to reflection, for what one reflects upon is a hitherto unreflected experience.[4]

Prereflective bodily self-consciousness is evident in touch; not only do we feel the things we touch, but we feel ourselves touching them and touched by them. When I pick up a cup of hot tea, I feel the hot, smooth surface of the porcelain and the heat penetrating my fingers, and these sensations linger for a time after I have put the cup back down on the table. Such bodily experience offers not only the experience of physical events that relate one's body to things, but also the experience of sensorial events that relate one's subjectively lived body to itself. Usually these sensorial events are those in which one's body does not sense itself explicitly. In picking up the teacup, I live through the heat in my fingers, but the perceptual object is the teacup, not myself. But one's body can also sense itself explicitly, as when one hand touches the other. In this case, the one touching is the thing touched, and the thing touched senses itself as the one being touched.

Phenomenologists have reflected on this sort of bodily self-experience for a number of important reasons. There is a dynamic linkage of outward perception and inward feeling, so that one encounters one's own bodily sentience directly. One's body shows itself to be a material thing, but one animated from within by sensation and motility (Husserl 1989, p. 153). This form of bodily self-consciousness makes vividly apparent the lived body's unique status as a physical subject:

> When my right hand touches my left, I am aware of it as a "physical thing." But at the same moment, if I wish, an extraordinary event takes place: here is my left hand as well starting to perceive my right, *es wird*

Leib, es empfindet [it becomes body, it senses].[5] The physical thing becomes animate. Or, more precisely, it remains what it was (the event does not enrich it), but an exploratory power comes to rest upon or dwell in it. Thus I touch myself touching: my body accomplishes "a sort of reflection." In it, through it, there is not just the unidirectional relationship of the one who perceives to what he perceives. The relationship is reversed, the touched hand becomes the touching hand, and I am obliged to say that the sense of touch here is diffused into the body—that the body is a "perceiving thing," a "subject-object." (Merleau-Ponty 1964, p. 166)

Yet the touching and being-touched experiences never absolutely coincide. The two hands are never simultaneously touched and touching in relation to each other, but instead alternate their roles spontaneously (Merleau-Ponty 1962, p. 93). This spontaneous alternation is an expression of the body's dynamic sensorimotor relation to its own subjectivity, and this kind of self-relation distinguishes one's body from other things disclosed to one in perception (Husserl 1960, p. 97; Merleau-Ponty 1962, p. 93).

In this experience we can also catch a glimpse of how sensorimotor subjectivity can implicate a kind of sensorimotor intersubjectivity. A dynamic process of "self-othering" takes place in this experience, so that one's body becomes other to itself. When my left hand touches my right (or when I experience my body in other ways), there arises the possibility of experiencing myself in a way that anticipates both the way in which another bodily subject would experience me and the way in which I would experience the other. Bodily self-awareness is in this way conditioned by a form of otherness or alterity. According to Husserl, this self-othering dynamic is a crucial precondition for empathy, in the broad sense of being able to recognize others as subjects like oneself on the basis of their bodily presence (Zahavi 2003a, p. 113). It is precisely the body's double status of being a "subject-object," a subjectively lived body and a physical living body, as well as the dynamic interplay between ipseity (I-ness) and alterity (otherness) inherent in this ambiguity, that grounds one's ability to recognize other bodies as bodily subjects like oneself. I will return to these ideas in the last chapter of this book.

These brief phenomenological reflections are enough to show that consciousness involves the body in a unique double way. One experiences one's body as both subject and object. One's body is the intentional object of one's consciousness when one attends to one or another aspect or part of it. The content of this kind of bodily awareness corresponds to the body image or one's body-as-object. Bodily consciousness cannot be reduced to this sort of experience, however, because one also prereflectively and nonintentionally experiences one's body-as-subject while experiencing objects in the world (one's body-as-object included). The challenge for any scientific account of consciousness is to preserve this unique double character of bodily self-consciousness. Hence any scientific account must meet these two criteria: it must account for the ways in which one's body is intentionally directed toward the world, and it must account for a form of self-awareness that does not imply identification of one's body as an object.

Dorothée Legrand (2006) has worked to give an account of bodily self-consciousness that meets these criteria. She argues that bodily consciousness in the case of action consciousness is reducible neither to awareness of one's intentions to act nor to proprioception understood as an internal mode of identification of the body. Therefore bodily consciousness, she concludes, cannot be based on either efferent or afferent mechanisms alone. Bodily consciousness consists in experiencing one's body as a locus of the convergence of perception and action, and therefore depends on a matching of sensory and motor information, so that perception and action are coherent (see also Hurley 1998, pp. 140–143). There must be a specific match between (1) the intention to act, (2) the motor consequences of this intention, including the guidance of bodily movements during the executed action, and (3) the sensory consequences of this action, including both proprioception and exteroception.

An important implication of this account is that neural correlates of self-consciounsess will remain explanatorily opaque with respect to mental life as long as we understand them only in terms of their intrinsic neural properties and not in the dynamic sensorimotor context of the body as a whole (Hurley and Noë 2003; Legrand 2003; Thompson and Varela 2001). This point brings us to dynamic senorimotor accounts of perceptual experience and their significance for the body-body problem.

The Dynamic Sensorimotor Approach to
Perceptual Consciousness

In a recent article on neural plasticity and the dynamic sensorimotor approach to perceptual experience, Susan Hurley and Alva Noë (2003) distinguish three different types of explanatory gap for consciousness. The first they call the *absolute gap:* "Why should neural processes be 'accompanied' by any conscious experience at all?" (Hurley and Noë 2003, p. 132). The second and third types are *comparative gaps.* The *intermodal* comparative gap, on the one hand, is the question of why a certain neural activity gives rise to visual experience, for example, rather than auditory experience. The *intramodal* comparative gap, on the other hand, is the question of why a certain neural activity gives rise to experience as of red, say, rather than green. Hurley and Noë present the dynamic sensorimotor approach as concerned with these two comparative gaps, not the absolute gap. In other writings, J. Kevin O'Regan and Noë (2001b) present the sensorimotor appproach as also addressing the absolute gap (see also Myin and O'Regan 2002). I will look first at the sensorimotor approach to the comparative gaps and then examine the sensorimotor approach to the absolute gap.

Hurley and Noë address the comparative gaps by examining cases of neural plasticity. They distinguish between two ways in which qualities of perceptual experience can be affected by changes to the normal relation between sensory stimulation and neural activity.

1. "Cortical dominance" occurs when "cortical activation from a new peripheral input source gives rise to experience with a qualitative character normally or previously associated with cortical activity in that area" (Hurley and Noë 2003, p. 133). For example, in certain patients who experience phantom limbs, a stroke to the face is also felt as a stroke to the phantom arm. According to Ramachandran, who has studied such patients, the explanation for this experience is that after the amputation, the tactile area of somatosensory cortex subserving the face takes over the deafferented arm area (Ramachandran and Blakeslee 1998; Ramachandran and Hirstein 1998). When this arm area receives stimulation from its new, nonstandard source (the face), it retains its normal qualitative expression as a touch-to-arm feeling. Thus this cortical area "dominates" in the sense that it "retains its 'natural sign' or normal qualitative expression" (Hurley and Noë 2003, p. 133).

2. "Cortical deference" occurs when "cortical activity in a given area appears to take its qualitative expression from the character of its non-standard or new input source" (ibid.). When congenitally blind persons read Braille, for example, the tactile feeling of reading is mediated by activity in the visual cortex (Sadato et al. 1996). In this case, the qualitative expression of activity in visual cortex apparently "defers" to its new input source.

These cases of cortical dominance and deference raise explanatory-gap sorts of questions. Why does activity in somatosensory cortex or visual cortex feel one way rather than another? Why in the phantom-limb case is there touch-to-arm feeling rather than only touch-to-face feeling? Why in congenitally blind Braille readers is activity in visual cortex experienced as tactile feeling rather than visual feeling? "What explains whether qualitative expression goes one way or the other in particular cases? What explains why activity in a certain cortical area is experienced as *like this* rather than *like that*?" (Hurley and Noë 2003, p. 139).

The dynamic sensorimotor hypothesis is that "changes in qualitative expression are to be explained not just in terms of the properties of sensory inputs and of the brain region that receives them, but in terms of dynamic patterns of interdependence between sensory stimulation and embodied activity" (Hurley and Noë 2003, pp. 145–146). According to the dynamic sensorimotor approach, in particular O'Regan and Noë's (2001a) "sensorimotor contingency theory," perceptual experience is not an inner event or state of the brain but a skillful activity constituted in part by the perceiver's implicit, practical knowledge of the way sensory stimulation varies with movement. Different senses have different patterns of sensorimotor dependence, and perceivers have an implicit, skillful mastery of these differences. In vision, for example, when the eyes rotate, the sensory stimulation on the retina shifts and distorts in precise ways, determined by the size of the eye movement, the spherical shape of the retina, the varying density of the retinal photoreceptors from fovea to parafovea, and so on. When the body moves forward, the optic flow pattern on the retina expands; when the body moves backward, it contracts. When the eyes close during blinks, stimulation becomes uniform (the retinal image goes blank). These sensorimotor dependencies are distinctively visual, whereas those characteristic of hearing and touch have different structures. To perceive is to rely implicitly and fluently on these patterns of sensorimotor dependencies.

Hurley and Noë use this framework to explain the dominance/deference distinction. They take deference to be the norm and dominance the exception. There are other cases of deference besides tactile sensation being mediated by visual cortex in proficient Braille readers. For example, auditory neurons can develop visual properties as a result of surgical neural rerouting of visual stimulation to auditory cortex in newborn ferrets (Roe et al. 1990, 1992; Sur, Angelecci, and Sharma 1999). Another example comes from tactile-vision subsitution systems (TVSS), in which visual input to a camera that produces tactile stimulation on the skin leads to a kind of "tactile seeing" once subjects are able to control the camera's movements (Bach-y-Rita 2002). Such cases cannot be explained simply by reference to which particular cortical areas are activated because the endogenous or exogenous rerouting of sensory-cortical pathways changes the dynamic sensorimotor patterns in which those cortical areas participate.

According to this account, deference is predicted when sensorimotor patterns are systematically transformed by rerouting, and the agent is able to learn the new patterns and their relations to the old ones (as happens, for example, with TVSS). When either of these conditions is not met, however, then dominance is predicted. The second condition is not met when the agent is passive or unable to move. For example, TVSS brings about quasivisual experiences of being able to perceive the shape and movement of objects at a distance only if the subject is able to exercise active control of the camera and thereby integrate it into his or her sensorimotor repertoire. If, however, the rerouted sensory stimulation gives rise only to "dangling" cortical activity—activity that is not integrated into a dynamic sensorimotor pattern—then the first condition is not met and again dominance is predicted. For example, phantom-limb sensations can arise when a particular area of somatosensory cortex is taken over by an adjacent area as a result of deafferentation. If such dangling activity could be reintegrated into a dynamic sensorimotor pattern, then dominance would be predicted to give way to deference. This sort of reintegration seems to occur partially and temporarily in Ramachandran's mirror-box experiments, in which the patient is given illusory visual feedback from his intact hand when instructed to move his phantom hand (Ramachandran and Blakeslee 1998).

The psychologist Nicholas Humphrey, in his writings on the explanatory gap, has remarked that "there can be no hope of scientific progress so long as we continue to write down the identity [mental state m = brain state b] in such a way that the mind terms and the brain terms are patently *incommensurable* . . . We shall need to work on both sides to define the relevant mental states and brain states in terms of concepts that really do have dual currency—being equally applicable to the mental and the material" (Humphrey 2000, pp. 7, 10).

This strategy of working on both sides of the gap is precisely the strategy pursued by the dynamic sensorimotor approach.[6] Rather than looking to the intrinsic properties of neural activity—for example, the firing patterns of neurons in a given cortical area—this approach looks to the dynamic sensorimotor relations among neural activity, the body, and the world. The concept that has dual currency for this approach is the concept of dynamic sensorimotor activity. On the mental side, perceptual experiences are explicated as ways of acting, constituted in part by the perceiver's implicit and practical knowledge, or skillful mastery, of the relation between sensory experience and movement (Noë 2004; O'Regan and Noë 2001a). The senses have different characteristic patterns of sensorimotor dependence, and perceivers have an implicit, skillful mastery of these differences.

It is important to note that this account of the mental side does not identify perceptual experience with the occurrence of the sensorimotor dependencies themselves, but instead with the perceiver's exercising his or her skillful mastery of the invariant patterns of sensorimotor dependencies. Contrary to behaviorism, perceptual experience, being in part constituted by endogenous knowledge (skillful mastery), mediates between sensory stimulation and motor behavior. Contrary to cognitivism, however, experience does not intervene in a linear causal fashion between sensory "input" and motor "output." Sensory stimulation does not *cause* experience in us, which in turn *causes* our behavior, because "skillful activity (consisting of behavior and sensory stimulation) *is* the experience" (O'Regan and Noë 2001b, p. 1015). In other words, as a skillful activity of the whole animal or person, perceptual experience emerges from the continuous and reciprocal (nonlinear) interactions of sensory, motor, and cognitive processes, and is thereby constituted by motor behavior, sensory stimulation, and practical knowledge. On the brain side, neural states are described not at the level of their intrinsic neurophysiological properties or as mere neural correlates of mental states, but rather in terms of how they participate in dynamic sensorimotor patterns involving the whole active organism.

The dynamic sensorimotor approach is best understood not as an attempt to close the comparative explanatory gaps in a reductionist sense, but instead as an attempt to bridge these gaps by deploying new theoretical resources for understanding perceptual experience and neural processes in a coherent and overarching sensorimotor framework. For each modality of perceptual experience—seeing, hearing, touching, and so on—there is a corresponding pattern of sensorimotor interdependence that is constitutive of that modality. What it is to experience the world perceptually is to exercise one's bodily mastery or know-how of certain patterns of sensorimotor dependence between one's sensing and moving body and the environment. If distinct sensorimotor patterns are in this way constitutive of seeing, hearing, and so forth, then it does not make sense to ask, "Why do these sensorimotor patterns go with what it is like to see, rathen than to hear or to touch?" By contrast, one can always raise this sort of question with regard to neural activity in a particular brain area: "Why should brain activity in this region of cortex go with what it is like to see, rather than to hear or to touch?" The way to satisfy the hunger behind this sort of question is to give an account that embeds local neural activity in its dynamic sensorimotor context. For these reasons, sensorimotor patterns (encompassing endogenous neural activity) seem more promising than mere neural correlates of consciousness (Hurley and Noë 2003, pp. 146–147; Noë and Thompson 2004a, 2004b).

In working to bridge the comparative explanatory gaps, the sensorimotor approach contributes to the body-body problem. Yet Hurley and Noë's account does not fully address the core of the body-body problem—the problem of sentience. They admit that to use a dynamic sensorimotor approach to bridge the comparative explanatory gaps is not to bridge the absolute gap of why there is experience at all. Their aim is to explain why the agent has experience like this rather than like that, but not to explain what makes the agent a conscious subject in the first place. Indeed, their account presupposes sentience because they start from the assumption that the agent already has experience of one sort or another.

O'Regan and Noë (2001b), however, argue that the sensorimotor approach is also able to explain why the agent has experience at all, and

Myin and O'Regan (2002) repeat this argument.[7] Their proposal is relevant to the body-body problem. Examining their account will serve to indicate why and how the dynamic sensorimotor account should be combined with both an enactive account of autonomous selfhood and a phenomenological account of bodily self-consciousness.

O'Regan, Noë, and Myin's strategy is to give a sensorimotor account of certain characteristic properties of sensory experience. These properties are "ongoingness," "forcible presence," "ineffability," and "subjectivity," and they are supposed to constitute the phenomenal character of conscious experience:

> *Ongoingness* means that an experience is experienced as occurring to me, or happening to me here, now, as though I was inhabited by some ongoing process like the humming of a motor. *Forcible presence* is the fact that, contrary to other mental states like my knowledge of history, for example, a sensory experience imposes itself upon me from the outside, and is present to me without my making any mental effort, and indeed is mostly out of my voluntary control. *Ineffability* indicates that there is always more to the experience than what we can describe in words. Finally, *subjectivity* indicates that the experience is, in an unalienable way, *my* experience. It is yours or mine, his or hers, and cannot be had without someone having it. But subjectivity also indicates that the experience is something *for me*, something that offers me an opportunity to act or think with respect to whatever is experienced. (Myin and O'Regan 2002, p. 30)

Ongoingness and forcible presence are to be explained in terms of "bodiliness" and "grabbiness," two complementary features of the operation of sensorimotor systems. These features distinguish perceptual awareness from nonperceptual awareness or thought (O'Regan and Noë 2001b). Bodiliness is the dependence of sensory stimulation on one's bodily movements. The greater the change is to sensory stimulation as a result of bodily movement, the higher the degree of bodiliness. Thus our visual experience of a book that is in front of us has a high degree of bodiliness, compared with our nonperceptual awareness of a book in the next room. Blinking, eye movements, and head and torso movements modulate the way the book affects one's sensory apparatus, but they make no difference to the book in the next room. Grabbiness is the tendency of something to attract one's attention. Vision has high grabbiness, for sudden changes in the visual scene around us immediately attract our attention. Thus movements or changes in the book in front of us will immediately affect our sensory apparatus in an attention-grabbing way, whereas movements of the book in the next room will not. Bodiliness and grabbiness are supposed to explain forcible presence and ongoingness in the following way:

> (1) the book forces itself on us because any movement of the book causes us to direct our attention (our processing resources) to it. (2) The slightest movement of the relevant parts of our bodies modifies the sensory stimulation in relation to the book. Metaphorically, it is as if we are in *contact* with the book . . . [W]e can explain ongoingness in a similar way . . . The sense of an ongoing qualitative state consists, (a) in our understanding that movements of the body can currently give rise to the relevant pattern of sensory stimulation (bodiliness), and (b) in our understanding that the slightest change in what we are looking at will grab our attention and in that way force itself on us. In this way we explain why it seems to us as if there is something ongoing in us without actually supposing that there is anything ongoing, and in particular, without supposing that there is a corresponding ongoing physical mechanism or process. (O'Regan and Noë 2001b, p. 1012)

There remain the two characteristics of ineffability and subjectivity. According to the sensorimotor approach, perceptual experiences are active manifestations of a kind of skillful knowledge and are defined in terms of potential for action. In general, it is difficult to describe the knowledge underlying a skill. Thus ineffability is explained by our being unable to describe verbally our implicit, practical knowledge of the sensorimotor patterns constitutive of perceptual experience. Subjectivity is explained in the following way:

> Someone is perceptually aware of something because she is interacting with it. It is her putting all the resources she has onto whatever she is conscious of that makes her conscious of it. So, once she is conscious of it, it is "for her"—it is her subjective project to which she is devoting all her capacities. So, consciousness is, by definition, "for the subject." (Myin and O'Regan 2002, p. 39)

This account is illuminating to the extent that it accounts for important characteristics of experience in dynamic sensorimotor terms. It is incomplete in two ways, however. First, it needs to be underwritten by an enactive account of selfhood or agency in terms of autonomous systems. Second, it needs to enrich its account of subjectivity to include prereflective bodily self-consciousness.

The dynamic sensorimotor approach needs a notion of autonomous selfhood or agency because to explain perceptual experience it appeals to sensorimotor knowledge. Knowledge implies a knower or agent or self that embodies this knowledge. What organization does a sensorimotor system need to have in order to be a genuine sensorimotor agent with a correlative sensorimotor environment?

According to the enactive approach, agency and selfhood require that the system be autonomous. The minimal case of autonomy, as we have seen, is a living cell. A cell is an autopoietic system. It is a self-organizing network of biochemical reactions that produces a membrane boundary that regulates external boundary conditions and makes possible the internal reaction network. A cell actively relates to its environment so as to satisfy a viability constraint. Its "sensory" responses serve to trigger "motor" behaviors subject to the maintenance of autopoiesis (robustness) and regulated by internal norms of adaptivity (flexibility). We have also seen that this circular organization and mode of coupling with the environment are recapitulated in a more complex form by the nervous system. The nervous system establishes and maintains a sensorimotor cycle, whereby what one senses depends directly on how one moves, and how one moves depends directly on what one senses. Whereas biological selfhood in its core cellular form is brought forth by the operational closure of the autopoietic network, sensorimotor selfhood results from the operational closure of the nervous sytem (Varela 1997a). In either case, it is legitimate to invoke the notion of "self" because the dynamics of the system is characterized by an invariant topological pattern that is recursively produced by the system and that defines an outside to which the system is actively and normatively related.

Compare these cases to O'Regan and Noë's example of a missile guidance system. They write that this system " 'knows all about' or 'has mastery over' the possible input/output relationships that occur during airplane tracking" (O'Regan and Noë 2001a, p. 943). In this case, however, unlike the case of a motile bacterium or metazoan organism, the "sensorimotor knowledge" is merely attributed to the system by the observer, not original to the system itself. There is no genuine sensorimotor knowledge or mastery in this system because the system is not autonomous (does not have an autonomous organization). It is not a self-producing and self-maintaining system that actively regulates its own boundary conditions so as to ensure its continued viability. It does not produce and maintain its own sensorimotor identity as an invariant of its sensorimotor interactions with the environment. Hence it has no genuine sensorimotor agency or selfhood, and it cannot be said to be actively and normatively related to the world.

Adding an enactive account of selfhood to the dynamic sensorimotor approach goes only part way toward addressing the body-body problem. In addition, we need to include subjectivity in the sense of prereflective bodily self-awareness.

When I pick up a bottle and grasp it with my hands, I experience the bottle as other to me, but the feeling of grasping the bottle is immediately and noninferentially experienced as mine.[8] The intentional object of my tactile experience is the bottle, but at the same time I live through my grasping feeling in a nonintentional (non-object-directed) manner. To experience the feeling as mine I do not have to identify it as mine. Rather, the feeling comes with an intrinsic "mine-ness" or "first-personal givenness" or "ipseity" (I-ness) that constitutes its subjectivity (Kriegel 2003a, 2003b; Zahavi 2002a, 2003c).

Myin and O'Regan (2002), as we have seen, claim to account for the subjectivity of perceptual experience. Their strategy, following O'Regan and Noë (2001b), is to "de-reify" experience by teasing apart its different phenomenal characteristics—subjectivity, ongoingness, forcible presence, and ineffability. Yet ongoingness and forcible presence involve subjectivity in a constitutive way: "Ongoingness means that an experience is experienced *as occurring to me,* or *happening to me* here, now, as though *I was inhabited* by some ongoing process like the humming of a motor. Forcible presence is the fact that . . . a sensory experience *imposes itself upon me* from outside, and is *present to me* without any mental effort, and indeed is mostly under *my voluntary control*" (Myin and O'Regan 2002, p. 30; emphasis added). Each italicized phrase describes an aspect of the subjectivity or first-personal character of experience. Similarly, ineffability means that *my* perceptual experience seems indescribable *to me* in certain respects.

Myin and O'Regan devote most of their efforts to explaining ongoingness and forcible presence. What they write about subjectivity does not address the first-personal character and non-object-directed or intransitive self-awareness proper to experience (or experiencing), but instead deals with the subject's conscious access to the intentional objects of perceptual experience. They propose that consciousness is "for the subject," because to be conscious of X is to put all one's skillful sensorimotor and attentional resources onto X, such that one is aware not simply of X but also of the opportunities for further action or thinking that X affords. This explanation is plausible as an account of what it is for *a given object X* to be "for the subject" (or accessible to the subject): X is the intentional object of the subject's attention (or is available to attention). But this account does not explain what it is for one's *perceptual experience of X* to be intransitively self-aware and thus to have first-personal givenness. For example, this account might explain what it is for the woolly red of the carpet to be the content of my current visual experience, but it does not explain what it is for the experience of seeing the woolly red of the carpet to be phenomenally manifest as mine. In other words, we are given an account of conscious access to the intentional objects of perceptual experience, but not of subjectivity in the sense of the first-personal quality of experience as such. Thus there remains a significant gap in this account.

A related problem is that this account identifies all consciousness with transitive or object-directed experience and all consciousness with attention (O'Regan and Noë 2001a, pp. 944, 955, 960). These identifications are too narrow.

Consider first the identification of consciousness with attention. Ned Block gives the example of being engaged in an intense conversation while a drill rattles away outside the window (Block 1997, pp. 386–387). Engrossed in the conversation, one does not notice the noise, but then eventually and all of sudden one does notice it. Block uses this example to illustrate the distinction between a mental state's being "phenomenally conscious" (subjectively experienced) and its being "access conscious" (accessible to thought, verbal report, and action guidance). His proposal is that insofar as one is aware of the noise all along, one is phenomenally conscious of it but not necessarily access conscious of it. When one notices the noise, one becomes access conscious of it (and perhaps also realizes that one has been hearing it all

along), so that one now has both phenomenal consciousness and access consciousness of the sound.

O'Regan and Noë (2001a, p. 964) dispute this description, claiming
that one does not hear the drill until one notices and attends to it.
One's auditory system may respond selectively to the noise, but one
makes no use of the information provided thereby, nor is one poised
to make any use of that information until one notices the drill. Hence
there is no ground for thinking we have a case of phenomenal consciousness without access consciousness. In the absence of access,
there is no phenomenal consciousness.

From the point of view of phenomenological analysis, both descriptions seem rather flat. The experiential difference between not noticing
and then noticing a noise is treated statically, as if it were a discrete state
transition, with no extended temporal dynamics, and there is no differentiation within the temporal dynamics of the experience between implicit and explicit aspects. One may notice a noise in an implicit way, in
which case one lives through the sound without grasping it as a distinct
object. One may also notice a noise in the sense of turning one's attention to it or having one's attention be captured by it, in which case the
noise is grasped as a distinct object. Finally, at an implicit level, it is important to differentiate between moments of comparatively weak and
strong affective force on the part of the noise as the experience unfolds.[9]

Two distinctions from Husserlian phenomenology, mentioned in
Chapter 2, are relevant here. The first is between *activity* and *passivity*.
"Activity" means taking a cognitive position in acts of attending,
judging, valuing, wishing, and so forth. "Passivity" means being involuntarily influenced and affected by something. The second distinction
is between *receptivity* and *affectivity*. "Receptivity" means responding to
something that is passively affecting one and hence presupposes a
prior affection (Zahavi 1999, p. 116). "Affection" means being affectively influenced or perturbed. The idea is that whatever becomes noticeable must already have been affecting one and must have some
kind of affective force or allure, or affective "grabbiness," in relation to
one's attention. As psychologists know, typically attention is affectively
motivated (Derryberry and Tucker 1994). Affective allure or grabbiness implies a dynamic gestalt or figure-ground structure: something
becomes noticeable, at whatever level, owing to the strength of its allure or grabbiness, emerging into affective prominence, salience, or

relief, while other things become less noticeable owing to the comparative weakness of their allure. This dynamic interplay of passivity and activity, affectivity and receptivity, expresses an ongoing "operative intentionality" underlying object-directed or intentional consciousness (Merleau-Ponty 1962, pp. xviii, 418).

These considerations suggest that hearing the sound before noticing it should be counted as a case of phenomenal consciousness. One does consciously hear the sound before noticing it, if "noticing" means turning one's attention to it. The sound is experienced implicitly and prereflectively. One lives through the state of being affected by the sound without thematizing the sound or one's affectedness by it. This prereflective consciousness counts as phenomenal consciousness because the sound's appearance and affective influence have a phenomenal character, though an indeterminate one. As Merleau-Ponty states, "attention . . . is the active constitution of a new object which makes explicit and articulate what was until then presented as no more than an indeterminate horizon" (Merleau-Ponty 1962, p. 30). Hence it does not seem right to say that one has no experience of the sound at all until one notices it. Nevertheless, there is no reason to believe that this experience is not also a case of access consciousness. After all, one is poised to make use of one's implicit and prereflective hearing of the sound. The content of the experience is at least accessible, even if it is not accessed explicitly.[10] If we imagine, however, that one is not cognitively poised in any way to rely on the sound, then we would need a reason to believe that one is nonetheless phenomenally conscious of it rather than simply discriminating or differentially responding to it nonconsciously, but no reason is forthcoming simply from this example.

Consider now the claim that all consciousness is transitive consciousness. We have already seen that intransitive or nonintentional bodily self-consciousness is constitutive of perceptual experience. When I see the woolly red of the carpet, I am transitively conscious of the woolly-red carpet, but I also consciously experience my seeing (my seeing is intransitively self-aware). When I grasp the bottle, I am transitively aware of the bottle, but I also consciously experience my grasping (my grasping is intransitively self-aware). It does not seem right to maintain either that my seeing or grasping is not conscious or that I am merely poised to become transitively conscious of them.

The first interpretation looks incoherent. It is hard to make sense of the idea that one could have a conscious perception of X without experiencing one's perception of X.

The second interpretation is conceptually and phenomenologically unclear. Does one's being poised to become transitively aware of one's perceiving (through an attentional shift) itself have a phenomenal or subjective character? If it does not, then it would seem to be an unconscious disposition or a subpersonal disposition of one's nervous system. The problem then is to explain how a completely unconscious or subpersonal disposition can account for the apparently occurrent character of nonintentional bodily self-consciousness. But if one's being thus poised does have a phenomenal and subjective character—if one feels thus poised—then that feeling needs to be accounted for as part of the subjective character of experience. This feeling cannot be accounted for simply in terms of transitive consciousness, precisely because it does not have a transitive or subject-object structure. On the contrary, it would seem to be another way of describing or getting at the phenomenon of intransitive and nonintentional bodily self-consciousness.

These reflections show that a complete account of perceptual experience requires an account of nonintentional (intransitive, non-object-directed), prereflective bodily self-consciousness. Although the dynamic sensorimotor approach has made significant progress in accounting for transitive perceptual consciousness, further work needs to be done to address bodily self-consciousness. This work will be crucial for progress on the body-body problem.

In this chapter I hope to have shown that the dynamic sensorimotor approach to perceptual experience can be profitably combined with an enactive account of selfhood and a phenomenological account of bodily self-consciousness. I also hope to have shown that this synthesis is needed in order to make headway on the explanatory gap recast as the body-body problem.

Central to the enactive approach is the idea that mind science and phenomenology can be linked in a reciprocal and mutually illuminating way (Varela, Thompson, and Rosch 1991). The enactive approach uses phenomenology to explicate mind science and mind science to explicate phenomenology. Concepts such as lived body and organism, bodily selfhood and autonomous agency, the intentional arc and dynamic sensorimotor dependencies, can thus become mutually illuminating rather than merely correlational concepts (Gallagher 1997; Varela 1996). This idea of the mutual illumination between phenomenology and mind science figures prominently in the remaining chapters of this book.

The next chapter continues the phenomenological analysis of consciousness begun in this chapter and puts this analysis to work in the scientific debate about mental imagery.

◆ ◆ ◆

TEN

Look Again

Consciousness and Mental Imagery

A LOT HAS HAPPENED in mind science and philosophy since the heyday of the mental imagery debate in the 1970s and 1980s.[1] The computer model or computational theory of mind, once considered to be "the only game in town," is now called classical cognitive science and coexists, separately and in various hybrid forms, with connectionism and embodied dynamicism. Consciousness, once dismissed as marginal to the scientific understanding of the mind, is now a subject of great interest. More striking still is the new and growing appreciation for the usefulness of introspection in the scientific investigation of cognition (Jack and Roepstorff 2002, 2003, 2004).

Given these developments, it is regrettable that the recent reappearance of the imagery debate takes no account of them (Kosslyn, Ganis, and Thompson 2003; Kosslyn, Thompson, and Ganis 2006; Pylyshyn 2002, 2003a, 2003b, 2003c). In particular, no effort is made to clarify the conscious experience of mental imagery. Instead, researchers assume that the subjective character of imagery experience is obvious and that there is no need for a careful phenomenological analysis of the way we experience this type of mental activity. Yet debate still reigns about the nature of mental imagery and its relation to cognition and the brain. If there is to be progress in understanding mental imagery as a form of human experience, and not merely as a form of mental representation, then we need to do better.

Using mental imagery research, I aim to show how mind science stands to gain from phenomenological analysis of experience. Let me explain what I mean by phenomenological analysis.

Earlier in this book, I distinguished three types of phenomenological analysis—static, genetic, and generative. It is the first of these three, static phenomenology, that will mainly concern us in this chapter. (Genetic phenomenology will occupy us in Chapters 11 and 12, and generative phenomenology will play a role in Chapter 13.) Static phenomenology analyzes how the intentional objects of experience are constituted or brought to awareness by virtue of certain invariant formal structures of consciousness. Henceforth, in this chapter, when I describe phenomenological analysis, I am referring to static phenomenology.

One of the central concerns of phenomenology is to uncover what belongs to the subjective experience of a given sort of mental activity, such as perceiving, imagining, or remembering. Phenomenology focuses not simply on the qualitative character of what is experienced, the objects of experience, but also on the subjective character of the mental activity itself, the acts of experience. A phenomenological analysis of visual perception, for example, focuses not only on the qualitative character of what we see—objects arrayed in space with various perceptible qualities—but also on what the activity of seeing is like, on what it feels like to encounter the world visually. Phenomenology is concerned with what seeing is like, as compared with hearing, or imagining, or remembering. What experience is like in this sense is constitutive of what experience is. Phenomenology is thus concerned with the constitutive features of experience.

Phenomenological analysis operates at the personal level. When we describe experience we are describing it as belonging to the whole person, and our descriptions have a holistic and normative character. We describe the interrelations of perceiving, intending, feeling, imagining, and acting, and we try to make sense of these interrelations in various norm-governed ways. By contrast, when we describe the neural processes on which experience depends, we are describing subpersonal phenomena, and our descriptions do not have this holistic and normative character. When, for example, in an experiment on mental imagery, I attribute to you a certain mental state, such as visualizing the rotation of some geometrical figure, I make an attribution at the personal level. Whether this attribution makes sense depends partly on what else I take you to believe (for example, about object geometry and spatial properties, but also about your understanding of the task instructions). When I attribute to an area of your brain a certain pattern of electromagnetic activity, however, I make an attribution at the subpersonal level, and this attribution is not subject to these holistic and normative considerations.

Phenomenological analysis can do important philosophical and scientific work. It can help to clarify the conceptual relation between accounts of experience at the personal level and accounts of cognitive and neural processes at the subpersonal level, and it can help to guide and inform experimental research in mind science.

In this chapter, I sketch a phenomenological analysis of imagery experience. The main point of this analysis is to call into question the usual conception of a "phenomenal mental image" as some kind of mental picture inspected by the mind's eye. Both "pictorialists" and "descriptionalists," the two main rivals of the imagery debate, assume that imagery experience seems subjectively to be the experience of mental pictures. What they disagree about is whether the subpersonal mental representations used in visual problem solving are depictive or propositional in form. Thus both theories agree in their assumptions about the phenomenology of mental imagery. What they disagree about is whether that phenomenology corresponds to or accurately reflects the underlying representational structures and processes. Yet both theories, I suggest, get the phenomenology wrong. According to the phenomenological account to be presented in this chapter, which closely follows Husserl's phenomenological analyses of imagination (Husserl 2006) and the elaboration of these analyses by Marbach (1993), in visual imaging or visualizing, we do not experience mental pictures. Instead we visualize an object or scene by mentally enacting or entertaining a possible perceptual experience of that object or scene. This phenomenological account of imagery experience, as we will see, provides important constraints on theories of mental imagery in psychology and cognitive neuroscience and supports an enactive approach to mental imagery. It also provides a vantage point from which to raise certain critical questions about Dennett's exclusively third-person phenomenological method or "heterophenomenology," which he first proposed in the context of the mental imagery debate (Dennett 1978).

Experience and the Imagery Debate

The subjective experience of mental imagery has occupied a problematic place in the imagery debate since this debate's inception in the early 1970s. On the one hand, everyone agrees that the experience of

imagery exists and that any adequate theory of imagery must ultimately be able to account for it. On the other hand, the main concern
of imagery theories has not been to explain imagery experience but
rather to explain the ability of individuals to solve problems in various
kinds of cognitive tasks in which they report using imagery. Classic examples are judging whether two objects of different orientation have
identical shapes by "mentally rotating" one to see whether it can be
brought into correspondence with the other, or "mentally scanning" a
visualized map in order to determine whether a particular object is
present on it (see Kosslyn 1980, 1994; Kosslyn et al. 1981). Although
imagery research relies on reports of imagery experience as a source
of data, the two main rival theories of the mental representations involved in imagery, pictorialism and descriptionalism, have left imagery
experience as such unaccounted for.

Pictorialism and descriptionalism are theories about the subpersonal representations and processes that are supposed to be causally
implicated in imagery tasks. According to pictorialism (whose principal exponent is Stephen Kosslyn), these representations are depictive (or "quasipictorial"), which means that they represent by virtue of
their spatial format. In a depictive representation, each part of the object is represented by a pattern of points, and the spatial relations
among these patterns correspond to the spatial relations among the
object's parts.[2] It is well known, for example, that in primates, the first
cortical area to receive signals from the retina, known as V1, is organized retinotopically. In other words, neurons in this area are organized in a way that roughly preserves the spatial structure of the retina.
Although this cortical representation of the retina is laid out in physical space, a depictive space need not be physical, according to
Kosslyn, but could be specified purely functionally, like an array in a
computer.

According to descriptionalism (whose principal exponent is Zenon
Pylyshyn), the mental representations involved in vision and imagery
represent by virtue of their propositional structure. Pylyshyn argues
that the notion of a purely functional space has no explanatory value
in accounting for the actual format of mental representations (2003a,
pp. 359–368). He also contends that the activation of retinotopically
organized brain areas in certain types of visual mental imagery tasks
does not show that imagery or vision involves depictive representations

laid out in the physical space of the brain, for mental images and top-ographical patterns of activation in cortical visual areas fail to cor-respond in a number of ways. (For example, the 3D spatial structure of what we perceive or imagine was never present on the 2D retina or its retinotopic cortical projection in V1) (Pylyshyn 2003a, pp. 387–426). In Pylyshyn's descriptionalist view, mental imagery is the mental repre-sentation of how things look or would look, based on our tacit propo-sitional knowledge of visual properties and relations.

Although scientific research on imagery designed to test these two theories must rely on first-person reports of imagery experience as an in-dispensable source of data, neither descriptionalism nor pictorialism has provided any explanatory bridge back to imagery experience at the personal level from their subpersonal representational theories. Im-agery experience is used on the way in but is left in limbo on the way out.

We can trace this situation back to Pylyshyn's opening round of the debate in 1973 (Pylyshyn 1973). Pylyshyn acknowledged that "imagery is a pervasive form of experience" and that "[w]e cannot speak of con-sciousness without, at the same time, implicating the existence of im-ages" (1973, p. 2). But he argued that imagery experience does not re-veal the content of mental representations or the information processing functions operating on those representations. Imagery ex-perience is not so much silent as positively misleading. The ordinary or commonsense conception of an image is that of a picture, but the mental representations mobilized in imagery tasks are best character-ized as descriptive and propositional, not pictorial. Pylyshyn's conclu-sion was that the concept of a mental image is not a useful explanatory construct in psychology.

Kosslyn and Pomerantz, in their reply to Pylyshyn in 1977, defended the explanatory importance of imagery (Kosslyn and Pomerantz 1981). They argued that introspection, when taken together with behavioral performance data, is an important source of evidence. They also re-marked that the experience of imagery is undeniable and that studying it in its own right is a legitimate enterprise (Kosslyn and Pomerantz 1981, p. 159; see also Kosslyn, Thompson, and Ganis 2006, p. 48). Yet they offered no such study or any scientific explanation of mental im-agery informed by this kind of study. Instead, they sketched a theory of imagery that seemed to rely on the problematic assumption that the *content* of imagery experience corresponds to the *format* of the underlying representation. This type of assumption has been called *analytical isomorphism* (Pessoa, Thompson, and Noë 1998; Thompson, Noë, and Pessoa 1999). Analytical isomorphism is the idea that successful explanation requires there be an isomorphism (one-to-one correspondence) between the phenomenal content of subjective experience and the structure or format of the underlying neural representations. This idea involves conflating properties of what is *represented* (representational *contents*) with properties of the *representings* (representational *vehicles*).

Kosslyn and Pomerantz seem to have implicitly relied on analytical isomorphism when they proposed that an image is a temporary depictive representation in active memory generated from more abstract information in long-term memory. In this view, an image is a spatial pattern of activation in a visual buffer. (In the most recent statement of Kosslyn's theory, the visual buffer is a single functional structure comprising the topographically organized areas of the occipital cortex; see Kosslyn, Thompson, and Ganis 2006, p. 136.) Kosslyn and Pomerantz implied that the images the person experiences *are* these "surface images" in the visual buffer.

In a subsequent paper, Kosslyn and his colleagues qualified the relation by explaining that the term *image* refers to representations in active memory, not an experience. In this way, the meaning of "image" becomes primarily subpersonal. Thus they wrote: "The experience of 'having an image' is taken as an indication that an image representation is present in active memory; the question whether one can have an image representation without the experience is left open" (Kosslyn et al. 1981, p. 133). Over the years Kosslyn has enlarged and refined his theory, but this gap between subpersonal representation and experience has not gone away. Thus, in his 1994 book, *Image and Brain,* he writes:

> [M]ost interest in psychology has focused on only one facet of imagery—its role in information processing, not its phenomenology or role in emotional life. In this book we will focus on the nature of the internal events that underlie the experience of "seeing with the mind's eye"; we shall not consider the qualities of the experience itself. The term "image" will refer to the internal representation that is used in information processing, not the experience itself. The experience of imagery is a sign that the underlying brain events are taking place, and hence plays an invaluable role in the research—but is not in its own right the present topic of study. (Kosslyn 1994, p. 3)

Here we can easily see that the concept of a mental image has become almost completely subpersonal, while imagery experience at the personal level remains mainly a heuristic for getting at the subpersonal level.

This divergence between the personal and subpersonal levels is closely related to the familiar explanatory gap for consciousness. There is a conceptual and epistemological gap between accounts of neural and cognitive processes at biological and functional levels, and consciousness in the sense of subjective experience. Thus, in the case of mental imagery, no current scientific account of the mechanisms of imagery ("the internal representation that is used in information processing") is sufficient to account for the subjective experience of imagery ("the experience itself").

This chasm between the personal and subpersonal levels, and the related explanatory gap between subjective experience and internal representation, are also evident in Pylyshyn's recent restatement of the descriptionalist view (Pylyshyn 2002, 2003a, 2003c). What is distinctive about mental imagery, according to Pylyshyn, is not that it involves a special depictive form of representation; rather, it is that the contents of the thoughts we experience as images represent how things look or would look to us. Pylyshyn is aware that how things look is a matter of the content of our conscious experience. He admits that "[a]s scientists we cannot ignore the contents of our conscious experience, because this is one of the principal ways of knowing what we see and what our thoughts are about" (Pylyshyn 2003a, p. xi). Nevertheless, he believes that the contents of experience are "insidious" and "misleading," and "contaminate" many scientific theories of perception and imagery (2003a, pp. xi, 2). In his view, to allow subjective experience to guide or constrain scientific theories of the mind is to fall prey to a "phenomenological snare" (2003b, p. 112). Hence he does not allow that a phenomenological account of seeing and imagining could be profitably linked to a scientific account of perception and imagery.

I disagree. It is not only possible, but also necessary, to pursue phenomenology and experimental science as mutually constraining and enlightening projects. If our aim is to have a comprehensive understanding of the mind, then focusing on the nature of the internal events that underlie imagery experience, without considering the qualities of the experience itself, will not take us far.

A good way to start is by scrutinizing the phenomenological assumptions made by imagery theorists. Although descriptionalists and picto-rialists adopt different attitudes toward imagery experience, they share a deeper view of its phenomenal character, and they assume a certain conception of what imagining is as an intentional act. Descriptionalists argue that our subjective experience of imagery is no guide to the format of the underlying mental representations, whereas pictorialists argue that our imagery experience does correspond, at least partially, to this representational format (see Kosslyn, Thompson, and Ganis 2006, p. 48). Nevertheless, theorists of both camps seem to agree that in imagery we experience "phenomenal mental images." The term *phenomenal mental image* has been used to refer to the "seeming objects of image experiences," by contrast with the term *functional mental image*, which refers to the internal representations involved in imagery (Rey 1981, p. 124). Usually, phenomenal mental images are assumed to be pictorial or depictive objects we *see* "with our mind's eye," though it is also sometimes said that phenomenal mental images are not things we see but things we *have* (Block 1983). In either case, it is usu-ally taken for granted that the subjective experience of mental imagery is properly characterized as the experience of having (seeing or un-dergoing) a phenomenal mental picture.

It is important to notice that this assumption is a conceptual and phenomenological one about what constitutes imagery experience at the personal level. One way to put this assumption is that our imagery experience involves the belief that in such experience we see or have images in the mind. Descriptionalists think this belief is, strictly speaking, false. According to descriptionalism, the mental representa-tions involved in imagery are not pictorial, introspection is misleading and unreliable, and our experience of imagery is a kind of "grand illu-sion." Pictorialists, however, think this belief is true or at least partially accurate. According to pictorialism, the mental representations in-volved in imagery are depictive, and introspection is sometimes reli-able. As Kosslyn, Thompson, and Ganis state in their recent case for the pictorialist view: "from the time of Plato at least up to William James . . . philosophers and psychologists have relied on their intro-spections to argue that depictive images play a functional role in psy-chology. If this view is correct, we will gain important insight into the nature of consciousness—given the striking correspondences between some aspects of phenomenology and the underlying representational format" (2006, p. 20).

We thus arrive at two deeper assumptions these theories share. First, our imagery experience subjectively seems to us to be pictorial, and so any phenomenological characterization of imagery experience must describe this experience as pictorial. Second, if how things seem to us subjectively at the personal level does not match or correspond to the internal representations at the subpersonal level, then our subjective experience is a kind of illusion—it is not really what it subjectively seems to be.

We can also find these assumptions, particularly the second one, in the study of visual perception. Let me mention two examples relevant to imagery research.

The first is Dennett's discussion of visual filling-in or perceptual completion (Dennett 1991a, pp. 344–356; see also Pessoa, Thompson, and Noë 1998; Thompson, Noë, and Pessoa, 1999). There is a blind spot in each eye corresponding to the region where the optic nerve leaves the retina and there are no photoreceptors. We are not usually aware of the blind spot. The blind spots of the two eyes do not overlap; something that falls on the blind spot of one retina falls outside the blind spot of the other; and our eyes are in constant motion. But the blind spot can be revealed using simple visual demonstrations. In these demonstrations, an object (such as small black dot on a white page) that falls within the area of the blind spot disappears from view, while this area seems to be filled in with the color and brightness of its surround. Dennett pointed out that from the fact that one has no awareness of a gap in one's visual field, it does not follow that there must be a neural representation of a gapless visual field, for the brain might simply ignore the absence of receptor signals at the blind spot. The absence of a representation is not the same as a representation of an absence. Even if the brain does represent the information as absent, there is no necessity that it actively fill in the missing information.

Nevertheless, there is neurophysiological and psychophysical evidence for active neural filling-in processes (Pessoa and de Weerd 2003; Pessoa, Thompson, and Noë 1998). What concerns me now, however, is the inference Dennett went on to make on the assumption that there is no filling-in. He argued that because there is no filling-in, there is a gap in our visual experience of the world but one we do not notice. Our experience seems continuous and gapless when it is really gappy and discontinuous. In Dennett's words: "One of the most striking features about consciousness is its discontinuity—as revealed in the blind spot, and saccadic gaps, to take the simplest examples. The discontinuity of consciousness is striking because of the *apparent* continuity of consciousness" (Dennett 1991a, p. 356). Dennett's conclusion is well known: we are all in the grip of a subjective illusion about our own consciousness.

Here is my second example. It is well known that perceivers often fail to notice large changes in visual scenes even when those changes are fully open to view. This phenomenon is called change blindness and is usually taken to show (among other things) the attention-dependent character of perception (O'Regan and Noë 2001a; Simons and Levin 1997). Unless you actively attend to detail in your environment, you do not perceive that detail. One striking example is a video clip of six people, three in black and three in white, who pass around two basketballs. You are instructed to count the number of passes made by the players in white. Once the clip is finished, you are asked if you noticed anything strange. The clip is then replayed, and you are told not to count the passes but to watch for anything unusual. This time you notice that a person dressed in a gorilla suit walks through the players, stops in the middle and beats his chest, and then slowly walks away (Simons and Chabris 1999).[3] It is hard to believe that you could have missed such a striking event the first time around. On the basis of such demonstrations, as well as other studies of visual attention (see Mack and Rock 1998), a number of scientists and philosophers have concluded that despite our impression of seeing a rich and detailed visual environment, we see very little of what is there before us. Our subjective impression that our visual experience is rich in detail is a "grand illusion" (see Noë 2002c).

This way of thinking about experience—as being illusorily pictorial in one's own subjective first-person case—is widespread in contemporary mind science. Consider the following statements about perception and imagery:

> Open your eyes and look around. It probably seems as though you see a rich, detailed and ever-changing picture of the world: a "stream of vision." (Blackmore 2003, p. 79)

> [D]espite the poor quality of the visual apparatus, we have the subjective impression of great richness and "presence" of the visual world. But this richness and presence are actually an illusion. (O'Regan 1992, p. 484)

We believe that we see a complete, dynamic picture of a stable, uniformly detailed, and colourful world . . . [but] our stable visual world
may be constructed out of a brief retinal image and a very sketchy,
higher-level representation along with a pop-out mechanism to redirect
attention. The richness of our visual world is, to this extent, an illusion.
(Blackmore et al. 1995, p. 1075)

One reason why understanding vision is so difficult is that we who are
attempting to understand the process are so embedded in the phenomenology of perception: We know what it *feels* like to see. We look
out and see the world, and we cannot escape the impression that what
we have in our heads is a detailed, stable, extended, and veridical display that corresponds to the scene before us. (Pylyshyn 2003a, pp. 2–3)

Kosslyn's view has great initial plausibility. For we seem to be aware of
images—pictures in the mind—playing an important role in thought.
(Sterelny 1990, p. 608)

The fact that we seem to use representations in our head in the same way
that we use maps and diagrams is a special case of the similarity between
perception and imagination. Just as we perceive the relative locations of
two cities on a real map without apparent effort or inference, so too we
seem to be able to employ the inner eye to perceive these locations on an
inner, memory-generated, representation. (Sterelny 1990, p. 615)

Cognitive science is rife with ideas that offend our intuitions. It is ar-
guable that nowhere is the pull of the subjective stronger than in the
study of perception and mental imagery. It is not easy for us to take seriously the proposal that the visual system creates something like
symbol structures in our brain since it seems intuitively obvious that
what we have in our mind when we look out onto the world, as well as
when we close our eyes and imagine a scene, is something that *looks like*
the scene, and hence whatever it is that we have in our heads must be
much more like a *picture* than a description. Though we may know that
this cannot be literally the case, that it would do no good to have an
inner copy of the world, this reasoning appears to be powerless to dis-
suade us from our intuitions. (Pylyshyn 2003a, p. 157)

Nobody denies that when we engage in mental imagery we seem to be
making pictures in our head—in some sense. The question is: Are we

really? That is, do the properties in our brains have any of the properties of pictures? (Dennett 2002a, p. 189)

In these statements, we see theorists committing themselves to the
following problematic ideas:

1. The phenomenal character of visual experience in general and
   imagery experience in particular is pictorial (what we see and visualize seems to us like the content of a picture); hence, any
   phenomenological account of imagery experience must describe this experience as pictorial.
2. If the phenomenal character of experience at the personal level
   does not match or correspond to the internal representations in
   our brains at the subpersonal level, then our experience is illusory (it is not really what it subjectively seems to be).
3. Visual experience is permeated by the belief that certain kinds
   of representations are created in our brains during perception
   and imagery, namely, depictive or pictorial representations ("pictures in the head").
4. The phenomenal character of visual experience, whether in perception or mental imagery, is intuitively obvious or evident to ca-
   sual reflection; hence, there is no need for careful phenomenological analysis. (Visual experience obviously seems pictorial.)

These ideas deserve to be criticized for a variety of reasons. First, it is
not obvious that the phenomenal character of perceptual experience
is pictorial, especially in the photographic sense assumed in some of
the above passages. On the contrary, the content of our experience is
not picture-like in a number of ways (see Noë 2004, Chapter 2). For example, we do not take ourselves to see the whole scene before us in
sharp focus and uniform detail from the center to the periphery of our
field of view. Rather, we know we can bring things into view by moving
our eyes, turning our head, and changing our bodily position. Another
difference is that our visual field, unlike a picture, is unbounded; there
is a sense in which it has no limit.

Second, there is no need for a precise match between what we experience in perception and whatever internal representations there are
in our brains. For example, we visually experience the world to be rich
in detail not because we must represent all that detail inside our heads

at any given moment, but because we have constant access to the presence and detail of the world, and we know how to make use of this access (O'Regan 1992; O'Regan and Noë 2001a).

Third, whatever impression we supposedly have of there being pictorial representations in our head when we perceive is not a first-person impression of experience but a third-person theoretical belief. Hence the illusion is a theorist's illusion, not an experiential one.

Dennett's response to this point is that the belief may be a theorist's belief, "but it turns out we are all theorists" (Dennett 1998, p. 754; see also Dennett 2002b). According to his view, perceivers tacitly believe they have pictorial representations in their heads corresponding to what they perceive, and perceptual experience is partly constituted by this belief. But this view seems misguided. Perceptual experience is directed toward the world, not toward the brain. Beliefs about what goes on in the brain are no part of ordinary perceptual experience. In particular, perceptual experience involves no commitment to the belief that we have pictures (or any other kind of representation) in our brains when we see (Noë 2002b, 2004, pp. 55–59; Noë, Pessoa, and Thompson 2000).

Finally, the foregoing points are not immediately obvious but emerge from careful phenomenological considerations (sometimes in tandem with experimental investigation). Although subjective experience is intimate and familiar, it hardly follows that its phenomenal character is easy to specify. We need to distinguish between what seems intuitively obvious and what requires careful phenomenological analysis to discern.

In the rest of this chapter, I build on these ideas and apply them to the phenomenological analysis of visual mental imagery. According to this analysis, visual experience is not pictorial in the way many theorists assume. The phenomenal content of perceptual experience is dissimilar from the content of a picture in certain crucial respects, and visualizing is not an experience in which we seem to see or have a mental picture. Visualizing is rather the activity of mentally representing an object or a scene by way of mentally enacting or entertaining a possible perceptual experience of that object or scene. If this analysis is correct, then contrary to what pictorialists assume, the phenomenology of imagery experience provides no particular reason to suppose that there are depictive representations in the brain corresponding to the content of what we see or visualize. Of course, this point hardly rules out the possibility that depictive representations in the brain play a functional role in perception and imagery. This possibility is an empirical matter to be determined by cognitive neuroscience. What the point does rule out, however, is that the depictive format of these representations corresponds to (or is identical with or constitutes) the content of what we experience when we see or visualize.

Picturing Visual Experience

To frame my discussion I propose to make use of Ernst Mach's famous attempt to portray his own visual field (Figure 10.1) (Mach 1959).[4] Lying on a divan with his right eye shut, Mach tried to depict not his room, but the content of his (monocular) visual field. We can consider his drawing on several levels. First, the drawing exemplifies a certain pictorial conception of visual experience. The content of perception is like that of a realistic picture. Second, given this conception, it is natural to think that were Mach to close his eyes and imagine his view of the room, he would, on the basis of memory, be creating or calling up a mental image, a picture in the head (probably sketchy and indistinct by comparison with perception). Third, Mach's drawing is itself a pictorial object; it is a material entity that depicts a certain scene. It is thus not simply an object of perceptual experience but an object of pictorial experience. We need to look more closely at these three aspects of Mach's drawing.

Mach's drawing is meant to be a depiction of what it is like for him to see his study (with one eye), a depiction of the phenomenal content of his visual experience. The drawing also invites us, the external viewer of the picture, to imagine taking up Mach's position as the internal viewer of the represented scene, so that our visual experience would, as it were, coincide with his. Yet readily available phenomenological evidence shows that our visual experience is not like this depiction (see Noë 2004, pp. 49–50, 69–72). Consider that we have poor peripheral vision. Hold a playing card at arms length just within your field of view; you will not be able to tell its color, suit, or number. Stare at a word or phrase on a page of text, and you will be able to make out only a few of the other words. These simple demonstrations show, contrary to Mach's drawing, that we do not experience the entirety of our visual field as having the clarity and detail of what we focally attend to.

Figure 10.1. Ernst Mach's depiction of the visual field. From E. Mach, *Die Analyse der Empfindungen und das Verhältniss des Physischen zum Psychischen* (Jena: Gustav Fischer, 1900), 13.

Barry Smith has interpreted Mach's drawing as a depiction of Ewald Hering's definition of the visual field as "the totality of real objects imaged at a given moment on the retina of the right or left eye" (Hering 1964, p. 226, as quoted by Smith 1999, p. 324). But this interpretation cannot be right. Given the poor resolution of peripheral vision, Mach must have moved his eye in order to draw the detail at the periphery. Furthermore, besides these overt shifts of visual attention involving eye movements, he must have made covert shifts of mental attention while holding his eye still, thereby changing his mental focus while holding peripheral vision constant. His drawing is thus a representation that abstracts and combines the contents of many attentional phases of visual experience. It is a static representation of a temporally extended, dynamic process of sensorimotor and mental exploration of the scene. It tries to present all at once visual contents that at any given moment are not present to one in the way of a detailed picture.[5]

Another important feature of Mach's drawing is his attempt to depict the indeterminacy of the peripheral visual field by means of fading to white.[6] This feature may also be an attempt to depict the field as unbounded or topologically open, in the sense that there is no boundary that is part of the field itself (Smith 1999, p. 324). Yet it seems impossible to depict these kinds of features of experience in a picture. The visual field is unbounded and indeterminate in various ways but not by becoming white in the periphery. How to characterize these features is a difficult matter, but they do not seem to be pictorial properties. Rather than qualities representable within experience, they are structural features of experience.

What these brief considerations indicate is that our visual experience of the world at any given moment lacks many of the properties typical of pictures, such as uniformity of detail, qualitative determinateness at every point, and geometrical completeness. Although most vision scientists would accept this statement, many would also regard it as inconsistent with how our visual experience subjectively seems to us (see Pylyshyn 2003a, pp. 4–46). It is important to notice, therefore, that the foregoing considerations have been entirely phenomenological and have not appealed to any facts beyond what is available for one to experience in one's own first-person case.

Transparency and Experience

Mach's attempt to depict his visual field presupposes that we experience or can introspectively attend to our visual field. Yet what Mach could not help but depict is his room and a portion of his body from a certain vantage point. Experience is in this way often said to be "diaphanous" or "transparent."[7] In trying to attend to the qualities of experience, we as it were see right through them to the qualities of what is experienced.

Some philosophers rely on this idea to argue for representationalism, the thesis that the phenomenal character of experience is entirely a matter of the representational content of experience, or to put it another way, that the qualities of experience are one and the same as the qualities of the world represented by experience (Harman 1997; Tye 1991, 1995, 2000). What it is like for me to see the gray expanse of the winter sky, for example, is entirely a matter of the way my visual perceptual experience represents the sky. Most versions of representationalism are externalist. They maintain that the representational content of experience is given by the external properties of the objects represented by the experience (Dretske 1995a; Tye 1995). Philosophers who maintain that experience has intrinsic sensational properties or qualia, in addition to representational content, reject representationalism. I wish to present a different criticism of representationalism. This criticism is phenomenological and is directly relevant to the task of clarifying the phenomenal character of mental imagery.

The phenomenal character of experience includes both the qualitative character of what we experience (for example, sensory qualities of the world and our body) and the subjective character of the mental acts whereby we experience (perceiving, remembering, imagining, and so on). Here I use the term *subjective character of experience* somewhat differently from Nagel (1974). Nagel, as we have seen, introduced this term to refer to what a subject's experience is like for that subject. What experience is like in this sense involves both the qualitative properties of the subject's experience (qualia) and the subject's first-person perspective. I am using the term, however, to refer specifically to how a given type of mental activity, such as seeing or visualizing, is experienced in one's own case. Such experience is typically not reflective or introspective but rather prereflective (see Chapter 9). In seeing an object, I prereflectively experience my seeing, and in visualizing an object, I prereflectively experience my visualizing. In this intransitive and prereflective way, my mental activity manifests subjectively with a certain character.[8]

Representationalism neglects the subjective character of experience.[9] By contrast, phenomenological analysis focuses explicitly on the linkage between the qualitative character of what we experience and the subjective character of the mental activity whereby we experience it.

To bring out the import of this point we need to consider more carefully the claim that experience is transparent. Its *locus classicus* in recent philosophy is the following passage from Gilbert Harman:

When Eloise sees a tree before her, the colors she experiences are all experienced as features of the tree and its surroundings. None of them are experienced as intrinsic features of her experience. Nor does she experience any features of anything as intrinsic features of her experience. And that is true of you too. There is nothing special about Eloise's visual experience. When you see a tree, you do not experience any features as intrinsic features of your experience. Look at a tree and try to turn your attention to intrinsic features of your visual experience. I predict you will find that the only features there to turn your attention to will be features of the presented tree, including relational features of the tree "from here." (Harman 1997, p. 667)

Harman's main concern in this passage is to undercut the sense-datum theory of perception, according to which the colors we are aware of are internal mental properties, not properties of external objects. Nevertheless, it is not clear what the exact argument of this passage is supposed to be (see Kind 2003; Stoljar 2004). Let us focus on two core phenomenological claims that can be extracted from this passage. The first concerns experience in the sense of *awareness* (presented in the third person about Eloise); the second concerns *attention* (presented as a prediction about what one will find in one's own first-person case):

Extreme transparency of awareness: We are not aware of (intrinsic mental features of) our experience, but only of the objects and properties presented by that experience.

Extreme transparency of attention: We cannot attend to (intrinsic mental features of) our experience, but only to the objects and properties presented by that experience.

Harman's passage clearly suggests these extreme transparency claims.[10] I call them extreme in order to distinguish them from the following two moderate transparency claims:[11]

Moderate transparency of awareness: We are not usually aware of (intrinsic mental features of) our experience, but only of the objects and properties presented by that experience.

Moderate transparency of attention: We can (with effort) attend to (intrinsic mental features of) our experience, but not by turning our attention away from what that experience is *of* (that is, what is presented by that experience).

I submit that the extreme transparency claims are demonstrably false and the moderate ones true.

Consider visual experience. When I see the bottle of wine in front of me on the table, I experience (am visually aware of) the wine bottle. But I also experience my seeing. In experiencing my seeing in this way I do not need to introspect or reflect; my awareness is instead an implicit and nonreflective one. I experience my seeing by living it nonreflectively. Suppose now that I close my eyes and visualize the wine bottle. The intentional object of my mental act is still the bottle (the bottle is "the seeming object of my image experience," not a mental picture of the bottle). But now what I implicitly and nonreflectively experience is my visualizing.

Several points are important here. First, there is clearly a significant difference in the intentional content of the visualization and the perception. The most striking is that the bottle as visualized does not have the immediacy and presence of the bottle as perceived; rather, it has a peculiar kind of phenomenal absence. As Sartre puts it: "in so far as he *appears to me as imaged,* this Pierre who is present in London, *appears to me as absent.* This fundamental absence, this essential nothingness of the imaged object, suffices to differentiate it from the objects of perception" (Sartre 2004, p. 180; emphasis in original).

Second, this difference in intentional content is not, however, a difference in descriptive content; it is not a difference in the features or properties the two experiences represent the object to have. Thus, there can be phenomenal differences in intentional content between experiences that are otherwise identical with respect to the object properties they represent.

Third, it is important also to notice the distinct experiential features of the intentional acts themselves. For example, the visual perception feels involuntary and effortless, whereas the visualization feels voluntary, effortful, and needing to call upon memory.[12] In these ways, I am aware not simply of the intentional objects and properties presented by my experience, but also of features of my experience, or rather of my ongoing activity of experiencing. These features include the specific intentional act or attitude component of the experience (perceiving or visualizing or remembering), associated qualities of this act (being effortless or effortful), and the invariant phenomenal quality of "mineness" or "for-me-ness" that characterizes all my experiencing (it is my seeing and my visualizing).[13]

We could summarize this last point by saying that the extreme transparency of awareness thesis neglects precisely the prereflective self-consciousness constitutive of subjective experience. In my visual experience of the wine bottle, I am explicitly aware of the bottle, but I am also implicitly aware of my visual experience of the bottle.[14] This sort of implicit awareness is a kind of self-consciousness (I am implicitly aware of the visual experience as *mine*). But it is not a reflective or introspective self-consciousness because there is no phenomenally conscious reflection or introspection that takes the experience as its object.[15] Rather, the experience itself is prereflectively self-aware. In Sartre's words: "every positional consciousness of an object is at the same time a non-positional [non-object-directed or intransitive] consciousness of itself" (Sartre, 1956, p. liii).

As I argued in Chapter 9, this type of self-consciousness is a constitutive feature of phenomenal consciousness. It is hard to make sense of the thought that one could have a conscious perception without experiencing one's perceiving, or that one could have a conscious mental image without experiencing one's imagining, or that one could have a conscious memory without experiencing one's remembering. But if conscious experience is necessarily self-aware in this way, then contrary to the extreme transparency thesis, we are implicitly aware of constitutive features of our experience and not simply of the objects and properties our experience presents.

It also seems clear, contrary to the extreme transparency of attention thesis, that we can become aware of features of our experience by attending to them (instead of attending simply to the objects presented by that experience). In seeing, I attend to features of what there is to see. But I can also attend to how seeing feels, to what the activity of seeing is like for me, and to the ways it feels different from freely imagining and from remembering. In attending to experience in this way, I can become aware of features I do not normally notice (attend to), precisely because they usually remain implicit and prereflective.

The moderate transparency of attention thesis is compatible with these points. It acknowledges that we can (with effort) attend to experience. But it also makes the point that we cannot do so by turning our attention away from what that experience presents. Some philosophers do talk about turning attention away from the experienced object to the intentional experience itself. But this way of speaking does not seem apt. Usually when we talk about turning our attention away from one thing to another we imply that we ignore or look away from the first in favor of the second. It seems impossible, however, to ignore the experienced object when we attend to features of the experience (Siewert 2004, pp. 35–37). This truth is what the transparency metaphor aims to convey. Thus the right way to think about phenomenological analysis is not that we turn our attention inward (as the notion of introspection implies) but that we direct our attention to the appearance of the object, or the appearance of the world more generally, while vigilantly keeping in mind that appearances are objective correlates of subjective intentional acts. (How something looks is correlated to and is a function of how one looks at it.)

Clearly, the sort of attention in play here is cognitive or mental attention, not perceptual attention. In attending to features of my visual experience, I do not (and cannot) look away from what that experience presents. Rather, I shift my mental or cognitive attention to how things look given my perceptual attitude. In this way, features of experience on the side of the intentional act, which usually remain implicit or latent, can be made explicit and available for phenomenological consideration. In sum, the way to think about what we do when we attend directly to features of our experience is not that we turn away from the outer and ignore it in favor of the inner, but rather that we make explicit or manifest features that are usually implicit or latent.[16]

Picture-Viewing

With these ideas in hand, let us return to Mach's drawing, considering it now as a picture seen by us. Following Husserl (2006), we can distinguish three types of intentional object implicit in the experience of picture-viewing (see Bernet, Kern, and Marbach 1993, pp. 150–152). First, there is the physical and perceptible *pictorial vehicle*, in our case, Mach's drawing on paper (the original and its reproductions). Second, there is the *pictorial image*, which also appears perceptually but is not apprehended as a real thing like the pictorial vehicle. In our example, the pictorial image is Mach's field of view *as depicted*. Whereas the pictorial vehicle is something we can touch or move, the pictorial image as such is not. It is irreal, or as Sartre more provocatively puts it, it is "a nothingness" (Sartre 2004, pp. 11–14, 125–136). Finally, there is the *pictorial subject* or referent—the person himself or herself who is the subject of the depiction (in a portrait), or the scene itself (in a landscape painting). In our example, the pictorial subject is Mach's actual field of view. The pictorial subject is absent and may or may not exist.

The phenomenological problem of the intentionality of picture-viewing is the problem of how these distinct types of intentional objects and their correlative intentional acts combine to form the unified experience of seeing something as a picture.

We now need to recall from Chapter 2 the phenomenological distinction between intentional acts of *presentation* and *re-presentation*. Perception is presentational; imagination, memory, and picture-viewing are re-presentational. We can approach this distinction from two sides—the side of the intentional object and the side of the intentional act. In a perceptual experience, the object is experienced as present in its "bodily being" and thus as directly accessible. In a re-presentational experience, the object is not experienced as present and accessible in this way but rather as absent. Yet this absence is precisely a *phenomenal absence,* for the experience is of the object *precisely as absent.* This difference on the side of the intentional object between bodily presence and absence corresponds to the difference on the side of the intentional act between presentation and re-presentation. A re-presentational experience constitutes its object precisely as both phenomenally absent in its bodily being and as mentally evoked or brought forth. In this way, the object is said to be mentally re-presented rather than perceptually presented. What makes the experience re-presentational is precisely that its object is mentally evoked or brought forth while also phenomenally absent; it is not that the object is mentally evoked or brought forth *again*. The latter characteristic belongs to memory but not to every type of re-presentational experience (such as fantasy).

Picture-viewing comprises both presentation and re-presentation in a complex way. The physical picture is present to perception, while the absent pictorial subject is re-presented, brought to presence by the pictorial image. In viewing and appreciating a picture, we are interested mainly in neither the physical picture nor the pictorial subject as such, but rather in the pictorial image that appears in the physical picture and represents the pictorial subject. The intentional object of picture-viewing is thus in a way double, for it comprises both the pictorial subject and the pictorial image of that subject appearing in the physical vehicle of the picture. One could argue that this physical vehicle counts as a pictorial entity thanks to the apprehension of an image appearing in it. In this view, imagination, in the sense of the mental apprehension of an image, is a necessary constituent of pictorial experience.

My concern here is not to defend this claim about pictorial experience, but rather to make the point that imagining in the sense of visualizing has a different intentional structure from picture-viewing.[17] This point can be introduced by first considering the mental activity of remembering.

Remembering

Suppose Mach, having finished his drawing, later remembers having drawn his visual field while seated in his study. In what does the experience of this sort of mental activity consist? How is remembering different in its subjective character from perceiving and picture-viewing?

As I noted earlier, perceptual experience has a directness and immediacy that makes it presentational in character rather than re-presentational.[18] In episodic or autobiographical remembering, however, a situation or event is experienced not as present but as past. The past situation or event is thus necessarily re-presented. The phenomenological question is how this re-presentation subjectively works. According to the classical image theory of memory, in remembering one apprehends a mental image of something experienced in the past. One problem with this theory is that in memory one does not take oneself to be imagining something that seems like what one remembers; one takes oneself to be remembering something as it occurred. The standard way to deal with this problem is to insist that what one remembers is the past occurrence, not the mental image, but that one remembers the past by way of the mental image. But this move highlights a deeper problem: the image theory fails to account for how an image had in the present can yield a memory experience as of something past. Husserl's account of memory as the re-presentation of a past experience aims to overcome this difficulty (Bernet 2002; Marbach 1993, pp. 78–83).

Consider that when you remember a past occurrence, situation, or event, you also implicitly remember your earlier experience of it. Mach remembers his field of view as it appeared to him from his couch, but in doing so he also implicitly remembers his earlier visual perception. Thus, in memory, one apprehends something absent (the past) not by means of an image, in the sense of a present mental picture, but through the activity of re-presenting an experience believed to have occurred in the past. Of course, one does not have to entertain this belief explicitly in the episodic or autobiographical memory experience. Rather, in remembering, the re-presented experience is simply subjectively given as having occurred in the past. In memory, one reproduces and relives, as it were, this past experience, but in a modified way, namely, precisely as re-presented, and thus as not occurring now, but posited as past. In other words, the past experience is not literally or really reproduced in the present; rather, it is reproduced as part of the intentional content of the memory (Marbach 1993, p. 61). In Husserl's formulation, the present memory does not "really" contain the contain the past experience but instead "intentionally implicates" it (Husserl 1983, §99, p. 294; Marbach 1993, pp. 34–36, 69–70).

In this view, to say that I remember X is to say that I intend (or refer or mentally direct myself to) X by re-presenting an experience of X that is subjectively given as having occurred in the past (or in a more cognitivist vein, that is believed to have occurred in the past). Notice that the intentional object of the memory is usually the past occurrence, not the past experience (unless the two are one and the same, as in the case of remembering a past emotion or feeling). If the intentional object of the memory is the past experience itself, then the act of remembering is a reflective one. Usually, however, the re-presenting of the past experience operates only implicitly and prereflectively in one's memory of the past event or situation.

A tempting way to link these ideas to mind science would be to say that memory does not involve "online" sensory experience—sensory experience appropriately constrained by current sensorimotor interaction with the environment—but rather "offline," simulated or emulated sensory experience. An emulation represents an activity by reenacting it in a circumscribed and modified way—for example, as an internal process that models but does not loop through peripheral sensory and motor systems (Grush 2004). Remembering could involve emulating earlier sensory experiences and thus reenacting them in a modified way.

The experience of remembering thus involves a kind of doubling of consciousness, for in being the conscious re-presentation of a past occurrence, remembering is also the conscious re-presentation of a previous consciousness (Bernet 2002). (Here we touch on the complexities of internal time-consciousness, which are the subject of the next chapter.) At the same time, seeing something as a picture involves a double intentional object—the pictorial subject plus the pictorial image appearing in the physical picture. There is thus a clear sense in which picture-viewing can be said to involve a phenomenal mental image, for the image in a picture is arguably nothing other than an intentional correlate of the mental activity of picture-viewing. This image has a clearly identifiable vehicle, namely, the physical material of the picture. Remembering, however, lacks this threefold structure of vehicle/image/referent. Moreover, appealing to mental images does not explain the intentionality of memory. The problem with the classical image theory of memory is that it turns memory experience into a kind of picture-viewing, thereby distorting its intentional structure and subjective character.

Visualizing

The same points hold for imagining in the sense of visual imaging or visualizing: imagery experience is not a species of picture-viewing. In visual imagining, one apprehends an object not by means of a phenomenal mental picture but by re-presenting that object as given to a possible perceptual experience. What needs to be clarified is how this sort of mental re-presentation differs from remembering.

Suppose Mach, while drawing his visual field, becomes distracted and visualizes his books rearranged on the shelves. We can suppose that he is not remembering any particular past arrangement and that he has no intention of actually rearranging them. He simply visualizes how they would look in a different arrangement. In this way, imagining does not require belief in the factual reality of the perceptual experi-

ence it intentionally implicates in its mental re-presentation of the
scene. In other words, there is no implication either that such an experience has occurred in the past (as in remembering) or that it will
occur in the future (as in anticipation or expectation). Rather, in
imagining, this doxastic feature of belief in the actual (past or future)
occurrence of the intentionally implicated experience is "neutralized."[19]

In this view, to say that I imagine X is to say that I mentally re-present
X as given to a neutralized perceptual experience of X (see Marbach
1993, p. 75). For example, in right now freely visualizing the Eiffel
Tower, I re-present the Eiffel Tower as given to a perceptual experience whose actual (past or future) occurrence I am in no way committed to. What makes this mental act re-presentational is that the
Eiffel Tower is phenomenally absent and mentally evoked or brought
forth. What makes the act different from remembering is that I mentally re-present the Eiffel Tower as given to a perceptual experience
that I do not posit as having occurred in the past. (Of course, the visualization in this case depends on memory, but that is another matter.)
In sum, we could say that to visualize X is to mentally re-present X by
subjectively simulating or emulating a neutralized perceptual experience of X.

This account thus comes close to what Martin calls "The Dependency
Thesis," which states, "to imagine sensorily a φ is to imagine experiencing a φ" (Martin 2002, p. 404). According to this thesis, when we visualize objects we imagine visually experiencing them. Martin takes this
thesis to imply that "one kind of phenomenally conscious state, an
event of imagining, takes as its object another type of conscious state of
mind, a sensory experience" (ibid.). On the Husserlian-inspired view
proposed here, however, although visualizing an object entails imagining visually experiencing the object, the visual experience is not the
object of the imagining; the intentional object is the visualized object.
As visualized, however, that object must be given visually in some way or
other, and this mode of visual givenness on the part of the object entails
a correlative mode of visual experience on the part of the subject. The
visual experience co-imagined in visualizing an object is thus simply the
intentional correlate of the imaged object's mode of visual appearance
in the visualization. The intentional object of the transitive imaging
consciousness is the imaged object; the correlative and co-imagined vi-

sual experience is experienced only intransitively and prereflectively. In other words, this experience is "lived through" without usually being noticed, attended to, or reflected upon. (If it is taken notice of in these ways, then the imaging experience becomes a reflective one.) I take this intentional structure to be the reason why, as Martin puts it, "imagery seems to give us the presence of an imagined scene rather than a mere imagined experience of the scene" (2002, p. 416) (though, as noted earlier, this presence is also a kind of phenomenal absence; see Sartre 2004, pp. 11–14, 126–127, 180).

Several comments about the noncommittal quality of imagining are in order. First, the neutralization or suspension of belief that makes for this noncommittal quality belongs to the co-imagined visual experience of the imaged object. It is thus independent of the belief in the existence or nonexistence of the imaged object or scene. I believe that the Eiffel Tower exists in Paris. Nevertheless, in visualizing the Eiffel Tower as given to (say) a perception from Trocadero, I also mentally evoke a visual experience whose actual occurrence at any time in the past or future I am in no way committed to. Alternatively, if I visualize a flute-playing centaur (see Husserl 1983, §23), then not only is my mentally evoked visual experience a neutralized one, but I also take the object of my visualization to be purely fictional. Thus, in visualizing, there remain various ways in which the object or scene can be mentally re-presented. For example, I can take it to exist (the Eiffel Tower), to not exist but to be possible in this world (a fantasy house in which I could live), or to not exist and to be purely fictional (a flute-playing centaur).[20]

Second, neutralization does not imply that one is noncommittal with respect to the imagined scene. For example, in visualizing the Eiffel Tower from Trocadero, I am not noncommittal about whether the imagined scene contains a tower seen from across the River Seine. In other words, my commitment to these features is not itself imagined but actual.[21]

Nevertheless, third, the visualizing act can posit its object in different ways. Sartre distinguishes four ways: "it can posit the object as nonexistent, or as absent, or as existing elsewhere; it can also 'neutralize' itself, which is to say not posit its object as existent" (2004, p. 12). The first three types of positing concern the imagined object and are all variations on the way it appears as absent in imagining. The

fourth type concerns the positing act itself and has a different structure.

In the first type, the object is posited as nonexistent and hence as
not able to be perceptually present at all. Such objects are fictions (like
the flute-playing centaur) (Sartre 2004, p. 20).[22] In the second and
third types, the object is posited as existing and as something that
could be brought into one's presence and perceived in its bodily
being. On the one hand, the object could be posited simply as absent
with no further qualification; on the other hand, it could be posited as
absent and elsewhere. For example, in now imagining my friend Alva,
I can posit him simply as absent, or as absent and in Berkeley.

The fourth type of positing is suspension of belief in the existence of
the object but without positing its nonexistence. So defined, suspension can occur not only in imagination but also in perception: "This is
what happens in perception when I see a man coming towards me and
I say 'It is possible this man is Pierre'. But, precisely, this suspension of
belief, this abstention, concerns *the man approaching*. Of this man, I
doubt that he is Pierre; I do not thereby doubt that he is a man. In a
word, my doubt necessarily implies a positing of existence of the type:
a man coming towards me" (Sartre 2004, p. 13). Sartre's example of
neutralization in imagination is a case of picture-viewing: "if I look at
the photos in a magazine, they can very well 'say nothing to me', which
is to say I look at them without positing their existence. Thus, the
people whose photographs I see are indeed reached through these
photographs, but without my positing their existence, just as the
Knight and Death are reached through Dürer's engraving, but without
my positing them" (Sartre 2004, p. 24).[23] Sartre's point is that I can
look at the photographs and see them as photographs of people, not
simply as glossy papers, but without thinking that these people are
alive or dead, existent or nonexistent. Rather, I remain noncommittal;
my pictorial experience simply does not go into or broach this
matter.[24]

There is thus a difference between the way Sartre employs the idea
of neutralization and the way I have presented it. On the one hand, as
Sartre makes clear, "what distinguishes the different positional types is
the thetic character of the intention, not the existence or nonexistence of the object" (2004, p. 24). In other words, the noncommittal
quality belongs to the intentional *act* rather than the intentional *content*. On the other hand, what Sartre takes to be neutralized is belief in

the existence or nonexistence of the imagined *object* (as in his example of the people in the photograph), whereas in my presentation what is neutralized is belief in the actuality of the *visual experience* that is implied in one's re-presenting the imaged object. That is, the noncommittal quality belongs to the mentally simulated or emulated seeing that is constitutive of visual imagining. It is thus firmly on the act-side rather than the content-side of the intentional structure.

The foregoing analysis of visual imagining tries to capture both the important similarities and differences between perceptual experience and imagery experience. Whereas visual imagining involves visual experience, this visual experience is only intentionally implied, not actual. That it is internal to the nature of visual imagining that there is a re-presented visual experience whenever one visually imagines an object or scene may account for the important similarities between visual perception and visualization (such as shared perspectival content). That the visual experience is only intentionally implied, however, means that its content is determined primarily by the imagining intention and the knowledge that intention contains.[25]

Given this point, we might be tempted to hypothesize that whereas our current sensorimotor activities constrain what we perceive, they do not constrain what we imagine. According to this hypothesis, there is no correlation (or merely a temporary, accidental one) between what one is visualizing and how one is sensing and moving in relation to one's environment. Elisabeth Pacherie appears to make this claim when she writes: "I can, for instance, close my eyes and imagine a cube, I can even imagine myself turning around the cube, I can during this exercise move my head and my body in different ways, but unless by coincidence or because of my deliberately intending it to be so, my movements will not be correlated with the sequence of images of the cube that I imagine I am moving around" (Pacherie 1999, p. 158).

Nevertheless, as Mark Wexler points out (personal communication), experimental results on the effects of hand and body movements on mental imagery count against this hypothesis. Rather, these results support the hypothesis that motor processes guide mental image transformations (Wexler, Kosslyn, and Berthoz 1998; see also Grush 2004). More precisely, sensory anticipations of the effects of motor actions that are overtly inhibited drive mental image transformations. For example, Wexler, Kosslyn, and Berthoz (1998) found that executing an unseen, clockwise manual rotation aids the simultaneous visualization of a clockwise rotation, whereas executing an unseen, counterclockwise manual rotation hinders the simultaneous visualization of a clockwise rotation. This result, combined with others (Simons and Wang 1998; Simons, Wang, and Roddenberry 2002; Wexler and Klam 2001; Wohlshläger and Wohlschläger 1998), indicates that one's bodily motion strongly constrains the visualizations one can perform while moving one's body or manipulating objects. These results also suggest that motor mechanisms drive at least some types of mental imagery even when one is not moving.

Although sensorimotor processes thus influence what we can visualize, there remains an important difference in the sensorimotor content of imagery experience and perceptual experience: An imagined object cannot be explored in the way a perceptual object can (see Casey 2000, pp. 91–93). In perception, objects not only appear perspectivally, but present profiles that vary with one's movement. We experience objects as having "sensorimotor profiles," as things whose appearances would vary in precise ways as we move around them, or as they move in relation to us (Noë 2004, p. 117). Perception thus implies "the necessity of *making a tour* of objects" (Sartre 2004, p. 8). At the same time, although the object as imagined appears perspectivally, "we no longer need to make a tour of it: the imaged cube is given immediately for what it is" (Ibid., p. 9). Whereas my seeing something as a cube is revocable—I could be mistaken, the object could show itself to be something else as I explore it—my imagining a cube is not revocable in this way. There is no possibility of still-to-be-disclosed profiles that could show the object not to be a cube, for to say it is no longer a cube, but rather (say) a diamond, is to say that I am now imagining a diamond. In other words, the intention of my imagining has changed and now determines a new intentional object. Exactly the same is true if I visualize a cube now from this angle, now from that angle: I do not explore or make a tour of the cube, but I change what I imagine by changing my imaginative intention.[26] Nevertheless, such intentions clearly embody sensorimotor knowledge. Furthermore, sensorimotor processes strongly influence the movement from one visualizing intention to the next one.

We are now in position to summarize the main point of this phenomenological analysis of imagery experience: this analysis makes no mention of phenomenal mental images, in the sense of phenomenal mental pictures inspected by the mind's eye. In visual imaging or visu-alizing, we do not inspect a phenomenal mental picture; instead we mentally re-present an object by subjectively simulating or emulating a perceptual experience of that object.

One might object that phenomenal mental images or pictures, though not the intentional objects of remembering and imagining ex-periences, and thus not inwardly "seen," are nonetheless "had" or "un-dergone" in those types of experience. How we should respond to this objection depends on what we understand a phenomenal mental image to be. If the proposal is that a phenomenal mental image is simply a subjectively simulated or emulated perceptual experience, then the foregoing analysis can be taken to support this proposal. No-tice, however, that this proposal amounts to an important conceptual and phenomenological clarification of the notion of a phenomenal mental image: a phenomenal mental image is not a phenomenal pic-ture in the mind's eye, nor indeed is it any kind of static image or de-piction; it is, rather, the mental activity of re-presenting an object by mentally evoking and subjectively simulating a perceptual experience of that object.

Alternatively, if the proposal is that this simulated visual experience is itself a kind of mental picture, or more precisely that its intentional content is pictorial, then the fate of this proposal hangs on whether perceptual experience is pictorial. Earlier in this chapter, we saw that there are ways in which the content of perceptual experience is unlike any picture. If perceptual experience is not pictorial, then there is no reason to think that the content of the simulated visual experience in imagining and remembering is pictorial. Hence there is no reason to think that this experience is some kind of mental picture. In sum, ac-cording to the view I am proposing, the only time visual experience is straightforwardly pictorial is when one has the visual experience of looking at a picture, or the experience of remembering or imagining looking at a picture.

The Imagery Debate Revisited

What is initially striking about the phenomenological analysis of im-agery experience, from the perspective of the imagery debate, is that it supports the claim, made by descriptionalists, though not proprietary to them, that visualizing is not the inspection of a mental image, but rather the mental representation of what it is like, or was like, or would be like, to see something, given one's tacit knowledge of how things look, how that knowledge is organized, and one's sensorimotor skills. The phenomenological analysis thus undermines a principal motivation for analytical isomorphism in imagery research, namely, the assumption that imagery experience is the experience of a phenomenal mental image or that the content of imagery experience is given by an image. Analytical isomorphism seeks to find depictive structures in the brain corresponding to the supposedly imagistic or pictorial content of imagery experience. It is, of course, an empirical question whether topographically organized areas of the cortex are involved in one or another type of visual imagining. But the evidence for their involvement cannot be taken to mean that activity in these areas corresponds to the content of what we experience when we visually imagine an object. In visualizing an object, we subjectively simulate a visual experience of the object, and the content of this experience is not given by an image or picture.

Although this line of thought is critical of pictorialism—to the extent that pictorialism maintains that activity in topographical cortical areas corresponds to the content of imagery experience—it should not be taken as favoring descriptionalism. Descriptionalism does not maintain simply that visualizing is the mental representation of what it is like to see something; it also maintains that the relevant tacit knowledge is propositional in form and that the subpersonal format of the neural representations is symbolic (language-like). The phenomenological analysis presented here is not directly relevant to this hypothesis about the subpersonal representational format. As we have seen, this analysis aims to clarify the subjective character and phenomenal content of imagery experience at the personal level. Whether such experience is neurally mediated by depictive or propositional structures is not something phenomenology on its own is in a position to answer.

One might wonder, however, whether the tacit knowledge to which the descriptionalist appeals is largely skillful and sensorimotor, rather than descriptive and propositional (Noë 2004; O'Regan and Noë 2001a; Thomas 1999, 2002). According to the dynamic sensorimotor approach to perception, discussed in the previous chapter, in perceiving we exercise our skillful bodily mastery of sensorimotor contingencies or ways that sensory experience varies as a function of bodily movement. Such bodily mastery may be largely a matter of practical, rather than propositional, sensorimotor knowledge. Furthermore, as we saw earlier, in visualizing we exercise the same skillful sensorimotor knowledge used in perception, and motor processes guide what we visualize. From an enactive perspective, therefore, visualizing is not a disembodied exercise of abstract sensorimotor skill, but rather a genuine sensorimotor act.

The foregoing phenomenological analysis does have some critical implications for descriptionalism: it suggests that the descriptionalist, tacit-knowledge account of mental imagery is vague and underspecified. According to Pylyshyn, the "null hypothesis" is that all cognition makes use of the same representational format.[27] What is distinctive about imagery is that the content of one's thoughts concern how things look. To decide, however, whether to reject this null hypothesis in any given case, we need to know exactly what the subject is mentally doing. According to the tacit knowledge proposal, when subjects are asked to visualize something, they in effect ask themselves what it is like to see it, and then they simulate as many of the relevant aspects as they can, given their knowledge of how things look, how that knowledge is organized, and their repertoire of psychophysical skills. The problem with this proposal, from a phenomenological point of view, is that does not specify in nearly enough detail what the individual subject is mentally doing during a particular episode of imagery experience. As we have seen, one can simulate seeing something in various ways—by imagining it (where this means noncommittal re-presentation according to various "positing attitudes"), by remembering it, and by seeing it in a picture. One can also reiterate these types of mental activities in complicated ways: one can remember imagining something; one can imagine remembering something; one can visualize looking at a picture; one can remember visualizing looking at a picture, and so forth. All these mental activities have different subjective characters and intentional and cognitive structures.

This point casts light on the intentional structure of imagery experience in standard imagery tasks. Consider Shepard and Metzler's well-known mental rotation task (Shepard and Metzler 1971). Subjects looked at pairs of two-dimensional, perspective line-drawings of three-dimensional shapes. The shapes were at different orientations, and the task was to determine whether the two shapes were the same. Shepard and Metzler found that the time it takes to decide whether the two shapes are identical increases linearly as the angle between them increases, no matter whether the rotation is in the plane or in depth. Although introspective reports were not collected in the original study, many people report visualizing one or both shapes being rotated in order to perform the task. This task involves a combination of picture-viewing and visual imagining because one sees the 2D display as a 3D image and then visualizes movement in the picture. In other words, one visualizes the rotation of a pictorial image.

Consider now Kosslyn's well-known map scanning experiments (described in Kosslyn et al. 1981). Subjects memorize a simple picture of an island with various objects on it. Once they have learned to draw the map from memory, they are asked to visualize it, fix their attention on one landmark, mentally "scan" to another landmark, and report when they can "see" this second landmark in their "mind's eye." The reaction time to report "seeing" the second landmark is measured and found to be a linear function of the distance between the two landmarks in the original map. This task combines picture-viewing, remembering, and visualizing, for one must *visualize a remembered picture.* Thus, in these imagery tasks, subjects appear to be simulating or mentally representing the perception of a picture. What these tasks elicit, therefore, is neither simply perception, nor visual remembering, nor visual imagining, but both actual and imagined pictorial experience.

As Pylyshyn has discussed, there is a widespread tendency to interpret the results of these experiments according to analytical isomorphism—in other words as showing that we rotate and scan phenomenal mental images isomorphic to depictive structures in the brain (Pylyshyn 2002, p. 180; 2003a, p. 356). One wonders to what extent this tendency is influenced by the fact that in these experiments subjects are perceiving and visualizing pictures. By contrast, in the case of motor imagery, there seems to be less temptation to assume that one is moving a motor image instead of emulating what it is like to perform a motor action.

The idea that phenomenal mental images are pictorial items contained within the mind was already criticized by Sartre in 1940, at the outset of his phenomenological study, *The Imaginary.* There he used phenomenological analysis to expose what he called "the illusion of immanence," by which he meant the cognitive illusion of taking mental images to be pictorial items in consciousness. One form this illusion can take is supposing that the qualities of the object one imagines also belong to one's mental image, or as we would say today, confusing properties of what is represented with properties of the representing. But Sartre went further than this familiar point. He argued that a mental image properly understood is not a content contained in consciousness; rather, it is a dynamic and relational act of consciousness:

> The word "image" could only indicate therefore the relation of consciousness to the object; in other words, it is a certain way in which the object appears to consciousness, or, if one prefers, a certain way in which consciousness presents to itself an object. To tell the truth, the expression "mental image" gives rise to confusion. It would be better to say "consciousness-of-Pierre-as-imaged" or "imaging-consciousness-of-Pierre." As the word "image" is long-standing, we cannot reject it completely. But, to avoid all ambiguity, I repeat here that an image is nothing other than a relation. (Sartre 2004, p. 7)[28]

This passage is relevant to today's imagery debate. Suppose we replace the concept of the mental image as a picture in the mind inspected by an inner eye with the concept of the mental image as the way an object appears to the imaging or visualizing consciousness. Suppose, furthermore, as I have argued here, that the way the object appears to this type of consciousness is not pictorial in certain crucial respects. It follows that we should not go looking in the brain for depictive representations corresponding to the content of what we see or visualize.

The foregoing phenomenological analysis also has methodological implications for empirical research. At the personal level, we need more refined and precise descriptions of what subjects are subjectively doing in various imagery tasks. Such descriptions should include the overall intentional structure of a given imagery task, as well as variations in subjective experience across individuals and from trial to trial for a given individual. Producing such descriptions requires incorporating a distinct phenomenological level of investigation into experimental psychology and neuroscience (Lutz and Thompson 2003; Varela 1996). On the one hand, we need to gather more precise descriptive first-person reports from subjects about how they experience their cognitive activity from trial to trial in a given experiment. On the other hand, collecting this type of data requires that subjects attend to their experience in an open and nonjudgmental way. First-person methods are methods that foster this ability to be present to one's own experience (Varela and Shear 1999a, 1999b). These methods need to be complemented with second-person methods of interviewing subjects so that the reports they produce are maximally descriptive of experience and minimally conjectural about the causes of experience (Petitmengin, in press).

After collecting descriptive first-person reports, we need to work with subjects to discern whether there are any invariant phenomenal structures of their experience. Experimental work on the neurodynamics of conscious visual perception has shown that phenomenal invariants of experience produced in this first-person/second-person phenomenological manner can be used to detect and interpret novel patterns of neural activity that correlate with cognitive activity and behavior (Lutz et al. 2002). Without this phenomenological window on brain activity, these patterns would remain lost in the highly variable neural signals, usually treated as noise. This approach of combining first-person reports informed by phenomenological analysis with third-person neurophysiological and behavioral data defines the research program known as neurophenomenology (see Chapter 11).

A neurophenomenological approach to imagery experience would dispense with the construct of the phenomenal mental image, understood as a pictorial entity or content in consciousness, and instead direct us to study imagining as a type of mental activity whereby we relate to something phenomenally absent. Such an approach would not aim to find representations in the brain that match phenomenal mental pictures. Instead, it would try to relate the experiential structure of the visualizing act to the dynamical structure of brain activity. It would use first-person and second-person methods to investigate how subjects experience the visualizing act in a given experimental protocol, pursue a phenomenological analysis of the experiential structure of visualizing, and use this analysis to guide investigation of the neurodynamics of the visualizing act.

In this chapter, I have stressed for heuristic purposes the differences between acts of visualizing, remembering, picture-viewing, and perceiving. These differences are largely static, conceptual ones, having to do with the different intentional structures of these mental activities. If we were to analyze perception, memory, and imagination from a more dynamic and genetic phenomenological perspective, however, then we would need to take account of how they dynamically affect each other, how they alternate and feed each other in our mental lives. This important topic lies beyond the scope of this book, but I hope to have shown how we might begin to approach it neurophenomenologically by using the combined resources of mind science and phenomenological analysis.

Phenomenology and Heterophenomenology

To conclude this chapter, I would like to examine the relation between the phenomenological approach to mental imagery, including the neurophenomenological proposal just sketched, and Dennett's heterophenomenology.

In his 1978 paper "Two Approaches to Mental Images," Dennett distinguished between what he called the scientific approach and the phenomenological approach to mental images (Dennett 1978). He later renamed the phenomenological approach "heterophenomenology," in order to emphasize the resolutely third-person approach taken by this sort of phenomenology (Dennett 1982, 1991a). The scientific approach to mental imagery defines mental images as the *normal causes* of the beliefs subjects have about what they call their experienced mental images. This approach guarantees the existence of mental images so defined and then investigates whether the normal causes of these beliefs include anything that has the properties of images ordinarily understood, such as a depictive representational format.

The heterophenomenological approach, in contrast, defines images as the *intentional objects* of the subjects' beliefs. It guarantees the existence of mental images as logical or intentional constructs. The aim of this approach is to assemble from the third-person point of view a comprehensive recording of the beliefs subjects express about their images; then it seeks to extrapolate and describe the corresponding intentional objects. Subjects have final authority over the content of their beliefs, but not over the status of the intentional objects of those beliefs (the mental images posited by their beliefs). The heterophenomenologist regards these intentional objects as occupants of the "heterophenomenological world" of the subjects. This world is to be treated by the heterophenomenologist as a purely notional realm, or as Dennett also describes it, as a kind of fictional world (1991a, pp. 78–81). The scientific task is then to determine whether these intentional objects correspond in a sufficient number of their properties with the real structural and functional properties of what goes on in the brains of subjects when they report having images. If there is enough of a correspondence, then we can identify the intentional objects with the underlying neural representations, and the beliefs of the subjects turn out to be largely true. If there is not sufficient correspondence, then the beliefs turn out to be mistaken (Dennett 1991a, p. 85). In this case, the individuals are subject to a kind of systematic illusion.

From the standpoint of this book, we can raise a number of critical points about heterophenomenology.

1. Heterophenomenology interprets first-person reports about experience as expressions of the subjects' beliefs about their experience. Then it evaluates the truth or falsity of those beliefs by determining whether they match or fail to match what is really going on in the brain. Later in this chapter I will suggest that attributing beliefs to subjects about their experience on the basis of what they say about their experience is misguided as a general interpretive policy. Let us set that issue aside for the moment, however, to focus initially on the proposal that the truth or falsity of what subjects report about their experience should be determined in relation to what is really going on in their brains. Let us also limit ourselves to experimental contexts in which subjects are instructed to give descriptive reports about their experience, and hence may be required to introspect and/or retrospect (see Jack and Roepstorff 2002). The critical point to be made is that this evaluative procedure is inappropriate for most first-person reports and certainly for those that are properly descriptive in form, as opposed to reports that indulge in conjecture about the underlying causes of experience.

Descriptive reports carry no particular commitments from the subject about what is going on in his or her brain. When one says, "I decided the two figures had the same shape by visualizing one of them being rotated," one is describing one's subjective experience of one's own mental activity and not expressing a belief about what is really going on in one's brain considered as a cognitive system. One is describing one's subjectivity at the personal level in a way that is completely noncommittal about the subpersonal workings of one's brain.[29] Therefore, we should not try to evaluate such reports by comparing what they assert to what is going on in the brain. And we should certainly not try to evaluate such reports by asking whether their *content* matches or fails to match the properties of the representational *format* of the relevant neural systems. In other words, it is a mistake to assume that the only way the subjects' beliefs about their imagery experience could turn out to be true is if the neural representations had a depictive format.

To make this assumption is tantamount to assuming analytical isomorphism: we assume that the subpersonal representational format must be depictive, given that we experience mental images. Then we decide that we do not really experience mental images, but only think or believe we do, because the representational format turns out not to be depictive. The remedy for this predicament is to keep in clear view the conceptual difference between experiential content at the personal level and representational format at the subpersonal level.

2. Heterophenomenology focuses on specifying the intentional objects of subjects' expressed beliefs but does not try to trace those intentional objects back to the intentional acts that are necessarily correlated to those objects. Instead, it construes those intentional objects as posits of the subjects' beliefs. From a phenomenological standpoint, however, there is no such thing as an intentional or notional object without a corresponding intentional act, and intentional acts are not to be identified with beliefs. Intentional acts are subjectively lived through mental (and bodily) acts of intending (relating or directing oneself to) objects, events, and states of affairs, and believing is only one type of intentional act. Furthermore, the intentional act is related constitutionally to its object, for the way the object appears or is disclosed depends on how it is intended (an imaged object appears differently to an act of remembering and an act of pure fantasy). For a phenomenological analysis to be comprehensive, it needs to bring into view this correlational structure of intentional experience and inten-

tional object, and it needs to analyze the constitutional relation between them.

3. The next critical point arises when we ask exactly how we are to gain access to these intentional acts themselves. In phenomenology, the mode of access is first-personal, specifically the awareness one has of one's own mental activities.[30] Given that we aim to gain access to intentional acts of imagining, remembering, and so on, as they are subjectively lived, we simply cannot forego this mode of access.

The foregoing point concerns the unavoidable need to make use of first-personal modes of access to mental phenomena. It also stands to reason that such modes of access are not static and fixed, but exhibit degrees of plasticity, and might be trainable in various ways. In other words, attention and meta-awareness could be flexible and trainable skills, so that through various first-person and second-person methods, individuals could become more attuned or sensitized to aspects of their experience that might otherwise remain inaccessible to them (see Chapter 11). Developing this type of awareness and putting it to work in an experimental context could be especially relevant to the science of consciousness, for individuals skilled in this way might be able to provide more informative first-person reports about their experience. These reports could in turn significantly constrain the interpretation of neurophysiological data (Lutz and Thompson 2003).

The critical question for heterophenomenology is how it relates both to the ineliminable need to rely on the first-person perspective and to the possibility of putting the first-person perspective directly to work in science in a more careful phenomenological way. There seems to be nothing in the heterophenomenological method itself that disallows using the first-person perspective in this phenomenological way. On the contrary, if the material on which heterophenomenology goes to work is first-person reports about experience, and if the production of such reports sometimes requires that subjects attend to and describe their experience, then heterophenomenology already depends on the first-person mode of access to mental phenomena being put to work in an experimental setting.

On the other hand, given its resolutely third-person attitude, nothing in heterophenomenology would lead it to envision—let alone take the step—of working with experience in this direct phenomenological way. Hence, this step, which is simply unavoidable if progress is to be made in the science of consciousness, must come from outside heterophenomenology, with phenomenological concepts and procedures that heterophenomenology cannot provide. Heterophenomenology, therefore, must be deemed methodologically incomplete. In short, phenomenology from its start has already encompassed heterophenomenology (or its possibility), but heterophenomenology on its own is insufficient.

4. Dennett's view is that the "primary interpreted data" for the science of consciousness are subjects' expressed beliefs about their experiences, and not the experiences themselves. In the context of an experiment in which subjects are required to make introspective reports, it may be legitimate to treat those reports as belief expressions (though it does not follow that the experiences they report are themselves beliefs). In more ordinary cases, however, to take statements about experience as expressions of beliefs about experience seems strained. This sort of interpretation distorts experience by overintellectualizing it. A belief, in the canonical philosophical sense, is a mental state having the form "S believes that p," or in first-person form, "I believe that p." A state of this type contains a subject term, or an "I," as well as a whole propositional content. We should not assume *a priori*, however, that any given experience has to have these features. In interpreting first-person reports as expressions of belief, the heterophenomenologist runs the risk of over-interpreting subjects, thereby distorting their experience.

Dennett offers the following argument for why subjects' expressed beliefs should be the primary (interpreted) data for a science of consciousness: "if you have conscious experiences you don't believe you have—those extra conscious experiences are just as inaccessible *to you* as to the external observers. So a first-person approach garners you no more usable data than heterophenomenology does. Moreover . . . if you believe you have conscious experiences that you don't in fact have—then it is your beliefs that we need to explain, not the nonexistent experiences!" (Dennett 2005, p. 45). The problem with this argument is that it collapses the crucial distinction between conscious experience and belief about conscious experience. One can insist on the importance of this distinction without supposing that there are qualia of the sort Dennett is concerned to attack (private, ineffable, and possibly inaccessible qualities of experience). Consider that we can indeed have experiences we do not believe we have. Examples are pervasive moods, our experience during absorbed and fluid skillful activities, and rapid and transient emotional experiences. Such experiences are not inaccessible in principle; therefore they do not have to be construed as cases of phenomenal consciousness divorced from any possibility of access consciousness. First-person and second-person methods work directly with these sorts of experience and thus do indeed garner more usable data than heterophenomenology does.

This thinking indicates that the assimilation of experience to belief about experience also makes experience too static and determinate. Lived experience is dynamic and indeterminate in multiple ways, and thus always outstrips whatever beliefs we may happen to have about our experience. The question of what we believe about our experience arises when we take a reflective or deliberative stance, but most of experience is prereflective and spontaneous, not reflective and deliberative. (This point also indicates the limits of static phenomenology and signals the need for genetic and existential phenomenologies of experience.)

These considerations lead to the conclusion that we should not equate conscious experiences with beliefs about conscious experiences. We find that to limit the science of consciousness to what subjects believe about their experience is too constricting.

5. Dennett advertises heterophenomenology as a purely third-person approach, a neutral method for the study of consciousness, and the standard practice of scientists studying consciousness. Questions can be raised about each of these purported features.

Is heterophenomenology really a purely third-person approach? Consider an experiment in which we are interested specifically in what subjects report about their experiences. For example, we may wish to learn exactly what experiences subjects report having when they perform a cognitive task apparently requiring visualization and "mental rotation." Dennett allows that to investigate consciousness scientifically we need to make use of first-person reports about experience. To obtain such reports, however, we need to instruct subjects to attend to their experience and/or to recall their experience retrospectively. Such instructions belong to the "script" given by the experimenter to the subjects (Jack and Roepstorff 2002). This script is addressed to the subject in the second-person; the sort of attention it is meant to induce is a cognitive act that has to be put into play in the first-person singular; the response the subject gives is addressed to the experimenter in the second-person; and the entire context of this communication and endeavor is an intersubjective one (Jack and Roepstorff 2002; Roepstorff 2001).

In light of these considerations, what are we to make of Dennett's insistence that heterophenomenology is a purely third-person endeavor? If the natural sciences are supposed to be the model of what it means to take a purely third-person approach to one's subject matter, then heterophenomenology cannot be a purely third-person approach. Perhaps it is an "extension" of the third-person approach taken in the natural sciences (Dennett 2003, p. 19). Yet this way of putting things masks two crucial points.

First, heterophenomenology is no mere extension because it employs methods fundamentally different from the methods of the natural sciences. As Dennett himself emphasizes, heterophenomenology requires that we adopt the "intentional stance," whereby we interpret behavior as speech acts, and speech acts as expressions of belief. Notice that such interpretation also requires talking things over with the subjects. Heterophenomenology thus stands in an interpretive, intersubjective, and interpersonal relation to its subject matter. These features make it fundamentally different from (say) particle physics, organic chemistry, and molecular biology. Indeed, these sciences are not really third-personal but impersonal.

Second, talking things over with the subjects (if it is to be effective and respectful) is not a purely third-person endeavor but a second-person one. Heterophenomenology depends on this second-person approach, particularly when it comes to devising experimental scripts and working with subjects to make sure they understand them (and are willing to participate in them).

Heterophenomenology, therefore, simply cannot be a purely third-person approach in the way Dennett advertises. If physics, chemistry, and biology set the standard for what counts as a third-person approach, then heterophenomenology qualifies as a kind of critical second-person approach. If physics, chemistry, and biology are more properly seen as impersonal, then heterophenomenology qualifies as a kind of hybrid third-person/second-person approach. Either way, heterophenomenology winds up looking different from Dennett's presentation of it as more of the same old "objective science" (a conception that basically amounts to a kind of positivism).

Is heterophenomenology really a neutral method? The foregoing discussion has brought to light two ways in which heterophenomenology is not a neutral method.

First, Dennett builds into heterophenomenology a biased conception of how to interpret first-person descriptive reports about experience in relation to brain activity, namely, that they are to be evaluated for their truth and falsity according to how well their content matches the properties of neural activity. The bias of this approach is that it demands that we interpret subjects' reports as expressing beliefs not simply about "what is going on inside them," but about "what is going on inside them *subpersonally.*"

Second, Dennett builds into heterophenomenology a biased conception of the relation between conscious experiences and beliefs about conscious experiences, and hence about what the proper data for a science of consciousness are supposed to be.

Is heterophenomenology really the standard practice in the science of consciousness? Alvin Goldman (1997, 2004) has challenged Dennett's assertion that heterophenomenology, specifically its adoption of agnosticism about the truth of subjects' verbal reports, is standard practice in the science of consciousness (see also Goldman 2000). In Goldman's view, "scientists make a practice of relying 'substantially' on subjects' introspective reports" (Goldman 2004, p. 11). Dennett disputes this point (2003, pp. 24–25; 2005, pp. 50–54), but I concur with Goldman.[31] As Jack and Roepstorff (2002) write in an important article on introspection:

> Introspective observation is not just a pervasive feature of our personal lives. Cognitive scientists use this source of evidence to inform virtually every stage of their work. From the moment we conceive of an experimental paradigm, through piloting and refinement, to the interpretation of results, we are guided by considerations of our own experience and the experiences we attribute to others, understood by proxy to our own. The very language of cognitive science is, in substantial part, the language of experience. Discussions are laden with terms that we understand first and foremost by reference to our own internal states: "consciousness," "awareness," "attention," "recollection," "perception," "imagery," "rehearsal," "recognition," "effort," "dreaming," etc. Many psychological constructs, but by no means all, have an agreed upon "op-

erational" behavioural definition. Nonetheless, the question of whether the same construct can be applied to other situations is often difficult to determine. Behavioural paradigms can often be formalized in several different ways. Judgements of similarity and difference between paradigm are open to dispute. It is a simple fact that the cognitive characterization of behavioural paradigms ("task analysis") remains a matter of subjective judgement. Further, it is clear that these judgements are frequently, and sometimes explicitly, informed by introspective observation. Discussions of results are frequently sprinkled with hypotheses whose only direct method of verification is introspection. (Jack and Roepstorff 2002, p. 333)

The crucial point here is twofold: scientists rely substantially not only on subjects' introspective reports, but also on their own first-person experience. Without relying on their own experience, scientists would not only be unable to make sense of what subjects are saying; they would also be unable to grasp what cognitive phenomena are. Heterophenomenology claims that it can do justice to all the first-person phenomena from an entirely third-person perspective. What we are now in position to appreciate is that the heterophenomenologist will not be able to make sense of his third-person data without drawing on his own first-person experience of mental phenomena.

ELEVEN

Temporality and the Living Present

THE AIM OF THIS CHAPTER is to deepen the enactive approach to experience by addressing the relation between time and experience. The experience of time is a long-standing and core theme of phenomenological philosophy. Recently, a number of theorists have combined phenomenological treatments of time-consciousness with dynamic-systems approaches to the mind and brain (Gallagher and Varela 2003; Lloyd 2002, 2003; van Gelder 1999b; Varela 1999). This synthesis plays a central role in the approach to consciousness known as neurophenomenology, proposed originally by Francisco Varela (1996). Neurophenomenology is an offshoot of the enactive approach. Its aim is to incorporate phenomenological investigations of experience into neuroscientific research on consciousness. Neurophenomenology focuses especially on the temporal dynamics of conscious experience and brain activity (Lutz 2002; Lutz and Thompson 2003; Thompson, Lutz, and Cosmelli 2005). In this chapter, I discuss neurophenomenology and its relation to phenomenological accounts of time and experience.

Experience and the Flow of Action

In everyday life we usually act purposively, effectively, and spontaneously, without deliberation, reflection, or explicitly entertaining a purpose. We open the door, greet a friend, make tea, answer the phone, clear the table, and so on. Such actions have a unity or coherence in the present moment, while flowing one into another in a seamless way. Yet there is discontinuity too. We shift rapidly from one activity to another, creating and responding to new situations. Disturbances and breakdowns can happen, disrupting the flow of activity and forcing us to engage anew in what we need to be doing. These continuities and discontinuities testify to the complex relation between embodied action and the temporal structure of experience.

For Merleau-Ponty, as we saw in Chapter 9, embodied action is based on a kind of bodily intentionality he calls motor intentionality. Motor intentionality is the sort of intentionality that characterizes habitual actions and bodily skills, or what Hubert Dreyfus (1991, 2002, 2005) calls absorbed skillful coping. Skillful coping does not have a subject-object structure: one's experience is not that of standing over against an independent object and then acting on it or finding out about it. Rather, as Merleau-Ponty says, the intentionality in play "is *at* its object rather than positing it" (1962, p. 446). As Dreyfus explains:

> According to Merleau-Ponty, in absorbed, skillful coping, I don't need a mental representation of my goal. Rather, acting is experienced as a steady flow of skillful activity in response to one's sense of the situation. Part of that experience is a sense that when one's situation deviates from some optimal body-environment relationship, one's activity takes one closer to that optimum and thereby relieves the "tension" of the deviation. One does not need to know, nor can one normally express, what that optimum is. (Dreyfus 2002, p. 378)

In describing the kinesthetic experience of bodily movement in intentional action, Husserl had already stated that its intentional structure is "I can" (move this way) rather than "I think" (a particular thought) (1989, pp. 266–277). Merleau-Ponty takes up this formulation and applies it to motor intentionality: "Consciousness is in the first place not a matter of 'I think that' but of 'I can'" (1962, p. 137). Consider his example (cited in Chapter 4) of the football player in action:

> For the player in action the football field is not an "object" . . . It is pervaded with lines of force (the "yard lines"; those which demarcate the "penalty area") and articulated in sectors (for example, the "openings" between the adversaries) which call for a certain mode of action and

which initiate and guide the action as if the player were unaware of it. The field itself is not given to him, but present as the immanent term of his practical intentions; the player becomes one with it and feels the direction of the "goal," for example, just as immediately as the vertical and the horizontal planes of his own body. It would not be sufficient to say that consciousness inhabits this milieu. At this moment consciousness is nothing other than the dialectic of milieu and action. Each maneuver undertaken by the player modifies the character of the field and establishes in it new lines of force in which the action in turn unfolds and is accomplished, again altering the phenomenal field. (1963, pp. 168–169)

This passage contains a number of important ideas. As already mentioned, experience does not have a subject-object structure in immersed skillful action. Instead, experience is the phenomenal flow of one's body-environment coupling. Furthermore, consciousness here is not detached observation or reflective self-awareness, but rather a nonreflective attunement to the interplay of action and milieu. Finally, this interplay has a certain temporal form or structure. There is clearly a phenomenal flow, but there are also changes from moment to moment. Consciousness has the structure of a nonreflective "I can" in the flow of habitual action, but the leading "I can" can change from moment to moment and modify the character of the flow (Rietveld 2004). As Merleau-Ponty says, "Each maneuver undertaken by the player modifies the character of the field and establishes in it new lines of force in which the action in turn unfolds and is accomplished, again altering the phenomenal field."

This last idea raises a number of important questions: How do such momentary changes occur? What is the relationship between them and the flow overall? What sort of awareness or consciousness is proper to this experience of punctuated flow? These questions will occupy us throughout this chapter and the next one.

To prepare the way, we need to look more closely at the relation between experience and absorbed skillful action. Dreyfus states (in the passage quoted above) that in absorbed skillful coping "acting is *experienced* as a steady flow of skillful activity" (emphasis added). This characterization seems exactly right. In skillful coping, we experience our activity (it is not unconscious), and we experience it as a steady flow (unless there is some disruption or breakdown). Yet Dreyfus also suggests in other writings that "absorbed action in the world does not involve *an experience of acting*" (1991, p. 58; emphasis added). Sometimes he suggests that skillful coping is largely unconscious (2000, pp. 322–323) and that any subsequent report we feel inclined to make about our experience during absorbed action is "a retroactive rationalization of our ongoing activity" (1991, p. 57). This view seems inconsistent with the previous one and phenomenologically questionable. What accounts for this discrepancy?

The basic problem is that Dreyfus seems to think that the only kind of self-awareness is reflective awareness and hence that there is no prereflective self-awareness in skillful coping (see Poellner 2003, pp. 48–51). In this view, in skillful coping we experience a steady flow of activity, but we are unaware of our acting because we are absorbed in acting and do not reflect on it. Indeed, were we to reflect, we would no longer be immersed in the flow of activity but would have arrested it so as to comment on it after the fact. Although we should grant this point about reflection, it does not follow that we are completely unaware of our acting in skillful coping. The reason is that reflective self-awareness is not the only kind of self-awareness. As argued in the previous chapters, experience also comprises a prereflective self-awareness—including in particular a prereflective bodily self-consciousness—that is passive (involuntary) and intransitive (not object-directed). There is every reason to think that this sort of prereflective self-awareness animates skillful coping. If skillful coping were not prereflectively self-aware, then it would not be different from unconscious automaticity and would have no experiential character whatsoever. And if it had no experiential character, then there could be no genuine phenomenology of skillful coping, but only a logical reconstruction of it.

The most phenomenologically plausible way of interpreting the claim that absorbed action does not involve experience of acting is that it does not involve transitive consciousness of acting. To say that skillful coping does not have a subject-object structure means that there need be no transitive or object-directed awareness of either the environment or one's acting in skillful coping. As Dreyfus says, "in active coping I need not be thematically aware of my current activity," and although some skillful activities require me to be "explicitly aware of the environment . . . for most skills I can simply respond to the overall gestalt or affordance and need not be aware of it at all" (2000, pp. 322–323). Notice, however, that the kind of awareness being considered here is thematic or explicit awareness. It does not follow from the absence of this kind of awareness that there is no experience of acting at all. On the contrary, it makes sense to suppose that skillful coping, by contrast with mindless automaticity, involves a nonthematic and implicit experience of acting. More precisely, it makes sense to suppose that skillful coping involves—indeed requires—prereflective bodily experience.

Dreyfus appears to deny this idea when he writes, "background coping is necessarily nonthematic and largely unconscious" (2000, p. 323). But we need to draw the necessary phenomenological distinctions. First, there is clearly a crucial difference between activities that we nonthematically experience and activities that are unconscious. The former have an experiential character, and the latter are not experiential in any sense. Second, nonthematic experience can be transitive (object-directed) or intransitive (non-object-directed). Perceptual experience of one's surroundings, for example, involves a transitive and nonthematic or marginal awareness of the background, as well as a thematic or focal awareness of the foreground. Recall the case of hearing the hum of a refrigerator while focusing intently on a conversation one is having with a friend. One's awareness of the hum is marginal and nonthematic; one's awareness of the conversation is focal and thematic.

One's prereflective and nonthematic experience of one's body, however, is not a transitive awareness of a marginal or background *object*, but rather an intransitive and direct acquaintance with one's bodily *subjectivity,* an acquaintance whose form is that of a nonintentional and nonobservational bodily self-awareness (Gallagher 2003; Legrand 2006; Zahavi 2002a). If skillful coping were devoid of any experience of acting, if our activities in skillful coping had no experiential character whatsoever, then skillful coping would lack such bodily self-awareness. But then skillful coping would be completely nonsentient. If that were the case, then there could be no phenomenology of skillful coping and Dreyfus's project would have no foundation.

The implication of this line of thought is that absorbed action in the world does involve experience of acting—or perhaps we should say *acting experience*—but this experience is usually lived in a prereflective way without becoming the focus of attentive awareness. Our ability to report without observation or inference what we are doing and experiencing depends on such prereflective experience and cannot be explained away simply as retroactive rationalization. Rather, this ability is an ability to make explicit or manifest aspects of our experience that are implicit or latent. Making aspects of experience explicit in this way unavoidably involves interpretation and the creation of meaning (Gendlin 1997). It also presupposes a pregiven background of tacit and unreflective experience that can never be made fully explicit. In these respects, accounts of prereflective experience are interpretive and not merely descriptive. It hardly follows, however, that they are nothing more than retroactive rationalization. Indeed, to claim that they are is ultimately self-defeating because it logically requires some criterion by which to distinguish retroactive rationalization from accurate phenomenological description, and what could the basis for such a criterion be other than some kind of prereflective acquaintance with lived experience?

These considerations reinforce the importance of the idea, shared by phenomenologists from Husserl to Heidegger to Sartre to Merleau-Ponty, that our experience or existence or manner of being comprises an immediate and nonreflective self-awareness, one in which we are acquainted with ourselves prior to any reflection (Zahavi 2005a). In the next section, we will see that this type of self-awareness or self-acquaintance is intimately connected to time-consciousness and the temporal structure of experience.

Time-Consciousness and Prereflective Self-Awareness

The analysis of time-consciousness occupies a special place in phenomenology. Any comprehensive analysis of intentionality must take into account the temporal character of the intentional objects of experience. Objects persist and undergo change and transformation; processes unfold and develop in time; and events arise, endure, and cease. Certain things, such as melodies, have different aspects that cannot exist simultaneously, but only across time. Furthermore, at a deeper level, there are temporal "syntheses of identity" at work in experience. A tree along your path presents different profiles as you walk by, but you experience them as belonging to one and the same tree, not as disconnected and momentary fragments. As Merleau-Ponty says, "the perceptual synthesis is a temporal synthesis" (1962, p. 239). In addition, we remember past objects and events, and anticipate future ones. You can remember the bare tree of the winter as you pass by and admire its flowering in the spring, and you can anticipate its changing colors in the fall. The tree as remembered, the tree as perceived, and the tree as anticipated are all intended as one and the same tree. In general, for something to be experienced as objective, it must be experienced as exceeding or transcending the particular act that intends it, and such transcendence in turn requires that we experience it as having an identity across different intentional acts and appearances.

Furthermore, experience itself is temporal, and particular experiences are temporally related to each other. We are aware of our experiences and mental activities as arising, enduring, and ceasing, and as followed by other experiences and mental activities, all related to one another in complex ways. Time-consciousness thus comprises both awareness of external things and their temporal characters, and awareness of experience itself as temporal and as unified across time. Husserl's account of the structure of time-consciousness is meant to explain both sorts of awareness—how we can be aware of temporal objects (outer time-consciousness) and how we can be aware of our own ebbing and flowing experiences (inner time-consciousness). This account and the myriad analyses it comprises remain the reference point for any phenomenological consideration of time-consciousness.[1]

Husserl argues that it would be impossible to experience temporal objects if our consciousness of the present moment were the experience of a punctual or instantaneous now. Consciousness of the present moment must rather be an experience of the present as having temporal width. Husserl thus agrees with William James that "the practically cognized present is no knife-edge," but instead a "duration-block," a temporal expanse containing past and future phases, or as James says, "a bow and a stern . . . a forward- and rearward-looking part" (1981, p. 574). But whereas James takes this duration-block, which he calls, following E. R. Clay, "the specious present," as a basic datum of experience needing neurological explanation, Husserl takes it as requiring further phenomenological analysis (Gallagher 1998, pp. 32–52). More precisely, the duration-block of the present moment is an *intentional object* of time-consciousness. Hence it needs to be analyzed by tracing it back to the structure of the *intentional processes* that *constitute* it—that bring it to awareness, in the sense of enabling us to experience it in the way that we do.

According to Husserl, time-consciousness has a threefold structure. Three intentional processes, called primal impression, retention, and protention, work together in any intentional act and cannot operate on their own apart from one another. Husserl's favorite example is listening to a melody. For each now-phase of the melody, each currently sounding note, there is a corresponding primal impression directed exclusively toward it. (There are also, of course, primal impressions of the now-phases prior to and after completion of the melody.) Primal impression involves no reference to either past or future, and so by itself is insufficient for the perception of the melody (and for the experience of any temporal object, no matter how brief its duration). Primal impression must be accompanied by retention and protention.

Retention is directed toward the just-elapsed phase of the melody, the just-heard note, which though no longer actual, is still being heard in the mode of just-past. The note still subjectively sounds not because it is really present to consciousness; on the contrary, it is no longer actual. It is present only intentionally; it is mentally intended as just-past.

Protention, by contrast, is directed in a more indefinite way toward the immediate future, in this case toward the notes of the melody sensed as just-about-to-occur. Unlike retention, which is intentionally filled or determinate in content, protention is unfilled or indeterminate. This openness, however, does involve a sense of anticipation, for were the melody to stop abruptly or were a wrong note to sound, we would be surprised. It is always possible in principle for us to be surprised in this way, no matter what the content of our present experience. Thus our consciousness always involves an open and forward-looking horizon.

The unified operation of protention, primal impression, and retention underlies our experience of the present moment as having temporal width. Primal impression is the continuous intending of the new, even if it be only the newly unchanging (as in the case of a continually sounding tone); retention is the continuous holding onto the present as slipping away and sinking into the past; and protention is the continuous going beyond the present as opening into the future. This threefold structure is invariant and present synchronically as a unified whole throughout the course of experience. Although the specific experiential contents of this structure change from moment to moment, the structure itself does not (unless consciousness suffers a radical breakdown).

It is important to distinguish retention and protention (intentional processes proper to the structure of any intentional act) from recollection and expectation (understood as specific types of intentional acts). There is a clear difference between retentional consciousness of the just-played notes of a melody and recollection of a past and finished hearing of the melody. Similarly, there is a clear difference between protentional consciousness of the about-to-be-played notes and expectation of hearing the melody at some time in the future. Retention and protention are structural features of any occurrent experience, and therefore recollection (the remembering of a past experience) and expectation (the anticipation of a future experience) themselves presuppose the work of retention and protention. For this reason, Husserl sometimes calls retention *primary memory* and recollection *secondary memory*, and protention *primary anticipation* and expectation *secondary anticipation*.

These secondary types of intentional act are *re-presentational*, whereas the primary forms of experience are *presentational*. Retention and protention function to make the immediate past and the immediate future intentionally available in our perceptual experience of the now. Recollection and expectation function to bring something absent into a kind of presence by mentally evoking a perceptual experience of it. We recollect a past playing of a melody by recollecting our previous experience of it, and we anticipate a future playing of the melody by anticipating our future experience of it. Finally, whereas recollection and expectation are intentional acts that we can initiate deliberately, retention and protention are passive and involuntary processes that operate continuously.

Figure 11.1 illustrates this continuous operation of primal impression-retention-protention. The horizontal line ABCD represents a temporal object, such as a stretch of a familiar melody. The vertical lines represent abstract momentary phases of an enduring act of consciousness. Each phase is structured by the three intentional processes of primal impression (pi), retention (r), and protention (p). If we let phase 3 be the actual now-phase, then there is a primal impression (pi_3) of the now sounding note C, a protention (p_3) of the next impending phase of consciousness (to be filled by note D), and a retention (r_3) of

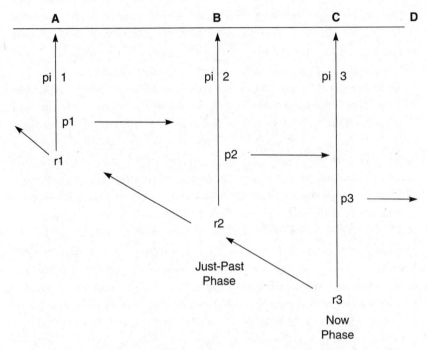

Figure 11.1. Time-consciousness according to Husserl. Reprinted with permission from Shaun Gallagher, *The Inordinance of Time* (Evanston, IL: Northwestern University Press, 1998), 79, fig. 5.1.

the just-past phase 2 of consciousness, whose primal impression (pi$_2$) was of note B.

As this figure illustrates, any given now-phase of consciousness retains the whole just-past phase of consciousness, specifically this phase's primal impression, retention, and protention. This just-past phase in turn retains its whole immediately prior phase, this prior phase its immediately prior phase, and so on, so that at any given moment there is a retentional continuum stretching back over past experience. Of course, this stretching back is intentional, not real. Present consciousness does not literally reach back into the past, nor are past phases really inherent in the present phase. Rather, the past is only intentionally contained in the present. The present phase intends the past ones and thereby keeps them in view. Yet the past phases are also perpetually slipping away and disappearing from view. The retentional continuum is characterized by decreasing clarity and affective force as it sinks back into the past, but it is also renewed at each moment, simultaneously being filled with new content while old content perpetually slips away into a sedimented and ultimately unconscious substratum.

Two important types of intentionality belong to this retentional continuum. The first type is the intentional unification of consciousness over time. This unification happens automatically because retention retains the previous phases of consciousness, specifically their interlocking primal impressions, retentions, and protentions. Husserl calls this retention of consciousness the *horizontal* or *lengthwise intentionality* of time-consciousness. Thanks to this lengthwise intentionality, consciousness is internally related to itself and self-affecting.

The second type of intentionality ensures the continuity of the experienced temporal object. This intentional process also happens automatically, because the retention of consciousness necessarily includes the retention of the intentional object belonging to the previous phases of consciousness. Husserl calls this type of intentionality the *transverse intentionality* of time-consciousness. Notice that the transverse intentionality, the retention of the temporal object, is founded on the lengthwise intentionality, the retention of the previous phases of consciousness. In other words, any given now-phase of consciousness retains the just-past phase of its temporal object by virtue of retaining the just-past phase of consciousness. To be aware of intentional objects across time, consciousness must also be retentionally aware of itself.

We can now begin to appreciate the relation between time-consciousness and prereflective self-awareness. As we have seen, each phase of experience retains not only the intentional contents of the just-past experience, but also the just-past phase of the experience itself, including its retentional-impressional-protentional structure. The retention of the just-past notes happens through the retention of one's just-past experience of them. In other words, retention explicitly grasps the just-past intentional content by implicitly holding onto the just-past experience. Thus the threefold structure of time-consciousness entails prereflective self-consciousness. At the same time one is aware of the melody, one is implicitly co-aware of one's ongoing experience of that melody, thanks to the threefold temporal structure of one's experience.

At this point, however, a problem arises. Our focus so far has been on the experience of external temporal objects, such as melodies. But we are also aware of our own transitory intentional acts or experiences and their temporal relations. Indeed, we just saw that in being aware of a melody, we are also implicitly aware of our enduring act of listening. Here then is the problem. In analyzing how there can be such things as melodies for our consciousness (how melodies are constituted), we have appealed to the threefold structure of time-consciousness. But what about our intentional acts or experiences themselves? Is their constitution for consciousness also to be analyzed in terms of the threefold structure of primal impression-retention-protention? But then what is to prevent such an analysis from leading to an infinite regress? If the phenomenal duration and unity of a melody are constituted by time-consciousness, and if our act of listening to the melody is itself also experienced with duration and unity, then are we not forced to posit yet another consciousness to account for this inner duration and unity? Is there any way to stop this regress?

Husserl grappled with this problem throughout his writings on time-consciousness. According to the standard interpretation of his views, Husserl distinguishes among three levels of temporality—*external temporal objects* (such as melodies), *experiences* of those objects or *intentional acts* directed at them, and the *experiencing of those intentional acts themselves*. Given that we are or can become aware of our experiences and intentional acts as unfolding in time, they also have a temporal character, but one belonging to subjective or immanent time, by contrast with the objective or transcendent time of external temporal objects. Whereas these external temporal objects are brought to awareness or constituted by intentional acts existing in immanent time, these intentional acts are brought to awareness or constituted by a deeper level of inner time-consciousness, which Husserl calls the absolute consciousness or the absolute flow. The absolute flow is supposed to be the deepest level of time-consciousness, a bedrock stratum that is presupposed by every other type of consciousness and intentional performance, and that makes all of them possible.

Given this framework, two questions immediately arise. The first concerns subjective or immanent time. Is it right to think of our intentional acts and experiences as *objects* of inner time-consciousness (i.e., as *internal temporal objects*) on analogy with objects of outer time-consciousness or external temporal objects? Does this way of thinking not distort self-awareness and how we experience ourselves in time? The second question concerns the absolute consciousness. Is this consciousness itself experienced? If it is not experienced, then it seems a theoretical construction, with no intuitable content. If it is, then it too must somehow be brought to awareness or constituted by consciousness, but then there looms an infinite regress.

To address the first question properly, it will help to know more about Husserl's conception of the absolute consciousness. So let me set this first question aside for the moment and return to it after addressing the second one.

Husserl's view is that consciousness as sheer flow is phenomenologically discernible. We can see, if we look closely and carefully enough (adhering to the epoché and phenomenological reduction), a flowing or streaming belonging to our consciousness that is distinct from the objects or contents of consciousness, that is, from whatever our experience is about or directed toward, whether in the objective and transcendent world, or the subjective and immanent sphere of our own intentional acts and experiences (Husserl 1991, p. 389). This flowing or streaming consciousness is absolute, ultimate, or original, in the sense that it is a condition of possibility for every other kind of consciousness, but is not itself made possible by some other, still deeper level of consciousness.

But given this idea, how can we avoid an infinite regress? If the absolute flow is itself experienced as flowing or unfolding in time, then its temporal phases must be brought to awareness or constituted by some still deeper level of consciousness. In this case the absolute flow is not really absolute, and the whole problem arises once more, with no end in sight.

Husserl tries to deal with this problem in two striking ways. First, he tries to make plausible the idea that the absolute flow is *self-constituting*, thanks to its horizontal or lengthwise intentionality (Husserl 1991, pp. 390–394). The flow of consciousness retains and protends itself—including retaining its protending of itself and protending its retaining of itself—and is in this way self-unifying. The absolute flow, it is tempting to say, is *self-organizing*. Second, Husserl denies that the absolute flow is a process unfolding *in* time or moving *through* time. The absolute time-consciousness is not one or another temporal process located in the flow of phenomenal time; it is the self-constituting flow of phenomenal time itself. Temporal predicates—"before," "after," "simultaneous," and so on—apply to the temporal objects of our experience, to the enduring, changing, and temporally ordered intentional objects of time-consciousness. But they do not apply literally and univocally to the absolute time-consciousness whereby we experience those objects. Although the absolute flow is temporal or has a kind of temporality, it is not in time in any familiar or ordinary sense. Thus the infinite regress is blocked.

The line of argument here is conceptual, transcendental, and phenomenological. It is a familiar conceptual point that an experience of something as red or loud, for example, is not itself red or loud. Similarly, the timing of what is experienced is not the same as the timing of the experience. For example, an experience whose temporal content is "A before B" does not have to take the form of an experience of A followed by an experience of B (see Dennett 1991a, pp. 148–149). To borrow an example from William James, in experiencing the silence before the thunder, we do not need to have first an experience of silence and then an experience of thunder. As James writes: "Into the awareness of the thunder itself the awareness of the previous silence creeps and continues; for what we hear when the thunder crashes is not thunder pure, but thunder-breaking-upon-silence-and-contrasting-with-it" (1981, p. 234). In general, an experience that presents something as having a beginning, an end, and a duration cannot itself be assumed to have a beginning, an end, and a duration in the same way (see Dennett 1991a, pp. 101–170; Dennett and Kinsbourne 1992; Pylyshyn 2003, pp. 369–370). Husserl recognizes this point, but applies it in a radical way consistent with his transcendental phenomenology.

In general, one cannot assume that concepts and terms applicable to the *constituted* (that which is given to experience) apply univocally to the *constituting* (that which makes such experience possible). If phenomenal or lived time (including scientifically understood time) is constituted by the structure of time-consciousness, then the concepts and terms applicable to phenomenal time are not univocally transposable to time-consciousness. But—and this is the crucial point—all our familiar temporal concepts pertain to time as *constituted*, and hence they cannot apply literally to the time-*constituting* absolute flow. With this thought in mind, Husserl admits that even the term *flow* here is metaphorical: "For all of this, we have no names" (1991, p. 382).

This line of thought is also phenomenological. We can distinguish within experience between what changes or varies and what remains invariant. The contents of the present moment—the particular things of which we are aware—arise and perish. But the present moment as a structure of awareness does not change or vary. No matter what we experience, it is always there, or rather always here. It is not a changing content of experience, but an unchanging structure of experience, the threefold structure of primal impression-retention-protention. Husserl calls the present moment understood this way the "living present." The living present does not flow through time; time "wells up" within it. Husserl describes the living present as "standing-streaming." It is standing because it does not move in or through time; it is streaming because as the continuous operation of primal impression-retention-protention, it underlies any appearance of flow whatsoever, including the appearance of consciousness to itself as flow.

We can now return to the question about whether it is right to think of our intentional acts and experiences as objects of inner time-consciousness or internal temporal objects. The discussion so far has been premised on the idea that we need to distinguish within experience overall between the experienced external object and the experienced intentional act—between our experience of the melody proceeding in time and our simultaneous experience of our listening act unfolding in time. But in what sense do we experience our listening as distinct from the melody? In particular, does it make sense to say that we experience our listening (or any intentional act) as a temporal *object,* albeit one of a special, immanent sort?

To address this question, let us return to the point that we experience absorbed activity not as having a subject-object structure, but instead as an immediate coupling or dynamic attunement to our environment. From this perspective, Husserl's classic descriptions of listening to a melody seem disembodied and abstract. He does not tell us whether the experience is an absorbed listening to a familiar and cherished piece of music or a hearing of a new and unfamiliar work, whether the performance is live or a recording, whether the setting is a celebratory event in the company of others or a solitary and contemplative listening. Of course, Husserl is interested in precisely the invariant structure of time-consciousness, which presumably constitutes the listening experience as such in any possible situation. It is important to grant and recognize the force of this point. Nevertheless, in abstracting away from the concrete setting of the experience, we run the risk of objectifying the experience and thereby misdescribing it. Especially if the listening is an absorbed or immersed one, there will not be any explicit or thematic awareness of the melody as a distinct object, or any explicit or thematic awareness of our ongoing listening.

This observation seriously challenges the idea that we ordinarily experience our listening as any kind of internal temporal object distinct from the heard melody. Recall that object-directed consciousness is transitive. To suppose that we experience our listening as an inner temporal object is accordingly to suppose that in being transitively conscious of the melody we are also transitively conscious of our listening. But this supposition seems mistaken, for the way we ordinarily experience our listening (and our intentional activities generally) is prereflectively and intransitively, not reflectively and transitively.

This point brings us back to the topic of prereflective self-awareness. Dan Zahavi (2003a, 2003b, 2005a) has proposed a different reconstruction of Husserl's account of temporality, one that equates inner time-consciousness with prereflective self-awareness. According to this view, transitive consciousness of intentional acts and experiences happens only in reflection and certain sorts of recollection. Prior to reflection or recollection there is no transitive or object-directed awareness of experience, certainly no explicit or thematic awareness, but also not even a marginal one. Rather, there is only experience of temporal objects and events in the world, as well as the prereflective and intransitive self-awareness of those very experiences. When we listen to a melody we hear the melody (transitive consciousness), but we also subjectively live through our listening (intransitive consciousness). The listening has a subjective character that makes it immediately manifest, without observation or inference, as one's own experience. In this way, we experience our listening implicitly, without its becoming an object of awareness—not even a marginal or background one, for the first-personal quality of the experience is precisely its subjectivity and not a type of object-consciousness. The subjectivity of the experience consists essentially in its being intransitively and nonreflectively self-aware. Or rather it consists in its being prereflectively self-aware, for it can come to be reflected upon but is necessarily prior to any such reflection. Only when reflected upon does it come to figure in awareness as a temporal unity of its own in immanent or subjective time.[2] Otherwise, it is simply lived through without being individuated as an experience.

Earlier we saw that prereflective self-awareness is a necessary condition for the experience of temporal phenomena. To be aware of phenomena across time, consciousness must be retentionally and protentionally aware of itself across time. Therefore, time-consciousness entails prereflective self-awareness. In other words, our being conscious of external temporal phenomena entails that our temporally enduring experiences of those phenomena are self-aware. Inner time-consciousness is thus nothing other than prereflective self-awareness.

If we understand inner time-consciousness this way, then what becomes of the absolute consciousness or absolute flow? How does it fit into this account?

In answering this question, we arrive at the following fundamental idea: "The absolute flow of experiencing simply is the pre-reflective self-manifestation of our experiences" (Zahavi 2003b, p. 169). Put another way, the structure of inner time-consciousness—primal impression-retention-protention—is exactly the structure of prereflective self-awareness and also precisely the absolute flow. We can appreciate this equivalence in the following way. The absolute flow is the standing-streaming living present. On the one hand, the living present is streaming because it is the continuous transformation (intentional modification) of the about-to-happen into the happening into the just-happened. On the other hand, the living present is standing, because the threefold structure of protention-primal impression-retention that constitutes the streaming is always present and unchanging.

The crucial point now is that this description of the absolute flow or standing-streaming living present also applies precisely to prereflective self-awareness. Preflective self-awareness is streaming because it is constitutive of the streaming or flowing experiences themselves, not a pure and empty awareness that appears on its own. By the same token, it is standing because it is an ever-present and unchanging feature of consciousness. As Zahavi writes, "Whereas we live through a number of different experiences, our self-awareness remains as an unchanging dimension. It stands—to use the striking image of James—permanent, like the rainbow on the waterfall, with its own quality unchanged by the events that stream through it" (2003b, p. 170).

Neurophenomenology and Time-Consciousness

In recent years, scientists and philosophers interested in the temporal dynamics of consciousness have rediscovered Husserl's analyses of time-consciousness (Lloyd 2002, 2003; van Gelder 1999b; Varela 1999). Varela in particular puts these analyses to use in his neurophenomenological approach to consciousness and offers a neurophenomenological account of time-consciousness as "an acid test of the entire neurophenomenological enterprise" (Varela 1999, p. 267).

Varela formulates the "working hypothesis" of neurophenomenology in the following way: "Phenomenological accounts of the structure of experience and their counterparts in cognitive science relate to each other through reciprocal constraints" (1996, p. 343). By "reciprocal constraints" he means that phenomenological analyses can help guide and shape the scientific investigation of consciousness, and that scientific findings can in turn help guide and shape the phenomenological investigations. A crucial feature of this approach is that dynamic systems theory is supposed to mediate between phenomenology and neuroscience. Neurophenomenology thus comprises three main elements (see Figure 11.2): (1) phenomenological accounts of the structure of experience; (2) formal dynamical models of these structural invariants; and (3) realizations of these models in biological systems.

Given that time-consciousness is supposed to be an acid test of the neurophenomenological enterprise, we need to see whether phenomenological accounts of the structure of time-consciousness and neurodynamical accounts of the brain processes relevant to consciousness can be related to each other in a mutually illuminating way. This task is precisely the one Varela undertakes in his neurophenomenology of time-consciousness and in his experimental research on the neurodynamics of consciousness.

Varela's strategy is to find a common structural level of description that captures the dynamics of both the impressional-retentional-protentional flow of time-consciousness and the large-scale neural processes thought to be associated with consciousness. We have already seen how the flow of time-consciousness is self-constituting. What we now need to examine is how this self-constituting flow is supposed to be structurally mirrored at the biological level by the self-organizing dynamics of large-scale neural activity.

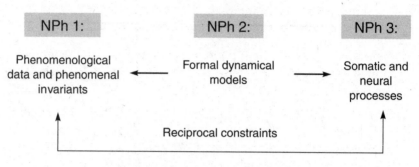

Figure 11.2. Neurophenomenology.

There is now little doubt in cognitive neuroscience that specific cognitive acts, such as the visual recognition of a face, require the rapid and transient coordination of many functionally distinct and widely distributed brain regions. Neuroscientists also increasingly believe that moment-to-moment, transitive (object-directed) consciousness is associated with dynamic, large-scale neural activity rather than any single brain region or structure (Cosmelli, Lachaux, and Thompson, 2007). Hence, any model of the neural basis of mental activity, including consciousness, must account for how large-scale neural activities can operate in an integrated or coherent way from moment to moment.

This problem is known as the large-scale integration problem (Varela et al. 2001). According to dynamical neuroscience, the key variable for understanding large-scale integration is not so much the activity of the individual neural components, but rather the nature of the dynamic links among them. The neural counterparts of mental activity are thus investigated at the level of collective variables that describe emergent and changing patterns of large-scale integration. One recent approach to defining these collective variables is to measure transient patterns of synchronous oscillations between different populations of neurons (Engel, Fries, and Singer 2001; Varela et al. 2001). According to Varela (1995, 1999), these synchrony patterns define a temporal frame of momentary and transient neural integration that corresponds to the duration of the present moment of experience.

Varela presents the reasoning behind this view in the form of three connected, but logically independent, working hypotheses (1995, 1999, pp. 274–277):

Hypothesis 1: For every cognitive act, there is a singular, specific neural assembly that underlies its emergence and operation.

According to this hypothesis, the emergence of any cognitive act requires the rapid coordination of many different capacities (attention, perception, memory, motivation, and so on) and the widely distributed neural systems subserving them. The neurophysiological substrate for this large-scale coordination is assumed to be a neural assembly, which can be defined as a distributed subset of neurons with strong reciprocal connections.[3]

In the context of large-scale integration, a dynamic neural assembly engages vast and disparate regions of the brain. There are reciprocal connections within the same cortical area or between areas at the same level of the network; there are also reciprocal connections that link different levels in different brain regions. Because of these strong interconnections across widely distributed areas, a large-scale neural assembly can be activated or ignited from any of its smaller subsets, whether sensorimotor or internal. These assemblies have a transient, dynamic existence that spans the time required to accomplish an elementary cognitive act and for neural activity to propagate through the assembly.

Various empirical and theoretical considerations suggest that the time-scale of such neurocognitive activity—whether it be a perception/action state (such as an eye or head movement), passing thought or memory, or emotional appraisal—is in the range of a fraction of a second, roughly 250–500 milliseconds or more (see Dennett and Kinsbourne 1992; Pöppel 1988). Varela (1999) calls this scale of duration the "1 scale" of large-scale integration and he distinguishes it from the "1/10 scale" of elementary sensorimotor and neural events (10–100 milliseconds), and the "10 scale" of descriptive-narrative assessments involving memory. During successive time intervals at the 1/10 and 1 scale, there is competition between different neural assemblies: when a neural assembly is ignited from one or more of its smaller subsets, it either reaches coherence or is swamped by the competing activations of other overlapping assemblies. If the assembly holds together after its activation, then one can assume it has a transitory efficacy. This holding time is bound by two simultaneous constraints: (1) it must be larger than the time (at the 1/10 scale) for spike transmission either directly or through a small number of synapses; and (2) it must be smaller than the time (at the 1 scale) it takes for a cognitive act to be completed. Thus the relevant neuronal processes are distributed not only in space, but also over periods of time that cannot be compressed beyond a certain limit (a fraction of a second).

Given Hypothesis 1, the question arises of how large-scale dynamic integration actually happens in the brain so as to make possible a flow of coherent and adaptive cognitive acts. One answer currently being explored in neuroscience is that large-scale integration happens through some form of temporal coding, in which the precise time at which individual neurons fire determines whether they participate in a given assembly. The most well-studied candidate for this kind of temporal coding is *phase synchrony*. Populations of neurons exhibit oscillatory discharges over a wide range of frequencies and can enter into precise synchrony or phase-locking over a limited period of time (a fraction of a second).[4] A growing body of evidence suggests that phase synchrony is an indicator (perhaps a mechanism) of large-scale integration (Engel, Fries, and Singer 2001; Varela et al. 2001). Varela states this idea in the form of a second hypothesis:

> *Hypothesis 2:* A specific neural assembly is selected through the fast, transient phase-locking of activated neurons belonging to subthreshold, competing neural assemblies.

Neural phase synchrony (the phase-locking of oscillatory discharges) occurs at various scales in the brain. Short-range synchronies occur within local networks (columns in primary visual cortex, for example), long-range synchronies over widely separated brain regions. In keeping with Hypothesis 2, long-range synchronization has been proposed as a mechanism for (or at least indicator of) the transient formation of a coherent large-scale neural assembly that selects and integrates multimodal networks (for example, between occipital and frontal lobes, or across hemispheres, which are separated by dozens of milliseconds in transmission time). Animal and human studies demonstrate that specific changes in synchrony occur during arousal, sensorimotor integration, attentional selection, perception, and working memory (Engel, Fries, and Singer 2001; Varela et al. 2001). It has also been hypothesized that whether a local neural process participates directly in a particular (transitive) conscious state depends on whether it participates in a coherent, synchronous large-scale assembly (Dehaene and Naccache 2001; Engel and Singer 2001; Tononi and Edelman 1998; Varela 1995).

Phase synchronies occur in a broad range of frequencies. Fast rhythms (above 15 hertz) in beta and gamma frequencies meet the requirement for rapid integration, and have been shown to play an important role in perceptual and attentional processes on the time-scale of fractions of a second (the 1 scale) (Engel, Fries, and Singer 2001; Varela et al. 2001). Slow rhythms (4–12 hertz) in alpha and theta bands have been shown to play important roles in attention and working memory and in sensorimotor integration.[5] These slow rhythms probably also play an important role in motivation and emotion (Lewis 2005), and may provide the context or carrier for fast-rhythm processes (VanRullen and Koch 2003). Taken together, these ideas and evidence support the general notion that phase synchrony subserves the overall integration of all aspects of a cognitive act, including associative memory, affective tone, emotional appraisal, and motor planning (Damasio 1990; Varela 1995; Varela et al. 2001).

Large-scale integration must involve not only the establishment of dynamic links, but also their active uncoupling or dismantling, in order to make way for the next cognitive act. Therefore, not only phase synchrony, but also desynchrony or "phase scattering" is thought to play an important role in large-scale integration (Varela 1995; Rodriguez et al. 1999; Varela et al. 2001, p. 236).[6]

Varela's third hypothesis is that this dynamic of synchronization and desynchronization is the neural basis for what we experience as the present cognitive moment:

Hypothesis 3: The integration-relaxation processes at the 1 scale are strict correlates of present-time consciousness.

To explain this hypothesis we need to go back to the distinction between the 1/10 scale and the 1 scale. Elementary sensorimotor and neural events at the 1/10 scale (10–100 milliseconds) are integrated into the 1 scale (250 milliseconds to several seconds) thanks to long-range integration and the formation of large-scale neural assemblies. In the language of dynamic systems theory, a neural assembly must have a "relaxation time," a time span during which it arises and stabilizes, followed by a bifurcation or phase-transition to a new assembly (a new pattern of long-range integration).

Varela's hypothesis is that this relaxation time (which is variable and dynamically dependent on a host of factors, such as fatigue, interest, motivation, affect, age, and so on) defines a temporal frame or window of simultaneity, such that whatever falls within this window counts as happening "now" for the system (Varela, Thompson, and Rosch 1991, pp. 72–79; see also VanRullen and Koch 2003). This neurodynamical "now" has an incompressible width or thickness, corresponding to the (variable) frame or window of the 1 scale, within which it incorporates elementary events of the 1/10 scale. It is therefore precisely not a knife-edge present, but a duration-block, having forward and rearward ends, a bow and a stern. According to Varela, this neurodynamical "now" is the neural basis for the present cognitive moment. In other words, the temporal structure of experience, specifically the rearward and forward-looking "now," depends on the way the brain dynamically parses its own activity. The term *strict correlates* in Hypothesis 3 is thus misleading because this hypothesis is meant to be causal, not merely correlative. The aim is to explain how the temporal structure of experience is caused by and realized in the dynamic structure of biological processes.

An experimental study by Varela and his colleagues can be used to illustrate these ideas (Rodriguez et al. 1999). This study used the visual recognition of high-contrast, black-and-white patterns as faces (so-called Mooney figures) as a paradigmatic example of a moment of consciousness. This study showed that conscious perception of meaningful complex forms is accompanied by synchronous activities in distant brain regions as recorded at the scalp level by EEG (electroencephalogram) (see Plate VI). Subjects were shown upright and upside-down Mooney figures, which are easily perceived as faces when presented upright, but usually perceived as meaningless black and white forms when presented upside-down. Subjects had to decide as rapidly as possible whether or not they perceived a face at first glance, and then they were asked to report accordingly by pressing on a two-choice button.

When the pattern of phase synchrony between pairs of electrodes in the gamma frequency band (30–45 hertz) was directly measured, it showed marked quantitative and qualitative differences between the "perception" and "no perception" conditions. Between 200 and 260 milliseconds, a first period of significant synchronization was observed in the perception condition but not in the no-perception condition. The synchrony involved left parieto-occipital and frontotemporal regions. Notice that this phase synchrony pattern is long-distance (between pairs of electrodes over widely separated regions of the scalp), unfolds at the 1 scale of duration (roughly 250 milliseconds after stimulus presentation), and corresponds to the moment of perceptual recognition (seeing the face "now"). This synchronization was followed by a period of massive loss of synchronization or phase scattering that peaked at around 500 milliseconds and was observed between parietal and occipitotemporal regions bilaterally. This finding suggests that an active uncoupling or desynchronization may be necessary for the transition from one synchronous neural assembly (and cognitive moment) to another.

Finally, a second period of synchrony increase appeared around 700 milliseconds. This final period coincided with the subject's button pressing and appears to be related to the motor response in both conditions. This second period is the only period of time in which some similarity between the phase synchrony patterns in the perception and no-perception conditions was noted. Although this study is correlative, not causal, it provides suggestive evidence that long-distance phase synchronization and desynchronization may subserve the temporal parsing of cognition into coherent and momentary acts.[7]

A crucial feature of this approach is that cognitive time is not based on any external or internal uniformly ticking clock, but rather arises from an endogenous and self-organizing neurodynamics. According to Varela, this dynamics can be described as having a retentional-protentional structure. Each emergent assembly arises as a bifurcation from the immediately previous one and is attracted along a certain forward trajectory, while containing the trace of its predecessor. At one level, each assembly can be seen as an individual pattern that arises, stabilizes, and subsides, thereby giving way to the next assembly. At another level, there is one itinerant trajectory, which wanders among various intrinsically unstable, attractor regions (corresponding to transient neural assemblies), without ever settling down to any one of them, illustrating a type of behavior known as chaotic itinerancy (Tsuda 2001). Varela's proposal is that the threefold structure of time-consciousness can be redescribed using these concepts of dynamic-systems theory, and that the resulting dynamical description can be grounded in biological features of the brain. In this way, he proposes to "naturalize" the phenomenological account of the structure of time-consciousness.

The key to this naturalized account is the principle of emergence through collective self-organization. As we have seen, emergence through self-organization has two sides: local-to-global determination (the formation of macrolevel patterns through microlevel interactions) and global-to-local determination (the constraining of microlevel interactions by macrolevel patterns). In the present case, the microlevel corresponds to arrays of neurons that behave as coupled nonlinear oscillators (at the 1/10 scale) thanks to their intrinsic cellular properties (see Le Van Quyen, Schuster, and Varela 1996). These oscillators enter into a synchrony or phase-locking that is described by the collective variable of relative phase (at the 1 scale). This collective or large-scale phase-synchrony pattern is a global indicator of the large-scale integration underlying a particular cognitive act.

This emergent act or behavior arises on the basis of the elementary components, but these components act as they do because of the global pattern in which they participate. As Varela observes (1999, p. 283), this sort of neurocognitive self-organization is not an abstract computation, but an embodied behavior subject to initial conditions (what the agent has just done and intends to do) and various exogenous and endogenous parameters (changes in environmental conditions, attentional modulation, motivation, and so on). Neural assemblies and large-scale integration are thus always embedded in and modulated by particular bodily and environmental contexts (Thompson and Varela 2001). Gallagher and Varela summarize this approach in the following way:

> The fact that an assembly of coupled oscillators attains a transient synchrony and that it happens within a certain temporal window is the explicit substrate of the living present. The dynamical models and the data show that this synchronization is dynamically unstable and will thus constantly and successively give rise to new assemblies (these transformations define the trajectories of the system). Each emergence bifurcates from the previous ones determined by its initial and boundary

conditions. Thus the preceding emergence is still present in the succeeding one as the trace of the dynamical trajectory (*retention* on the phenomenological level). The order parameters (initial conditions and boundary conditions) are important here. They are defined by the embodiment and experiential context of the action, behaviour, or cognitive act. The boundary conditions shape the action at the global level and include the contextual setting of the task performed, as well as the independent modulations arising from the contextual setting where the action occurs (i.e., new stimuli or endogenous changes in motivation). (Gallagher and Varela 2003, p. 123; see also Varela 1999, p. 283)

So far we have seen that neural coherence (phase synchrony) at the 1 scale is supposed to be the neurobiological correlate of the present cognitive moment and that the dynamical trajectory of neural coherence—the way each transient pattern of coherence contains a trace of its predecessor and is attracted along a certain trajectory—is supposed to be the neurobiological correlate of retention-protention. What about the self-constituting absolute flow or standing-streaming structure of time-consciousness? How is it supposed to be dynamically described and biologically realized?

Recall that the absolute flow is an invariant structure of experience, not a changing content of experience. This point suggests that, in dynamic-systems terms, the absolute flow cannot correspond to any particular attractor region (synchrony pattern) or trajectory in phase space. Rather, it must correspond to an invariant and generic feature of the dynamics, which needs to be described in terms of the geometry of the entire phase space.

Varela proposes that this generic feature is the self-organizing nature of the system's dynamics, in particular the intrinsic instability or metastability of the system's dynamics. There are two important aspects to this idea. First, the absolute flow has to be described in terms not of any particular trajectory, but of the collection of all trajectories (all possible behaviors)—in other words at the level of what is known as the system "flow" in dynamic systems theory. Second, the dynamics that shapes this flow, in the case of the brain, is self-generating and metastable. Metastability means that the surface or manifold over which a trajectory courses is unstable, so that the trajectory shifts constantly from one unstable region to another without ever settling down

to any one of them. In a metastable system, noise and dynamic instability are intrinsic to the system, so that the system can switch au-
tonomously from one behavior to another, without any external in-
struction.[8] On the one hand, the system is constantly self-moving,
transiting from one local instability to another, without ever settling
down or staying put. On the other hand, the self-movement that manifests in any trajectory is generically the same. There is thus a kind of
standing-streaming character to the dynamics. Self-movement is the
nature of the system and is generically the same for any trajectory
(standing), but this self-movement exists or manifests itself only in the
individual, unstable trajectories (streaming).

So far I have presented neurophenomenology as a theoretical proposal to naturalize the phenomenological account of time-
consciousness by redescribing the structure of time-consciousness in
the language of dynamic systems theory and mapping this description
onto biological processes going on in the brain. But neurophenomenology is not meant to be only a theoretical proposal; it is also meant
to be an empirical research program for the experimental investigation of consciousness in cognitive and affective neuroscience (Lutz
and Thompson 2003; Varela 1996). In the next section, I discuss experimental neurophenomenology. Then, in the remainder of this
chapter, I address some conceptual issues about the neurophenomenological project overall.

Experimental Neurophenomenology

There is growing awareness in cognitive and affective neuroscience that
detailed and precise first-person descriptions of subjective experience
are needed in order to relate moment-to-moment experience to the
complexity of brain activity (Jack and Roepstorff 2002).[9] Experimental
neurophenomenology stresses the importance of collecting descriptive
first-person reports of experience from phenomenologically trained
subjects as a heuristic strategy for uncovering the physiological processes relevant to consciousness. Such first-person descriptive reports
can be called "first-person data," for they record observations made by
individual subjects of their experiences from their first-person perspective.[10] Biobehavioral data, by contrast, are "third-person data," for they
record observations of biobehavioral phenomena made by scientists

from their third-person perspective. The neurophenomenological approach is to obtain detailed first-person data through careful phenomenological investigation of experience and to use these original first-person data to uncover new third-person data about the physiological processes crucial for consciousness. One central aim of experimental neurophenomenology is thus to generate new data by incorporating careful phenomenological forms of investigation into the experimental protocols of neuroscientific research on consciousness.[11]

To this end, experimental neurophenomenology employs first-person phenomenological methods in order to obtain original and refined first-person data. Individuals vary in their abilities as observers and reporters of their own experiences, and these abilities can be enhanced through various phenomenological methods. First-person methods are disciplined practices individuals can use to increase their sensitivity to their experience at various time-scales (Depraz, Varela, and Vermersch 2000, 2003; Varela and Shear 1999a, 1999b). These practices involve the systematic training of attention, mindfulness, and self-regulation of emotion. Such methods exist in phenomenology (Moustakas 1994), psychology (Petitmengin-Peugeot 1999; Price and Barrell 1980; Price, Barrell, and Rainville 2002), psychotherapy (Epstein 1995; Gendlin 1981; Stern 2004), and contemplative traditions of mental training (Wallace 1998, 1999). Some are routinely used in clinical and health programs (Kabat-Zinn 1990), and physiological correlates and effects of some of these practices have been investigated (Austin 1998; Lutz, Dunne, and Davidson 2007).

The relevance of these practices to neurophenomenology derives from the capacity for sustained attentiveness to experience they systematically cultivate. This capacity enables tacit and prereflective aspects of experience, which typically are either inaccessible or reconstructed after the fact according to various biases, to become subjectively accessible and describable in more accurate ways. Using first-person methods, individuals may be able to gain access to aspects of their experience (such as transient affective state and quality of attention) that otherwise would remain unnoticed and hence unavailable for verbal report and description. The experimentalist, however, using the phenomenological accounts produced with these methods, may be able to gain access to physiological processes that otherwise would remain opaque, such as the variability in brain response recorded in neuroimaging experiments, often treated as noise. Thus one rationale for using first-person methods in an experimental context is to generate new data (both first-person and third-person) for the science of consciousness.

The working hypothesis of experimental neurophenomenology is that phenomenologically precise first-person data, produced by employing first-person methods, strongly constrain the analysis and interpretation of the physiological processes relevant to consciousness. Moreover, third-person data produced in this manner might eventually constrain first-person data, so that the relationship between the two would become one of dynamic, "mutual," or "reciprocal constraints" (Varela 1996; Lutz 2002). Reciprocal constraints means (1) that the subject is actively involved in generating and describing specific phenomenal features of his or her experience, (2) that the neuroscientist is guided by these first-person data in the analysis and interpretation of physiological data, and (3) that the (phenomenologically enriched) neuroscientific analyses can provoke revisions and refinements of the phenomenological accounts, as well as facilitate the subject's becoming aware of previously inaccessible aspects of his or her mental life.[12]

To establish such reciprocal constraints, both an appropriate candidate for the neurophysiological basis of consciousness and an adequate theoretical framework to characterize it are needed. Experimental neurophenomenology is guided by the theoretical proposal (discussed in the previous section) that the most promising current candidate for the neurophysiological basis of consciousness is a flexible repertoire of dynamic large-scale neural assemblies that transiently link multiple brain regions and areas. This theoretical proposal is shared by a number of neuroscientists, though specific models vary in their details (for a review, see Cosmelli, Lachaux, and Thompson 2007). In this approach, the framework of dynamic systems theory is essential for characterizing the neurophysiological processes relevant to consciousness.

In summary, experimental neurophenomenology is based on the following threefold synergy (compare to Figure 11.2):

1. (NPh1) First-person data from the careful examination of experience with specific first-person methods.
2. (NPh2) Formal models and analytic tools from dynamic systems theory.

3. (NPh3) Neurophysiological data from measurements of large-scale, integrative processes in the brain.

I turn now to review two experimental studies of consciousness and large-scale cortical dynamics based on this approach. Each study concerned the temporal dynamics of visual perception. In the first study, individual subjects gave detailed, trial-by-trial accounts of their experience, and these descriptions were used to define original and stable experiential categories or phenomenal invariants for each individual subject. These phenomenal invariants were then used to detect and interpret neurodynamic activity (Lutz et al. 2002). In the second study, a strict structural invariant of experience for all subjects was defined and then used as a heuristic to reveal a corresponding structural invariant of cortical dynamics (Cosmelli et al. 2004). Both studies were explicitly motivated by the methods and hypotheses of neurophenomenology.

Perception and Ongoing Subjective Mental Activity

When an awake and alert human subject is stimulated during an experiment, his or her brain is not idling or in a state of suspension, but engaged in cognitive activity. The way the brain responds derives from the interaction between its ongoing activity and the afferent stimulation. Yet because this ongoing activity has not been carefully studied, most of the brain response is not understood. Successive exposure to the same stimulus elicits highly variable responses; this variability is usually treated as unintelligible noise (and may be discarded by techniques that average across trials and/or subjects). The source of this variability is thought to reside mainly in fluctuations of the subject's attentional state, spontaneous thought processes, strategy to carry out the task, motivation, and so on. Although it is common to control, at least indirectly, for some of these subjective factors, the ongoing subjective mental activity is not usually analyzed systematically.

One strategy would be to describe in more detail this ongoing activity by obtaining first-person reports about its subjective character. These reports should reveal subtle changes in the subject's experience, whether from trial to trial or across individuals. This type of qualitative first-person data is usually omitted from brain-imaging studies, yet if methodological precautions are taken in gathering such data, they can be used to shed light on cognition via a joint analysis with quantitative measures of neural activity. Following this approach, in a pilot neurophenomenological study, Lutz et al. (2002) investigated variations in subjective experience for one limited aspect of visual perception—the emergence of an illusory 3D figure during the perceptual fusion of 2D random-dot images with binocular disparities.

The task began with subjects fixating for seven seconds a dot pattern containing no depth cues (see Figure 11.3). At the end of this "preparation period," the pattern was changed to a slightly different one with binocular disparities. Subjects then had to press a button as soon as the 3D shape had completely emerged. Throughout the trial EEG signals were recorded, and immediately after the button-press subjects gave a brief verbal report about their experience. In these reports, they labeled their experience using phenomenal categories or invariants that they themselves had found and stabilized during a prior training session. The recording session thus involved the simultaneous collection of first-person data (phenomenological reports) and third-person data (electrophysiological recordings of neural activity and behavioral measures of button-pressing reaction time).

In the training session, subjects intensively practiced performing the task in order to improve their perceptual discrimination and to enable them to explore carefully variations in their subjective experience during repeated exposure to the task. Subjects were instructed to attend to their own immediate mental processes during the task and to the felt-quality of the emergence of the 3D image. In phenomenological terms, the aim was to induce awareness not simply of the "what" or object-pole of experience (in this case the 3D image), but also of the correlated "how" or act-pole of experience (in this case the performance of perceptual fusion and its subjective character).

In this pilot study, this phenomenological attitude was either self-induced by subjects familiar with it or facilitated by the experimenter through the method of open questions (Petitmengin, in press; Petitmengin-Peugeot 1999). For example: *Experimenter:* "What did you feel before and after the image appeared?" *Subject:* "I had a growing sense of expectation but not for a specific object; however, when the figure appeared, I had a feeling of confirmation, no surprise at all." Or "It was as if the image appeared in the periphery of my attention, but then my attention was suddenly swallowed up by the shape."

Protocol

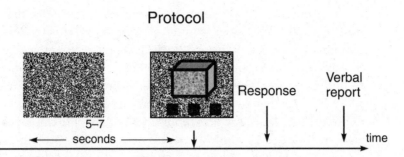

Figure 11.3. Visual task for neurophenomenological pilot study of ongoing conscious perception. Reprinted with permission from Antoine Lutz, Jean-Philippe Lachaux, Jacques Martinerie, and Francisco J. Varela, "Guiding the Study of Brain Dynamics by Using First-Person Data," *Proceedings of the National Academy of Sciences USA* 99 (copyright 2002, National Academy of Sciences, U.S.A.), 1587, fig. 1.

Subjects were repeatedly exposed to the stimuli, and trial by trial they described their experience through verbal accounts, which were recorded on tape. In dialogue with the experimenters, they defined their own stable experiential categories or phenomenal invariants to describe the main elements of the subjective context in which they perceived the 3D shapes. The descriptive verbal reports from a total of four subjects were classified according to the common factor of *degree of preparation* felt by the subject and *quality of perception*. This factor was used to cluster the trials into three main categories: Steady Readiness, Fragmented Readiness, and Unreadiness. Subcategories (describing the unfolding of the visual perception, for example) were also found in individual subjects, but were not investigated in the pilot study.

- *Steady Readiness.* In most trials, subjects reported that they were "ready," "present," "here," or "well-prepared" when the image appeared on the screen, and that they responded "immediately" and "decidedly." Perception was usually experienced with a feeling of "continuity," "confirmation," or "satisfaction." These trials were grouped into a cluster SR, characterized by the subjects being in a state of "steady readiness."
- *Fragmented Readiness.* In other trials, subjects reported that they had made a voluntary effort to be ready but were prepared either

less "sharply" (due to a momentary "tiredness") or less "focally" (due to small "distractions," "inner speech," or "discursive thoughts"). The emergence of the 3D image was experienced with a small feeling of surprise or "discontinuity." These trials formed a second cluster corresponding to a state of "fragmented readiness."

- *Unreadiness (Spontaneous Unreadiness, Self-Induced Unreadiness).* In the remaining trials, subjects reported that they were unprepared and saw the 3D image only because their eyes were correctly positioned. They were surprised by it and reported that they were "interrupted" by the image in the middle of a thought (memories, projects, fantasies). This state of distraction occurred spontaneously for subjects S1 and S4, whereas S2 and S3 triggered it either by fantasizing or by thinking about plans (S3), or by visualizing a mental image (S2). To separate passive and active distraction, these trials were divided into two different clusters: "spontaneous unreadiness" for S1 and S4, and "self-induced unreadiness" for S2 and S3.

These phenomenal invariants found in the training session were used to divide the individual trials of the recording session into corresponding "phenomenological clusters." The EEG signals were analyzed to determine the transient patterns of local and long-distance phase synchronies between electrodes, and separate dynamical analyses of the signals were conducted for each cluster. The phenomenological clusters were thus used as a heuristic to detect and interpret neural activity. The hypothesis was that distinct phenomenological clusters would be characterized by distinct "dynamical neural signatures" before stimulation (reflecting state of preparation), and that these signatures would then differentially condition the neural and behavioral responses to the stimulus. To test this hypothesis, the behavioral data and the EEG data were analyzed separately for each cluster.

The overall result was that original dynamical categories of neural activity were detected, and hence the opacity in brain responses (due to their intrinsic variability) was reduced. For an example, we can consider the contrast between the two clusters of Steady Readiness and Spontaneous Unreadiness for one of the subjects (see Plate VII). In the first cluster (A), the subject reported being prepared for the stimulus presentation, with a feeling of continuity when the stimulation occurred and an impression of fusion between himself and the percept. In the second cluster (B), the subject reported being unprepared, distracted, and having a strong feeling of discontinuity in the flux of his mental states when the stimulus was presented. He described a clear impression of differentiation between himself and the percept. These distinct features of subjective experience were correlated with distinct dynamical neural signatures (transient patterns of local and long-distance phase synchrony and frequency amplitude).

During steady preparation, a frontal phase-synchronous ensemble emerged early between frontal electrodes and was maintained on average throughout the trial, correlating with the subject's impression of continuity. The average reaction time for this group of trials was short (300 milliseconds on average). The energy in the gamma band (30–70 Hz) increased during the preparation period leading up to the time of stimulus presentation. This energy shift toward the gamma band occurred in all subjects and was specific to the "prepared" clusters. The energy in the gamma band was always higher in anterior regions during the prestimulus period for subjects in the "prepared" clusters than for subjects in the "unprepared" clusters, whereas the energy in the slower bands was lower. These results suggest that the deployment of attention during the preparation strategy was characterized by an enhancement of the fast rhythms in combination with an attenuation of the slow rhythms.

In the unprepared cluster, however, no stable phase-synchronous ensemble can be distinguished on average during the prestimulus period. When stimulation occurred, a complex pattern of weak synchronization and massive desynchronization or phase-scattering between frontal and posterior electrodes was revealed. A subsequent frontal synchronous ensemble slowly appeared while the phase-scattering remained present for some time. In this cluster the reaction time was longer (600 milliseconds on average). This complex pattern of synchronization and phase-scattering could correspond to a strong reorganization of the brain dynamics in an unprepared situation, delaying the constitution of a unified cognitive moment and an adapted response. This discontinuity in the brain dynamics was strongly correlated with a subjective impression of discontinuity.

Apart from these patterns common to all subjects, it was also found that the precise topography, frequency, and time course of the synchrony patterns during the preparation period varied widely across subjects. These variations should not be treated as noise, however, because they reflect distinct dynamical neural signatures that remained stable in individual subjects throughout several recording sessions over a number of days (see Plate VIII).

In summary, this study demonstrated that (1) first-person data about the subjective context of perception can be related to stable phase-synchrony patterns measured in EEG recordings before the stimulus; (2) the states of preparation and perception, as reported by the subjects, modulated both the behavioral responses and the dynamic neural responses after the stimulation; and (3) although the precise shape of these synchrony patterns varied among subjects, they were stable in individual subjects throughout several recording sessions and therefore seem to constitute a consistent signature of a subject's cognitive strategy or aptitude to perform the perceptual task.

Waves of Consciousness

As we saw earlier in this chapter, time-consciousness has the phenomenal structure of a standing-streaming, an unceasing yet continually changing flow of moments of awareness. Is it possible to take account of this phenomenal temporality while studying the brain processes relevant to consciousness? This question motivated the second experimental study, in which binocular rivalry and magnetoencephalography (MEG) were used to investigate the temporal dynamics of brain activity during conscious perception (Cosmelli et al. 2004).

When two different visual patterns are presented simultaneously, one to each eye, they seem to alternate back and forth at irregular intervals, in a phenomenon known as binocular rivalry. In binocular rivalry, as in other forms of multistable perception such as ambiguous figures, the perception changes while the visual stimulation remains the same. For this reason, binocular rivalry has been used as a probe for finding the neural processes associated specifically with the content of a moment of conscious perception (see Blake 2001; Blake and Logothetis 2002). Yet binocular rivalry also offers an ideal experimental condition to assess the dynamics of cortical activity during ongoing conscious perception, because the perception of a given stimulus fluctuates spontaneously and unpredictably in time.

The rivalrous stimuli used in this experiment were an image of a face and an image of a series of expanding checkerboard rings. The subject was instructed to indicate when one or the other image became visually dominant by pressing one or the other of two buttons. The expanding rings spanned from 0 to 4 degrees of visual eccentricity at a rate of five times per second (5 hertz). Stimuli such as this one that have an intrinsic frequency will produce a concomitant, evoked cortical response (a posterior-anterior wave of activation) at the same frequency. Thus the 5 hertz spanning velocity of the checkerboard stimulus was used as a "frequency tag" to mark neural activity and thereby guide the localization of both the cortical network specifically evoked by this pattern and the modulation of this network throughout successive dominance and suppression periods.

Prior to the recording session, subjects familiarized themselves extensively with the rivalry experience for these stimuli. They gave detailed phenomenological accounts, guided by the method of open questions asked by the experimenter. From these descriptions, the following structural invariant of experience was found to be strictly valid for all subjects: during binocular rivalry, periods of dominance are *recurrent* through time, while the transitions between periods of dominance are *highly variable* in the way they arise. Though quite general, this invariant is nonetheless a significant constraint on the detection and interpretation of the underlying neural activity. In particular, one can hypothesize that in binocular rivalry, cortical activity during conscious perception may exhibit a corresponding structure of recurrent dynamic patterns with highly variable transitions.

Testing this hypothesis requires novel tools. One needs to be able to map recurrent brain sources with no restrictions on the temporal sequence of their activation. One also needs to be able to take explicitly into account the variable dynamics of each perceptual transition without averaging (which could destroy potentially relevant information). For these reasons, novel source localization techniques (for inferring underlying cortical source activity from MEG scalp data) and novel statistical analyses (for studying recurrence and variability without averaging) were developed and tested (David et al. 2002; David, Cosmelli, Hasboun, and Garnero 2003).

Using these tools, phase synchrony analysis was performed on the underlying cortical signals reconstructed from the MEG scalp data.

The hypothesis was that during conscious perception of the expanding checkerboard rings, phase synchrony in this frequency band would rise and fall in concert with perceptual dominance. A consistent correlation was found between the time-course of the synchronization of the cortical network and the transitions in conscious perception. Thus the overall evoked cortical synchrony correlated with the conscious perception.

To analyze the spatiotemporal dynamics of the specific cortical networks engaged during conscious perception, the ongoing pattern of synchronous brain activity throughout a series of perceptual transitions was followed. A dynamic buildup of the synchronous network was apparent throughout the perceptual transitions. At the beginning of each transition, few synchronous pairs were evident. As perceptual dominance developed, the occipital pole showed an increase in local synchrony involving primary visual cortex and more dorsal occipital areas. Long-range coactivation was then established between occipital regions and more frontal areas, including mainly medial frontal regions. This pattern of an occipitofrontal distributed network was maintained for several seconds and coincided with full perceptual dominance of the frequency tagged, expanding checkerboard rings. Then, as suppression began, long-range synchronous activity fell apart, leaving coactive areas in the occipital pole and, in some cases, inferotemporal regions up to the temporal pole. During full suppression, few coactive regions were left and the brain patterns returned to the pretransition situation. This study thus presented ongoing patterns of cortical synchronous activation correlated to the spontaneous stream of conscious perception.

By using first-person methods to generate new first-person data, and then using these data to make sense of the highly variable brain responses, these two studies illustrate the potential of neurophenomenology for the neuroscience of consciousness. Nevertheless, these studies do not fully embody the neurophenomenological aim to create mutual constraints between phenomenology and neuroscience. Although novel phenomenological data are used to uncover new patterns of brain activity, there is no reciprocal use of biological data to uncover novel phenomenal features of experience. Furthermore, although these studies provide temporally extended, dynamic neural correlates of ongoing conscious states (unlike most studies to-date of the neural correlates of consciousness), they nevertheless remain correlational. Hence they do not cast light on the nature of the relation (beyond correlation) between experiential and biological properties.

In the remainder of this chapter, I address some conceptual issues about neurophenomenology. I begin with how we should think about neurophenomenology in relation to the current scientific aim to discover the neural correlates of consciousness (Metzinger 2000; Rees, Kreiman, and Koch 2002).

Neurophenomenology and the Neural Correlates of Consciousness

In his article "What Is a Neural Correlate of Consciousness?" David Chalmers (2000) distinguishes between two types of neural correlates of consciousness or NCCs—neural correlates of background states of consciousness (background NCCs), such as wakefulness, dreaming, and so on, and neural correlates of the specific contents of consciousness (content NCCs). He defines a content NCC as follows:

> An NCC (for content) is a minimal neural representational system N such that representation of a content in N is sufficient, under conditions C, for representation of that content in consciousness. (Chalmers 2000, p. 31)

As this definition indicates, the content-NCC approach is based on the assumption that the contents of consciousness match the contents of neural representational systems. Alva Noë and I call this assumption (which we criticize) the "matching content doctrine" (Noë and Thompson 2004a, 2004b). According to the matching content doctrine, for every conscious experience E, there is a neural representational system N, such that (i) N is the minimal neural representational system whose activation is sufficient for E, and (ii) there is a match between the content of E and the content of N.

The matching content doctrine can be called into question. Although neural correlates of various types of conscious states have been found experimentally, these correlates do not provide any case of a match between the content of a neural system and the content of a conscious state ("match" means equivalence, not mere correlation or correspondence, as can be seen from the above definition of a content

NCC) (Noë and Thompson 2004a). Moreover, the very idea that neural systems described neurophysiologically could match conscious states in their content seems inadequate. Experiential content and neural content are different kinds of content, and so it is a category mistake to confuse the two. Experience is intentional (world-presenting), holistic (constituted by interrelated perceptions, intentions, emotions, and actions), and intransitively self-aware (has a nonreflective subjective character). Neural content as standardly described has none of these features. Although there are various sorts of systematic relations between experiences and neural processes, we need not assume that these relations include any content match (Noë and Thompson 2004a, 2004b).

In this context, we need to remember that the neurophenomenology of time-consciousness is not supposed to be a proposal about the neural correlates of the *contents* of time-consciousness, but rather a proposal about the neural basis of the phenomenological *structure* of time-consciousness. The proposal is a formal or structural one, not one about representational content. Neurophenomenology derives from embodied dynamicism in its enactive version and thus does not assume the standard representationlist view of the brain (see Chapter 3).

Furthermore, unlike the content-NCC approach, neurophenomenology is not committed to there being a minimally sufficient neural substrate of consciousness.[13] It is possible (as argued in Chapter 8) that the minimally sufficient condition for consciousness includes bodily processes. This possibility is not consistent with the NCC view, according to which the neural correlates of conscious states are minimally sufficient for those states. It is consistent, however, with the neurophenomenological proposal that the formal structure of time-consciousness depends on the dynamic structure of brain activity. Neurophenomenology maintains that large-scale integration is necessary, but not minimally sufficient, for time-consciousness. In Varela's view, bodily processes of emotion and motor activity are crucial to the flow of experience and act as global order parameters for neural events at the 1 and 1/10 scales of duration (Varela 1999; Varela and Depraz 2005). Thus, according to Varela, bodily activity in skillful coping sculpts the entire dynamical landscape of time-consciousness. I discuss this idea in the next chapter.

The content-NCC approach goes hand in hand with a particular research strategy that Searle (2000a) calls the building block model of consciousness. This model is aggregative: it assumes that ordinary multimodal experience can be analyzed into individual sensory experiences (visual experiences, auditory experiences, and so on). The building block approach tries to isolate content NCCs for specific types of individual sensory experiences, such as the visual experience of a perceptually dominant stimulus in binocular rivalry. The ultimate aim is to determine not mere correlates of particular types of conscious states, but the causally necessary and sufficient conditions of these states, including a theory or model of the neurophysiological mechanisms involved. The conjecture is that if we could determine the content NCCs for a particular sort of sensory experience, such as the visual experience of color or visual experience in general, this finding might generalize to other sorts of conscious experiences. To put it another way, if we could determine for color vision or vision in general what makes a given content a phenomenally conscious content, then we might be able to determine what makes a content conscious for any modality.

The building block model also can be criticized. It is problematic to assume that consciousness is made up of various building blocks corresponding to constituent individual sensory experiences, which are then somehow bound together to constitute the unity (or apparent unity) of consciousness. As Searle points out, "Given that a subject is conscious, his consciousness will be modified by having a visual experience, but it does not follow that the consciousness is made up of various building blocks of which the visual experience is just one" (2000a, p. 572).

In criticizing the building block model, Searle singles out another approach to the brain basis of consciousness, which he calls the unified field model. According to this model, the neural substrates of individual conscious states should not be considered sufficient for the occurrence of those states, for those states themselves presuppose the background consciousness of the subject. Any given conscious state is a modulation of a preexisting conscious field. An individual experience or conscious state (such as visual recognition of a face) is not a constituent of some aggregate conscious state, but rather a modification within the field of a basal or background consciousness: "Conscious experiences come in unified fields. In order to have a visual experience, a subject has to be conscious already, and the experience is a modifica-

tion of the field" (Searle 2000a, p. 572).[14] The unified field approach
accordingly investigates (1) the neural basis of the whole unified field
at the level of large-scale activity, (2) the neurophysiological processes
that characterize the dynamic modulation of the conscious field in
time, and (3) the differences in brain activity across basal or background states (sleeping, dreaming, wakefulness, and so on).

Experimental neurophenomenology is better interpreted in light of
the unified field model than the building block model. Consider the
study using binocular rivalry. Binocular rivalry is one of the main experimental paradigms for the content-NCC approach. In the NCC literature, binocular rivalry is usually presented as revealing a competition between two separate and distinct states that alternately become
conscious. The research task is to discover the neural activity that represents what the subject sees (the content NCC) for each distinct conscious state (Crick 1994). Each conscious state is treated, in effect, as a
building block of a composite rivalry experience. Careful phenomenological examination of the rivalry experience, however, suggests that
this experience is not composite in the building block sense. It is not a
composite experience having the normal (nonrivalrous) experience
of one image and the normal (nonrivalrous) experience of the other
image as constituent repeating elements (Noë and Thompson 2004a,
pp. 24–25). Rather, it is better described as one bistable experience. In
other words, the bistable experience of seeing a face/expanding
checkerboard ring is not equivalent to the normal experience of
seeing a face, plus the normal experience of seeing an expanding
checkerboard ring, plus the two alternating with the appropriate temporal dynamics. As a bistable perception, it is a unique sort of experience, which accordingly must be assessed on its own terms.

Kelso (1995) takes precisely this approach to the perception of multistable figures such as the Necker cube, describing this kind of perception as a metastable state. Similarly, the neurophenomenological
study of binocular rivalry takes a dynamic structural approach rather
than a building-block content approach. The temporal dynamics of rivalry is considered to be constitutive of the experience rather than an
added element in building block fashion. By taking into account detailed phenomenological accounts of the temporal structure of rivalry,
a dynamic pattern of recurrence with highly variable transitions is revealed to be a structural invariant of the rivalry experience, a pattern

irreducible to an alternation of two stable and clearly differentiated perceptual experiences. By using this structural invariant as a guide to detect and interpret neural activity, the neurophenomenological approach is able to show that ongoing patterns of cortical synchronization and desynchronization correlate with fluctuations of conscious perception.

The neurophenomenological study of depth perception and ongoing mental activity also provides a nice case for the unified field model. This study can be interpreted as an investigation of the dynamic structure of the field of consciousness at phenomenological and neurophysiological levels. It examines "modifications of the already existing field of qualitative subjectivity" (Searle 2000a, p. 563), in the form of modifications of perceptual experience that depend on the subjective experience of readiness or unreadiness. To map the neurodynamics of ongoing conscious states, the study makes use of both proximal and distant baselines, corresponding respectively to the one-second period immediately before stimulation and the seven-second preparation period leading up to stimulation. Using the proximal baseline enhances the contrast between the synchronous process immediately preceding the arrival of the stimulation and the processes triggered by the stimulation. Using the distant baseline reveals a resemblance in synchrony patterns between prestimulus activity and the response induced by the stimulation.

From a unified field perspective, these two baselines correspond to different time slices of the conscious field. The distant baseline takes in more of the preexisting field of subjective experience and thus reveals patterns of dynamic activity that are not seen using the proximal baseline. It also enables one to show that the preexisting conscious field is not only modified by, but also differentially conditions, the emergence of the 3D image. In phenomenological terms, the subjective context of readiness/unreadiness leading up to perception is a noetic factor of the field of consciousness, which differentially conditions the noematic factor of the depth image.

In addition, this study suggests that we need to reconsider the temporal interval of interest for the neural correlate of a conscious cognitive act. The correlate of depth perception clearly occurs between the appearance of the stimulus and the motor response. Yet this momentary conscious state extends from a previous one and finds its place within a temporal horizon defined by retention and protention. This horizon is not neutral but has a certain subjective character (minimally characterized here as readiness/unreadiness). Hence, in order to describe the dynamics of a transitory conscious state, we need to characterize not only the activity following the stimulus, but also the ongoing activity preceding the stimulus and this activity's protentional character.

According to the unified field approach, "what we have to look for is some massive activity of the brain capable of producing a unified holistic conscious experience" (Searle 2000a, p. 574). One of the working hypotheses of neurophenomenology is that this massive activity involves large-scale integration via phase synchrony (or other forms of "generalized synchrony" across different frequencies; see Friston 2000a, 2000b; Schiff et al. 1996). Large-scale integration is metastable (new patterns constantly arise without the system settling down to any one of them) and rapid (occurring at the 1 scale of 100 milliseconds or more), and it defines a global reference pole for the selection and modulation of local neural activity (Le Van Quyen 2003).

Searle's proposal is that states of consciousness arise as modifications of the field of basal consciousness, but he does not always clearly distinguish between the two notions of state consciousness and background consciousness. The distinction is important for conceptual, phenomenological, and neurophysiological reasons.

On the one hand, there is good reason to believe that the coherent large-scale activity characterizing transient conscious states occurs in thalamocortical networks (Llinas et al. 1998; Tononi and Edelman 1998). Strong corticocortical and corticothalamic projections can generate a coherent neural process on a fast time scale (the 1 scale), through ongoing reentrant and highly parallel interactions among widely distributed brain areas.

On the other hand, background consciousness depends crucially on brainstem structures and processes (Parvizi and Damasio 2001). Background consciousness is inextricably tied to the homeodynamic regulation of the body and includes a primary affective awareness or core consciousness of one's bodily selfhood (Damasio 1999; Panksepp 1998b). Background consciousness in this fundamental sense is none other than sentience, the feeling of being alive, the affective backdrop of every conscious state. Sentience—or primal consciousness (Panksepp

1998b) or core consciousness (Damasio 1999)—is evidently not organized according to sensory modality, but rather according to the regulatory, emotional, and affective processes that make up the organism's
basic feeling of self. For this reason, the search for content NCCs in a
particular sensory modality such as vision runs the risk of missing the
biologically and phenomenologically more fundamental phenomenon
of sentience, whose affective character and ipseity (nonreflective self-
awareness) underlie and pervade all sensory experience.

Given the dependence of sentience on midbrain and brainstem
structures, as well as regulatory systems of the whole body, it is unsatisfactory to say that consciousness, in the sense of a single and unified
conscious field, "is in large part localized in the thalamocortical
system" (Searle 2000a, p. 574). Although the thalamocortical system is
crucial for transient conscious states, midbrain and brainstem structures are crucial for affective core consciousness or sentience. Thus virtually the entire neuraxis seems essential for consciousness in the
widest sense of the term (Watt 1998).

In addition to producing new data about the dynamic neural activity
relevant to consciousness, neurophenomenology might be able to
shed light on the causal structure of this activity. For example, it seems
natural to interpret the depth perception study in terms of the
dynamic-systems principle of circular causality, in which local events
collectively self-organize into coherent global patterns that in turn
constrain and modulate local events. Thus the antecedent and
"rolling" experiential context of perception modulates the way the object appears or is experientially lived during the moment of perception, and the content of this transient conscious state reciprocally affects the flow of experience. At the neurodynamical level, the brain
response presumably results from the intertwining of the endogenous
brain activity and the peripheral afferent activity evoked by the stimulus. Therefore the way the stimulus is directly lived by the subject (as
indicated by rigorous phenomenological reports using first-person
methods) could serve as a heuristic to shed light on the causal structure by which local afferent activity both modulates and is modulated
by the contextual influence of the current large-scale neural pattern,
such that this local activity either participates in or is discarded from
the emergence of the large-scale pattern.

In summary, according to this neurophenomenological perspective, a transitory conscious state is neurally embodied as a dynamic large-scale state that shapes local activities. This transitory state is embedded within a more encompassing state of background consciousness configured by dynamic integration along the entire neuraxis (Thompson and Varela 2001). These multiple level, large-scale states not only emerge from lower level activities, but also mobilize and channel these activities along particular trajectories. In Kelso's words, "Mind itself is a spatiotemporal pattern that molds the metastable dynamic patterns of the brain" (1995, p. 288).

Neurophenomenology and Naturalism

From the perspective of phenomenological philosophy, an important question to ask about neurophenomenology is what sort of naturalism its naturalized account of time-consciousness presupposes or requires. I will conclude this chapter by addressing this issue.

As a starting point, we can consider the following statement from Husserl's 1925 lectures on phenomenological psychology:

> [T]he synthesis of consciousness is completely different from the external combinations of natural elements . . . instead of spatial mutual externality, spatial intermingling and interpenetration, and spatial totality, it pertains to the essence of conscious life to contain an intentional intertwining, motivation, mutual implication by meaning, and this in a way which in its form and principle has no analogue at all in the physical. (1977, p. 26)

The thought expressed here is that the forms or structures that phenomenology discerns as constitutive of consciousness are completely different from the forms or structures that empirical science discerns in nature. Science treats nature as a realm of entities located in space and interacting causally; phenomenology treats consciousness as a temporal flow of intentional experiences related to each other motivationally. According to Husserl, no analogue of the synthetic unity proper to consciousness is to be found in physical nature.

The neurophenomenology of time-consciousness directly challenges this claim. As we have seen, according to neurophenomenology, the formal structure of time-consciousness or phenomenal temporality has an analogue in the dynamic structure of neural processes. This analogue is revealed by a nonlinear dynamical form of description, a kind of description not available to Husserl (see Roy et al. 1999). This kind of description sees in nature more than simply externally related spatial elements, but also forms or structures that are irreducibly relational (see Chapters 3 and 4) and immanently purposive (see Chapter 6). In this respect, we can say that the kind of phenomenological antinaturalism espoused in the above passage has been outstripped by science (in a way not unlike the way autopoietic biology has outstripped the limits of reason as Kant saw them in relation to the organism and self-organization).[15]

Yet, according to Varela (1997b), the naturalism neurophenomenology offers is not a reductionist one. Because dynamic systems theory is concerned with geometrical and topological forms of activity, it possesses an ideality that makes it neutral with respect to the distinction between the physical and the phenomenal, but also applicable to both. Dynamical descriptions can be mapped onto biological systems and shown to be realized in their properties (for example, the collective variable of phase synchrony can be grounded in the electrophysiological properties of neurons), and dynamical descriptions can be mapped onto what Husserl calls eidetic features, the invariable phenomenal forms or structures of experience. One reason the naturalism of neurophenomenology is supposed to be nonreductive is that these three types of analysis—phenomenological, biological, and dynamical—are equally needed, and no attempt is made to reduce one to the other or eliminate one in favor of another. For this reason, Varela (1997b) describes neurophenomenology as "triple-braided."

The question we now face is whether neurophenomenology offers anything more than an isomorphism or one-to-one correspondence between the phenomenological and biological domains, revealed by applying a formal dynamical model to both (Bayne 2004). It is undeniable that Varela's Hypotheses 1–3 are isomorphic in form, for they propose a one-to-one correspondence between the structure of dynamic neural activity and the structure of time-consciousness. In this respect, neurophenomenology is reminiscent of Wolfgang Köhler's principle of isomorphism. In *Gestalt Psychology* Köhler writes: "The principle of isomorphism demands that in a given case the organization of experience and the underlying physiological facts have the same structure" (Köhler 1947, p. 301). Köhler seems to have meant this principle to be a working hypothesis subject to empirical test, not an *a priori* postulate that any explanation must be isomorphic in form (Scheerer 1994). For this reason, and also because it pertains to *structural* or *organizational* features, Köhler's principle is not equivalent to analytical isomorphism, which assumes that the *content* of experience is isomorphic to the *representational format* of brain processes (see Chapter 10). Varela, like other dynamic-systems theorists (Kelso 1995), seems to rely on this structural version of the isomorphism idea as a heuristic to guide the search for dynamic patterns of neural activity pertinent to the structure of consciousness, specifically its temporal structure. Isomorphism serves as a working tool for tracking brain dynamics at the level of large-scale integration but not as an explanatory principle.

Yet neurophenomenology also aims to go beyond this sort of structural isomorphism. Isomorphism suggests an epistemological parallelism in which the biological and phenomenological accounts run on parallel tracks, with no mutual interaction or influence. Neurophenomenology, following Merleau-Ponty's lead, proposes a more daring idea—that biology and phenomenology can stand in a mutually enlightening, explanatory relation.[16] The idea that biology can stand in an explanatory relation to phenomenology is familiar and widely accepted; it is a basic premise of mind science. The idea that phenomenology could stand in an explanatory relation to biology, however, will sound odd to many readers. What could phenomenology possibly explain in this domain? The answer is nothing less than how certain biological processes are also realizations of selfhood and subjectivity, as argued throughout this book.

Clearly, "how" here does not have a causal meaning; the job of phenomenology is not to give a causal account of how selfhood and subjectivity arise in the natural world. Nor does phenomenology aim to give a logical derivation of phenomenal concepts from natural concepts. Rather, phenomenology provides a way of observing and describing natural phenomena that brings out or makes manifest their properly phenomenological features—selfhood, purposiveness, normativity, subjectivity, intentionality, temporality, and so on—which otherwise would remain invisible to science. Put another way, phenomenology offers a way of seeing the inner life of biological systems. That the autopoietic form of an organism realizes a kind of purposive selfhood normatively related to the world, that the dynamic form of neural activity realizes a special structure of temporality—these insights become available only if we bring the resources of phenomenology to bear on biological phenomena. In this way, phenomenology helps to make intelligible the relation between biological life, and mind and consciousness.

We thus arrive at another reason the naturalism of neurophenomenology is nonreductive: in bringing the resources of phenomenology to bear on our understanding of nature, the very idea of nature is transformed (Roy et al. 1999, p. 54; Zahavi 2004b). The physicalist conception of nature as an objective reduction base for the phenomenal no longer holds sway, and instead nature is reexamined from a phenomenological angle. In this way, we find ourselves needing to use certain concepts, most notably that of the lived body, that are essentially mixed or heterogeneous, in the sense that they cannot be factored into the dichotomous categories of the physical and the phenomenal, or the objective and the subjective. It is the possibility of such a mixed discourse—one already actualized in Merleau-Ponty's writings—that Varela anticipates in describing neurophenomenology as triple-braided. The next chapter pursues this sort of mixed discourse in a discussion of emotion, valence, and consciousness.

TWELVE

◆ ◆ ◆

Primordial Dynamism

Emotion and Valence

AS MY STARTING POINT in this chapter, I explore an aspect of time-consciousness that was neglected in the previous chapter—the future-oriented aspect of protention. As we will see, there is a strong link between protention and emotion, so that affect plays an important role in the generation of the flow of experience and action.

Protention

In thinking about the structure of time-consciousness, it is easy to assume that protention is simply the reverse or inverse of retention and thus that the threefold structure of temporality is symmetrical. But this cannot be the case for several reasons (Gallagher 1998, p. 68; Varela 1999, p. 296).

First, protention is intentionally "unfulfilled," which means that what it targets is absent or not fully present. Protention aims at the "not yet," and so its content has yet to be determinately filled in. Retention, in contrast, is "fulfilled," for it targets what was just there, and hence its content is determinate. Protention is intentionally directed toward a nonactual and immediately imminent phase of what is happening, retention toward an immediately elapsed and previously actual phase. Retention is thus determinate in its content in a way protention cannot be. Although protention intends the future in a more or less definite way, it is nonetheless open and indeterminate, for what it intends has yet to occur.

Second, it follows that protention is a bounded domain, though not a continuum. Retention always involves a continuum, the retention of previous retentions. Protentions cannot form a continuum in this way, for the protentions that would be intended by the currently operating protention have not yet occurred. In Gallagher's words: "Protention cannot be a gradual and orderly falling into obscurity; it must be an unregulated, relatively indeterminate, and temporally ambiguous sense of what is to come" (1998, p. 68). Whereas retentions continually recede into the past and intentionally contain each other, protention is an open horizon of anticipation.

Finally, emotion is integral to protention, for protention always involves motivation, an affective tone, and an action tendency or readiness for action. It is this link to emotion that I intend to explore in this chapter.

Let us begin with the idea that protention is motivated. On the one hand, retention motivates protention, or more precisely, retentional contents motivate protentional contents, for one's anticipation of what is about to happen in the immediate future is based on one's retention of what has just happened. For example, my current experience of watching a flock of birds fly across the sky continually protends a certain direction to their flight, based on my continual retention of where they have just been. On the other hand, protentions motivate retentions, for what is protended affects what is retained. I protend the flight path of the birds, and these protentions are retained as fulfilled (if the flight path is as I anticipate) or unfulfilled (if something unexpected happens). Retention thus includes not simply retention of what has just occurred, but also retention of just-having-been protending in this or that way. Retention always includes retention of protention and of the way protention is fulfilled or unfulfilled (Rodemeyer 2003).

The motivational relation between retention and protention is thus highly nonlinear. Retention motivates protention, which affects retention, which motivates protention, and so on and so forth, in a self-organizing way that gives temporal coherence to experience. If we abstract away from the specific retentional and protentional contents, and consider retention and protention at a purely formal or structural level, then we can say that, regardless of their contents, retention continually modifies protention and protention continually modifies retention. This mutual modification is reciprocal, though not symmetrical. Retention modifies the "style" of protention, but protention cannot retroactively influence retentions that have already occurred. Rather, "actual protentioning will affect retentioning that has not yet occurred, in the sense that retentioning will always be a retentioning of just-having-been protentioning, but not vice-versa" (Gallagher 1998, p. 68). In this way, the flow of experience is self-organizing, forward moving, irreversible, and motivationally structured.

In this chapter, I look at the role of affect and action tendencies in the generation of this flow. Their importance in relation to protention can be indicated now by noting that the protentional "not yet" is always suffused with affect and conditioned by the emotional disposition (motivation, appraisal, affective tone, and action tendency) accompanying the flow (Varela 1999, p. 296). From a neurophenomenological perspective, these emotional aspects of protention act as major boundary and initial conditions for the neurodynamical events at the $1/10$ and 1 scales described in the previous chapter. For this reason, Varela describes protention as a global order parameter that shapes the dynamics of large-scale integration in the brain.[1] Whereas retention corresponds to the dynamical trajectories as realized by the current state of the system, protention corresponds to the global order parameters for anticipation that condition the subsequent directions of the trajectories.

Before going more deeply into these ideas, let me connect them to the theme of this book, the deep continuity of life and mind. In Chapter 6 we saw that biological time is fundamentally forward-looking and arises from autopoiesis and sense-making. Life is asymmetrically oriented toward the future because the realization of the autopoietic organization demands incessant metabolic self-renewal. As Jonas (1968) declares, echoing Spinoza, life's basic "concern" is to keep on going. This immanent purposiveness of life is recapitulated in the temporality and intentionality of consciousness. Consciousness is a self-constituting flow inexorably directed toward the future and pulled by the affective valence of the world. What I wish to explore now is how this forward trajectory of life and mind is fundamentally a matter of emotion.

Enactive Emotion

In a groundbreaking paper on emotion and consciousness, neuropsychologist Douglas Watt (1998) describes emotion as a "prototype whole brain event," a global state of the brain that recruits and holds together activities in many regions, and thus cannot have simple neural correlates. We can take this point one step further by saying that emotion is a prototype whole-organism event, for it mobilizes and coordinates virtually every aspect of the organism. Emotion involves the entire neuraxis of brain stem, limbic areas, and superior cortex, as well as visceral and motor processes of the body. It encompasses psychosomatic networks of molecular communication among the nervous system, immune system, and endocrine system. On a psychological level, emotion involves attention and evaluation or appraisal, as well as affective feeling. Emotion manifests behaviorally in distinct facial expressions and action tendencies. Although from a biological point of view emotion comprises mostly nonconscious brain and body states, from a psychological and phenomenological point of view it includes rich and multifaceted forms of experience.[2]

In the face of this complexity, some scientists (LeDoux 1996) and philosophers (Griffiths 1997) have argued that although there are *emotions,* there is no such thing as *emotion.* The reason they cite is the absence of a unified category of phenomena to which the word "emotion" refers. Although one can point to particular emotions, notably the so-called basic emotions of fear, surprise, anger, disgust, sadness, and joy (according to one list), and to neural systems that mediate them, there is no emotion "natural kind" to which they belong. Nevertheless, these theorists continue to use the word "emotion" to describe their subject matter and to relate biological and psychological levels of explanation, thereby showing the theoretical or at least expository usefulness of the term.[3]

It is still an open question, however, which theoretical framework can best account for the diverse aspects of emotion—from the biological to psychological to phenomenological—in conceptually and empirically profitable ways. Dynamic systems approaches to emotion look especially promising in this light (Lewis 2000, 2005; Lewis and Granic 2000). Besides the affinity between these approaches and the enactive approach, there are important points of convergence between dynamic systems approaches to emotion and phenomenological ones, as we will see later in this chapter.

Etymology tells us that the word "emotion" (from the Latin verb *emovere*) literally means an outward movement. Emotion is the welling up of an impulse within that tends toward outward expression and action. There is thus a close resemblance between the etymological sense of emotion—an impulse moving outward—and the etymological sense of intentionality—an arrow directed at a target, and by extension the mind's aiming outward or beyond itself toward the world. Both ideas connote directed movement. This image of movement remains discernible in the abstract, cognitive characterization of intentionality in phenomenology. As discussed in Chapter 2, intentionality is no mere static relation of aboutness, but rather it is a dynamic striving for intentional fulfillment. In genetic phenomenology, this intentional striving is traced back to its roots in "originally instinctive, drive related preferences" of the lived body (Husserl 2001, p. 198). Husserl calls this type of intentionality "drive-intentionality" *(Triebintentionalität)* (see Mensch 1998). Patočka calls it "e-motion." This term connotes movement, its instigation by "impressional affectivity," and the dynamic of "constant attraction and repulsion" (Patočka, 1998, p. 139). Walter Freeman recognizes this bond between emotion and intentionality, making it the starting point for his enactive or "activist-pragmatist" approach to emotion:

> A way of making sense of emotion is to identify it with the intention to act in the near future, and then to note increasing levels of the complexity of contextualization. Most basically, emotion is outward movement. It is the "stretching forth" of intentionality, which is seen in primitive animals preparing to attack in order to gain food, territory, or resources to reproduce, to find shelter, or to escape impending harm . . . The key characteristic is that action wells up from within the organism. It is not a reflex. It is directed toward some future state, which is being determined by the organism in conjunction with its perceptions of its evolving condition and its history. (Freeman 2000, p. 214)

It is illuminating to compare this starting point with a different neuroscientific one, that of Joseph LeDoux (1996). According to LeDoux, "the word 'emotion' does not refer to something that the mind or brain really has or does," because "There is no such thing as the 'emotion' faculty and there is no single brain system dedicated to this phantom function." Instead, "the various classes of emotions are mediated by separate neural systems that have evolved for different reasons . . . and the feelings that result from activating these systems . . . do not have a common origin" (1996, p. 16). In short, although there are lots of emotions, there is no such thing as emotion (p. 305). LeDoux states explicitly the premise on which this line of reasoning rests: "the proper level of analysis of a psychological function is the level at which that function is represented in the brain" (p. 16). From an enactive perspective, however, this conception of a function—a mechanism that implements some mapping from input (sensory stimulation) to output (motor response)—presupposes that we are treating the brain as a heteronomous device, not an autonomous system. As Freeman writes, linear input-output models leave "no opening for self-determination" (1999b, p. 147).

Self-determining or autonomous systems, as we have seen, are defined by their organizational and operational closure, and thus do not have inputs and outputs in the usual sense. For these systems, the linear input/output distinction must be replaced by the nonlinear perturbation/response distinction. From an enactive perspective, brain processes are understood in relation to the circular causality of action-perception cycles and sensorimotor processes. Hence emotion is not a function in the input-output sense, but rather a feature of the action-perception cycle—namely, the endogenous initiation and direction of behavior outward into the world. Emotion is embodied in the closed dynamics of the sensorimotor loop, orchestrated endogenously by processes up and down the neuraxis, especially the limbic system.[4] The enactive approach can thus provide a theoretically significant, superordinate concept of emotion and can ground that concept in large-scale dynamic properties of brain organization.

The guiding question for an enactive approach to emotion is well put by Freeman: "How do intentional behaviors, all of which are emotive, whether or not they are conscious, emerge through self-organization of neural activity in even the most primitive brains?" (Freeman 2000, p. 216).

Consideration of this question needs to begin with features of brain organization. The overall organization of the brain reflects a principle of reciprocity: if area A connects to area B, then there are reciprocal connections from B to A (Varela 1995; Varela et al. 2001). Moreover, if B receives most of its incoming influence from A, then it sends the larger proportion of its outgoing activity back to A and only a smaller proportion onward (Freeman 2000, p. 224). Nevertheless, traditional neuroscience has tried to map brain organization onto a hierarchical, input-output processing model in which the sensory end is taken as the starting point. Perception is described as proceeding through a series of feedforward or bottom-up processing stages, and top-down influences are equated with back-projections or feedback from higher to lower areas. Freeman aptly describes this view as the "passivist-cognitivist view" of the brain.

From an enactive viewpoint, things look rather different. Brain processes are recursive, reentrant, and self-activating, and do not start or stop anywhere. Instead of treating perception as a later stage of sensation and taking the sensory receptors as the starting point for analysis, the enactive approach treats perception and emotion as dependent aspects of intentional action, and takes the brain's self-generated, endogenous activity as the starting point for neurobiological analysis. This activity arises far from the sensors—in the frontal lobes, limbic system, or temporal and associative cortices—and reflects the organism's overall protentional set—its states of expectancy, preparation, affective tone, attention, and so on. These states are necessarily active at the same time as the sensory inflow (Engel, Fries, and Singer 2001; Varela et al. 2001).

The working hypothesis of experimental neurophenomenology, as we saw in the previous chapter, is that aspects of these states can be phenomenologically tracked in humans, and the resulting first-person data can be used to guide neurodynamical experimentation. Whereas a passivist-cognitivist view would describe such states as acting in a top-down manner on sensory processing, from an enactive perspective top down and bottom up are heuristic terms for what in reality is a large-scale network that integrates incoming and endogenous activities on the basis of its own internally established reference points. Hence, from an enactive viewpoint, we need to look to this large-scale dynamic network in order to understand how emotion and intentional action emerge through self-organizing neural activity.

A Neurodynamical Model

Walter Freeman's work is especially relevant here. Building on his pioneering research in neurodynamics over many years, he has proposed

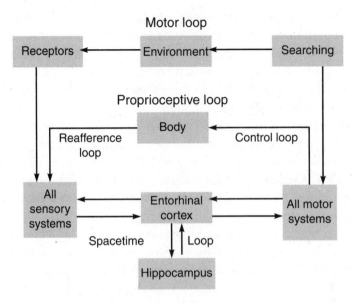

Figure 12.1. Walter Freeman's model of the intentional arc arising from the dynamic architecture of the limbic system. Reprinted with permission from Walter Freeman, "Consciousness, Intentionality, and Casuality," *Journal of Consciousness Studies* 6/11–12 (1999): 150, fig. 4.

an enactive and neurodynamical model of what Merleau-Ponty calls "the intentional arc subtending the life of consciousness" (see Chapter 9). Freeman's model contains five circular causal loops, comprising brain, body, and environment, but centered on the limbic system, the brain area especially associated with emotion (see Figure 12.1). Emotion, intention, and consciousness emerge from and are embodied in the self-organizing dynamics of these nested loops.

At the most global level is the "motor loop" between organism and environment. This loop consists of the sensorimotor circuit leading from motor action in and through the environment, and back to the sensory stimulation resulting from movement. Motor action involves directed arousal and search, and expresses the organism's states of expectancy. The sensory stimuli that the organism receives depend directly on its motor action, and how the organism moves depends directly on the sensory consequences of its previous actions. Merleau-Ponty, in *The Structure of Behavior*, recognized the importance of this loop: "since all stimulations which the organism receives have in turn been possible only by its preceding movements which have culminated in exposing the receptor organ to the external influences, one could . . . say that . . . behavior is the first cause of the stimulations. Thus the form of the excitant is created by the organism itself, by its proper manner of offering itself to actions from outside" (1963, p. 13).

Whereas the motor loop travels outside the brain and body into and through the environment, the "proprioceptive loop" travels outside the brain but is closed within the body. This loop consists of pathways from sensory receptors in the muscles and joints to the spinal cord, cerebellum, thalamus, and somatosensory cortex. Freeman (2000) also describes this loop as an interoceptive one. Interoception in this context is best understood as the sense of the physiological condition of the entire body, not just the viscera, and involves distinct neural pathways in the spinal cord, brainstem, thalamus, and insula (Craig 2002).

The three remaining loops of the model are all within the brain. If we begin on the sensory side, then we first need to remember that sensory stimuli occur in a context of expectancy and motor activity. When a stimulus arrives, the activated receptors transmit pulses to the sensory cortex, where they induce the construction by nonlinear dynamics of an activity pattern in the form of a large-scale spatial pattern of coherent oscillatory activity. This pattern is not a representation of the stimulus but an endogenously generated response triggered by the sensory perturbation, a response that creates and carries the meaning of the stimulus for the animal. This meaning reflects the individual organism's history, state of expectancy, and environmental context.

These meaningful dynamic patterns constructed in the cortex converge into the limbic system through the entorhinal cortex, an area of multisensory convergence that receives and combines activity from all primary sensory areas of the cortex. The dynamic activity patterns are spatially and temporally sequenced in the hippocampus, an area known to be involved in memory and the orientation of behavior in space and time. Reciprocal interaction between the entorhinal cortex and the hippocampus (the "spacetime loop") creates a unified gestalt (in the form of a large-scale, coherent oscillatory pattern), which is transmitted both to the motor systems (the "control loop"), thereby mobilizing the visceral and musculoskeletal activities needed for action and emotional expression, and back to the sensory systems through corollary discharges (the "reafference loop"), thereby preparing them for the expected consequences of motor actions.

Freeman calls this sensory preparation process "preafference" and sees it as the neural basis for what we subjectively experience as attention and expectancy (1999a, p. 34). Expectancy, in Freeman's sense, corresponds closely to the phenomenological notion of protention: it is not a distinct cognitive act, but rather an intentional aspect of every cognitive process. Freeman holds that preafference "provides an order parameter that shapes attractor landscapes, making it easier to capture expected or desired stimuli by enlarging or deepening the basins of their attractors" (1999a, p. 112). This view of preafference agrees with Varela's idea that protention provides an order parameter for the neurodynamics of sensorimotor and neural events at the 1/10 and 1 scales of duration.

Figure 12.1 shows the flow of activity going in both feedforward (counterclockwise) and feedback (clockwise) directions. Freeman hypothesizes that the forward direction consists of microlevel fluctuations in neuronal activity that engender new macroscopic states, whereas the feedback direction consists of macroscopic order parameters that constrain the microlevel activities of the forwardly transmitting neuronal populations. These feedforward and feedback flows thus correspond, respectively, to the local-to-global and global-to-local sides of emergence. Cutting this circular causality into forward and feedback arcs is heuristic, for at any moment there is only system causation, whereby the system moves as a whole (see Appendix B).

Freeman also relates this model to consciousness. He proposes that in addition to the large-scale activity patterns that emerge through the nonlinear dynamics of the spacetime loop, there is another higher-order pattern at the hemispheric level of the brain, in which the lower-order activity patterns of the limbic system and sensory cortices are components. This higher-order pattern organizes and constrains the lower-order ones. Freeman hypothesizes that this type of globally coherent, spatiotemporal pattern of activity, which takes on the order of a tenth to a quarter of a second to arise (Varela's 1/10 and 1 scales), is the brain correlate of a state of "awareness," and that "consciousness" consists of a sequence of such states. While emotion (the internal im-

petus for action) and intentional action constitute the cognitive flow
in the feedforward direction (see Figure 12.1), awareness and consciousness constitute the cognitive flow in the feedback direction.
Awareness, according to this model, far from being epiphenomenal,
plays an important causal role. Its role is not as an internal agent or homunculus that issues commands, but as an order parameter that organizes and regulates dynamic activity. Freeman and Varela thus agree
that consciousness is neurally embodied as a global dynamic activity
pattern that organizes activity throughout the brain. Freeman describes consciousness as a "dynamic operator that mediates relations
among neurons" and as a "state variable that constrains the chaotic activities of the parts by quenching local fluctuations" (1999a, pp. 132,
143). What Varela's neurophenomenology of time-consciousness adds
to this view is a proposal about how the sequence of such transitory activity patterns (corresponding to discrete states of awareness) can also
constitute a flow thanks to their retentional-protentional structure.

Let us return to emotion. As Freeman's model indicates, "emotion is
essential to all intentional behaviors" (Freeman 2000). Consider perception. According to the dynamic sensorimotor approach (see
Chapter 9), in perceiving we exercise our skillful mastery of sensorimotor contingencies—how sensory stimulation varies as a result of
movement. This approach to perception focuses on the global sensorimotor loop of organism and environment. We can now appreciate,
however, that this loop contains numerous neural and somatic loops,
whose beating heart (in mammals) is the endogenous, self-organizing
dynamics of cortical and subcortical brain areas. Sensorimotor processes are motivated and intentionally oriented thanks to endogenous
neural gestalts that emerge from depths far from the sensorimotor surface. Hence, according to the enactive approach, sensorimotor processes modulate, but do not determine, an ongoing endogenous activity, which in turn infuses sensorimotor activity with emotional
meaning and value for the organism.

Emotional Self-Organization

My aim now is to sketch a neurophenomenological way of thinking
about emotion by connecting these neurodynamical ideas to the phenomenology of emotion experience. To frame the discussion, I will

draw from emotion theorist Marc Lewis's dynamic systems model of emotional self-organization (Lewis 2000, 2005).

Lewis (2000) proposes a developmental model of emotional self-organization at three time-scales—the microdevelopment of emotion episodes at a time-scale of seconds or minutes, the mesodevelopment of moods at a time-scale of hours or days, and the macrodevelopment of personality at a time-scale of months and years (see Table 12.1). At each scale, emotional self-organization is modeled as an emergent cognition-emotion interaction. Cognition includes perception, attention, evaluation, memory, planning, reflection, and decision making, all of which are aspects of what emotion theorists call "appraisal," the evaluation of a situation's significance. Emotion includes arousal, action tendencies, bodily expression, attentional orientation, and affective feeling.

Yet cognition and emotion are not separate systems, for two reasons (Lewis 2005). First, there is a large amount of anatomical overlap between the neural systems mediating cognition and emotion processes, and these systems interact with each other in a reciprocal and circular fashion, up and down the neuraxis. Second, the emergent global states to which these interactions give rise are "appraisal-emotion amalgams," in which appraisal elements and emotion elements modify each other continuously. Such modification happens at each time-scale, through reciprocal interactions between local appraisal and emotion elements, and circular causal influences between local elements and their global organizational form.

To explore the parallels between this model and phenomenological ideas, we need to look at the model's three time-scales of emotional self-organization in more detail. At the microlevel, emotional self-organization takes the form of an emergent "emotional interpretation" (or EI), a rapid convergence of a cognitive interpretation of a situation and an emotional state (happiness, anger, fear, shame, pride, sympathy, and so forth). Cognitive and emotional processes modify each other continuously on a fast time-scale, while simultaneously being constrained by the global form produced by their coupling in a process of circular causality. This emergent form, the emotional interpretation, is a global state of emotion-cognition coherence, comprising an appraisal of a situation, an affective tone, and an action plan. Lewis also describes this higher-order form, drawing on

Table 12.1 Three scales of emotional self-organization, showing parallels and distinctions across scales and hypothesized psychological and neurobiological mechanisms.

	Emotional interpretation (EI)	Mood	Personality
Development scale	Micro	Meso	Macro
Duration	Seconds–minutes	Hours–days	Months–years
Description	Rapid convergence of cognitive interpretation with emotional state	Lasting entrainment of interpretive bias with narrow emotional range	Lasting interpretive-emotional habits specific to classes of situations
Dynamic-systems formalism	Attractor	Temporary modification of state space	Permanent structure of state space
Psychological mechanism	Cognition-emotion coupling or resonance, successful goal-directed action	Cognition-emotion coupling, goal preoccupation, inhibited or unsuccessful action	Cognition-emotion complementarities that arise from and constrain coupling in EIs and moods
Possible neurobiological mechanism	Cortical coherence mediated by orbitofrontal organization entrained with limbic circuits	Orbitofrontal-corticolimbic entrainment, motor rehearsal and pre-afference, sustained neurohormone release	Selection and strengthening of some corticocortical and corticolimbic connections, pruning of others, loss of plasticity
Higher-order form in circular causality	Intention, goal	Intentional orientation	Sense of self

Source: Marc D. Lewis, "Emotional Self-Organization at Three Time-Scales," in Marc D. Lewis and Isabela Granic, eds., *Emotion, Development, and Self-Organization* (Cambridge, 2000), p. 59. Reprinted with the permission of Cambridge University Press.

Freeman's ideas, as a global intention for acting on the world. This global intention is not only a whole-brain event, but also a whole-organism event. As Freeman writes, "Considering the rapidity with which an emotional state can emerge—such as a flash of anger, a knife-like fear, a surge of pity or jealousy—whether the trigger is the sight of a rival, the recollection of a missed appointment, an odor of smoke, or the embarrassing rumble of one's bowel at tea, the occasion is best understood as a global first-order state transition involving all parts of the brain and body acting in concert" (2000, p. 224).

According to Lewis's (2005) model, the emergence of an emotional interpretation begins as a fluctuation in the flow of intentional action, triggered by a perturbation (external or internal), which eventually disrupts the orderliness of the current emotional interpretation. Rapid processes of self-amplification through positive feedback ensue, followed by self-stabilization through negative feedback and entrainment, leading to the establishment of a new orderliness in the form of a new momentary emotional interpretation and global intention. This self-stabilization phase is the precondition for learning, the consolidation of long-term emotion-appraisal patterns.

There are thus three principal phases in the emergence of an emotional interpretation—a trigger phase, a self-amplification phase, and a self-stabilization phase—as well as an additional fourth learning phase that extends the influence of the present emotional interpretation to future ones. Lewis likens the whole process to a bifurcation from one attractor to another in an emotion-cognition state space. He has recently presented a neuropsychological model of some of the brain areas and large-scale neural-integration processes involved (Lewis 2005).[5]

Although Lewis emphasizes the importance of affective feeling as a motivational component of emotion, he does not explore the phenomenology of affect in relation to the emergence of an emotional interpretation. It is therefore worth investigating the resonance between Lewis's model and the genetic phenomenology of affect.

To explore this resonance, we need to recall a few key ideas from genetic phenomenology. *Passive synthesis* is the term Husserl uses to describe how experience comes to be formed as one is affected precognitively. He draws a distinction between "passivity" and "receptivity" (Husserl 2001, p. 105). Passivity means being involuntarily affected while engaged in some activity. Receptivity means responding to an involuntary affection (affective influence) by noticing or turning toward it. Every receptive action presupposes a prior affection (2001, p. 127). Husserl writes: "By affection we understand the allure given to consciousness, the peculiar pull that an object given to consciousness exercises on the ego" (2001, p. 196). "Allure" does not refer to a causal stimulus-response relation but to an intentional "relation of motivation" (Husserl 1989, p. 199). Attention at any level is motivated by virtue of something's affective allure. Depending on the nature and force of the allure, as well as one's motivations, one may yield to the allure passively or involuntarily, voluntarily turn one's attention toward it, or have one's attention captured or repulsed by it.

Receptivity is the lowest active level of attention, at the fold, as it were, between passivity and activity—a differentiation that can be made only relatively and dynamically, not absolutely and statically. Allure implies a dynamic gestalt or figure-ground structure: something becomes noticeable, at whatever level of attention, owing to the strength of its allure; it emerges into affective prominence, salience, or relief; while something else becomes unnoticeable owing to the weakness of its allure (Husserl 2001, p. 211). This dynamic interplay of passivity and activity, affection and receptivity, expresses a "constantly operative" intentionality (Husserl 2001, p. 206) that does not have an articulated subject-object structure (Merleau-Ponty 1962, p. xviii).

With these ideas in place, we can turn to investigate the microdynamics of affect at the 1 scale. In the previous chapter, we saw that our experience of the present moment depends on how the brain dynamically parses its own activity by forming transient, large-scale neural assemblies that integrate sensorimotor and neural events occurring at the 1/10 scale. Recall also that in the flow of habitual activity changes can occur, sometimes as smooth transitions, sometimes as breakdowns and disruptions. In Merleau-Ponty's terms, the leading "I can" can change from moment to moment as we rapidly switch activities.

From a neurodynamical perspective, when such switches occur the global neural assembly that is currently dominant comes apart through desynchronization, and a new moment of global synchronization ensues. Varela proposes that these switches are driven by emotion and manifest themselves in experience as dynamic fluctuations of affect (Varela 1999; Varela and Depraz 2005). In the flow of skillful coping, we switch activities as a result of the attractions and repulsions we experience prereflectively (Rietveld 2004). Such emotional fluctuations act as control parameters that induce bifurcations from one present moment of consciousness to another. In this way, emotion plays a major role in the generation of the flow of consciousness, and this role can be phenomenologically discerned in the microtemporality of affect.[6]

Varela and Depraz (2005) present such a phenomenology of affect in their paper, "At the Source of Time: Valence and the Constitutional Dynamics of Affect." Their analysis proceeds on the basis of two examples of emotion experience. One is a singular experience of Varela's—a "musical exaltation" experience while listening to the first few notes of a sonata at a concert.[7] The other is a generic experience of "averting the gaze," of shielding or hiding one's eyes (se cacher les yeux), described evocatively by Merleau-Ponty in the early pages of The Visible and the Invisible (which are devoted to the "perceptual faith," our everyday belief in the veracity of perception):

> It is said that to cover one's eyes so as to not see a danger is to not believe in the things, to believe only in the private world; but this is rather to believe that what is for us is absolutely, that a world we have succeeded in seeing as without danger is without danger. It is therefore the greatest degree of our belief that our vision goes to the things themselves. Perhaps this experience teaches us better than any other what the perceptual presence of the world is: . . . beneath affirmation and negation, beneath judgment . . . it is our experience, prior to every opinion, of inhabiting the world by our body . . . (1968, p. 28).

Varela and Depraz ask the reader to take a moment to reenact one's own examples of this averting-the-gaze experience. Examples come readily to my mind—avoiding meeting someone's eyes on the street who is about to ask for money; averting my eyes from a headline I can tell is upsetting before I have fully taken it in from the morning newspaper at my doorstep; or reflexively recoiling from a solitary angry face, snarling at me in bitter loneliness from a restaurant window as I walk by one sunny Christmas afternoon and inadvertently peer too long.

Following Watt (1998), Varela and Depraz point to a number of concurrent components of affect in such momentary emotion episodes. (In what follows I combine and rephrase elements from both Watt's original presentation, which is given from the perspectives of emotion theory and affective neuroscience, and Varela and Depraz's, which is more phenomenologically oriented.)

- A *precipitating event* or trigger, which can be perceptual or imaginary (a memory, fantasy), or both. (This component corresponds to the trigger phase in Lewis's model of an emotional interpretation.)
- An emergence of *affective salience,* involving an evident sense of the precipitating event's meaning. In emotion theory, this aspect of emotion is described as reflecting an appraisal, which can take form before the experience of affect (as part of the precipitating process), just after (as a post-hoc appraisal), and can interact continually and reciprocally with affect, through processes of self-amplification and self-stabilization (as emphasized by Lewis). The appraisal can be fleeting or detailed, realistic or distorted, empathetic or insensitive (and typically reflects some combination of these features). Much of the appraisal will be prereflective and/or unconscious.
- A *feeling-tone,* described in psychology as having a valence or hedonic tone along a pleasant/unpleasant polarity.
- A *motor embodiment,* in the form of facial and posture changes, and differential action tendencies or global intentions for acting on the world.
- A *visceral-interoceptive embodiment,* in the form of complex autonomic-physiological changes (to cardiopulmonary parameters, skin conductance, muscle tone, and endocrine and immune system activities).

Each of these five components can be discerned in my averting-the-gaze examples, especially the recoil from the angry face. Inadvertently seeing an angry face is a *precipitating event* or trigger. Faces, especially angry ones, have strong affective allure. Seeing a face as an angry face is an example of the rapid emergence of affective salience and appraisal, an emotional interpretation. The salience increases with the realization that the anger is directed at me—an elaboration of the emotional interpretation. A complex *feeling-tone* of startle, surprise, fear, and distress strikes like an electric shock. I turn my eyes and head to look away, and I quickly speed up my pace *(motor embodiment)*. My global intention is to get away, though not to the point of feeling the need to escape physical danger (another appraisal). My gut contracts, my breathing becomes faster and shallower, my face becomes flushed and hot, and my muscles tense as I turn away and speed up my walk *(visceral-interoceptive embodiment)*. At the same time I am overcome with the realization that Christmas is a painful and lonely time for many people, while feelings of sadness and sympathy for the lonely man, shame at my own insensitivity, and defensiveness at his aggression—all complex emotional interpretations with their own triggers, saliencies, appraisals, feeling-tones, and associated motor and visceral embodiments—rapidly alternate, reverberate, and seemingly reinforce one another, in a matter of seconds. As distance from the episode in space and time increases over the next few minutes and hours, a melancholy mood sets in, which affects me for the rest of the day, along with a feeling of resistance and an attempt to push the experience, now in the form of memory, from my mind. These longer-term, emotion-appraisal patterns arise at the mesoscale of mood, and condition and modulate my emotions for some time to come.

We can now see that the microdevelopment of an emotional interpretation contains within it a complex microdevelopment of affect. Husserl's detailed phenomenological descriptions of this microdevelopment are highly suggestive of a self-organizing, dynamic process. He describes experience as subject to "affective force." Affective force manifests as a rapid, dynamic transformation of experience, mobilizing one's entire lived body. The transformation is one in the "vivacity of consciousness" or the "varying vivacity of a lived-experience" (Husserl 2001, §35, pp. 214–221). There are relative differences of vivacity belonging to an experience, depending on what is affectively efficacious and salient. There is a "gradation of affection," from the affectively ineffective or nil to the affectively salient or prominent, with various intermediate gradations. The transformation in vivacity takes the form of a dynamic transition from the arousal or awakening of a responsive tendency to the emergence of affective salience. If we were to phrase this account in dynamic systems terms, then we could say that affective allure amounts to a parameter that at a certain critical threshold induces a bifurcation from passive affection ("passivity") to an active and motivated orienting ("receptivity") toward something emerging as affectively salient or prominent.[8]

Varela and Depraz maintain that this dynamics of affect has its "germ" or "source" in a "primordial fluctuation" of the body's feeling and movement tendencies. This fluctuation manifests in any given instance as a particular movement tendency or motion disposition inhabited by a particular affective force. Patočka calls it an "e-motion" and describes it as a manifestation of the "primordial dynamism" of the lived body (Patočka 1998, pp. 40–42, 139). These fluctuations are *valenced* in the following sense. As movement tendencies, they exhibit movement and posture valences—toward/away, approach/withdrawal, engage/avoid, receptive/defensive. As feeling tendencies, they exhibit affective and hedonic valences—attraction/repulsion, like/dislike, pleasant/unpleasant, and positive/negative. As socially situated, they exhibit social valences—dominance/submission, nurturance/rejection. And as culturally situated, they exhibit normative and cultural valences, that is to say, values—good/bad, virtuous/unvirtuous, wholesome/unwholesome, worthy/unworthy, praiseworthy/blameworthy.

In summary, the dynamics of affect in an emotional interpretation can be traced back to fluctuations in valence, but valence needs to be understood not as a simple behavioral or affective plus/minus sign, but rather as a complex space of polarities and possible combinations (as in the chemical sense of valence) (see Colombetti 2005).

Having explored affect at the microscale of emotional interpretations, we can now turn to the mesoscale of moods. In Lewis's model, moods comprise emotional continuity together with prolonged appraisal patterns. Whereas the movement from one emotional interpretation to another corresponds to a bifurcation from one attractor to another, the onset of a mood corresponds to a temporary modification of the entire emotion-cognition state space. Moods involve changes to the surface or global manifold of the state space, and thereby alter the landscape of possible attractors corresponding to possible emotional interpretations. "Self-organizing moods," Lewis proposes, "at least negative moods—may arise through the entrainment of an interpretive bias with a narrow range of emotional states. This entrainment may evolve over occasions from the coupling of components in recurrent EIs, augmenting cooperativities that favor particular emotions and interpretations" (Lewis 2000, p. 48). Whereas the higher-order form of an emotional interpretation is a global intention for acting on the world, the higher-order form of a mood is an enduring intentional orientation.

An emotional interpretation, having the form of a global intention for action, can resolve itself in action (or an action type such as engagement or avoidance), but Lewis suggests that the intentional orientation of a negative mood persists because no action can be taken to resolve it: "Intentions (or real-time goals) prepare for actions, and actions dissipate intentions. But if actions are not attempted or are not effective, then emotional engagement with goal-relevant associations and plans may keep the goal alive, not as an immediate prospect but as a need or wish extending over time" (Lewis 2000, p. 49). Moods thus involve intentional and goal-directed content that cannot be reduced simply to the goal-directed content of the specific emotional interpretations they comprise.

If an emotional interpretation reflects a bifurcation or phase transition in the psychological (emotion-cognition) state space, whereas the global manifold of this space at any time reflects some mood, then it follows that mood is always present as a background setting or situation within which transient emotional interpretations occur.

This view of mood as an enduring, background intentional orientation is reminiscent of Heidegger's description of mood as the most fundamental awareness one has of being in a world (1996, pp. 126–131). Yet there are differences too. For Heidegger, mood is not a form of object-directed experience, but rather a non-object-directed "attunement" *(Stimmung)* or "affectedness" (Dreyfus 1991, p. 168). Mood is omnipresent and primordial. It is always present, rather than being intermittent, and it is our original (most basic) way of being in the world. It preexists and is the necessary precondition for specific moods, such as fearfulness, depression, and contentment, which emerge out of primordial mood. Thus, from a Heideggerian point of view, the enduring intentional orientation of a specific mood, such as depression, could not arise unless we were already attuned to the world, that is to say, unless the world were already disclosed to us through primordial mood.

From a neurophenomenological point of view, Heidegger's account is unsatisfying. For one thing, it is strangely disembodied, for the body plays no role in his account of mood and attunement, despite the attention he gives to fear and to the "fundamental mood" of anxiety. Second, in completely neglecting the microtemporality of affect in favor of a macroscopic analysis of mood and temporality, Heidegger provides no links from one scale to the other. Third, as Patočka points out, because mood for Heidegger involves understanding our place in the world in time, his account excludes animals, infants, and young children (1998, pp. 132–133). Mood is proper to "Dasein," Heidegger's term for individual human existence. Heidegger's analysis of the "existential structures" constitutive of Dasein clearly indicates that Dasein is individual human existence of a mature and socialized adult form. Dasein is that being for whom being is an issue; that being who hides from the possibility of its own death, surrendering itself in everyday life to "the they," the anonymous other, and who thereby lives inauthentically. In the case of animals and children, however, there is also subjectivity relating to the world (Patočka 1998, p. 133). Gallagher makes a similar observation:

> on Heidegger's description, it's difficult to classify the neonate as an instance of Dasein, ontologically or experientially. If Dasein is *das Man* ["the they"], the infant has not yet had the chance to become *das Man* since it is only at the beginning of a socialization process. If Dasein has the possibility of authenticity as an alternative to inauthenticity, the infant has no such possibility. It can hardly be authentic or inauthentic since the possibility of its own death is not yet an issue for it. Perhaps the very young Dasein is not Dasein at all. (Gallagher 1998, p. 119)

There are two critical points here. First, as an "existential structure," Heideggerian mood is largely static, for it has little if any genetic phenomenological depth. Second, if attunement or affectedness is supposed to be the most basic way of being in the world, then it would seem that Heidegger is leaving out something still more primordial, namely, the sensorimotor and affective sensibility of our bodily subjectivity (Patočka 1998, pp. 133–135). In short, Heidegger's account neglects the lived body.

There remains the emotion macroscale of personality formation to consider in Lewis's model. Emotional self-organization at this level is the formation of lasting interpretive-emotional habits specific to classes of situations. It involves permanent or long-lasting alterations to the basic shape of the emotion-cognition state space: "These include the initial establishment of attractors for recurrent EIs in infancy and the reconfiguration or replacement of those attractors during periods of personality transition" (Lewis 2000, p. 54). The emotional self-organization of personality development is explicitly intersubjective. Its higher-order form, which, due to circular causality, both emerges from and constrains moods and emotional interpretations, is a sense of personal self—"a subjective, intentional, thrusting forward into the world—this time lasting for months and years" (Lewis 2000, p. 57). According to this model, the sense of personal self is constituted by temporally extended, long-term patterns of habitual emotions linked with habitual appraisals, built up especially from moods.

In phenomenology, this sense of a personal self corresponds to what Husserl calls the "concrete ego." By this he means the "I" that is constituted by "habitualities"—dispositional tendencies to experience things one way rather than another—as a result of general capabilities and sedimented experiences formed through active striving. Yet although this conception of self is of great importance for Husserl, and although his phenomenology is rich in analyses of affect and association, empathy and intersubjectivity, the Husserlian "concrete ego" is strangely lacking in personality. Overall there has been regrettably little analysis of emotion at the level of personality in phenomenology (unlike the Freudian or psychodynamic tradition).

In exploring the parallels and convergences between dynamic systems approaches to emotion and phenomenological approaches, I have been trying to sketch in a preliminary way what a neurophenomenology of emotion might look like. Lewis's model is helpful in this regard because it describes emotion at a structural or formal level that is open to phenomenological and biological interpretation. Relying on the morphodynamical notion of form or structure, we can explore phenomenological accounts of the structure of emotion experience, while relating these accounts to psychological processes described by emotion theory and to neurobiological processes described by neurodynamics. Weaving together these multiple strands in this mutually enlightening way provides another example of the neurophenomenological approach to the structure of experience.

✦ ✦ ✦

Empathy and Enculturation

IN EXPLORING EMOTION in the previous chapter, we began with ab-stract considerations about the structure of the flow of experience and then moved to the more tangible topic of emotional self-organization and the dynamics of affect. As we followed this path, the intersubjec-tivity of human experience gained increasing visibility, becoming espe-cially prominent in the example of seeing an angry face and averting one's gaze.

Yet so far in this book I have only alluded to intersubjectivity without giving it the attention it deserves. Intersubjectivity is a vast and impor-tant theme of phenomenological philosophy, with numerous ramifica-tions. It is also a central concern for developmental psychology, social psychology, and clinical psychology, for psychoanalysis, and more re-cently for affective and cognitive neuroscience. To explore the rela-tions among the many phenomenological, clinical, and scientific treat-ments of intersubjectivity in any comprehensive way would require another book. My aim in this final chapter is accordingly far more modest. It is to build a bridge between mind science and Husserl's ge-netic and generative phenomenology of intersubjectivity. This bridge is meant as a preliminary step to future investigations that would draw from both other important phenomenological discussions of intersub-jectivity and scientific and clinical research.

This chapter is organized around two ideas. The first idea is that self and other enact each other reciprocally through empathy.[1] One's con-sciousness of oneself as a bodily subject in the world presupposes a certain empathetic understanding of self and other. The second idea is that human subjectivity emerges from developmental processes of enculturation and is configured by the distributed cognitive web of symbolic culture. For these reasons, human subjectivity is from the outset intersubjectivity, and no mind is an island.

Intentionality and Open Intersubjectivity

My first step is to introduce an important idea from Husserl's later reflections on intersubjectivity—the idea that the intentionality of consciousness is "intersubjectively open" (Zahavi 1997, 2001a, 2001b). Consciousness is not solipsistically closed in upon itself; rather, it is structurally open to the other in advance of any actual encounter between self and other.

We have already seen (in Chapter 2) that intentionality in the broadest phenomenological sense is openness toward the world. What needs emphasis now is that this openness is also implicitly intersubjective, for the world is disclosed to us as intersubjectively accessible. On the one hand, the types of things we encounter in our dealings with the world are first and foremost cultural artifacts and equipment, not indifferent physical objects (Heidegger 1996, pp. 62–67). On the other hand, even objects, considered abstractly simply as objects of perception, appear to us as perceivable by other possible subjects. It is this latter thought I want to introduce here.[2]

When we perceive an object, it appears as having sides or profiles that are not currently in view. We see the side facing us, while the other sides are hidden. Although we do not directly see an object's hidden profiles, we nonetheless have a distinctly perceptual sense of their presence. In Husserl's language, perception automatically "appresents" the hidden profiles in and through its presentation of the visible ones. The term *appresentation* refers to one's intending the presence of something not directly given on the basis of something that is directly given. In perception, we appresent or co-intend the backside of an object, which is not immediately visible, on the basis of the front side, which is directly visible. How to understand this relation between presence and absence in perceptual experience is a longstanding topic of phenomenological philosophy. The relevance of intersubjectivity to this topic can be brought out in the following way: can we account for

this relation between presence and absence in perceptual experience
without referring to another possible perceptual consciousness besides
one's own? Husserl's answer is negative. In perception, or more precisely in its appresenting function, we implicitly understand the absent
profiles to be also the objective correlates of the possible perceptions
of another subject (see Zahavi 1997, 2001a).

The thought here is that the very meaning or sense "object"
(namely, something standing over against oneself as a subject), which
is implicit in the intentionality of the perceptual act, implies being simultaneously perceivable by a plurality of subjects. To retrace the main
steps leading to this thought, consider that if there is no need to refer
to other perceivers besides myself in characterizing the intentionality
of my perception, then the absent or hidden profiles of an object must
be appresented as correlates simply of my perception. The following
two alternatives, therefore, suggest themselves. First, the absent profiles might be appresented as profiles given either in my past perceptions or my possible future perceptions of the object. Second, the
hidden profiles might be appresented as the correlates of the perceptions I would have right now were I looking at the thing from vantage
points different from my present one. Both accounts seem unsatisfactory. The first one makes the unity of the object for perception the result of a series of temporally separated profiles, only one of which (the
visible one) is actual. But I do not experience the profile facing me as
present with respect to a past or future absent profile; I experience it
as present with respect to the other co-present but hidden profiles. According to the second account, however, I appresent the absent profiles as correlates of my co-present, but nonactual, perceptions. This
account makes the unity of the object for my perception a composite
of actual and nonactual profiles (the correlates of my nonactual perceptions), whereas it needs to be a unity of actual profiles, some visible
and some hidden.

Thus the appresented and hidden profiles seem better understood
not as correlates of one's own possible perceptions, but as the correlates of the possible perceptions of other subjects, who could perceive
the object simultaneously with oneself, though from a different vantage point.[3] For one to be able to appresent the hidden profiles of an
object, no other subjects need be actually present, nor need any other
subjects be present in the world at all. (As Husserl says, I might be the

last survivor of a universal plague.) Rather, the point is that the intentional structure of perception discloses objects as transcending one's individual consciousness of them in such a way as to imply their presence to and perceptibility by other possible subjects. In this way, the intentionality of consciousness is intersubjectively open and incompatible with any solipsism that would deny the possibility in principle of a plurality of subjects who view the same world as I do.

In addition to the open intersubjectivity of intentionality, which is a structural feature of consciousness, two other kinds of intersubjectivity can be distinguished in Husserl's analyses. The first is the experience of the bodily presence of the other, or the face-to-face experience of self and other. The second is the generative intersubjectivity of communally handed-down norms, conventions, and historical traditions. Both types of intersubjectivity will play a role in this chapter. To prepare the way, we need to examine the relation between the open intersubjectivity of consciousness and intersubjectivity as the face-to-face encounter of self and other.[4]

One might suppose that the intersubjective openness of consciousness depends on the perceptual experience of the other, that one's perceptual experience of the other's expressive bodily presence is the basis for the intersubjectivity of consciousness. One could argue, for example, that when I experience another person experiencing me, I tacitly realize that I am an other for the other, that I am disclosed to the other as the other is disclosed to me, and thus that I am only one among many in a context of others. In this way, my consciousness would become intersubjectively opened, as it were, from the outside.

This account, however, gets things backwards. For me to perceive the other—that is, for the other's bodily presence to be perceptually disclosed to me—the open intersubjectivity of perceptual experience must already be in play. Thus one's actual experience of another bodily subject is based on an *a priori* openness to the other. For the same reason, the intersubjective openness of consciousness cannot be reduced to any contingent and factual relation of self and other, for this openness belongs to the very structure of subjectivity in advance of any such encounter. Nevertheless, there is clearly much more to our experience of other subjects than the mere dependence of this experience on the open intersubjectivity of consciousness. Whereas open intersubjectivity is primarily a feature of the formal structure of intentionality, the concrete experience of self and other allows for dissension and thus an experience of the alterity of the other (Zahavi 1997, p. 317). What I propose to do now is to consider the structure of this concrete experience in more detail by examining the experience of empathy.

The Phenomenological Concept of Empathy

Psychologists use the term *empathy* to describe three distinguishable and interrelated affective and cognitive processes involving self and other (Levenson and Reuf 1992). The first is feeling what another person is feeling; the second is knowing what another person is feeling; and the third is responding compassionately to another person's distress—a response better described as sympathy (Eisenberg 2000).

Phenomenologists approach empathy in a somewhat different way (Stein 1989). Empathy is a unique form of intentionality in which we are directed toward the other's experience. Any intentional act that discloses or presents "foreign experience" counts as empathy. Although empathy, thus understood, is based on perception (of the other's bodily presence) and can involve inference in difficult or problematic situations (when one has to work out how another person feels about something), it is not reducible to some additive combination of perception and inference. The phenomenological conception of empathy thus stands opposed to any theory according to which we understand others by first perceiving their bodily behavior and then inferring or hypothesizing that their behavior is caused by experiences or inner mental states similar to those that apparently cause similar behavior in us. Rather, in empathy we experience another human being directly as a person—that is, as an intentional being whose bodily gestures and actions are expressive of his or her experiences or states of mind. The task for phenomenology is to analyze the modes or ways in which the other is disclosed as another subjectivity, as well as the intentional structures of consciousness that make this disclosure possible.

Edith Stein, in her book *On the Problem of Empathy*, draws attention to a number of formal structural features of empathy, understood as the awareness of another's experience (Stein 1989, pp. 6–11).[5] We can begin with the relation between perception and empathy. In both perception and empathy, the intentional object is presented as there itself right now, but in different ways. Whereas perception presents an object as there in its concrete and individual being, empathy does not present the experience of another subject in this way. When one becomes aware of the sorrow of another person, the sorrow is not given as a concrete and individual being, standing right there before one, as when one sees or touches something. Rather, the sorrow is given in and through the sorrowful countenance or pained expression. There is thus "a close, yet very loose, parallel between empathic acts and the averted sides of what is seen" (Stein 1989, p. 6). In perception, the averted sides, though hidden, and thus in one sense unperceived, have a kind of perceptual presence, a perceptual presence-in-absence. Similarly, in empathy, the feeling of sorrow, though not present as it is originally for the subject who experiences the sorrow, has a perceptual presence in the sorrowful countenance. In phenomenological language, whereas an object's averted sides are appresented on the basis of its perceived side, a person's feeling is appresented on the basis of her empathetically grasped countenance and comportment. Similarly, whereas the visible side is there itself right now and grasped as such in perception, so the sorrowful countenance is there itself right now and grasped as such in empathy.

Yet this parallel only goes so far. In perception, the averted sides can in principle always be brought into view. In empathy, although hidden or concealed aspects of the sorrowful countenance can be brought into view, the sorrow itself as a subjective feeling cannot be made perceptually present in this way. In Stein's words: "I can consider the expression of pain, more accurately, the change of face I empathically grasp as an expression of pain, from as many sides as I desire. Yet, in principle, I can never get an 'orientation' where the pain itself is primordially given" (1989, p. 7).

This "nonprimordiality" of empathy—the fact that an experience cannot be disclosed in its original first-person subjectivity from the second-person perspective of empathy—means there is also a parallel or an analogy between empathy and memory and imagination. When one remembers a joy, the joy is not "primordially and bodily there," but rather is given in memory "as having once been alive" (Stein 1989, p. 8). The joy is absent, but it is not simply absent, for it has a kind of presence-in-absence for the remembering experience. It is, as we saw in Chapter 10, phenomenally absent. Yet once again the parallel or

analogy only goes so far. In the case of memory, the subject who is remembering is the same as the subject remembered. In the case of empathy, however, the subject who is empathizing is not the same as the
subject empathized.

> And this is what is fundamentally new in contrast with the memory, ex-
> pectation, or the fantasy of our own experiences. These two subjects are
> separate and not joined together, as previously, by a consciousness of
> sameness or a continuity of experience. And while I am living in the
> other's joy, I do not feel primordial joy. It does not issue live from my
> "I." Neither does it have the character of once having lived like remem-
> bered joy. But still much less is it merely fantasized without actual life.
> This other subject is primordial although I do not experience it as pri-
> mordial [as I do myself]. In my non-primordial experience [of the
> other's feeling] I feel, as it were, led by a primordial one not experi-
> enced by me but still there, manifesting itself in my non-primordial ex-
> perience. (Stein 1989, p. 11)

Empathy, like perception, memory, imagination, and expectation, is
thus a *sui generis* kind of intentional experience. Empathy shares certain structural features with perception and certain other structural
features with memory, imagination, and expectation, but it cannot be
reduced to these intentional acts or constructed out of them. Therefore, in addition to the foregoing comparisons, empathy needs to be
analyzed on its own terms.

Stein describes empathy as the experience of feeling led by an experience that is not one's own but that is given in one's experience of another's expressive bodily presence. She distinguishes "three levels or
modalities of accomplishment" in empathy, "even if in a concrete case
people do not always go through all levels but are often satisfied with
one of the lower ones" (Stein 1989, p. 10). First, the experience of another emerges before me: "When it arises before me all at once, it
faces me as an object (such as the sadness I 'read in another's face')"
(p. 10). Second, I can inquire into the content of the experience and
"its implied tendencies," in which case "the content, having pulled me
into it, is no longer really an object" (ibid.). I am now directed toward
the object of the empathized experience, that is, I mentally transpose
myself to the other's place to comprehend the object of the subject's
experience from his or her point of view. Third, once this clarification

of the other's experience has taken place, the experience faces me again, but now in a clarified or an explicated way. Stein refers to these three levels as "(1) the emergence of the experience, (2) the fulfilling explication, and (3) the comprehensive objectification of the explained experience" (ibid.).

These levels of empathy can also be reiterated back onto me, so that I have an empathetic experience of the other's empathetic experience of me. In other words, "among the acts of another that I comprehend empathically there can be empathic acts in which the other comprehends another's acts. This 'other' can be a third person or me myself. In the second case we have [what Theodor Lipps calls] 'reflexive sympathy' where my original experience returns to me as an empathized one" (Stein 1989, p. 18).

Throughout these levels, empathy is based on the experience of the other as a living bodily subject like oneself:

> This individual is not given as a physical body, but as a sensitive, living body belonging to an "I," an "I" that senses, thinks, feels, and wills. The living body of this "I" not only fits into my phenomenal world but is itself the center of orientation of such a phenomenal world. It faces this world and communicates with me. (Stein 1989, p. 5)

Following Stein, we can explicate in more detail this empathetic experience of the other as a living bodily subject. We experience the other's bodily presence as (1) animated by its own fields of sensation; (2) animated by general feelings of life or vitality (growth, development, aging, health, sickness, vigor, sluggishness, and so on); (3) expressive of subjective experience; (4) another center of orientation in space; and (5) capable of voluntary action.

Stein calls the empathetic perception of the other's bodily presence as animated by its own fields of sensation "sensual empathy" or "sensing-in." To take her example: "The hand resting on the table does not lie there like the book beside it. It 'presses' against the table more or less strongly; it lies there limpid or stretched; and I 'see' the sensations of pressure and tension" (1989, p. 58). So far this example includes only the first level of accomplishment in empathy—the emergence of the experience of another. The second level involves delving into the content of the other's experience. If this happens, then there is a movement from empathy as an involuntary sensorimotor and affective coupling of our two lived bodies to empathy as the imaginative movement of myself to the other's place: "my hand is moved (not in reality but 'as if') to the place of the foreign one. It is moved into it and occupies its position and attitude, now feeling its sensations, though not primordially and not as being its own . . . the foreign hand is continually perceived as belonging to the foreign physical body so that the empathized sensations are continually brought into relief as foreign in contrast with our own sensations" (1989, p. 58).

For this kind of sensual empathy to happen, one's own body and the other's body must be of a similar type or have comparable body schemas. What the limits of this body type or schema are is an open and important question. Stein notes, "empathy is quite successful with men's and children's hands which are very different from mine" (p. 58). Then she raises the crucial point: "The type 'human physical body' does not define the limits of the range of my empathic objects, more exactly, of what can be given to me as a living body." For example: "Should I perhaps consider a dog's paw in comparison with my hand, I do not have a mere physical body, either, but a sensitive limb of a living body . . . I may sense-in pain when the animal is injured." Nevertheless, Stein maintains, "the further I deviate from the type 'man,' the smaller does the number of possibilities of fulfillment become' (1989, p. 59).

Interwoven with sensual empathy is the perception of the other's bodily presence as expressive of subjective thoughts and feelings: "we 'see' shame 'in' blushing, irritation in the furrowed brow, anger in the clenched fist" (1989, p. 75). These examples of blushing and irritation show that the empathetic perception of facial expressions is paradigmatic of this aspect of empathy. As Jonathan Cole writes in an article on facial embodiment:

> [T]he face involves an injunction not only to express, and to observe expressions, but to immerse oneself in what is expressed and to feel something of it oneself. Though complementary to body language, in this it may go beyond what is usually considered to be expressed through posture. Expressions actually help in constituting what is within. A face, therefore, is not only an expression of a self available for others to read, but to some extent the self is constituted in the face and developed, and experienced, in the interaction between faces. (Cole 1997, p. 482)

Another aspect of empathy is the perception of the other as being another center of orientation in a common spatial world. Our experience of space and our sense of bodily selfhood are intertwined: We perceive things to be arrayed around us, while we are "here," at what Husserl calls the "zero-point" of spatial orientation. This differentiation between "here" and "there" does not belong to space considered as a medium independent of one's body; it belongs to our egocentric bodily space. When we perceive another, we perceive her as "there" in relation to us "here," and we grasp her as having her own egocentric space defined by her own body. Furthermore, we perceive her body as a locus of intentional agency and voluntary movement. We do not experience another's movements as mechanical but as alive, spontaneous, and volitional. Neither sentience (having fields of sensation) nor spatial orientation (having an egocentric space) can be separated from voluntary movement in our empathetic perception of another. In empathetically perceiving another person as a sentient being capable of voluntary movement, we perceive her as occupying her own "here," in relation to which we stand "there."

Once again, this sort of empathetic experience can remain at the first level of accomplishment (empathetically perceiving the other over there), or it can proceed to the second level where it unfolds according to the imaginative movement of putting oneself in the other's place. This imaginative self-transposition allows us to gain a new spatial perspective on the world, the perspective of the other. At the same time, we continue to have our own center of spatial orientation. Thus empathy enables us to grasp space as an intersubjective medium in which there is no single zero-point or bodily center of orientation. To put the point another way, empathy is a precondition for our experience of inhabiting a common and intersubjective spatial world. Empathy provides a viewpoint in which one's center of orientation is one among others. Clearly, the space correlated to such a viewpoint cannot be one's own egocentric space, for that space is defined by one's own zero-point, whereas the new spatial perspective contains one's zero-point as simply one spatial point among many others.

According to both Husserl and Stein, this experiential grasp of an intersubjective space is a condition of possibility for one's ability to experience one's own living body as a physical body like other bodies in the world. If one were confined to one's own first-person singular point of view, such that one had absolutely no empathetic openness to others, including how one is an other for the other, one could not grasp that one's own body is a physical object perceivable by a plurality of subjects. A physical object is something that can stand before one in perception and be examined from a multiplicity of points of view. One's own living body, however, from one's exclusively first-person singular point of view, cannot stand before one in this way. No matter how one turns, one's body is always "here," at the zero-point, never "there." One cannot walk around it to behold it from all sides (Merleau-Ponty 1962, pp. 90–97). In general, one's body, as that by which one perceives the world, cannot be perceptually disclosed to one as simply another object in the world. Thus, as long as we consider the living body simply from the first-person singular perspective, it is phenomenally unlike any other physical object. It is phenomenally "the strangest object" (Stein 1989, p. 41), something radically incomplete. In Husserl's words: "The same Body [lived body] which serves me as means for all my perception obstructs me in the perception of it itself and is a remarkably imperfectly constituted thing" (1989, p. 167). Through empathy, specifically the experience of oneself as an other for the other, one gains a view of one's own bodily being beyond one's first-person singular perspective.

Stein elaborates this important point in terms of what she calls reiterated empathy. In reiterated empathy, I see myself from your perspective. Stated more precisely, I empathetically grasp your empathetic experience of me. In this way, I acquire a view of myself not merely as something perceivable by others but as something empathetically perceivable by others as a living bodily subject. In other words, I no longer merely experience sentience from within, but I also experience myself as recognizably sentient from without, from the perspective of the other. In this way, my sense of personal selfhood, even at a basic bodily level, is tied to recognition by another and to the ability to grasp that recognition empathetically.

Implicit in the foregoing account are three distinguishable empathetic processes or types of empathy, to which we can also add a fourth (Depraz 2001b; Thompson 2001, 2005):

1. The passive or involuntary coupling or pairing of my living body with your living body in perception and action.

2. The imaginary movement or transposition of myself into your place.
3. The understanding of you as an other to me, and of me as an other to you.
4. The moral perception of you as a person.

In the next sections, I use this phenomenological typology of empathetic experience as a way to organize and make sense of recent empirical studies of empathy and social cognition from developmental psychology, ethology, and cognitive and affective neuroscience. In this way, I sketch a neurophenomenological framework for the scientific study of empathy.[6]

Affective and Sensorimotor Coupling

The first type of empathy is the dynamic coupling or pairing of the living bodies of self and other. It is passive in the sense of not being initiated voluntarily or as a result of deliberation or reflection, and it serves as a support for the other aspects of empathy. "Coupling" or "pairing" means an associative bonding or linking of self and other on the basis of their bodily similarity. This similarity operates not so much at the level of visual appearance, which forms part of the body image as an intentional object present to consciousness, but at the level of gesture, posture, and movement—that is, at the level of the unconscious body schema (Gallagher 1986b). Thus bodily coupling or pairing allows empathy to be not simply the comprehension of another's particular emotions (sadness, joy, and so on), but on a more fundamental level the experience of another as a living bodily subject like oneself.

This phenomenological conception of the bodily basis of empathy can be linked to mind science by referring to the growing body of psychological and neurophysiological evidence for coupling mechanisms linking self and other at sensorimotor and affective levels (Decety in press; Decety and Sommerville 2003; Gallese, Keysers, and Rizzolatti 2004; Preston and de Waal 2002). For example, according to the common-coding theory of perception and action, perceived events and planned actions share a common neural format (Prinz 1997). Thus perception of an action automatically activates not simply processes of perceptual recognition for that action, but also various aspects of the motor processes for generating it.

Evidence supporting this idea comes from the discovery of so-called mirror neurons in area F5 of the premotor cortex of monkeys (di Pellegrino et al. 1992). These neurons display the same pattern of activity both when the animal accomplishes certain goal-directed hand movements and when the animal observes another individual performing the same actions. The activity of the neurons is correlated with specific intentional motor acts (defined by the presence of a goal) and not with the execution of particular movements (defined by the contraction of particular muscle groups). The neurons can be classified according to the type of action, such as "grasp with the hand," "grasp with the hand and mouth," and "reach." All the neurons of the same type correlate with actions that meet the same objective. On the basis of these properties, mirror neurons appear to form a cortical system that matches the observation of motor actions performed by another individual with performance of the same type of actions by oneself (Gallese, Keysers, and Rizzolatti 2004).

These findings at the level of single neurons have been complemented by brain-imaging studies in humans using functional magnetic resonance imaging (fMRI). One study showed that activity in two different cortical areas—the right anterior parietal cortex, and Broca's area in the left inferior frontal cortex (which is the motor area for speech and the human homologue of area F5 in the monkey)—became more intense when an individual simultaneously performed the same finger movements he observed being performed by another individual (Iacoboni et al. 1999). The authors of this study suggest that the left frontal area is concerned with the motor goal of the observed action, and hence with understanding the meaning of the action, whereas the right parietal area is concerned with the precise kinesthetic aspects of the movement, and hence with the details needed to memorize or repeat the exact movement. Another brain-imaging study showed that when one individual observes another execute actions with different body parts (mouth actions, hand actions, and foot actions), the neural patterns of activation in the observer's brain correspond to those that would be active were the observer performing the same bodily actions (Buccino et al. 2001). Thus mirror systems comprise a rich repertoire of body actions besides hand actions.

Neural studies of these mirror systems provide evidence for the dynamic co-constitution of perception and action at the level of intentional agency (Hurley 1998, pp. 413–419). In the context of social cognition, this constitutive interdependency shapes the social domain on the basis of a sensorimotor resonance between self and other in the perception and execution of action. In Gallese's words: "when we observe actions performed by other individuals our motor system 'resonates' along with that of the observed agent" (Gallese 2001, p. 38).

Such mirroring and resonance also occur in the case of pain and emotion. Neurons in the anterior cingulate cortex that respond when a patient receives an unpleasant stimulus to his hand also respond when the patient watches a pinprick applied to the examiner's hand (Hutchinson et al. 1999). It has also been shown that perception of emotion activates neural mechanisms that play a key role in generating emotions (Adolphs 2003) and that many of the same brain areas are activated both when subjects imitate and when they observe facial expressions of various emotions (Carr et al. 2003).

In addition to sensorimotor coupling, emotive coupling and affective resonance also occur between self and other. In affective resonance, two or more individuals affect each other's emotional states. A classic example is crying in newborn infants (which is usually labeled with the misleading term *emotional contagion*). Newborn babies cry in response to the sound of another baby's cry, a reaction that is thought to provide some of the underpinnings for the later development of cognitive empathy (Eisenberg and Strayer 1987; de Waal 1996, p. 121). Affective resonance also occurs when two individuals engage in direct interaction and one actively seeks to affect the other, as when a rejected youngster throws a tantrum at its mother's feet—a behavior seen not only in humans but also in apes (de Waal 2002).

Imaginary Transposition

The second type of empathy is the imaginary transposition of oneself to the other's place. This process is more active and cognitive than sensorimotor and affective resonance. Instead of simply the involuntary, bodily pairing of self and other, cognitive perspective-taking processes enable one to imagine or mentally transpose oneself into the place of the other.

Comparative studies of empathy from cognitive ethology provide an important window on cognitive empathy. The presence and extent of empathy among nonhuman animals, especially primates, is a subject of much debate. According to an "all-or-none" view, cognitive empathy (the only kind of empathy, according to this view) requires the cognitive ability to attribute mental states to another individual and to understand the other's behavior in light of them. This ability, usually called mind-reading, is taken by many theorists to require the possession of a "theory of mind," a theoretical body of knowledge about mental states and their role in generating behavior. Advocates of this way of thinking have argued that chimpanzees fail certain mind-reading tests and therefore do not possess a theory of mind. Accordingly, they are said to be incapable of cognitive empathy (Povinelli 1998; Povinelli and Preuss 1995). Yet, as I have suggested here and as others have proposed, most notably Frans de Waal (1996), empathy should not be seen as an all-or-nothing phenomenon. In de Waal's words: "Many forms of empathy exist intermediate between the extremes of mere agitation and distress of another and full understanding of their predicament. At one end of the spectrum, rhesus infants get upset and seek contact with one another as soon as one of them screams. At the other end, a chimpanzee recalls a wound he has inflicted, and returns to the victim to inspect it" (de Waal 1996, p. 69).

Other intermediate cases are consolation behavior and tailored-helping behavior. Consolation behavior is friendly contact by an uninvolved and less distressed bystander toward a victim of a previously aggressive encounter. For example, de Waal, in his book *Good Natured,* presents a photograph of a juvenile chimpanzee comforting a distressed adult. Consolation behavior has been extensively documented in great apes only (and has not been found in monkey species despite great efforts to find it). Tailored helping is coming to the aid of another (either a conspecific or a member of another species) with behaviors tailored to the other's particular needs (as when one ape helps another out of a tree or tries to help an injured bird fly). Such behavior, in de Waal's words, "probably requires a distinction between self and other that allows the other's situation to be divorced from one's own while maintaining the emotional link that motivates behavior" (de Waal 2002). There exists a large number of anecdotal reports of tailored helping in apes.

Cognitive empathy at its fullest, however, is achieved when one individual can mentally adopt the other's perspective by exchanging places with the other in imagination. Described phenomenologically: I am here and I imagine going there and being at the place where you are right now. Conversely, you are here (the "there" where I imagine being) and you imagine you are going there, to the place where I am (my "here"). Through this imagined movement and spatial transposition, we are able to exchange our mental perspectives, our thoughts and feelings. Whether apes possess this kind of mental ability is unclear and a subject of debate (Gallup 1998; Povinelli 1998).

In human children, the mental ability to transpose self and other seems to be linked to the emergence, at around nine to twelve months of age, of a whole cluster of cognitive abilities known collectively as joint attention (Tomasello 1999, pp. 62–63). "Joint attention" refers to the triadic structure of a child, adult, and an object or event to which they share attention, and comprises the activities of gaze following (reliably following where adults are looking), joint engagement with shared objects or events, using adults as social reference points, and imitative learning (acting on objects as adults do). At around the same time, infants also begin to point to things and hold them up for someone to see, gestures that serve to direct adult attention actively and intentionally. As Michael Tomasello argues, "infants begin to engage in joint attentional interactions when they begin to understand other persons as intentional agents like the self" (1999, p. 68). He proposes that the infant uses her primal understanding of others as "like me" and her newly emerging understanding of her own intentional agency, as the basis on which to judge analogically and categorically that others are intentional agents "like me" as well.

According to this view, experience of the self comes first and serves as a basis for developing understanding of the other (Decety and Sommerville 2003; Meltzoff and Moore 1998). Contrary to this view is the view that self and other arise together. Thus, Baressi and Moore (1996) propose that self-understanding and other-understanding develop together out of a prior experience of intentional relations that does not differentiate between first-person and third-person sources of information. The differences between these views and their relation to comparable differences in phenomenological accounts of intersubjectivity are beyond the scope of this chapter and stand out as an important topic for further research.

Mutual Self and Other Understanding

The third type of empathy involves not simply imagining myself in your place but understanding you as an other who accordingly sees me as an other to you. In other words, the imaginary transposition in this kind of empathy involves the possibility of seeing myself from your perspective, that is, as you empathetically perceive me. Empathy thus becomes reiterated, so that I empathetically imagine your empathetic experience of me and you empathetically imagine my empathetic experience of you. We also talk to each other about our experiences, and so linguistic communication and interpretation participate in and structure this exchange. As a result, each of us participates in an intersubjective viewpoint that transcends our own first-person singular perspectives.

We can turn again to developmental psychology for insight into the genesis of this third aspect of empathy and the role it plays in constituting an intersubjective perspective. Tomasello, in his book *The Cultural Origins of Human Cognition,* describes this genesis in the human infant:

> As infants begin to follow into and direct the attention of others to outside entities at nine to twelve months of age, it happens on occasion that the other person whose attention an infant is monitoring focuses on the infant herself. The infant then monitors that person's attention to her in a way that was not possible previously, that is, previous to the nine-month social-cognitive revolution. From this point on the infant's face-to-face interactions with others—which appear on the surface to be continuous with her face-to-face interactions from early infancy—are radically transformed. She now knows she is interacting with an intentional agent who perceives her and intends things toward her. When the infant did not understand that others perceive and intend things toward an outside world, there could be no question of how they perceived and intended things toward me. After coming to this understanding, the infant can monitor the adult's intentional relation to the world including herself . . . By something like this same process infants at this age also become able to monitor adults' emotional attitudes toward them as well—a kind of social referencing of others' attitudes to the self. This new understanding of how others *feel* about me opens up the possibility for the development of shyness, self-consciousness, and a

sense of self-esteem . . . Evidence for this is the fact that within a few months after the social-cognitive revolution, at the first birthday, infants begin showing the first signs of shyness and coyness in front of other persons and mirrors. (Tomasello 1999, pp. 89–90)

As Tomasello goes on to discuss, once the infant understands other individuals as intentional beings and herself as one participant among others in a social interaction, then whole new cognitive dimensions arise. The child comes to be able to participate in joint attentional scenes—social interactions in which the child and the adult jointly attend to some third thing, and to one another's attention to that third thing, for an extended period of time, and in which the child can conceptualize her own role from the same "outside" perspective as the other person. Joint attentional scenes in turn provide the framework for the acquisition of language, symbolic representation, and communicative conventions.

There are a number of parallels between Tomasello's analysis of joint attentional scenes and the phenomenological analysis of empathy. Although he does not use the term *empathy* in this context, the cognitive achievement he describes of being able to conceptualize oneself from the perspective of another person corresponds to what Edith Stein calls "reiterated empathy." In reiterated empathy, one sees oneself from the perspective of another and thereby grasps oneself as one individual participant in an intersubjective world. Similarly, the child's participation in a joint attentional scene requires that she be able to monitor the intentional acts of another person, including those acts directed toward her own intentional acts, for she herself is often the object of joint attention. This ability on the part of the child corresponds to being able to engage in reiterated empathy, in which the child empathetically grasps not simply the other as an intentional agent like herself, but the other's empathetic experience of herself as an intentional agent. Without this empathetic ability to understand oneself as an other for the other, it is hard to see how one could come to have a nonegocentric and intersubjective perspective on oneself as a participant in a social interaction:

[J]oint attention is sometimes characterized as the child coordinating attention between just two things: the object and the adult. But . . . as the child begins to monitor adults' attention to outside entities, that outside entity sometimes turns out to be the child herself—and so she begins to monitor adults' attention to her and thus to see herself from the outside, as it were. She also comprehends the role of the adult from this same outside vantage point, and so, overall, it is as if she were viewing the whole scene from above, with herself as just one player in it. This is as opposed to the way other primate species and six-month-old human infants view the social interaction from an "inside" perspective, in which the other participants appear in one format (third-person exteroception) and "I" appears in another different format (first-person proprioception . . .). (Tomasello 1999, pp. 99–100)

Tomasello's discussion of the child's achievement of this intersubjective perspective emphasizes the developmental progression from the neonate's understanding of the other as an animate being to the infant's understanding of the other as an intentional agent with attention and goal-directed behavior, to the four-year-old child's understanding of the other as a mental agent with thoughts and beliefs (which need not be expressed in behavior and can fail to match the world).

Phenomenologists, without neglecting the intentional and mental aspects of the self, draw attention to the first-person/third-person ambiguity of the lived body in reiterated empathy. My body is lived by me in the first person, but it also appears to you in the third person (or second person), and in empathetically grasping that experience of yours, I experience myself as an other to you. Here a connection can be made to the point about the difference between first-person (proprioceptive) and third-person (exteroceptive) cognitive formats in social interactions. If the "I" were to appear only in a first-person singular format, then it would not be possible to have any nonegocentric understanding of the "I" as a bodily individual in a public intentional world that transcends the self. My egocentric (proprioceptive and kinesthetic) experience of myself does not present my body to me as a perceptual thing equivalent to other perceptual things that stand before me—for my body does not stand before me in this way. Therefore, as we remarked earlier, if the lived body were disclosed only from a first-person singular perspective, it would seem unlike any other object and strangely incomplete. Through reiterated empathy in joint attentional scenes—the experience of oneself as an other for the other—

one can gain a nonegocentric and intersubjective view of one's own lived body as an individual intentional agent in a public world.

Moral Perception

The fourth type of empathy is the perception of the other as a being who deserves concern and respect. This type of empathy is not the same as any particular feeling of concern for another, such as sympathy, love, or compassion. Rather, it is the underlying capacity to have such other-directed and other-regarding feelings of concern (Vetlesen 1994). We cultivate this capacity in each other—for instance, from parent to child—and thereby constitute each other as persons in a moral sense.

This type of empathy can also be introduced from a developmental perspective. As we have seen, there is a progression from the infant's understanding of others as intentional agents (with attention, behavioral strategies, and goals) to the young child's understanding of others as mental agents (with beliefs, desires, and plans). According to Piaget and Tomasello, moral understanding begins to emerge at around the same time as the child comes to understand others as mental agents. It derives not from the rules adults impose on behavior but from empathizing with other persons as mental agents and being able to see and feel things from their point of view (Tomasello 1999, pp. 179–181).

Within Western moral philosophy there is a long tradition going back to Kant that emphasizes reason over feeling. To act out of duties legislated by reason is thought to have greater moral worth than acting on the basis of feeling or sentiment. Yet as de Waal observes, echoing David Hume and Adam Smith: "Aid to others in need would never be internalized as a duty without the fellow-feeling that drives people to take an interest in one another. Moral sentiments came first; moral principles second" (1996, p. 87).

Empathy in the moral sense is a basic cognitive and emotional capacity underlying all the moral sentiments and emotions one can have for another. The point here is not that empathy exhausts moral experience, for it certainly does not, but that empathy provides the source of that kind of experience and the entry point into it. Without empathy, concern and respect for others as persons in the moral sense—

as ends-in-themselves—would be greatly impoverished. As Mark
Johnson has argued:

> [T]he Kantian imperative always to treat others (and oneself) as ends-
> in-themselves has no practical meaning independent of our imagina-
> tively taking up the place of the other. Contrary to Kant's explicit
> claims, we cannot know what it means to treat someone as an end-in-
> himself, in any concrete way, unless we can imagine his experience,
> feelings, plans, goals, and hopes. We cannot know what respect for
> others demands of us, unless we participate imaginatively in their expe-
> rience of the world. (Johnson 1993, p. 200)

The four types of empathy presented here occur together in face-to-
face intersubjective experience. They intertwine through the lived
body and through language. You imagine yourself in my place on the
basis of the expressive similarity and spontaneous coupling of our lived
bodies. This experience of yours contributes to the constitution of me
for myself, for I experience myself as an intersubjective being by empathetically imagining your empathetic experience of me. Conversely,
I imagine myself in your place, and this experience of mine contributes to the constitution of you for yourself. As we communicate in
language and gesture, we interpret and understand each other dialog-
ically. This dialogical dynamic is not a linear or additive combination
of two preexisting, skull-bound minds. It emerges from and reciprocally shapes the nonlinear coupling of oneself and another in perception and action, emotion and imagination, and gesture and speech. In
this way, self and other bring forth each other reciprocally through
empathy.

Enculturation

In taking up empathy at the end of this book, our focus has shifted
from individual cognition and subjectivity to social cognition and intersubjectivity. Empathy, however, is only one aspect of intersubjectivity, one that operates at the level of the face-to-face encounter between individuals in a social group. For a fuller perspective on
intersubjectivity we need to take account of culture, history, and the
life-world. We need to look not only at formal structures of empathetic
experience and their embodied development, but also at the cultural

and historical becoming of human experience within and across generations. In phenomenological terms, we need to move from static and genetic analyses to generative ones.

One of the most important reasons that human mentality cannot be reduced simply to what goes on inside the brain of an individual is that human mental activity is fundamentally social and cultural. Culture is no mere external addition or support to cognition; it is woven into the very fabric of each human mind from the beginning. Symbolic culture in particular shapes the "cognitive architecture" of the human mind. Stripped of culture, we simply would not have the cognitive capacities that make us human. In the words of the neuropsychologist Merlin Donald:

> Our dependency on culture is very deep and extends to the very existence of certain kinds of symbolic representation and thought. Socially isolated humans do not develop language or any form of symbolic thought and have no true symbols of any kind. In fact, the isolated human brain does not act like a symbolizing organ, any more than an ape brain does. It is apparently unable to generate symbolic representations on its own. It does so only through intensive enculturation. (Donald 2001, p. 150)

We can adopt the developmental term *enculturation* to describe this constitutive power of culture. Human mentality emerges from developmental processes of enculturation and is configured by the distributed cognitive web of symbolic culture.

In recent years, a few cognitive scientists in different fields have drawn attention to the constitutive role that culture plays in human cognition (Donald 1991, 2001; Hendriks-Jansen 1996; Hutchins 1995; Tomasello 1999). Although their studies clearly imply that it makes no sense to think of culture and nature as separate developmental domains, there remains a persistent tendency in mind science to conceptualize human cognitive development in the dichotomous framework of "nature versus culture" or "nature versus nurture." Hence right from the start we need to situate the enculturation thesis in a developmental framework that explicitly rejects these dichotomous categories.

Developmental systems theory, discussed in Chapter 7, gives us the framework we need. Developmental systems theory rejects accounts of evolution and development that are conceptually structured by the innate-versus-acquired, nature-versus-nurture, and nature-versus-culture dichotomies. The developmental system of an organism or life cycle is the matrix of resources necessary for its development. Any resource that reliably recurs in each generation and plays a role in reconstructing the life cycle counts as something inherited. Such resources include not simply genes, but many other elements of the organism and its niche, from cytoplasmic components within the cell, which must be passed on with the genes, to symbiont organisms, social structures, and cultural practices.

In addition, developmental systems theory rejects the "master molecule" conception of genes: genes are not distinctly informational causes of development different in kind from other developmental factors that do not qualify as informational. Rather than unfolding according to a transmitted genetic blueprint or program, the developmental process of a life cycle reconstructs itself from generation to generation by way of myriad interdependent causal pathways on multiple levels—genetic, cellular, social, and cultural. Evolution is not simply change in gene frequencies, but "change in the distribution and constitution of developmental (organism-environment) systems" (Oyama 2000b, p. 77). Nor is ontogeny the outcome of two mutually exclusive classes of inherited and acquired developmental factors. Phenotypic traits are as much acquired as inherited because they must be developmentally constructed anew in each generation and thus acquired in ontogeny; and environmental resources are as much inherited or transmitted as they are acquired, for they are passed on inseparably with the genes and thus enter into the formation of the organism from the very beginning. From a developmental systems perspective then, it makes no sense to divide the traits of the human organism into the separate categories of nature and culture. As Griffiths and Gray state:

> Many species typical features of human psychology depend critically on stably replicated features of human culture. Many psychological features that are specific to certain human cultures may nevertheless have evolutionary explanations, since this variation may reflect differentiation among lineages of developmental systems. An obvious research program within developmental systems theory is an attempt to locate critical developmental resources in human culture(s), and to study

their influence on development, and how they are themselves replicated. (Griffiths and Gray 1994, p. 302)

The critical developmental resources provided by human culture
have long been of central concern to the field of cultural psychology
(Bruner 1990; Tomasello 1999; Vygotsky 1978). A good example from
this field—one that enables us to build on the discussion of empathy—
is the study of joint attention and cultural learning. Donald describes
joint attention as a "primary cultural guidance device" that "allows
children to follow cultural signals that will become increasingly more
abstract as they expand their horizons" (2001, p. 205). The nature of
these expanding horizons has been thoroughly reviewed by Tomasello
(1999), who describes how joint attentional scenes are the basis for the
acquisition of language and symbolic representation. They are also the
basis for a whole host of associated cognitive capacities and structures,
such as the ability to examine one's own thinking from the perspective
of the other and thereby redescribe one's own cognitive representations of the world. By drawing from his work, we can show how the genetic phenomenological analysis of empathy and the lived body can be
placed within a more encompassing generative analysis of culture and
the intersubjective life-world.

Let me begin by going back to the face-to-face coupling of infant
and adult in joint attentional interaction. In this characteristically
human form of structural coupling (but see Savage-Rumbaugh, Fields,
and Taglialatela 2001 on apes), two (or more) individuals jointly attend to some shared thing, and to one another's attention to that
thing, through the reciprocal coupling of their lived bodies—eye contact, facial expressions, voice, touch, and gesture—and their capacities
for temporally extended conscious awareness and the voluntary attentional control of action (Donald 2001, pp. 194–204).

We need to note two crucial features of the joint attentional scenes in
which infants and young children come to participate with adults
(Tomasello 1999, pp. 97–98). The first is that these scenes occupy a
middle ground of shared social reality between the larger perceptual
world and the smaller linguistic world: they include only a subset of
things in the child's perceptual world, but more things than those indicated in any set of linguistic symbols. The second is that the child's understanding of this shared social reality includes not simply the adult

and the object of their shared attention, but the child herself, "concep-tualized from the same 'outside' perspective as the other person and the object so that they are all in a common representational format" (Tomasello 1999, pp. 97–98). We have seen how this external and none-gocentric representational format is related to empathy, in particular to the reiterated empathy whereby one comprehends another's experi-ence of oneself (for example, another's attention to one's own inten-tional and attentional acts in a joint attentional scene). What we need to examine now is how this nonegocentric format provides the intersubjec-tive context for cultural learning and the acquisition of language and symbolic representation.

According to Tomasello, the acquisition of language and symbolic representation in joint attentional scenes proceeds on the basis of the child's abilities to understand communicative acts and intentions, as well as to engage in a particular kind of imitative and cultural learning called role-reversal imitation (1999, pp. 100–107). Communicative in-tentions are intentions to direct the attention of another person to something in the joint attentional scene. For the child to understand communicative intentions, she has to be able to monitor the inten-tional states of others toward her own intentional/attentional states. To produce the communicative acts she understands, however, she has to learn to use communicative symbols toward the adult in the same way the adult uses them toward her. This kind of imitative and cultural learning requires not simply that the child substitute herself for the adult as actor, but that she substitute the adult for herself as the target of the intentional act (otherwise she would wind up directing the symbol toward herself). She is able to effect this substitution because she can understand the whole joint attentional scene from an external perspective, in which she and the adult are represented in the same nonegocentric format and hence are interchangeable. (This would not be the case were she represented in a first-person or egocentric format, and the adult in a third-person format.) This process of role-reversal imitation in communication, Tomasello believes, "actually cre-ates the intersubjectively understood communicative convention or symbol" (1999, p. 107). Thus communicative conventions or symbols are enacted or generated for the infant by role-reversal imitation.

One feature that distinguishes the communicative symbols of lan-guage from other intersubjective and communicative symbols is that they are perspectival—they embody the variety of perspectives that human beings can take on things for communicative purposes. Consider one of Tomasello's examples:

> An individual language user looks at a tree and, before drawing the attention of her interlocuter to that tree, must decide, based on her assessment of the listener's current knowledge and expectations, whether to use That tree over there, It, The oak, That hundred-year old oak, The tree, The bagswing tree, That thing in the front yard, The ornament, The embarrassment, or any number of other expressions. She must decide if the tree is in / is standing in / is growing in / was placed in / is flourishing in the front yard. And these decisions are not made on the basis of the speaker's direct goal with respect to the object or activity involved, but rather on the basis of her goal with respect to the listener's interest and attention to that object or activity. This means that the speaker knows that the listener shares with her these same choices for construal—again, all available simultaneously. Indeed, the fact that the speaker is, while she is speaking, monitoring the listener's attentional status (and vice versa) means that both participants in a conversation are always aware that there are at least their two actual perspectives on a situation, as well as the many more that are symbolized in unused symbols and constructions. (Tomasello 1999, pp. 126–127; emphasis omitted)

Language acquisition involves the internalization of such multiple perspectives and communicative intentions. As one acquires a language, one internalizes, through imitative and cultural learning, the communicative intentions of others to get one to share their attention, as well as the perspectives they take on things in joint attentional scenes. In other words, language acquisition involves the internalization of joint attention into symbolic representation (Tomasello 1999, pp. 125–129).

The enculturation of the mind in language fundamentally transforms the nature of human cognition. Tomasello details three main interrelated ways in which language builds on basic human cognitive skills and fashions them into far more complex ones: (1) Linguistic communication is the vehicle for the "transmission" of most cultural knowledge: "Beyond fundamental primate skills of cognition . . . children's domain-specific knowledge and expertise depend almost totally on the accumulated knowledge of their cultures and its 'transmission' to them via linguistic and other symbols, including both writing and pictures" (p. 165). (2) Linguistic communication influences children's construction of cognitive categories, relations, analogies, and metaphors. In English, for instance, we can construe objects and properties as events or activities *(He iced the puck; She colored the picture);* activities and properties as objects *(Skating is fun; Green is my favorite color);* and objects and events as if they were other objects and events *(Time is an arrow; Love is a journey)* (p. 157; see also Johnson 1987; Lakoff 1987; Lakoff and Johnson 1980). (3) Linguistic interaction with others or discourse induces children to take different conceptual perspectives, including the perspective of the other on their own discourse. The child's internalization of the adult's instructional "voice" and perspective on herself plays a key role in the development of dialogical representations (representations of the intersubjective dialogue itself) as well as self-reflective and metacognitive representations (pp. 170–200).

It is interesting to speculate about the relationship between the human mind's enculturation into symbolic systems and the brain. One might think to apply the logic of emergence to this relationship. On the one hand, the properties of distributed symbolic systems cannot be predicted from what individual brains can do in isolation, for they emerge from the complex interactions of many individuals (Donald 2001, pp. 152–153). On the other hand, it seems reasonable to hypothesize that the cultural environment of symbolic representation, which provides the scaffolding for the construction of complex cognitive representations and skills, can alter the neural architecture of the developing brain (Donald 2001, pp. 153, 212). Indeed, neuroscientific evidence is now accumulating that experience-dependent brain activity in particular environmental contexts plays a huge role in the development of the individual brain. Rather than being a collection of prespecified modules, the brain appears to be an organ that constructs itself in development through spontaneously generated and experience-dependent activity (Quartz 1999; Quartz and Sejnowski 1997), a developmental process made possible by robust and flexible developmental mechanisms conserved in animal evolution (see Chapter 7).

Given this "neural constructivist" viewpoint—and the consilient one of developmental systems theory—it seems reasonable to believe that, as Donald puts it, "symbolizing cultures own a direct path into our brains and affect the way major parts of the executive brain become wired up during development. This is the key idea of deep enculturation . . . Culture effectively wires up functional subsystems in the brain that would not otherwise exist" (2001, p. 212). In this way, "culture begins in the womb" (Savage-Rumbaugh, Fields, and Taglialatela 2001, p. 278).

In phenomenological terms, this power of culture and language to shape human subjectivity and experience belongs not simply to the genetic constitution of the individual, but to the generative constitution of the intersubjective community. Individual subjectivity is from the outset intersubjectivity, as a result of the communally handed down norms, conventions, symbolic artifacts, and cultural traditions in which the individual is always already embedded. Thus the internalization of joint attention into symbolic representations is not simply an ontogenetic phenomenon, but a historical and cultural one:

One of the most interesting things about the process of language acquisition is that the adults from whom the child is learning went through the same process earlier in their lives, and across generations the symbolic artifacts that comprise English, Turkish, or whatever language, accumulate modifications as new linguistic forms are created by grammaticization, syntacticization, and other processes of language change—so that today's child is learning the whole historically derived conglomeration. Consequently, when the child learns the conventional use of these well-traveled symbols, what she is learning is the ways that her forebears in the culture have found it useful to manipulate the attention of others in the past. And because the people of a culture, as they move through historical time, evolve many and varied purposes for manipulating one another's attention (and because they need to do this in many different types of discourse situations), today's child is faced with a panoply of different linguistic symbols and constructions that embody many different attentional construals of any given situation. Consequently, as the child internalizes a linguistic symbol—as she learns the human perspectives embodied in a linguistic symbol—she cognitively represents not just the perceptual or motoric aspects of a situation but also one way, among other ways of which she is aware, that the current situation may be attentionally construed by "us," the users of that symbol. The way that human beings use linguistic symbols thus

creates a clear break with straightforward perceptual or sensory-motor
representations, and it is due entirely to the social nature of linguistic
symbols. (Tomasello 1999, pp. 125–126)

The intersubjective symbolic representations that configure the
human mind are the product of generative and generational processes
on three time scales—phylogeny, history, and ontogeny (Tomasello
1999, pp. 10, 202–203). Phylogenetic time is the time during which the
human primate species evolved its distinctive form of social cognition,
on the basis of identification with other members of the species as intentional and mental beings. This evolutionary process also included
the evolution of a distinctive form of consciousness—an expanded
"conscious capacity" for long-term awareness, cognitive and emotional
self-regulation, and voluntary attentional control, on a time-scale of
minutes and hours, not simply seconds (Donald 2001). These evolutionary expansions of the human mind were a precondition for imitative learning and innovation, and hence for the generation of culture.
Historical time is the time of cumulative cultural evolution, which in
turn requires ontogenetic time for its realization. Children learn
things from their forebears and then modify them (in ontogenetic
time), and these modifications accumulate over the generations (in
historical time). Tomasello dubs this process the "ratchet effect" of cumulative cultural evolution: innovations accumulate over the generations thanks to imitative cultural learning. The ratchet effect has "radically changed the nature of the ontogenetic niche in which human
children develop so that, in effect, modern children encounter and interact with their physical and social worlds almost totally through the
mediating lenses of preexisting cultural artifacts" (Tomasello 1999, p.
202).

Tomasello and Donald both see phylogeny as equivalent to biological
evolution, as opposed to cumulative cultural evolution, which happens
over historical and ontogenetic time on the basis of the biological adap-
tations of the human primate species (intentional understanding and
enlarged conscious capacity) as evolved in phylogenetic time. The
trouble with this way of dividing things up is that it tends to fall back
into the nature/culture and innate/acquired dichotomies. Under-
neath the cultural clothes acquired in history and ontogeny, there is the
naked human primate of phylogeny (an image contrary to Tomasello's

and Donald's intentions). To solve this problem we need to link cultural psychology to developmental systems theory. Evolution is the evolution of developmental systems; human evolution includes the evolution of a new stage of development, namely, childhood, which is linked to a new form of social cognition; and this new form of social cognition crucially depends on the generative and generational processes of human culture.

In this final section of this chapter, I have sketched only the barest beginnings of a generative perspective on human experience that aims to combine phenomenology and mind science. Much work remains to be done, but I hope to have shown how we can trace a path from life to consciousness to intersubjectivity and culture that can do justice to our existence as living bodily subjects. The individual human subject is the enculturated bodily subject. In this way, the knowing and feeling subject is not the brain in the head, or even the brain plus the body, but the socially and culturally situated person, the enculturated human being.

◆ ◆ ◆

Husserl and Cognitive Science

READERS FAMILIAR WITH MY EARLIER BOOK, *The Embodied Mind: Cognitive Science and Human Experience* (Varela, Thompson, and Rosch 1991), might be surprised by the importance I give to Husserlian phenomenology here, given the critical attitude toward Husserl that book expressed. What accounts for this change of attitude? The purpose of this Appendix is to clarify this matter.

In *The Embodied Mind*, we asserted (i) that Husserl was a methodological solipsist (p. 16); (ii) that his theory ignored "both the consensual aspect and the direct embodied aspect of experience" (p. 17); (iii) that his theory of intentionality was a representational theory (p. 68); (iv) that his theory of the life-world was reductionistic and representationalist (that he tried to analyze the life-world "into a more fundamental set of constituents" (p. 117) consisting of beliefs understood as mental representations (p. 18)); and (v) that his phenomenology was a purely abstract, theoretical project lacking a pragmatic dimension (pp. 19, 117). We concluded that the Husserlian project was a "failure" (p. 19) and even wrote about the "breakdown of phenomenology" more generally (p. 19). This assessment then motivated our turn to the tradition of Buddhist philosophy and mindfulness-awareness meditation as a more promising phenomenological partner for cognitive science.

As Chapter 2 indicates, however, I no longer subscribe to this assessment of Husserlian phenomenology. Our earlier interpretation of Husserl was mistaken. Husserlian phenomenology has far more resources than we realized for productive cross-fertilization with both the sciences of mind (Petitot et al. 1999; Varela 1996) and Buddhist thought (Thompson 2005; Varela 2000b; Varela and Depraz 2003). In particular, I now believe (i) that Husserl was not a methodological solipsist; (ii) that he was greatly concerned with the intersubjective and embodied aspects of experience; (iii) that his theory of intentionality was not a representational theory; and (iv) that his theory of the life-world was not reductionistic and representationalist. Furthermore, although I think phenomenology has tended to overemphasize theoretical discussion in the form of textual interpretation (to the neglect of phenomenological pragmatics as well as original phenomenological analyses and philosophical argumentation), I think it is too facile to say simply that phenomenology is a purely abstract, theoretical project lacking a pragmatic dimension. It follows that I would now not characterize Husserlian phenomenology as a "failure." Nor would I assert that phenomenology suffered a "breakdown" owing to its neglect of phenomenological pragmatics.

My viewpoint has changed for two reasons. The first is that when Varela and I were writing *The Embodied Mind* (during 1986–1989; Eleanor Rosch joined the project near the end of 1989) our knowledge of Husserl was limited. We were familiar with the main published works in English translation (*Logical Investigations, Ideas I, Cartesian Meditations, The Crisis of European Sciences and Transcendental Phenomenology*) but had not studied them carefully enough, and we did not know about Husserl's writings on passive synthesis (then untranslated) and intersubjectivity (still untranslated). We were both more familiar with Heidegger and were influenced by his (largely uncharitable) reading of Husserl. We also had little knowledge of other phenomenological thinkers who were deeply influenced by Husserl (Merleau-Ponty excepted), and we had studied only a little of the secondary literature on Husserl.

The second reason is that we accepted Hubert Dreyfus's (1982) influential interpretation of Husserl as a representationalist and protocognitivist philosopher, as well as his Heideggerian critique of Husserl thus interpreted. Dreyfus has been a pioneer in bringing the phenomenological tradition into the heartland of the cognitive sciences through his important critique of artificial intelligence (Dreyfus 1972, 1992) and his groundbreaking studies on skillful knowledge and action (Dreyfus 2002; Dreyfus and Dreyfus 1986). Yet his work is also marked by a peculiar interpretation of Husserl. Dreyfus presents Husserl's phenomenology as a form of representationalism that anticipates cognitivist and computational theories of mind. He then rehearses Heidegger's criticisms of Husserl thus understood and deploys them against cognitivism and artificial intelligence. Dreyfus reads Husserl largely through a combination of Heidegger's interpretation and a particular analytic (Fregean) reconstruction of one aspect of Husserl's thought—Husserl's notion of the noema. Thus the Husserl Dreyfus presents to cognitive science and analytic philosophy of mind is a problematic interpretive construct and should not be taken at face value.

For a while Dreyfus's interpretation functioned as a received view in the cognitive science community of Husserl's thought and its relationship to cognitive science. This interpretation has since been seriously challenged by a number of Husserl scholars and philosophers.[1] This is not the place to review these controversies at length. Suffice it to say that I take these studies to have demonstrated the following points:

1. Husserl does not subscribe to a representational theory of mind, and certainly not a representational theory of the sort Dreyfus wishes to criticize. Intentional experiences do not acquire their directedness in virtue of "a special realm of representational entities" (Dreyfus 1982, p. 1). Rather, the intentional openness of consciousness is an integral part of its being (Zahavi 2003a, p. 21).[2]

2. Husserl is not a methodological solipsist. The transcendental phenomenological reduction is not a way of trying to characterize the contents of consciousness purely internally, apart from their relation to the world. It is a way of characterizing the world, namely, at the phenomenal level at which it is experienced, and of studying the relation of the world so characterized to our subjectivity.

3. Husserl does not assimilate all intentionality to object-directed intentionality; he does not "claim that all mental life, even our awareness of practical activity and our sense of existing in a shared world, must be a form of object-directedness" (Dreyfus 1982, p. 9; see also Dreyfus 1988). On the contrary, as the above discussion of passive synthesis indicates, the notion of a precognitive and non-object-directed "operative intentionality" is central to the subject matter of Husserl's phenomenology in its genetic register.[3]

4. Husserl does not treat the "background" presupposed by object-directed intentional experiences as simply a system of beliefs understood as mental representations (Dreyfus 1982, p. 23). In *Ideas II*, for instance, Husserl distinguishes between consciousness of objects and comportment toward objects, and then he states, "The ultimate, however, is a *background that is prior to all comportment* and is instead presupposed by all comportment" (Husserl 1989, p. 291; emphasis in original). There is no suggestion that this background consists of beliefs in the sense of distinct object-directed mental states. Rather, he goes on to write, "In a certain sense, there is, in the obscure depths, a root soil"; he speaks of this root soil as our "natural side," "the underlying basis of subjectivity," and then he states, "To the natural side there belongs immediately the lower life of feelings, the instinctual life, and indeed the function of attention as well . . ." (p. 292). There is no suggestion that this "root soil" of instinctual life is fully recoverable at the level of reflective intentional analysis (see Sheets-Johnstone 1999a, pp. 249–252; see also Mensch 1998).

5. Husserl's treatment of the life-world cannot be reduced to an attempt to analyze the life-world into a set of sedimented background "assumptions" or "hypotheses" (equivalent to a system of "frames" in artificial intelligence) (Dreyfus 1982, pp. 23–24; 1988). Rather, Husserl recognizes that the life-world as pregiven horizon and ground is precisely not objectifiable in this way. This realization leads him to envision the possibility of a generative phenomenology of the life-world (see Steinbock 1995, pp. 104–122; Welton 2000, pp. 331–392).[4]

In summary, although Dreyfus is to be credited for bringing Husserl into the purview of cognitive science, it is important to go beyond his interpretation and to reevaluate Husserl's relationship to cognitive science on the basis of a thorough assessment of his life's work. This reevaluation is already underway (see Petitot et al. 1999). It can be seen as part of a broader appropriation of phenomenology in contemporary thought, in relation to both other movements of twentieth-century philosophy and the rich potential for cross-fertilization with Asian philosophical traditions.[5] These new developments have greatly influenced my thought in this book.

◆ ◆ ◆

Emergence and the Problem of
Downward Causation

A NUMBER OF QUESTIONS can be raised about the relationship between the conception of emergence presented in Chapter 3 and other conceptions of emergence. My purpose in this appendix is to review these issues, to sharpen my account of emergence, and to rebut some well-known and influential objections to emergence that have appeared in the philosophical literature.

Discussions of emergence are structured by the classical opposition between reductionism and emergentism (Silberstein 2002). These positions have epistemological and ontological components. Epistemological reductionism states that the best understanding of a system is to be found at the level of the structure, behavior, and laws of its component parts and their relations; ontological reductionism states that the relations between the parts of the system are all determined without remainder by the intrinsic properties of the most basic parts. Epistemological emergentism states that the best understanding of a system is to be found at the level of the structure, behavior, and laws of the whole system, and ontological emergentism that a whole is more than the sum of its parts and their intrinsic properties.

As one might gather from my discussion of emergence in Chapter 3 this opposition between parts versus whole, or between basic features (conceived as intrinsic properties of microscopic particulars) versus emergent features, is part of the problem, not part of the solution.

Beyond the classical opposition between reductionism and emergentism tricky issues arise because there are now so many different

senses of "reduction" and "emergence" in the scientific and philosophical literature. Many different kinds of phenomena have been
considered emergent, and different epistemological and/or ontological criteria of emergence have been used to classify them as emergent.[1] There seems to be no good reason, therefore, to search for any
single and neatly analyzable concept of emergence independent of
particular explanatory contexts. The focus here will accordingly be on
the notion of emergence implicit in the theory of autonomous systems
and on the application of this notion to biological and cognitive phenomena by the enactive approach.

Let me begin by setting up a framework in the form of the following
provisional definition of emergence in the case of complex systems
(Thompson and Varela 2001). This definition is meant to capture the
main features of emergence that researchers in complex systems
theory seem to have in mind when they talk about emergence.

Definition: A network, N, of interrelated components exhibits an emergent process, E, with emergent properties, P, if and only if:

(1) E is a global process that instantiates P, and arises from the cou-
     pling of N's components and the nonlinear dynamics, D, of
     their local interactions.
(2) E and P have a global-to-local ("downward") determinative in-
     fluence on the dynamics D of the components of N.

And possibly:

(3) E and P are not exhaustively determined by the intrinsic proper-
     ties of the components of N, that is, they exhibit "relational
     holism."

Terminology: Emergent Processes and Properties

Although the term *emergent property* is widespread, I prefer *emergent process.* Strictly speaking, it does not make sense to say that a property
emerges, but only that it comes to be realized, instantiated, or exemplified in a process or entity that emerges in time. Emergence is a temporal process, but properties (whether considered as universals or as
linguistic abstractions) are atemporal. For instance, the property of
being alive did not emerge when life originated on Earth; rather, it

came to be instantiated as a result of the emergent process of autopoiesis that constitutes living cells. This example also points to the importance of the causal characteristics of emergent processes: the emergent network of autopoiesis constitutes a biological individual (a cell) that brings about changes in the external environment. It also creates a structured context in which new kinds of events can take place, such as protein synthesis and RNA/DNA replication, which cannot occur apart from or outside of the protected intracellular environment.

Proposition 1: Nonlinear Dynamics

The emergent processes covered by this definition occur in networks whose coupled elements have nonlinear interactions. The distinction between nonlinear and linear interactions provides one way of distinguishing between systems that have emergent processes and systems that do not (Campbell and Bickhard 2002). Linear interactions are additive or proportional. They typically give rise (except in the quantum domain) to systems that are "aggregative" (Wimsatt 1986)—systems whose causal features derive from aggregating the properties of the components. Nonlinear interactions are nonadditive or nonproportional. They give rise (by definition) to systems whose activities cannot be derived aggregatively from the properties of their components. It is therefore tempting to say, borrowing the terminology of the classical British emergentists (Samuel Alexander, C. Lloyd Morgan, and C. D. Broad), that nonlinear processes generate "emergents," whereas linear processes produce only "resultants."

Nonlinearity results from positive and negative feedback relationships. These relationships bring about patterns of behavior, which can be described as constrained alternatives in the space of all possible global states of the system (as attractors in phase space). To understand such activity patterns we need to model them in the language of collective variables and order parameters, while at the same time showing how these collective variables and order parameters are biophysically realized in natural phenomena.

The emergent processes of concern to the enactive approach occur in complex systems that need to be seen as autonomous, such as unicellular and multicellular organisms, the immune system, and the brain.

An autonomous system has operational closure and accordingly dynamically maintains its own organization as the crucial invariant. "Organizational-operational closure" characterizes the system's invariant form through structural and material change, and thus is a topological and morphodynamic notion (Deffuant et al. 1995; Petitot 1992). Yet because this invariant form is precisely the dynamic pattern of a circular network whose constituent processes operate under closure (every product of the network stays within the network), the morphodynamics in this case defines not merely a formal identity through time but a formal *self-identity*. This type of morphodynamics marks an important difference between emergence in autonomous systems and other oft-cited examples of emergence (such as convection rolls). In the case of autonomy (organizational-operational closure), what emerges is simultaneously a "self" or "individual" and a correlative niche (the domain or set of interactions possible for such a system given its organization and concrete structural realization). The exemplar and minimal case of this kind of emergence is the living cell (see Chapters 5 and 6).

Another way to characterize autonomous systems is in relation to the contrast between "decomposable" and "nondecomposable" systems (Bechtel and Richardson 1993; Simon 1969). Decomposable systems have a clear hierarchical organization. Each component or subsystem operates according to its own intrinsic principles independent of the others, making the system strongly modular. In a "nearly decomposable" system, higher levels interact with lower levels through top-down or feedback relations. The nature of these interactions determines the extent to which the system is nearly decomposable: "A system will be nearly decomposable to the extent that the causal interactions *within* subsystems are more important in determining component properties than are the causal interactions *between* subsystems" (Bechtel and Richardson 1993, p. 27). As the components of the system become less governed by intrinsic factors and more by the system's organization, then the system is "minimally decomposable." A nondecomposable system is one in which the connectivity and interrelatedness of the components give rise to global processes that subsume the components so that they are no longer clearly separable. In such a system, the distinction between preexisting parts and supervening whole becomes problematic. Not only does the whole emerge from the components, but also the components emerge from the whole.

An autonomous system is at least minimally decomposable, if not nondecomposable. More precisely, when one adopts an autonomy perspective, one *ipso facto* characterizes the system as at least minimally decomposable. The reason is that an autonomous system is an organizationally and operationally closed network; hence it is the connectivity of its constituent processes that determines its operation as a network.

Neural assemblies can be used to illustrate these ideas. With only a few exceptions, the brain is organized on the basis of a principle of reciprocity: if area A connects to area B, then there are reciprocal connections from B to A (Varela 1995; Varela et al. 2001). The traditional practice in neuroscience is to map these reciprocally interconnected brain areas onto a hierarchy of processing levels from peripheral (lower) to central (higher) areas (measured in terms of synaptic distance from sensory stimulation). The sensory end is taken as the starting point, and perception is described as proceeding through a series of feedforward or bottom-up processing stages. Top-down influences are equated with back-projections and feedback from higher to lower areas. This scheme treats the brain as a nearly decomposable or minimally decomposable system (depending on the extent to which the top-down influences are emphasized).

From a dynamicist point of view, however, the picture looks different. First, the dynamicist does not depict the brain as a processing hierarchy that starts at the sensory end. Strictly speaking, brain processes are always ongoing and do not start or stop anywhere. A better entry point for many purposes of analysis can be found in the brain's own endogenous activity, as reflected in the organism's states of preparation, expectation, emotional tone, and attention, which are necessarily active at the same time as the sensory inflow (Varela et al. 2001, p. 230; see also Engel, Fries, and Singer 2001; Freeman 1999a, 1999b, 2000; Lutz et al. 2002). Such activity arises far from the sensors—from the frontal lobes or limbic system, or in the middle of the whole network from temporal and associative cortices. There is considerable evidence that this kind of endogenous activity participates even in the early stages of sensory perception. Although this sort of activity is usually described as top-down or feedback, "top down" and "bottom up" are heuristic terms for what is in reality a large-scale network that integrates both incoming and endogenous activity. It is precisely at this network level that collective-variable dynamics and order parameters become important for characterizing the large-scale integration of widely distributed neuronal activities.

Second (and to anticipate the discussion of Proposition 2), this large-scale dynamics can modulate local neuronal activity by entraining or "pulling" the behavior of individual neurons into a particular pattern of global activity (see the discussion of the neurodynamics of epilepsy in Chapter 3). This dynamic-systems form of global-to-local influence neither requires nor is equivalent to top-down control in a sequential hierarchy of processing stages (Engel, Fries, and Singer 2001; Thompson and Varela 2001).

To look at the brain in this way is to characterize it as at least a minimally decomposable system—a system in which the behavior of the components is determined largely by the system's organization. Yet it is also important to consider that the brain—in its dynamic operation as a large-scale network—might need to be characterized as a nondecomposable system. No doubt it is useful for certain explanatory purposes to characterize the brain as a (nearly or minimally) decomposable system. Yet problems can arise when one assumes that the explanatory strategies of decomposition and localization (differentiating a system into separable components and assigning responsibility for specific tasks to those components) are adequate to characterize brain activity (Bechtel and Richardson 1993; Uttal 2001). In particular, decomposition and localization are insufficient to characterize the operational closure of the brain as a dynamic neuronal network. In Maturana and Varela's words:

> Since, due to its constitution as a network of lateral, parallel, sequential, and recursive interactions, the nervous system closes on itself at all levels, the mutilations that it may suffer generally leave a closed neuronal network with a changed structure. Accordingly, the organization of the nervous system is essentially invariant under mutilations, while its domain of possible states, which depends on its structure, and, hence, on its architecture, is not. Yet, due to its closed organization, whatever is left of the neuronal network after a partial ablation necessarily operates as a different whole with different properties than the original, but not as a system from which some properties have been selectively subtracted ... There is intrinsically no possibility of operational localization in the nervous system in the sense that no part of it can be deemed

responsible for its operation as a closed network, or for the properties which an observer can detect in its operation as a unity. However, since every nervous system has a definite architecture, every localized lesion in it necessarily produces a specific disconnection between its parts and, hence, a specific change in its domain of possible states. (Maturana and Varela 1980, p. 129)

This characterization implies that the brain—understood operationally as a dynamic network of processes or "brainweb" (Varela et al. 2001)—is a nondecomposable system. We still lack a theoretical language for expressing the complex behaviors of such systems in dynamic-systems terms (see Le Van Quyen 2003). In the brain case, nondecomposability would mean that the brainweb generates global processes that subsume their components so that they are no longer clearly separable as components. At this dynamic level, the distinction between preexisting parts and supervening whole has no clear application: One might as well say that the components (local neuronal activities) emerge from the whole as much as the whole (dynamic patterns of large-scale integration) emerges from the components.

"Nondecomposability" and "decomposability" are heuristic, epistemological categories, not ontological ones. It is not my intention to argue for a metaphysical thesis of ontological holism on the basis of nondecomposability (which is not to say that nondecomposability is merely epistemological in the sense an ontological reductionist would assert). At the moment my point is rather to call attention to the nondecomposability perspective in order to correct a strong bias in much of classical and contemporary neuroscience toward a modular (localizationist) view of the brain (see also Uttal 2001). Ultimately, it is the interplay between these heuristic categories within and across various explanatory contexts that is important, not one heuristic versus the other. As Le Van Quyen states:

Following Simon (1973), it is important to consider this interplay as a "loose vertical coupling," permitting the distinction between levels, and a "loose horizontal coupling," allowing the separation between subsystems at each level. While the word "loose" suggests "decomposable," the word "coupling" implies resistance to decomposition. In my view, the characterization of this "loose coupling" represents one of the essential challenges for future developments. (Le Van Quyen 2003, p. 84)

Proposition 2: Global-to-Local Influence

Complex systems theorists, as we have seen, appeal to the idea of circular or reciprocal causality, by which they mean that global patterns both arise from local interactions and govern or constrain those interactions. In synergetics, a branch of complex systems theory, a vivid but unappealing metaphor is used to describe this global-to-local influence. The global, collective-variable dynamics is said to influence local behavior by "enslaving" the network elements into a particular dynamic régime (Haken 1983).

The term *downward causation* is also often used to describe this sort of global-to-local influence. One of the earliest uses of the term in a scientific context was in an article by Donald Campbell (1974), called "'Downward Causation' in Hierarchically Organized Biological Systems." Campbell's view was that in hierarchically organized biological systems, downward causation from higher to lower levels of organization occurs in the form of natural selection: "Where natural selection operates through life and death at a higher level of organization, the laws of the higher-level selective system determine in part the distribution of lower-level events and substances . . . all processes at the lower levels of a hierarchy are restrained by and act in conformity to the laws of the higher levels" (p. 180). This idea that higher-level processes "restrain" lower-level processes so that they "act in conformity" to them corresponds to the idea that global processes (collective-variable dynamics) constrain or govern local interactions.

What exactly does "constraint" mean in this context? In complex systems theory, constraints can be understood as relational properties that the parts possess in virtue of their being integrated or unified (not aggregated) into a systemic network. "Constraint" is therefore a formal or topological notion (Deacon 2003). The form, configuration, or topology of a system limits or prevents certain possible behaviors the parts could have on their own, while simultaneously opening up new possibilities for them in virtue of the states the system as a whole can access (Juarrero 1999, pp. 132–133).

Let us examine this notion of constraints in more detail, beginning with the difference between "context-free constraints" and "context-sensitive constraints" (Gatlin 1972, as cited by Juarrero 1999, pp. 6–7, 131–140). A context-free constraint is one that is externally imposed and alters the probabilities of the available behavioral alternatives of the system's components. For instance, a container filled with evenly diffused molecules of gas at room temperature is at thermodynamic equilibrium, but inserting a piston (a context-free constraint) into the container and moving the piston so that the molecules are compressed to one side imposes an orderly arrangement on them. If the pressure on the piston is removed, the system will move back toward equilibrium in accordance with the second law of thermodynamics. A context-sensitive constraint, on the other hand, is one that synchronizes and correlates previously independent parts into a systemic whole. Catalysis is a good example (Juarrero 1999, pp. 139–141). Imagine a primeval soup with several types of molecules (A, B, and C) randomly floating around in it. As a result of externally imposed, context-free constraints (e.g., the weather), there will be more of some molecules in certain areas than in others. Now imagine that A catalyzes the formation of B. This relationship between A and B imposes a context-sensitive constraint on both of them:

> Once the probability that something will happen depends on and is altered by the presence of something else, the two have become systematically and therefore internally related. As a result of the operations of context-sensitive constraints and the conditional probabilities they impose, A is now part of B's external structure. Because A is no longer "out there" independent of B, to which it is only externally related, the interdependence has created a larger whole, the AB system. Insofar as it is part of B's new context or external structure, A has been imported into B. (Juarrero 1999, p. 139)

Juarrero calls this kind of context-sensitive constraint a "first-order contextual constraint" because it operates at the same level of organization as the individual components (A and B). A "second-order contextual constraint" is established when the organization of the whole system emerges as a constraint on the system's components. Thus, in a simplified and idealized autocatalytic network, A catalyzes the formation of B, B catalyzes the formation of C, C of D, and D closes the loop and catalyzes the formation of A. The relationship between each pair of catalyzing and catalyzed molecules is a first-order contextual constraint. Once autocatalytic closure occurs, however, these first-order relationships become subject to the second-order contextual constraint of the organization as a whole.

A still more striking example is autopoiesis. A minimal autopoietic system corresponds not simply to an autocatalytic network, but to an autocatalytic network housed within and interdependently linked to a semipermeable membrane-boundary. Autocatalytic networks do not qualify as autopoietic systems because they do not self-produce their own topological boundaries (see Chapter 5).[2] Autocatalytic networks either have no boundaries or their boundaries are set by an externally imposed, context-free constraint (such as the walls of an experimental container). In an autopoietic system, however, the membrane forms part of the second-order contextual constraint of the system's organization. In this type of system, the entire self-producing organization of membrane-plus-internal-autocatalytic-network operates as a second-order contextual constraint from the whole to the parts. Furthermore, in multicellular organisms, the autopoiesis of the individual cells becomes subject to the higher-order contextual constraints of the multicellular organization (second-order autopoiesis). In other words, the autopoiesis of the individual cells becomes subordinated to the maintenance of the higher-order autopoiesis or autonomy of the multicellular organism (Maturana and Varela 1980, pp. 107–111; 1987, pp. 73–89).

We now have in hand an answer to the question of what downward causation means in the context of complex systems theory. According to the line of thought just sketched, downward causation corresponds to the second-order contextual constraint of a system's organization restricting or limiting the degrees of freedom of the system's components. Downward causation corresponds to the influence the relatedness of the system's components has on the behavior of those components. More precisely, it corresponds to the influence of the system's topological organization on its constituent processes (Varela 1979; see also Deacon 2003). "Downward" is thus a metaphor for the formal or topological influence of a whole with respect to its parts.

It is questionable whether this metaphor is a good one. Although there are clearly empirical differences in scale and logical differences in order between the topology of a system and its constituent processes and elements, the two levels do not move in parallel, with one acting upward and the other acting downward, because the whole system moves at once. John Searle makes this point in a related discussion: "The right way to think of this is not so much 'top down' but as system causation. The system, as a system, has causal effects on each element, even though the system is made up of the elements" (Searle 2000b, p.

17). From this perspective, the term *downward causation* is symptomatic of a partial recognition of system causation together with an inability to shift completely to a system-causation perspective.

Some philosophers might wonder whether the topological influence of a system on its elements should be considered a causal influence. This issue is inseparable from broader conceptual issues about causation. Philosophical debates about emergence and downward causation tend to be structured not only by a strong ontology of part and whole (or basic features versus emergent features), but also by a strong ontology of "causal powers"—the causal powers of basic features versus the causal powers (or lack thereof) of emergent features. Rather than get caught up in the philosophical debates about causal-power views of causation, I am content to explicate what dynamic systems theorists have in mind when they talk about whole-to-part influence in complex systems. As we have seen, this influence corresponds to the organizational constraint of a system with respect to its components. Such influence is topological. It is therefore not an external force that acts on something, but an interconnectedness or relatedness among processes. This interrelatedness structures the context and background of local interactions, such that certain kinds of events can take place that otherwise would not occur. Some authors describe the constraint of a system's organization as a standing or ongoing, "structuring" cause, by contrast with an episodic "triggering" cause (see Dretske 1995b for this distinction), and liken organizational constraints so understood to Aristotle's formal cause (Emmeche, Køppe, and Stjernfelt 2000; Juarrero 1999, pp. 125–128). This recuperation of formal causation gains support from the phenomenological and morphodynamic analysis of form presented in Chapter 4.

Proposition 3: Relational Holism

According to the ontological thesis of part/whole reductionism ("mereological supervenience"), all the properties of a whole are determined by the intrinsic (nonrelational) properties of its most fundamental parts. (Hence the whole is said to supervene on the intrinsic properties of its parts.) In contrast, according to holism ("mereological emergence") certain wholes possess emergent features that are not determined by the intrinsic properties of their most basic parts.

Such emergent features are irreducibly relational. They are constituted by relations that are not exhaustively determined by or reducible to the intrinsic properties of the elements so related. These holistic relations do not simply influence the parts, but supersede or subsume their independent existence in an irreducibly relational structure.[3]

One might think that relational holism could be invoked to legitimize the notion of downward causation. Downward causation is supposed to be the determinative influence that the relatedness of the system's components has on their behavior. If this relatedness were holistic, then this fact would presumably account for the determinative influence of the system as a whole on its parts. The problem with this line of thought is that relational holism implies that the relation is the most basic unit and therefore that the terms of the relation have no independent (nonrelational) status. Hence the components could not constitute an independent lower level subject to higher-level "downward" influence, as the term *downward causation* cannot help but suggest. In other words, given relational holism, downward causation seems a misnomer. The presence of relational holism would thus provide another reason for doubting that the concept of downward causation is appropriate for describing the influence of a whole on its parts.

The concept of relational holism was introduced largely in connection with nonseparability or entanglement in quantum mechanics, in which the state of the system is not constituted by the states of its parts and only the whole system can be said to be in a definite state (Teller 1986; see also Belousek 2003). On the basis of nonseparability, a number of philosophers have argued that quantum mechanical systems are holistic or mereologically emergent.[4] Silberstein and McGeever (1999) have proposed that nonseparability is a paradigm of "ontological emergence." By this they mean (i) that it is a kind of emergence that belongs to a system or whole in itself, as opposed to being an artifact of our theories or models; and (ii) that it violates the metaphysical doctrine of (atomistic) mereological supervenience, which states that every property of the whole is exhaustively determined by the intrinsic properties of its most fundamental parts.[5] Silberstein and McGeever's question with regard to complex dynamic systems is whether they, too, exhibit ontological emergence or only epistemological emergence.[6]

The main reason usually given for thinking that nonlinear dynamic systems are not holistic or ontologically emergent is that they are classical deterministic systems. In a deterministic nonlinear dynamic system, at all times (i) every variable has a definite value, and (ii) any change in the value of any variable is nonstochastic. As Silberstein states: "It is hard to imagine how any system that is 'deterministic' in both these ways could exhibit mereological emergence" (Silberstein 2001, p. 83). Nevertheless, because it is impossible for us to deduce mathematically the behavior or global dynamic properties (attractors) of the system, these behaviors and properties can be described as epistemologically emergent. For instance, chaotic systems are deterministic, but they can appear random and are unpredictable in the long run. They are highly sensitive to initial conditions (small differences in perturbations produce exponentially divergent effects), and we are able to specify the values of their variables only to a finite degree of precision. Stephen Kellert expresses this notion of epistemological emergence: "chaos theory argues against the universal applicability of the method of micro-reductionism, but not against the philosophical doctrine of reductionism. That doctrine states that all properties of a system are reducible to properties of its parts. Chaos theory gives no examples of 'holistic' properties which could serve as counter-examples to such a claim" (Kellert 1993, p. 90).

More recent discussions may cast doubt on this statement. Frederick Kronz (1998) proposes that the key to chaos in classical systems is the nonseparability of the Hamiltonian energy function (see also Kronz and Tiehen 2002, pp. 332–333). Whereas the Newtonian formulation of classical mechanics takes forces as fundamental, the Hamiltonian formulation takes energies as fundamental. The Hamiltonian of a system corresponds to the total energy of the system (kinetic energy plus potential energy). In classical mechanics, the Hamiltonian describing a linear system is separable into a sum of Hamiltonians, with one element in the sum for each constituent of the system. If there are nonlinear terms in the equations of motion, however, then the Hamiltonian is nonseparable. Building on Kronz's discussion, Robert Bishop (2002) proposes that the nonseparability of the Hamiltonian is crucial for understanding the emergent global coherence of a complex system:

[T]he properties of integrity, integration and stability exhibited by Bénard cells are global properties and involve the nonlocal relation of all fluid elements to each other. This global behavior differs from holistic entanglement in quantum mechanics in the sense that fluid elements may be distinguished from each other while they are simultaneously identified as members of particular Bénard cells and participate in interaction with fluid elements throughout the system. In this context focusing on the nonseparability of the Hamiltonian may be more appropriate because, in contrast to the quantum case, classical states are always separable even when the Hamiltonian is nonseparable. (Bishop 2002, p. 7)

According to this proposition, there is a kind of holism proper to complex systems that does not seem compatible with the philosophical doctrine of reductionism. At the same time, this form of holism (nonseparability of the Hamiltonian) is not incompatible with determinism.

What determinism means, however, is a whole other matter (see Atmanspacher and Bishop 2002). I do not intend to enter this thicket here, but two basic points are worth making. First, it is important to distinguish between determinism as a feature of a scientific model and determinism as a metaphysical thesis about nature. According to the metaphysical thesis, all physical properties in nature are definite and determinate, and the evolution of the natural world is fixed uniquely. (The complete and instantaneous state of the world fixes its past and future with no alternatives.) This thesis hardly follows from the fact that we can construct nonstochastic dynamic-system models of observable phenomena. Second, it is also important to distinguish between nonlinear dynamic systems as abstract mathematical models and as observable biophysical systems. Any concrete empirical system will involve some degree of randomness in the form of stochastic fluctuations (Kelso 1995). For any given empirical system, the analytical techniques most appropriate for characterizing the system's behavior depend on the hypotheses one makes about its degree of nonlinearity and its degree of stochasticness (Le Van Quyen 2003; Schreiber 1999). Metastable dynamic systems display different mixes of nonlinearity and stochasticness at different spatial and temporal scales (Friston 2000b; Kelso 1995; Le Van Quyen 2003).

Science has barely begun to chart this vast sea of nonlinearity and stochasticness. Within this context, "deterministic" seems best understood as describing certain nonlinear analysis techniques (those in which there are no noise terms), not as an ontological characteristic of nature (in a classical observer-transcendent sense).

Résumé: Dynamic Co-emergence

The discussion up to this point provides further support for a conception of emergence as dynamic co-emergence. Dynamic co-emergence means that part and whole co-emerge and mutually specify each other. Kronz and Tiehen (2002), in their discussion of emergence and quantum mechanics (with reference also to nonlinear dynamic systems), advocate the same idea, which they call dynamic emergence:

> Emergent wholes have contemporaneous parts, but these parts cannot be characterized independently from their respective wholes. Emergent wholes are produced by an essential, ongoing, interaction of its [*sic*] parts. These are the central features of the new view sketched here; the nonseparable Hamiltonian constitutes an essential ongoing interaction . . . By adopting [this] view, we can say that it does not make sense to talk about reducing an emergent whole to its parts, since the parts are in some sense constructs of our characterization of the whole. (Kronz and Tiehen 2002, p. 345)

Objections to Emergence and Downward Causation

My last task in this appendix is to examine some recent and well-known objections to emergence and downward causation raised by the philosopher Jaegwon Kim (1993, 1998, 1999). Kim argues that "reflexive downward causation"—the causal influence of a whole on its own microconstituents—is incoherent when understood to happen simultaneously or synchronically, and is either otiose or violates the "causal closure of the physical" when understood to happen diachronically (Kim 1999, pp. 28–33). If Kim is right, then emergence and downward causation turn out to be to merely epistemological in the ontological reductionist's sense. For this reason, it will be instructive to consider his arguments.

Here is Kim's description of the first case of synchronic reflexive downward causation:

> At a certain time t, a whole W, has emergent property M, where M emerges from the following configuration of conditions: W has a complete decomposition into parts $a_1, \ldots, a_n$; each a_i has property P_i; and relation R holds for the sequence $a_1, \ldots, a_n$. For some a_j, W's having M at t causes a_j to have P_j at t. (Kim 1999, p. 28)

What Kim finds troubling and ultimately incoherent about this case is the synchronic way in which it combines upward determination and downward causation. The upward determination of W's having M at t as an effect of a_j's having P_j at t is simultaneous with the downward causation of a_j's having P_j at t as an effect of W's having M at t.

Nevertheless, there is no obvious incoherence in this case yet. Simultaneous causation, though counterintuitive to commonsense, is not obviously incoherent. For instance, certain theories in physics postulate instantaneous action at a distance; whether such influences exist, and whether they should qualify as causal, are difficult empirical and conceptual issues. Furthermore, simply to pronounce causal circularity in general "unacceptable," as Kim does (p. 28), is too facile, given that the notion of circular causality plays a central role in complex systems theory. Whether the circular causality of complex systems theory is best seen as synchronic and/or diachronic, or as simply a shorthand for reciprocal causal explanation, is an open and difficult question, which cannot be decided simply by armchair pronouncements.

Hence it comes as no surprise that Kim has to derive the incoherence he discerns by introducing an additional metaphysical principle about causation—the "causal-power actuality principle"—to which he thinks "we tacitly subscribe" (though he does not tell us whether "we" means metaphysicians, scientists, or the ordinary person in the street):

> For an object x, to exercise, at time t, the causal/determinative powers it has in virtue of having property P, x must *already* possess P at t. When x is caused to acquire P at t, it does not already possess P at t and is not capable of exercising the causal/determinative powers inherent in P. (Kim 1999, p. 29)

With this principle applied to the case, synchronic reflexive downward causation is incoherent. W's having M at t is supposed to be an effect of a_j's having P_j at t, which implies (by the causal-power actuality principle) that a_j must already possess P_j at t, but a_j's having P_j at t is supposed to be an effect of W's having M at t, which implies that a_j does not already have P_j at t.

The notion of downward causation as global-to-local structuring influence casts doubt on the generality of Kim's principle. The problem with the principle can be seen in the case of Rayleigh-Bénard convection rolls. The orderly rolling motions (which in a closed container form parallel cylinders called "Bénard cells") emerge from the local dynamics of the fluid molecules and *at the same time* constrain the states of motion available to those molecules. As Robert Bishop states:

> When the cells are established at t, this governing property is established at t; it did not exist prior to t. Likewise, prior to t, the trajectories of fluid elements had the property of accessing various states of motion, a property they lose at t due to the global governing effects of Bénard cells. The causal constraints/modifications on the motion of the fluid elements in this case are synchronic: The emergence of the self-regulating global pattern is simultaneous with the modifications of the accessible states of the system. If it were not synchronic, the pattern would not arise. (Bishop 2002, p. 9)

Contrary to Kim, therefore, synchronic reflexive downward causation seems perfectly coherent, as long as it is not conceptualized as efficient causation (in which cause and effect are external to one another), but rather as global-to-local structuring influence.

Let us turn to Kim's argument against diachronic downward causation. Here matters require still more disentangling. Kim distinguishes between two kinds of downward causation—one in his view ordinary and unproblematic, the other highly problematic—but neither kind fits the kind of downward causation found in complex systems theory.

The first kind is simply causation from the properties of a whole to properties of its parts—where Kim leaves the notions of "whole" and "part" unanalyzed. A whole causes one of its microconstituents to change in a certain way, and there is a time-delay between cause and effect. Kim interprets Roger Sperry's (1969) analogy of a rolling wheel constraining the motion of its own molecules as a case of this kind of diachronic downward causation. The structural properties of the wheel constrain the movements of the molecules composing it, so that the molecules are caused to move in a particular way as the wheel rolls downhill. Here are Kim's other examples and his verdict about this kind of diachronic downward causation:

> I fall from the ladder and break my arm. I walk to the kitchen for a drink of water and ten seconds later, all my limbs and organs have been displaced from my study to the kitchen. Sperry's bird flies into the blue yonder, and all of the bird's cells and molecules, too, have gone yonder. It doesn't seem to me that these cases present us with any special mysteries rooted in self-reflexivity, or that they show emergent causation to be something special and unique. (1999, p. 30)

Kim concludes that "emergent downward causation should not simply be identified with causation from properties of the whole to properties of its own parts, that is, reflexive downward causation" (1999, p. 31). What emergent downward causation requires is not simply whole-to-part influence, but a difference in kind between the macrolevel and microlevel events. In other words, the causal relations between the two levels must implicate different properties—unlike the rolling wheel or the flying bird, in which the property of motion is common to the whole and its constituent parts.

Kim seems right about these cases. But there is a shortcoming to his analysis: none of the examples he gives in the passage above contains the kind of global-to-local influence found in complex systems. Nowhere in these examples is there the sort of nonlinear coupling of system components typical of a self-organizing system. This absence is particularly evident in the case of Sperry's wheel, which is an aggregative system, not a self-organizing one. Nowhere is there any dynamic global pattern formation (as in convection rolls and Bénard cells). Nor is there any self-reflexivity because there is no complex system with operational closure and second-order contextual constraints (as in autopoiesis). Kim neglects the most important and relevant cases for emergence and downward causation. He draws the right general conclusion, but not for the right reason. It is true that emergent downward causation should not be identified simply with whole-to-part causation, but that is because emergent downward causation (at least in the complex systems context) is not meant to describe any kind of whole-to-part influence. Rather, it should describe the specific kind of reflexive global-to-local influence that happens in a system that has dynamic global coherence in and through collective self-organization.

Kim's next step is to examine the sort of downward causation in which the macrolevel and microlevel events have different character-istic properties. His model is mental-to-physical causation, but the form of his argument has nothing to do with the mental and the phys-ical as such; it could just as easily apply to the relationship between bi-ological and physical events. The argument he advances rests on three principles (see Kim 1993, pp. 336–357):

1. *The Physical Realization Principle:* Every emergent event or prop-erty M must be realized by (or determined by, or supervenient on) some physical event or property P (its "emergence base").
2. *The Causal Inheritance Principle:* If M is instantiated on a given oc-casion by being realized by P, then the causal powers of this in-stance of M are identical with (or a subset of) the causal powers of P.
3. *The Principle of the Causal Closure of the Physical Domain:* Any phys-ical event that has a cause at time t has a physical cause at t. Hence, "if we trace the causal ancestry of a physical event, we need never go outside the physical domain" (1993, p. 280).

The critical question Kim then asks is why the physical emergence base of the emergent cannot displace the emergent as a cause of any of its putative effects. Here is the basic form of his argument. Suppose emergent M causes M^* (which may or may not be an emergent). M^* has its own physical emergence base P^*. Therefore M's causation of M^* presupposes M's causation of P^*. In other words, the only way for M to bring about M^* is by bringing about its physical emergence base P^* (a case of downward causation). Now, M has its own physical emer-gence base P. The presence of P is sufficient for the presence of M. (Note that P is supposed not to cause M, but synchronically to realize M.) But M is causally sufficient for P^* and thereby M^*. It follows that P is causally sufficient for both P^* and M^*. But then M's status as a cause is preempted by P, thus making M "otiose and dispensable" as a cause of P^* and M^*. The upshot of this argument is a dilemma for the emergentist who believes in downward causation: either downward causation is otiose, because the putative causal power of the emergent is preempted by the causal power of the physical elements on which the emergent is based, or downward causation violates the principle that the physical domain is causally closed.

This argument, when applied to the case of emergent downward causation in self-organizing systems, is tantamount to denying that the system's organization exerts any influence on the system's components. The thought seems to be that all of what we call the macrolevel and emergent causation really happens at the microlevel (by the Causal Inheritance Principle). Talk of the system's organization having an emergent causal influence is simply a macrolevel description of the microlevel causal events. Such a description can be epistemologically useful for us, even though ontologically speaking all the real causal action goes on at the microlevel of the emergence base (Kim 1999, p. 33). In this view, the system's organization is in fact epiphenomenal—an effect of lower level causal transactions with no significant causal status of its own—although it can still be useful for us to talk about the system as if its organization did play a causal role in bringing about certain events (see Kim 1993, pp. 92–108).

The problem with this way of thinking is its refusal to countenance the causal importance of a system's organization (the relations that define it as a system). It does not acknowledge that the microlevel interactions happen as they do because of the way the local processes are organized, which is a macrolevel, relational characteristic of the system. That the macrolevel organization of a complex system is not simply epiphenomenal is evident in at least two respects.

First, it is multiply realizable: the very same organization can obtain, even though the constituents that realize it can vary. Indeed, in the case of any dissipative (energetically open) self-organizing system, not only *can* the particular constituents vary, but they also *must* vary, because they have to be incessantly renewed as the system dissipates energy into its environment. This kind of material renewal is especially striking in autopoiesis. There is and must be a constant turnover of material constituents in the cell while the autopoietic organization remains invariant (otherwise the cell dies). This aspect of a complex system is part of its robustness or dynamic stability, which means that the organization of the system is resilient to small changes or perturbations at the microlevel, and adaptive to large changes.

Second, the dynamic stability of a complex system is reflected in the fact that different counterfactual statements are true for the macrolevel organization and for the microlevel processes. The organization is necessary for certain subsequent events, but the particular constituents are not. If the organization had been different and those constituents the same, the events would not have occurred; but if the constituents had been different (within certain limits) and the organization the same, the events would still have occurred (because of the way the constituents were organized).[7] Given that different counterfactual statements are true of the microlevel constituents and the macrolevel organization, the two cannot be identified.

Kim recognizes some of these points, but he goes through contortions to deal with them. In a footnote at the very end of his article, "Making Sense of Emergence," he admits that "complex systems obviously bring new causal powers into the world, powers that cannot be identified with causal powers of the more basic simpler systems. Among them are the causal powers of microstructural, or micro-based, properties of a complex system" (1999, p. 36). By a microstructural or micro-based property, he means a macrolevel property that is completely decomposable into a collection of microconstituents plus the microlevel properties and relations that characterize them (Kim 1998, p. 84). (Given this characterization, it would seem that Kim simply assumes that the microlevel does not include holistic relations, such as quantum entanglement or nonseparability of the Hamiltonian in nonlinear dynamic systems, but this is left unclear.) In this footnote (and the corresponding lengthier treatment in his book *Mind in a Physical World*), Kim gives away many of the issues at stake in the debate about emergence without ever acknowledging that he has done so (Campbell and Bickhard 2002). Thus he admits that "macroproperties can, and in general do, have their own causal powers, powers that go beyond the causal powers of their microconstituents" (1998, p. 85, emphasis omitted). Nevertheless, he declares, "these properties are not themselves emergent properties; rather, they form the basal conditions from which further properties emerge (for example . . . consciousness is not itself a microstructural property of an organism, though it may emerge from one)" (1999, p. 36).

The reasons Kim denies emergence to these macroproperties are complicated and problematic. First, his conception of emergent properties is derived from the British emergentists, who held that it is simply an inexplicable brute fact of nature—to be accepted in an "attitude of natural piety" in Samuel Alexander's phrase—that a certain organization of lower-level elements gives rise to some emergent quality.

According to this way of thinking, an emergent property is not to be identified with the macrolevel organization itself, but with a qualitatively distinct property that supervenes on and has as its emergence base that organization (see Kim 1998, pp. 85–86). There is no compelling reason today to endorse this peculiar conception of emergence. The British emergentists rightly drew attention to the significance of organization and relational structure, but did not have the scientific tools for studying them that we now do. It is not classical British emergentism but contemporary science that should guide our thinking about emergence.[8]

Second, Kim apparently accepts part/whole reductionism. Hence for him all macrolevel, micro-based properties are decomposable into the intrinsic properties of microlevel entities (although, as I mentioned earlier, this is left unclear). But part/whole reductionism as an ontological thesis about nature is unacceptable because (among other things) it presupposes a conceptual framework (of preexisting particulars with intrinsic properties) that apparently has no coherent formulation in the language of microphysical theory (which is, after all, supposed to be the ground floor on which everything else rests, according to the reductionist). Macrolevel characteristics can be micro-dependent and micro-involving, without being micro-based in Kim's sense (analytically decomposable into preexisting microlevel entities and their intrinsic properties).

Third, Kim's approach to emergence is entirely dominated by the Cartesian mind-body problem and its procrustean framework of the mental versus the physical. Given part/whole reductionism about the physical domain (a basically Cartesian conception of nature), and a very wide and problematic conception of "physical" that includes all of biology and psychology save phenomenal consciousness (which is excluded not as something immaterial but as something that resists physicalistic reductive analysis), the only candidates left over for emergence are "qualia," the qualitative or phenomenal properties of conscious experience. By contrast, the approach to emergence presented in this book is oriented not by the Cartesian mind-body problem but by the Kantian problem of self-organization (see Chapter 6) and its relation to the threefold order of matter, life, and mind.[9]

Let me close this discussion by making a few comments about the three principles at the base of Kim's argument. His argument is as strong as these principles, and although they have force against classical British emergentism, each one is dubious when applied to emergence in the context of contemporary science.

According to the first principle, every emergent is determined by its physical realization base or emergence base; according to the second, every emergent inherits its causal powers from its emergence base. These principles are simply an expression of physicalistic ontological reductionism. This position claims science for its support, but it is metaphysical in the sense of going beyond anything science itself tells us. I see no good reason to believe in such a thing as an "emergence base," where this means a configuration of preexisting microphysical entities with intrinsic properties and causal powers that ground the macrophysical level. This image of nature as a mereologically ordered hierarchy grounded on a base level of particulars is a metaphysical picture projected onto science, whereas the image science projects is of networks of processes at various spatiotemporal scales, with no base-level particulars that "upwardly" determine everything else (Bickhard and Campbell 2002; Hattiangadi 2005).

What about Kim's third principle, the causal closure of the physical? The precise meaning and status of this principle are not clear. The main problem is that it is far from clear what "physical" means—what it includes and excludes—and it is hard to see how one could go about answering this question short of having a complete and true physics (whatever that means and assuming it even makes sense to suppose such a thing). Suppose at some point in the future physicists felt compelled to include mental properties (*qua* mental) as fundamental properties of physical theory (Montero 1999, 2001). Given that we cannot accurately predict the future course of physics, we have to at least allow for this possibility. In fact, some physicists and philosophers already believe such inclusion to be necessary to account for both mental and physical phenomena (Shimony 1997). But in that case, the closure of physics would include the mental *qua* mental (as opposed to the mental *qua* reduced to the physical). This possibility illustrates that the Cartesian mental/physical distinction has become useless.

As for Kim, he embraces a very wide sense of "physical" that includes every classical example of an emergent property from physics, chemistry, biology, and psychology, save qualia. Nowhere in my discussion of emergence and downward causation have I appealed to anything outside the physical domain so broadly conceived. If the principle of the causal closure of the physical is instead construed more narrowly to mean the causal closure of the microphysical, then the principle is not obviously true and may even be false or incoherent (Dupré 1993; Hattiangadi 2005). For instance, according to Bohr's interpretation of quantum mechanics, macrophysical concepts are as indispensable to characterize microphysical phenomena as microphysical phenomena are to explain certain macrophenomena (Hattiangadi 2005). Moreover, the causal closure of physics has traditionally been linked to the ideal of the unity of science via intertheoretic reduction—that biology is in principle reducible to chemistry, and chemistry to physics. But such unity via intertheoretic reduction seems nowhere in sight (Dupré 1993; Garfinkel 1981). As Nancy Cartwright says about the classic case of the supposed intertheoretic reduction of physical chemistry to quantum mechanics: "Notoriously we have nothing like a real reduction of the relevant bits of physical chemistry to physics—whether quantum or classical. Quantum mechanics is important for explaining aspects of chemical phenomena but always quantum concepts are used alongside of *sui generis*—that is, unreduced—concepts from other fields. They don't explain the phenomena on their own" (Cartwright 1997, p. 163).

One final remark about Kim's conception of the "physical" is in order here. Part/whole reductionism goes hand in hand with an atomistic metaphysics of basic physical particulars and their mereological configurations, a metaphysics to which Kim apparently subscribes (1993, pp. 77, 96–97, 337). At the same time, he also apparently believes that nothing in the philosophical dispute about emergence depends on precise general definitions of "physical" (1993, p. 340). But this seems wrong on both counts. In the context of contemporary science, as we have seen, "nature" does not consist of basic particulars, but fields and processes, and this difference between a process-viewpoint and an elementary-particle-version of Cartesian substance metaphysics does make a difference to the philosophical issues about emergence (Campbell and Bickhard 2002; Hattiangadi 2005). In the former view, there is no bottom level of basic particulars with intrinsic properties that upwardly determines everything else. Everything is process all the way "down" and all the way "up," and processes are irreducibly relational—they exist only in patterns, networks, organizations, configurations, or webs. For the part/whole reductionist, "down" and "up" describe more and less fundamental levels of reality. Higher levels are realized by and determined by lower levels (the "layered model of reality;" see Kim 1993, pp. 337–339). In the process view, "up" and "down" are context-relative terms used to describe phenomena of various scale and complexity. There is no base level of elementary entities to serve as the ultimate "emergence base" on which to ground everything. Phenomena at all scales are not entities or substances but relatively stable processes, and since processes achieve stability at different levels of complexity, while still interacting with processes at other levels, all are equally real and none has absolute ontological primacy.

Notes

1. Cognitive Science and Human Experience

1 For overviews see Clark (1997, 2001); Franklin (1995); and Varela, Thompson, and Rosch (1991).

2 What counts as computation is actually a difficult conceptual and empirical question. What I am summarizing here is the received or formalist view of computation in classical cognitive science and philosophy of mind. If Brian Cantwell Smith (1996) is right, however, then this received view is seriously defective. Readers are referred to Smith's book for an important reconceptualization of computation from an embodied and situated perspective.

3 The term *explanatory gap* was originally introduced by Levine (1983) to describe the conceptual and epistemological gap between the qualitative characteristics of conscious states (qualia) and brain states. See Roy et al. (1999) for a broader discussion of the explanatory gap in cognitive science.

4 Not all cognitive theorists with strong ties to the cognitivist tradition share this view, however. Jerome Bruner, for instance, a founding father of the cognitive revolution, has long argued that cognitive science must include culture, embodiment, subjectivity, and the experience of meaning (Bruner 1990). In addition, in the 1990s a number of computational theorists began to advocate embodied and situated approaches to computation that departed from the classical view in various ways (see Agre 1995; Smith 1996; Wilson 1994).

5 See Dupuy (2000) for an account of cybernetics and its influence on cognitive science.

443

6 See Freeman (1995, 1999a); Kelso (1995); Port and van Gelder (1995); Thelen and Smith (1994); and Varela, Thompson, and Rosch (1991).

7 See Dreyfus and Dreyfus (1986); Johnson (1987); Lakoff (1987); Varela, Thompson, and Rosch (1991); and Winograd and Flores (1986). Dreyfus (1972) was a pioneering antecedent for much of this work.

8 See Freeman (1995, 1999a) and Varela, Thompson, and Rosch (1991).

9 Varela first thought of the name "the enactive approach" in the summer of 1986 in Paris when he and Thompson began writing *The Embodied Mind*. At one point before introducing the term *enactive*, Varela had been using "the hermeneutic approach" to emphasize the affiliation of his ideas to the philosophical school of hermeneutics—an affiliation also emphasized by other theorists of embodied cognition at the time (Johnson 1987; Varela, Thompson, and Rosch 1991, pp. 149–150; Winograd and Flores 1986). The first and second ideas summarized above were presented in Varela's 1979 book, *Principles of Biological Autonomy*. They were developed with Humberto Maturana and grew out of Maturana's earlier work on the biology of cognition (Maturana 1969, 1970; Maturana and Varela 1980, 1987). The third, fourth, and fifth ideas were presented by Varela, Thompson, and Rosch (1991) and by Thompson, Palacios, and Varela (1992), and were elaborated by Varela and Thompson in a number of subsequent papers (Thompson 2001; Thompson and Varela 2001; Varela 1991, 1997a; Varela and Thompson 2003).

10 *The Embodied Mind* briefly discussed and criticized Husserlian phenomenology (Varela, Thompson, and Rosch 1991, pp. 15–21). Although I still stand by some of those critical points, I also believe our treatment was too hasty. At the time we lacked sufficient knowledge of the depth and breadth of Husserl's writings. We were also influenced by Hubert Dreyfus's (1982) interpretation of Husserl as a cognitivist and proto-computationalist, an interpretation I no longer accept and that Varela too disavowed in his subsequent work on naturalizing phenomenology (see Petitot et al. 1999). For further discussion of this matter see Appendix A.

2. The Phenomenological Connection

1 Does Husserl thereby succumb to the idea that there is an uninterpreted and theory-neutral "given" in experience, the so-called philosophical myth of the given? This is a difficult and complicated question. Philosophy offers us not one but several different notions of the "given," and Husserl's thought developed considerably over the course of his life. In

fact, he held different views at different times regarding what might be meant by the given. Suffice it to say that it is a mistake to label Husserl as a philosopher of the given in the sense originally targeted by Wilfrid Sellars (1956) or by critics of the notion of theory-neutral observation, such as Thomas Kuhn (1970), for at least four reasons. First, the given in the phenomenological sense is not nonintentional sense-data but the world as it appears to us. Second, the phenomenality of the world is not understandable apart from the constitutive relation that subjectivity and consciousness bear to it. Third, as discussed in this chapter, whatever counts as given has to be seen as dynamically emergent in relation to what is pregiven, and the transition from pregiven to given depends on the subject's motivations, interests, and attentional capacities. Finally, the given comprises not simply phenomenal presence in a narrow sense (what is facing me right now), but also absence and possibility (the sides of the bottle I cannot see but that are available for me to see through movement). For recent discussions of some of these issues see Botero (1999); Roy (2003); and Steinbock (1999).

2 These features of the epoché closely parallel the basic mental skills cultivated in Buddhist mindfulness (shamatha-vipashyana) meditation (see Wallace 1998, 1999; see also Depraz, Varela, and Vermersch 2003).

3 This sense of the epoché is well expressed by the noted phenomenologist J. N. Mohanty (1989, pp. 12–13): "I need not emphasize how relevant and, in fact, necessary is the method of phenomenological epoche for the very possibility of genuine description in philosophy. It was Husserl's genius that he both revitalized the descriptive method for philosophy and brought to the forefront the method of epoche, without which one cannot really get down to the job. The preconceptions have to be placed within brackets, beliefs suspended, before philosophy can begin to confront phenomena as phenomena. This again is not an instantaneous act of suspending belief in the world or of directing one's glance towards the phenomena as phenomena, but involves a strenuous effort at recognizing preconceptions as preconceptions, at unraveling sedimented interpretations, at getting at presuppositions which may pretend to be self-evident truths, and through such processes aiming asymptotically at the prereflective experience."

4 See Depraz (1995, 2001a); Steinbock (1995); Welton (2000, 2003); and Zahavi (2003a).

5 Some scholars have argued that Husserl's mature philosophical thinking about history and the life-world derives from Heidegger's influence. It is possible, however, that the substantial (but unacknowledged) influence goes in precisely the opposite direction (Smith 2003,

pp. 10, 14). Merleau-Ponty himself declares on the very first page of his *Phenomenology of Perception* (1962, p. vii) that the whole of Heidegger's *Being and Time* "springs from an indication given by Husserl" and amounts to nothing more than an explication of Husserl's notion of the life-world. A few pages later Merleau-Ponty states: "Far from being, as has been thought, a procedure of idealistic philosophy, phenomenological reduction belongs to existential philosophy: Heidegger's 'being-in-the-world' appears only against the background of the phenomenological reduction" (p. xiv). It has long been said that Merleau-Ponty's interpretation of Husserl as anticipating not simply the spirit but much of the substance of his own *Phenomenology of Perception* is nothing more than an inaccurate reading of his own views back into Husserl. Recent scholarship, however, indicates that Merleau-Ponty's interpretation of Husserl is for the most part correct (Zahavi 2002b).

6 This paragraph and the next three are indebted to Zahavi (2003a, 2003c).

7 Another important category of experiences that do not have a subject-object structure are various types of contemplative or meditative states (see Austin 1998; Lutz, Dunne, and Davidson 2007; and Forman 1990). In a future work, I plan to explore the relation between Western phenomenology and the epistemological and phenomenological accounts of conemplative states found in Asian philosophical traditions.

8 My use of this example is due to Gallagher (1986b) and Zahavi (2003c).

9 A huge amount of scholarly discussion has been lavished on the proper way to interpret the Husserlian notion of the noema. The discussion concerns the relation between the *object-as-intended* (the noema) and the *object-that-is-intended* (the object itself)—the wine bottle-as-perceived (as felt and seen) and the bottle itself. According to the representationalist interpretation, the noema is a type of representational entity, an ideal sense or meaning, that mediates the intentional relation between the mental act and the object. In this view, consciousness is directed toward the object only by means of the noema and thus achieves its openness to the world only in virtue of the representational noema. According to the rival nonrepresentationalist interpretation, the noema is not any intermediate, representational entity; the noema is the object itself, but the object considered phenomenologically, that is, precisely in its givenness. In other words, *the object-as-intended is the object-that-is-intended,* but considered under the operation of suspending the realistic positing of the natural attitude. The noema can thus be grasped only in a phenomenological

or transcendental attitude. This view rejects the representationalism of the former view. Consciousness is intrinsically self-transcending. Accordingly, it does not achieve reference to the world by virtue of intermediate entities that bestow intentionality upon it. It would take me too far afield to review the twists and turns of this debate. I shall therefore simply state that for a variety of reasons I think the representationalist interpretation is mistaken and the nonrepresentationalist interpretation is correct, both as an interpretation of Husserl and as a philosophical account of (object-directed) intentionality (see Drummond 2003; Zahavi 2003a, pp. 53–68, 2004a).

10 Cf. Susan Hurley (1998), who proposes a "two-level interdependence view" of animals and people as "dynamic singularities" at the subpersonal level and as normatively understood intentional agents at the personal level.

11 For simplicity of exposition, I am here setting aside phenomenologists, most notably Sartre (1960), who maintain a nonegological conception of intentional consciousness. According to this conception, the ego is a constituted object of an egoless consciousness and thus belongs on the noematic and not the noetic side of the correlational structure. For an important discussion showing how Husserl already recognized Sartre's insights, see Stawarska (2002).

12 In 1949 the psychologist Donald Hebb proposed what is now known as Hebb's Rule (Hebb 1949). He suggested that learning could be based on changes in the brain that stem from the degree of correlated activity between neurons: if two neurons tend to be active together, their connection is strengthened; otherwise it is diminished. Therefore, the system's connectional architecture becomes inseparable from its history of transformation. In 1890 James had already written in his *Principles of Psychology:* "When two elementary brain-processes have been active together or in immediate succession, one of them, on reoccurring, tends to propagate its excitement into the other" (1981, p. 534; emphasis omitted).

13 It is often assumed that Heidegger was the source of Husserl's idea of the pregiven life-world that cannot be made explicit as an object. Yet Husserl had already been working on the notion of the life-world in the early 1920s (Heidegger's *Being and Time* was published in 1927), and his work in the 1930s does not show any direct influence of Heidegger's notion of the world. See Welton (2000, pp. 120, 339).

14 For an important contemporary reflection on this point as it relates to the metaphysics of intentionality, see Brian Cantwell Smith (1996, pp. 103–104).

3. Autonomy and Emergence

1 For a brief introduction to dynamic-systems theory see Norton (1995).
   A now classic exposition from a visual and geometric perspective is
   Abraham and Shaw (1982–1988). See also Kellert (1993) for a useful
   philosophical treatment.

2 See Freeman (1999a); Friston (2000a, 2000b); Kauffman (1993); Kelso
   (1995); Le Van Quyen (2003); So et al. (1998); and Solé and Goodwin
   (2000).

3 This book contains Varela's reworking of his collaborative work with
   Maturana as well as his early attempts to formalize the notion of autonomy.

4 "Closure" is used here in its algebraic sense: an operation K exhibits closure in a domain D if every result of its operation yields results within D.
   Thus the operation of a system has operational closure if the results of its
   activity remain within the system itself. This notion of operational closure
   has nothing to do with the idea of a materially closed system—a system
   that is closed to interactions with what lies beyond it. Autonomous systems are and must be coupled to their surroundings; the issue is the nature of the dynamics that defines them and determines how they interact
   with what lies beyond them (Varela 1979, 1997a; Varela and Bourgine
   1991). Varela in his writings does not distinguish between organizational
   and operational closure; he uses the two terms more or less interchangeably. My usage follows Rudrauf et al. (2003, p. 34).

5 The quotation at the end is from Goldstein's 1934 work, *The Organism*
   (Goldstein 1995, p. 85).

6 Varela (1979) indicates that this thesis is meant to be analogous to
   Church's Thesis that any calculation is formally equivalent to a recursive
   function. "Recursive function" is a technical notion used to define the
   imprecise notion of a calculation. Similarly, "organizational closure" is a
   technical notion used to define the imprecise notion of autonomy. In
   either case the thesis is not subject to proof (hence is not a theorem),
   but it can be taken as a challenge to find a counterexample (something
   that intuitively counts as a calculation but is not formally equivalent to a
   recursive function; something that intuitively counts as autonomous but
   does not have organizational closure).

7 "Self" in this setting means identity through change in the form of an
   invariant topological form that is recursively produced by the system
   and that defines a domain of interactions. Hence this notion of self
   does not imply consciousness. These points are discussed at greater
   length in Parts II and III.

8 See Varela (1979, p. 12): "If one says that there is a machine *M* in which there is a feedback loop through the environment, so that the effects of its output affect its input, one is in fact talking about a larger machine *M'* which includes the environment and the feedback loop in its defining organization."

9 The following discussion combines a number of points made by Freeman (1995, 1999a, 1999b, 2003); Maturana and Varela (1980, 1987); Skarda and Freeman (1987); and Varela (1979, 1984).

10 See Freeman (1999a); Friston (2000b); Kelso (1995); Le Van Quyen (2003); Tononi and Edelman (1998); and Varela et al. (2001). The article by Le Van Quyen provides a very useful overview.

11 See Le Van Quyen, Adam et al. (1997); and Le Van Quyen, Martinerie et al. (1997). For discussion, see Le Van Quyen and Petitmengin (2002) and Thompson and Varela (2001).

12 Cf. Varela and Goguen (1978): "The wholeness of a system is embodied in its organizational closure. The whole is not the sum of its parts; it is the organizational closure of its parts."

4. The Structure of Behavior

1 My discussion here is indebted to Priest (1998, pp. 162–163).

2 Merleau-Ponty takes human symbolic behavior as paradigmatic of mind—hence his alignment of matter, life, and mind with the physical, vital, and human orders. Missing from this typology is any animal order. Although Merleau-Ponty does not single out an animal order explicitly in *The Structure of Behavior* (whereas he does later in his lecture course *Nature*), he does recognize one within the vital and human orders. Earlier in the book he classifies behavior according to the degree to which its structure (and hence the organism) is submerged in or emergent from the organism's concrete situation (1963, p. 103). The more emergent the structure of behavior is with respect to the milieu, the more effectively the organism can dominate situations and learn. The more effectively the organism can withdraw from and exercise control over its immersion in the milieu, the more it triumphs over immediacy and achieves individuality.

Merleau-Ponty presents a hierarchy of three forms of behavior, which he calls "syncretic," "amovable" (removable or detachable), and "symbolic" (1963, pp. 104–124), and explains, "These three categories do not correspond to three groups of animals: there is no species of animal whose behavior *never* goes beyond the syncretic level nor any whose behavior *never* descends below the symbolic forms. Nevertheless, animals can be distributed along this scale according to the type of behavior which is most typical of them" (1963, p. 104). "Syncretic" means a structure whose elements are blended, fused, or united in some way; hence syncretic behavior is largely fused or united with its milieu. Syncretic behavior is typical of simple animals, such as invertebrates, whose responses to situations seem largely prescribed and inflexible. "Amovable" (removable or detachable) behavior is exemplified in higher animals that are not so tightly bound to their immediate material situation because they can interact with it on the basis of "signals" that are not "instinctual" (1963, p. 105). Signals of this sort "are founded on structures that are relatively independent of the materials in which they are realized" (ibid.). Amovable behavior is signal behavior: the situation to which the organism responds is a signal and its signification, as in the simple temporal or spatial contiguity of a conditioned and an unconditioned stimulus (1963, pp. 105–106).

Unlike the reflex theorists he criticizes, however, Merleau-Ponty argues that the organism responds to the stimulus because of the form or structure it has for the organism. The stimulus as signal is a structure, a gestalt, and the organism's response is always to a structure-for-the-animal (a stimulus informed by the sensorimotor structure of the animal), not to an animal-independent, physicochemical element (1963, pp. 10–15). Yet signals are not signs or symbols: "The true sign represents the signified, not according to an empirical association, but inasmuch as its relation to other signs is the same as the relation of the object signified by it to other objects" (1963, pp. 121–122). Thus the third form of behavior is symbolic behavior: "Here behavior no longer *has* only one signification, it *is* itself signification" (1963, p. 122). Merleau-Ponty asserts that "In animal behavior signs always remain signals and never become symbols" (1963, p. 120), but cognitive ethology today challenges this view (see Deacon 1997; Savage-Rumbaugh and Lewin 1994). In any case, symbolic forms of behavior are most typical of human beings and thus distinguish the human order (see Tomasello 1999).

3 It would be fruitful to compare Merleau-Ponty's typology, in particular his conception of the human order, with Heidegger's treatment of the fundamental difference between animal and human life, in his lecture course *The Fundamental Concepts of Metaphysics* (Heidegger 1995). Heidegger distinguishes between stones as being "worldless," animals as being "poor in world," and humans as being "world-forming." Whereas humans have a "comportment" *(Verhalten)* toward a "world," animals merely display "behavior" *(Benehmen)* in relation to an "encircling ring"

of animal desires and drives. Thus, for Heidegger, there can be no disclosure of the "world" or "objects in the world" to the animal. It is, however, beyond the scope of this chapter to undertake an examination of Heidegger's view in relation to Merleau-Ponty's. Moreover, this undertaking would also need to cover the development of Merleau-Ponty's views on animal and human life, as represented especially by his lectures on the idea of nature (Merleau-Ponty 2003).

4 I have discussed this issue extensively elsewhere. See Pessoa, Thompson, and Noë (1998); Thompson, Noë, and Pessoa (1999); and Noë and Thompson (2004a, 2004b).

5. Autopoiesis

1 The theory of autopoiesis was first presented in Spanish in Maturana and Varela (1973). Maturana and Varela (1980) contains a translation of this text, as well as an important earlier article by Maturana (Maturana 1970, which is a revision of Maturana 1969). The first English-language presentation of autopoiesis appeared in Varela, Maturana, and Uribe (1974). For useful discussions and elaborations of autopoiesis see Fleischaker (1988), Luisi (2003), and Mingers (1995).

2 Compare Maturana (1980a, pp. 52–53): "A dynamic system that is defined as a composite unity as a network of productions of components that, a) through their interactions recursively regenerate the network of productions that produced them, and b) realize this network as a unity by constituting and specifying its boundaries in the space in which they exist, is an *autopoieitic system.*"

3 For instance, some social theorists have argued that human social systems such as the family are autopoietic. In this case it is not at all clear that "boundary" and "internal network" have a clear sense. For Maturana's and Varela's differing views on autopoiesis and social relations, see Maturana (1980b) and Varela (1989). For discussion see Luisi (2003) and Mingers (1995).

4 The history of the original model and its reimplementation is an interesting story of its own. See McMullin (1997a, 1997b).

5 As McMullin and Varela (1997) point out, the spontaneous formation of an autopoietic network cannot occur unless the artificial chemistry actually supports the realization of the autopoietic organization. Thus the phenomenon of spontaneous formation is logically secondary (though prior chronologically) to that of the realization of the autopoietic organization.

6 Letelier, Marín, and Mpodozis (2003) interpret the need for the chain-

based bond inhibition interaction as implying that "the closure exhibited by tesselation automatas [*sic*] is not a consequence of the 'network' of simulated processes, but rather an artifact of coding procedures" (p. 270). But in the revised McMullin and Varela (1997) model, chain-based bond inhibition is a purely local rule of the qualitative chemistry. It is not clear, therefore, why the closure of the network is supposed to be an artifact of coding procedures.

7 For the background of this work see Luisi and Varela (1989). For recent overviews see Luisi (1993, 2003).

8 It is interesting to note that Mikulecky (2000) reaches the same conclusions by applying Robert Rosen's (1991, 2000) theory of living systems to the Gaia hypothesis. For an important discussion of the relation between Rosen's metabolic-repair (M,R) systems and autopoiesis, see Letelier, Marín, and Mpodozis (2003). I discuss Rosen's ideas in Chapter 6.

9 For a wide-ranging literary and philosophical reflection that brings together the work of Lovelock, Margulis, Varela, and mathematician Ralph Abraham, see W. I. Thompson (1989). See also the essays collected in W. I. Thompson (1987b, 1991a).

10 This invocation of norms goes beyond Maturana's (1970) characterization, quoted above, of what makes a living system a cognitive system. See Chapter 6 for further discussion of this point.

6. Life and Mind

1 This line of reasoning is similar to the one behind contemporary formulations of the explanatory gap or hard problem of consciousness. It is argued that the laws of nature do not suffice to explain the presence of consciousness in a physical world because consciousness is contingent with respect to those laws. Hence novel psychophysical principles are required (see Chalmers 1996, 1997).

2 To the best of my knowledge, Kant was the first to introduce the term *self-organizing* and apply it to organisms. It is surprising there has been so little reconsideration of Kant's *Critique of Judgment* in relation to contemporary scientific theories of self-organizing biological systems. Notable exceptions are Juarrero-Roqué (1985) and Weber and Varela (2002).

3 See Jantsch (1980); Kauffman (1993); Kelso (1995); Prigogine and Stengers (1984); and Solé and Goodwin (2000).

4 Recall Bitbol's words, quoted in Chapter 4: "Here science is not supposed to reveal anything of a preexistent underlying absolute reality, nor is it a more or less random aggregate of efficient recipes. Science is

rather the stabilized byproduct of a dynamic reciprocal relation between reality as a whole and a special fraction of it. Defining this special fraction of reality qua subject is the reverse side of its actively extracting objectlike invariant clusters of phenomena" (Bitbol 2003, p. 337).

5 Varela writes: "In this book 'machines' and 'systems' are used interchangeably. They obviously carry different connotations, but the differences are inessential, for my purpose, except in seeing the relation between the history of biological mechanism and the modern tendency for systemic analysis. Machines *and* systems point to the characterization of a class of unities in terms of their organization" (1979, p. 7, note 4).

6 In a Darwinian context, such functions are thought to be determined by natural selection. A structure has the function it does because its playing that role increased the reproductive success of ancestral organisms that possessed it. I discuss this idea in the next chapter.

7 Philosophers often confuse these two senses of intrinsic. The point is that something can be intrinsic in the sense of constitutive while also being relational. For example, orange is intrinsically (constitutively) a mixture of red and yellow, and red is intrinsically (constitutively) opposed to green. These constitutive properties of the colors are also relational ones.

8 Varela and I discussed these issues in e-mail exchanges over a period of several months in 1999. Our discussion began because I pointed out to him that his commitment to the explanatory role that phenomenology could play in relation to biology seemed inconsistent with his older position on teleology with Maturana. We had both independently been reading Kant and Jonas, and I asked him whether he would still maintain his earlier antiteleological stance in light of Jonas's argument (discussed below) that one cannot recognize something to be a living being unless one recognizes it as purposive and that one cannot recognize something as purposive unless one is an embodied agent who experiences purposiveness in one's own case. Varela replied that he was "still quite suspicious" about this appeal to teleology, and hence about this way of linking phenomenology and biology, and that he preferred to "shift the accent" from teleology to original intentionality, understood as the sense-making capacity proper to autopoietic units. He saw this shift as a refinement of the " 'Santiago school' move to introduce the equation life = cognition." It is clearly "silly," he said, to make cellular cognition just like animal cognition, but their "common root" is this basic sense-making capacity proper to autopoietic life. Appealing to sense-making, he suggested, was more "constructive" than appealing to the "elusive principle of purpose." Sense-making provides a strong link

to intentionality, but "whether this turns into teleology," he said, "is another matter."

This line of thought struck me as unsatisfactory because "original intentionality" and "sense-making" are themselves teleological notions. The issue is precisely how to analyze this teleology. Although the proposition "living is sense-making" may be an important elaboration of the equation life = cognition, it is insufficient to establish any antiteleological stance with respect to Kant's and Jonas's notions of intrinsic purposiveness. I pressed Varela on this issue, and he later indicated that as time had gone by he had come to have a "broader view." He had begun to see that "in a funny way you do recover a full fledged teleology . . . but this teleology . . . is intrinsic to life in action," and "does not require an extra transcendental source" in the Kantian sense. In other words, teleology, in the sense of self-organized, intrinsic purposiveness, can be seen as a constitutive feature of the organism, on the basis of its autonomy and sense-making, rather than only a form of our judgment, as Kant had held. It is precisely this conception that Weber and Varela (2002) advance and call *immanent teleology*.

9 Di Paolo (2005, p. 438) defines adaptivity as "a system's capacity, in some circumstances, to regulate its states in relation to its boundary of viability with the result that, if the states are sufficiently close to the boundary, (1) tendencies are distinguished and acted upon depending on whether the states approach or recede from the boundary in some scale-invariant measure and, as a consequence, (2) tendencies of the first kind are moved closer to or transformed into tendencies of the second and so future states are prevented from reaching the boundary with outward velocity." As he goes on to note, "This capacity may result from the action of dedicated mechanisms or it may be an emergent aspect of specific ways of realizing autopoiesis. But importantly, it is not a direct consequence of the definition of autopoiesis but an elaboration of it from which it is possible to recover the homeostatic [as opposed to merely conservational] interpretation." See also Ruiz-Mirazo and Moreno (2004) for related considerations in the context of the thermodynamic requirements for the realization of basic autonomy.

10 Of course, from a transcendental phenomenological perspective this statement needs qualification. Physicochemical phenomena, considered from the first-order vantage point of physics and chemistry, do not implicate a point of view in the way that biological phenomena do. When seen from a second-order, transcendental perspective, however, physical and chemical phenomena also have to be understood in terms of the conditions of possibility for their disclosure to science, and thus

do implicate a point of view, namely, that of the scientific tradition itself.

11 Heidegger, for his part, distinguishes sharply between nonliving and
living things, and characterizes living things in a way that serves to elucidate the phenomenological meaning of being-in-the-world: "A stone
never finds itself but is simply on hand. A very primitive unicellular
form of life, on the contrary, will already find itself, where this disposition can be the greatest and darkest dullness, but for all that it is in its
structure of being essentially distinct from merely being on hand like a
thing" (Heidegger 1985, p. 255). This notion of "finding itself" or "disposition" *(Befindlichkeit)* defines the phenomenological meaning of
being-in-the-world (see also pp. 165–166, where Heidegger explains "in-
being" as analogous to the being proper to life, by contrast with nonliving things). Heidegger characterizes animal being (understood as including unicellular organisms) as "poor in world," by contrast with
human being, which is "world forming" (Heidegger 1995).

12 Merleau-Ponty, in discussing von Uexküll, writes that the "reactions of
the animal in the milieu . . . behaviors . . . deposit a surplus of signification on the surfaces of objects" (Merleau-Ponty 2003, pp. 172–173).

13 Boden apparently finds this usage objectionable. She writes: "ascrip-
tions of knowledge and cognition normally presuppose the possession
of perceptual and motor capacities, integrated in adaptive ways" (2000,
p. 137). There is no need to dispute this claim. Instead, we can point
out that what counts as possession of perceptual and motor capacities is
not obvious and seems to be a graded matter. Consider again the
humble bacterium. As we have seen, motile bacteria engage in complex
sensorimotor-style behaviors. Some of the most basic features of animal
brains and sensorimotor coordination can be found in these tiny organisms (see Allman 1999, pp. 3–8; Bonner 1980, p. 68; Koshland 1977;
and Maturana and Varela 1987, pp. 147–150). As Harold Morowitz
writes: "The first biological emergence where there is a hint of *mind* is
in the swimming of motile bacteria uphill in a food gradient and downhill in a gradient of toxic substance. This is not well understood. It requires a cell to sense concentration and to interpret the time derivative
as a spatial gradient. By randomly changing direction with a frequency
that responds to the gradient, the cell can statistically swim in the appropriate direction. The cognitive feel about this is that the cell can let
its profits run and cut its losses" (Morowitz 2001, pp. 51–52).

14 One could appeal here to Heidegger for support (see note 11 above):
living being, even in its simplest unicellular form, involves a kind of
being-in-the-world, unlike the "worldess" being of nonliving things

(even if for Heidegger living being is "poor in world," in contrast to the "world-forming" being of Dasein).

15 I thus agree with Damasio when he describes Spinoza's idea of *conatus* as containing the thought "that of necessity, all living organisms endeavor to preserve themselves without conscious knowledge of the undertaking and without having decided, as individual selves, to undertake anything. In short, they do not know the problem they are trying to solve. When the consequences of such natural wisdom are mapped back in the central nervous system, subcortically and cortically, the result is feelings, the foundational component of our minds" (Damasio 2003, p. 79). The phrase "natural wisdom" strikes me as problematic in this context, and we cannot yet be said to understand how the brain's mapping of vital processes results in feelings (for a hypothesis, see Rudrauf and Damasio 2005).

16 One might think this situation is not unlike cellular automata models of autopoiesis (see Chapter 5), in which every unit is local and discrete, and the global pattern may simply be in the eye of the beholder. The status of such models is a difficult matter. We could follow Dennett (1991b) and see the global patterns as "real paterns." If Rosen (1991, 2000) is right, however, that the self-referential organization of living beings makes them noncomputable, then these models cannot capture the living organization.

17 Of course, one can always argue that firsthand experience of how things seem to one does not necessarily count as valid knowledge of how things are. But the point above is rather that experience itself needs to be accounted for. To deny firsthand experience outright would, in the present context, be tantamount to "sacrificing an evidence (purposiveness) to a theorem (exclusiveness of *causa efficiens*) which was derived by generalization from another evidence" (Jonas 1966, p. 90).

7. Laying Down a Path in Walking

1 The following discussion is based on Maturana and Varela (1987). See also Fleischaker (1994).

2 Proteins are produced from their constituent amino acids according to the sequence of nucleotide triplets of DNA on the chromosomes (the so-called genetic code). From this DNA sequence is "transcribed" a complementary sequence in messenger RNA (mRNA). This RNA sequence is then "translated" into an amino acid chain through the action of ribosomes and transfer RNA (tRNA) molecules. In addition,

each step along the way depends on the participation of many other molecular elements, such as RNA polymerase enzymes, and negative and positive regulatory proteins, to name just a few.

3 In DNA replication, the hydrogen bonds between the complementary bases on the two strands of the parent DNA molecule break apart and the strands of the double helix uncoil, with each strand serving as a template for the synthesis of a new strand complementary to itself. The copying mechanism involves many molecular elements, such as the enzyme DNA polymerase, which moves down the two single strands linking free nucleotides to their complementary bases on the templates; DNA-binding proteins, which stabilize the single DNA strands so that they do not coil back up; and DNA-repair mechanisms, which remove damaged sections of the strands so that they can be replaced with the correct sections by DNA polymerases.

4 Strictly speaking, the process of natural selection has a fourth requirement, namely, that the mechanism producing phenotypic variations be independent of requirements (2) and (3), so that (2) and (3) can have no directional effect on the mechanism producing variations.

5 Chromatin is the substance of which eukaryotic chromosomes are made; it consists primarily of a kind of protein called histone. DNA methylation is the attachment of methyl chemical groups to the DNA sequence, which block the transcription of the genes to which they are attached, and thereby regulate gene activity.

6 This point is not new, having been made many times by biologists over the years. One of the earliest criticisms of the genetic-program metaphor came from the embryologist Paul Weiss (1969; see Dupuy 2000, pp. 132–133). Another early criticism was made by Maturana and Varela (1980, pp. 90, 102). For recent critical discussions see Goodwin (1994); Keller (1995, 2000); Lewontin (1993); Moss (1992, 2003); Oyama (2000b, first edition published in 1985); Rose (1997); and Sarkar (1996).

7 For recent debate about the notion of information in this context, see Maynard Smith (2000a) and the replies by Godfrey-Smith (2000a); Sarkar (2000); Sterelny (2000); plus Maynard Smith's rejoinder (2000b).

8 Dennett relies here on an argument developed by the philosophers Sterelny and Kitcher, according to which a length of DNA can be said to "code for" a phenotypic trait relative to a "standard" background of other genes and a "standard environment" (Sterelny and Kitcher 1988). To which Griffiths and Gray reply: "But consider the DNA in an acorn. If this codes for anything, it is for an oak tree. But the vast majority of

acorns simply rot. So 'standard environment' cannot be interpreted statistically. The only interpretation of 'standard' that will work is 'such as
to produce evolved developmental outcomes' or 'of the sort possessed
by successful ancestors.' With this interpretation of 'standard environment,' however, we can talk with equal legitimacy of cytoplasmic or
landscape features coding for traits in standard genic backgrounds. No
basis has been provided for privileging genes over other developmental
resources" (Griffiths and Gray 1994, p. 283).

9 Jonas made this point long ago in *The Phenomenon of Life* (1966, pp. 52–
53).

10 Compare Dawkins's allowance that "a billion discrete, digital characters
carved in tablets of crystal" is a metaphor, whereas in the passage
quoted earlier he avows that "it is raining instructions out there; it's
raining programs" is not a metaphor. Both are metaphors, and both express informational dualism.

11 The classic text of developmental systems theory is Oyama (2000b). See
also Griffiths and Gray (1994); Oyama (2000a, 2000c); Oyama, Griffiths, and Gray (2001); and Sterelny and Griffiths (1999, Chapter 5).
Griffiths and Stotz (2000) explore some of the parallels and mutual
support between developmental systems theory and enactive cognitive
science.

12 I have omitted Oyama's references (many of which I have already
cited).

13 The distinction here is between biological evolution, conceived of as
driven by natural selection (with separation of germ line and soma, and
one-way "information flow" from DNA to protein) and cultural evolution, conceived of as operating according to the acquisition of traits by
learning.

14 This point about the inseparability of nature and culture links developmental systems theory to discussions in the social sciences and humanities, in particular to those cultural theorists who have criticized the
"modernist project" of trying to separate culture and nature (see Latour
1993; W. I. Thompson 1987a, 1987b, 1991a, 1991b).

15 Oyama (1999) has expressed dissatisfaction with the "internalist
predilection" she discerns in earlier formulations of the autopoietic
perspective. The formulations to which she objects, however, have
played no role in my presentation of the autopoietic perspective in this
book.

16 The common terminology of "regulatory genes" "controlling" development is misleading. First, the genes do not control the particular kind of
structure that develops: Mouse *pax-6* transferred to the fruitfly leads to

the development of the *fruitfly* eye at that site; thus the surrounding cellular context is essential. Second, the genes act not alone but as participants of a network or system (involving transcription factors and other genes); hence regulatory properties can be properly assigned only at the level of the system, not at the level of the individual gene. As Stearns observes: "the concept of 'regulatory genes' often comes up in discussions of developmental constraints . . . There is, however, no such thing as a regulatory gene, only regulatory systems with genes embedded in them. Some genes make products that have direct control over the expression of other genes, and some genes make products that have indirect control over the expression of other genes. At times, gene products may be primarily structural in their impact. At other times, the same products may be primarily regulatory in their impact. Since the same gene product can play various context-dependent roles, it is a mistake to assign to the genes a property that is properly applied to the different roles their products can play in different contexts . . . The technical distinction between regulatory and structural is worth preserving, so long as one remembers that they refer to context-dependent roles, not to a property of a gene as fixed as its DNA sequence" (Stearns 1986, p. 40).

17 "Selector genes" are genes that specify so-called selector proteins, which are transcription factors that play a crucial role in the formation and patterning of body parts. The term *selector gene* unfortunately suggests that these genes themselves select a particular outcome, whereas the outcome is rather the result of the network or system consisting of these genes and their transcription factors (as well as other genes and proteins). See the previous note.

18 One might wonder: how could skeletal considerations serve as the basis for the proposal that arthropods and vertebrates have a common body layout, given that arthropods have no bones? The answer, according to Coen, is as follows: "Geoffroy proposed that these apparently different types of organisation were really two sides of the same coin; it was just that vertebrates were organised around a skeleton whereas insects lived within theirs. To turn yourself into an insect you have to imagine your skeleton expanding outwards, whilst your body remains the same size. Eventually the bones reach and enclose the skin, and all the soft tissues and vital organs end up interior to them, like a very elaborate bone marrow. He believed that once this was appreciated, detailed correspondences between insect and vertebrate structures fell into place according to his principle of connections. For example, the main trunk of the insect would correspond to the vertebral column (backbone), and its legs would be equivalent to our ribs" (Coen 1999, p. 114).

19 In Maturana and Varela (1987) and Varela, Thompson, and Rosch
    (1991), this view of evolution was called *evolution by natural drift*. *Enactive*
    evolution makes explicit the homology with *enactive cognition*.

20 A morphogenetic field is a region in the developing organism that or-
    ganizes itself spatiotemporally according to various precise biochemical
    processes.

21 The notion of persistence has been technically defined as a measure of
    fitness in terms of risk minimization: "A single-generation measure of
    risk minimization expresses the idea of minimizing the probability of
    leaving no offspring that survive to maturity, for example, while a long-
    term measure of risk minimization expresses the idea of minimizing the
    probability that a gene, clone, or species would go extinct" (Stearns
    1986, p. 30). Risk-minimization measures of fitness contrast with abun-
    dance measures, such as measures of lifetime reproductive success.

22 A nice case of reverse engineering is Simon Conway Morris's attempts
    to figure out the anatomy and mode of life of *Hallucigenia sparsa*, a
    worm that lived in the seas during the Cambrian period about 500 mil-
    lion years ago. At first he thought that the seven pairs of stilt-like spines
    along its body enabled it to rest and walk on the ocean bottom, but
    later he realized he had reconstructed the animal upside-down and that
    the spines served as a defensive array on top of the animal. This case is
    telling because its object is a fossil, that is, a static form, not a living
    being. Given a frozen form, reverse engineering becomes a pragmati-
    cally necessary stance to adopt. But it is important not to confuse the in-
    terpretive stance with the thing itself being interpreted. See Conway
    Morris (1998, pp. 54–56) and Gould (1989, pp. 153–157).

23 The Argument from Design has a long philosophical history, going
    back to St. Thomas Aquinas, Aristotle, and Plato. The version of the ar-
    gument presented above is the one that directly influenced Darwin; it
    appeared in William Paley's 1805 work *Natural Theology* (Paley 1996).
    Paley's argument is best understood to be an inference to the best ex-
    planation: given the two hypotheses of intelligent design and random
    formation, which is better supported by the evidence of the complex or-
    ganization of living beings? Just as the complex organization of a watch
    is better evidence that the watch is the product of intelligent design
    rather than of random formation, so too is the complex organization of
    living beings better evidence that they are the product of intelligent de-
    sign than of random formation. There is another version of the Argu-
    ment from Design, the analogical or inductive version. It states that or-
    ganisms and artifacts are similar (both seem well organized); artifacts
    are the product of intelligent design; therefore organisms are the

product of intelligent design. David Hume had already subjected this version of the argument to devastating criticism in his *Dialogues Concerning Natural Religion* (1779). See Sober (1993, pp. 30–36).

24 Indeed, the very term *Design Space*, which Dennett uses to refer to the logical space of possible forms or organizations for living things, is not theoretically neutral (as it ought to be if it is to demarcate the phenomena needing explanation). It is biased because it takes for granted the functionalist assumption that organisms are designed entities. It would be preferable to use the term *morphospace*. Similarly, Dennett's functionalist argument against Goodwin's structuralism—that when Goodwin says there are laws of form in biology he says something as implausible as that there are laws of form in automotive engineering—misses the key point that organisms are different from heteronomous entities such as automobiles. Therefore any analysis of them premised on an analogy to that sort of entity is of limited value.

At one point Dennett even goes so far as to say that "Adaptationist reasoning is not optional; it is the heart and soul of evolutionary biology. Although it may be supplemented, and its flaws repaired, to think of displacing it from [its] central position in biology is to imagine not just the downfall of Darwinism but the collapse of modern biochemistry and all the life sciences and medicine" (1995a, p. 238). This defense of adaptationism turns it into an *a priori* condition of evolutionary theory (or indeed of all biology) and thereby empties the adaptationist research program of empirical content. As Sober writes: "Adaptationism is first and foremost a research program. Its core claims will receive support if specific adaptationist hypotheses turn out to be well confirmed. If such explanations fail time after time, eventually scientists will begin to suspect that its core assumptions are defective. Phrenology waxed and waned according to the same dynamic. Only time and hard work will tell whether adaptationism deserves the same fate" (1993, p. 129). Contrary to Dennett, modern biochemistry and the life sciences and medicine are not based on the adaptationist research program in evolutionary theory. Therefore they would not collapse were the core assumptions of adaptationism shown to be defective.

25 As Stearns writes: "One could describe all of biology as the consequence of constraints—not just reductionist biology [in which the constraints flow directly from physics and chemistry], but natural selection itself, viewed as a mechanism. The meaning of the word would vanish. We can preserve it in a relative sense if we recognize that it only has meaning in a local context where one concentrates on the possibilities latent in certain processes and views the limitations on those possibilities as arising from outside that context. One could always stand the problem on its

head, switch contexts, and what had been constraints would become a set of possibilities, and what had been possibilities would become constraints. Thus life histories can constrain the evolution of behavior, and behavior can constrain the evolution of life histories. Development can constrain the evolution of biochemistry, and biochemistry can constrain the evolution of development" (Stearns 1986, pp. 35–36).

8. Life beyond the Gap

1 Aristotle did hesitate over whether intellectual thought requires a body. Later, the medieval Christian Aristotelians held that whereas sensation requires a body, intellectual cognition does not.

2 It is not clear whether Descartes would have allowed that his argument for a "real distinction" between mind and body could be turned around in this way. He argued in his *Discourse on Method* that consciousness is required in order to be able to reason and express one's thoughts in langauge, including being able to put together physical signs in the right synactic patterns so as to express a given meaning. Therefore, in his view, it would seem that there could not be a being functionally and behaviorally identical to a human being—in particular, identical with regard to linguistic behavior—that lacked consciousness.

3 As in Descartes's "Second Meditation:" "if I look out of the window and see the men crossing the square, as I just happen to have done, I normally say that I see the men themselves . . . Yet do I see any more than hats and coats which could conceal automatons? I *judge* that they are men" (Descartes 1986, p. 21).

4 Nagel's original formulation, quoted at the beginning of this chapter, reads: "If mental processes are physical processes, then there is something it is like, intrinsically, to undergo certain physical processes. What it is for such a thing to be the case remains a mystery" (1979, p. 175).

5 In Husserl's words: "*The lived-body is at one with the physical body*, membered thus and so, and, through the actual and potential kinaestheses belonging [to it] in their special way, [it is] precisely organ and system of organs" (Husserl 1973, p. 643, as quoted and translated by Welton 1999, p. 51; emphasis in original).

6 Thus Husserl uses the following terms: *physischer Körper, physischer Leib, leiblicher Körper, Leibkörper, körperlicher Leib, körperliche Leiblichkeit,* and *Körperleib* (Depraz 1997, 2001a, p. 3).

7 Husserl (1970) makes this point at length in his famous discussion of the "Galilean style" of modern natural science in *The Crisis of European Sciences and Transcendental Phenomenology.*

8 I think it would be better to say that the appearances exist only *for* consciousness. To say that consciousness consists in the appearances themselves could lead one to think that appearances are contents of consciousness in the sense of being contained within consciousness. Appearances are relational: they correspond to the phenomenality of the world for conscious subjects.

9 Searle's position that the irreducibility of consciousness is a trivial consequence of our definitional practices suggests that it might be possible to change those practices so that consciousness would be reducible. Yet, although intellectual revolutions giving rise to new conceptions of reduction and consciousness are certainly possible, any conception or method of reduction, and any definitional practice, will presuppose consciousness or (inter)subjectivity as a condition of possibility, and so there will always remain a nontrivial sense in which consciousness is irreducible. Searle comes close to allowing this sort of point when he writes: "the main point of having the concept of consciousness is to capture the first-person, subjective features of the phenomenon and this point would be lost if we redefine consciousness in third-person, objective terms. We would still need a name for the first-person ontology" (Searle 2004, p. 120).

10 I ignore here the complicated question of what counts as the brain's or nervous system's proper parts. See Swanson (2000).

11 I am greatly indebted to Diego Cosmelli for ongoing collaboration and discussion concerning these points.

12 See Hurley and Noë (2003); Noë (2004); Noë and Thompson (2004a, 2004b); and Thompson and Varela (2001).

9. Sensorimotor Subjectivity

1 I have slightly modified the English translation. The French reads: "Mais je ne suis pas devant mon corps, je suis dans mon corps, ou plutôt je suis mon corps."

2 Prereflective bodily self-consciousness is close to Hurley's notion of "perspectival self-consciousness" (Hurley 1998, pp. 140–143). Perspectival self-consciousness is awareness of one's own intentional motor agency in perception. This sort of awareness is constitutive of having a unified perspective on the world, such that one is able to keep track of the interdependence of one's perception and action. According to Hurley, perspectival self-consciousness does not involve conceptually structured thought or inference (but see Noë 2002a and 2004). Perspectival self-consciousness is not equivalent to everything phenomenol-

ogists mean by the notion of prereflective bodily self-consciousness; rather, it is equivalent to that part of bodily self-consciousness that involves action consciousness.

3 Prereflective self-consciousness is consciousness of one's body-as-subject and therefore is not equivalent to proprioception, if proprioception is understood as a mode of perceptual awareness of one's body-as-object. Whether proprioception should be understood this way is a matter of debate among philosophers. Bermúdez (1998) argues that proprioception is a form of perception; Gallagher (2003) argues that it is a form of non-perceptual bodily awareness; Legrand (2006) contends that it is a form of perception and is not sufficient for prereflective self-consciousness.

4 One might try to argue that one's impression that there is such an unreflected experience prior to reflection is a kind of illusion, that reflection creates what it reflects upon (this seems to be the view of Blackmore 2002). But I see little to recommend this line of thought. Reflection comprises attention and meta-awareness, and although these mental functions modify experience, there is no compelling reason to think that they invariably create their own content out of material that is completely nonconscious or has no phenomenal character whatsoever. On the contrary, this position leaves reflection unmotivated and thus inexplicable. What could motivate reflection, in the ongoing course of one's mental life, other than one's being prereflectively affected? Another problem is that prereflective self-awareness is entailed by the structure of time-consciousness, as we will see in Chapter 11.

5 Merleau-Ponty here alludes to a passage from Husserl's *Ideas II:* "Touching my left hand, I have touch-appearances, that is to say, I do not just sense, but I perceive and have appearances of a soft, smooth hand, with such a form. The indicational sensations of movement and the representational sensations of touch, which are Objectified as features of the thing, 'left hand,' belong in fact to my right hand. But when I touch the left I also find in it, too, series of touch-sensations, which are '*localized*' in it, though these are not constitutive of properties (such as roughness or smoothness of the hand, this physical thing). If I speak of the *physical* thing, 'left hand,' then I am abstracting from these sensations (a ball of lead has nothing like them and likewise for every 'merely' physical thing, everything that is not my Body). If I do include them, then it is not that the physical thing is now richer, but instead *it becomes Body, it senses*" (Husserl 1989, p. 152; emphasis in the original).

6 See (Noë 2004) for critical discussion of Humphrey's view from the perspective of the dynamic sensorimotor approach. See also Humphrey

(2001) and O'Regan and Noë (2001b) for a critical exchange on these issues.

7 Noë (2004), however, no longer maintains this view.

8 I do not mean to imply that something is experienced as other simply because it is external to one's biological membrane. As Merleau-Ponty writes: "The blind man's stick has ceased to be an object for him, and is no longer perceived for itself; its point has become an area of sensitivity, extending the scope and active radius of touch, and providing a parallel to sight. In the exploration of things, the length of the stick does not enter expressly as a middle term: the blind man is rather aware of it through the position of objects than of the position of objects through it . . . To get used to a hat, a car or a stick is to be transplanted into them, or conversely, to incorporate them into the bulk of our own body" (Merleau-Ponty 1962, p. 143).

9 Compare Husserl's description of this sort of case: "a soft noise becoming louder and louder takes on a growing affectivity in this materially relevant transformation; the vivacity of it in consciousness increases. This means that it exercises a growing pull on the ego. The ego finally turns toward it. However, examining this more precisely, the modal transformation of affection has already occurred prior to the turning toward. Along with a certain strength that is at work under the given affective circumstances, the pull proceeding from the noise has so genuinely struck the ego that it has come into relief for the ego, even if only in the antechamber of the ego. The ego already detects it now in its particularity even though it does not yet pay attention to it by grasping it in an attentive manner. This 'already detecting' means that in the ego a positive tendency is awakened to turn toward the object, its 'interest' is aroused—it becomes an acutely active interest in and through the turning toward in which this positive tendency, which goes from the ego-pole toward the noise, is fulfilled in the striving-toward. Now we understand the essential modal transformation that has occurred here. First an increasing affection; but the affective pull is not yet, from the standpoint of the ego, a counter-pull, not yet a responsive tendency toward the allure issuing from the object, a tendency that for its part can assume the new mode of an attentively grasping tendency. There are further distinctions that can be made here, but they do not concern us at this time" (Husserl 2001, p. 215). This description is explicitly temporal and dynamic; it displays phenomenal consciousness as characterized by continual, graded transformations of accessibility or access potential; and it roots modal transformations of consciousness in the dynamics of affect and movement tendencies (emotion).

10 Jennifer Church makes a similar point: "the access*ibility* (i.e., the access *potential*) of the hearing experience is evident from the fact that I do eventually access it. Further, it seems that I *would* have accessed it sooner had it been a matter of greater importance—and thus, in a still stronger sense, it was accessible all along. Finally, it is not even clear that it was not *actually* accessed all along insofar as it rationally guided my behaviour in causing me to speak louder, or move closer, and so forth" (Church 1997, p. 426).

10. Look Again

1 For this debate, see the articles collected in Block (1981a, 1981b). See also Rollins (1989) and Tye (1991).

2 How to specify precisely what makes a representation depictive is a difficult matter. Kosslyn (1994, p. 5) defines a depictive representation as "a type of picture, which specifies the locations and values of configurations of points in a space. For example, a drawing of a box would be a depictive representation. The space in which the points appear need not be physical, such as this page, but can be like an array in a computer, which specifies spatial relations purely functionally. That is, the physical locations in the computer of each point in an array are not themselves arranged into an array; it is only by virtue of how this information is 'read' and processed that it comes to function as if it were arranged into an array (with some points being close, some far, some falling along a diagonal, and so on). In a depictive representation, each part of an object is represented by a pattern of points, and the spatial relations among these patterns in the functional space correspond to the spatial relations among the parts themselves. Depictive representations convey meaning via their resemblance to an object, with parts corresponding to parts of the object." For critical discussion of this concept of depictive representation, see Pylyshyn (2002, 2003a, pp. 328–333). See also Tye (1991, pp. 33–60) for helpful clarifications.

3 This clip can be viewed at:
http://viscog.beckman.uiuc.edu/grafs/demos/15.html

4 My use of Mach's picture builds on Noë (2004, Chapter 2) and Thompson, Noë, and Pessoa (1998, pp. 194–195).

5 Of course, picture-viewing also involves sensorimotor and mental exploration of the picture. My point, however, is that visual experience is not determinate in its contents in the way the surface of a picture is determinate in its qualitative features.

6 Wittgenstein comments on this feature of Mach's drawing in his *Philo-*

sophical Remarks (267). According to Wittgenstein, Mach confuses a (visual) phenomenological mode of representation and a physical mode of representation. See Noë (2004, pp. 71–72).

7 This idea goes back to G. E. Moore: "When we try to introspect the sensation of blue, all we can see is the blue; the other element is as if it were diaphanous. Yet it *can* be distinguished if we look attentively enough, and if we know there is something to look for" (Moore 1993, p. 25). Note that Moore here states that the visual sensation is *as if it were* diaphanous but that it *can* be distinguished, a view in keeping with his sense-data theory of perception. H. P. Grice, however, in his expression of the diaphanous idea, implied that we cannot introspectively distinguish any sensation distinct from what we see: "such experiences (if experiences they be) as seeing and feeling seem to be, as it were, diaphanous: if we were asked to pay close attention, on a given occasion, to our seeing or feeling as distinct from what was being seen or felt, we should not know how to proceed; and the attempt to describe the differences between seeing and feeling seems to dissolve into a description of what we see and what we feel" (Grice 2002, p. 45). For discussion of the transparency thesis, see Kind (2003); Martin (2002); Siewert (2004); and Stoljar (2004).

8 My usage of "subjective character of experience" is close to Kriegel's (2005). He uses the phrase to mean the implicit and nonreflective "for-me-ness" of conscious experience. For both Kriegel and me, the phenomenal character of experience is the compresence (to use his formulation) of qualitative character and subjective character (for-me-ness). In this view, every conscious mental state (every mental state with phenomenal character) is implicitly and nonreflectively self-aware (see Chapter 9).

9 This statement needs qualification. By "representationalism" I mean externalist representationalism. For a representationalist model of subjectivity, defined as the possession of a phenomenal first-person perspective, see Metzinger (2003). This model focuses on the phenomenal content of the first-person perspective, but it does not analyze the intentionality of mental acts as these are experienced in their subjective performance. It would take me too far afield to consider Metzinger's account here. For incisive criticism of this account from a phenomenological perspective, see Zahavi (2005b), and from an embodied dynamicist perspective consistent with phenomenology, see Legrand (2005).

10 Thus Harman says, "Nor does she experience any features of anything as intrinsic features of her experience. And that is true of you too." Similarly, Ian Gold, citing Harman, writes: "Experience, it is sometimes

said, is 'diaphanous': one sees through it to the object or property the experience is representing. The experience itself has no properties accessible to the experiencer" (Gold 2002, p. 190).

11 See Kind (2003, p. 230). She distinguishes between "strong" and "weak" transparency claims, whose formulations differ from mine.

12 I do not mean to imply that all imagining is voluntary and effortful in this way. Daydreaming, reverie, and fantasy are usually not. See Sartre (2004 pp. 18–19): "In most cases, no doubt, the [mental] image springs from a deep spontaneity that cannot be assimilated to the will . . . But involuntary and voluntary images represent two closely related types of consciousness, of which one is produced by a voluntary spontaneity and the other by a spontaneity without will."

13 Dainton (2000, 2002) has criticized what he calls *awareness-content dualism* in theories of consciousness. Crucial to this dualism as Dainton describes it is the view that awareness is a bare act devoid of any intrinsic phenomenal characteristics. The phenomenological differentiation of experience into intentional-act and intentional-object poles involves no commitment to this notion of bare awareness.

14 Kriegel (2004) interprets this implicit self-awareness as a form of marginal or peripheral awareness. This view can also be found in Gurwitsch (1964). The problem with this view is that it treats one's nonreflective awareness of one's experiences on the model of one's implicit awareness of objects in the background of perception. Various arguments show, however, that experiences are not given as *objects* to self-awareness and that prereflective self-consciousness does not have a subject/object structure. See Chapter 11 and Zahavi (2005a).

15 Notice I say that the experience is not the object of another higher-order phenomenally conscious mental state. The reason is that I do not wish to beg the question against the higher-order thought theory of consciousness. According to this theory, a conscious mental state is one that is the object of an accompanying higher-order cognitive state that is not itself a conscious state. Thus this theory attempts to explain *intransitive* consciousness (a mental state's being a conscious mental state) in terms of *transitive* consciousness. (A mental state is intransitively conscious just in case one is transitively conscious of it, and to be transitively conscious of it is to have an accompanying higher-order thought that one is in that very state.) This theory is meant to be a substantive hypothesis about what intransitive consciousness is, not a phenomenological description. My point, however, is a phenomenological one: it is that experience involves an implicit self-awareness that is not a function of conscious reflection or introspection. The higher-order thought

theory is free to acknowledge this phenomenological point, but would aim to explain or analyze implicit self-awareness in terms of transitive consciousness and accompanying (nonconscious) higher-order thoughts. I think such accounts are unsuccessful, but I do not intend to argue for this point here. For the higher-order thought theory, see Rosenthal (1997). For rebuttals of the higher-order thought theory on behalf of a one-level account of consciousness as intransitive self-consciousness, see Kriegel (2003a) and Zahavi and Parnas (1998).

16 There is a large phenomenological literature on whether this activity of making features of experience explicit and available for phenomenological consideration is primarily descriptive or interpretive, and whether it must involve an objectifying (and hence distorting) form of reflection. For some recent discussions, see Poellner (2003); Stawarska (2002); and Zahavi (2005a).

17 The claim that imagination is a necessary constituent of pictorial experience is controversial. Now classic discussions are Walton (1990) and Wolheim (1980, 1987). For recent discussions, see Hopkins (1998); Levinson (1998); Lopes (1996); and Wolheim (1998).

18 Cf. Searle (1983, pp. 45–46): "If, for example, I see a yellow station wagon in front of me, the experience I have is directly of the object. It doesn't just 'represent' the object, it provides direct access to it. The experience has a kind of directness, immediacy and involuntariness which is not shared by a belief which I might have about the object in its absence. It seems therefore unnatural to describe visual experiences as representations . . . Rather, because of the special features of perceptual experiences I propose to call them 'presentations.' The visual experience I will say does not just represent the state of affairs perceived; rather, when satisfied, it gives direct access to it, and in that sense it is a presentation of that state of affairs."

19 For this notion of the "neutrality modification" applied to belief, see Husserl (1983, §109, pp. 257–259). For discussion of the role that neutralization plays in imagination, see Marbach (1993, pp. 75–76).

20 See Marbach (1993, pp. 76–77). He distinguishes between "imagining a real possibility concerning, e.g., a thing, event, situation, etc. that one believes to exist in the real world" and "imagining a mere possibility, i.e. something purely fictional."

21 Martin (2002) makes this point and uses it to construct an argument against representationalism analogous to the representationalist's phenomenal-transparency argument against the sense-datum theory.

22 The status of fiction in relation to the imagination is a distinct problem in its own right and is beyond the scope of this chapter. As Stawarska

(2001, p. 101) observes: "One wonders . . . whether it is . . . justified to subsume the *non-existence* of purely fictional characters under the heading of 'absence.' It seems more appropriate to take *non-existence* as the contrary of *existence* and to ascribe *absence* and *presence* (existential categories) to beings that are posited as *existent* only. A centaur cannot be absent (nor present) since it does not belong to the class of things posited as existent." Indeed, Sartre himself notes, "It is only on the ground of sensory intuition that the words 'absent,' 'far from me,' can have a sense, on the ground of a sensory intuition that gives itself as not being able to take place" (2004, p. 13).

23 Earlier in the text (2004, p. 20), Sartre uses the figures of the Knight and Death in Dürer's engraving as an example of objects that are posited as nonexistent, that is, as fictions. Sartre's account of imagination actually contains a tension between assimilating imagining to a kind of pictorial consciousness and conceiving of imagining as a *sui generis* type of mental activity that cannot be analyzed in pictorial terms. See Stawarska (2001) and McCulloch (1994, Chapter 5).

24 Nevertheless, Sartre states in a footnote: "This suspension of belief remains a positional act" (2004, p. 197, n. 10). As he also makes clear later in the text: "one of the essential factors of the imaging consciousness is belief. This belief aims at the object of the image. All imaging consciousness has a certain positional quality in relation to its object. An imaging consciousness is, indeed, consciousness of an *object as imaged*, and not consciousness *of an image*" (p. 86; emphasis in original). Suspension of belief is positional because it is a feature of what Sartre calls positional or thetic consciousness, that is, object-directed consciousness (consciousness that posits an object). But image consciousness also includes (as does all consciousness) a nonpositional or nonthetic consciousness of itself, that is, an intransitive (non-object-directed) and prereflective self-consciousness: "the imaging consciousness that we produce before a photograph is an act and this act includes a nonthetic consciousness of itself as spontaneity. We have consciousness, of some sort, of *animating* the photo, of lending life to it in order to make an image of it" (p. 25). This remark indicates that, for Sartre, prereflective self-consciousness does not have a subject/object structure, and therefore it cannot be analyzed as a form of marginal, peripheral, or background awareness.

25 See Sartre (2004, p. 57): "The image is defined by its intention. It is the intention that makes it the case that the image of Pierre is consciousness of Pierre. If the intention is taken at its origin, which is to say as it springs from our spontaneity, it already implies, no matter how naked and bare it may seem, a certain knowledge: it is, hypothetically, the

knowledge *(connaissance)* of Pierre . . . But the intention does not limit itself, in the image, to aiming at Pierre in an indeterminate fashion: he is aimed at as blond, tall, with a snub or aquiline nose, etc. It must therefore be charged with knowledge *(connaissances)*, it must aim through a certain layer of consciousness that we can call the layer of knowledge. So that, in the imaging consciousness, one can distinguish knowledge and intention only by abstraction. The intention is defined only by the knowledge since one represents in image only what one knows in some sort of way and, reciprocally, knowledge here is not simply knowledge, it is an act, it is what I want to represent to myself . . . Naturally, this knowledge should not be considered as added to an already constituted image to clarify it: it is the active structure of the image."

26 Because of these characteristics of imagining—the determination of its content by knowledge and intention, as well as the essential unexplorability of the imagined object—Sartre describes the intentional attitude of imagining as one of "quasi-observation," by which he means an attitude of observation, but an observation that does not teach anything (2004, p. 10). As McGinn (2004, pp. 19–20) notes, this formulation should be modified to allow for the possibility of cognitive enhancement (for example, problem solving) by imagining.

27 Pylyshyn routinely conflates this hypothesis with the substantive hypothesis that all cognition involves the same propositional format, namely, a "language of thought." But to pretend that the language of thought hypothesis does not have its own deep conceptual problems (where does the semantics of the symbols come from?), analogous to those that dog pictorialism, is sheer bluster.

28 Sartre compromised this insight, however, by falling back into treating imaging consciousness as a species of pictorial consciousness. See Stawarska (2001).

29 Indeed, although it is unlikely in our day and age, it is certainly imaginable that there could be a subject who gave such a report and did not even know he had a brain, or thought that mental processes were really carried out by the heart.

30 Recall that the sort of phenomenology I am concerned with in the context of this chapter is static phenomenology. Other forms of phenomenology would not describe their mode of access to phenomena in this way. To equate phenomenology with one particular way of doing phenomenology would be a leveling misrepresentation. Different ways of doing phenomenology are appropriate in different contexts. In this respect, phenomenology is no different from science or philosophy

overall. The conviction animating this chapter is simply that static phenomenological analysis is directly relevant to the imagery debate in cognitive science.

31 Dennett writes: "[O]f course experimenters on illusions rely on subjects' introspective beliefs (as expressed in their judgments) about how
things seem to them, but that is the agnosticism of heterophenomenology; to go beyond it would be, for instance, to assume that in size illusions there really are visual images of different sizes somewhere in
subjects' brains (or minds), which of course no researcher would dream
of doing" (2005, p. 54). In this last statement, we see the same bias
toward interpreting first-person reports as expressions of belief about
what is going on in the brain or mind considered as a subpersonal cognitive system. Goldman (2004) usefully terms this sort of interpretation
"architecturally loaded" (because it interprets subjects as expressing beliefs about their subpersonal cognitive architecture). He writes: "The
following . . . seems like a reasonable rule of thumb: 'When considering
an introspective report, and a choice is available between an *architecturally loaded* interpretation of the report and an *architecturally neutral* interpretation, always prefer the latter.' This is just the opposite of Dennett's practice. His proclivity is to interpret ordinary introspective
reports in architecturally loaded terms" (Goldman 2004, p. 12).

11. Temporality and the Living Present

1 Husserl's writings on time-consciousness include the famous "Lectures
on the Consciousness of Internal Time from the Year 1905," published
together with other writings from the years 1893–1917 (Husserl 1991).
In addition are Husserl's still untranslated "Bernauer Manuscripts" on
time-consciousness, written during 1917–1918, as well as the so-called
unpublished C manuscripts in the Husserl archives from the years
1929–1935. For important treatments of Husserl's account of time-
consciousness, see John Barnett Brough's "Translators Introduction" to
Husserl's *On the Phenomenology of the Consciousness of Internal Time*
(Husserl 1991, pp. xi–lvii), and Bernet, Kern, and Marbach (1993, pp.
101–114); Brough (1972, 1989); Gallagher (1998); Rodemeyer (2003);
Smith (2003, pp. 86–100); and Zahavi (2003a, pp. 80–98, 2003b,
2005a). See also Sokolowski (2000, pp. 130–145) for a clear and elo-
quent introduction to the Husserlian phenomenology of time-
consciousness.

2 I say temporal *unity,* not temporal *object,* for we should not assume that
any experience of which we become reflectively aware should be de-

scribed (at least phenomenologically) as an *internal object* (though re-
solving this matter will clearly depend on what we mean by "object").

3 Varela does not indicate whether the correspondence here is type-type
or merely token-token—that is, whether every type of cognitive act corresponds to a specific type of neural assembly, or merely whether any
particular token cognitive act corresponds to a particular token neural
assembly (such that there can be variation in the token neural assemblies corresponding to token cognitive acts of the same type). He does
indicate, however, that the hypothesis is meant to be a strong one that
predicts that only one dominant or major neural assembly is present
during a cognitive act and that physiological correlates associated with
the assembly should be repeatedly detected for different instances of
the same act. This demand suggests that the hypothesis is meant to
imply a type-type correspondence. Nevertheless, the hypothesis needs
to be taken in a statistical sense to allow for the fact that endogenous
neural activity is highly variable and modulates responses to a given
stimulus (see David et al. 2002, p. 56).

4 Synchrony in this context refers to the relation between the temporal
structures of the signals regardless of signal amplitude. Two signals are
said to be synchronous if their rhythms coincide. In signals with a dominant oscillatory mode, synchronization means the adjustment of the
rhythmicity of two oscillators in a *phase locking*: $n\phi_1(t) - m\phi_2(t) = const$,
where $\phi_1(t), \phi_2(t)$ are the instantaneous phases of the oscillators, and
n, m are integers indicating the ratios of possible frequency locking. It is
usually assumed for simplicity that $n = m = 1$, but there is also evidence
for 1:2 and 1:3 phase synchrony (see Varela et al. 2001; Le Van Quyen
2003).

5 For attention and working memory, see Fries et al. (2001); Sarntheim et
al. (1998); von Stein and Sarntheim (2000); and von Stein, Chiang, and
König (2000). For sensorimotor integration, see Kahana, Seelig, and
Madsen (2001); O'Keefe and Burgess (1999).

6 Complex nonlinear forms of cross-band synchrony, so-called generalized
synchrony (Schiff et al. 1996), are also to be expected and may prove
more relevant in the long run to understanding large-scale integration
than strict phase synchrony (Friston 2000a, 2000b; Le Van Quyen 2003).

7 In a subsequent study, Rodriguez and colleagues have shown using a
masking paradigm that conscious perception correlates mainly with
phase synchrony and not gamma oscillations (Melloni and Rodriguez
2005).

8 For further discussion, see Faure and Korn (2001); Friston (2000a,
2000b); Kelso (1995); Korn and Faure (2003); and Tsuda (2001).

9 This section draws from the detailed treatments in Lutz and Thompson (2003), and Thompson, Lutz, and Cosmelli (2005).

10 Metzinger (2003, p. 592) concludes that "first-person data do not exist" because "first-person access to the phenomenal content of one's own mental states does not fulfill the defining criteria for the concept of 'data.'" According to Metzinger, these criteria are, first, extraction from the physical world by technical measuring devices with well-defined public procedures; and second, collection or generation among groups of human beings, specifically "scientific communities open to criticism and constantly seeking independent means of verification."

This conception is faulty, however. Data are something given (from the Latin *datum*). What is given in a scientific context are observations and records of observations. Not all recorded observations are measurements. (Think of a naturalist who observes and describes animal behavior in its natural setting, or an anthropologist recording the customs of a people.) Metzinger is right to call attention to the intersubjective nature of data, but he is mistaken to think that first-person reports about experience based on first-person access to one's own mental states cannot be intersubjective and open to critical evaluation. Finally, first-person data are precisely what psychologists and psychiatrists are collecting when they ask subjects in interviews or through questionnaires to describe their experience.

11 The term *phenomenology* in this context is not limited to phenomenology in the European sense stemming from Husserl, but includes any systematic project of investigating and describing experience. So understood, phenomenology includes Asian traditions, in particular the various Buddhist and Hindu philosophical analyses of the nature of the mind and consciousness, based on contemplative mental training. The relationship of these schools to Western phenomenology and mind science is beyond the scope of this book, and will be the subject of future work. For further discussion, see Dreyfus and Thompson (2007); Lutz, Dunne, and Davidson (2007); and Varela, Thompson, and Rosch (1991).

12 Preliminary examples of this third step can be found in neurophenomenological studies of epilepsy (Le Van Quyen and Petitmengin 2002; Petitmengin 2005) and pain (Price, Barrell, and Rainville 2001; Rainville 2005).

13 Chalmers (2000, p. 25) defines minimal sufficiency as follows: "(1) the states of N suffice for the corresponding states of consciousness, and (2) no proper part M of N is such that the states of M suffice for the corresponding states of consciousness."

14 The idea of consciousness as a unified field of subjective experience has long been central to phenomenology (see Gurwitsch 1964).

15 Ronald Bruzina, in his review of *Naturalizing Phenomenology* (Petitot et al. 1999), argues that the neural analogue of the formal structure of temporality cannot be taken to provide an account of the specifically temporal character of experience because the threefold structure of temporality is an intentional structure, not a spatially extended one like the neural analogue (Bruzina 2004, p. 76). This point about the intentional structure of temporality not being spatial is crucial. Yet although the brain as a physical entity is clearly laid out in space, the dynamical form or structure of its processes is not itself a spatially extended structure (a point already seen by Merleau-Ponty 1963, p. 72). It is at this level of dynamical form that we are supposed to find the neural analogue of the threefold structure of time-consciousness. We use the geometrical techniques of phase space to represent this dynamical form to ourselves, but this is analogous to Husserl's use of geometrical diagrams to represent the threefold structure of temporality.

16 Varela introduces the notion of "generative passages" between phenomenology and science to describe this idea. See Varela (1997b) and Roy et al. (1999, p. 68). See also Lutz (2002), and for critical discussion see Bayne (2004).

12. Primordial Dynamism

1 Varela's dynamical account of protention is close to Kelso's dynamical account of intention in which intention is an order parameter for the coordination dynamics of intentional behavior (see Kelso 1995, pp. 137–158). See also Walter Freeman's (1999a, 1999b, 2000) neurodynamical model of emotion, intention, and consciousness, discussed in this chapter.

2 For the neuroscience of emotion, see Panksepp (1998a). For comprehensive collections of neuroscientific and psychological discussions of emotion, see Davidson, Scherer, and Goldsmith (2003); Ekman and Davidson (1994); Lane and Nadel (2000); and Lewis and Haviland-Jones (2000). For psychoneuroimmunological views of emotion, see Maier and Watkins (1998); Pert (1997); and Pert et al. (1985). For affect and consciousness, see Damasio (1999). For emotion experience, see Lambie and Marcel (2002), and the articles collected in Colombetti and Thompson (2005a).

3 For a thorough critical discussion and rebuttal of the position that there is no such thing as emotion, see Charland (2001).

4 LeDoux is well known for his rejection of the concept of the limbic system and the associated limbic system theory of emotion (see LeDoux 1996, pp. 98–103). Freeman's view of the limbic system as a neurodynamic source of intentional action, described in this chapter, is significantly different from the limbic system theory of emotion criticized by LeDoux. For a spirited defense of the limbic system concept see Panksepp (2002).

5 For further discussion of the relation between Lewis's model of emotion and the enactive approach, see Colombetti (in press); Colombetti and Thompson (2005b, 2006).

6 It can also be discerned psychotherapeutically through what Daniel Stern (2004) calls the "micro-analytic interview." His study *The Present Moment in Psychotherapy and Everyday Life* offers many interesting points of convergence with the neurophenomenological approach to time and affect presented here.

7 Varela and Depraz (2005, pp. 67–68) provide a description of the experience from Varela's notes: "Today went to the concert at 11, a certain heaviness in my eyelids, and a bit of a moody blues as setting. I'm sitting leaning forward onto the edge of the 2nd balcony. The musicians (sublime Italian ensemble) arrive, tune up, and settle, a short silence and then begin with the sonata of the *Musical Offering,* which I love. Instantly, within the first five or six notes of the main theme, the break in mood and feeling tone arises: suddenly my chest heaves a little, my skin becomes goose-bumpy and it is as if the body is brought into position. Almost at the same time there is a wave of beauty, of poignancy which brings sudden tears into my eyes, an intensified breathing. Without premeditation, I feel my eyes close and I lean backwards to relax my body into complete receptivity. My mental-space seems to spread out and my ego-center to become almost imperceptible. By the time the first variation of the musical theme starts the feeling tone is fully formed and the first waves of thought-wandering have begun, the first being a memory of another occasion when the very same music also touched me to tears. The whole thing has lasted a mere fraction of a second."

8 At one point, Husserl's description is strikingly reminiscent of the state-space descriptions of dynamic systems theory: "I have already employed the quite suitable expression, affective relief. On the one hand, this alludes to a unity [the content of the 'living present' of experience], on the other hand, to a difference of 'peaks' for the different particular moments [the distinct contents synthesized within the living present], finally, too, the possibility of entire augmentations or entire diminutions insofar as the affective relief can arch out more prominently or be-

come more flattened depending upon the alterations of the living present" (2001, p. 216).

13. Empathy and Enculturation

1 My discussion of empathy in this chapter draws heavily, with revision, from Thompson (2001, 2005).

2 The following discussion is based on Zahavi (1997).

3 One might argue that although the co-intended absent profiles cannot be intended as the correlates of my fictitious co-present perceptions, they can be intended as the correlates of my perceptions were I to walk around the thing and look at it from over there. The problem with this interpretation, however, is that it makes the absent profiles the correlates of my possible future perceptions, which has already been shown to be inadequate. Moreover, this interpretation itself involves the open intersubjectivity of consciousness, in the form of the alterity or otherness built into consciousness, for it requires that one imagine or otherwise mentally grasp oneself as altered or othered in relation to one's present self.

4 Here I follow Zahavi (1997, pp. 313–319).

5 This work was Stein's 1916 doctoral dissertation, prepared under Husserl's supervision. Stein draws from Husserl's discussion of empathy in his *Ideas II* (Husserl 1989), but develops Husserl's ideas in her own unique way. For discussion of the similarities and differences between Stein's and Husserl's views on empathy, see Leask (2002).

6 Heidegger (1995, pp. 201–209) rejects the concept of empathy *(Einfühlung)* as an erroneous way of understanding human relations because it presupposes "that we must first 'feel our way into' the other being in order to reach it. And this implies that we are 'outside' in the first place" (p. 203). For Heidegger, "being-with" belongs to the essence of our existence, and we are always already "transposed" into one another, prior to any particular attempt to grasp the feelings of another. Heidegger's criticism of the concept of empathy is insightful and important. In my view, however, Husserl's concept of empathy remains important, particularly when the overall framework of Husserl's view of intersubjectivity is taken into account (see Zahavi 2001b). In completely rejecting empathy, Heidegger loses touch with the affective and corporeal aspects of intersubjectivity. In this connection, it is worth noting that Merleau-Ponty, in his lecture course *Nature*, explicitly retakes Husserl's notion of empathy *(Einfühlung)* and uses it to describe how the body in its esthesiological and libidinal being both projects into and

introjects other bodies, thereby constituting an "intercorporeity" (Merleau-Ponty 2003, pp. 210, 218, 225).

Appendix A

1 See Langsdorf (1985); Marbach (1993); Roy (1995); Roy et al. (1999, pp. 57–60); Welton (2000, pp. 393–404); and Zahavi (2003a, pp. 53–68, 2004a).

2 Here I follow the nonrepresentationalist interpretation of Husserl. Dreyfus is an exponent of the representationalist interpretation. See Drummond (2003) and Zahavi (2004a).

3 This point bears further elaboration: (1) "Operative intentionality [*fungierende Intentionalität*] designates prereflective experience that is functional without having to be thematic or engaged in an explicit epistemic acquisition. It constitutes the prepredicative unity of objects, of the world, and of our life. This dimension of experience is described by Husserl under the aegis of 'aesthetic experience,' and more particularly with the expressions 'passive synthesis' and 'instinct' or 'drive-intentionality' [*Triebintentionalität*]. For Merleau-Ponty operative intentionality includes the intentionality of movement, erotic intentionality, the habitual body, etc. Phenomenological analyses of these modes of intentionality take place on the level of the lived-body [*Leib, le corps propre*]" (Steinbock 1999, p. 183; see also Mensch 1998). (2) Dreyfus cites a passage from Husserl's *Crisis* (1970, p. 149) and describes him as there asserting the possibility of gaining access to a "dormant intentionality" corresponding to "the 'intentional history' of what we now simply take for granted" (Dreyfus 1982, p. 24). Yet the dormant intentionality with which Husserl is concerned in this passage is operative intentionality, not object-directed intentionality. (3) Husserl does not assert in this passage, as Dreyfus puts it, "that we always have access to the content of our intentional states" (Dreyfus 1982, p. 24). Rather, Husserl explicitly states: "every straightforwardly performed validity in natural world-life always presupposes validities extending back, immediately or mediately, into a necessary subsoil of obscure but *occasionally available* reactivatable validities . . ." [emphasis added]. Of course, there remains the important problem of what it means to gain access to the emergence of the given (object-directed intentionality) from the pregiven (operative intentionality). But Dreyfus's interpretation of Husserl (according to which all intentionality is object-directed and we have straightforward access to the content of all such intentional states) does not allow for the proper formulation of this problem. (4) Given the strong linkage between Husserl

and Merleau-Ponty on the topic of operative intentionality (and given
that Husserl does not subscribe to a representational theory of mind), it
is inaccurate to state that "Merleau-Ponty . . . developed [his] views in
opposition to Husserl's insistence on the philosophical priority of the
analysis of the representational content of individual intentional states"
(1982, pp. 2–3). On the contrary, Merleau-Ponty (in his *Phenomenology of
Perception*) can be seen as a direct descendant of Husserl's genetic phenomenology of the lived body (see Zahavi 2002b).

4 Dreyfus states that Husserl learned from Heidegger the idea "that all
cognition depends on a world in which we are involved and which can
never be made explicit as an object" (Dreyfus 1982, p. 23). Yet he provides no evidence for this relationship between Husserl and Heidegger.
According to Welton (2000, pp. 120, 339), Husserl had been working
on the notion of the life-world already in the early 1920s (Heidegger's
Being and Time was published in 1927) and his work in the 1930s does
not show any direct influence of Heidegger's notion of the world.

5 See Depraz (1999a); Gupta (1998, 2003, 2004); Laycock (1994);
Lusthaus (2002); and Yamaguchi (1997).

Appendix B

1 See Andersen et al. (2000); Schröder (1998); Silberstein (2001, 2002);
Silberstein and McGeever (1999); and Van Gulick (2001).

2 Juarrero treats autopoietic and autocatalytic systems as if they were
equivalent, but they are not.

3 Another holistic view of emergence goes further by seeing emergence
as a kind of fusion (Humphreys 1996, 1997a, 1997b). The difference between fusion and relational holism is that a fusion is not a relational
structure because the previously unrelated elements are "used up" in
the fusion.

4 See Belousek (2003); Hawthorne and Silberstein (1995); Healey
(1991); Humphreys (1996, 1997a, 1997b); Kronz and Tiehen (2002);
and Maudlin (1998).

5 Ontological emergence in the form of relational holism violates atomistic mereological supervenience, but perhaps not every form of mereological supervenience. Atomism states that every property of a whole is
logically supervenient on, or logically determined by, the intrinsic properties of the whole's most fundamental parts. In this view, every relation
is a reducible relation. Yet, if mereological supervenience were taken
more liberally to mean that every property of a whole is logically supervenient on, or logically determined by, the properties of the parts and

their relations—where this allows for nonatomistic or irreducible relations—then mereological supervenience would be consistent with relational holism. This differentiation of versions of mereological supervenience is not too important at this stage of the discussion. It becomes relevant when we discuss emergence as understood by the classical British emergentists (Samuel Alexander, C. D. Broad, and C. Lloyd Morgan) and its influence on contemporary philosophy of mind (see Kim 1999). The British emergentists apparently believed, according to Jaegwon Kim's (1999) interpretation, that emergent properties are not identical with macrolevel, organizational properties (whether or not holistic), but are additional distinct properties that supervene on those organizational properties as their emergence bases. The emergence of such distinct, irreducible properties (such as "life" or "consciousness") given a sufficient macrolevel organization, and their supervenience on that macrolevel, were taken as brute facts of nature, to be accepted in an "attitude of natural piety" in Samuel Alexander's phrase.

6 If one criterion of ontological emergence is that it not be an artifact of our theories or models, and if quantum mechanics is supposed to be the best case of ontological emergence, then it would seem a realist interpretation of quantum mechanics is being assumed. Whether there is a coherent realist interpretation of quantum mechanics is an unresolved matter. Bitbol (in press) presents a critical discussion of the realist premises of philosophical treatments of emergence in quantum mechanics. His de-ontologized conception of emergence is close to my conception of dynamic co-emergence.

7 Therefore it would seem that Kim is mistaken when he writes: "A whole has a certain emergent property, M, at a given time, t, and the fact that this property emerges at t is dependent on its having a certain microconfiguration at t, and this includes a given constituent of it, a_j, having P_j at t. That is, unless a_j had P_j at t, W could not have had its emergent property M at t" (1999, p. 29). But if W is a complex system with structural stability, then it could well have had its emergent property M at t, without its constituent a_j having had P_j at t.

8 Cf. Kronz and Tiehen (2002, pp. 332–333): "the British emergentists may have placed too much emphasis on the Newtonian formulation of classical physics in motivating their metaphysical doctrine by regarding forces as fundamental, and then developing their metaphysics by analogy with the way in which forces behave . . . If they had modeled their metaphysical doctrines on the Hamiltonian formulation of classical mechanics, in which energies (both kinetic and potential) are fundamental, the associated metaphysical doctrine may have had a very

different character. Poincaré was aware of chaotic classical models, and that they involved nonseparable Hamiltonians; but it is unclear whether the British emergentists were familiar with them."

9 In a mere three sentences in his "Making Sense of Emergence" Kim confronts the Kantian problematic of self-organization (from Kant's *Critique of Judgment*) and casually dismisses it without so much as a mention: "But how is it possible for the whole to causally affect its constituent parts on which its very existence and nature depend? If causation or determination is transitive, doesn't this ultimately imply a kind of self-causation, or self-determination—an apparent absurdity? It seems to me that there is reason to worry about the coherence of the whole idea" (1999, p. 28).

References

Abraham, R., and Shaw, C. (1982–1988). *Dynamics: A Visual Introduction.* Santa Cruz, CA: Ariel Press.

Adolphs, R. (2003). Cognitive neuroscience of human social behavior. *Nature Reviews Neuroscience* 4: 165–178.

Agre, P. E. (1995). Computational research on interaction and agency. *Artificial Intelligence* 72: 1–52.

Allman, J. M. (1999). *Evolving Brains.* New York: Scientific American Library.

Andersen, P. B., Emmeche, C., Finnemann, N. O., and Christiansen, P. V., eds. (2000). *Downward Causation. Minds, Bodies and Matter.* Aarhus, Denmark: Aarhus University Press.

Arendt, D., and Jung, K. N. (1994). Inversion of dorso ventral axis? *Nature* 371: 26.

Arthur, W. (2002). The emerging conceptual framework of evolutionary developmental biology. *Nature* 415: 757–764.

Atmanspacher, H., and Bishop, R., eds. (2002). *Between Chance and Choice: Interdisciplinary Perspectives on Determinism.* Thorverton, UK: Imprint Academic.

Austin, J. H. (1998). *Zen and the Brain.* Cambridge, MA: MIT Press.

Bachman, P. A., Luisi, P. L., and Lang, J. (1992). Autocatalytic self-replicating micelles as models for prebiotic structures. *Nature* 357: 57–59.

Bach-y-Rita, P. (2002). Sensory substitution and qualia. In A. Noë and E. Thompson, eds., *Vision and Mind: Selected Readings in the Philosophy of Perception,* pp. 497–514. Cambridge, MA: MIT Press.

Barresi, J., and Moore, C. (1996). Intentional relations and social understanding. *Behavioral and Brain Sciences* 19: 107–154.

483

Bateson, G. (1972). *Steps toward an Ecology of Mind.* New York: Ballantine
   Books.
Bayne, T. (2004). Closing the gap? Some questions for neurophenome-
   nology. *Phenomenology and the Cognitive Sciences* 3: 349–364.
Bechtel, W., and Richardson, R. C. (1993). *Discovering Complexity: Decomposi-
   tion and Localization as Strategies in Scientific Research.* Princeton, NJ:
   Princeton University Press.
Beer, R. D. (2000). Dynamical approaches to cognitive science. *Trends in
   Cognitive Sciences* 4: 91–98.
Belousek, D. W. (2003). Non-separability, non-supervenience, and quantum
   ontology. *Philosophy of Science* 70: 791–811.
Bermúdez, J. L. (1998). *The Paradox of Self-Consciousness.* Cambridge, MA:
   MIT Press.
Bernet, R. (2002). Unconscious consciousness in Husserl and Freud. *Phe-
   nomenology and the Cognitive Sciences* 1: 327–351.
Bernet, R., Kern, I., and Marbach, E. (1993). *An Introduction to Husserlian
   Phenomenology.* Evanston, IL: Northwestern University Press.
Bishop, R. C. (2002). Downward causation in complex systems. British So-
   ciety for the Philosophy of Science Annual Meeting, Glasgow, Scotland,
   4–5 July 2002.
Bitbol, M. (2003). A cure for metaphysical illusions: Kant, quantum mechanics, and the Madhyamaka. In B. Alan Wallace, ed., *Buddhism and
   Science: Breaking New Ground,* pp. 325–361. New York: Columbia University Press.
———. (in press). Ontology, matter and emergence. *Phenomenology and the
   Cognitive Sciences.*
Bitbol, M., and Luisi, P. L. (2005). Autopoiesis with or without cognition:
   defining life at its edge. *Journal of the Royal Society Interface* 1: 99–107.
Blackmore, S. (2002). There is no stream of consciousness. *Journal of Consciousness Studies* 9: 17–28.
———. (2003). *Consciousness: An Introduction.* Oxon: Hodder & Stoughton.
Blackmore, S. J., Brelstaff, G., Nelson, K., and Troscianko, T. (1995). Is the
   richness of our visual world an illusion? Transaccadic memory for complex scenes. *Perception* 24: 1075–1081.
Blake, R. (2001). A primer on binocular rivalry, including current controversies. *Brain and Mind* 2: 5–38.
Blake, R., and Logothetis, N. (2002). Visual competition. *Nature Reviews
   Neuroscience* 3: 1–11.
Block, N., ed. (1981a). *Imagery.* Cambridge, MA: MIT Press/A Bradford Book.
———, ed. (1981b). *Readings in the Philosophy of Psychology,* vol. 2. Cambridge, MA: Harvard University Press.

———. (1983). Mental pictures and cognitive science. *Philosophical Review* 93: 499–542.

———. (1997). On a confusion about a function of consciousness. In N. Block, O. Flanagan, and G. Güzeldere, eds., *The Nature of Consciousness: Philosophical Debates*, pp. 375–416. Cambridge, MA: MIT Press/A Bradford Book.

Boden, M. (2000). Autopoiesis and life. *Cognitive Science Quarterly* 1: 117–145.

Bonner, J. T. (1980). *The Evolution of Culture in Animal Societies*. Princeton, NJ: Princeton University Press.

Botero, J.-J. (1999). The immediately given as ground and background. In J. Petitot, F. J. Varela, B. Pachoud, and J.-M. Roy, eds., *Naturalizing Phenomenology: Issues in Contemporary Phenomenology and Cognitive Science*, pp. 440–463. Stanford, CA: Stanford University Press.

Bourgine, P., and Stewart, J. (2004). Autopoiesis and cognition. *Artificial Life* 20: 327–345.

Bressler, S., and Kelso, J. A. S. (2001). Cortical coordination dynamics and cognition. *Trends in Cognitive Sciences* 5: 26–36.

Brockman, J. (1995). *The Third Culture*. New York: Simon & Schuster.

Brough, J. B. (1972). The emergence of an absolute consciousness in Husserl's early writings on time-consciousness. *Man and World* 5: 298–326.

———. (1989). Husserl's phenomenology of time-consciousness. In J. N. Mohanty and W. R. McKenna, eds., *Husserl's Phenomenology: A Textbook*, pp. 249–289. Washington, DC: Center for Advanced Research in Phenomenology.

Bruner, J. (1990). *Acts of Meaning*. Cambridge, MA: Harvard University Press.

Bruzina, R. (2004). Phenomenology and cognitive science: moving beyond the paradigms. *Phenomenology and the Cognitive Sciences* 20: 43–48.

Buccino, G., Binkofski, F., Fink, G. R., Fadiga, L., Fogassi, L., Gallese, V., Seitz, R. J., Zilles, K., Rizzolatti, G., and Freund, H.-J. (2001). Action observation activates premotor and parietal areas in a somatotopic manner: an fMRI study. *European Journal of Neuroscience* 13: 400–404.

Burian, R. M., and Richardson, R. C. (1996). Form and order in evolutionary biology. In M. Boden, ed., *The Philosophy of Artificial Life*, pp. 146–172. Oxford: Oxford University Press, 1996.

Buss, L. W. (1987). *The Evolution of Individuality*. Princeton, NJ: Princeton University Press.

Campbell, D. (1974). "Downward causation" in hierarchically organized biological systems. In F. J. Ayala and T. Dobzhansky, eds., *Studies in the Philosophy of Biology*, pp. 179–186. Berkeley: University of California Press.

Campbell, R. J., and Bickhard, M. H. (2002). Physicalism, emergence, and downward causation. Unpublished. URL: http://www.lehigh.edu/~mhb0/physicalemergence.pdf

Carr, L., Iacoboni, M., Dubeau, M.-C., Mazziotta, J. C., and Lenzi, J. L. (2003). Neural mechanisms of empathy in humans: a relay from neural systems for imitation to limbic areas. *Proceedings of the National Academy of Sciences USA* 100: 5497–5502.

Cartwright, N. (1997). Why physics? In R. Penrose, A. Shimony, N. Cartwright, and S. Hawking, *The Large, the Small, and the Human Mind,* pp. 161–168. Cambridge: Cambridge University Press.

Casey, E. (2000). *Imagining: A Phenomenological Study,* 2d ed. Bloomington: Indiana University Press.

Chalmers, D. J. (1996). *The Conscious Mind: In Search of a Fundamental Theory.* New York: Oxford University Press.

———. (1997). Moving forward on the problem of consciousness. *Journal of Consciousness Studies* 4: 3–46.

———. (2000). What is a neural correlate of consciousness? In T. Metzinger, ed., *Neural Correlates of Consciousness,* pp. 18–39. Cambridge, MA: MIT Press.

———. (2002). Consciousness and its place in nature. In D. J. Chalmers, ed., *Philosophy of Mind. Classical and Contemporary Readings,* pp. 247–272. New York: Oxford University Press.

Charland, L. C. (2001). In defence of "emotion": Critical notice of Paul E. Griffiths, *What Emotions Really Are: The Problem of Psychological Categories. Canadian Journal of Philosophy* 31: 133–154.

Chiel, H., and Beer, R. (1997). The brain has a body: adaptive behavior emerges from interactions of nervous system, body and environment. *Trends in Neurosciences* 20: 553–557.

Church, J. (1997). Fallacies or analyses? In N. Block, O. Flanagan, and G. Güzeldere, eds., *The Nature of Consciousness: Philosophical Debates,* pp. 425–426. Cambridge, MA: MIT Press/A Bradford Book.

Clark, A. (1997). *Being There: Putting Brain, Body, and World Together Again.* Cambridge, MA: MIT Press/A Bradford Book.

———. (2001). *Mindware. An Introduction to the Philosophy of Cognitive Science.* New York: Oxford University Press.

Clark, A., and Chalmers, D. (1998). The extended mind. *Analysis* 58: 7–19.

Coen, E. (1999). *The Art of the Genes: How Organisms Make Themselves.* Oxford: Oxford University Press.

Cole, J. (1997). On being "faceless": selfhood and facial embodiment. *Journal of Consciousness Studies* 4: 467–484.

Cole, J., Depraz, N., and Gallagher, S. (2000). Unity and disunity in bodily awareness: phenomenology and neuroscience. Association for the Scientific Study of Consciousness IV. Workshop. Brussels. URL: http://pegasus.cc.ucf.edu/~gallaghr/brus3.html

Colombetti, G. (2005). Appraising valence. In G. Colombetti and E. Thompson, eds., *Emotion Experience*, pp. 103–126. Thorverton, UK: Imprint Academic. Also published in *Journal of Consciousness Studies* 12: 103–126.

———. (in press). Enactive appraisal. *Phenomenology and the Cognitive Sciences.*

Colombetti, G., and Thompson, E., eds. (2005a). *Emotion Experience.* Thorverton, UK: Imprint Academic. Also published as a special issue of the *Journal of Consciousness Studies* 12(8–9).

———. (2005b). Enacting emotional interpretations with feeling. *Behavioral and Brain Sciences* 28: 200–201.

———. (2006). The feeling body: Toward an enactive approach to emotion. In W. Overton, U. Mueller, and J. Newman, eds., *Body in Mind, Mind in Body: Developmental Perspectives on Embodiment and Consciousness.* Mahwah, NJ: Lawrence Erlbaum.

Conway Morris, S. (1998). *The Crucible of Creation: The Burgess Shale and the Rise of Animals.* Oxford: Oxford University Press.

Cornell, J. F. (1986). A Newton of the grassblade? Darwin and the problem of organic teleology. *Isis* 77: 405–421.

Cosmelli, D., David, O., Lachaux, J.-P., Martinerie, J., Garnero, L., Renault, B., and Varela, F. J. (2004). Waves of consciousness: ongoing cortical patterns during binocular rivalry. *Neuroimage* 23: 128–140.

Cosmelli, D., Lachaux, J.-P., and Thompson, E. (2007). Neurodynamical approaches to consciousness. In P. D. Zelazo, M. Moscovitch, and E. Thompson, eds., *The Cambridge Handbook of Consciousness.* New York: Cambridge University Press.

Cottrell, A. (1999). Sniffing the camembert: on the conceivability of zombies. *Journal of Consciousness Studies* 6: 4–12.

Coutinho, A. (2003). A walk with Francisco Varela from first- to second-generation networks: in search of the structure, dynamics and metadynamics of an organism-centered immune system. *Biological Research* 36: 17–26.

Craig, A. D. (2002). How do you feel? Interoception: the sense of the physiological condition of the body. *Nature Reviews Neuroscience* 3: 655–666.

Crick, F. (1958). On protein synthesis. *Symposium of the Society for Experimental Biology* 12: 138–163.

———. (1994). *The Astonishing Hypothesis: The Scientific Search for the Soul.* New York: Scribner's.

Crowell, S. (in press). Phenomenological immanence and semantic externalism: a rapprochement. *Synthese,* in press.

Dainton, B. (2000). *Stream of Consciousness: Unity and Continuity in Conscious Experience.* London: Routledge Press.

———. (2002). The gaze of consciousness. *Journal of Consciousness Studies* 9: 31–48.

Damasio, A. R. (1990). Synchronous activation in multiple cortical regions: a mechanism for recall. *Seminars in the Neurosciences* 2: 287–297.

———. (1999). *The Feeling of What Happens: Body and Emotion in the Making of Consciousness.* New York: Harcourt Brace.

———. (2003). *Looking for Spinoza: Joy, Sorrow, and the Feeling Brain.* New York: Harcourt.

Darwin, C. (1996). *On Evolution: The Development of the Theory of Natural Selection.* Indianapolis, IN: Hackett Publishing Company.

David, O., Cosmelli, D., Hasboun, D., and Garnero, L. (2003). A multitrial analysis for revealing significant corticocortical networks in magentoencaphalography and electroencephalography. *Neuroimage* 20: 186–201.

David, O., Cosmelli, D., Lachaux, J.-P., Baillet, S., Garnero, L., and Martinerie, J. (2003). A theoretical and experimental introduction to the non-invasive study of large-scale neural phase-synchronization in human beings (invited paper). *International Journal of Computational Cognition* 1: 53–77. URL: http://www.YangSky.com/yangijcc.htm

David, O., Garnero, L., Cosmelli, D., and Varela, F. J. (2002). Estimation of neural dynamics from MEG/EEG cortical current density maps: application to the reconstruction of large-scale cortical synchrony. *IEEE Transactions on Biomedical Engineering* 49: 975–987.

Davidson, R. J., Scherer, K. R., and Goldsmith, H. H., eds. (2003). *Handbook of Affective Science.* Oxford: Oxford University Press.

Dawkins, R. (1982). *The Extended Phenotype.* Oxford: Oxford University Press.

———. (1986). *The Blind Watchmaker.* London: Penguin Books.

———. (1989). *The Selfish Gene,* new ed. Oxford: Oxford University Press.

———. (1995). *River out of Eden: A Darwinian View of Life.* New York: Basic Books.

Deacon, T. W. (1997). *The Symbolic Species: The Co-Evolution of Language and the Brain.* New York: W. W. Norton.

———. (2003). The hierarchic logic of emergence: untangling the interdependence of evolution and self-organization. In B. Weber and D. Depew, eds., *Evolution and Learning: The Baldwin Effect Reconsidered,* pp. 273–308 Cambridge, MA: MIT Press.

Decety, J. (in press). A social cognitive neuroscience model of human empathy. In E. Harmon-Jones and P. Winkielman, eds., *Fundamentals of Social Neuroscience*. New York: Guilford Press.

Decety, J., and Sommerville, J. A. (2003). Shared representations between self and other: a social cognitive neuroscience view. *Trends in Cognitive Sciences* 7: 527–533.

Deffuant, G., Fuhs, T., Monnert, E., Bourgine, P., and Varela, F. J. (1995). Semi-algebraic networks: an attempt to design geometric autopoietic networks. *Artificial Life* 2: 157–177.

Dehaene, S., and Naccache, L. (2001). Towards a cognitive neuroscience of consciousness: basic evidence and a workspace framework. *Cognition* 79: 1–37.

Dennett, D. C. (1978). Two approaches to mental images. In D. C. Dennett, *Brainstorms: Philosophical Essays on Mind and Psychology,* pp. 174–189. Cambridge, MA: MIT Press/A Bradford Book.

———. (1982). How to study consciousness empirically, or nothing comes to mind. *Synthese* 59: 159–180.

———. (1991a). *Consciousness Explained.* Boston: Little, Brown.

———. (1991b). Real patterns. *Journal of Philosophy* 88: 27–51.

———. (1995a). *Darwin's Dangerous Idea: Evolution and the Meanings of Life.* New York: Simon & Schuster.

———. (1995b). The unimagined preposterousness of zombies. *Journal of Consciousness Studies* 2: 322–326.

———. (1998). No bridge over the stream of consciousness. *Behavioral and Brain Sciences* 21: 753–756.

———. (2002a). Does your brain use the images in it, and if so, how? *Behavioral and Brain Sciences* 25: 189–190.

———. (2002b). How could I be wrong? How wrong could I be? *Journal of Consciousness Studies* 9: 13–16.

———. (2003). Who's on first? Heterophenomenology explained. In A. Jack and A. Roepstorff, eds., *Trusting the Subject? The Use of Introspective Evidence in Cognitive Science. Volume 1,* pp. 19–30. Thorverton, UK: Imprint Academic.

———. (2005). *Sweet Dreams: Philosophical Obstacles to a Science of Consciousness.* Cambridge, MA: MIT Press/A Bradford Book.

Dennett, D. C., and Kinsbourne, M. (1992). Time and the observer: the where and when of consciousness in the brain. *Behavioral and Brain Sciences* 15: 183–247.

Depraz, N. (1995). *Transcendence et incarnation: le statut de l'intersubjectivité comme altérité à soi chez Husserl.* Paris: Librarie Philosophique J. Vrin.

———. (1997). La traduction de *Leib,* une *crux phaenomenologica. Etudes Phénoménologiques* 3.

———. (1999a). Review of Ichiro Yamaguchi, *Ki als leibhaftige Vernunft*. *Alter* 7: 63–68.

———. (1999b). The phenomenological reduction as praxis. *Journal of Consciousness Studies* 6: 95–110.

———. (1999c). When transcendental genesis encounters the naturalization project. In J. Petitot, F. J. Varela, B. Pachoud, and J.-M. Roy, eds., *Naturalizing Phenomenology: Issues in Contemporary Phenomenology and Cognitive Science*, pp. 464–489. Stanford, CA: Stanford University Press.

———. (2001a). *Lucidité du corps. De l'empiricisme transcendental en phénoménologie*. Dordrecht: Kluwer Academic Publishers.

———. (2001b). The Husserlian theory of intersubjectivity as alterology: emergent theories and wisdom traditions in the light of genetic phenomenology. In E. Thompson, ed., *Between Ourselves: Second-Person Issues in the Study of Consciousness*, pp. 169–178. Thorverton, UK: Imprint Academic. Also published in *Journal of Consciousness Studies* 8 (2001): 169–178.

Depraz, N., Varela, F. J., and Vermersch, P. (2000). The gesture of awareness: an account of its structural dynamics. In M. Velmans, ed., *Investigating Phenomenal Consciousness*, pp. 121–136. Amsterdam: John Benjamins Press.

———. (2003). *On Becoming Aware: A Pragmatics of Experiencing*. Amsterdam: John Benjamins Press.

De Preester, H. (2003). Meaning: what's the matter? Intrinsic relations and the organism. *Theoria et Historia Scientiarum* 7: 195–205.

DeRobertis, E. M., and Sasai, Y. (1996). A common plan for dorsoventral patterning in bilateria. *Nature* 380: 37–40.

Derryberry, D., and Tucker, D. M. (1994). Motivating the focus of attention. In P. M. Niedenthal and S. Kitayama, eds., *The Heart's Eye: Emotional Influences in Perception and Attention*, pp. 167–196. New York: Academic Press.

Descartes, R. (1986). *Meditations on First Philosophy, with Selections from the Objections and Replies*, trans, J. Cottingham. Cambridge: Cambridge University Press.

de Waal, F. B. M. (1996). *Good Natured: The Origins of Right and Wrong in Humans and Other Animals*. Cambridge, MA: Harvard University Press.

———. (2002). On the possibility of animal empathy. In T. Manstead, N. Fridja, and A. Fischer, eds., *Feelings and Emotions: The Amsterdam Symposium*, pp. 381–401. Cambridge: Cambridge University Press.

Di Paolo, E. A. (2005). Autopoiesis, adaptivity, teleology, agency. *Phenomenology and the Cognitive Sciences*, 4: 429–452.

Donald, M. (1991). *Origins of the Modern Mind: Three Stages in the Evolution of Culture and Cognition*. Cambridge, MA: Harvard University Press.

———. (2001). *A Mind So Rare: The Evolution of Human Consciousness.* New York: W. W. Norton.

Doolittle, W. F. (1981). Is nature really motherly? *CoEvolution Quarterly* 29: 58–63.

———. (1987). From selfish DNA to Gaia: one molecular biologist's view of the evolutionary process. In J. M. Robson, ed., *Origin and Evolution of the Universe: Evidence for Design?*, pp. 59–76. Kingston, Ontario: McGill-Queen's University Press.

Dretske, F. (1995a). *Naturalizing the Mind.* Cambridge, MA: MIT Press/A Bradford Book.

———. (1995b). Mental events as structuring causes of behavior. In J. Heil and A. Mele, eds., *Mental Causation,* pp. 121–136. Oxford: Clarendon Press.

Dreyfus, G., and Thompson, E. (2007). Asian perspectives: Indian theories of mind. In P. D. Zelazo, M. Moscovitch, and E. Thompson, eds., *The Cambridge Handbook of Consciousness.* New York: Cambridge University Press.

Dreyfus, H. (1972). *What Computers Can't Do.* New York: Harper and Row.

———. (1982). Introduction. In H. Dreyfus and H. Harrison, eds., *Husserl, Intentionality and Cognitive Science.* Cambridge, MA: MIT Press.

———. (1988). Husserl's epiphenomenology. In H. R. Otto and J. A. Tuedio, eds., *Perspectives on Mind,* pp. 85–104. Dordrecht: D. Reidel.

———. (1991). *Being-In-The-World: A Commentary on Heidegger's Being and Time, Division I.* Cambridge, MA: MIT Press.

———. (1992). *What Computers Still Can't Do.* Cambridge, MA: MIT Press.

———. (2000). Responses. In M. Wrathall and J. Malpas, eds., *Heidegger, Coping, and Cognitive Science. Essays in Honor of Hubert L. Dreyfus,* vol. 2, pp. 311–349. Cambridge, MA: MIT Press.

———. (2002). Intelligence without representation—Merleau-Ponty's critique of mental representation. *Phenomenology and the Cognitive Sciences* 1: 367–383.

———. (2005). Merleau-Ponty and recent cognitive science. In T. Carman and M. B. N. Hansen, eds., *The Cambridge Companion to Merleau-Ponty,* pp. 129–150. Cambridge: Cambridge University Press.

Dreyfus, H., and Dreyfus, S. (1986). *Mind over Machine.* New York: Free Press.

Drummond, J. J. (2003). The structure of intentionality. In D. Welton, ed., *The New Husserl: A Critical Reader,* pp. 65–92. Bloomington: Indiana University Press.

Dupré, J. (1993). *The Disorder of Things.* Cambridge, MA: Harvard University Press.

Dupuy, J.-P. (2000). *The Mechanization of the Mind: On the Origins of Cognitive Science.* Princeton, NJ: Princeton University Press.

Dyson, F. (1985). *Origins of Life.* Cambridge: Cambridge University Press.

Eisenberg, N. (2000). Empathy and sympathy. In M. Lewis and J. M. Haviland-Jones, eds., *Handbook of Emotions,* 2d ed., pp. 677–691. New York: Guilford Press.

Eisenberg, N., and Strayer, J. (1987). *Empathy and Its Development.* New York: Cambridge University Press.

Ekman, P., and Davidson, R. J., eds. (1994). *The Nature of Emotion. Fundamental Questions.* Oxford: Oxford University Press.

Elman, J. (1991). Representation and structure in connectionist models. In G. Altman, ed., *Cognitive Models of Speech Processing.* Cambridge, MA: MIT Press.

Emmeche, C., Køppe, S., and Stjernfelt, F. (2000). Levels, emergence, and three versions of downward causation. In P. B. Andersen, C. Emmeche, N. O. Finnemann, and P. V. Christiansen, eds., *Downward Causation: Minds, Bodies and Matter,* pp. 13–34. Aarhus, Denmark: Aarhus University Press.

Engel, A. K., Fries, P., and Singer, W. (2001). Dynamic predictions: oscillations and synchrony in top-down processing. *Nature Reviews Neuroscience* 2: 704–716.

Engel, A. K., and Singer, W. (2001). Temporal binding and the neural correlates of sensory awareness. *Trends in Cognitive Sciences* 5: 16–25.

Epstein, M. (1996). *Thoughts without a Thinker: Psychotherapy from a Buddhist Perspective.* New York: Basic Books.

Faure, P., and Korn, H. (2001). Is there chaos in the brain? I. Concepts of nonlinear dynamics and methods of investigation. *Comptes Rendus de l'Académie des Sciences* 324: 773–793.

Fleischaker, G. R. (1988). Autopoiesis: the status of its system logic. *Biosystems* 22: 37–49.

———. (1990a). Origins of life: an operational definition. *Origins of Life and Evolution of the Biosphere* 20: 127–137.

———. (1990b). Symbols and dynamics: two different system ideas. *Perceiving-Acting Workshop Review* [*PAW Review*], Center for the Study of Perception and Action [CEPSPA] 5: 30–32.

———. (1994). A few precautionary words concerning terminology. In G. R. Fleischaker, S. Colonna, and P. L. Luisi, eds., *Self-Production of Supramolecular Structures. From Synthetic Structures to Models of Minimal Living Systems,* pp. 33–41. Dordrecht: Kluwer Academic Publishers.

Fodor, J. (1975). *The Language of Thought.* Cambridge, MA: Harvard University Press.

————. (1981). *Representations. Philosophical Essays on the Foundations of Cognitive Science.* Cambridge, MA: MIT Press/A Bradford Book.

Fontana, W., and Buss, L. W. (1994). What would be conserved if "the tape were played twice"? *Proceedings of the National Academy of Sciences USA* 91: 757–761.

Fontana, W., Wagner, G., and Buss, L. W. (1994). Beyond digital naturalism. *Artificial Life* 1: 211–227.

Forman, R. K. C., ed. (1990). *The Problem of Pure Consciousness.* New York: Oxford University Press.

Franklin, S. (1995). *Artificial Minds.* Cambridge, MA: MIT Press.

Freeman, W. J. (1995). *Societies of Brains: A Study in the Neuroscience of Love and Hate.* Mahwah, NJ: Lawrence Erlbaum.

————. (1999a). *How Brains Make Up Their Minds.* London: Weidenfeld and Nicolson.

————. (1999b). Consciousness, intentionality, and causality. *Journal of Consciousness Studies* 6: 143–172.

————. (2000). Emotion is essential to all intentional behaviors. In M. D. Lewis and I. Granic, eds., *Emotion, Development, and Self-Organization: Dynamic Systems Approaches to Emotional Development,* pp. 209–235. Cambridge: Cambridge University Press.

————. (2003). The wave packet: an action potential for the 21st century. *Journal of Integrative Neuroscience* 2: 3–30.

Freud, S. (1915). The unconscious (1915). In S. Freud, *On Metapsychology: The Theory of Psychoanalysis,* pp. 159–222. The Pelican-Freud Library, vol. 11. London: Penguin Books, 1984.

————. (1923). The Ego and the Id (1923). In S. Freud, *On Metapsychology: The Theory of Psychoanalysis,* pp. 339–407. The Pelican-Freud Library, vol. 11. London: Penguin Books, 1984.

Fries, P., Reynolds, J. H., Rorie, A. E., and Desimone, R. (2001). Modulation of oscillatory neuronal synchronization by selective visual attention. *Science* 291: 1560–1563.

Friston, K. J. (2000a). The labile brain. I. Neuronal transients and nonlinear coupling. *Philosophical Transactions of the Royal Society of London. B.* 355: 215–236.

————. (2000b). The labile brain. II. Transients, complexity, and selection. *Philosophical Transactions of the Royal Society of London. B.* 355: 237–252.

Gallagher, S. (1986a). Body image and body schema: a conceptual clarification. *The Journal of Mind and Behavior* 7: 541–554.

————. (1986b). Lived body and environment. *Research in Phenomenology* 16: 139–170.

————. (1995). Body schema and intentionality. In J. L. Bermúdez, A.

Marcel, and N. Eilan, eds., *The Body and the Self,* pp. 225–244. Cambridge, MA: MIT Press.

———. (1997). Mutual enlightenment: recent phenomenology in cognitive science. *Journal of Consciousness Studies* 4: 195–214.

———. (1998). *The Inordinance of Time.* Evanston, IL: Northwestern University Press.

———. (2003). Bodily self-awareness and object perception. *Theoria et Historia Scientarium: International Journal for Interdisciplinary Studies* 7: 53–68.

Gallagher, S., and Varela, F. J. (2003). Redrawing the map and resetting the time: phenomenology and the cognitive sciences. In E. Thompson, ed., *The Problem of Consciousness: New Essays in Phenomenological Philosophy of Mind. Canadian Journal of Philosophy,* supplementary vol. 29, pp. 93–132. Calgary: University of Alberta Press.

Gallese, V. (2001). The "shared manifold" hypothesis: from mirror neurons to empathy. In E. Thompson, ed., *Between Ourselves: Second Person Issues in the Study of Consciousness,* pp. 33–50. Thorverton, UK: Imprint Academic. Also published in *Journal of Consciousness Studies* 8 (2001): 33–50.

Gallese, V., Keysers, C., and Rizzolatti, G. (2004). A unifying view of the basis of social cognition. *Trends in Cognitive Sciences* 8: 396–403.

Gallup, G., Jr. (1998). Can animals empathize? Yes. *Scientific American* 9: 65–75.

Gardner, H. (1985). *The Mind's New Science: A History of the Cognitive Revolution.* New York: Basic Books.

Garfinkel, A. (1981). *Forms of Explanation: Rethinking the Questions in Social Theory.* New Haven, CT: Yale University Press.

Garrett, B. (in press). What the history of vitalism teaches us about consciousness and the "hard problem." *Philosophy and Phenomenological Research.*

Gatlin, L. (1972). *Information and the Living System.* New York: Columbia University Press.

Gendlin, E. T. (1981). *Focusing.* New York: Bantam.

———. (1997). *Experiencing and the Creation of Meaning: A Philosophical and Psychological Approach to the Subjective.* Evanston, IL: Northwestern University Press.

Gerhart, J., and Kirschner, M. (1997). *Cells, Embryos, and Evolution: Toward a Cellular and Developmental Understanding of Phenotypic Variation and Evolutionary Adaptability.* Malden, MA: Blackwell Science Publications.

Gibson, J. J. (1979). *The Ecological Approach to Visual Perception.* Boston: Houghton Mifflin.

Gilbert, S. F., Opitz, J. M., and Raff, R. A. (1996). Resynthesizing evolutionary and developmental biology. *Developmental Biology* 173: 357–372.

Godfrey-Smith, P. (1996). Spencer and Dewey on life and mind. In M.

Boden, ed., *The Philosophy of Artificial Life,* pp. 314–331. Oxford: Oxford University Press.

———. (2000a). Information, arbitrariness, and selection: comments on Maynard Smith. *Philosophy of Science* 67: 202–207.

———. (2000b). On the theoretical role of "genetic coding." *Philosophy of Science* 67: 26–44.

Gold, I. (2002). Interpreting the neuroscience of imagery. *Behavioral and Brain Sciences* 25: 190–191.

Goldman, A. I. (1997). Science, publicity, and consciousness. *Philosophy of Science* 64: 525–545.

———. (2000). Can science know when you're conscious? Epistemological foundations of consciousness research. *Journal of Consciousness Studies* 7: 3–22.

———. (2004). Epistemology and the evidential status of introspective reports. In A. Jack and A. Roepstorff, eds., *Trusting the Subject? The Use of Introspective Evidence in Cognitive Science.* vol. 2. pp. 1–16. Thorverton, UK: Imprint Academic.

Goldstein, K. (1995). *The Organism: A Holistic Approach to Biology Derived from Pathological Data in Man.* New York: Zone Books.

Goodwin, B. (1994). *How The Leopard Changed Its Spots: The Evolution of Complexity.* New York: Scribner's.

Gould, S. J. (1989). *Wonderful Life: The Burgess Shale and the Nature of History.* New York: W. W. Norton.

Gould, S. J., and Lewontin, R. C. (1978). The spandrels of San Marco and the Panglossian paradigm: a critique of the adaptationist programme. *Proceedings of the Royal Society of London* 205: 581–598. Page references in the text are to the version reprinted in E. Sober, ed., *Conceptual Issues in Evolutionary Biology,* pp. 252–270. Cambridge, MA: MIT Press/A Bradford Book, 1984.

Gray, R. D. (1992). Death of the gene: developmental systems strike back. In P. E. Griffiths, ed., *Trees of Life: Essays in Philosophy of Biology,* pp. 165–209. Dordrecht: Kluwer Academic Publishers.

Grice, H. P. (2002). Some remarks about the senses. In A. Noë and E. Thompson, eds., *Vision and Mind: Readings in the Philosophy of Perception,* pp. 35–54, Cambridge, MA: MIT Press/A Bradford Book.

Griffiths, P. E. (1997). *What Emotions Really Are: The Problem of Psychological Categories.* Chicago: University of Chicago Press.

Griffiths, P. E., and Gray, R. D. (1994). Developmental systems and evolutionary explanation. *Journal of Philosophy* 91: 277–304.

Griffiths, P. E., and Knight, R. D. (1998). What is the developmentalist challenge? *Philosophy of Science* 65: 253–258.

Griffiths, P. E., and Stotz, K. (2000). How the mind grows: a developmental perspective on the biology of cognition. *Synthese* 122: 29–51.

Grush, R. (2004). The emulation theory of representation: motor control, imagery, and perception. *Behavioral and Brain Sciences* 27: 377–396.

Gupta, B. (1998). *The Disinterested Witness: A Fragment of Advaita Vedanta Phenomenology.* Evanston, IL: Northwestern University Press.

———. (2003). *Cit. Consciousness.* New Delhi: Oxford University Press.

———. (2004). Advaita Vedanta and Husserl's Phenomenology. *Husserl Studies* 20: 119–134.

Gurwitsch, A. (1964). *The Field of Consciousness.* Pittsburgh, PA: Dusquesne University Press.

Güzeldere, G. (1997). The many faces of consciousness: a field guide. In N. Block, O. Flanagan, and G. Güzeldere, eds., *The Nature of Consciousness: Philosophical Debates,* pp. 1–67. Cambridge, MA: MIT Press/A Bradford Book.

Haken, H. (1983). *Synergtics: An Introduction.* Berlin: Springer-Verlag.

Haken, H., Kelso, J. A. S., and Bunz, H. (1985). A theoretical model of phase transitions in human hand movements. *Biological Cybernetics* 51: 347–356.

Hall, B. K., and Olson, W. M. (2003). *Keywords and Concepts in Evolutionary Developmental Biology.* Cambridge, MA: Harvard University Press.

Hanna, R., and Thompson, E. (2003). The mind-body-body problem. *Theoria et Historia Scientiarum: International Journal for Interdisciplinary Studies* 7: 24–44.

Harman, G. (1997). The intrinsic quality of experience. In N. Block, O. Flanagan, and G. Güzeldere, eds., *The Nature of Consciousness: Philosophical Debates,* pp. 663–676. Cambridge, MA: MIT Press/A Bradford Book.

Hattiangadi, J. (2005). The emergence of minds in space and time. In D. M. Johnson and C. Ernelling, eds., *The Mind as a Scientific Object: Between Brain and Culture,* pp. 79–100. New York: Oxford University Press.

Hawthorne, J., and Silberstein, M. (1995). For whom the Bell arguments toll. *Synthese* 102: 99–138.

Healey, R. A. (1991). Holism and nonseparability. *Journal of Philosophy* 88: 393–421.

Hebb, D. (1949). *The Organization of Behavior.* New York: John Wiley.

Heidegger, M. (1982). *The Basic Problems of Phenomenology,* trans. A. Hofstadter. Bloomington: Indiana University Press.

———. (1985). *History of the Concept of Time,* trans. T. Kisiel. Bloomington: Indiana University Press.

———. (1995). *The Fundamental Concepts of Metaphysics: World, Finitude, Solitude,* trans. W. McNeill and N. Walker. Bloomington: Indiana University Press.

————. (1996). *Being and Time,* trans. J. Stambaugh. Albany: State University of New York Press.

Held, K. (2003). Husserl's phenomenological method. In D. Welton, ed., *The New Husserl: A Critical Reader,* pp. 3–31. Bloomington: Indiana University Press.

Hendriks-Jansen, H. (1995). *Catching Ourselves in the Act: Situated Activity, Interactive Emergence, Evolution, and Human Thought.* Cambridge, MA: MIT Press/A Bradford Book.

Hering, E. (1964). *Outlines of a Theory of the Light Sense,* trans. L. M. Hurvich and D. Jameson. Cambridge, MA: Harvard University Press.

Ho, M.-W., and Saunders, P. (1984). *Beyond Neo-Darwinism.* New York: Academic Press.

Holland, P. W. H. (1999). The future of evolutionary developmental biology. *Nature* 402: Supplement: C41–C44.

Hopkins, R. (1998). *Picture, Image, and Experience.* New York: Cambridge University Press.

Humphrey, N. (2000). How to solve the mind-body problem. *Journal of Consciousness Studies* 4: 5–20.

————. (2001). Seeing it my way: sensation, perception—and feeling red. *Behavioral and Brain Sciences* 24: 997.

Humphreys, P. (1996). Aspects of emergence. *Philosophical Topics* 24: 53–70.

————. (1997a). Emergence, not supervenience. *Philosophy of Science* 64 (Proceedings): S337–S345.

————. (1997b). How properties emerge. *Philosophy of Science* 64: 1–17.

Hurley, S. L. (1998). *Consciousness in Action.* Cambridge, MA: Harvard University Press.

Hurley, S. L., and Noë, A. (2003). Neural plasticity and consciousness. *Biology and Philosophy* 18: 131–168.

Husserl, E. (1960). *Cartesian Meditations: An Introduction to Phenomenology,* trans. Dorian Cairns. Dordrecht: Kluwer Academic Publishers.

————. (1970). *The Crisis of European Sciences and Transcendental Phenomenology,* trans. D. Carr. Evanston, IL: Northwestern University Press.

————. (1973). *Zur Phänomenologie der Intersubjektivität, Dreiter Teil: 1929–1935. Husserliana,* vol. 15. The Hague: Martinus Nijhoff.

————. (1975). *Experience and Judgment,* trans. J. S. Churchill. Evanston, IL: Northwestern University Press.

————. (1977). *Philosophical Psychology,* trans. J. Scanlon. The Hague: Martinus Nijhoff.

————. (1980). *Phenomenology and the Foundations of the Sciences: Ideas Pertaining to a Pure Phenomnology and to a Phenomenological Philosophy. Third Book,* trans. T. E. Klein and W. E. Pohl. The Hague: Martinus Nijhoff.

———. (1983). *Ideas Pertaining to a Pure Phenomenology and to a Phenomenological Philosophy, First Book,* trans. F. Kersten. The Hague: Martinus Nijhoff.

———. (1989). *Ideas Pertaining to a Pure Phenomenology and to a Phenomenological Philosophy, Second Book,* trans. R. Rojcewicz and A. Schuwer. Dordrecht: Kluwer Academic Publishers.

———. (1991). *On the Phenomenology of the Consciousness of Internal Time (1893–1917),* trans. J. B. Brough. Dordrecht: Kluwer Academic Publishers.

———. (1997). *Thing and Space: Lectures of 1907,* trans. R. Rojcewicz. Dordrecht: Kluwer Academic Publishers.

———. (2000). *Logical Investigations,* vols. 1 and 2, trans. J Findlay. New York: Humanity Books/Prometheus Books. English translation originally published in 1970.

———. (2001). *Analyses Concerning Passive and Active Synthesis: Lectures on Transcendental Logic,* trans. A. J. Steinbock. Dordrecht: Kluwer Academic Publishers.

———. (2006). *Phantasy, Image Consciousness, and Memory (1898–1925),* trans. J. B. Brough. Berlin: Springer.

Hutchins, E. (1995). *Cognition in the Wild.* Cambridge, MA: MIT Press/A Bradford Book.

Hutchinson, W., Davis, K., Lozano, A., Tasker, R., and Dostrovsky, J. (1999). Pain related neurons in the human cingulate cortex. *Nature Neuroscience* 2: 403–405.

Iacoboni, M., Woods, R. P., Brass, M., Bekkering, H., Mazziotta, J. C., and Rizzolatti, G. (1999). Cortical mechanisms of human imitation. *Science* 286: 2526–2528.

Isles, A. R., and Wilkinson, L. S. (2000). Imprinted genes, cognition and behavior. *Trends in Cognitive Sciences* 4: 309–318.

Jablonka, E. (2001). The systems of inheritance. In S. Oyama, P. E. Griffiths, and R. D. Gray, eds., *Cycles of Contingency: Developmental Systems and Evolution,* pp. 99–116. Cambridge, MA: MIT Press.

Jablonka, E., and Szathmáry, E. (1995). The evolution of information storage and heredity. *Trends in Ecology and Evolution* 10: 206–211.

Jack, A. I., and Roepstorff, A. (2002). Introspection and cognitive brain mapping: from stimulus-response to script-report. *Trends in Cognitive Sciences* 6: 333–339.

———, eds. (2003). *Trusting the Subject? Volume 1. The Use of Introspective Evidence in Cognitive Science.* Thorverton, UK: Imprint Academic.

———. (2004). *Trusting the Subject?* vol. 2. *The Use of Introspective Evidence in Cognitive Science.* Thorverton, UK: Imprint Academic.

Jackendoff, R. (1987). *Consciousness and the Computational Mind.* Cambridge, MA: MIT Press/A Bradford Book.

James, W. (1981). *The Principles of Psychology.* Cambridge, MA: Harvard University Press.

———. (1985). *Psychology: The Briefer Course.* Notre Dame, IN: University of Notre Dame Press.

Jantsch, E. (1980). *The Self-Organizing Universe: Scientific and Human Implications of the Emerging Paradigm of Evolution.* Oxford: Pergamon Press.

Johnson, M. (1987). *The Body in the Mind: The Bodily Basis of Imagination, Reason, and Meaning.* Chicago: University of Chicago Press.

———. (1993). *Moral Imagination: Implications of Cognitive Science for Ethics.* Chicago: University of Chicago Press.

Jonas, H. (1966). *The Phenomenon of Life: Toward a Philosophical Biology.* Chicago: University of Chicago Press. Reprinted by Northwestern University Press, 2000.

———. (1968). Biological foundations of individuality. *International Philosophical Quarterly* 8: 231–251.

———. (1996). *Mortality and Morality: A Search for the Good after Auschwitz.* Evanston, IL: Northwestern University Press.

Juarrero, A. (1999). *Dynamics in Action: Intentional Behavior as a Complex System.* Cambridge, MA: MIT Press/A Bradford Book.

Juarrero-Roqué, A. (1985). Self-organization: Kant's conception of teleology and modern chemistry. *Review of Metaphysics* 39: 107–135.

Kabat-Zinn J. (1990). *Full Catastrophe Living: Using the Wisdom of Your Body and Mind to Face Stress, Pain, and Illness.* New York: Dell.

Kahana, M. J., Seelig, D., and Madsen, J. R. (2001). Theta returns. *Current Opinion in Neurobiology* 11: 739–744.

Kant, I. (1987). *Critique of Judgment,* trans. W. S. Pluhar. Indianapolis, IN: Hacket Publishing Company.

Kauffman, S. A. (1991). Antichaos and adaptation. *Scientific American* 265: 78–84.

———. (1993). *Origins of Order: Self-Organization and Selection in Evolution.* New York: Oxford University Press.

———. (1995). *At Home in the Universe.* New York: Oxford University Press.

———. (2000). *Investigations.* New York: Oxford University Press.

Keller, E. F. (1984). *A Feeling for the Organism: The Life and Work of Barbara McClintock.* New York: W. H. Freeman.

———. (1995). *Refiguring Life: Metaphors of Twentieth Century Biology.* New York: Columbia University Press.

———. (2000). *The Century of the Gene.* Cambridge, MA: Harvard University Press.

Kellert, S. H. (1993). *In the Wake of Chaos*. Chicago: University of Chicago Press.

Kelso, J. A. S. (1995). *Dynamic Patterns: The Self-Organization of Brain and Behavior*. Cambridge, MA: MIT Press/A Bradford Book.

Kelso, J. A. S., Fuchs, A., Lancaster, R., Holroyd, T., Cheyne, D., and Weinberg, H. (1998). Dynamic cortical activity in the human brain reveals motor equivalence. *Nature* 392: 814–818.

Kelso, J. A. S., and Kay, B. A. (1987). Information and control: a macroscopic analysis of perception-action coupling. In H. Heuer and A. F. Sanders, eds., *Perspectives on Perception and Action*, pp. 3–32. Hillsdale, NJ: Lawrence Erlbaum.

Kim, J. (1993). *Supervenience and Mind: Selected Philosophical Essays*. Cambridge: Cambridge University Press.

———. (1998). *Mind in a Physical World: An Essay on the Mind-Body Problem and Mental Causation*. Cambridge, MA: MIT Press/A Bradford Book.

———. (1999). Making sense of emergence. *Philosophical Studies* 95: 3–36.

Kind, A. (2003). What's so transparent about transparency? *Philosophical Studies* 115: 225–244.

Köhler, W. (1947). *Gestalt Psychology*. New York: Liveright.

Korn, H., and Faure, P. (2003). Is there chaos in the brain? II. Experimental evidence and related models. *Comptes Rendus Biologie* 326: 787–840.

Koshland, D. E., Jr. (1977). A response regulator model in a simple sensory system. *Science* 196: 1055–1063.

Kosslyn, S. M. (1980). *Image and Mind*. Cambridge, MA: Harvard University Press.

———. (1994). *Image and Brain: The Resolution of the Imagery Debate*. Cambridge, MA: MIT Press/A Bradford Book.

Kosslyn, S. M., Ganis, G., and Thompson, W. L. (2003). Mental imagery: against the nihilistic hypothesis. *Trends in Cognitive Sciences* 7: 109–111.

Kosslyn, S. M., Pinker, S., Smith, G. E., and Schwartz, S. P. (1981). On the demystification of mental imagery. In N. Block, ed., *Imagery*, pp. 131–150. Cambridge, MA: MIT Press/A Bradford Book.

Kosslyn, S. M., and Pomerantz, J. R. (1981). Imagery, propositions, and the form of internal representations. In N. Block, ed., *Readings in the Philosophy of Psychology, vol. 2*, pp. 150–169. Cambridge, MA: Harvard University Press.

Kosslyn, S. M., Thompson, W. L., and Ganis, G. (2006). *The Case for Mental Imagery*. New York: Oxford University Press.

Kriegel, U. (2003a). Consciousness as intransitive self-consciousness: two views and an argument. *Canadian Journal of Philosophy* 33: 103–132.

———. (2003b). Consciousness as sensory quality and as implicit self-awareness. *Phenomenology and the Cognitive Sciences* 2: 1–26.

———. (2004). The functional role of consciousness: a phenomenological approach. *Phenomenology and the Cognitive Sciences* 3: 171–193.

———. (2005). Naturalizing subjective character. *Philosophy and Phenomenological Research* 71: 23–57.

Kronz, F. M. (1998). Nonseparability and quantum chaos. *Philosophy of Science* 65: 50–75.

Kronz, F. M., and Tiehen, J. T. (2002). Emergence and quantum mechanics. *Philosophy of Science* 69: 324–347.

Kuhn, T. (1970). *The Stucture of Scientific Revolutions.* Chicago: University of Chicago Press.

Lachaux, J. P., Rodriguez, E., Martinerie, J., and Varela, F. J. (1999). Measuring phase-synchrony in brain signals. *Human Brain Mapping* 8: 194–208.

Lakoff, G. (1987). *Women, Fire and Dangerous Things: What Categories Reveal about the Mind.* Chicago: University of Chicago Press.

Lakoff, G., and Johnson, M. (1980). *Metaphors We Live By.* Chicago: University of Chicago Press.

Lambert, D. M., and Hughes, A. J. (1988). Keywords and concepts in structuralist and functionalist biology. *Journal of Theoretical Biology* 133: 133–145.

Lambie, J. A., and Marcel, A. J. (2002). Consciousness and the varieties of emotion experience: a theoretical framework. *Psychological Review* 109: 219–259.

Lane, R. D., and Nadel, L., eds. (2000). *Cognitive Neuroscience of Emotion.* Oxford: Oxford University Press.

Langsdorf, L. (1985). Review of Dreyfus 1982. *Husserl Studies* 3: 303–311.

Langton, C. G., ed. (1989). *Artificial Life.* Santa Fe Studies in the Sciences of Complexity, vol. 6. Redwood City, CA: Addison-Welsey.

Latour, B. (1993). *We Have Never Been Modern,* trans. C. Porter. Cambridge, MA: Harvard University Press.

Laycock, S. W. (1994). *Mind as Mirror and the Mirroring of Mind. Buddhist Reflections on Western Phenomenology.* Albany: State University of New York Press.

Leask, I. (2002). Edith Stein and others. *Journal of the British Society for Phenomenology* 33: 286–298.

LeDoux, J. (1996). *The Emotional Brain.* New York: Simon Schuster.

———. (2002). *Synaptic Self: How Our Brains Become Who We Are.* London: Penguin Books.

Legrand, D. (2003). How not to find the neural signature of self-consciousness. *Consciousness and Cognition* 12: 544–546.

———. (2005). Transparently oneself. *Psyche* 11 (5), June 2005. URL: http://psyche.cs.monash.edu.au/symposia/metzinger/LEGRAND.pdf

———. (2006). The bodily self: the sensori-motor roots of pre-reflexive self-consciousness. *Phenomenology and the Cognitive Sciences* 5: 89–118.

Lennox, J. G. (1992). Teleology. In E. F. Keller and E. Lloyd, eds., *Keywords in Evolutionary Biology*, pp. 324–333. Cambridge, MA: Harvard University Press.

Letelier, J. C., Marín, G., and Mpodozis, J. (2003). Autopoietic and (*M,R*) systems. *Journal of Theoretical Biology* 222: 261–272.

Le Van Quyen, M. (2003). Disentangling the dynamic core: a research program for neurodynamics at the large-scale. *Biological Research* 36: 67–88.

Le Van Quyen, M., Adam, C., Lachaux, J.-P., Martinerie, J., Baulac, M., Renault, B., and Varela, F. J. (1997). Temporal patterns in human epileptic activity are modulated by perceptual discriminations. *Neuroreport* 8: 1703–1710.

Le Van Quyen, M., Martinerie, J., Adam, C., and Varela, F. J. (1997). Unstable periodic orbits in human epileptic activity. *Physical Review* E 56: 3401–3411.

Le Van Quyen, M., and Petitmengin, C. (2002). Neuronal dynamics and conscious experience: an example of reciprocal causation before epileptic seizures. *Phenomenology and the Cognitive Sciences* 1: 169–180.

Le Van Quyen, M., Schuster, H., and Varela, F. J. (1996). Fast rhythms can emerge from slow neuronal oscillators. *International Journal of Bifurcation and Chaos* 6: 1807–1816.

Levenson, R., and Reuf, A. M. (1992). Empathy: a physiological substrate. *Journal of Personality and Social Psychology* 63: 234–246.

Levine, J. (1983). Materialism and qualia: the explanatory gap. *Pacific Philosophical Quarterly* 64: 354–361.

Levins, R., and Lewontin, R. (1985). *The Dialectical Biologist.* Cambridge, MA: Harvard University Press.

Levinson, J. (1998). Wolheim on pictorial representation. *Journal of Aesthetics and Art Criticism* 56: 227–233.

Lewis, M. D. (2000). Emotional self-organization at three time scales. In M. D. Lewis and I. Granic, eds., *Emotion, Development, and Self-Organization: Dynamic Systems Approaches to Emotional Development*, pp. 37–69. Cambridge: Cambridge University Press.

———. (2005). Bridging emotion theory and neurobiology through dynamic systems modeling. *Behavioral and Brain Sciences* 28: 169–194.

Lewis, M. D., and Granic, I., eds. (2000). *Emotion, Development, and Self-Organization: Dynamic Systems Approaches to Emotional Development.* Cambridge: Cambridge University Press.

Lewis, M. L., and Haviland-Jones, J. M., eds. (2000). *Handbook of Emotions*, 2d ed. New York: Guilford Press.

Lewontin, R. (1978). Adaptation. *Scientific American* 239: 212–230.

———. (1993). *Biology as Ideology: The Doctrine of DNA*. New York: Harper-Collins.

Llinas, R., Ribary, U., Contreras, D., and Pedroarena, C. (1998). The neuronal basis for consciousness. *Philosophical Transactions of the Royal Society of London Series B* 353: 1801–1818.

Lloyd, D. (2002). Functional MRI and the study of human consciousness. *Journal of Cognitive Neuroscience*, 14: 818–831.

———. (2003). *Radiant Cool: A Novel Theory of Consciousness*. Cambridge, MA: MIT Press/A Bradford Book.

Lopes, D. (1996). *Understanding Pictures*. Clarendon: Oxford University Press.

Lovelock, J. E. (1979). *Gaia: A New Look at Life on Earth*. New York: Oxford University Press.

———. (1987). The ecopoiesis of daisy world. In J. M. Robson, ed., *Origin and Evolution of the Universe: Evidence for Design?* pp. 153–166. Kingston, Ontariol: McGill-Queen's University Press.

———. (1988). *The Ages of Gaia*. New York: W. W. Norton.

———. (1991). Gaia: a planetary emergent phenomenon. In W. I. Thompson, ed., *Gaia 2: Emergence. The New Science of Becoming*, pp. 30–49. Hudson, NY: Lindisfarne Press.

Lovelock, J. E., and Margulis, L. (1974). Homeostatic tendencies of the earth's atmosphere. *Origins of Life* 5: 93–103.

Luisi, P. L. (1993). Defining the transition to life: self-replicating bounded structures and chemical autopoiesis. In W. D. Stein and F. J. Varela, eds., *Thinking about Biology*. Santa Fe Studies in the Sciences of Complexity, Lecture Notes, vol. 3, pp. 17–39. NJ: Addison-Wesley.

———. (1998). About various definitions of life. *Origins of Life and Evolution of the Biosphere* 28: 613–622.

———. (2003). Autopoiesis: a review and a reappraisal. *Naturwissenschaften* 90: 49–59.

Luisi, P. L., Lazcano, A., and Varela, F. J. (1996). What is life? Defining life and the transition to life. In M. Rizzotti, ed., *Defining Life: The Central Problem in Theoretical Biology*, pp. 146–167. Padua: Edizione Università di Padova.

Luisi, P. L., and Varela, F. J. (1989). Self-replicating micelles—a chemical version of a minimal autopoietic system. *Origins of Life and Evolution of the Biosphere* 19: 663–643.

Lusthaus, D. (2002). *Buddhist Phenomenology: A Philosophical Investigation of*

Yogacara Buddhism and the Ch'eng Wei-shih tun. London: Routledge/ Curzon Press.

Lutz, A. (2002). Toward a neurophenomenology as an account of generative passages: a first empirical case study. *Phenomenology and the Cognitive Sciences* 1: 133–167.

Lutz, A., Dunne, J. D., and Davidson, R. J. (2007). Meditation and the neuroscience of consciousness: an introduction. In P. D. Zelazo, M. Moscovitch, and E. Thompson, eds., *The Cambridge Handbook of Consciousness.* New York: Cambridge University Press.

Lutz, A., Lachaux, J.-P., Martinerie, J., and Varela, F. J. (2002). Guiding the study of brain dynamics by using first-person data: synchrony patterns correlate with ongoing conscious states during a simple visual task. *Proceedings of the National Academy of Sciences USA* 99: 1586–1591.

Lutz, A., and Thompson, E. (2003). Neurophenomenology: integrating subjective experience and brain dynamics in the neuroscience of consciousness. *Journal of Consciousness Studies* 10: 31–52.

Mach, E. (1959). *The Analysis of Sensations and the Relation of the Physical to the Psychical,* trans. C. A. Williams. New York: Dover Publications.

Mack, A., and Rock, I. (1998). *Inattentional Blindness.* Cambridge, MA: MIT Press.

Maes, P., ed. (1990). *Designing Autonomous Agents.* Cambridge, MA: MIT Press.

Maier, S. F., and Watkins, L. R. (1998). Cytokines for psychologists: implications of bi-directional immune-to-brain communication for understanding behavior, mood, and cognition. *Psychological Review* 105: 83–107.

Marbach, E. (1993). *Mental Representation and Consciousness: Towards a Phenomenological Theory of Representation and Reference.* Dordrecht: Kluwer Academic Publishers.

Margulis, L. (1984). *Early Life.* Boston: Jones and Bartlett.

———. (1991). Biologists can't define life. In C. Barlow, ed., *From Gaia to Selfish Genes: Selected Writings in the Life Sciences,* pp. 236–238. Cambridge, MA: MIT Press.

———. (1993). *Symbiosis in Cell Evolution,* 2d ed. San Francisco: W. H. Freeman.

———. (1998). *Symbiotic Planet: A New Look at Evolution.* New York: Basic Books.

———. (2001). The conscious cell. In P. C. Marijúan, ed., *Cajal and Consciousness: Scientific Approaches to Consciousness on the Centennial of Ramon y Cajal's* Textura, pp. 55–70. Annals of the New York Academy of Sciences, vol. 929. New York: New York Academy of Sciences.

Margulis, L., and Lovelock, J. E. (1974). Biological modulation of the Earth's atmosphere. *Icarus* 21: 471–489.

Margulis, L., and Sagan, D. (1986). *Microcosmos: Four Billion Years of Microbial Evolution.* New York: Summit Books.

———. (1995). *What Is Life?* New York: Simon & Schuster.

———. (2002). *Acquiring Genomes. A Theory of the Origins of Species.* New York: Basic Books.

Margulis, L., and Schwartz, K. V. (1988). *Five Kingdoms: An Illustrated Guide to the Phyla of Life on Earth,* 2d ed. San Francisco: W. H. Freeman.

Martin, M. G. F. (2002). The transparency of experience. *Mind and Language* 17: 376–425.

Matthews, G. B. (1991). Consciousness and life. In D. M. Rosenthal, ed., *The Nature of Mind,* pp. 63–70. Oxford: Oxford University Press.

Maturana, H. R. (1969). The neurophysiology of cognition. In P. Garvin, ed., *Cognition: A Multiple View,* pp. 3–23. New York: Spartan Books.

———. (1970). Biology of cognition. In H. R. Maturana and F. J. Varela, *Autopoiesis and Cognition: The Realization of the Living,* pp. 2–58. Boston Studies in the Philosophy of Science, vol. 43. Dordrecht: D. Reidel, 1980.

———. (1975). The organization of the living: a theory of the living organization. *International Journal of Man-Machine Studies* 7: 313–332.

———. (1980a). Autopoiesis: reproduction, heredity and evolution. In M. Zeleny, ed., *Autopoiesis, Dissipative Structures, and Spontaneous Social Orders,* pp. 45–79. Boulder, CO: Westview Press.

———. (1980b). Man and society. In F. Benseler, P. M. Hejl, and W. K. Köck, eds., *Autopoiesis, Communication, and Society.* New York: Campus Verlag.

Maturana, H. R., and Varela, F. J. (1973). *De máquinas y seres vivos: Una teoría de la organizacíon biológica.* Santiago, Chile: Editorial Universitaria.

———. (1980). *Autopoiesis and Cognition: The Realization of the Living.* Boston Studies in the Philosophy of Science, vol. 42. Dordrecht: D. Reidel.

———. (1987). *The Tree of Knowledge: The Biological Roots of Human Understanding.* Boston: Shambala Press/New Science Library.

Maudlin, T. (1998). Part and whole in quantum mechanics. In E. Castellani, ed., *Interpreting Bodies: Classical and Quantum Objects in Modern Physics,* pp. 46–60. Princeton, NJ: Princeton University Press.

Maynard Smith, J. (1986). *The Problems of Biology.* Oxford: Oxford University Press.

———. (1993). *The Theory of Evolution,* 2d ed. Cambridge: Cambridge University Press.

———. (1998). *Shaping Life: Genes, Embryos and Evolution.* London: Weidenfeld and Nicholson.

————. (2000a). The concept of information in biology. *Philosophy of Science* 67: 177–194.

————. (2000b). Reply to commentaries. *Philosophy of Science* 67: 214–218.

Maynard Smith, J., Burian, R., Kauffman, S., Alberch, P., Campbell, J., Goodwin, B., Lande, R., Raup, D., and Wolpert, L. (1985). Developmental constraints and evolution. *Quarterly Review of Biology* 60: 265–287.

McClelland, J., Rummelhart, D., and the PDP Research Group. (1986). *Parallel Distributed Processing: Explorations in the Microstructure of Cognition*, vols. 1 and 2. Cambridge, MA: MIT Press.

McCulloch, G. (1994). *Using Sartre: An Analytical Introduction to Early Sartrean Themes*. London: Routledge Press.

McGinn, C. (1991). *The Problem of Consciousness*. Oxford: Basil Blackwell.

————. (2004). *Mindsight: Image, Dream, Meaning*. Cambridge, MA: Harvard University Press.

McMullin, B. (1997a). Computational autopoiesis: the original algorithm. Working Paper 97–01–001, Santa Fe Institute, Santa Fe, NM 87501, USA. Available at: http://www.eeng.dcu.ie/~alife/bmcm-ecal97/

————. (1997b). Modelling autopoiesis: harder than it may seem! Presented at Biology, Cognition, Language & Society: An International Symposium on Autopoiesis, Belo Horizonte, Brazil, November 1997. Available at: http://www.eeng.dcu.ie/~mcmullin

————. (1999). Some remarks on autocatalysis and autopoiesis. Presented at the workshop *Closure: Emergent Organizations and Their Dynamics*, May 3–5, 1999. University of Ghent, Belgium. Available at: http://www.eeng.dcu.ie/~mcmullin/

————. (2001). An intriguing journey: a review of *Investigations* by Stuart Kauffman. *Complexity* 6: 22–23. Available at: http://www.eeng.dcu.ie/~mcmullin/

McMullin, B., and Varela, F. J. (1997). Rediscovering computational autopoeisis. In P. Husbands and I. Harvey, eds., *Fourth European Confrence on Artificial Life*, pp. 38–48. Cambridge, MA: MIT Press/A Bradford Book. Available at: http://www.eeng.dcu.ie/~mcmullin/

Melloni, L., and Rodriguez, E. (2005). Phase synchronization but not gamma oscillations correlates with conscious perception. Poster Presentation. Association for the Scientific Study of Consciousness, 9th Annual Meeting, Pasadena, CA, June 23–27, 2005.

Meltzoff, A. N., and Moore, M. K. (1998). Infant intersubjectivity: broadening the dialogue to include imitation, identity, and intention. In S. Braten, ed., *Intersubjective Communication and Emotion in Early Ontogeny*, pp. 47–62. Cambridge: Cambridge University Press.

Mensch, J. R. (1996). *After Modernity: Husserlian Reflections on a Philosophical Tradition*. Albany: State University Press of New York.

———. (1998). Instincts—a Husserlian account. *Husserl Studies* 14: 219–237.

Merleau-Ponty, M. (1962). *Phenomenology of Perception,* trans. Colin Smith. London: Routledge Press.

———. (1963). *The Structure of Behavior,* trans. A. Fisher. Pittsburgh, PA: Dusquene University Press.

———. (1964). *Signs,* trans. Richard C. McCleary. Evanston, IL: Northwestern University Press.

———. (1968). *The Visible and the Invisible,* trans. A. Lingis. Evanston, IL: Northwestern University Press.

———. (2001). *The Incarnate Subject: Malebranche, Biran, and Bergson on the Union of Body and Soul,* trans. P. B. Milan. Amherst, NY: Humanity Books.

———. (2003). *Nature: Course Notes from the Collège de France.* Compiled with notes by D. Ségard, trans. R. Vallier. Evanston, IL: Northwestern University Press.

Metzinger, T., ed. (2000). *Neural Correlates of Consciousness.* Cambridge, MA: MIT Press.

———. (2003). *Being No One: The Self-Model Theory of Subjectivity.* Cambridge, MA: MIT Press/A Bradford Book.

Mikulecky, D. C. (2000). Robert Rosen: the well-posed question and its answer—why are organisms different from machines? *System Research and Behavioral Science* 17: 419–432.

Mingers, J. (1995). *Self-Producing Systems: The Implications and Applications of Autopoieisis.* New York: Plenum Press.

Mohanty, J. N. (1989). *Transcendental Phenomenology.* Oxford: Basil Blackwell.

Monod, J. (1971). *Chance and Necessity,* trans. A. Wainhouse. New York: Vintage Books.

Montero, B. (1999). The body problem. *Nous* 33: 183–200.

———. (2001). Post-physicalism. *Journal of Consciousness Studies* 8: 61–80.

Moody, T. (1994). Conversations with zombies. *Journal of Consciousness Studies* 1: 196–200.

Moore, G. E. (1993). The refutation of idealism. In G. E. Moore, *Selected Writings,* pp. 23–44. London: Routledge and Kegan Paul.

Moran, D. (2000). *Introduction to Phenomenology.* London: Routledge Press.

Moreno, A., and Barandiaran, X. (2004). A naturalized account of the inside-outside dichotomy. *Philosophica* 73: 11–26.

Morowitz, H. J. (1992). *Beginnings of Cellular Life: Metabolism Recapitulates Biogenesis.* New Haven, CT: Yale University Press.

———. (2001). The epistemic paradox of mind and matter. In P. C. Marijúan, ed., *Cajal and Consciousness: Scientific Approaches to Consciousness on the Centennial of Ramon y Cajal's Textura,* pp. 50–54. Annals of the New

York Academy of Sciences, vol. 929. New York: New York Academy of Sciences.

Morowitz, H. J., Heinz, B., and Deamer, D. W. (1988). The chemical logic of a minimum protocell. *Origins of Life and Evolution of the Biosphere* 18 (1988): 281–287. Reprinted in D. W. Deamer and G. R. Fleischaker, eds., *Origins of Life: The Central Concepts,* pp. 263–269. Boston: Jones and Bartlett, 1994.

Moss, L. (1992). A kernel of truth? On the reality of the genetic program. In D. Hull, M. Forbes, and K. Okruhlik, eds., *Proceedings of the Philosophy of Science Association* [PSA] 1: 335–348.

———. (2003). *What Genes Can't Do.* Cambridge, MA: MIT Press/A Bradford Book.

Moustakas, C. (1994). *Phenomenological Research Methods.* Thousand Oaks, CA: Sage Publications.

Murphy, M. P., and O'Neil, L. A. J., eds. (1995). *What Is Life? The Next Fifty Years: Speculations on the Future of Biology.* Cambridge: Cambridge University Press.

Myin, E., and O'Regan, J. K. (2002). Perceptual consciousness, access to modality, and skill theories: a way to naturalize phenomenology? *Journal of Consciousness Studies* 9: 27–46.

Nagel, T. (1974). What is it like to be a bat? *Philosophical Review* 83: 435–450. (Quoted passages in the text are from the reprinted version in T. Nagel, *Mortal Questions,* pp. 165–180. New York: Cambridge University Press, 1979.)

———. (1979). *Mortal Questions.* New York: Cambridge University Press.

———. (1980). Armstrong on the mind. In N. Block, ed., *Reading in the Philosophy of Psychology,* vol. 1, pp. 200–206. Cambridge, MA: Harvard University Press. Originally published in *Philosophical Review* 79 (1970): 394–403.

Newell, A., and Simon, H. (1976). Computer science as empirical inquiry: symbols and search. *Communications of the Association for Computing Machinery* 19: 113–126. Reprinted in J. Haugeland, ed., *Mind Design II,* pp. 81–110. Cambridge, MA: MIT Press/A Bradford Book, 1997.

Noë, A. (2002a). Is perspectival self-consciousness non-conceptual? *Philosophical Quarterly* 52: 185–195.

———. (2002b). Is the visual world a grand illusion? *Journal of Consciousness Studies* 9: 1–12.

———, ed. (2002c). *Is the Visual World a Grand Illusion?* Thorverton, UK: Imprint Academic.

———. (2004). *Action in Perception.* Cambridge, MA: MIT Press.

Noë, A., Pessoa, L., and Thompson, E. (2000). Beyond the grand illusion:

what change blindness really teaches us about vision. *Visual Cognition* 7: 93–106.

Noë, A., and Thompson, E. (2004a). Are there neural correlates of consciousness? *Journal of Consciousness Studies* 11: 3–28.

———. (2004b). Sorting out the neural basis of consciousness: Authors' reply to commentators. *Journal of Consciousness Studies* 11: 87–98.

Norton, A. (1995). Dynamics: an introduction. In R. F. Port and T. Van Gelder, eds., *Mind as Motion: Explorations in the Dynamics of Cognition*, pp. 45–68. Cambridge, MA: MIT Press/A Bradford Book.

Odling-Smee, F. J. (1988). Niche-constructing phenotypes. In H. C. Plotkin, ed., *The Role of Behavior in Evolution*, pp. 73–132. Cambridge, MA: MIT Press.

O'Keefe, J., and Burgess, N. (1999). Theta activity, virtual navigation and the human hippocampus. *Trends in Cognitive Sciences* 11: 403–406.

Oparin, A. (1938). *The Origin of Life on Earth*. London: Macmillan.

O'Regan, J. K. (1992). Solving the "real" mysteries of visual perception: the world as an outside memory. *Canadian Journal of Psychology* 46: 461–488.

O'Regan, J. K., and Noë, A. (2001a). A sensorimotor account of vision and visual consciousness. *Behavioral and Brain Sciences* 24: 939–1011.

———. (2001b). Authors' response: acting out our sensory experience. *Behavioral and Brain Sciences* 24: 1011–1031.

Oyama, S. (1992a). Is phylogeny recapitulating ontogeny. In F. J. Varela and J.-P. Dupuy, eds., *Understanding Origins*, pp. 227–232. Dordrecht: Kluwer Academic Publishers.

———. (1992b). Ontogeny and phylogeny: a case of metarecapitulation? In P. Griffiths, ed., *Trees of Life: Essays in Philosophy of Biology*, pp. 211–239. Dordrecht: Kluwer Academic Publishers.

———. (1993). Constraints and development. *Netherlands Journal of Zoology* 43: 6–16.

———. (1999). Locating development: locating developmental systems. In K. K. Scholnik, K. Nelson, S. A. Gelman, and P. H. Miller, eds., *Conceptual Development: Piaget's Legacy*, pp. 185–208. Hillsdale, NJ: Lawrence Erlbaum.

———. (2000a). *Evolution's Eye: A System's View of the Biology-Culture* Divide. Durham, NC: Duke University Press.

———. (2000b). *The Ontogeny of Information: Developmental Systems and Evolution*, 2d ed. Durham, NC: Duke University Press. First edition published by Cambridge University Press, 1985.

———. (2000c). Causal democracy and causal contributions in developmental systems theory. *Philosophy of Science* 67 (Proceedings): S332–S347.

Oyama, S., Griffiths, P. E., and Gray, R. D., eds. (2001). *Cycles of Contingency: Developmental Systems and Evolution*. Cambridge, MA: MIT Press.

Pacherie, E. (1999). *Leibhaftigkeit* and representational theories of perception. In J. Petitot, F. J. Varela, B. Pachoud, and J.-M. Roy, eds., *Naturalizing Phenomenology: Issues in Contemporary Phenomenology and Cognitive Science*, pp. 148–160. Stanford, CA: Stanford University Press.

Paley, W. (1996). Natural theology. In M. Ruse, ed., *But Is It Science? The Philosophical Question in the Creation/Evolution Controversy*, pp. 46–69. New York: Prometheus Books.

Panksepp, J. (1998a). *Affective Neuroscience: The Foundations of Human and Animal Emotions*. Oxford: Oxford University Press.

———. (1998b). The periconscious substrates of consciousness: affective states and the evolutionary origins of self. *Journal of Consciousness Studies* 5: 566–582.

———. (2002). The MacLean legacy and some modern trends in emotion research. In G. A. Cory and R. Gardner, eds., *The Evolutionary Neuroethology of Paul MacLean: Convergences and Frontiers*, pp. ix–xxviii. Westport, CT: Praeger Publishers.

Parvizi, J., and Damasio, A. (2001). Consciousness and the brainstem. *Cognition* 79: 135–159.

Patočka, J. 1998. *Body, Community, Language, World*, trans. E. Kohák. Chicago: Open Court.

Pattee, H. H. (1977). Dynamic and linguistic modes of complex systems. *International Journal of General Systems Theory* 3: 259–266.

di Pellegrino, G., Fadiga, L., Fogassi, L., Gallese, V., and Rizzolatti, G. (1992). Understanding motor events: a neurophysiological study. *Experimental Brain Research* 91: 176–180.

Penfield, W. (1938). The cerebral cortex in man. I. The cerebral cortex and consciousness. *Archives of Neurology and Psychiatry* 40: 417–442.

Penfield, W., and Jasper, H. (1954). *Epilepsy and the Functional Anatomy of the Human Brain*. Boston: Little, Brown.

Pert, C. B. (1997). *Molecules of Emotion*. New York: Simon & Schuster.

Pert, C. B., Ruff, M. R., Weber, R. J., and Herkenham, M. (1985). Neuropeptides and their receptors: a psychosomatic network. *Journal of Immunology* 135: 820s–826s.

Pessoa, L., and de Weerd, P., eds. (2003). *Filling-In: From Perceptual Completion to Cortical Reorganization*. Oxford: Oxford University Press.

Pessoa, L., Thompson, E., and Noë, A. (1998). Finding out about filling-in: a guide to perceptual completion for visual science and the philosophy of perception. *Behavioral and Brain Sciences* 21: 723–802.

Petitmengin, C. (2001). *L'expérience intuitive*. Paris: L'Harmattan.

———. (2005). Un exemple de recherche neuro-phénoménologique, l'anticipation des crises d'épilepsie. *Intellectica* 40: 63–89.

———. (in press). Describing one's subjective experience in the second person: an interview method for the science of consciousness. *Phenomenology and the Cognitive Sciences.*

Petitmengin-Peugeot, C. (1999). The intuitive experience. In F. J. Varela and J. Shear, eds., *The View from Within: First-Person Approaches to the Study of Consciousness,* pp. 43–78. Thorverton, UK: Imprint Academic.

Petitot, J. (1992). *Physique du sens.* Paris: Editions du CNRS.

———. (1994). Phenomenology of perception, qualitative physics, and sheaf mereology. In R. Casati, B. Smith, and G. White, eds., *Philosophy and the Cognitive Sciences,* pp. 387–408. Hölder-Pichler-Tempsky.

———. (1995). Morphodynamics and attractor syntax: constituency in visual perception and cognitive grammar. In R. F. Port and T. van Gelder, eds., *Mind as Motion: Explorations in the Dynamics of Cognition,* pp. 227–282. Cambridge, MA: MIT Press/A Bradford Book.

———. (1999). Morphological eidetics for a phenomenology of perception. In J. Petitot, F. J. Varela, B. Pachoud, and J.-M. Roy, eds., *Naturalizing Phenomenology: Issues in Contemporary Phenomenology and Cognitive Science,* pp. 330–371. Stanford, CA: Stanford University Press.

Petitot, J., and Smith, B. (1996). Physics and the phenomenal world. In R. Poli and P. Simons, eds., *Formal Ontology,* pp. 233–253. Dordrecht: Kluwer Academic Publishers.

Petitot, J., Varela, F. J., Pachoud, B., and Roy, J.-M., eds. (1999). *Naturalizing Phenomenology: Issues in Contemporary Phenomenology and Cognitive Science.* Stanford, CA: Stanford University Press.

Poellner, P. (2003). Nonconceptual content, experience, and the self. *Journal of Consciousness Studies* 10: 32–57.

Pöppel, E. (1988). *Mindworks: Time and Consciousness Experience.* Boston: Harcourt, Brace Jovanovich.

Port, R. F., and van Gelder, T., eds. (1995). *Mind as Motion: Explorations in the Dynamics of Cognition.* Cambridge, MA: MIT Press/A Bradford Book.

Povinellli, D. J. (1998). Can animals empathize? Maybe not. *Scientific American* 9: 65–75.

Povinelli, D. J., and Preuss, T. M. (1995). Theory of mind: evolutionary history of a cognitive specialization. *Trends in Neurosciences* 18: 418–424.

Preston, S. D., and de Waal, F. B. M. (2002). Empathy: its ultimate and proximate bases. *Behavioral and Brain Sciences* 25: 1–20.

Price, D., and Barrell, J. (1980). An experiential approach with quantitative methods: a research paradigm. *Journal of Humanistic Psychology* 20: 75–95.

Price, D., Barrell, J., and Rainville, P. (2002). Integrating experiential-phenomenological methods and neuroscience to study neural mechanisms of pain and consciousness. *Consciousness and Cognition* 11: 593–608.

Priest, S. (1998). *Merleau-Ponty.* London: Routledge Press.

Prigogine, I., and Stengers, I. (1984). *Order out of Chaos: Man's New Dialogue with Nature.* New York: Bantam.

Prinz, W. (1997). Perception and action planning. *European Journal of Cognitive Psychology* 9: 129–154.

Pylyshyn, Z. W. (1973). What the mind's eye tells the mind's brain: a critique of mental imagery. *Psychological Bulletin* 80: 1–24.

———. (1984). *Computation and Cognition: Towards a Foundation for Cognitive Science.* Cambridge, MA: MIT Press/A Bradford Book.

———. (2002). Mental imagery: in search of a theory. *Behavioral and Brain Sciences* 25: 157–238.

———. (2003a). *Seeing and Visualizing: It's Not What You Think.* Cambridge, MA: MIT Press/A Bradford Book.

———. (2003b). Explaining mental imagery: now you see it, now you don't. *Trends in Cognitive Sciences* 7: 111–112.

———. (2003c). Return of the mental image: are there really pictures in the brain? *Trends in Cognitive Sciences* 7: 113–118.

Quartz, S. (1999). The constructivist brain. *Trends in Cognitive Sciences* 3: 48–57.

Quartz, S., and Sejnowski, T. J. (1997). The neural basis of cognitive development: a constructivist manifesto. *Behavioral and Brain Sciences* 20: 537–596.

Raff, R. A. (1996). *The Shape of Life: Genes, Development, and the Evolution of Animal Form.* Chicago: University of Chicago Press.

Rainville, P. (2005). Neurophénoménologie des états et des contenus de conscience dans l'hypnose et l'analgésie hypnotique. *Théologique* 12: 15–38.

Ramachandran, V. S., and Blakeslee, S. (1998). *Phantoms in the Brain.* New York: William Morrow.

Ramachandran, V. S., and Hirstein, W. (1998). The perception of phantom limbs. *Brain* 121: 1603–1630.

Rees, G., Krieman, G., and Koch, C. (2002). Neural correlates of consciousness in humans. *Nature Reviews Neuroscience* 3: 261–270.

Rey, G. (1981). Introduction: what are mental images? In N. Block, ed., *Readings in Philosophical Psychology,* vol. 2, pp. 117–127. Cambridge, MA: Harvard University Press.

Rietveld, E. (2004). The nature of everyday coping: reinterpreting Merleau-Ponty's phenomenology of concrete habitual coping in the light of Varela's naturalization of time-consciousness. Presented at the ASSC-8

(Association for the Scientific Study of Consciousness) Conference, June 26–28, 2004, Antwerp, Belgium.

Rodemeyer, L. (2003). Developments in the theory of time-consciousness: an analysis of protention. In D. Welton, ed., *The New Husserl: A Critical Reader,* pp. 125–154. Bloomington: Indiana University Press.

Rodriguez, E., George, N., Lachaux, J. P., Martinerie, J., Renault, B., and Varela, F. J. (1999). Perception's shadow: long-distance synchronization of human brain activity. *Nature* 397: 430–433.

Roe, A. W., Pallas, S. L., Kwon, Y. H. and Sur, M. (1990). A map of visual space induced in primary auditory cortex. *Science* 250: 818–820.

———. (1992). Visual projections routed to the auditory pathway in ferrets. *Journal of Neuroscience* 12: 3651–3664.

Roepstorff, A. (2001). Brains in scanners: an *Umwelt* of cognitive neuroscience. *Semiotica* 134: 747–765.

Rollins, M. (1989). *Mental Imagery: On the Limits of Cognitive Science.* New Haven, CT: Yale University Press.

Rose, S. (1997). *Lifelines: Biology Beyond Determinism.* Oxford: Oxford University Press.

Rosen, R. (1991). *Life Itself: A Comprehensive Inquiry into the Nature, Origin, and Fabrication of Life.* New York: Columbia University Press.

———. (2000). *Essays on Life Itself.* New York: Columbia University Press.

Rosenthal, D. (1997). A theory of consciousness. In N. Block, O. Flanagan, and G. Güzeldere, eds., *The Nature of Consciousness: Philosophical Debates,* pp. 729–753. Cambridge, MA: MIT Press/A Bradford Book.

Rowlands, M. (2003). Consciousness: the transcendentalist manifesto. *Phenomenology and the Cognitive Sciences* 2: 205–221.

Roy, J.-M. (1995). Le "Dreyfus Bridge": Husserlianisme et Fodorisme. *Archives de Philosophie* 58: 533–548.

———. (2003). Phenomenological claims and the myth of the given. In E. Thompson, ed., *The Problem of Consciousness: New Essays in Phenomenological Philosophy of Mind. Canadian Journal of Philosophy,* supplementary vol. 29, pp. 1–32. Calgary University of Alberta Press.

Roy, J.-M., Petitot, J., Pachoud, B., and Varela, F. J. (1999). Beyond the gap: an introduction to naturalizing phenomenology. In J. Peitot, F. J. Varela, B. Pachoud, and J.-M. Roy, eds., *Naturalizing Phenomenology: Issues in Contemporary Phenomenology and Cognitive Science,* pp. 1–80. Stanford, CA: Stanford University Press.

Rudrauf, D., and Damasio, A. (2005). A conjecture regarding the biological mechanism of subjectivity and feeling. *Journal of Consciousness Studies* 12: 236–262.

Rudrauf, D., Lutz, A., Cosmelli, D., Lachaux, J.-P., and Le Van Quyen, M.

(2003). From autopoiesis to neurophenomenology: Francisco Varela's exploration of the biophysics of being. *Biological Research* 36: 27–66.

Ruiz-Mirazo, K., and Moreno, A. (2004). Basic autonomy as a fundamental step in the synthesis of life. *Artificial Life* 10: 235–259.

Rummelhart, D., Smolensky, P., McClelland, J., and Hinton, G. (1986). Schemata and sequential thought processes in PDP models. In J. McClelland, D. Rummelhart, and the PDP Research Group, *Parallel Distributed Processing: Explorations in the Microstructure of Cognition,* vol. 2, pp. 7–58. Cambridge, MA: MIT Press.

Ruse, M. (1996). The relationship between science and religion in Britain, 1830–1870. In M. Ruse, ed., *But Is It Science? The Philosophical Question in the Creation/Evolution Controversy,* pp. 50–70. New York: Prometheus Books.

Sadato, N., Pascual-Leone, A., Grafman, J., Ibanez, V., Deiber, M. P., Dold, G., and Hallet, M. (1996). Activation of the primary visual cortex by braille reading in blind subjects. *Nature* 380: 526–528.

Sarkar, S. (1996). Biological information: a skeptical look at some central dogmas of molecular biology. In S. Sarkar, ed., *The Philosophy and History of Molecular Biology: New Perspectives,* pp. 187–232. Dordrecht: Kluwer Academic Publishers.

———. (2000). Information in genetics and developmental biology: comments on Maynard Smith. *Philosophy of Science* 67: 208–213.

Sarntheim, J., Petsche, H., Rappelsberger, P., Shaw, G. L., and von Stein, A. (1998). Synchronization between prefrontal and posterior association cortex during human working memory. *Proceedings of the National Academy of Sciences USA* 95: 7092–7096.

Sartre, J.-P. (1956). *Being and Nothingness,* trans. Hazel Barnes. New York: Philosophical Library.

———. (1960). *The Transcendence of the Ego: An Existentialist Theory of Consciousness.* New York: Noonday Press.

———. (2004). *The Imaginary: A Phenomenological Psychology of the Imagination,* trans. J. Webber. London: Routledge Press.

Savage-Rumbaugh, S., Fields, W. M., and Taglialatela, J. P. (2001). Language, speech, tools and writing: a cultural imperative. In E. Thompson, ed., *Between Ourselves: Second-Person Issues in the Study of Consciousness,* pp. 273–292. Thorverton, UK: Imprint Academic. Also published in *Journal of Consciousness Studies* 8 (2001): 273–292.

Savage-Rumbaugh, S., and Lewin, R. (1994). *Kanzi: The Ape at the Brink of the Human Mind.* New York: John Wiley.

Scheerer, E. (1994). Psychoneural isomorphism: historical background and current relevance. *Philosophical Psychology* 7: 183–210.

Schiff, S. J., So, P., Chang, T., Burke, R. E., and Sauer, T. (1996). Detecting dynamical interdependence and generalized synchrony through mutual prediction in a neural ensemble. *Physical Reviews E* 54: 6708–6724.

Schmid-Schonbein, C. (1998). Improvements of seizure control by psychological methods in patients with intractable epilepsy. *Seizure* 7: 261–270.

Scholz, B. C. (2002). Innateness. *Nature* 415: 739.

Schreiber, T. (1999). Interdisciplinary application of nonlinear time series methods. *Physics Reports* 308: 1–40.

Schröder, J. (1998). Emergence: non-deducibility or downwards causation? *Philosophical Quarterly* 48: 432–452.

Searle, J. R. (1983). *Intentionality: An Essay in the Philosophy of Mind.* Cambridge: Cambridge University Press.

———. (1992). *The Rediscovery of the Mind.* Cambridge, MA: MIT Press/A Bradford Book.

———. (2000a). Consciousness. *Annual Review of Neuroscience* 23: 557–578.

———. (2000b). Consciousness, free action and the brain. *Journal of Consciousness Studies* 7: 3–22.

———. (2004). *Mind: A Brief Introduction.* New York: Oxford University Press.

Sejnowski, T., and Rosenberg, C. (1986). *NETtalk: A Parellel Network that Learns to Read Aloud.* Technical Report JHU/EEC-86/01. Baltimore, MD: Johns Hopkins University Press.

Sellars, W. (1956). Empiricism and the philosophy of mind. In H. Feigl and M. Scriven, eds., *Minnesota Studies in the Philosophy of Science. Vol. 1. The Foundations of Science and the Concepts of Psychology and Psychoanalysis,* pp. 253–329. Minneapolis: University of Minnesota Press.

Sheets-Johnstone, M. (1999a). *The Primacy of Movement.* Amsterdam: John Benjamins Press.

———. (1999b). Emotion and movement: analysing their relationship. *Journal of Consciousness Studies* 6: 259–277.

Shepard, R., and Metzler, J. (1971). Mental rotation of three-dimensional objects. *Science* 171: 701–703.

Shimony, A. (1997). On mentality, quantum mechanics, and the actualization of potentialities. In R. Penrose, A. Shimony, N. Cartwright, and S. Hawking, *The Large, the Small, and the Human Mind,* pp. 144–160. Cambridge: Cambridge University Press.

Shoemaker, S. (1968). Self-reference and self-awareness. *Journal of Philosophy* 65: 555–567.

———. (1984). *Identity, Cause and Mind: Philosophical Essays.* Cambridge: Cambridge University Press.

Siewert, C. (2004). Is experience transparent? *Philosophical Studies* 117: 15–41.

Silberstein, M. (2001). Converging on emergence: consciousnesss, causation, and explanation. *Journal of Consciousness Studies* 8: 61–98.

———. (2002). Reduction, emergence, and explanation. In P. Machamer and M. Silberstein, eds., *The Blackwell Guide to the Philosophy of Science*, pp. 80–107. Oxford: Basil Blackwell.

Silberstein, M., and McGeever, J. (1999). The search for ontological emergence. *Philosophical Quarterly* 49: 182–200.

Simon, H. (1955). A behavioral model of rational choice. *Quarterly Journal of Economics* 59: 99–118.

———. (1969). *The Sciences of the Artificial.* Cambridge, MA: MIT Press.

———. (1973). The organization of complex systems. In H. H. Pattee, ed., *Hierarchy Theory: The Challenge of Complex Systems*, pp. 1–27. New York: George Braziller.

Simons, D. J., and Chabris, C. R. (1999). Gorillas in our midst: sustained inattentional blindness for dynamic events. *Perception* 28: 1059–1074.

Simons, D. J., and Levin, D. T. (1997). Change blindness. *Trends in Cognitive Sciences* 1: 261–267.

Simons, D. J., and Wang, R. F. (1998). Perceiving real-world viewpoint changes. *Psychological Science* 9: 315–320.

Simons, D. J., Wang, R. F., and Roddenberry, D. (2002). Object recognition is mediated by extraretinal information. *Perception and Psychophysics* 64: 521–530.

Skarda, C., and Freeman, W. J. (1987). How brains make chaos in order to make sense of the world. *Behavioral and Brain Sciences* 10: 161–195.

Skuse, D. H., James, R. S., Bishop, D. V. M., Coppins, B., Dalton, P., Aamodt-Leeper, G., Bacarese-Hamilton, M., Creswell, C., McGurk, R., and Jacobs, P. A. (1997). Evidence from Turner's Syndrome of an imprinted X-linked locus affecting cognitive functions. *Nature* 387: 705–708.

Slack, J. M., Holland, P. W. H., and Graham, C. F. (1993). The zootype and the phylotypic stage. *Nature* 361: 490–492.

Smith, A. D. (2003). *Husserl and the Cartesian Meditations.* London: Routledge Press.

Smith, B. (1999). Truth and the visual field. In J. Petitot, F. J. Varela, B. Pachoud, and J.-M. Roy, eds., *Naturalizing Phenomenology: Issues in Contemporary Phenomenology and Cognitive Science*, pp. 317–329. Stanford, CA: Stanford University Press.

Smith, B. C. (1996). *On the Origin of Objects.* Cambridge, MA: MIT Press/A Bradford Book.

Smith, K. C. (1994). The Emperor's New Genes: The Role of the Genome in Development and Evolution. Doctoral Dissertation. Department of Philosophy, Duke University.

Smolensky, P. (1988). On the proper treatment of connectionism. *Behavioral and Brain Sciences* 11: 1–74.

So, P., Francis, J. T., Netoff, T. I., Gluckman, B. J., and Schiff, S. J. (1998). Periodic orbits: a new language for neuronal dynamics. *Biophysical Journal* 74: 2776–2785.

Sober, E. (1993). *Philosophy of Biology.* Boulder, CO: Westview Press.

Sober, E., and Wilson, D. S. (1998). *Unto Others: The Evolution and Psychology of Altruism.* Cambridge, MA: Harvard University Press.

Sokolowski, R. (2000). *An Introduction to Phenomenology.* Cambridge: Cambridge University Press.

Solé, R., and Goodwin, B. (2000). *Signs of Life: How Complexity Pervades Biology.* New York: Basic Books.

Sonea, S., and Panisset, M. (1983). *A New Bacteriology.* Boston: Jones and Bartlett.

Spiegelberg, H. (1994). *The Phenomenological Movement: A Historical Introduction,* 3d rev. and enlarged ed. Dordrecht: Kluwer Academic Publishers.

Sperry, R. (1969). A modified concept of consciousness. *Psychological Review* 76: 532–536.

Stawarska, B. (2001). Pictorial representation or subjective scenario? Sartre on imagination. *Sartre Studies International* 7: 87–111.

———. (2002). Memory and subjectivity: Sartre in dialogue with Husserl. *Sartre Studies International* 8: 94–111.

Stearns, S. C. (1982). On fitness. In D. Mossakowski and G. Roth, eds., *Environmental Adaptation and Evolution,* pp. 3–17. Suttgart: Gustav Fischer.

———. (1986). Natural selection and fitness, adaptation and constraint. In D. M. Raup and D. Jablonski, eds., *Patterns and Processes in the History of Life,* pp. 23–44. Berlin: Springer-Verlag.

———. (1992). *The Evolution of Life Histories.* Oxford: Oxford University Press.

Stein, E. (1989). *On the Problem of Empathy,* trans. Waltraut Stein. Washington, DC: ICS Publications.

Steinbock, A. J. (1995). *Home and Beyond: Generative Phenomenology after Husserl.* Evanston, IL: Northwestern University Press.

———. (1999). Saturated intentionality. In Donn Welton, ed., *The Body,* pp. 178–199. Oxford: Basil Blackwell.

———. (2004). On the phenomenology of becoming aware. *Continental Philosophy Review* 37: 21–43.

Sterelny, K. (1990). The imagery debate. In W. Lycan, ed., *Mind and Cognition,* pp. 607–626. Cambridge, MA: Basil Blackwell.

———. (2000). The "genetic program" program: a commentary on Maynard Smith on information in biology. *Philosophy of Science* 67: 195–201.

Sterelny, K., and Griffiths, P. E. (1999). *Sex and Death: An Introduction to the Philosophy of Biology.* Chicago: University of Chicago Press.

Sterelny, K., and Kitcher, P. (1988). The return of the gene. *Journal of Philosophy* 85: 339–360.

Stern, D. N. (2000). *The Interpersonal World of the Infant,* 2d ed. New York: Basic Books.

———. (2004). *The Present Moment in Psychotherapy and Everyday Life.* New York: W. W. Norton.

Stoljar, D. (2004). The argument from diaphanousness. In M. Ezcurdia, R. Stainton, and C. Viger, eds., *New Essays in the Philosophy of Language and Mind. Canadian Journal of Philosophy,* supplementary vol. 30, pp. 341–390. Calgary: University of Alberta Press.

Sur, M., Angelecci, A., and Sharma, J. (1999). Rewiring cortex: the role of patterned activity in development and plasticity of neocortical circuits. *Journal of Neurobiology* 41: 33–43.

Swanson, L. W. (2000). What is the brain? *Trends in Neurosciences* 23: 519–527.

Szostak, J. W., Bartel, D. P., and Luisi, P. L. (2001). Synthesizing life. *Nature* 409: 387–390.

Teller, P. (1986). Relational holism and quantum mechanics. *British Journal for the Philosophy of Science* 37: 71–81.

Thelen, E., Schöner, G., Scheler, C., and Smith, L. B. (2001). The dynamics of embodiment: a field theory of infant perseverative reaching. *Behavioral and Brain Sciences* 24: 1–86.

Thelen, E., and Smith, L. B. (1994). *A Dynamic Systems Approach to the Development of Cognition and Action.* Cambridge, MA: MIT Press.

Thom, R. (1975). *Structural Stability and Morphogenesis.* Reading, MA: W. A. Benjamin.

Thomas, L. (1974). *The Lives of a Cell: Notes of a Biology Watcher.* New York: Viking Press.

Thomas, N. J. T. (1999). Are theories of imagery theories of imagination? An active perception approach to conscious mental content. *Cognitive Science* 23: 207–245.

———. (2002). The false dichotomy of imagery. *Behavioral and Brain Sciences* 25: 211.

Thompson, E. (1997). Symbol grounding: a bridge from artificial life to artificial intelligence. *Brain and Cognition* 34: 48–71.

———. (2001). Empathy and consciousness. In E. Thompson, ed., *Between Ourselves: Second-Person Issues in the Study of Consciousness,* pp. 1–32. Thorverton, UK: Imprint Academic. Also published in *Journal of Consciousness Studies* 8 (2001): 1–32.

———. (2004). Life and mind: from autopoiesis to neurophenomenology. A tribute to Francisco Varela. *Phenomenology and the Cognitive Sciences* 3: 381–398.

———. (2005). Empathy and human experience. In J. D. Proctor, ed., *Science, Religion, and the Human Experience,* pp. 261–285. New York: Oxford University Press.

Thompson, E., Lutz, A., and Cosmelli, D. (2005). Neurophenomenology: an introduction for neurophilosophers. In A. Brook and K. Akins, eds., *Cognition and the Brain: The Philosophy and Neuroscience Movement,* pp. 40–97. New York: Cambridge University Press.

Thompson, E., Noë, A., and Pessoa, L. (1999). Perceptual completion: a case study in phenomenology and cognitive science. In J. Petitot, F. J. Varela, B. Pachoud, and J.-M. Roy, eds., *Naturalizing Phenomenology: Issues in Contemporary Phenomenology and Cognitive Science,* pp. 161–195. Stanford, CA: Stanford University Press.

Thompson, E., Palacios, A., and Varela, F. J. (1992). Ways of coloring: comparative color vision as a case study for cognitive science. *Behavioral and Brain Sciences* 15: 1–74. Reprinted in Alva Noë and Evan Thompson, eds., *Vision and Mind: Readings in the Philosophy of Perception.* Cambridge, MA: MIT Press, 2002.

Thompson, E., and Varela, F. J. (2001). Radical embodiment: neural dynamics and consciousness. *Trends in Cognitive Sciences* 5: 418–425.

Thompson, W. I. (1987a). The cultural implications of the new biology. In W. I. Thompson, ed., *Gaia: A Way of Knowing. Political Implications of the New Biology,* pp. 11–34. Hudson, NY: Lindisfarne Press.

———, ed. (1987b). *Gaia: A Way of Knowing.* Hudson, NY: Lindisfarne Press.

———. (1987c). Gaia and the politics of life. In W. I. Thompson, ed., *Gaia: A Way of Knowing. Political Implications of the New Biology,* pp. 167–214. Hudson, NY: Lindisfarne Press.

———. (1989). *Imaginary Landscape: Making Worlds of Myth and Science.* New York: St. Martin's Press.

———, ed. (1991a). *Gaia 2: Emergence. The New Science of Becoming.* Hudson, NY: Lindisfarne Press.

———. (1991b). The imagination of a new science and the emergence of a planetary culture. In W. I. Thompson, ed., *Gaia 2: Emergence. The New Science of Becoming,* pp. 11–29. Hudson, NY: Lindisfarne Press.

———. (1991c). Politics becoming planet. In W. I. Thompson, ed., *Gaia 2: Emergence. The New Science of Becoming,* pp. 249–269. Hudson, NY: Lindisfarne Press.

Tomasello, M. (1999). *The Cultural Origins of Human Cognition.* Cambridge, MA: Harvard University Press.

Tononi, G., and Edelman, G. (1998). Consciousness and complexity. *Science* 282: 1846–1851.

Trevarthen, C., and Aitken, K. J. (2001). Infant intersubjectivity: research, theory, and clinical applications. *Journal of Child Psychology and Psychiatry* 42: 3–48.

Tsuda, I. (2001). Toward an interpretation of dynamic neural activity in terms of chaotic dynamical systems. *Behavioral and Brain Sciences* 24: 793–847.

Turvey, M. T., and Shaw, R. E. (1999). Ecological foundations of cognition I. Symmetry and specificity of animal-environment systems. *Journal of Consciousness Studies* 6: 95–110.

Tye, M. (1991). *The Imagery Debate.* Cambridge, MA: MIT Press/A Bradford Book.

———. (1995). *Ten Problems of Consciousness.* Cambridge, MA: MIT Press/A Bradford Book.

———. (2000). *Color, Content, and Consciousness.* Cambridge, MA: MIT Press/A Bradford Book.

Uttal, W. R. (2001). *The New Phrenology: The Limits of Localizing Cognitive Processes in the Brain.* Cambridge, MA: MIT Press/A Bradford Book.

van Gelder, T. (1998). The dynamical hypothesis in cognitive science. *Behavioral and Brain Sciences* 21: 615–665.

———. (1999a). Dynamic approaches to cognition. In R. Wilson and F. Keil, eds., *The MIT Encyclopedia of Cognitive Sciences,* pp. 244–246. Cambridge, MA: MIT Press.

———. (1999b). Wooden iron: Husserlian phenomenology meets cognitive science. In J. Petitot, F. J. Varela, B. Pachoud, and J.-M. Roy, eds., *Naturalizing Phenomenology: Issues in Contemporary Phenomenology and Cognitive Science,* pp. 245–265. Stanford, CA: Stanford University Press.

Van Gulick, R. (2001). Reduction, emergence and other recent options on the mind-body problem: a philosophic overview. *Journal of Consciousness Studies* 8: 1–34.

VanRullen, R., and Koch, C. (2003). Is perception discrete or continuous? *Trends in Cognitive Sciences* 7: 207–213.

Varela, F. J. (1979). *Principles of Biological Autonomy.* New York: Elsevier North Holland.

———. (1984). Living ways of sense-making: a middle path for neuroscience. In P. Livingston, ed., *Disorder and Order: Proceedings of the Stanford International Symposium,* pp. 208–224. Stanford Literature Series, vol. 1, Anma Libri.

———. (1987). Laying down a path in walking. In W. I. Thompson, ed., *Gaia: A Way of Knowing. Political Implications of the New Biology,* pp. 48–64. Hudson, NY: Lindisfarne Press.

———. (1989). Reflections on the circulation of concepts between a biology of cognition and systemic family therapy. *Family Process* 28: 15–24.

———. (1991). Organism: a meshwork of selfless selves. In A. Tauber, ed., *Organism and the Origin of Self,* pp. 79–107. Dordrecht: Kluwer Academic Publishers.

———. (1995). Resonant cell assemblies: a new approach to cognitive functions and neuronal synchrony. *Biological Research* 28: 81–95.

———. (1996). Neurophenomenology: a methodological remedy for the hard problem. *Journal of Consciousness Studies* 3: 330–350.

———. (1997a). Patterns of life: intertwining identity and cognition. *Brain and Cognition* 34: 72–87.

———. (1997b). The naturalization of phenomenology as the transcendence of nature: searching for generative mutual constraints. *Alter* 5: 355–381.

———. (1999). The specious present: a neurophenomenology of time consciousness. In J. Petitot, F. J. Varela, B. Pachoud, and J.-M. Roy, eds., *Naturalizing Phenomenology: Issues in Contemporary Phenomenology and Cognitive Science,* pp. 266–314. Stanford, CA: Stanford University Press.

———. (2000a). *El fénomena de la vida.* Santiago, Chile: Dolmen Essayo.

———. (2000b). Pour une phénoménologie de la *shunyata* I. In N. Depraz and J.-F. Marquet, eds., *La gnose: une question philosophique.* Paris: Editions du Cerf.

Varela, F. J., and Bourgine, P., eds. (1991). *Toward a Practice of Autonomous Systems. Proceedings of the First European Conference on Artificial Life.* Cambridge, MA: MIT Press.

Varela, F. J., and Cohen, A. (1989). Le corps evocateur: une relecture de l'immunité. *Nouvelle Revue de Psychanalyse* 40: 193–213.

Varela, F. J., and Coutinho, A. (1991). Second generation immune networks. *Immunology Today* 12: 159–166.

Varela, F. J., and Depraz, N. (2003). Imagining: embodiment, phenomenology, and transformation. In B. A. Wallace, ed., *Buddhism and Science: Breaking New Ground,* pp. 195–232. New York: Columbia University Press.

———. (2005). At the source of time: valence and the constitutional dynamics of affect. In G. Colombetti and E. Thompson, eds., *Emotion Experience,* pp. 64–81. Thorverton, UK: Imprint Academic, 2005. Also published as a special issue of *Journal of Consciousness Studies* 12: 64–81.

Varela, F. J., and Goguen, J. (1978). The arithmetic of closure. In R. Trappl, ed., *Progress in Cybernetics and Systems Research,* vol. 3, pp. 48–63. New York: Wiley Hemisphere.

Varela, F. J., Lachaux, J.-P., Rodriguez, E., and Martinerie, J. (2001). The brainweb: phase synchronization and large-scale integration. *Nature Reviews Neuroscience* 2: 229–239.

Varela, F. J., Maturana, H. R., and Uribe, R. (1974). Autopoiesis: the orga-
    nization of living systems, its characterization and a model. *Biosystems* 5:
    187–196.

Varela, F. J., and Shear, J. (1999a). First-person accounts: why, what, and
    how. In F. J. Varela and J. Shear, eds., *The View from Within: First-Person
    Approaches to the Study of Consciousness*, pp. 1–14. Thorverton, UK: Im-
    print Academic.

———, eds. (1999b). *The View from Within: First-Person Approaches to the Study
    of Consciousness*. Thorverton, UK: Imprint Academic.

Varela, F. J., and Thompson, E. (2003). Neural synchrony and the unity of
    mind: a neurophenomenological perspective. In A. Cleeremans, ed.,
    The Unity of Consciousness: Binding, Integration and Dissociation, pp. 266–
    287. New York: Oxford University Press.

Varela, F. J., Thompson, E., and Rosch, E. (1991). *The Embodied Mind: Cog-
    nitive Science and Human Experience*. Cambridge, MA: MIT Press.

Vetlesen, A. J. (1994). *Perception, Empathy, and Judgment: An Inquiry into the
    Preconditions of Moral Performance*. University Park: Pennsylvania State
    University Press.

Virchow, R. (1967). The cell doctrine. In E. A. Carlson, ed., *Modern Biology:
    Its Conceptual Foundations*, pp. 22–25. New York: George Brazilier.

von Stein, A., Chiang, C., and König, P. (2000). Top-down processing medi-
    ated by interareal synchronization. *Proceedings of the National Academy of
    Sciences USA* 97: 14748–14753.

von Stein, A., and Sarntheim, J. (2000). Different frequencies for different
    scales of cortical intergration: from local gamma to long range alpha/theta
    synchronization. *International Journal of Psychophysiology* 38: 301–313.

von Uexküll, J. (1957). A stroll through the worlds of animals and men. In
    K. S. Lashley, ed., *Instinctive Behavior: The Development of a Modern Con-
    cept*, pp. 5–80. New York: International Universities Press.

Vygotsky, L. (1978). *Mind in Society: The Development of Higher Psychological
    Processes*. Ed. M. Cole. Cambridge, MA: Harvard University Press.

Wake, D. B., Roth, G., and Wake, M. H. (1983). On the problem of stasis in
    organismal evolution. *Journal of Theoretical Biology* 101: 211–224.

Wallace, A. B. (1998). *The Bridge of Quiescence: Experiencing Tibetan Buddhist
    Meditation*. La Salle, IL: Open Court.

———. (1999). The Buddhist tradition of *shamatha:* methods for refining
    and examining consciousness. In F. J. Varela and J. Shear, eds., *The View
    from Within: First-Person Approaches to the Study of Consciousness*, pp. 175–
    188. Thorverton, UK: Imprint Academic.

Walton, K. L. (1990). *Mimesis as Make-Believe: On the Foundations of the Repre-
    sentational Arts*. Cambridge, MA: Harvard University Press.

Watt, D. F. (1998). Emotion and consciousness: implications of affective neuroscience for extended reticular thalamic activating system theories of consciousness. Target Article, Association for the Scientific Study of Consciousness Electronic Seminar. Unpublished.

Weber, A., and Varela, F. J. (2002). Life after Kant: natural purposes and the autopoietic foundations of biological individuality. *Phenomenology and the Cognitive Sciences* 1: 97–125.

Weber, B. H., and Depew, D. J. (1995). *Darwinism Evolving: Systems Dynamics and the Genealogy of Natural Selection.* Cambridge, MA: MIT Press.

———. (1996). Natural selection and self-organization. *Biology and Philosophy* 11: 33–65.

Webster, G., and Goodwin, B. (1996). *Form and Transformation: Generative and Relational Principles in Biology.* Cambridge: Cambridge University Press.

Weiss, P. (1969). The living system: determinism stratified. In A. Koestler and J. R. Smythies, eds., *Beyond Reductionism: New Perspectives in the Life Sciences.* London: Hutchinson.

Welton, D. (1999). Soft, smooth hands: Husserl's phenomenology of the lived body. In D. Welton, ed., *The Body,* pp. 38–56. Oxford: Basil Blackwell.

———. (2000). *The Other Husserl: The Horizons of Transcendental Phenomenology.* Bloomington: Indiana University Press.

———, ed. (2003). *The New Husserl. A Critical Reader.* Bloomington: Indiana University Press.

Wexler, M. and Klam, F. (2001). Movement prediction and movement production. *Journal of Experimental Psychology: Human Perception and Performance* 27: 48–64.

Wexler, M., Kosslyn, S. M., and Berthoz, A. (1998). Motor processes in mental rotation. *Cognition* 68: 77–94.

Wheeler, M. (1997). Cognition's coming home: the reunion of life and mind. In P. Husbands and I. Harvey, eds., *Proceedings of the 4th European Conference on Artificial Life,* pp. 10–19. Cambridge, MA: MIT Press.

Williams, G. C. (1966). *Adaptation and Natural Selection.* Princeton, NJ: Princeton University Press.

Wilson, R. A. (1994). Wide computationalism. *Mind* 103: 351–372.

Wimsatt, W. C. (1985). Developmental constraints, generative entrenchment and the innate-acquired distinction. In W. Bechtel, ed., *Integrating Scientific Disciplines,* pp. 185–208. Dordrecht: Martinus Nijhoff.

———. (1986). Forms of aggregativity. In A. Donagan, A. Perovich, and M. Wedin, eds., *Human Nature and Human Knowledge,* pp. 259–291. Dordrecht: D. Reidel.

Winograd, T., and Flores, F. (1987). *Understanding Computers and Cognition. A New Foundation for Design,* NJ: Ablex Press.

Wohlshläger, A., and Wohlschläger, A. (1998). Mental and manual rotation. *Journal of Experimental Psychology: Human Perception and Performance* 24: 397–412.

Wolheim, R. (1980). *Art and Its Objects,* 2d ed. New York: Cambridge University Press.

———. (1987). *Painting as an Art.* Princeton, NJ: Princeton University Press.

———. (1998). On pictorial representation. *Journal of Aesthetics and Art Criticism* 56: 217–226.

Yamaguchi, I. (1997). *Ki als leibhaftige Vernunft. Beitrag zur interkulturellen Phänomenologie der Leiblichkeit.* Munich: W. Fink Verlag.

Zahavi, D. (1997). Horizontal intentionality and transcendental intersubjectivity. *Tijdschrift Voor Filosofie* 59: 304–321.

———. (1999). *Self-Awareness and Alterity. A Phenomenological Investigation.* Evanston, IL: Northwestern University Press.

———. (2001a). *Husserl and Transcendental Intersubjectivity: A Response to the Linguistic-Pragmatic Critique,* trans. E. A. Benke. Athens, OH: Ohio University Press.

———. (2001b). Beyond empathy. Phenomenological approaches to intersubjectivity. In E. Thompson, ed., *Between Ourselves: Second-Person Issues in the Study of Consciousness,* pp. 151–167. Thorverton, UK: Imprint Academic. Also published in *Journal of Consciousness Studies* 8: 151–167.

———. (2002a). First-person thoughts and embodied self-awareness: Some reflections on the relation between recent analytical philosophy and phenomenology. *Phenomenology and the Cognitive Sciences* 1: 7–26.

———. (2002b). Merleau-Ponty on Husserl: a reappraisal. In T. Toadvine and L. Embree, eds., *Merleau-Ponty's Reading of Husserl,* pp. 3–29. Dordrecht: Kluwer Academic Publisher.

———. (2003a). *Husserl's Phenomenology.* Stanford, CA: Stanford University Press.

———. (2003b). Inner time-consciousness and pre-reflective self-awareness. In D. Welton, ed., *The New Husserl: A Critical Reader,* pp. 157–180. Bloomington: Indiana University Press.

———. (2003c). Intentionality and phenomenality: a phenomenological take on the hard problem. In E. Thompson (ed.), *The Problem of Consciousness: New Essays in Phenomenological Philosophy of Mind. Canadian Journal of Philosophy,* supplementary vol. 29, pp. 63–92. Calgary: University of Alberta Press.

———. (2004a). Husserl's noema and the internalism-externalism debate. *Inquiry* 47: 42–66.

————. (2004b). Phenomenology and the project of naturalization. *Phenomenology and the Cognitive Sciences* 3: 331–347.

————. (2005a). *Subjectivity and Selfhood: Investigating the First-Person Perspective.* Cambridge, MA: MIT Press/A Bradford Book.

————. (2005b). Being someone. *Psyche* 11 (5), June 2005. URL: http://psyche.cs.monash.edu.au/symposia/metzinger/Zahavi.pdf

Zahavi, D., and Parnas, J. (1998). Phenomenal consciousness and self-awareness: a phenomenological critique of representational theory. *Journal of Consciousness Studies* 5: 687–705.

Zaretzky, A. N., and Letelier, J. C. (2002). Metabolic networks from (*M,R*) systems and autopoiesis perspective. *Journal of Biological Systems* 10: 265–284.

Index

355; Kantian, 136; of multicell organisms, 105–107; of sentience, 354–355; of single-cell organisms, 97–105. *See also* autopoiesis; autopoietic organization

Organizational characterization of life, 97

Organizational closure: defined, 45, 448n6; Goguen's view of, 449n12; in Rosen's theory, 143; Varela's view of, 449n12

Original intentionality, 453n8

The other and intentionality, 22

Oyama, S.: on autopoiesis, 458n15; on evolution, 188; on the genetic "code," 184–185; on genocentrism, 201–202; on inheritance, 178; on neo-Darwinism, 193; response to genocentrism, 188–190

Pacherie, E., 295

Pain and object-directedness, 23

Paley, W.: on the Argument from Design, 460n23; on divine artifacts, 133; mechanical perspective, 211

Panisset, M., 119

Parity thesis, 191

Passive bodily coupling, 392–395

Passive genesis, 29–30, 32–33

Passive synthesis, 29–30, 373

Passivist-cognitivist view of the brain, 366

Passivity, 263–264, 373–374

Patočka, J.: on e-motion, 364, 378; on feeling of existence, 229–230; on mood, 380

Pattee, H. H., 54–56

Pattern dynamics, 58

Penfield, W., 62–63

Perceived situation-work, 76–78

Perception: and empathy, 386–387; Husserl's view of, 232; moral, 393; simultaneous, by others, 384–385, 477n3

Perception experiment, 341–346

Perceptual completion, 275–276

Perceptual synthesis, 317–318

Peripheral vision, 280–282

Personality, 371–372, 380–381

Personal vs. subpersonal, 6, 447n10

Perturbation/response distinction in autonomous systems, 365

Petitot, J., 72–73

Phantom limbs: and dominance vs. deference, 255; Merleau-Ponty's view of, 32–33; Ramachandran's view of, 253

Phase synchrony, 332–333

Phenomenological analysis, 267–269

Phenomenological attitude, 18–21, 81–87

Phenomenological psychology, 20

Phenomenological reduction, 17–22

Phenomenology, 14–15, 474n11

Pheno-physics, 85

Phenotypic traits, 192–193, 202

Phenotypic variation, 170

Philosophy distinguished from cognitive science, 3–4

Philosophy of life, 128–129

Phylogeny, 191–192

Phylotypic body plan, 197–201

Physical orders, 72–76

Physical realization principle, 435

Physical-symbol-system model, 8

Physical vs. living structure, 73–75

Physicochemical phenomena, 454n10

Physics of phenomenality, 72–73

Piaget, J., 401

Pictorialism compared with descriptionalism, 270–275

Picture-viewing, 287–289

Plants, 94, 221

Poincaré, H., 40

Pomerantz, J. R., 271

Preafference and expectancy, 369

Precipitating event, 376

Preformation, 175–176

Pregiven, 30, 35–36. *See also* given

Prereflective experience, 250–251, 261

Prereflective self-awareness, 322–328

Prereflective self-consciousness, 464n3

Prereflective vs. reflective awareness, 315

The present, 318–319

Presentation: and re-presentation, 25–26, 288, 320; in time-consciousness, 320

Presistence, 460n21